T&T CLARK HANDBOOK OF JOHN OWEN

Forthcoming titles in this series include

T&T Clark Handbook of Christology, *edited by Darren O. Sumner and Chris Tilling*

T&T Clark Handbook of Public Theology, *edited by Christoph Hübenthal and Christiane Alpers*

T&T Clark Handbook of Election, *edited by Edwin Chr. van Driel*

T&T Clark Handbook of Modern Theology, *edited by Philip G. Ziegler and R. David Nelson*

T&T Clark Handbook of the Doctrine of Creation, *edited by Jason Goroncy*

T&T Clark Introduction to Asian American Christian Ethics, *edited by Grace Yia-Hei Kao*

T&T Clark Handbook of Theology and the Arts, *edited by Imogen Adkins and Stephen M. Garrett*

T&T Clark Handbook of Intercultural Theology and Mission Studies, *edited by John G. Flett and Dorottya Nagy*

Titles already published include

T&T Clark Handbook of Christian Theology and Climate Change, *edited by Ernst M. Conradie and Hilda P. Koster*

T&T Clark Handbook of Political Theology, *edited by Rubén Rosario Rodríguez*

T&T Clark Handbook of Pneumatology, *edited by Daniel Castelo and Kenneth M. Loyer*

T&T Clark Handbook of Ecclesiology, *edited by Kimlyn J. Bender and D. Stephen Long*

T&T Clark Handbook of Christian Theology and the Modern Sciences, *edited by John P. Slattery*

T&T Clark Handbook of Christian Ethics, *edited by Tobias Winright*

T&T Clark Handbook of Analytic Theology, *edited by James M. Arcadi and James T. Turner, Jr*

T&T Clark Handbook of Theological Anthropology, *edited by Mary Ann Hinsdale and Stephen Okey*

T&T CLARK HANDBOOK OF JOHN OWEN

Edited by
Crawford Gribben and John W. Tweeddale

t&tclark
LONDON • NEW YORK • OXFORD • NEW DELHI • SYDNEY

T&T CLARK
Bloomsbury Publishing Plc
50 Bedford Square, London, WC1B 3DP, UK
1385 Broadway, New York, NY 10018, USA
29 Earlsfort Terrace, Dublin 2, Ireland

BLOOMSBURY, T&T CLARK and the T&T Clark logo are trademarks of
Bloomsbury Publishing Plc

First published in Great Britain 2022
Paperback edition published 2024

Copyright © Crawford Gribben, John W. Tweeddale and contributors, 2022

Crawford Gribben and John W. Tweeddale have asserted their right under the Copyright, Designs and Patents Act, 1988, to be identified as Editors of this work.

For legal purposes the Acknowledgements on p. vii constitute an extension of this copyright page.

Cover image: Dr John Owen by John Whessell, ca.1830, engraver.
The National Library of Wales.

All rights reserved. No part of this publication may be reproduced or transmitted in any form or by any means, electronic or mechanical, including photocopying, recording, or any information storage or retrieval system, without prior permission in writing from the publishers.

Bloomsbury Publishing Plc does not have any control over, or responsibility for, any third-party websites referred to or in this book. All internet addresses given in this book were correct at the time of going to press. The author and publisher regret any inconvenience caused if addresses have changed or sites have ceased to exist, but can accept no responsibility for any such changes.

A catalogue record for this book is available from the British Library.

Library of Congress Cataloging-in-Publication Data
Names: Gribben, Crawford, editor. | Tweeddale, John W., editor.
Title: T&T Clark handbook of John Owen / edited by Crawford Gribben and John W. Tweeddale.
Description: London ; New York : T&T Clark, 2022. | Series: T&t clark handbooks | Includes bibliographical references and index. |
Identifiers: LCCN 2021048754 (print) | LCCN 2021048755 (ebook) | ISBN 9780567688743 (hardback) | ISBN 9780567705976 (paperback) | ISBN 9780567688767 (pdf)
Subjects: LCSH: Owen, John, 1616-1683–Criticism and interpretation.
Classification: LCC BX5207.O88 T23 2022 (print) | LCC BX5207.O88 (ebook) | DDC 285/.9092 [B]–dc23/eng/20211221
LC record available at https://lccn.loc.gov/2021048754
LC ebook record available at https://lccn.loc.gov/2021048755

ISBN: HB: 978-0-5676-8874-3
PB: 978-0-5677-0597-6
ePDF: 978-0-5676-8876-7
eBook: 978-0-5676-8875-0

Series: T&T Clark Handbooks

Typeset by Deanta Global Publishing Services, Chennai, India

To find out more about our authors and books visit www.bloomsbury.com and sign up for our newsletters.

CONTENTS

Acknowledgements		vii
List of Contributors		viii
List of Abbreviations		xi
1	Introduction *Crawford Gribben and John W. Tweeddale*	1

Part I Owen's contexts

2	Owen's life *Michael A. G. Haykin*	13
3	Owen as a theologian *Ryan M. McGraw*	25
4	Owen's intellectual context *Richard A. Muller*	53
5	Owen and politics *Crawford Gribben*	81
6	Owen the preacher *Martyn C. Cowan*	118
7	Owen and education *Eric Newton*	146
8	Owen and the Church of England *Lee Gatiss*	170

9	Owen the polemicist Paul C.-H. Lim	197
10	Owen and scientific reform Katherine Calloway	223
11	Owen and philosophy Paul Helm	251

Part II Owen's writings

12	Θεομαχία αυτεξουσιαστικη: *or, A display of Arminianisme* (1643) Christopher Cleveland	275
13	*Salus electorum, sanguis Jesu: or, The death of death in the death of Christ* (1648) Timothy Robert Baylor	303
14	*Of the mortification of sinne in believers* (1656) Joel R. Beeke	336
15	*Exercitations on the epistle to the Hebrews* (1668) John W. Tweeddale	364
16	Πνευματολογια: *or, A discourse concerning the Holy Spirit* (1674) Andrew M. Leslie	384
17	*The nature of apostasie* (1676) Tim Cooper	414
18	*The doctrine of justification by faith* (1677) Whitney Gamble-Smith	439
19	*Meditations and discourses on the glory of Christ* (1684) Suzanne McDonald	461

Part III Owen today

20	Retrieving Owen Kelly M. Kapic	489

BIBLIOGRAPHY	517
OWEN'S WORKS INDEX	558
AUTHOR AND SUBJECT INDEX	561

ACKNOWLEDGEMENTS

As editors, we would like to thank our contributors, who have together produced what we hope will be a defining text in scholarship on John Owen. The colleagues at T&T Clark have been unfailingly helpful during the book's production. We would also like to thank our families, who have 'borne the burden and heat of the day.'

CONTRIBUTORS

Timothy Robert Baylor is a lecturer in theology and religion at the University of Wales Trinity Saint David. He has contributed chapters on Owen in the volumes *'In Christ' in Paul* (2014) and *Trinity without hierarchy* (2019).

Joel R. Beeke is a professor of systematic theology and homiletics at and the president of Puritan Reformed Theological Seminary and a pastor of the Heritage Reformed Congregation in Grand Rapids, Michigan. He is author of *Assurance of faith: Calvin, English Puritanism, and the Dutch Second Reformation* (1991), *Debated issues in sovereign predestination: Early Lutheran predestination, Calvinian reprobation, and variations in Genevan lapsarianism* (2017) and the multivolume *Reformed systematic theology* (2019).

Katherine Calloway is an assistant professor in English at Baylor University. She is the author of *Natural theology in the scientific revolution: God's scientists* (2014).

Christopher Cleveland is a humanities teacher at Veritas Academy in Savannah, Georgia. He is the author of *Thomism in John Owen* (2013) and a contributor to *The Oxford handbook of Reformed theology* (2020).

Tim Cooper is a professor of church history and the head of the School of Arts at the University of Otago. He is the author of *Fear and polemic in seventeenth-century England: Richard Baxter and antinomianism* (2001) and *John Owen, Richard Baxter and the formation of Nonconformity* (2011), and a co-editor of Richard Baxter's *Reliquiae Baxterianae* (2020).

Martyn C. Cowan is a lecturer in historical theology at Union Theological College. He is the author of *John Owen and the civil war apocalypse: Preaching, prophecy and politics* (2017).

Lee Gatiss is the director of Church Society and a lecturer in church history at the Union School of Theology. He is the author of *From life's first cry: John Owen on infant baptism and infant salvation* (2008) and a senior editor of *The NIV Proclamation Bible* (2013).

Crawford Gribben is a professor of early modern British history at Queen's University Belfast. He is the author of *John Owen and English Puritanism: Experiences of defeat* (2016) and *An introduction to John Owen: A Christian vision for every stage of life* (2020).

Michael A. G. Haykin is the chair of and a professor of church history at the Southern Baptist Theological Seminary. He is the general editor of *The complete works of Andrew Fuller*, a co-editor of *Drawn into controversie: Reformed theological diversity and debates within seventeenth-century British Puritanism* (2011) and co-author of *Owen on the Christian life: Living for the glory of God in Christ* (2015).

Paul Helm was a professor of the history and philosophy of religion, King's College, London, from 1993 to 2000. Before that he taught philosophy at the University of Liverpool for thirty years, and afterwards at Regent College, Vancouver, from 2001 to 2005. He is the author of *Calvin at the centre* (2009), *Human nature from Calvin to Edwards* (2018) and *Reforming free will* (2020).

Kelly M. Kapic is a professor of theological studies at Covenant College. He is a co-editor of *The Ashgate research companion to John Owen's theology* (2012), co-editor of *John Owen between orthodoxy and modernity* (2019) and the author of *Communion with God: The divine and the human in the theology of John Owen* (2007).

Andrew M. Leslie is the head of theology, philosophy, and ethics and a lecturer in Christian doctrine at Moore Theological College. He is the author of *The light of grace: John Owen on the authority of Scripture and Christian faith* (2015).

Paul C.-H. Lim is an associate professor of the history of Christianity at Vanderbilt University. He is a co-editor of *The Cambridge companion to Puritanism* (2008) and the author of *In pursuit of purity, unity, and liberty:*

Richard Baxter's Puritan ecclesiology in its seventeenth-century context (2004) and *Mystery unveiled: The crisis of the Trinity in early modern England* (2012).

Suzanne McDonald is a professor of historical and systematic theology at the Western Theological Seminary. She is the author of *Re-imaging election: Divine election as representing God to others and others to God* (2010) and *John Knox for armchair theologians* (2013).

Ryan M. McGraw is the academic dean of and Morton H. Smith professor of systematic theology at Greenville Presbyterian Theological Seminary. He is the author of *A heavenly directory: Trinitarian piety, public worship and a reassessment of John Owen's theology* (2014), *John Owen: Trajectories in Reformed Orthodox theology* (2017) and *Reformed scholasticism: Recovering the tools of Reformed theology* (2019).

Richard A. Muller is P. J. Zondervan professor of historical theology emeritus and a senior fellow of the Junius Institute for Digital Reformation Research at Calvin Theological Seminary. He is the author of the multivolume *Post-Reformation Reformed dogmatics: The rise and development of Reformed Orthodoxy, ca. 1520 to ca. 1725* (2003), *Divine will and human choice: Freedom, contingency, and necessity in early modern thought* (2017) and *Grace and freedom: William Perkins and the early modern Reformed understanding of free choice and divine grace* (2020).

Eric Newton is an adjunct professor of theology at BJU Seminary, Greenville, South Carolina. He serves as the managing editor of the *Journal of Biblical theology & worldview*.

Whitney Gamble-Smith is the director of interdisciplinary studies and adjunct professor at the Master's University in Santa Clarita, California. She is the author of *Christ and the law: Antinomianism at the Westminster Assembly* (2018) and a contributor to *The history of Scottish theology* (2019).

John W. Tweeddale is the vice president of academics and a professor of theology at Reformation Bible College in Sanford, Florida. He is the author of *John Owen and Hebrews: The foundation of Biblical interpretation* (2019) and a co-editor of *John Calvin: For a new reformation* (2019).

ABBREVIATIONS

Note: Works are listed in chronological order.

A display of Arminianisme (1643)
Θεομαχία αυτεξουσιαστικη [*Theomachia autexousiastikē*]: *or, A display of Arminianisme. Being a discovery of the old Pelagian idol free-will, with the new goddesse contingency, advancing themselves, into the throne of the God of heaven to the prejudice of his grace, providence, and supreme dominion over the children of men. Wherein the maine errors of the Arminians are laid open, by which they are fallen off from the received doctrine of all the Reformed churches, with their opposition in divers particulars to the doctrine established in the Church of England. Discovered out of their owne writings and confessions, and confuted by the word of God* (London, 1643).

The duty of pastors and people distinguished (1644)
The duty of pastors and people distinguished: or, A briefe discourse, touching the administration of things commanded in religion. Especially concerning the means to be used by the people of God (distinct from church-officers) for the increasing of divine knowledge in themselves and others. Wherein bounds are prescribed to their performances, their liberty is enlarged to the utmost extent of the dictates of nature and rules of charity, their duty laid down in directions, drawn from Scripture precepts, and the practice of Gods people in all ages. Together with the severall wayes of extraordinary calling to the office of publicke teaching, with what assurance such teachers may have of their calling, and what evidence they can give of it, unto others (London, 1644).

Two short catechismes (1645)	*The principles of the doctrine of Christ: Unfolded in two short catechismes, wherein those principles of religion are explained, the knowledge whereof is required by the late ordinance of Parliament, before any person bee admitted to the sacrament of the Lords Supper. For the use of the congregation at Fordham, in the county of Essex* (London, 1645).
A vision of unchangeable free mercy (1646)	*A vision of unchangeable free mercy, in sending the means of grace to undeserved sinners: wherein Gods uncontrollable eternall purpose, in sending, and continuing the Gospel unto this nation, in the middest of oppositions and contingencies, is discovered: his distinguishing mercy, in this great work, exalted, asserted, against opposers, repiners: in a sermon preached before the Honourable House of Commons, April 29, being the day of publike humiliation. Whereunto is annexed, a short defensative about church-government, (with a countrey essay for the practice of church-government there) toleration and petitions about these things* (London, 1646).
Eben-ezer (1648)	*Eben-ezer: A memoriall of the deliverance of Essex, county, and committee, being an exposition on the first ten verses of the third chapter of the prophesie of Habakkuk in two sermons. The first preached at Colchester before his Excellency on a day of thanksgiving for the surrender thereof. The other at Rumford unto the committee who were imprisoned by the enemy Sep. 28. A day set apart unto thanksgiving for their deliverance* (London, 1648).
Eshcol (1648)	*Eshcol: A cluster of the fruit of Canaan; brought to the borders, for the encouragement of the saints, travelling thither-ward, with their faces towards Syon. Or, rules of direction, for the walking of the saints in fellowship, according to the order of the Gospel. Collected and explained for the use of the Church at Coggeshall* (London, 1648).
The death of death in the death of Christ (1648)	*Salus electorum, sanguis Jesu: or, The death of death in the death of Christ. A treatise of the redemption and reconciliation that is in the blood of Christ with the merit thereof, and the satisfaction wrought thereby. Wherin the proper end of the death of Christ is asserted: the immediate effects and fruits thereof assigned, with their extent in respect of it's object; and the whole controversie about universall redemption fully discussed in foure parts, whereof the 1. Declareth the eternall counsell, and distinct actuall concurrence of Father, Sonne, and Holy Spirit unto the worke of redemption in the blood of Christ, with the covenanted intendment, and accomplished end of God therein. 2. Removeth false and supposed ends of the death of Christ; with the distinctions invented to salve the manifold contradictions of the pretended universal atonement; rightly stating the controversie. 3. Containeth arguments against universall redemption from the word, with an affection of the satisfaction and merit of Christ. 4. Answereth all considerable objections as yet brought to light either by Arminians, or others (their late followers as to this point) in the behalfe of universall redemption; with a large unfolding of all the texts of Scripture by any produced and wrested to that purpose* (London, 1648).

ABBREVIATIONS

A sermon preached to the Honourable House of Commons, in Parliament assembled: on January 31 (1649)	*A sermon preached to the Honourable House of Commons, in Parliament assembled: on January 31. A day of solemne humiliation. With a discourse about toleration, and the duty of the civill magistrate about religion, thereunto annexed. Humbly presented to them, and all peace-loving men of this nation* (London, 1649).
Certaine treatises (1649)	*Certaine treatises written by John Owen M.A. Sometimes of Queens College in Oxford, now pastor of the church at Coggsehall in Essex. Formerly published at severall times, now reduced into one volume, viz. 1. A display of the errours of the Arminians concerning the old Pelagian idoll free-will, &c. in 14 chapters. 2. Salus electorum sanguis Jesu. A treatise of the redemption and reconciliation that is in the blood of Christ, with the merit thereof, and the satisfaction wrought thereby; wherein the whole controversie of universall redemption is fully discussed, in foure books, in 31 chapters; with an appendix uppon accasion of a late booke published by Mr. Joshua Sprigge containing erroneous doctrine. 3. The duty of pastors and people distinguished, touching the meanes to bee used by the people (distrinct from church-officers) for encreasing of divine knowledge, prescribing, 1. The bounds of their performance. 2. The extent of their liberty according to the dictates of nature, and rules of charity. 3. Their duty according to Scripture, and practice in all ages, with the severall waies of extraordinary calling to the office of publique teaching, the assurance to be had, and the evidence to be given, of such calling, in 8. Chapters* (London, 1649).
The shaking and translating of heaven and earth (1649)	Ουρανων ουρανια [*Ouranōn Ourania*]. *The shaking and translating of heaven and earth. A sermon preached to the Honourable House of Commons in Parliament assembled: on April 19. A day set apart for extraordinary humiliation* (London, 1649).
The branch of the Lord, the beauty of Sion (1650)	*The branch of the Lord, the beauty of Sion: or, The glory of the Church, in its relation unto Christ. Opened in two sermons; one preached at Berwick, the other at Edinburgh* (Edinburgh, 1650).
Of the death of Christ (1650)	*Of the death of Christ, the price he paid, and the purchase he made. Or, the satisfaction, and merit of the death of Christ cleared, the universality of redemption thereby oppugned: and the doctrine concerning these things formerly delivered in a treatise against universal redemption vindicated from the exceptions, and objections of Mr Baxter* (London, 1650).
The stedfastness of promises, and the sinfulness of staggering (1650)	*The stedfastness of promises, and the sinfulness of staggering: Opened in a sermon preached at Margarets in Westminster before the Parliament Febr. 28. 1649. Being a day set apart for solemn humiliation throughout the nation* (London, 1650).

The advantage of the kingdome of Christ (1651)	*The advantage of the kingdome of Christ in the shaking of the kingdoms of the world: or, Providentiall alterations in their subserviency to Christ's exaltation. Opened, in a sermon preached to the Parliament Octob. 24. 1651. A solemne day of thankesgiving for the destruction of the Scots army at Worcester with sundry other mercies, by John Owen minister of the Gospell* (Oxford, 1651).
The labouring saints dismission to rest (1652)	*The labouring saints dismission to rest. A sermon preached at the funeral of the Right Honourable Henry Ireton Lord Deputy of Ireland: In the Abbey Church at Westminster, the 6th day of February 1651* (London, 1652).
The primer (1652)	*The primer: or, An easie way to teach children the true reading of English. With a necessary catechisme, to instruct youth in the grounds of Christian religion. Also choice places of Scripture for that purpose. Composed by John Owen, minister of the Gospel. Approved and allowed by a committee of Parliament* (London, 1652).
A sermon preached to the Parliament, Octob. 13. 1652 (1652)	*A sermon preached to the Parliament, Octob. 13. 1652. A day of solemne humiliation. Concerning the kingdome of Christ, and the power of the civile magistrate about the things of the worship of God* (Oxford, 1652).
Diatriba de justitia divina (1653)	*Diatriba de justitia divina. Seu iustitiæ vindicatricis vindiciæ quibus, essentialis illa naturæ divinæ proprietas, ex Sacris Literis demonstrator, & contra Socinianos, imprimis authores catech. Racov. Io. Crellium, ipsumq; F. Socinum asseritur: nec non exercitium ejus necessarium, unà cum indispensabili satisfactionis Jesu Christi ad salutem peccatorum necessitate, adversus virorum doctiss. G. Twissi, G. Vossii, &. S. Rhetorfortis, aliorumq; impugnationes, preterea astruitnr* (Oxford, 1653).
The doctrine of the saints perseverance (1654)	*The doctrine of the saints perseverance, explained and confirmed. Or, the certain permanency of their 1. Acceptation with God, & 2. Sanctification from God. Manifested & proved from the 1. Eternal principles 2. Effectuall causes 3. Externall meanes thereof. In, 1. The immutability of the 1. Nature 2. Decrees 3. Covenant and 4. Promises of God. 2. The oblation and intercession of Jesus Christ. 3. The 1. Promises 2. Exhortations 3. Threats of the Gospell. Improved in its genuine tendency to obedience and consolation. And vindicated in a full answer to the discourse of Mr John Goodwin against it, in his book entituled Redemption redeemed. With some digressions concerning 1. The immediate effects of the death of Christ. 2. Personall indwelling of the Spirit. 3. Union with Christ. 4. Nature of Gospell promises, &c. also a preface manifesting the judgement of the antients concerning the truth contended for: with a discourse touching the epistles of Ignatius; the Episcopacy in them asserted; and some animadversions on Dr. H.H. his dissertations on that subject* (Oxford, 1654).

Vindiciae evangelicae (1655)	Vindiciae evangelicae, or, The mystery of the Gospell vindicated, and Socinianisme examined, in the consideration, and confutation of a catechisme, called a Scripture Catechisme, written by J. Biddle M.A. and the Catechisme of Valentinus Smalcius, commonly called the Racovian Catechisme. With the vindication of the testimonies of Scripture, concerning deity and satisfaction of Jesus Christ, from the perverse expositions, and interpretations of them, by Hugo Grotius in his Annotations on the Bible. Also an appendix, in vindication of some things formerly written about the death of Christ, & the fruits thereof, from the animadversions of Mr. R.B (Oxford,1655).
Of the mortification of sinne in believers (1656)	Of the mortification of sinne in believers: The necessity, nature, and meanes of it. With a resolution of sundry cases of conscience, thereunto belonging (Oxford, 1656).
A review of the annotations of Hugo Grotius (1656)	A review of the annotations of Hugo Grotius, in reference unto the doctrine of the deity, and satisfaction of Christ. With a defence of the charge formerly laid against them (Oxford, 1656).
God's work in founding Zion (1656)	God's work in founding Zion, and his peoples duty thereupon. A sermon preached in the Abby Church at Westminster, at the opening of the Parliament Septemb. 17th 1656 (Oxford, 1656).
God's presence with a people (1656)	God's presence with a people, the spring of their prosperity; with their speciall interest in abiding with Him. A sermon, preached to the Parliament of the Commonwealth of England, Scotland, and Ireland, at Westminster, Octob. 30. 1656. A day of solemn humiliation (London, 1656).
Of communion with God (1657)	Of communion with God the Father, Sonne, and Holy Ghost, each person distinctly; in love, grace, and consolation: or, The saints fellowship with the Father, Sonne, and Holy Ghost, unfolded (Oxford, 1657).
Of schisme (1657)	Of schisme. The true nature of it discovered and considered, with reference to the present differences in religion (Oxford, 1657).
A review of the true nature of schisme (1657)	A review of the true nature of schisme, with a vindication of the congregationall churches in England, from the imputation thereof unjustly charged on them by Mr D. Cawdrey, preacher of the Word at Billing in Northampton-shire (Oxford, 1657).
An answer to a later treatise of Daniel Cawdrey about the nature of schisme (1658)	An answer to a later treatise of Daniel Cawdrey about the nature of schisme. In John Cotton, A defence of Mr. John Cotton from the imputation of selfe contradiction, charged on him by Mr. Dan. Cawdrey written by himselfe not long before his death. Whereunto is prefixed, an answer to a late treatise of the said Mr. Cawdrey about the nature of schisme. By John Owen: D.D. (Oxford, 1658).

Of temptation (1658)	Of temptation, the nature and power of it. The danger of entring into it. And the meanes of preventing the danger. With a resolution of sundry cases thereunto belonging (Oxford, 1658).
Pro Sacris Scripturis (1658)	Pro Sacris Scripturis adversus hujus tempom Fanaticos exercitaliones apologeticae Quatuor fanaticos (London, 1658).
Of the divine originall (1659)	Of the divine originall, authority, self-evidencing light, and power of the Scriptures. With an answer to that enquiry, how we know the Scriptures to be the word of God. Also a vindication of the purity and integrity of the Hebrew and Greek texts of the Old and New Testament; in some considerations on the prolegomena, & appendix to the late Biblia polyglotta. Whereunto are subjoyned some exercitations about the nature and perfection of the Scripture, the right of interpretation, internall Light, revelation, &c. (Oxford, 1659).
The glory and interest of nations professing the Gospel (1659)	The glory and interest of nations professing the Gospel. Opened in a sermon preached at a private fast, to the Commons assembled in Parliament. Published by their command (London, 1659).
Two questions (1659)	Unto the questions sent me last night, I pray accept of the ensuing answer, under the title of two questions concerning the power of the supream magistrate about religion, and the worship of God; with one about tythes, proposed and resolved (London, 1659).
Θεολογουμενα παντοδαπα (1661)	Θεολογουμενα παντοδαπα [Theologoumena pantodapa]. Sive de natura, ortu, progressu, et studio veræ theologiæ libri sex. Quibus etiam origines & processus verì & falsi cultus religiosi, casus & instaurationes ecclesiæ illustriores ab ipsis rerum primordiis, enarrantur. Accedunt digressiones De grati universali. Scientiarum ortu. Ecclesiæ Romanæ notis. Literarum origine. Antiquis literis Hebraicis. Punctatione Hebraica. Versionibus SS. Ritibus Judaicis. Aliísque (Oxford, 1661).
Animadversions on Fiat lux (1662)	Animadversions on a treatise intituled Fiat lux: or, A guide in differences of religion, between Papist and Protestant, Presbyterian and Independent. By a Protestant (London, 1662).
A discourse concerning liturgies (1662)	A discourse concerning liturgies, and their imposition (London, 1662).
A vindication of the animadversions on Fiat lux (1664)	A vindication of the animadversions on Fiat lux. Wherein the principles of the Roman church, as to moderation, unity and truth are examined: And sundry important controversies concerning the rule of faith, papal supremacy, the mass, images, &c. discussed (London, 1664).

Indulgence and toleration considered (1667)	*Indulgence and toleration considered. In a letter unto a person of honour* (London, 1667).
A peace-offering (1667)	*A peace-offering in an apology and humble plea for indulgence and liberty of conscience. By sundry Protestants differing in some things from the present establishment about the worship of God* (London, 1667).
A brief instruction in the worship of God (1667)	*A brief instruction in the worship of God, and discipline of the churches of the New Testament, by way of question and answer with an explication and confirmation of those answers* (London, 1667).
Hebrews (1668)	*Exercitations on the Epistle to the Hebrews also concerning the Messiah. Wherein the promises concerning him to be a spiritual redeemer of mankind are explained and vindicated. His coming and accomplishment of his work according to the promises is proved and confirmed. The person, or who he is, is declared. The whole oeconomy of the Mosaical law, rites, worship, and sacrifice is explained. And in all, the doctrine of the person, office, and work of the Messiah is opened; the nature and demerit of the first sin is unfolded; the opinions and traditions of the antient and modern Jews are examined; their objections against the Lord Christ and the Gospel are answered; the time of the coming of the Messiah is stated: And the great fundamental truths of the Gospel vindicated. With an exposition and discourses on the two first chapters of the said epistle to the Hebrews* (London, 1668).
Indwelling sin (1668)	*The nature, power, deceit, and prevalency of the remainders of indwelling-sin in believers. Together with the wayes of its working, and means of prevention. Opened, evinced and applyed, with a resolution of sundry cases of conscience thereunto appertaining* (London, 1668).
A practical exposition on the 130th Psalm (1669)	*A practical exposition on the 130th Psalm. Wherein the nature of the forgiveness of sin is declared, the truth and reality of it asserted. And the case of a soul distressed with the guilt of sin, and relieved by a discovery of forgiveness with God, is at large discoursed* (London, 1669).
Truth and innocence vindicated (1669)	*Truth and innocence vindicated: In a survey of a discourse concerning ecclesiastical polity; and the authority of the civil magistrate over the consciences of subjects in matters of religion* (London, 1669).
A brief declaration and vindication of the doctrine of the Trinity (1669)	*A brief declaration and vindication of the doctrine of the Trinity: As also of the person and satisfaction of Christ. Accommodated to the capacity and use of such as may be in danger to be seduced, and the establishment of the truth* (London, 1669).

An account of the grounds and reasons on which Protestant dissenters desire liberty (1670)	*An account of the grounds and reasons on which Protestant dissenters desire liberty* (London, 1670).
Sabbath (1671)	*Exercitations concerning the name, original, nature, use, and continuance of a day of sacred rest. Wherein the original of the Sabbath from the foundation of the world, the morality of the fourth commandment, with the change of the seventh day are enquired into. Together with an assertion of the divine institution of the Lord's Day, and practical directions for its due observation* (London, 1671).
A discourse concerning evangelical love, church-peace and unity (1672)	*A discourse concerning evangelical love, church-peace and unity. With the occasions and reasons of present differences and divisions about things sacred and religious. Written in the vindication of the principles and practise of some ministers and others* (London, 1672).
A vindication of some passages (1674)	*A vindication of some passages in a discourse concerning communion with God, from the exceptions of William Sherlock, rector of St. George Buttolph-Lane* (London, 1674).
Πνευματολογια (1674)	Πνευματολογια [*Pneumatologia*]: *or, A discourse concerning the Holy Spirit. Wherein an account is given of his name, nature, personality, dispensation, operations, and effects. His whole work in the old and new creation is explained; the doctrine concerning it vindicated from oppositions and reproaches. The nature also and necessity of Gospel-holiness; the difference between grace and morality, or a spiritual life unto God in evangelical obedience and a course of moral virtues, are stated and declared* (London, 1674).
Hebrews (1674)	*Exercitations on the epistle to the Hebrews, concerning the priesthood of Christ. Wherein the original, causes, nature, prefigurations, and discharge of that holy office, are explained and vindicated. The nature of the covenant of the redeemer, with the call of the Lord Christ unto his office, are declared. And the opinions of the Socinians about it are fully examined, and their opposition unto it refuted. With a continuation of the exposition on the third, fourth, and fifth chapters of said epistle to the Hebrews* (London, 1674).

The nature of apostasie (1676)	*The nature of apostasie from the profession of the Gospel, and the punishment of apostates declared, in an exposition of Heb.* 6. 4, 5, 6. *With an enquiry into the causes and reasons of the decay of the power of religion in the world; or the present general defection from the truth, holiness and worship of the Gospel. Also, of the proneness of churches and persons of all sorts unto apostasie. With remedies and means of prevention* (London, 1676).
The doctrine of justification by faith (1677)	*The doctrine of justification by faith through the imputation of the righteousness of Christ, explained, confirmed, & vindicated* (London, 1677).
The reason of faith (1677)	*The reason of faith. Or, an answer unto that enquiry, wherefore we believe the Scripture to be the word of God. With the causes and nature of that faith wherewith we do so. Wherein the grounds whereon the Holy Scripture is believed to be the word of God with faith divine and supernatural, are declared and vindicated* (London, 1677).
The causes, waies & means of understanding the mind of God (1678)	Σύνεσις πνευματική [*Synesis pneumatikē*]: *or, The causes, waies & means of understanding the mind of God as revealed in his word, with assurance therein. And a declaration of the perspicuity of the Scriptures, with the external means of the interpretation of them* (London, 1678).
Χριστολογια (1679)	Χριστολογια [*Christologia*]: *or, A declaration of the glorious mystery of the person of Christ, God and Man. With the infinite wisdom, love, and power of God in the contrivance and constitution thereof. As also of the grounds and reasons of his incarnation, the nature of his ministry in heaven, the present state of the church above thereon; and the use of his person in religion. With an account and vindication of the honour, worship, faith, love, and obedience due unto him, in and from the church* (London, 1679).
The Church of Rome, no safe guide (1679)	*The Church of Rome, no safe guide. Or, reasons to prove that no rational man, who takes due care of his own eternal salvation, can give himself up unto the conduct of that church in matters of religion* (London, 1679).
Some considerations about union among Protestants (1680)	*Some considerations about union among Protestants, and the preservation of the interest of the Protestant religion in this nation* (London, 1680).
A brief vindication of the non-conformists (1680)	*A brief vindication of the non-conformists from the charge of schism. As it was managed against them in a sermon preached before the Lord Mayor by Dr. Stillingfleet, Dean of St. Pauls* (London, 1680).

Hebrews (1680)	*A continuation of the exposition of the Epistle of Paul the Apostle to the Hebrews viz, on the sixth, seventh, eight, ninth, and tenth chapters. Wherein together with the explication of the text and context, the priesthood of Christ by those of Melchizedek and Aaron, with an account of their distinct offices, the nature and efficacy of the sacrifice of Christ, as typed by all the sacrifices of the law, the erection of the tabernacles according to the heavenly patter; with the institution of all its utensils and services, their especial signification and end, the nature and differences of the two covenants, the old and the new, with the preference of the latter above the former, the reasons and necessity of the taking away and abolishing of the old legal worship annexed unto the covenant of Sinai, and the means whereby it was removed, the glorious administration of the mediatory office of Christ in heaven, and sundry other evangelical truths of the highest importance, with the duty of believers in hearing the word in times of trial and persecution; the means and danger of apostacy from the profession of the Gospel, are declared, explained and confirmed: as also, the pleas of the Jews for the continuance and perpetuity of their legal worship, with the doctrine of the principal writers of the Socinians about these things, are examined and disproved* (London, 1680).
An enquiry into evangelical churches (1681)	*An enquiry into the original, nature, institution, power, order and communion of evangelical churches. The first part with an answer to the discourse of the unreasonableness of separation written by Dr. Edward Stillingfleet, Dean of Pauls, and in defence of the vindication of non-conformists from the guilt of schisme* (London, 1681).
An humble testimony (1681)	*An humble testimony unto the goodness and severity of God in his dealing with sinful churches and nations. Or, the only way to deliver a sinful nation from utter ruine by impendent judgments, in a discourse on the words of our Lord Jesus Christ, Luk. 13, 1, 2, 3, 4, 5* (London, 1681).
The grace and duty of being spiritually-minded (1681)	Φρόνεμα του πνεύματου [*Phronēma tou pneumatou*]: or, *The grace and duty of being spiritually-minded, declared and practically improved* (London, 1681).
A discourse of the work of the Holy Spirit in prayer (1682)	*A discourse of the work of the Holy Spirit in prayer. With a brief enquiry into the nature and use of mental prayer and forms* (London, 1682).
A brief and impartial account of the nature of the Protestant religion (1682)	*A brief and impartial account of the nature of the Protestant religion: Its present state in the world, its strength and weakness, with the ways and indications of the ruine or continuance of its publick national profession. By a Protestant* (London, 1682).

The chamber of imagery in the Church of Rome laid open (1683)	*The chamber of imagery in the Church of Rome laid open. In A continuation of morning exercises questions and cases of conscience, practically resolved by sundry ministers* (London, 1683).
Meditations and discourses on the glory of Christ (1684)	*Meditations and discourses on the glory of Christ, in his person, office, and grace, with the differences between faith and sight. Applied unto the use of them that believe* (London, 1684).
Hebrews (1684)	*A continuation of the exposition of the Epistle of Paul the Apostle to the Hebrews viz, on the eleventh, twelfth & thirteenth chapters, compleating that elaborate work: wherein, together with the explication of the text and context: the efficacy and operation of faith in them that are justified, with respect unto constancy in their profession in times of persecution: several special duties, necessary unto a due compliance with an exhortation unto constancy and perseverance: a cogent argument to the same purpose taken from a comparison between the two states, of the law and the Gospel; with their original, nature, and effects: the reasons for abolishing the mosaical ceremonies drawn from the necessity of one altar and sacrifice, and the nature of the Christian's altar and sacrifice: are declared, explained and confirmed. With an index of the Scriptures explained in this volume: as also a table of the principal matters therein contained. Together with a table to the third volume, preceding this: and an index of Scriptures explained in the same. By the late eminent and faithful servant of Jesus Christ, John Owen, D.D* (London, 1684).
Bibliotheca Oweniana (1684)	*Bibliotheca Oweniana, sive catalogus librorum plurimus facultatibus insignium, instructissimae bibliothecae Rev. Doct. Vir. D. Joan Oweni, (quondam Vice-Cancellarii & Decani Edis-Christi in Academia Oxoniensi) nuperrimè defuncti, cum variis manuscriptis Grecis, Latinis &c. propria manu doct. patric. junii aliorumq conscriptis, quorum auctio habebitur Londini apud domum auctionariam ex adverso Nigri Cygni, in vico vulgò dicto Ave-Mary-Lane, propè Ludgate-Street, vicesimo sexto die Maii, 1684*, ed. Edward Millington (London, 1684).
A treatise of the dominion of sin and grace (1688)	*A treatise of the dominion of sin and grace. Wherein sin's reign is discovered, in whom it is, and in whom it is not. How the law supports it, how grace delivers from it, by setting up its dominion in the heart* (London, 1688).
The true nature of a Gospel church and its government (1689)	*The true nature of a Gospel church and its government: Wherein these following particulars are distinctly handled. I. The subject matter of the church. II. The formal cause of a particular church. III. Of the polity, rule or discipline of the church in general. IV. The officers of the church. V. The duty of pastors of churches. VI. The office of teachers in the church. VII. Of the rule of the church, or of ruling elders. VIII. The nature of church polity or rule, with the duty of elders. IX. Of deacons. X. Of excommunication. XI. Of the communion of churches. The publishing whereof was mentioned by the author in his Answer to the unreasonableness of separation* (London, 1689).

Seasonable words for English Protestants (1690)	*Seasonable words for English Protestants. A sermon, from Jer. 51.5. Setting forth, 1. When a land is filled with sin? 2. What evidences we have that England is not forsaken yet by God? And 3. What is required of us, that we may not be given up to destruction* (London, 1690).
Meditations and discourses concerning the glory of Christ (1691)	*Meditations and discourses concerning the glory of Christ applyed unto unconverted sinners, and saints under spiritual decayes: in two chapters, from John XVII, xxiv* (London, 1691).
A guide to church-fellowship and order (1692)	*A guide to church-fellowship and order. According to the Gospel-institution: Wherein these following particulars are distinctly handled: I. The necessity of believers to joyn themselves in church-order, II. The subject matter of the church, III. The continuation of a church-state, and of the administration of evangelical ordinances of worship, briefly vindicated, IV. What sort of churches the disciples of Christ may and ought to joyn themselves unto as unto entire communion* (London, 1692).
Two discourses concerning the Holy Spirit, and his work (1693)	*Two discourses concerning the Holy Spirit, and his work. The one, of the Spirit as a comforter. The other, as He is the author of spiritual gifts. In the former discourse these particulars are distinctly handled. Chap. I. The Holy Ghost the comforter and advocate of the church. Chap. II. General adjuncts or properties of the office of a comforter. Chap. III. Unto whom the Holy Spirit is a comforter. Chap. IV. Of the inhabitation of the Spirit. Chap. V. Actings of the Spirit as a comforter. How he is an unction. Chap. VI. The Spirit a seal, and how. Chap. VII The Spirit an earnest, and how* (London, 1693).
Gospel grounds and evidences of the faith of God's elect (1695)	*Gospel grounds and evidences of the faith of God's elect: Shewing, I. The nature of true saving faith, in securing of the spiritual comfort of believers in this life, is of the highest importance, II. The way wherein true faith doth evidence itself in the soul and consciences of believers, unto their supportment and comfort, under all their conflicts with sin, in all their tryals and temptations, III. Faith will evidence it self, by a diligent, constant endeavour to keep it self and all grace in due exercise, in all ordinances of divine worship, private and publick, IV. A peculiar way whereby true faith will evidence it self, by bringing the soul into a state of repentance* (London, 1695).
An answer unto two questions (1720)	*An answer unto two questions: by the late judicious John Owen, D.D. With Twelve arguments against any conformity to worship, not of divine institution* (London, 1720).

Seventeen sermons (1720)	*Seventeen sermons preach'd by the late Reverend and learned John Owen, D. D. Sometime vice-chancellor of the University of Oxford, and dean of Christ-Church. Being all the sermons of his that ever were printed: With the dedications preceding each sermon.* 2 volumes (London, 1720).
A complete collection of the sermons of the Reverend and learned John Owen (1721)	*A complete collection of the sermons of the Reverend and learned John Owen, D.D. Formerly published: with an addition of many others never before printed. Also several valuable tracts, now first published from manuscripts: and some others, which were very scarce. To which are added his Latin Orations, whilst vicechancellor of Oxford, taken from his own copies. And to the whole are prefix'd memoirs of his life: some letters written by him upon special occasions: and his funeral sermon, preach'd by Mr. David Clarkson* (London, 1721).
The works of the late Reverend and learned John Owen (1721)	*The works of the late Reverend and learned John Owen, D.D. Sometime vice-chancellor of the University of Oxford, and dean of Christ-Church: Containing several scarce and valuable discourses, (viz.) I. A declaration of the glorious mystery of the person of Christ, God and man. II. Of communion with God the Father, Son, and Holy Ghost. III. Of in-dwelling sin in believers. IV. Of temptation; the nature and power of it. V. Of mortification of sin in believers. VI. Of the death of Christ, the price he paid, and purchase he made. With a display of Arminianism. First published in the Doctor's life-time; and now collected together in one volume; being very useful for families. To which is prefixed the doctor's effigies curiously engraven. Recommended by several Learned and Judicious Divines* (London, 1721).
Thirteen sermons (1756)	*Thirteen sermons preached on various occasions. By the Reverend and learned John Owen, D.D. Of the last Age. Never Before Printed* (London, 1756).
Twenty-five discourses suitable to the Lord's Supper (1760)	*Twenty-five discourses suitable to the Lord's Supper, delivered just before the administration of that sacred ordinance* (London, 1760).
Hebrews (1790)	*An exposition of the epistle to the Hebrews; with the preliminary exercitations, by John Owen, D. D., revised and abridged, with a full and interesting life of the author*, 4 vols., ed. Edward Williams (London, 1790).
Hebrews (1812)	*An exposition of the epistle to the Hebrews, with the preliminary exercitations*, 7 vols., ed. George Wright (Edinburgh, 1812–14).
Works (1826)	*The works of John Owen*, 21 vols., ed. Thomas Russell (London: Paternoster, 1826).

Evangelical theology (1837)	*Evangelical theology: A translation of the sixth book of Dr. Owen's Latin work entitled* Theologoumena, trans. John Craig (Edinburgh, 1837).
Works (1850)	*The works of John Owen*, 24 vols., ed. William H. Goold (London, 1850–55).
Works (1965 or 1991)	*The works of John Owen*, 16 vols., ed. William H. Goold (Edinburgh: Banner of Truth, vols. 1–16 in 1965; and vols. 17–23 [on Hebrews] in 1991).
The correspondence of John Owen	*The correspondence of John Owen (1616–1683): With an account of his life and work*, ed. Peter Toon (Cambridge: James Clarke, 1970).
The Oxford orations	*The Oxford orations of Dr. John Owen*, ed. Peter Toon (Cornwall: Gospel Communications, 1971).
Biblical theology	*Biblical theology: The history of theology from Adam to Christ*, trans. Stephen P. Westcott (Morgan, PA: Soli Deo Gloria, 1994).

****

One aim of this handbook is to standardize abbreviations and citations for Owen's writings. All citations to Owen's writings are first given in their original seventeenth-century form (with the date of the primary source in parenthesis) followed by the corresponding reference in the standard 24-volume Goold edition of Owen's works (1850–5). Volumes 1–17 in the Goold edition include Owen's general works, while volumes 18–24 contain Owen's commentary on Hebrews. References to this edition are given as *Works* (1850), with only the first year of publication given in parenthesis, representing the entire series. However, references to the Goold edition in secondary literature are often complicated due to the Banner of Truth Trust's reprinting, reordering and renumbering certain volumes of the original Goold edition. Due to the omission of Owen's Latin works in volumes 16 and 17 of the Goold edition, the Banner reprint consolidated the English works in both these volumes into a newly arranged volume 16. As a result, the Banner edition also renumbered the Hebrews volumes but preserved the original pagination of the Goold edition. Therefore, volumes 18–24 of the Goold edition correspond to volumes 17–23 in the Banner edition. Throughout the handbook, volumes 1–16 in the Banner edition are given as *Works* (1965), while volumes 17–23 of the Banner edition are given as *Works* (1991) – once again with only the first year of publication given in parenthesis. The relationship between the Goold and Banner editions can be seen as follows:

Goold edition	Banner edition
Volumes 1–17 of *Works* (1850) = Owen's general works, including his Latin writings in volumes 16 and 17.	Volumes 1–16 of *Works* (1965) = Owen's general works, excluding Owen's Latin writings and with a newly arranged volume 16. However, volumes 1–15 in the Banner edition are an exact reprint of the Goold edition.
Volumes 18–24 of *Works* (1850) = Owen's commentary on Hebrews.	Volumes 17–23 of *Works* (1991) = Owen's commentary on Hebrews. Although the volumes have been renumbered, the contents are an exact reprint of the Goold edition.

Here are examples of how these citations will be used in the handbook:

- Owen, Χριστολογια (1679), 107–11; *Works* (1850), 1:100–3.
- Owen, Χριστολογια (1679), 107–11; *Works* (1965), 1:100–3.
- Owen, Θεολογουμενα παντοδαπα (1661), 128 (lib. 2, cap. 1); *Works* (1850), 17:135 (2.1.4).
- Owen, *Hebrews* (1668), 86 (1.8.1); *Works* (1850), 18:142.
- Owen, *Hebrews* (1668), 86 (1.8.1); *Works* (1991), 17:142.

CHAPTER 1

Introduction

CRAWFORD GRIBBEN AND JOHN W. TWEEDDALE

Over the last two decades, John Owen (1616–83) has become one of the most widely discussed English theologians, and perhaps the most widely read theologian of the seventeenth century. After his death, his work was never forgotten, even if it was not rapidly gathered into a standard edition, like *The works of Thomas Goodwin* (1681) and those of many other Puritans and dissenters, examples of which appeared regularly into the early eighteenth century. While some of Owen's works faded into obscurity, others were regularly reprinted through the eighteenth and nineteenth centuries, with several of his titles on communion with God and sanctification becoming evangelical classics, and being recommended by such respected figures as John Wesley and William Wilberforce.[1] Owen's status as a theologian of choice was marked by the publication of two editions of his works in the nineteenth century. The first, edited by Thomas Russell, appeared in twenty-one volumes (1826), although Russell omitted some of Owen's works, including his massive commentary on Hebrews. Several decades later, the Scottish Reformed Presbyterian minister William H. Goold oversaw a much more ambitious attempt to publish what almost amounted to Owen's complete works, including many, but not all, of the auditors' notes on his preaching that remained in manuscript (1850–5). Goold's editorial practices, which modernized Owen's syntax, reflected those of his time, but they continue to serve modern readers. Readers still tend to access Owen through the Banner of Truth reprint of the Goold edition (1965, 1991),

---

[1] Gribben, 'Becoming John Owen: The making of an evangelical reputation', 311–25.

which itself took liberties in re-arranging his material between volumes and in omitting, for example, Goold's text of Θεολογουμενα παντοδαπα: Sive de natura, ortu, progressu, et studio veræ theologiæ (1661), arguably one of Owen's most important works. Stephen P. Westcott published an accessible translation of Θεολογουμενα παντοδαπα as *Biblical theology* (1994), putting into his debt a generation of readers who lack the linguistic competencies that Owen took for granted. The recent decision by Crossway to publish a new edition of Owen's works, in updated English, with a more fully comprehensive critical apparatus, and with new translations of the Latin material, is a signal of the continuing popular appeal of the so-called Atlas of Independency[2] of the increasingly sophisticated and ambitious scholarly work that seeks to explain his achievements, and of a widely shared concern that his often cumbersome seventeenth-century prose continues to be difficult. But even the Crossway edition will be incomplete: a large number of manuscript texts of Owen's preaching that remain in manuscript in Dr Williams's Library, London, are likely to remain unpublished.

Since the 1970s, Owen's reputation has grown among pious readers at the same time as his work has attracted increasing scholarly attention inside communities of religious readers and in the university at large. While several doctoral dissertations emerged in both the United States and Britain throughout the twentieth century, Sarah Cook's 'A political biography of a religious Independent: John Owen, 1616–1683' (1972), written at Harvard University, stands out for situating Owen's life in his political activity as a leading Independent minister. A growing number of monographs have been published by leading academic presses to address Owen's historical contexts and theological conclusions. Moving beyond older biographical accounts, Peter Toon advanced studies on Owen with his edited collection of *The correspondence of John Owen* (1970), a translation of *The Oxford orations of Dr. John Owen* (1971) and his critical biography *God's statesman: The life and work of John Owen* (1971). For understanding the shape of Owen's thought, Sinclair B. Ferguson's *John Owen on the Christian life* (1987), which popularized his doctoral thesis, introduced Owen's theological and pastoral insights to a broader audience. One of the most important early interventions was the discussion of Owen that appeared in Christopher Hill's *Experiences of defeat: Milton and some contemporaries* (1984). But the recovery of interest in Owen's work in the 1990s was more obviously driven by the methods of historical theology than by Hill's distinctive brand of social history. Most of the monographs published on Owen's work during this period investigated the significance of his ideas, situating his

---

[2]This phrase was originally used by George Vernon, a critic of Owen's, in *A letter to a friend concerning some of Dr. Owens principles and practices* (1670), 36; cf. Wood, *Athenae Oxonienses* (1692), 556.

conclusions in patristic, medieval or early modern theological contexts. Alan C. Clifford analysed Owen's soteriology in *Atonement and justification: English evangelical theology, 1640–1790* (1990), which was the subject of significant criticism in several books that drew upon the research of Richard A. Muller and considered the place of Owen within the so-called Calvin and the Calvinists debate. The trend of evaluating Owen within his theological contexts markedly increased after the appearance of Carl R. Trueman's *The claims of truth: John Owen's trinitarian theology* (1998), Sebastian Rehnman's *Divine discourse: The theological methodology of John Owen* (2002), Trueman's *John Owen: Reformed Catholic, Renaissance man* (2007), which appeared in Ashgate's 'Great Theologians' series, and Alan Spence's *Inspiration and incarnation: The coherence of Christology in John Owen* (2007), among several others.[3] The work of these historical-theological pioneers was most effectively consolidated by *The Ashgate research companion to John Owen's theology* (2012), which did more than anything else to underscore Owen's status as a subject of academic enquiry, and, as the title suggests, to emphasize that this enquiry was focused on theological ideas. However, since the publication of the Ashgate companion, studies of Owen have begun to shift focus. Owen scholars continue to publish distinguished work in the field of historical theology, with notable titles including Christopher Cleveland's *Thomism in John Owen* (2013), Ryan M. McGraw's *A heavenly directory: Trinitarian piety, public worship and a reassessment of John Owen's theology* (2014), Edwin E. M. Tay's *The priesthood of Christ: Atonement in the theology of John Owen* (2014), Andrew M. Leslie's *The light of grace: John Owen on the authority of Scripture and the Christian faith* (2015) and McGraw's *John Owen: Trajectories in Reformed Orthodox theology* (2017). Likewise, the collection of essays on *John Owen between orthodoxy and modernity* (2019) capture the thrust of many of these lines of inquiry and rightfully place Owen as a man who not only represents the 'high Calvinism' of the post-Reformation but also embodies aspects of the early modern era. Along these lines, other scholars have been pushing the field in the direction of the social history of ideas, by considering Owen's life and work in contexts outside the world of Reformed dogmatics, with notable titles including Tim Cooper's ground-breaking work on *John Owen, Richard Baxter and the formation of Nonconformity* (2011), Crawford Gribben's *John Owen and English Puritanism: Experiences of defeat* (2016), Martyn C. Cowan's *John Owen and the civil war apocalypse: Preaching, prophecy, and politics* (2017) and John W. Tweeddale's *John Owen and Hebrews: The foundation of biblical interpretation* (2019).

---

[3]For more comprehensive analysis of this literature, see Cooper, 'John Owen unleashed: Almost', 226–42; Gribben, *John Owen and English Puritanism*, 4–11; Kapic, 'Communion with God', 12–48; Tweeddale, *John Owen and Hebrews*, 4–22. See also Kapic's chapter in this volume.

The increasing interest of academic publishers in Owen's work reflects his status within the academy. Many universities teach courses on the mid-seventeenth-century British and Irish civil wars, on which Owen features as the most significant architect of the Cromwellian religious settlement. Some major evangelical seminaries have developed courses on Owen's theology, including Dallas Theological Seminary, Greenville Presbyterian Theological Seminary, Puritan Reformed Theological Seminary, Reformed Theological Seminary and Westminster Theological Seminary. The production of PhD theses on Owen continues apace. And there are signs that this interest is increasing. Owen's position as a subject of university and seminary teaching is now as assured as is his wider public appeal. In fact, the audience for Owen's work may never have been larger, and, with the publication of a new edition of his work as well as editions of key texts in modernized English, this audience will likely only increase in size.

By combining introductions to some of Owen's most significant publications with considerations of new scholarly themes in his work, this volume aims to move beyond the Ashgate companion to become the most obvious reference for teachers and general readers of his work. This volume both documents the existing scholarly consensus in and sets a new scholarly agenda for Owen studies. It draws together many of the best contributors from the emerging historical-theological and social-historical traditions in Owen scholarship. Its contributors are at different career stages, but each has already made a significant intervention within Owen studies, and several are among the most important voices in their respective fields. Collecting their work, this volume represents the variety of scholarly approaches to the study of Owen's work, and offers the fullest and most rounded account of the most studied theologian of the seventeenth century.

As its title suggests, this handbook has been designed to address the needs of new and established readers of Owen's work. New readers of his work will be guided into his canon by the contextual and thematic discussions in Part I and by the introductions to major works in Part II. More established readers of Owen will find that the material in Part I will stimulate new research agendas. The chapters in this section will defamiliarize some well-established contexts, such as Owen's relationship to the world of Reformed dogmatics. Other contributors will offer entirely new approaches to Owen's achievements – particularly in the chapters on the scientific revolution, education and philosophy. Part III offers agendas for theological professionals and lay readers of Owen, arguing for the importance of his work outside the academy and in the life of the church. These sections will develop as follows.

Part I of the handbook reviews Owen's life and thought and offers new assessments of his intellectual formation, political connections, understanding of preaching, views on education, relationship to the Church of England, theological debates, interaction with the scientific revolution and understanding of philosophy.

Chapters 2 and 3 outline the contours of Owen's biography and theology. They provide a helpful entry point into Owen studies. Michael A. G. Haykin considers Owen as the 'Calvin of England' and notes that his writings reflect many common Puritan emphases such as spiritual conversion, assurance of faith, life in the Spirit, biblical authority and orthodox Calvinism. This chapter sketches Owen's life against the backdrop of one of the most tumultuous eras in British history. It shows that he was not only a theologian of the first rank but also a leading nonconformist figure who was deeply involved in the political and ecclesial struggles of his day. In Chapter 3, Ryan M. McGraw treats the scope and character of Owen's work as a theologian, demonstrating that his writings span a variety of literary genres, including theological treatises, biblical commentaries, polemical exchanges, catechisms and sermons. Writing in both Latin and English, and addressing both academic and popular audiences, Owen's theological interests were wide-ranging. McGraw observes that Owen's pastoral and personal concerns led him increasingly to focus on trinitarian, pneumatological and Christological themes. Tracing the chronology of Owen's corpus, this chapter provides a concise but comprehensive overview of Owen's writings.

Building on these themes, Richard A. Muller and Crawford Gribben develop the intellectual and social contexts that give shape to Owen's thought and career. Muller argues that Owen was one of the most sophisticated English thinkers of the seventeenth century, rivalling notable counterparts such as John Davenant or Richard Baxter. This chapter demonstrates that Owen's literary output offers evidence of his awareness of the theological and philosophical tradition and his immersion in the issues of his times. Consistently Reformed or 'Calvinist' in his basic theological views, Owen altered the focus of his work throughout his life, as Muller explains, in response to a series of events, such as the rising and waning tide of English Puritanism; the development of an English version of Arminianism; the widespread distribution of Socinian writings during the Cromwellian era; the impact of new trends in biblical interpretation; and the issues of confessionality and ecclesiology after the restoration of the monarchy. His later writings, particularly after the Restoration, evidence a turn towards matters of Protestant union and fundamental articles of agreement. These themes are picked up in greater detail in Chapter 5.

Gribben makes the important, but overlooked, point that throughout his lifetime of work in church leadership and theological polemic, Owen was deeply engaged in politics. In some senses, this was inevitable, given the politicization of religion during the civil wars. Still, Owen took advantage of the rising fortunes of the Independents and the formation of the English republic to serve as an MP and to build relationships with the hard-liners who fomented the coup that brought down the Cromwellian regime and inadvertently paved the way for the Restoration. As dissenters worked out their relationship to the restored monarchy, Gribben observes that Owen published short-form political polemic that argued for religious toleration, while being associated with anti-government conspiracies, including, in the last months of his life, being arrested on suspicion that he was involved in the 'Rye House' plot against the life of the king and the Duke of York, his likely successor. This chapter shows that Owen's attitude to politics drew upon Reformed resistance theory, among other themes, to propose dangerous solutions to the political difficulties of his co-religionists, sometimes with unexpected results.

The following six chapters present a series of case studies that explore aspects of Owen's career. In Chapter 6, Martyn C. Cowan unpacks the theme of Owen as a preacher and contends that his sermons, while exemplifying the marks of the Puritan homiletical tradition, are best described as a form of prophetic preaching. With over one hundred extant sermons, many of which remain unpublished, Cowan chronicles how Owen preached across five turbulent decades to a wide variety of auditors: elites at Westminster (most notably to the Rump Parliament on the day after the regicide), an occupying Cromwellian army on foreign soil, the University of Oxford and to dissenters gathered in illegal conventicles in Restoration London. Chapter 7 takes up the underdeveloped topic of Owen's views of education. In 1651, shortly after Oliver Cromwell became chancellor of the University of Oxford, Parliament appointed Owen, who had served as one of Cromwell's chaplains, as dean of Christ Church. In the following year, Owen became vice-chancellor. As the senior administrator of the university from 1652 to 1657, Owen emerges as one of the Interregnum's most prominent figures. This leads Eric Newton to assess not only Owen's rise to national prominence but also his unique views on education. In Chapter 8, Lee Gatiss examines Owen's appreciation of the Thirty-nine Articles and other Anglican formularies, his conversion to and defence of Independency in church polity, and the tensions Owen experienced as a Puritan who had been ordained as an Anglican minister. While challenging prevailing notions of Owen's ecclesiology, Gatiss uncovers a theme repeated throughout this handbook, namely, that Owen was more than capable of changing his tactics for advancing the cause of Reformation depending on the prevailing political circumstances of the time.

Next, Paul C. H. Lim focuses on Owen's polemical writings against Arminianism and Socinianism and his defence of affective divinity and scriptural sufficiency, namely the Laudians and the radical Protestants, especially the Quakers. Although Owen's commitment to the main themes of high Calvinism can be seen throughout his career, Lim concentrates on a collection of writings that provide a more contextualized and nuanced understanding of the theological controversies of the day and the polemical vectors that exercised Owen and his co-religionists and antagonists. In Chapter 10, Katherine Calloway assesses for the first time Owen's complicated relationship to scientific reform and traces his connections with such figures as John Wilkins, Henry Stubbe, Thomas Hobbes, Lucy Hutchinson and Robert Boyle. She reveals that while he could downplay the value of the Royal Society, he also had positive relationships with some scientific reformers, emphasized points of theology that were consistent with the empirical method and exhibited a growing appreciation for the value of natural science. This chapter argues that Owen both corroborates and complicates standard accounts of a relationship between English Reformed Protestantism and the rise of natural science. Finally, Paul Helm concludes Part I with a sustained reflection on Owen's use of philosophy. While Owen was a theologian rather than a philosopher, he maintained a critical appreciation of the value of philosophy for theological discourse, seen most clearly in his use of the categories of scholasticism. To illustrate this basic point, Helm focuses his analysis on Owen's anthropology, the doctrine of the Holy Spirit and theological methodology.

Part II considers a small selection of Owen's prolific literary achievements. These chapters introduce a cross-section of well-known and neglected works that span the duration of his career. While McGraw's earlier chapter surveys the Owen canon, these chapters provide contextual expositions of representative works. Many of his other writings deserve similar attention, but these chapters illustrate the value of reading Owen in his own historical and theological contexts.

Chapters 12–14 feature three of Owen's most popular and well-recognized works. Opening this section of the handbook, Christopher Cleveland situates Owen's first book, Θεομαχία αυτεξουσιαστική: or, *A display of Arminianisme* (1643), within contemporary theological debates, including the Remonstrant controversy and the *congregatio de auxiliis* of the Roman Catholic Church. This chapter explains the background of *A display of Arminianisme*, reconstructs the issues with which it engages, considers the sources Owen referenced, summarizes the book's argument and evaluates the strengths and weaknesses of Owen's argumentation. In Chapter 13, Timothy Baylor explores what is perhaps Owen's most famous work, *Salus electorum, sanguis Jesu: or, The death of death in the death of Christ* (1648). Known for its defence of 'limited atonement', the book is significant not only for Owen's construal of an atonement theology but also for beginning a series of debates with Richard Baxter on the nature of the death of Christ. Perhaps more than any of his writings, *The death of death in the death of Christ* illustrates Owen's development as a theologian, as Baylor details Owen's later change of mind from what he argued in this classic work on the question of the relationship of the death of Christ to the nature of the divine will. In Chapter 14, Joel R. Beeke considers one of Owen's most beloved, and probing, devotional treatises. Based on a series of sermons given at the University of Oxford, Owen's *Of the mortification of sinne in believers* (1656) is widely regarded as a classic of Puritan spirituality. In this short work, Beeke shows that Owen sought to combat methods of personal holiness that drew upon Arminian and antinomian ideas, give practical guidance for 'mortifying' sin and outline a Reformed doctrine of sanctification.

The following five chapters review a selection of Owen's post-Restoration works, written in the final years of his life. In 1668, Owen published the first part of what would ultimately become a four-volume commentary on the book of Hebrews, a work that when finished exceeded two million words. John W. Tweeddale challenges older narratives by arguing that the first volume of *Hebrews* not only establishes the trajectory of his overall project but also recasts Owen as a biblical exegete and scholar. This chapter contends that Owen's life, ministry and writings cannot be understood fully apart from his commentary on Hebrews. Next, Andrew M. Leslie evaluates Πνευματολογια: or, A discourse concerning the Holy Spirit (1674), another literary milestone for Owen. This chapter explores how Owen regarded this book as a genuinely original undertaking, and more comprehensive in scope than anything that had been previously written on the subject, which helps explain why one leading contemporary theologian described the work as 'the greatest Reformed treatise on the Spirit'. In Chapter 17, Tim Cooper evaluates a lesser-known work titled *The nature of apostasie* (1676) to shed light on how much of Owen's later writing stems from experiences of personal defeat and failure. Cooper explains how the demise of Reformed Orthodoxy in England created a culture of winners and losers, where Owen provided but one perspective on what he believed to be England's moral and theological decline into apostasy. In Chapter 18, Whitney Gamble-Smith explains that while the doctrine of justification may have been a catalyst for the Protestant Reformation in the sixteenth century, it was in the seventeenth century that debates over the nature, cause and timing of justification grew into a tempest of elaborate arguments. Against this backdrop, she argues that Owen's *The doctrine of justification* (1677) established a benchmark for a Reformed understanding of the doctrine. Finally, Suzanne McDonald expounds upon the last work that Owen brought to publication, *Meditations and discourses on the glory of Christ* (1684). This chapter provides a sketch of Owen's Christology and reflects on the interwoven doctrinal rigour, pastoral heart and passion for discipleship that characterizes much of Owen's corpus, showing that the Christian life of faith, according to Owen, is best understood as a preparation for beholding the glory of Christ by sight in eternity.

Part III reflects on the importance of Owen for today by evaluating ways that Owen scholarship can benefit historians, theologians, biblical scholars, ministers and lay readers. In Chapter 20, Kelly M. Kapic considers the resurgence of interest in Owen that has taken place over the past fifty years. One surprising aspect of this interest is the remarkable breadth of people who read Owen, including scholars, pastors and popular, non-academic audiences. Even when disagreeing with some of Owen's theological or pastoral conclusions, many have come to believe that his insights deserve careful attention. Drawing the handbook to a close, this chapter points to some areas that have been particularly fruitful for contemporary readers of Owen. From his trinitarian theology to his advice on temptation, Owen's contributions remain relevant even centuries after his death. However, as Kapic observes, such enthusiasm is not without dangers, and so some caution is given for further attempts at retrieval.

As this handbook attempts to show, John Owen is one of the most significant figures in seventeenth-century England and the author of several Reformed and evangelical classics. His prolific literary output, pastoral ministry, educational reform at Oxford, political connections in the Cromwellian revolution, support of Nonconformity during the Restoration and experiences of defeat throughout his life make him a subject of both academic and general interest. We hope that this handbook will spark new avenues of research and encourage a new generation to read and study this Puritan divine. However, as editors, our goal for this volume is not merely to inform future interactions with Owen's work. After all, we have learned from our study of Owen that the final end of all Christian activity is the knowledge of God in the face of Jesus Christ (2 Cor. 4:6). It is to that end that we submit this work.

PART I
Owen's contexts

CHAPTER 2

Owen's life

MICHAEL A. G. HAYKIN

'I WOULD GLADLY RELINQUISH ALL MY LEARNING'

Charles II allegedly once asked one of the most learned scholars that he knew why any intelligent person should waste time listening to the sermons of an uneducated tinker and Baptist preacher by the name of John Bunyan (1628–88). 'Could I possess the tinker's abilities for preaching, please your majesty', replied the scholar, 'I would gladly relinquish all my learning'.[1] The scholar's name was John Owen (1616–83), and this small story says a good deal about the man and his character, even if it is apocryphal. His love of preaching and apparent humility reveals a man who was Puritan to the core.[2]

In his day, one of Owen's fellow Puritans called him the 'Calvin of England'.[3] At the outset of the revival of academic and popular interest in Owen's literary corpus in the twentieth century, Roger Nicole described Owen as 'the greatest divine who ever wrote in English', while J. I. Packer regarded him as 'England's foremost bastion and champion of Reformed evangelical orthodoxy'.[4] Despite his theological brilliance, though, Owen's chief interest was not in producing

---

[1] Portions of this essay have appeared in Barrett and Haykin, *Owen and the Christian life*. Used by permission.
[2] For the anecdote, see Thomson, 'Life of Dr. Owen', in *Works* (1965), 1:xcii; Toon, *God's statesman*, 162; Guelzo, 'John Owen, Puritan Pacesetter', 14.
[3] Barnes, *The memoirs of the life of Mr. Ambrose Barnes* (1867), 16; Greaves, 'Owen, John (1616–1683)', *ODNB*, s.v.
[4] Cited in Guelzo, 'John Owen', 14; Packer, *Quest for godliness*, 81.

theological treatises for their own sake but to advance the personal holiness of God's people.[5]

'BRED UP FROM MY INFANCY'

John Owen was born in 1616, the same year that William Shakespeare died. He grew up in an Anglican minister's home in a small village now known as Stadhampton, then called Stadham, about 5 miles southeast of Oxford.[6] His father, Henry Owen, was the pastor of the parish church. The names of three of his brothers have come down to us: his older brother, William, who became the Puritan minister at Remenham, just north of Henley-on-Thames; and his two younger brothers: Philemon, who was killed fighting under Cromwell in Ireland in 1649, and Henry (b. 1599), who fought as a major in the New Model Army of Oliver Cromwell, served as an Irish administrator and MP in the second Protectorate Parliament and was implicated in the Rye House Plot (1683).[7]

Owen seems to have recorded only one direct reference to his childhood years. 'I was bred up from my infancy', he remarked in 1657, 'under the care of my father, who was a Nonconformist [i.e. Puritan] all his daies, & a painful labourer [that is, diligent worker] in the vineyard of the Lord'.[8] If we take as our cue how other Puritans raised their children, we can presume that as a small boy Owen, along with his siblings, would have been taught to pray, read the Bible and obey its commandments. At least once a day, there would have been time set aside for family worship when he would have listened to his father explain a portion of God's Word and pray for their nation, his parishioners and each of his children.[9] It needs noting that this is the only personal remark about his family that Owen makes in any of his published works. There was clearly a profound reticence on Owen's part to open up his life to his readers. As James Moffatt rightly remarked at the turn of the twentieth century: 'Owen never trusts himself to his readers [. . .] Hence his private life and feelings remain for

---

[5]See, for example, Owen, *Of the mortification of sinne in believers* (1656), A4–A5; *Works* (1965), 6:4.
[6]For good accounts of Owen's life, see Toon, *God's statesman*, and Gribben, *John Owen and English Puritanism*. For his theology, see Ferguson, *John Owen on the Christian life*; Trueman, *The claims of truth*; Oliver (ed.), *John Owen*; and Kapic and Jones (ed.), *The Ashgate research companion to John Owen's theology*.
[7]Toon, *God's statesman*, 2; Gribben, *John Owen and English Puritanism*, passim; *History of parliament*, s.v. (forthcoming).
[8]Owen, *A review of the true nature of schisme* (1657), 38; *Works* (1965), 13:224.
[9]This insight about piety in the home and wording are adapted from Toon, *God's statesman*, 2.

the most part a mystery.'[10] In Crawford Gribben's words, he was a 'guarded writer'.[11]

At twelve years of age, Owen was sent by his father to Queen's College, the University of Oxford. Here he obtained his BA on 11 June 1632, when he was sixteen. He went on to study for the MA, which he was awarded on 27 April 1635. Everything seemed to be set for Owen to pursue an academic career. It was not, however, a good time to launch out into the world of academe. The Archbishop of Canterbury, William Laud (1573–1645), had set out to suppress the Puritan movement, which was seen as radical, even revolutionary, by the leadership of the state church. Laud sought to purge Puritans from churches and universities. By 1637 Owen had no alternative but to leave Oxford and to become, along with many other Puritans who refused to conform to the established church, a private chaplain. He eventually found employment in the house of John, Lord Lovelace, a nobleman sympathetic to the Puritan cause. Laud's policies, supported by Charles I (1600–1649), alienated the Puritan cause and pushed Puritans to the point where many of them believed they had no choice but to engage in a civil war against their sovereign. In the early stages of the English Civil War, which broke out in 1642, Lovelace decided to support the king, and Owen, whose sympathies were with Parliament, left his chaplaincy and moved to London.

A 'CLEAR SHINING FROM GOD'

Owen's move to London was providential in several ways. It brought him into contact with some of the leading defenders of the parliamentary cause, Puritan preachers who viewed the struggle between the king and Parliament in terms of the struggle between Christ and Antichrist. Moreover, during these days in London, he had an experience that deeply shaped both his subsequent career and thought. By 1642, Owen was convinced that the final source of authority in religion was Scripture and that the doctrines of orthodox Calvinism were biblical Christianity. But he had yet to experience on a personal level the assurance of his salvation.[12]

Owen found this assurance one Sunday when he decided to go with a cousin to hear Edmund Calamy, the elder (1600–1666), a famous Presbyterian preacher, at St Mary's Church, Aldermanbury. Upon arriving at this church, the visitors were informed that Calamy was not going to preach that morning. Instead, an unknown country preacher was going to fill in for the Presbyterian divine. His

---

[10]Moffatt, *The golden book of John Owen*, 19–20.
[11]Gribben, *John Owen and English Puritanism*, 10.
[12]Toon, *God's statesman*, 12.

cousin urged Owen to go with him to hear Arthur Jackson (c. 1593–1666), another notable Puritan preacher, at nearby St Michael's. But Owen decided to remain at St Mary's, where the preacher spoke from Mt. 8.26 (Geneva Bible): 'Why are ye fearful, O ye of little faith?' The sermon was a turning point in Owen's life. Through the preacher's words, Owen sensed God speaking to him and removing his doubts and fears as to whether he was truly regenerate.[13]

Peter Toon suggests that the impact of this spiritual experience for Owen cannot be overestimated. It gave Owen a deep, inner conviction that he was indeed a child of God and chosen in Christ before the foundation of the world, that God loved him and had a loving purpose for his life and that this God was the true and living God. In practical terms, it meant a lifelong interest in the work of God the Holy Spirit that would issue thirty years later in his monumental study of the Holy Spirit, Πνευματολογια: or, A discourse concerning the Holy Spirit (1674).[14] As he later reflected: 'Cleare shining from God, muste be at the bottome of deepe labouring with God.'[15]

'WHERE IS THE GOD OF MARSTON MOOR, AND THE GOD OF NASEBY?'

In 1643 Owen was offered the pastorate in the village of Fordham, 6 miles or so northwest of Colchester in Essex. Owen was here till 1646, when he became the minister of the church at the market town of Coggeshall, some 5 miles to the south. Here, as many as 2,000 people would fill the church each Lord's Day to hear Owen preach.[16]

It is noteworthy that this change in pastorates began an ecclesiological shift towards Congregationalism. Up to this point, Owen had been Presbyterian in his understanding of church government. However, Owen began to change his mind after reading *The keyes of the kingdom of heaven* (1644), by John Cotton (1584–1652), and by 1648 he was a confirmed Congregationalist. It was also at Coggeshall that he wrote the classic work on particular redemption, *Salus electorum, sanguis Jesu: or, The death of death in the death of Christ* (1648).[17] The backdrop for these early years of Owen's pastoral ministry was the English Civil War. However, it needs to be noted that little of the early fighting took place in Essex or remotely near Coggeshall; hence, at this point, Owen saw little of the bloody horrors of conflict.[18]

---

[13]Toon, *God's statesman*, 12–13.
[14]See discussion in Toon, *God's statesman*, 13.
[15]Owen, *Eben-ezer* (1648), 15; *Works* (1965), 8:90.
[16]Oliver, 'John Owen (1616–1683): His life and times', 16.
[17]For a study of this work, see Macleod, 'John Owen and *The death of death*', 70–87.
[18]Cooper, 'Why did Richard Baxter and John Owen diverge?' 507–11.

During these tumultuous days, Owen identified himself with the Parliamentary cause. Like others who ardently supported Parliament in their struggle against the king, Owen would look back on some of the decisive parliamentary victories in the mid-1640s as a clear vindication of their cause by God. As he once stated, 'Where is the God of Marstone-Moor, and the God of Naseby, is an acceptable expostulation in a gloomy day.'[19] He also developed a friendship with the rising military figure Oliver Cromwell and was invited to preach before Parliament on several occasions. By late 1648 some of the parliamentary army officers had begun to urge that Charles I be brought to trial on charges of treason since he had fought against his own people and Parliament. Charles was accordingly put on trial in January 1649. By the end of that month, a small and unrepresentative cadre of judges, sitting in an unconstitutional court, had found him guilty and sentenced their king to death. On 31 January, the day following the public execution of the king, Owen was asked to preach before Parliament.

Owen based his sermon on Jeremiah 15 and used the occasion to urge the Members of Parliament, now the de facto rulers of England, that they must remove from the nation all traces of false worship and superstition and wholeheartedly establish a religion based on Scripture alone. This was the only way for them to obtain God's favour. Owen made no direct reference to the events of the previous day, nor did he mention, at least in the version of his sermon that has come down to us, the name of the king. Nevertheless, his hearers and later readers would have been easily able to deduce from his use of the Old Testament how he viewed the religious policy and end of Charles. Working from the story of the wicked king Manasseh that is recorded in 2 Kings 21, and with cross-references to Jeremiah 15, Owen argued that the leading cause for God's judgements upon the Jewish people had been such abominations as idolatry and superstition, tyranny and cruelty. He then pointed to various similarities between the conditions of ancient Judah and the England of his day. At the heart of the sermon was a call to Parliament to establish a Reformed style of worship, disseminate biblical Christianity, uphold national righteousness and avoid oppression. He assured those who heard him that day that God's promise of protection to Jeremiah was also applicable to all who in every age stood firmly for justice and mercy.[20]

'EMINENT PROVIDENCES'

Later that same year, Owen accompanied Cromwell on his campaign in Ireland, where Owen remained from August 1649 until February 1650. Though ill for

---

[19] Owen, *Eben-ezer* (1648), 13; *Works* (1965), 8:88.
[20] Owen, *Righteous zeal encouraged by divine protection* (1649); *Works* (1965), 8:133–62; Toon, *God's statesman*, 33–4.

much of this time, he frequently preached to 'a numerous multitude, of as thirsting a People after the Gospel as ever yet I conversed withal'.[21] When he returned to England the following year, he confessed that 'the tears and cries of the inhabitants of Dublin after the manifestations of Christ are ever in my view'. Accordingly, he sought to convince Parliament of the spiritual need of this land and asked:

> How is it that Jesus Christ, is in Ireland only as a Lyon stayning all his garments with the bloud of his Enemies? and none to hold him out as a Lamb sprinkled with his own bloud to his friends? Is it the Sovereignty and Interest of England that is alone to be there transacted? For my part, I see no further into the MYSTERY of these things, but that I could heartily rejoyce, That Innocent blood being expiated, the Irish might enjoy Ireland so long as the Moon endureth, so that Jesus Christ might possess the Irish. I would there were for the present, one Gospel preacher, for every Walled Town in the English possession in IRELAND [. . .] If they were in the dark, and loved to have it so, it might something close a door upon the bowels of our compassion; but they cry out of their darkness, and are ready to follow every one whosoever, to have a Candle. If their being Gospelless, move not our hearts, it is hoped, Their importunate Cryes will disquiet our Rest: and wrest help, as a Beggar doth an Alms.[22]

Although Owen's pleas were heeded and this period saw the establishment of a number of Puritan congregations – both Congregationalist and Baptist – in Ireland, Crawford Gribben has shown that the Cromwellian reformation in Ireland that Owen envisioned was often marked by a variety of theological debates and was 'a profoundly dividing affair'.[23]

By the early 1650s, Owen had become one of Cromwell's leading advisors, especially in national ecclesiastical affairs. There is little doubt that Owen was a firm supporter of Cromwell in this period. As Owen told him on one occasion in 1654, for example: 'The Series and Chaine of eminent providences, whereby you have been carried on, and protected in all the hazardous worke of your Generation, which your God hath called you unto, is evident to all.'[24] Three years later, though, when Cromwell was urged to become the monarch of England, Owen was among those who opposed this move. As it turned out, Cromwell did not accept the crown. But Owen's friendship with Cromwell

---

[21]Owen, *Of the death of Christ* (1650), 97; *Works* (1965), 10:479.
[22]Owen, *The steadfastness of the promises, and the sinfulness of staggering* (1650), 42–4; *Works* (1965), 8:235–6.
[23]Gribben, *God's Irishmen*, 3, 11; Gribben, *The Irish Puritans*, 91–115.
[24]Owen, *The doctrine of the saints perseverance* (1654), n.p.; *Works* (1965), 11:5.

had been damaged, and in the final years of Cromwell's life – he died in 1658 – the two men were nowhere near as close as they had been.[25] Undoubtedly, this caused Owen distress, since he had once viewed Cromwell with enormous admiration. However, the rupture in his friendship with Cromwell probably reinforced a tendency in Owen's character to be self-reliant.[26]

Cromwell had appointed Owen as vice-chancellor of the University of Oxford in 1652. From this position Owen helped to re-assemble the faculty, who had been dispersed by the war, and to put the university back on its feet. He also had numerous opportunities to preach to the students at Oxford. Two important works on holiness came out of his preaching during this period. *Of temptation*, first published in 1658, was essentially an exposition of Mt. 26.4. It analysed the way in which believers fall into sin. A second work, *The mortification of sin in believers* (1656), was in some ways the richest of all of Owen's treatises on this subject. It was based on Rom. 8.13 and laid out a strategy for fighting indwelling sin and warding off temptation. Owen emphasized that in the fight against sin the Holy Spirit employs all of our human powers. In sanctifying us, Owen insisted, the Spirit works

> in us, and upon us, as we are fit to be wrought in, and upon, that is, so as to preserve our own liberty, and free Obedience. He works upon our Understandings, Wills, Consciences, and Affections, agreeably to their own Natures; He works in us, and with us, not against us, or without us; so that his Assistance is an Encouragement as to the facilitating of the Work, and no Occasion of neglect as to the work itself.[27]

Not without reason did Owen describe the Spirit in another place as 'the great Beautifier of souls'.[28]

'A SPIRIT OF BONDAGE'

Owen's pneumatology in Oxford was also shaped by encounters with Quakers. In June 1654, Elizabeth Fletcher (*c.* 1638–58) and Elizabeth Leavens (died 1665), two Quakers from Kendal, Westmoreland, visited Oxford, the first to

---

[25] Oliver, 'John Owen (1616–1683)', 26; Toon, *God's statesman*, 97–101.
[26] See the remarks on Owen's friendships by Moffatt, *Golden book of John Owen*, 19–20, and Cooper, 'Owen's personality: The man behind the theology', 215–26.
[27] Owen, *The mortification of sin in believers* (1656), 34; *Works* (1965), 6:20. See also the comments of Packer, '"Keswick" and the Reformed doctrine of sanctification', 156.
[28] Owen, *Indwelling sin* (1668), 58; *Works* (1965), 6:188. For further discussion of this area of Owen's teaching, see Haykin, 'The great beautifier of souls', 18–22.

bring their message to the university town.²⁹ They sought to warn students about the ungodly nature of academia and to convince them that their real need was not intellectual illumination but the inner light given by the Holy Spirit. Their message, though, fell largely on deaf ears. Elizabeth Fletcher felt led by God to resort to a more dramatic testimony to arrest the students' attention. She stripped off her clothing and walked semi-naked through the streets of Oxford as 'a signe against the Hippocriticall profession they then made there, being then Presbetereans & Independants, which profession she told them the Lord would strip them of, so that their Nakedness should appear'.³⁰ Fletcher's 'going naked as a sign', a practice not uncommon among the early Quakers, sparked a hostile reaction among the students.³¹ Some of the students seized her and her companion, dragged them through a miry ditch and then half-drowned them under the water pump on the grounds of St John's College. At some point, Fletcher was also either thrown over a gravestone or pushed into an open grave, sustaining injuries that plagued her for the rest of her short life.

It appears, though, that this ordeal did little to dampen the spirits of the two women. The following Sunday, they visited an Oxford church, where they interrupted the service in order to give a divine warning to the congregation. This time they were arrested and imprisoned in the Bocardo prison. The following day, Owen, who was responsible for discipline within the university as vice-chancellor, accused the two Quakers of blaspheming the Holy Spirit and profaning the Scriptures. Convinced that if the women's behaviour were left unpunished it would incite disorder in the university, he ordered the women to be whipped and expelled from the town.

Two years later, Owen had another memorable encounter with the Quakers. This time it was a theological debate in Whitehall Palace with the man who would be viewed as the foremost figure in the seventeenth-century British Quaker community, George Fox (1624–91). Fox later recounted what transpired when he and another Quaker, Edward Pyott (died 1670), visited Cromwell.

> Edward Pyott and I went to Whitehall after a time and when we came before him [i.e. Cromwell] there was one Dr. John Owen, Vice-Chancellor of Oxford with him: so we was moved to speak to Oliver Cromwell concerning

---

[29] For brief biographical sketches of these two women, see Greaves, 'Fletcher, Elizabeth', 1:292, and Ludlow, 'Leavens, Elizabeth', 2:182. For the following account of their visit to Oxford, see Sewel, *The history of the rise, increase and progress of the Christian people called Quakers*, 1:120–1, and Toon, *God's statesman*, 76.
[30] Carroll, 'Early Quakers and "going naked as a sign"', 80.
[31] For two excellent studies of this phenomenon, see Carroll, 'Going naked as a sign', 69–87, and Bauman, *Let your words be few*, 84–94. See also the related studies by Carroll, 'Sackcloth and ashes and other signs and wonders', 314–25; 'Quaker attitudes towards sign and wonders', 70–84.

the sufferings of Friends and laid them before him and turned him to the light of Christ who had enlightened every man that cometh into the world: and he said it was a natural light and we showed him the contrary and how it was divine and spiritual from Christ the spiritual and heavenly man, which was called the life in Christ, the Word and the light in us. And the power of the Lord God riz in me, and I was moved to bid him lay down his crown at the feet of Jesus. Several times I spoke to him to the same effect, and I was standing by the table; and he came and sat upon the table's side by me and said he would be as high as I was. And so he continued speaking against the light of Christ Jesus.[32]

Owen admitted that some 'Edification' could be found in the 'silent [worship] Meetings' of the Quakers.[33] On the whole, however, he saw them as 'poor deluded souls'.[34] Their teaching about the inner light was an attack on the work and person of the Holy Spirit, a 'pretended light', and possibly even 'a dark Product of Satan'.[35] When they pointed to the trembling and quaking that sometimes gripped men and women in their meetings as evidence of the Spirit's powerful presence, Owen saw only 'a Spirit of bondage' that threw them 'into an unsonlike frame'.[36] At the heart of the errors of the Quakers, Owen felt, was their failure to grasp the trinitarian nature of the work of redemption. As he wrote in 1674, 'Convince any of them of the Doctrine of the Trinity, and all the rest of their Imaginations vanish into Smoak.'[37] These encounters led to Owen's most concentrated attack on the Quakers in his *Pro Sacris Scripturis*, which was written in 1658.[38] In his biography of the Congregationalist theologian, Peter Toon suggests that Owen's writing of the treatise in Latin was a deliberate affirmation of traditional learning in the face of the Quakers' denigration of university education.[39] Toon may well be right, for Owen devoted a substantial portion of the second chapter of this treatise to a defence of sound exegesis and exegetical techniques, many of which would be learned in the university environment of the theological college.

Then Owen's world began to change. Oliver Cromwell died in September of 1658 and the 'rule of the saints', as some called it, began to fall apart. In the autumn of that year, Owen, now a key leader among the Congregationalists,

---

[32]Fox, *The journal of George Fox*, ed. Nickalls, 274–5.
[33]Owen, *A discourse of the work of the Holy Spirit in prayer* (1682), 194; *Works* (1965), 4:331.
[34]Owen, Πνευματολογια (1674), 45; *Works* (1965), 3:66.
[35]Owen, Πνευματολογια (1674), 19; *Works* (1965), 3:36–7.
[36]Owen, *Of communion with God* (1657), 300; *Works* (1965), 2:258.
[37]Owen, Πνευματολογια (1674), 45; *Works* (1965), 3:66.
[38]For a study of Owen's doctrine of the relationship of Scripture and the Spirit, see Campbell, 'John Owen's rule and guide'.
[39]Toon, *God's statesman*, 76, n.4.

played a vital role in drawing up what is known as the Savoy Declaration (1658), which would give the Congregationalist churches fortitude for the difficult days ahead. Only a few days after Cromwell's death, Owen met with around 200 other Congregationalist leaders, including men like Thomas Goodwin (1600–80), Philip Nye (*c.* 1596–1672) and William Bridge (*c.* 1600–71), in the chapel of the old Savoy Palace in London. One of the outcomes of this synod was a recommendation to revise the Westminster Confession of Faith for the Congregationalist churches. The lengthy preface that came before the Savoy Declaration – which has often been ascribed to Owen, but instead appears to have been written by Philip Nye and Thomas Goodwin[40] – argued that

> The Spirit of Christ is in himself too *free*, great and generous a Spirit, to suffer himself to be used by any human arm, to whip men into belief; he drives not, but *gently leads into all truth*, and *persuades* men to *dwell in the tents* of *like precious faith*; which would lose of its preciousness and value, if that sparkle of freeness shone not in it.[41]

The following year Owen preached again before Parliament. But the times were changing, and this proved to be the last of such occasions.

'LABOUR AFTER SPIRITUAL REVIVALS'

Within months of Cromwell's death, anarchic political conditions had so gripped the republic that one of Cromwell's generals, George Monck (1608–70), decided that the monarchy needed to be restored. At the head of the regiment he had created in the last years of the English Civil Wars, which came to be known as the Coldstream Guards, Monck entered London in February 1660 and began the political process that led to the restoration of the monarchy in the person of Charles II. Those who came to power with Charles were determined that those whom they associated with the republican regime would never again hold the reins of political authority or exercise cultural influence. During the early years of Charles's reign, the Puritan cause was savagely persecuted. After the Act of Uniformity in 1662, which required all religious worship to be according to the letter of the Book of Common Prayer, and other legislation enacted during the 1660s and early 1670s, all other forms of worship were illegal.

A number of Owen's close friends, including John Bunyan, suffered fines and imprisonment for not heeding these laws. Although Owen was shielded from actual imprisonment by some powerful friends like Lord Philip Wharton

---

[40]Nathaniel Mather states that 'Dr Goodwin and Mr Nye were the penmen' of 'the prefaces [*sic*] to the Savoy Confession'; BL Add Ms 23622, fol. 132.
[41]'A Preface' to *The Savoy declaration*, 3:709, emphasis original.

(1613–96), he led an often precarious existence until his death. He was on several occasions arrested and was once threatened by a mob, which surrounded his carriage.[42] Between 1663 and 1666, he was tempted to accept the offer of a safe haven in America when the Puritan leaders in Massachusetts offered him the presidency of Harvard.[43] Owen, though, recognized where he was needed most, and he wrote prodigiously in defence of Nonconformity.

This polemical defence, though, took its toll. In 1672, Owen told the New England Puritan John Eliot (1604–90) that 'there is scarce any one alive in the world that hath more reproaches cast upon him than I have'. As he was experiencing 'a dry and barren spirit', he begged Eliot to pray for him that God would 'water me from above'.[44] Two years later, in a letter to Charles Fleetwood (c. 1618–92), a close friend, and one of Cromwell's sons-in-law, he described himself as a 'poor withering soul' and expressed his fear that

> we shall die in the wilderness; yet ought we to labour and pray continually that the heavens would drop down from above, and the skies pour down righteousness – that the earth may open and bring forth salvation, and that righteousness may spring up together [see Ps. 85.10-11]. [. . .] I beseech you to contend yet more earnestly than ever I have done, with God, with my own heart, with the church, to labour after spiritual revivals.[45]

Owen's fears were not unfounded. He would die without seeing any turning of the tide for the Nonconformists, and the spiritual state of England in general would continue to decline until the evangelical revivals of the mid-1730s. And although Owen's call to 'labour after spiritual revivals' anticipated eighteenth-century evangelicalism's pursuit of spiritual renewal without the arm of the

---

[42]Barraclough, *John Owen*, 15.
[43]Greaves, 'Owen, John (1616–1683)', *ODNB*, s.v.
[44]John Owen to John Eliot [1672], in *The correspondence of John Owen*, 154.
[45]John Owen to Charles Fleetwood, 8 July [1674], in *The correspondence of John Owen*, 159. Owen was not the only Puritan leader urging prayer for revival in the 1670s. Four years after Owen wrote this letter, John Howe (1630–1705) preached a series of sermons based on Ezek. 39.29 in which he dealt with the subject of the outpouring of the Holy Spirit. In one of these sermons he told his audience (*The prosperous state of the Christian interest before the end of time, by a plentiful effusion of the Holy Spirit: Sermon IV*, 1:575):

> When the Spirit shall be poured forth plentifully I believe you will hear much other kind of sermons, or they will, who shall live to such a time, than you are wont to do now-a-days [. . .] It is plain, too sadly plain, there is a great retraction of the Spirit of God even from us; we not know how to speak living sense [i.e. felt reality] unto souls, how to get within you; our words die in our mouths, or drop and die between you and us. We even faint, when we speak; long experienced unsuccessfulness makes us despond; we speak not as persons that hope to prevail [. . .] When such an effusion of the Spirit shall be as is here signified [. . .] [ministers] shall know how to speak to better purpose, with more compassion and sense, with more seriousness, with more authority and allurement, than we now find we can.

state, there is firm evidence that Owen hoped for a political solution to the persecution of Nonconformity and was engaged in a number of plots against the government in the final years of his life.[46]

Owen's first wife, Mary, died in 1676, and he remarried the following year. His second wife, Dorothy D'Oyley, was the widow of a wealthy Oxfordshire landowner whom Owen would have known from his connections to his home village of Stadhampton.[47] She was already a member of his congregation.[48] Added to the toil, distresses and anxieties of Owen's later years were the physical challenges that he faced, especially asthma and kidney stones. But these years were also ones of prodigious literary fruitfulness. As Gribben has noted, he was one of the 'busiest writers' of his era. His voluminous commentary on Hebrews appeared between 1668 and 1684, which he regarded in many ways as his magnum opus.[49] *Πνευματολογία: or, A discourse concerning the Holy Spirit* came out in 1674 and an influential work on justification, *The doctrine of justification by faith*, in 1677. Owen's *Meditations and discourses on the glory of Christ*, which Robert Oliver has termed 'incomparable', was written under the shadow of death in 1683 and represents Owen's dying testimony to the unsurpassable value and joy of living a life for the glory of Christ.[50]

Owen fell asleep in Christ on 24 August 1683. His final literary work was a letter to his friend, Charles Fleetwood, written two days before his death. 'Dear Sir', he wrote,

> I am going to him whom my soul hath loved, or rather who hath loved me with an everlasting love; which is the whole ground of all my consolation. The passage is very irksome and wearysome through strong pains of various sorts which are all issued in an intermitting fever. All things were provided to carry me to London today attending to the advice of my physician, but we were all disappointed by my utter disability to undertake the journey. I am leaving the ship of the church in a storm, but whilst the great Pilot is in it the loss of a poore under-rower will be inconsiderable. Live and pray and hope and waite patiently and doe not despair; the promise stands invincible that he will never leave thee nor forsake thee.[51]

Owen was buried on 4 September in Bunhill Fields, the *campo santo* of English Nonconformity, and there awaits the resurrection of the saints.

---

[46]Gribben, *John Owen and English Puritanism*, 257–61.
[47]Oliver, 'John Owen (1616–1683)', 35.
[48]Crippen, 'Dr. Watts's church-book', 27.
[49]See Tweeddale, 'John Owen's commentary on Hebrews in context', 52, 54–5.
[50]Oliver, 'John Owen (1616–1683)', 35.
[51]John Owen to Charles Fleetwood, 22 August 1683, in *The correspondence of John Owen*, 174.

CHAPTER 3

Owen as a theologian

RYAN M. MCGRAW

This chapter treats the scope and character of John Owen's work as a theologian. The genres of his works include theological treatises, biblical commentaries, polemical exchanges, catechisms, sermons, academic orations, poetry and some letters. His audiences were both popular and academic, and he wrote both in Latin and in English. While his theological interests were wide-ranging, his pastoral and polemical concerns, such as countering English Arminianism and Socinianism, led him increasingly to focus his attention on trinitarian, pneumatological and Christological themes. This chapter will introduce students to the scope and character of Owen's theological output by tracing much of his work chronologically, thematically and stylistically. In doing so, this chapter will give attention to developments and changes in his thought throughout his career in order to give readers a sense of his theological character as a whole in light of his literary output and development.

OWEN'S CHRONOLOGICAL OUTPUT AS A THEOLOGIAN

Crawford Gribben has noted aptly, 'Whatever else Owen was, he was a thinker.'[1] Owen wrote eight and a half million words in eighty books. This makes it challenging to grasp the overarching scope of his theological output.

---

[1] Gribben, *John Owen and English Puritanism*, 1.

Even Gribben wrote, 'I am compelled to admit that Owen has defeated me.'[2] This section introduces Owen's character as a theologian by sketching the main ideas presented in his works as they appeared in print chronologically. It follows Peter Toon's chronological list of Owen's writings and largely restricts its scope to the works contained in the Goold edition. This means that his three volumes of unpublished sermons are omitted, as are other writings such as his Oxford orations and letters.[3] For the sake of organization, the material is divided between his writings during the English Civil War and Interregnum (1643–60), works following the restoration from roughly 1660 to 1679, and his final projects, some of which appeared in print posthumously. His increasing preoccupation with trinitarian, pneumatological and Christological themes will be clear in this narrative.

1643–59

Owen's first published work was Θεομαχία αυτεξουσιαστικη: or, *A display of Arminianisme* (1643).[4] In somewhat vitriolic tone, he opposed 'the idol of free will', which he viewed as the crux of the issue, in relation to rising concerns over Arminianism in the English church. He lumped together opponents from the Arminian-leaning Thomas Jackson (1595–1640) to the Reformed Orthodox Edward Reynolds (1599–1676). He also connected Arminian views of the atonement with Socinianism. Such emphases would carry with greater nuance into later works, such as *Vindiciae evangelicae*.[5] His views on other matters, such as the efficacy of baptism in removing habitual sin, disappear entirely from later works. The work was calculated to get the attention of the powers that be, achieving its effect by his being presented to a parish in Fordham, Essex.[6] His later emphases on the trinitarian nature of the covenant of redemption are absent in this work. This is likely due in part to the relative newness of the appeal to the intra-trinitarian covenant in English Reformed theology. Gribben has argued that *A display of Arminianisme* was Owen's most 'Thomistic book'.[7]

The duty of pastors and people distinguished followed in 1644 in order to instruct the Fordham congregation in worship and church government.[8] The political overtones present in *A display of Arminianisme* are largely muted here. Owen was an avowed Presbyterian at the time, though he bypassed the role

---

[2]Gribben, *John Owen and English Puritanism*, x.
[3]For the Oxford orations, which are not included in the standard set of Owen's *Works*, see Owen, *The Oxford orations*.
[4]Owen, *A display of Arminianisme* (1643).
[5]Trueman, *John Owen*.
[6]Gribben, *John Owen and English Puritanism*, 46.
[7]Gribben, *John Owen and English Puritanism*, 46.
[8]Owen, *The duty of pastors and people distinguished* (1644).

of synods in the church, which was the main point dividing Independents and Presbyterians. He soon shifted openly to an Independent platform of church government, largely following his reading of John Cotton's *The keyes of the kingdom* (1644).[9] Gribben rightly questions how robust Owen's Presbyterianism was in this early work, since he quotes Rutherford on Presbyterian government only to contradict his conclusions by defining the church in terms of gathered congregations. This stress on gathered congregations would become even more prominent in his writings following the Restoration.

In 1645, Owen published *The principles of the doctrine of Christ unfolded in two short catechismes* in order to better prepare his congregation for coming to the Lord's Supper. The *Greater catechism* presented his somewhat eccentric views of the Mosaic covenant as a republished covenant of works, which put him at odds with the forthcoming conclusions of the Westminster Assembly in its Confession of Faith (1647). The catechisms focused on Christology, which became a pervasive emphasis of Owen's work. A few years earlier, in 1643, he wrote a work on the priesthood of Christ, which he never published.[10]

After taking a pastoral charge in Coggeshall, Essex, Owen walked in more influential circles. Thomas Westrow used his patronage to invite Owen to preach *A vision of unchangeable free mercy* (1646) before Parliament.[11] Owen's sermon was politically charged, offering a theological interpretation of the progress of the English Civil War at many points. His concern, however, was primarily for the state of religion in the country. When Parliament recommended the sermon for publication, which was standard practice for such sermons, Owen took the liberty of appending his 'Country essay', which defended his Independent church polity against the charges of sectarianism. He also outlined his views on limited religious toleration in a way that would cause some trouble for the current establishment. At this time, such questions began to divide Parliament. Gribben argues that the 'Country essay' contradicted Owen's later views on defining heresy.[12] However, Coffey makes a compelling argument to the effect that while tensions existed in Owen's views of toleration and heresy, his later efforts to establish a broad-based confession of faith grounded on fundamentals was a development of, rather than a departure from, his earlier teaching.[13] *Eschol: A cluster of the fruit of Canaan* appeared in 1648.[14] Gribben notes that

---

[9]Cotton, *The keyes of the kingdom of heaven, and power thereof, according to the word of God* (1644).
[10]See Owen, *The duty of pastors and people distinguished* (1644), 16; cf. Gribben, *John Owen and English Puritanism*, 42–3.
[11]Owen, *A vision of unchangeable free mercy* (1646).
[12]Gribben, *John Owen and English Puritanism*, 79.
[13]Coffey, 'John Owen and the Puritan toleration controversy, 1646–59', 232.
[14]While Toon's list places this work in 1647, Gribben explains that the book was approved for publication on 30 December 1647, but was published in the spring of 1648. Gribben, *John Owen*

the book 'called for devotional and ethical renewal', and that its author was 'concerned by the growth of religious novelty'.[15]

In 1648, Owen produced *Salus electorum, sanguis Jesu: or, The death of death in the death of Christ*.[16] In spite of its notoriety in the twentieth century, this was not Owen's magnum opus, but it was his most significant work to date.[17] His opponent asserted election at the expense of redemption. Owen rejected eternal justification in this book, though Richard Baxter (1615–91) later accused him of maintaining this doctrine. Owen also interacted with the tradesman Thomas Moore, who argued for a universal atonement. Owen was the fourth author in two years to respond to Moore.[18] *The death of death in the death of Christ* included a chapter expanded from *A display of Arminianisme* that now outlined trinitarian themes more clearly. As Gribben notes, 'Calvinism had become Christianity's best defense against trinitarian heresy, for Arminian ideas were the gateway to a full-scale assault on classical theism.'[19] Owen's concern with Socinianism was growing at this time and would occupy much of the rest of his life. His views on Heb. 9.14 ('How much more shall the blood of Christ, who through the eternal Spirit offered himself without spot to God, purge your conscience from dead works to serve the living God?') shifted over time as well. Here he interpreted the text in a trinitarian vein, while later he did not. Richard Byfield (1598–1644), who was a member of the Westminster Assembly, endorsed the work, but he confessed that he did not know the author.

In 1648, Owen published *Eben-ezer: A memorial of the deliverance in Essex: Two sermons*.[20] He spent a large amount of time with the parliamentary army during the siege.[21] He wrote *Eben-ezer* to celebrate the liberation of Colchester in 1648.[22] This was the first time that he did not publish with Philemon Stephens, now taking responsibility for publishing costs himself.[23] *Eben-ezer* moved from recent history to reiterate Owen's views of toleration.[24] The Presbyterians' Blasphemy Act was passed in 1648, which required the execution of anti-trinitarians and atheists, and the imprisonment of those who challenged Presbyterian church government. Owen feared persecution from a Presbyterian Parliament. Through the influence of Owen's allies – and, in December 1648,

---

and English Puritanism, 83.
[15]Gribben, *John Owen and English Puritanism*, 83–4.
[16]Owen, *The death of death in the death of Christ* (1648).
[17]Gribben, *John Owen and English Puritanism*, 85.
[18]Gribben, *John Owen and English Puritanism*, 86.
[19]Gribben, *John Owen and English Puritanism*, 88.
[20]Owen, *Eben-ezer* (1648).
[21]Gribben, *John Owen and English Puritanism*, 92.
[22]Gribben, *John Owen and English Puritanism*, 93.
[23]Gribben, *John Owen and English Puritanism*, 94.
[24]Gribben, *John Owen and English Puritanism*, 95.

the army coup known as 'Pride's Purge' – the Blasphemy Ordinance was never enacted.[25]

In 1649 Owen published two sermons on *Righteous zeal: A sermon with an essay on toleration*[26] and Ουρανων ουρανια: *The shaking and translating of heaven and earth: A sermon*.[27] The first is the sermon that Owen preached the day after Charles I was executed. In comparison with other sermons preached that day, it is remarkably reserved, making little to no mention of the regicide. Gribben noted that Owen 'seemed more concerned to announce his theology of toleration than his beliefs about the regicide'.[28] The second sermon had political overtones while including references to the shaking of the Hebrew system of worship in transition to the New Testament. The following year (1650) he published *The branch of the Lord: Two sermons*.[29] These sermons both promoted his Congregationalist platform and developed his ecclesiology in conjunction with his Christology.

Of the death of Christ (1650) represents an expansion of Owen's views of the atonement presented in *The death of death in the death of Christ*.[30] It was largely sparked by Richard Baxter's criticism of the former work, and it marked the first time that Owen and Baxter clashed theological swords publicly. It augments the earlier book by distinguishing the impetation and application of redemption more clearly, showing the need for the entire Trinity to work in redemption.[31] Christ's death alone secured the salvation of the elect, but the Spirit called sinners to union and communion with Christ. The unified work of redemption by the entire Trinity alone could secure their salvation, including the application of redemption to them. This is a good example of how his increasing development of trinitarian theology deepened his theological emphases. The same year he preached another sermon before Parliament on *The steadfastness of the promises, and the sinfulness of staggering* in order to press the government to persevere in what he viewed as their righteous cause.[32]

Owen transitioned to serving as dean of Christ Church, Oxford, in 1651. In 1653, he became vice-chancellor of the university.[33] His work during this

---

[25] Gribben, *John Owen and English Puritanism*, 96; Hall, *The Puritans*, 303.
[26] Owen, *A sermon preached to the Honourable House of Commons, in Parliament assembled: on January 31* (1649).
[27] Owen, *The shaking and translating of heaven and earth* (1649).
[28] Gribben, *John Owen and English Puritanism*, 100.
[29] John Owen, *The branch of the Lord, the beauty of Sion* (1650). I will not note the publication of every sermon below, but will instead highlight those that are either historically or theologically significant.
[30] Owen, *Of the death of Christ* (1650).
[31] van den Brink, 'Impetation and application in John Owen's theology', 85–96.
[32] Owen, *The steadfastness of promises, and the sinfulness of staggering* (1650).
[33] Toon, *God's statesman*, 50.

period reflected his republican politics, his concern for religious establishment with limited toleration and his concerns to defend theological education at the university against Quakers and others. In 1652, he preached *The labouring saint's dismission to rest* at the funeral of Henry Ireton, who was one of Cromwell's military leaders in Ireland.[34] He also published *Christ's kingdom and the magistrate's power* and the *Humble proposals for the propagation of the Gospel*, the latter of which he co-authored with the Congregationalist leaders of the Westminster Assembly.[35] The former work reflected his concern for proper political boundaries for the magistrate's power in relation to public worship. The latter sought to promote church planting and to curtail the prevalence of heresies. All three of these works reveal Owen's increasingly prominent political role in the Interregnum.

Diatriba de justitia divina (1653; *Dissertation on divine justice*)[36] marked the first distinct change in Owen's views, at least at one point, and was one of the rare occasions on which he noted the change.[37] Previously, he held that Christ's death was necessary for the salvation of sinners by divine appointment only (a position known as 'hypothetical necessity'). Now he believed in the absolute necessity of Christ's atonement as satisfaction to divine justice. The key issue was whether one regarded justice as an absolute or relative attribute of God. While both categories of necessary divine attributes represented God's essential properties, some attributes found particular expression in relation to the creatures. William Twisse (1578–1646), Samuel Rutherford (1600–61) and others of Owen's targets argued that holiness was absolute in God and that justice was relative to creation. Owen countered that justice was God's disposition to give everyone their due. While the exercise of divine justice had respect to creation, divine justice was an absolute rather than a relative divine attribute. This doctrinal shift gave Owen more ammunition against Socinian views of the atonement.[38] *Diatriba de justitia divina* is very scholastic in tone, drawing much material from Aquinas as well as the Jesuit author, Franciscus Suarez (1548–1617). Goold included an eighteenth-century English translation in his edition of Owen's *Works*. Its original Latin form, however, shows that its intended audience was academic. It is more challenging than many of his English writings, and it shows that Owen was at home in the world of scholastic reasoning and categories.

---

[34]Owen, *The labouring saints dismission to rest* (1652).
[35]Owen, *A sermon preached to the Parliament, Octob. 13. 1652* (1652); Owen et al., *The humble proposals* (1652).
[36]Owen, *Diatriba de justitia divina* (1653).
[37]Trueman, 'John Owen's *Dissertation on divine justice*', 87–103. Owen noted the change in his views about halfway through the unpaginated preface to the reader of the *Diatriba*.
[38]Trueman, 'John Owen's *Dissertation on divine justice*', 87–103.

The doctrine of the saints perseverance explained and confirmed appeared in 1654 as an extended critique of John Goodwin's *Redemption redeemed* (1651).[39] This large volume illustrates the crossover between Owen's deepening trinitarian theology and the concern to counter Arminianism at the outset of his career. Owen opposed Goodwin's arguments for universal atonement and his denial of the final perseverance of all saints primarily by appealing to the unified work of the entire Trinity. His focus on Socinianism better enabled him to employ trinitarian arguments against other opponents. In 1655, he added *Vindicae evangelicae*, which targeted the Socinian threat directly.[40] Owen's primary targets were the recent English publication of the Racovian Catechism as well as two works by John Biddle (1615–62), who was a prominent English Socinian.[41] The book largely refutes the Socinian theological system point by point, making this book close to a full presentation of Owen's entire theological system. As one might expect, the primary emphases are on the Trinity, the identity of Jesus Christ as the God-man, and Christ's substitutionary atoning work. Goold reprinted Owen's review of the annotations of Hugo Grotius (1583–1645) alongside *Vindiciae evangelicae* since Owen grouped their views of Christ's atonement together. Grotius thought that his governmental view of the atonement was sufficient to refute Socinianism, while Owen argued that this view supported their cause by denying penal substitution and the satisfaction of divine justice. For good measure, Owen took a swipe at Richard Baxter's views of atonement and justification at the same time, implicating Baxter and Grotius with Socinian tendencies.

Owen combined his political and theological interests in 1656. He preached two sermons before Parliament, *God's presence with his people* and *God's work in founding Zion*, both of which pressed the nation to persevere in godliness in the present political climate.[42] The *Of the mortification of sinne in believers* has become one of Owen's best-known books.[43] This short work grew out of a series of sermons preached to students at Oxford. It aimed to give practical instruction on mortifying sin in believers, which was one-half of the Reformed doctrine of sanctification.[44] The other half was vivification, which stresses the need to replace sinful dispositions and practices with godly ones. For this reason, Owen notes the incomplete quality of sanctification throughout the

---

[39] Owen, *The doctrine of the saints perseverance* (1654).
[40] Owen, *Vindiciae evangelicae* (1655).
[41] For two in-depth studies of the rise of English Socinianism during this period, see Mortimer, *Reason and religion in the English revolution*, and Lim, *Mystery unveiled*.
[42] Owen, *God's presence with a people* (1656); Owen, *God's work in founding Zion* (1656).
[43] Owen, *Of the mortification of sinne in believers* (1656).
[44] For a fuller treatment of the Reformed view of sanctification, see Marshall, *The Gospel-mystery of sanctification*.

work, likening mortification to clearing the ground or pulling up the weeds of sin in order to replace them with godly habits and acts. Modern readers only expecting a list of practical directions might miss the Christological focus of the volume, even though union with Christ stood as the foundation of Owen's platform on mortification. His stress on the Holy Spirit in killing sin rounded out his trinitarian emphasis. There is no mention here of public worship or the public means of grace in sanctification, which is surprising in light of his consistent emphasis on public worship throughout many of his other writings.

Of communion with God developed from a series of sermons preached at Oxford in 1652, and only published in 1657.[45] This book presents a devotional model of trinitarian theology that stresses communion with all three divine persons jointly and each person particularly.[46] Most of the attention focuses on communion with Christ in his personal and purchased grace. Public worship features prominently in this book, as well as in the two sermons he preached on public worship in the 1670s.[47] Trinitarian devotion became a recurring theme in Owen's writings, largely in order to integrate the Trinity into the Gospel and Christian experience as a counter-point to the Socinians. Some have argued that this emphasis on distinct communion with each person was a radical innovation in Reformed theology. However, readers should remember Owen's dependence on Latin continental authors at this point. It was common in systematic works, like Amandus Polanus's (1561–1610) *Syntagma theologia*, to situate each theological locus in the appropriate works of each divine person.[48] Moreover, Owen's dependence on Dutch theologians, like Gisbertus Voetius (1589–1676) and Johannes Hoornbeeck (1617–66), may account for some of the distinct emphases on the divine persons.[49] Arminian theologians in the Netherlands, to which Voetius and Hoornbeeck responded, affirmed the doctrine of the Trinity, but denied its practical import.[50] Dutch *Nadere Reformatie* theologians responded to this in force by demonstrating that the Trinity was the foundation of theology and piety and that it was relevant to

---

[45]Owen, *Of communion with God* (1657).
[46]For recent analyses of this work, see Letham, 'John Owen's doctrine of the trinity in its catholic context', 185–98; Kapic, *Communion with God*; McGraw, *A heavenly directory*; Ferguson, *The Trinitarian devotion of John Owen*.
[47]These two sermons, entitled 'The nature and beauty of public worship', are found in *Works* (1965), vol. 9.
[48]Polanus, *Syntagma theologiae Christianae ab Amando Polano a Polansdorf* (1610).
[49]Owen cited both theologians as particularly noteworthy in Θεολογούμενα παντοδαπα (1661), 519, lib. VI, cap. 8, and page 522, for Hoornbeeck and Voetius, respectively. Voetius in particular referred to the Trinity as the *fundamentum fundamenti* in relation to all doctrine and practice. Voetius, *Selectarum disputationum theologicarum pars prima* (1648–67), 1:472.
[50]For an example of a prominent Arminian theologian who denied the practical import of the Trinity throughout his system, see Episcopius, *Antidotum contines pressiorem declaratioem propriae et genuine senetentiae quae in Synodo Nationali Dordracena est et stabilita* (1620), e.g., 135–6.

every area of Christian faith and life. While Owen expanded these themes even more fully, and with a Socinian rather than Arminian target primarily in view, his thought is not as novel as it seems in this light. These Dutch theologians also feared Socinian inroads through Arminian theology, as exemplified by Conrad Vorstius (1569–1622), who crossed over between the two groups.[51] Owen also likely drew from medieval precedent in which authors such as Aquinas stressed communion with the divine persons based on their processions, missions and appropriations.[52]

In 1657, Owen also wrote two works on the issue of schism: *A review of the true nature of schisme* and *Of schisme, The true nature of it discovered and considered, with reference to the present differences in religion*.[53] Both works sought to defend Independent churches against charges of schism by existing apart from the established Church of England. Liberty of conscience, particularly as related to public worship and the prayer book, features prominently in both works. The former responded to the Presbyterian, Daniel Cawdrey (1588–1664).[54] Cawdrey joined the litany of Presbyterians, pushing for an established Presbyterian church that left no room for Independents. While Owen's party was in political power at the time, he took the opportunity once again to justify his views on limited religious toleration. He included little material on the Trinity in these works.

In 1658, Owen wrote *Pro sacris Scripturis exercitationes adversus fanaticos*. This book targeted Quaker views on extra-biblical revelation. As such, it is a defence of the inspiration and sufficiency of Scripture. It is somewhat ironic that he wrote the book in Latin, since his opponents were both opposed to education for ministers and many of them could not read Owen's attack against them. This book not only set forth Owen's doctrine of Scripture, but it also protected the right of the University of Oxford to continue to exist as an educational institution.

In 1658, Owen also published *Of temptation: The nature and power of it*. Like *Of the mortification of sinne in believers*, it originated as a series of sermons to teenage students at the university. Goold's grouping of this book and *Of the mortification of sinne in believers* in volume six of Owen's *Works* has led subsequent readers to class them together. The association is not inappropriate, since the book addresses the importance of recognizing the power and subtlety of temptation to sin in believers.

---

[51]For the overlap between Socinianism and Arminianism, see Mulsow and Rohls (eds), *Socinianism and Arminianism*.
[52]For a clear treatment of this topic, see Legge, *The Trinitarian Christology of St Thomas Aquinas*.
[53]Owen, *A review of the true nature of schisme* (1657); Owen, *Of schisme* (1657).
[54]Cawdrey, *Independencie a great schism proved against Dr. Owen, his apology in his tract of schism* (1657).

This period of Owen's life closed in 1659 with him defending the doctrine of Scripture and the Mosaic origin of the Hebrew vowel points.[55] Owen was so concerned with Brian Walton's (1600–61) 'London Polyglot' that he began critiquing the work before reading it. His concern was that the number of manuscript variants present in the Polyglot threatened the divine preservation of the text of Scripture, leaving the door open for the doctrine of Rome in appealing to the authority of the church to decide the text of Scripture.[56] Ironically, Walton believed that he was defending the integrity of the original text against heretics.[57] Owen argued for the self-attesting and self-authenticating nature of the Bible, with heavy stress on the testimony of the Holy Spirit to convince believers of it. There is nothing remarkable here in terms of Reformed orthodoxy, but the perceived challenge to the text of Scripture struck at the first principles of the Protestant religion.[58] Gribben rightly notes, 'All other theological concerns paled beside this.'[59] Owen believed that the Hebrew vowel points were divinely inspired rather than coming through the Masoretic scribes because he believed that they were necessary for the intelligibility of the Hebrew text. Not all Reformed authors agreed with his position on this point, and many of them did not see the late addition of the vowel points as a threat to the integrity of Scripture. Owen, however, regarded this as an essential matter. He appropriately closed this period of his life with another parliamentary sermon pressing the godly to persevere in their cause and a short worship on the power of magistrates in matters of religious worship.[60] These works sought to further Owen's Congregationalist principles in an increasingly precarious political climate.

1660–79

In 1660, Charles II ascended the English throne.[61] His new regime retaliated against the Interregnum with a new Act of Uniformity in 1662. Somewhere around 2,000 ministers, university fellows and schoolmasters lost their positions during this time, and other measures made it hard for nonconformists to live safely. Some of those who were most closely connected with the execution of Charles I were executed. For this reason, Gribben observes, 'in the early 1660s,

---

[55]Owen, *Of the divine originall* (1659).
[56]Tyacke (ed.), *The history of the University of Oxford*, 4:600.
[57]Walton, *The considerator considered*.
[58]For the background behind the Reformed doctrine of Scripture in contrast to other views, see Fesko, 'The doctrine of scripture in Reformed orthodoxy', 429–64.
[59]Gribben, *John Owen and English Puritanism*, 195.
[60]Owen, *The glory and interest of nations professing the gospel preached* (1659); Owen, *Two questions* (1659).
[61]Keeble, *The Restoration: England in the 1660s*; Rose, *Godly kingship in Restoration England*.

Owen preferred to publish anonymously'.[62] He defended extemporaneous prayer in *A discourse concerning liturgies and their imposition* in 1662.[63] Gribben notes that the book 'almost certainly' appeared before the Act of Uniformity later that year. It is better to view this book as an intervention in a debate in which Owen had a personal stake instead of Goold's depiction of Owen dispassionately defending the Presbyterians. Owen had survived the Restoration, and he was concerned about defending the liberties needed to secure the liberty of conscience for his own party. While Presbyterians may have been an obvious target of royal authority during this period, they were not the only ones. The crux of the matter for Owen was that the word of God was the sole rule for public worship. Christ did away with the liturgical complexity of the Old Testament. In Owen's view, this happened decisively in AD 70 with the destruction of the Jewish temple.

Θεολογούμενα παντοδαπα, which appeared 1661, was arguably Owen's most significant theological work to date. Its nature and purpose have been debated among scholars in recent years.[64] It likely represented the fruits of some of his teaching at Oxford in the preceding decade. Yet the work is more negative regarding the usefulness of scholasticism than earlier books like *The death of death in the death of Christ* and the *Diatriba de justitia divina* would lead readers to believe. The book traces in tandem the knowledge of God as corrupted by sin (and exemplified in false religions and philosophies) and the true knowledge of God in light of divine covenants. This has led some authors to treat the work as a covenant theology. Stephen Westcott translated the title as *Biblical theology: A history of theology from Adam to Christ*.[65] The problem is that this translated title barely picks up a word of the original. I have argued elsewhere that the book's subtitle largely mirrors Franciscus Junius's work on Reformed prolegomena, which seems to be the best way to classify the work.[66] The first four chapters address the standard questions of prolegomena, such as the definition and nature of theology and the manner of theological studies, with the character of the theologian coming at the end (also like Junius).[67] The trinitarian and covenantal descriptions of the true knowledge of God present in *Of communion with God* pervade this volume. The length of the book and progression of themes through biblical history may reflect both Owen's curbing

---

[62] Gribben, *John Owen and English Puritanism*, 216.
[63] Owen, *A discourse concerning liturgies* (1662).
[64] For example, Rehnman, *Divine discourse*, 17; Trueman, *John Owen*, 5.
[65] Owen, *Biblical theology*, trans. Westcott. Subsequent editions include the subtitle as I list it in the text earlier.
[66] McGraw, *John Owen*, Chapter 7. See an alternative argument about the genre of this text in Richard Muller's chapter in this volume.
[67] Junius, *De theologia vera* (1594).

of scholasticism as well as simply his standard prolix style, filled with logically related digressions.

The *Animadversions on a treatise entitled Fiat lux* (1662) defended Protestant theology against a Roman Catholic attack. In an ironic twist, Edward Hyde, earl of Clarendon, appears to have asked Owen to reply to the book in the same year that the new Act of Uniformity was imposed. Gribben argues that this should, in some respects, be Owen's most controversial book, due to its high praise for the monarchy as well as his reticence towards imposing creeds and confessions. It is difficult to know where the later theme fits in Owen's views because it appears to be a single blip or anomaly in an otherwise continuous emphasis on creeds. It is hard to read his statements about the civil magistrate as anything other than either a shift in his republican views or an attempt to court royal favour. The theology of the book represents mainstream Reformed thought, defending Protestant views of Scripture and the church (with an eye to defending the Independents again), and a robust trinitarian and Christological view of the Gospel. *A vindication of the animadversions on Fiat lux* followed in 1664.

The *Discourse concerning liturgies and their imposition*, noted earlier, appeared in the same year. Goold mistakenly idealized this book, arguing that Owen was defending the liberty of Presbyterians, who were the prime targets of the impending Act of Uniformity. However, Owen's stress on allowing congregations the freedom to conduct public worship according to the teachings of Scripture alone and not according to the Book of Common Prayer represented an issue in which the Independents had a life-or-death stake. Some of the leading figures from the Interregnum had been executed and many more were excluded from the Restoration government and church settlement. Owen did not likely expect to live long after 1660. This makes his work on liturgies far from dispassionate and detached.

Owen's *A brief instruction in the worship of God* (1667) came to be known as 'the Independents' catechism'.[68] It sought to defend the soundness of Congregationalist practice by establishing from Scripture the denomination's principles of worship and church government. It served as a manual for Independent churches as well as a defence of their principles against the established Church of England. Like many of Owen's books during this period, it was first published anonymously, but his authorship was soon widely known, and he began to acknowledge it more publicly in replying to published objections against it. In the book, Owen outlines Reformed views of worship primarily through an exposition of the second commandment, and he sketches Congregational views of local congregations, their officers, synods and discipline

---

[68]Owen, *A brief instruction in the worship of God* (1667).

processes. If this work sketched the Congregationalist platform for worship and church government, his works on *Indulgence and toleration* and *A peace-offering*, both published the same year, defended the right of Congregational churches to exist in the face of persecution.[69] The next year, he wrote a book on *Indwelling sin in believers*, drawing from his trinitarian insights to help readers learn both to take the presence of sin in them seriously and to use the divinely appointed means to overcome it.[70]

In 1668, Owen published the first of four parts of what should be regarded as his magnum opus – *Exercitations on the epistle to the Hebrews*.[71] His work on Hebrews may have picked up themes from an unpublished and no longer extant manuscript on the priesthood of Christ that he prepared in 1643. The first two volumes included 'preliminary exercitations' arguing for the Pauline authorship of the book, the priesthood of Christ, Jewish conceptions of the Messiah as the background for the book and the perpetuity and spiritual character of the Sabbath. The work on Hebrews marked the climax of his theological writing career, and the commentary draws from almost all of Owen's major doctrinal treatises. His book on *The nature of apostasie* (1676) later appeared as a companion to his exposition of Hebrews 6, including large sections coupling his trinitarian theology with the theme of public worship.[72] The book begins with an exposition of the text, largely overlapping with the content of the commentary, with a stress on the idea that the people who fell away from grace in the passage had the non-saving influences and gifts of the Spirit as opposed to his saving graces. As such, the work focusing on the responsibility to use the light that one is given from the Lord and to beware of hardening one's heart under the Spirit's influences. It is a penetrating treatise, which tacitly defended the perseverance of the saints, while urging against the real temptations to abandon the faith and to fall away from the grace of the Gospel. It is thoroughly trinitarian and Christological, with a special eye to the way in which the Spirit works in the human soul. This reflected his continued concerns with the Socinians and devotional trinitarian theology with his aims to defend Independent views on the importance of liberty of conscience in public worship. While his defence of Independency is tacit only in these volumes, it is the most likely reason for his persistent coupling of public worship with his devotional trinitarian themes, which he did both in the Hebrews volumes and in his treatment of *The nature of apostasie*.

---

[69]Owen, *Indulgence and toleration* (1667); Owen, *A peace-offering* (1667).
[70]Owen, *Indwelling sin* (1668).
[71]For a treatment of the significance of this project in relation to Owen's theological career, see Tweeddale, *John Owen and Hebrews*.
[72]Owen, *The nature of apostasie* (1676).

Strangely, in this light, there is very little emphasis on the Trinity in his exercitation on the Sabbath, though public worship predominates there.[73] While Francis Cheynell included the Sabbath in his book on the Trinity, Owen did not stress the Trinity in his book on the Sabbath.[74] The remainder of the volumes on Hebrews appeared in 1674, 1680 and 1684, though he likely began work on them a decade prior to publishing the first volume. The Hebrews set represents Owen at his best, incorporating his most mature systematic, exegetical and practical theology. If the sermons contained in volume nine of Goold's edition of Owen's *Works* present a digest of key themes in Owen's theology, then the Hebrews commentary includes a compendium of such themes in the context of an extended exposition of Scripture. The block citations of Latin, Hebrew and Greek text make this work difficult to access for his envisioned broad audience, but it shows Owen's prowess as a theologian.[75]

The amount of Owen's writing output in this later period of his life is astonishing. At roughly the same time that the first volume on Hebrews appeared, he published a massive exposition of Psalm 130, with other books to follow in rapid succession.[76] This exposition aimed at practical divinity, primarily in relation to the assurance of God's pardoning grace. It placed the saving work of the triune God stood at the heart of the Gospel and Christian experience. A short letter entitled, *Truth and innocence vindicated*, came out in 1669, defending the right of Congregational churches to exist alongside the established church, and limiting the power of magistrates in matters of religious conscience.[77] During this period, in a strange turn of events, William Sherlock (1641–1707) wrote a critique of *Communion with God* almost two decades after its publication, primarily in relation to Owen's stress on communion with each divine person. Sherlock also appears to have held views inconsistent with the substitutionary nature of Christ's atoning death. This was important enough to Owen to respond with a vindication of his earlier work, which accused Sherlock of undermining the Gospel itself by altering the nature of Christ's atoning work.[78] Sherlock stood at the heart, promoting uniformity in religion against Independents. This calling attention to an older book on issues related to the Trinity and atonement provoked Owen to write a thorough reply. Also in 1669, he published a short work on the Trinity and Christ's person

---

[73] Owen, *Sabbath* (1671).
[74] Cheynell, *The divine triunity of the Father, Son, and Holy Spirit*, 399.
[75] Gribben observes that Owen 'was his own ideal reader'; Gribben, *John Owen and English Puritanism*, 270.
[76] Owen, *A practical exposition on the 130th Psalm* (1669).
[77] Owen, *Truth and innocence vindicated* (1669).
[78] Owen, *A vindication of some passages* (1674).

and work to counter Socinian trends in a way that would reach the broadest audience he could.[79]

For obvious reasons, books devoted to defending religious dissent and Congregational church government continued to appear during this period. Owen defended the right of Congregational churches to exist and to worship according to their consciences in both *Reflections on a slanderous libel* and in *A discourse concerning evangelical love, church-peace, and unity*.[80] The latter sought to ground the love, peace and unity of the church in union with Christ and communion in the Holy Spirit, drawing from Owen's trinitarian insights at key points.

Owen designed his Πνευματολογια (1674), on the person and work of the Holy Spirit, as an original contribution to theology. He argued that he knew of no one who had gone before him who had attempted a comprehensive treatment of the person and work of the Holy Spirit.[81] Goold grouped Owen's work on the Spirit together in seven parts, though Gribben argues that Owen did not intend all of these parts to hold together in a single piece. The first and primary part of the work situates the Holy Spirit in the Trinity, presenting a comprehensive trinitarian theology that is more robust and sophisticated even than that developed in *Of communion with God*. His concern was both anti-Socinian and devotional, contrasting the Spirit's work in regeneration and sanctification to mere 'moral virtue'. His primary courts of appeal were Scripture, church history and Christian experience. One feature that has stood out in this work to contemporary authors in particular is Owen's stress on the Spirit's work in the humanity of Christ as a pattern for his work in believers.[82] At least the books on the Spirit as Comforter, as a Spirit of prayer and his work in relation to spiritual gifts belong with this first instalment.[83] *The reason of faith* and Σύνεσις πνευματική: or, *The causes, waies & and means of understanding the mind of God* fit with it well, and Goold is justified in grouping these texts together to complete Owen's massive project on the Spirit.[84] The former argues for a 'faith divine and supernatural' wrought by the Spirit in believers as the grounds of believing in the divine inspiration of Scripture, while the latter rooted the proper interpretation of Scripture in the Spirit's work. I will address these latter two works in a later part of this chapter. If the Hebrews volumes

---

[79] Owen, *A brief declaration and vindication of the doctrine of the Trinity* (1669).
[80] Owen, *A discourse concerning evangelical love* (1672).
[81] Owen, Πνευματολογια (1674).
[82] For examples, see Spence, *Incarnation and Inspiration*; Webster, 'The place of Christology in systematic theology', 628–48; Ferguson, *The Holy Spirit*; Hoglund, *Called by triune grace*.
[83] Owen, *Two discourses concerning the Holy Spirit* (1693); Owen, *A discourse of the work of the Holy Spirit in prayer* (1682).
[84] Owen, *The reason of faith* (1677); Owen, *The causes, waies & means of understanding the mind of God* (1678).

were not Owen's magnum opus, then his work on the Holy Spirit would likely take this place. Together, these massive projects mark Owen's most thorough, mature and profound thought.

Owen wrote *The doctrine of justification by faith* (1677) in response to perceived threats to the doctrine.[85] Gribben argues that the book represents Owen's increasing return to his concerns with fundamental articles of the faith.[86] Owen certainly faced plenty of threats to the doctrine in his lifetime, stemming from Arminianism, Socinianism and more recent attempts to promote Roman Catholicism. Like his other works from this period, it is trinitarian, Christological and pneumatological in relation to the work of the Spirit. Perhaps surprising to some readers, Owen showed the breadth of his charity and toleration by stating that there were likely some people who were saved by faith in Christ alone who notionally denied the doctrine.[87] No one could question the importance of the doctrine in his estimation, given the fact that these comments preceded a roughly 500-page exposition of it. This fitted Protestant orthodoxy more broadly, and the book on justification represents one of the most robust treatments of the doctrine in seventeenth-century England, surpassing the treatments of authors like William Twisse and Anthony Burgess (1600–63).[88]

The reason of faith (1677) resumed and expanded Owen's earlier defence of the self-attesting and self-authenticating nature of Scripture. His primary contention was that the nature of saving faith is to accept the testimony of another. In the case of Scripture, this involved accepting the authority of God's testimony in Scripture to Scripture as the only formal ground on which believers receive the Bible as the word of God. A divine and supernatural faith was necessary in order to have this faith, which brought readers back to the regenerating power of the Holy Spirit. This approach to the doctrine of Scripture was standard in high orthodox Reformed theology, and did not begin to shift towards a dependence on external evidences clearly until later in the century with authors like Howe, Baxter and Bates.[89] The appeal to external evidences over the internal testimony of Scripture was a shift that did not come into full force until after the Enlightenment was in full bloom.

---

[85] Owen, *The doctrine of justification by faith* (1677).
[86] Gribben, *John Owen and English Puritanism*, 254.
[87] Owen, *The doctrine of justification by faith* (1677), 227–9; *Works* (1965), 5:163–4.
[88] William Twisse, *Vindiciae gratiae, potestatis ac providentiae Dei, hoc est, ad examen libelli Perkinsiani de praedestinationis mode et ordine, institutum a Jacobo Arminio, responsio scholastica* (1632); Burgess, *The true doctrine of justification in two parts* (1655). Both authors were members of the Westminster Assembly. While Twisse did not write a distinct treatise on justification, he included extended treatments of the doctrine in volumes like the one cited here.
[89] See the treatment of such authors in Wallace, *Shapers of English Calvinism, 1660–1714*.

The causes, waies & means of understanding the mind of God followed in 1678 and was related thematically to *The reason of faith*. If the Spirit led believers to Scripture, then he also led believers through Scripture. This book outlines rules for understanding the Scriptures based on the teaching and example of Scripture itself. Among other things, the New Testament's use of the Old Testament served as a model for the right use of Scripture. This was standard fare for Reformed orthodox theology. Owen also stressed the necessity of the Spirit's help in prayer for help in interpreting Scripture, thus making the Spirit the believer's teacher both objectively and subjectively.

With astonishing literary output, Owen simultaneously wrote and published a massive treatise on Christology – his Χριστολογια (1679).[90] His earlier scholasticism reappears in full force here, coupled with his robust biblical exposition and appeals to church history. His complex style makes it easy for readers to get lost, even in the preface, where one can become confused regarding which parts represent his views and which parts the views of his opponents. The book is, in some ways, a counterpart to Πνευματολογια, with similar trinitarian themes and stress on the Spirit's work on the incarnate Christ. The work marks the pinnacle of high orthodox Christology from the viewpoint of one of its most impressive proponents. The covenant theology, including the covenant of redemption, which marked his later work, is present clearly throughout, as is his periodic emphasis on public worship.

In the same year, Owen published *The Church of Rome, no safe guide*.[91] We have already seen that there were rising fears in England at the time of a resurgence of Roman Catholicism. This surfaced in Owen's response to *Fiat lux*, his book on justification (though the Socinians were his primary target there), and most directly in *The Church of Rome, no safe guide*. The book is a systematic treatment of Roman Catholic theology, focusing on matters of religious authority and the trinitarian nature of the Reformed Gospel. This should remind readers that Owen fought battles on many fronts simultaneously. Though his focus remained on the Socinian threat and on defending Congregationalism, he had time to focus on other threats to orthodox, Rome standing out among them. He also published a substantial sermon against Roman Catholicism titled, *The chamber of imagery in the Church of Rome laid open* (1683). This sermon contrasted the ways of salvation and worship in Protestantism and Roman Catholicism. Owen argued that while Protestantism was a religion of faith in Christ, Roman Catholicism was a religion of outward sense. He argued that the primary glory of new covenant worship did not lie in its outward form, but in communion with the whole Trinity.

---

[90] Owen, Χριστολογια (1679).
[91] Owen, *The Church of Rome, no safe guide* (1679).

1680s onwards

Owen died in 1683. It may seem in this light that he did not have much left to do in three years in comparison to his staggering number of publications during the previous decade. Yet this period marked the completion of some of the projects that were the most important to him and a trickling of publications followed his death, many of which continue to draw interest into the twenty-first century. Gribben argues that while Owen did not make a lasting mark on English Reformed theology in his lifetime, there would be a renewed spark of interest in his spiritual writings following the rise of the evangelical movement in the 1730s.[92] Appropriately, the third part of his work on Hebrews came to fruition in 1680 and the last part in 1684, shortly after his death.

Owen continued his defence of nonconformists in *Nonconformity vindicated* (1680). This rehashed old themes in a new situation. Owen's congregation in London had merged with Joseph Caryl's (1602–73) in 1673 during a time of relative toleration, yet troubled times loomed once again. The same year Owen sought to consolidate the nonconformists as a group with *Some considerations of union among Protestants*.[93] In line with his earlier writings, he argued that union among Protestants should consist in mutual love grounded in union with Christ and the Spirit's work. The following year, Owen added an ominous tone of looming judgement in *An humble testimony unto the goodness and severity of God*, which argued that repentance was the need of the hour for English Protestants.[94] The same year he wrote *An enquiry into the original, nature and communion of evangelical churches*, arguing that Congregational churches alone fitted the apostolic model of church order, defending his views against charges of schism by Edward Stillingfleet (1635–99).[95] Owen's thought meandered in the answer to Stillingfleet, devoting both the introduction and the appendix to refuting his opponent. His standard trinitarian themes are muted here, allowing Congregational principles to dominate. William Sherlock came to Stillingfleet's defence by attacking Owen and Baxter by name, with whom Owen was already annoyed by his assault on *Of communion with God* in 1674.[96]

Owen wrote Φρόνεμα του πνεύματου: or, *The grace and duty of being spiritually-minded* (1681) as a means of promoting a Christ-focused and Spirit-filled devotion to God.[97] His treatment of true and false affections in religion became a partial inspiration for the more famous work on *Religious affections* (1746)

---

[92]Gribben, *John Owen and English Puritanism*, 270–2.
[93]Owen, *Some considerations about union among Protestants* (1680).
[94]Owen, *An humble testimony* (1681).
[95]Owen, *An enquiry into evangelical churches* (1681).
[96]Sherlock, *A discourse about church-unity* (1681).
[97]Owen, *The grace and duty of being spiritually-minded* (1681).

by Jonathan Edwards (1703–58). Among other themes, Owen included several chapters on false and true affections in relation to public worship. Communion with the Trinity stood at the heart of the difference between the two in the context of the public means of grace. While it is true that Owen did not consistently appeal to the public means of grace in all his writings, the presence of such a strong push in this direction in this late work should temper those who believe that he favoured private devotion over the public means of grace. The themes of Trinity, Christ, Spirit and public worship do not tie together everything that Owen wrote, but they do appear consistently throughout his writing career, and they reflect his Puritan piety; his preoccupation with Socinianism; and his defence of Nonconformity and limited religious toleration. *A brief and impartial account of the Protestant religion* appeared in 1682, stressing his focus on fundamental articles of religion, his opposition to Roman Catholicism and his emphasis on communion with the triune God in the Gospel.[98]

Owen's *Letter concerning the matter of present excommunications* (1683) defended persecuted non-conformists against the religious establishment once again.[99] His platform of religious toleration would not bear fruit until after his death during the Glorious Revolution of 1689. Appropriately, Owen's fourth and final volume of his work on *Hebrews* was published in 1684, the year after he died. These works brought resolution to his primary theological and literary agendas.

One of the last things that Owen prepared for publication was his *Meditations and discourses on the glory of Christ* (1684).[100] This was a series of meditations that he wrote to help his congregation place the Saviour at the centre of Christian faith, life and experience. The book identified the primary reason why believers did not make more progress in holiness as their failure to meditate on the person of Christ in order to commune with him by faith. This is, in many respects, a shorter and popular-level attempt to present the material of Χριστολογια to a different audience. It contains new material, such as his robust treatment of Christ as the heart of the beatific vision of God, which was the goal of salvation.[101] An addition to the meditations appeared in 1691 and was appended to it thereafter, expanding its applications at greater length. Owen professed to take comfort from the publication of this volume prior to his death.[102]

---

[98] Owen, *A brief and impartial account of the nature of the Protestant religion* (1682).
[99] Owen, *A letter concerning the matter of the present excommunications* (1683).
[100] Owen, *Meditations and discourses on the glory of Christ* (1684).
[101] McDonald, 'Beholding the glory of God in the face of Jesus Christ', 141–58.
[102] See the account in Toon, *God's statesman*, 171.

Several of Owen's manuscripts appeared after his death. The first of these was *A treatise of the dominion of sin and grace* in 1688.[103] This volume seeks to guide readers in discerning whether they are living under a state of sin or of grace. The material is related closely to *Of the mortification of sinne in believers* and the treatise on *Indwelling sin*. In line with the latter, Owen sought to show that the presence of sin in believers did not indicate that they were in a state of sin rather than one of grace. The crucial difference between these two states lies in the work of the Holy Spirit in uniting believers to Christ, with the fruits accompanying this work. This means that the work drew from Owen's trinitarian, Christological and pneumatological emphases.

A more systematic work on Congregationalist principles appeared among Owen's posthumous publications. In many respects, *The true nature of a Gospel church and its government* (1689) presents Owen's fullest expression of his Congregationalist principles.[104] It includes a robust view of the office of ruling elder, which Baxter had mistakenly viewed as grounds of union between Presbyterians and Independents in the preceding decade.[105] What made Independents distinctive in their polity was not the presence or absence of elders, but their views that church power terminated in the local congregation.[106] While synods were still necessary under this view, they were not higher church courts but collegial associations of the godly. The term 'church' could apply only to local congregations. This makes untenable suggestions that Owen became Presbyterian again before his death. The mistake is somewhat forgivable in that Baxter made it as well, relating that if he and Owen agreed that the people in the church did not have the power of the keys while their officers did not, then they agreed in principle over church polity.[107] Owen stressed the pastoral work and spiritual qualifications for the eldership. This is somewhat ironic, since Gribben relates that Owen and his assistant ministers laboured without the help of ruling elders in the latter part of his life.[108]

Owen's small posthumous work on *Gospel grounds and evidences of the faith of God's elect* (1695) is remarkable for several reasons.[109] His basic contention was that the primary mark of saving faith is evidenced by one's view of God's glory as revealed in Christ.[110] Believers are pleased with this way of redemption

---

[103]Owen, *A treatise of the dominion of sin and grace* (1688).
[104]Owen, *The true nature of a gospel church and its government* (1689).
[105]Gribben, *John Owen and English Puritanism*, 229.
[106]Burroughs, *Irenicum* (1645), 43.
[107]Baxter, *Reliquiæ Baxterianæ: or, Mr. Richard Baxter's narrative of the most memorable passages of his life and times*, ed. N. H. Keeble et al. (2020), 2:403.
[108]Gribben, *John Owen and English Puritanism*, 259.
[109]Owen, *Gospel grounds and evidences of the faith of God's elect* (1695).
[110]Owen, *Gospel grounds and evidences of the faith of God's elect* (1695), 2, 18; *Works* (1965), 5:405, 415.

first and foremost because of the way in which this way glorifies God. This gave practical expression to the covenant theology in *Of communion with God*, the Spirit's regenerating work in *Πνευματολογια*, the spiritual affections in *The grace and duty of being spiritually-minded*, saving faith in *The doctrine of justification by faith*, the Christological beatific vision in *Meditations and discourses on the glory of Christ* and other areas of his thought. A treatment of things that do not rise to the marks of saving faith follow, though with a pastoral bent towards comforting believers. It is also remarkable that Jonathan Edwards's sermon, *True grace, distinguished from the experience of devils* (1753), followed the same procedure in inverse order.[111] While Owen began with delight in the glory of God, Edwards used this idea as his conclusion. While Owen closed with false marks of faith, Edwards opened with them. It is difficult to draw a direct line of dependence on Owen, though Edwards certainly read and used him. Owen's stress on the Trinity, Christ and the Spirit are clear here once again.

Other minor posthumous works followed, including an *Answer unto two questions with arguments against any conformity to worship not of divine institutions* (1720), *Complete collection of the sermons of J. Owen, also several tracts, to which are added his Latin orations* (1721), *Three discourses delivered at the Lord's Table* (1750), *Thirteen sermons preached on various occasions* (1756), *Twenty-five discourses suitable to the Lord's Supper* (1760) and others, all of which Goold included in his edition of Owen's writings.

The nineteenth century saw two sets of Owen's *Works*, illustrating his relevance to evangelicalism. The Russell edition of Owen's *Works* (1826) came first.[112] The collection was incomplete, though it included David Clarkson's funeral oration. The Goold edition was more complete and began to appear in 1850.[113] Goold arranged Owen's writings thematically rather than chronologically, which had advantages and disadvantages. Owen's books on Christ, the Trinity and the Spirit comprise the first four volumes. This has the advantage of putting Owen's best foot forward, gathering key themes of his writing career together. However, his writings on the church and toleration do not exactly correspond to the volumes bearing those names, since Goold scattered these works among others without a clearly communicated reason for doing so. This makes Owen's political labours as well as his Independent views more difficult to trace. The set did not include Owen's letters or Oxford orations, but it did include most of his major Latin works in volume 17. Yet, the dissertation on divine justice appears in its English translation rather than its Latin original. In the 1960s, Banner of Truth reprinted the Goold edition, minus the Latin works in volume 17,

---

[111]Edwards, *True grace, distinguished from the experience of devils* (1753).
[112]Owen, *The works of John Owen*, ed. Russell (1826).
[113]Owen, *The works of John Owen*, ed. Goold (1850).

while re-arranging the contents of volume 16.[114] Peter Toon produced editions of the letters in 1970 and the Oxford orations in English in 1971.[115] Recently, three volumes of unpublished sermons were discovered. Crossway intends to produce a critical edition of Owen's works, comparing the Goold edition with original printings, which will include enough additional material to make up thirty-five volumes. This is a massive leap forward over Goold's twenty-four volumes, and the new version will restore the original text, removing Goold's frequent modifications of Owen's writings.

Reading Owen is a daunting task due both to the sheer volume of his work and the complexity of his argumentation. The former chronological survey, while incomplete, gives readers a feel for the main contours of his thought and writing. The remainder of this chapter will examine more briefly some of the key features of the core of Owen's work as a theologian.

THEMATIC AREAS IN OWEN'S THEOLOGY

While the trinitarian, pneumatological and Christological foci of Owen's thought are clear from the chronological survey of his publications, the content of his *Works* deserves more particular analysis in order to round out his character as a theologian. After summarizing his primary emphases in relation to books stretching beyond places where readers might expect to find them, we will briefly analyse areas in which Owen's thought changed or developed with time.[116]

Primary emphases

The Trinity looms large in most of Owen's writings, with the exception of many of his works promoting Congregationalist polity, which also took up much of his attention for both political and personal reasons. Pneumatology and Christology can be regarded as sub-themes of his broader trinitarian emphasis. An anonymous poem appropriately eulogized Owen shortly after his death, praising his 'Theo-Christo-Pneumatology'.[117] While Owen wrote on a wide range of subjects and his theological emphases defy easy classification, the words of this poem come close to what was nearest and dearest to him.[118]

---

[114]Owen, *The works of John Owen*, ed. Goold (1965).
[115]*The correspondence of John Owen* (1970); *The Oxford orations* (1971).
[116]Much of the material below is summarized from my findings in *A heavenly directory*.
[117]Cited in Gribben, *John Owen and English Puritanism*, 265.
[118]Gribben, *John Owen and English Puritanism*, 270, citing Trueman's assessment to this end.

There is little question that these areas have captured the most attention from modern Owen scholars.[119]

However, the topic of public worship, as it were, draws a circle around Owen's trinitarianism, emphasis on the Holy Spirit and his Christology. As I have argued elsewhere, he regarded public worship as the highest expression of communion with the triune God and he tied trinitarian piety and worship together pervasively across the spectrum of his writings.[120] The Trinity and worship are also related to his Congregational principles in many respects. While Independents largely shared broader Reformed principles related to public worship, they urged a greater measure of toleration for some differences in this area than their Church of England and Presbyterian counterparts.

Some have suggested that Owen's Congregational principles led him to prioritize private over public worship, due to the stress on the need for individual church members to enter into covenant with God and with each other.[121] This is true in some works, like *Of the mortification of sinne in believers*, but it is not true in most of them. I have traced many of these connections throughout his *Works* in *A heavenly directory*. Here, it is sufficient merely to list a few overlapping and additional examples. In his two sermons on 'The nature and beauty of public worship', Owen couched his entire summary of Reformed worship in trinitarian terms around Eph. 2.18 ('For through him, we both have access to one Spirit, to the Father'). In *The chamber of imagery in the Church of Rome laid open*, Owen argued that the primary beauty of public worship under the new covenant consists in knowing God as triune.[122] His comments on Hebrews 12 are full of references to experiencing communion with the Trinity in public worship. His books on apostasy and spiritual-mindedness both include two full chapters coupling these themes.[123] His refutation of John Goodwin in *The doctrine of the saints perseverance* appeals to the unified work of the triune God as the primary refutation of his opponent consistently throughout the entire work. This hearkened back to his appeals to the intra-trinitarian covenant of redemption in *The death of death in the death of Christ*, as well

---

[119]Examples include Trueman, *The claims of truth*; Trueman, *John Owen*; Kay, *Trinitarian spirituality*; Kapic, *Communion with God*; Spence, *Incarnation and inspiration*; Wisse and Meijer, 'Pneumatology: Tradition and renewal', 465–518; McGraw, *A heavenly directory*; Lim, *Mystery unveiled*; Mortimer, *Reason and religion in the English revolution*; Letham, 'John Owen's doctrine of the trinity in its catholic context', 185–98. This does not include recent theological engagement with Owen's trinitarian Christology in authors like John Webster, Michael Allen, Michael Hoglund, Sinclair Ferguson and others, some of whom I cite above.
[120]McGraw, *A heavenly directory*.
[121]See especially Kay, *Trinitarian spirituality*.
[122]Owen, *Works* (1965), 8:451–2.
[123]Owen, *The nature of apostasie* (1676), chs. 11 and 13; Owen, *The grace and duty of being spiritually-minded* (1681), chs. 14–15; both books may be found in *Works* (1965), vol. 7.

as to the trinitarian arguments in his first book, *A display of Arminianisme*, even though the covenant of redemption does not appear there. It is fitting, therefore, that *Meditations and discourses on the glory of Christ*, which was one of the last works published in his lifetime, concludes with the Spirit leading believers to a Christological beatific vision of God.[124] This was a 'Theo-Christo-Pneumatology' indeed. Owen devoted his attention to much more than these three themes, yet they were rarely far from his mind in most of his writings.

Areas of change and development in Owen's theology

Detecting areas of change in Owen's theology is a daunting task, largely because Owen rarely acknowledged them in print. Some changes were stark and clear, while others may have been developmental shifts. This section groups these areas accordingly.

The two changes that stand out most clearly are Owen's views of divine justice and church polity.[125] The previous narrative noted that *A display of Arminianisme* taught that God was not obligated to save sinners by satisfying divine justice, though he chose to do so. Roughly a decade later, Owen changed his mind, probably in response to Socinianism. From the dissertation on divine justice onward, he argued that justice was an essential attribute of God that required satisfaction by Christ's death. Owen drew from scholastic precedents, old and modern, Protestant and Roman Catholic, as well as from a wealth of biblical data. Socinian views of the atonement appear to have been the occasion rather than the cause of this shift. As we have seen, respectable Reformed authors continued to hold both positions.

Owen also acknowledged his shift from Presbyterianism to Congregationalism. This shift, however, is subtler than it may appear at first. He gives no evidence of a Presbyterian view of synods in *The duties of pastors and people distinguished* in 1644, which was his only 'Presbyterian' publication. Gribben suggests with good evidence that Owen may have been a half-hearted Presbyterian.[126] He seemed to stress the nature of the church as a gathered congregation. In this respect, his Independent principles may represent a development of his views rather than a departure from an earlier stance.

---

[124]Owen, *Meditations and discourses on the glory of Christ* (1684), 172–247; *Works* (1965), 1:374–415.

[125]Gribben, *John Owen and English Puritanism*, 8. Gribben lists the question whether assurance is of the essence of faith as well as Congregational polity as Owen's two primary theological shifts. However, assurance in relation to faith is more complex than appears at first glance, and it is difficult to classify here. Almost all Reformed authors believed that assurance belonged to the essence of saving faith in some respect, while leaving room for the idea that assurance could fluctuate and that believers could have a weak faith.

[126]Gribben, *John Owen and English Puritanism*, 60.

Owen's views on toleration deserve careful attention. On the one hand, he never abandoned the idea of a broad-based established church with limited toleration. On the other hand, he fluctuated over the question of how to set the bounds for toleration. Gribben regards Owen as approving Calvin's involvement in the execution of Servetus for his anti-trinitarianism, making his later opposition to corporal punishment for heresy a departure from such statements.[127] Coffey argues that Owen did not condemn Calvin's actions, but that he never departed from his stance against the execution of heretics.[128] Owen's 'Country essay' expressed concerns over defining heresy, while he engaged in a failed effort at enforcing a confession of faith around twenty fundamentals in 1654, and another failed attempt to use the Savoy Declaration as a national settlement in 1658. His approach to toleration was more defensive in the 1660s and 1670s, as he struggled for the right to survive. He may not have entirely abandoned the quest, at least in principle, to incorporate Independents into a national church, though he argued that this church should consist of gathered congregations that received government recognition under a general confession of faith. Gribben's flagging Owen's support of the monarch in *Animadversions on Fiat lux* in his quest to do so deserves attention in this regard. In short, Owen's views on toleration and establishment remained relatively stable, with many bumps and fluctuations along the way.

Gribben also draws attention to Owen's assertion in *A display of Arminianisme* to the end that baptism removes the inherent corruption of sin without removing the guilt of original sin.[129] There is certainly no trace of this peculiar view in his later writings. While some English authors argued that baptism removed the guilt of original sin, Owen's early stance is difficult to trace.[130] For that matter, baptism rarely held a prominent place in most of Owen's *Works*, containing only some material defending infant baptism and a few scattered references throughout his works. Yet Owen held a high view of communion with Christ in the Lord's Supper, seen for example in his sermon on 'The chamber of imagery', and he argued in places for weekly communion.[131] Rather than having a decreasing sacramental theology, it appears more that he had a lopsided one.

Owen's covenant theology also remained relatively stable while undergoing maturation and further nuance. His early Christological *Greater catechism* stated the Mosaic covenant was a covenant of works, while the Savoy Declaration did not do so. His Hebrews commentary explained that the covenant of works

---

[127] Gribben, *John Owen and English Puritanism*, 101.
[128] Coffey, 'Toleration controversy'.
[129] Gribben, *John Owen and English Puritanism*, 51.
[130] For example, Burgess, *Baptismall regeneration of elect infants*.
[131] Gribben, *John Owen and English Puritanism*, 229.

was present under Moses declaratively, but not covenantally.[132] It was not the covenant of works. Yet neither was it the covenant of grace. He reflected, and approved of, the view of Samuel Petto (1624–1711), who treated the Mosaic covenant as neither the covenant of works nor the covenant of grace but a 'superadded covenant'.[133] The covenant of grace continued by virtue of God's covenant with Abraham under Moses until Christ abolished and fulfilled the 'old covenant', replacing it with the new. This resembled the trichotomous view of the covenants held by Moses Amyraut (1595–1644), John Cameron (1579–1625) and Samuel Bolton (1606–54), with Owen taking a nod to unnamed Lutheran influences.[134] Yet the covenant of works remained associated with the Mosaic covenant. This related ironically to baptism, since the Presbyterian John Flavel (1627–91) at least associated this position with his Baptist opponent.[135] Owen's Congregational principle of the church consisting of a covenanted body of regenerate believers resulted in tensions with his clearly paedobaptist stance as well.

Other areas of development and change in Owen's thought are harder to pin down. He fluctuated over a trinitarian and Christological reading of 'the eternal Spirit' in Heb. 9.14, but this was a difference of exegesis rather than of substance.[136] The covenant of redemption loomed large in most of his writings, but not in his early ones, though his trinitarianism persisted. This is best explained by the recent development of the idea in British Reformed theology in the 1640s.[137] The Trinity, with special emphases on Christology and pneumatology, comes close to constituting a core to Owen's theology. His extensive attention to these issues grew partly out of his concerns to counter Socinian theology. The fluctuations in his thought throughout his career appear to reflect in most cases a deepening of his earlier views, with some minor exceptions along the way. Owen was unambiguously a trinitarian Congregationalist theologian.

Owen's style as a theologian

Some brief observations about the style of Owen's writings will complete the picture of understanding the character of his theology as a whole as well as some of his individual books. It has almost become cliché to say that Owen is often hard to read. Even Gribben, whose biography shows as much mastery of Owen's thought as anyone could hope to achieve, wrote: 'Owen is a challenging

---

[132] Owen, *Hebrews* (1680), comm. Heb. 8.6; *Works* (1850), 23:77.
[133] Petto, *The difference between the old and new covenant stated and explained* (1674).
[134] Owen, *Hebrews* (1680), comm. Heb. 8.6; *Works* (1850), 23:76–7. See discussion in Tweeddale, *John Owen and Hebrews*, 123–43.
[135] Flavel, *Vindiciæ legis & foederis* (1690).
[136] Gribben, *John Owen and English Puritanism*, 88.
[137] Muller, 'Toward the *pactum salutis*', 11–65.

writer.'[138] This relates to a number of factors, related to language, intended audiences, personality and other things. For instance, he was a Latin speaker who spent much of his life studying and teaching in Latin at the University of Oxford, which often resulted in a highly Latinized style in his English works.[139] Gribben observes the large number of neologisms in Owen's works as well, in which he coined new English words.[140] Part of the editorial task of the scholarly edition of Owen's *Works* is to provide definitions of such terms.

In addition to linguistic issues, Owen wrote for a diverse group of audiences.[141] Some of his works, such as *The death of death in the death of Christ* or *Diatriba de justitia divina*, were very scholastic in tone and complex in structure and argument, intended primarily for a well-educated audience proficient in Latin as well as scholastic categories. Other publications aimed at broader audiences, such as his *Meditations and discourses on the glory of Christ* and *Of the mortification of sinne in believers*. Some occupied a middle category as illustrated by Θεολογουμενα παντοδαπα, which likely represents part of Owen's theological lectures to Oxford students, yet included some sharp criticisms of the scholastic method. His massive commentary on Hebrews was simultaneously exegetical and theological. While he intended this work to reach a broader audience of believers, it is encumbered with features that would have been unfriendly to such readers, including block citations in Hebrew from rabbinic sources, lengthy citations on Socinian authors in Latin, detailed analyses of the Greek text of the book and large section divisions on each part of the text, with many doctrinal digressions. Owen also preached numerous sermons, to churches and before Parliament. The sermons themselves serve as a miniature summary of his theological emphases and output.

The difficulty of reading Owen for many readers may stem from his personality. He could hardly resist a theological or practical digression if it was at all related to his text or topic. However, readers will find his popular works to be much easier to read than those with an academic audience in mind. Comparing *Meditations and discourses on the glory of Christ* to Χριστολογια sufficiently illustrates the difference this could make even when Owen was treating the same topic. Understanding these features of his style will better enable people to know what to expect and where to look in his *Works* for their areas of interest.

---

[138]Gribben, *John Owen and English Puritanism*, 2.
[139]Packer, *A quest for godliness*, 194.
[140]Gribben, *John Owen and English Puritanism*, 3.
[141]Gribben, *John Owen and English Puritanism*, 2.

CONCLUSION

This sketch of Owen's character as a theologian is surely imperfect, and readers with expertise in particular works will likely find holes in the narrative. Like Gribben, this author feels that Owen has defeated him. It is hard to master more than eight million words written by a complex thinker who did not ordinarily note areas of development in his thought. The purpose of this broad-brush assessment of Owen's writing career is to set readers on the right track. Though the way forward may be blurred at points, this chapter seeks to create a visible path through it nonetheless. Other students of Owen will fill in the details along the way. The narrative discussed earlier is a modest (and less than exhaustive) attempt to help them get a general feel for Owen's theological corpus, leaving significant room for expansion. In any case, the trinitarian, pneumatological and Christological themes should be clear, along with the ways in which his Congregational polity and politics pervaded his thought.

CHAPTER 4

Owen's intellectual context

RICHARD A. MULLER

TOWARDS DEFINING OWEN'S INTELLECTUAL CONTEXT

John Owen was one of the most well-read English thinkers of the seventeenth century, equalling and in some areas exceeding the broad grasp of John Davenant, William Twisse or Richard Baxter.[1] To examine Owen's intellectual context is, in effect, to review his understanding of issues and sources in relation to his patterns of production and the varied backgrounds, whether ecclesial, doctrinal or political, that led him to produce what he did and to present it as he did. By way of example, Owen produced a series of anti-Arminian works. Clearly, the presence of Arminian writings in the first half of the seventeenth century provides some sense of the context in which these works were produced. But Owen's responses to these writings were not simply intellectual exercises. They were statements of an ecclesiastical position that he perceived both to be the confessional norm for the English church and to be under threat, first primarily from continental, largely Dutch, sources and later from developed

---

[1] Owen's life and work are well presented in Gribben, *John Owen and English Puritanism*; Trueman, *John Owen*; Wallace, 'The life and thought of John Owen to 1660'; and Cook, 'A political biography of a religious independent'. On Owen's theology, see Kapic and Jones (eds), *The Ashgate research companion to John Owen's theology*, and relevant chapters in this volume.

forms of English Arminianism. The context for his argumentation also includes the available resources on which he could draw to establish and defend his position, whether biblical or churchly, and whether patristic, medieval or early modern.

Owen's education at Oxford provided him with a broad-based expertise in classical and patristic literature, as well as a refined grasp of ancient languages, Scripture and the necessary textual, analytical and lexical tools to engage in substantial writing projects. His literary career of some four decades from his first publication in 1643 to the last years of his life spanned the eras of Commonwealth and Restoration, as well as the decades that mark the flowering of high orthodoxy among Reformed writers in England and on the continent. His work offers evidence not only of his grasp of the theological and philosophical tradition but also his detailed immersion in the issues and developments of his times. Consistently Reformed or 'Calvinist' in his basic theological views, Owen altered the focus of his work in response to the rising and waning tide of English Puritanism, the rise of an English version of Arminianism and the widespread distribution of Socinian writings during the Cromwellian era, the impact of new trends in biblical interpretation and the issues of confessionality and ecclesiology after the Restoration of the monarchy. Owen's polemics against Arminian, Socinian and Roman opponents reveal wide knowledge of British and continental developments and, particularly in the case of the anti-Socinian polemic, a significant immersion in the writings that he opposed. His later writings, particularly those coming after the Restoration, evidence a turn towards issues of Protestant union and fundamental articles of agreement.

Also to be observed in Owen's work, in addition to and, to a certain extent, apart from other contextual concerns of polemic and politics, is his address to particular audiences. Owen was both a pastor and an academic. Some of his works, such as sermons and catechesis, were directed towards lay audiences, whereas others, such as his major dogmatic and exegetical efforts, were directed towards an erudite, academic, indeed, scholastic, audience. In all genres of his literary output, Owen was deeply committed to a particular understanding of Reformed orthodox doctrine and its companion, a Reformed ecclesiology. Baxter characterized him, together with Francis Cheynell, as one of the 'over-Orthodox doctors' of his era whose intention was to 'obviate the Heresies and Errours of the Divines'.[2] His style and approach changed, however, in differing contexts. His sermons, although clearly erudite, were not particularly burdened with technical terms or references to sources, authorities and opponents. By contrast, his more academic, even scholastic, works literally bristle with references and intentionally demonstrate a mastery of sources. As has been

---

[2]Baxter, *Reliquiae Baxterianae* (1696), 199.

remarked by various scholars who have examined his works, Owen was not an innovator, and he did not leave his mark by advancing new perspectives.³

The generalization is certainly true with reference to Owen's intentional stance within the boundaries of ecumenical and Reformed confessional orthodoxy. One of Owen's intellectual contexts, then, is the development of Protestant scholastic orthodoxy – reflected both in his commitment to Reformed orthodoxy and engagement in its debates and in his approach to the definitions, details and distinctions that were characteristic of early modern Protestant scholasticism, particularly as it transitioned from its early to its high orthodox form.⁴ He consistently added to the density of argument on all of the major topics he wrote, and in his major works, he added much by way of detail and nuance that was original. This density of argument with regard to historical sources and contemporary materials reflects the academic or scholastic context of Owen's efforts: his work on trinitarian and Christological issues, for example, reveals extensive use of and reliance on patristic sources, while his philosophical argumentation evidences his broad acquaintance with classical sources while illustrating the eclectic use of medieval materials characteristic of the Reformed writers of his era.⁵

In view of the vagueness of the term, it is certainly a mistake simply to identify Owen as a 'Puritan'. From the perspective of the varied contexts of his work, it is necessary also to describe him as an English Reformed theologian, Independent in his ecclesiology, devoted from the first to the Reformed doctrine of the English church in an era of confessional change and ecclesial disruption. Given the wide scope of his reading and his deep involvement, whether theological, ecclesial or political, in the religious movements of his time, his work reflects a series of contexts that were both English and European and evidences an immersion in the major controversies of the era. Given that he came to his work both as a pastor and academic, his writings also reflect both a concern for basic piety and instruction and a concern for technical detail and mastery of sources and argumentation. In his academic or technical works, he drew on continental Protestant sources and Roman Catholic sources, both positively and polemically. This is not to say that the more practical writings directed towards laity were devoid either of polemic or evidence of erudition – only that these writings, notably Owen's sermons, were composed in a less technical manner. Arguably, it was towards an academic or technically trained audience that Owen's major efforts were directed. These contexts can also be

---

³Cf. Gribben, *John Owen and English Puritanism*, 270; with Letham, 'John Owen's doctrine of the trinity', 185–97, here 190.
⁴See Muller, *Post-Reformation Reformed dogmatics*, 1:27–32.
⁵Cleveland, *Thomism in John Owen*.

inferred from the reception of his thought in the broader Reformed community as well as in England. The impact of his writings can also be assessed, at least in part, from their continued publication in the centuries after his death, including a significant number of posthumous works and translations into Dutch and other languages.

Owen began his prolific writing career at the age of twenty-seven with a weighty polemic against the 'maine errors of the *Arminians*', arguing their departure from 'the received Doctrine of all the Reformed Churches' and 'divers particulars' of their departures from 'the Doctrine established in the Church of *England*'.[6] These phrases, taken from the title of Owen's Θεομαχία αυτεξουσιαστικη: or, *A display of Arminianisme* (1643), already offer a sense of the breadth of Owen's intellectual context: not merely development and debate in the English church but also the broader continental engagement of Reformed theology – and, as his citations and arguments further evidence, a significant recourse to the riches of the Christian tradition, patristic and medieval.[7]

A steady stream of treatises, tracts, instructional works and sermons followed, yielding more than sixty titled works during his lifetime, some quite vast in scope, plus numerous sermons and prefaces, published at a rate of several per year up to the time of Owen's death, followed by a series of posthumous writings extending into the third decade of the eighteenth century. Whereas Owen's positive doctrinal and exegetical work appeared in massive tomes throughout his career, his polemics are highly contextualized, reflecting major issues that he confronted at particular times. This distinction does not lead to a separation of the various genres of Owen's works; rather, it permits a contextualized reading of the positive treatises in the light of Owen's own developing study and debate.

The larger part of Owen's earliest publications was polemical. His anti-Arminian writings are found mainly in five treatises written between 1643 and 1654; his anti-Socinian efforts are concentrated in three works dating from 1655 to 1656, with a final *Vindication* of the doctrine of the Trinity appearing in 1669; his defences of the text and doctrine of Scripture appeared in 1658 and 1659; and his anti-Papal polemic belongs largely to five volumes that appeared between 1662 and 1682 in reaction to the Catholicizing tendencies of the restored monarchy. To these might be added the treatise on justification (1677), in which the doctrine is vindicated primarily against Roman Catholic polemics. Other clearly temporally and contextually determined works are Owen's ecclesiological tracts and treatises – an extended series beginning in 1643 and extending to a number of posthumously published tracts. In these works,

---

[6]Owen, *A display of Arminianisme* (1643); *Works* (1965), 10:1–137.
[7]Cf. Trueman, *The claims of truth*, 29–34.

Owen considered issues of schism and Nonconformity, toleration and liberty, and – after the Restoration, related to his anti-Papal polemics – the problems of imposition of liturgies, church discipline and the issue of Protestant union.

Owen published positive treatises on the person of Christ and the Trinity in 1657, 1674 and 1679, followed by the posthumous publication of several related essays. His major work on the nature, history and study of theology appeared in 1661. Owen's most extended project, an *Exposition of the epistle to the Hebrews*, occupied him from 1668 to the end of his life, the last volume appearing in 1687. The vast work on the Holy Spirit began to appear in print in 1674 and also occupied Owen until the end of his life, with the final part appearing in 1693, a decade after his death. All of these works offer evidence of Owen's intellectual development, including the impact of his polemical writings, so that the progress of his polemics provides some access to the intellectual context of many of the non-polemical treatises as well.

Accordingly, this chapter approaches Owen's work with his intellectual preparation in view as providing one significant context for understanding his thought at the same time that the historical contexts of his ecclesio-political fortunes and major polemical battles are examined in three chronological divisions – his early formation and ministry to 1651; his years at Oxford, 1651–60; and his work during the Restoration era, 1660–83. References to Owen's works in the following must be selective, in the interest of illustrating his intellectual contexts rather than attempting to provide a survey of his works in each of the three divisions of his life.

EARLY CONTEXTS: ECCLESIAL AND ANTI-ARMINIAN WRITINGS TO 1651

Owen's earliest written efforts, both positive and polemical, were framed by his university experience, his early work in pastoral ministry at the close of the Laudian era, and his several years as chaplain and preacher associated with the parliamentary army under Fairfax. At Queen's College, Oxford, in the 1630s, Owen experienced the dilution of Reformed confessionality – with William Laud as chancellor of the university and Christopher Potter as provost of Queen's College, debates over major points of doctrine were ordered to be held without polemic against Arminian views, but as Potter's declarations made clear, with prejudice against the Canons of Dort and against the doctrine of reprobation in particular.[8] Owen left Oxford with a deep sense of interrelated theological and ecclesiological troubles in the Church of England and also with a dedication to disciplined writing that remained with him for his entire

---

[8] Gribben, *John Owen and English Puritanism*, 31.

life. On the theological side, Owen was convinced that Arminian tendencies were eroding the life and thought of the English church. In his second anti-Arminian work, *Salus electorum, sanguis Jesu: or, The death of death in the death of Christ* (1648), Owen noted that its content was the result of a 'serious inquiry . . . into the mind of God about these things . . . that the wit of man, in former or latter days, hath published in opposition to the truth'.[9] On the ecclesiological side he was convinced, with other Puritan pastors and writers, that Reformation had not gone far enough and that the polity of the church needed to be altered, whether in the direction of Presbyterian governance or Independency. Arguably, Owen saw these two problems as deeply intertwined in the Laudian church.

The first of Owen's anti-Arminian writings and his first published work, *A display of Arminianisme* (1643), belongs to the second phase of English reactions to what has been called Arminianism or, more polemically, semi-Pelagianism. The initial phase runs from the controversy over the views of Peter Baro to the time of the Dutch controversies over Arminianism.[10] A second phase, running roughly from the Synod of Dort into the Laudian era, concerned the British reception of the continental debate, its confessional resolution at Dort and the subsequent elaboration of Remonstrant theology.[11] A further development of debate, in which Owen would later immerse himself, arose during the Commonwealth era and took on distinctly more indigenous accents.[12]

Owen's first treatise was dedicated to the members of the Committee for Religion appointed in the House of Lords in 1640 and directed towards the preservation of 'the received doctrine of the Church of England'.[13] It achieved Owen's intention of gaining attention and patronage. The treatise reflects the second phase of English debate over Arminianism in its dense referencing of Arminius, the apology of the Remonstrants, Grevinchovius, Corvinus, Episcopius, Venator and Vorstius, but it also contains stray references to British Arminians, notably Thomas Jackson and Samuel Hoard.[14] The scant citations of Jackson's and Hoard's work of the previous decade not only evidences Owen's recognition of earlier debate in England but also his assumption that the focus of his argument should be elsewhere, namely, on the continental, largely Dutch,

---

[9] Owen, *The death of death in the death of Christ* (1648), sig. A4v; *Works* (1965), 10:149.
[10] See White, *Predestination, policy and polemic*, 101–74; Stanglin, 'Arminius *Avant la Lettre*', 51–74.
[11] Cf. White, *Predestination, policy and polemic*, 175–286.
[12] See Ollerton, 'The crisis of Calvinism and the rise of Arminianism'; see also Wallace, 'Life and thought', 35–112, on early English Arminian backgrounds to Owen's development.
[13] Owen, *A display of Arminianisme* (1643), sig. A3v; *Works* (1965), 10:9.
[14] E.g., Owen, *A display of Arminianisme* (1643), sig. A4r, 6–8, 10, 53–60; *Works* (1965), 10:10, 15–16, 19, 55–61.

Arminians.[15] The focus on continental Arminianism is evident, moreover, in the absence of any reference to John Davenant's response to Hoard.[16]

On the positive side of Owen's early work, there are his catechisms,[17] an essay on the distinction between the duties of pastors and laity,[18] and a work on Christian fellowship.[19] The 'lesser' of Owen's two catechisms occupies barely three pages in his collected works. The *Greater catechism*, however, is a more expansive work that surveys the entire scope of Christian doctrine from Scripture, God and Trinity, to the divine works of creation, and providence, sin, the law and redemption, the incarnation and work of Christ in his offices, the order of salvation, the church and the last things. Given the more topical and occasional character of the larger number of Owen's works, his *Greater catechism* is one of the few places in which one can glimpse Owen's approach, albeit an early approach, to the broader outlines of a Reformed body of divinity, reflective of both English and continental Reformed thought.

Owen's first ecclesiological work, *The duty of pastors and people distinguished* (1644),[20] has been characterized as representing a moderate or 'muted' Presbyterianism, but written as Owen was already moving towards Independency.[21] The treatise begins with chapters on the patriarchal and Mosaic administrations of worship and instruction, posed against an easy identification of Christian pastoral duties with Old Testament practice. The argument both draws on the typical Reformed view of distinctions between the Old and the New Testaments and adumbrates Owen's interest, later developed in his Θεολογούμενα παντοδαπά (1661), of using the eras of biblical history to argue a progress in revelation towards the New Testament. An immediate context of Owen's argument was the contrary position of Herbert Thorndike, then lecturer in history at Trinity College, Cambridge, known for his erudition and Roman Catholic sympathies.[22] The work also reflects Owen's early Presbyterianism in its critique of Hooker and Whitgift[23] – in some contrast

---

[15] Owen, *A display of Arminianisme* (1643), 8, 10; *Works* (1965), 10:17, 19. Cf. Jackson, *A treatise of the divine essence and attributes* (1628–9); Hoard, *Gods love to mankind manifested* (1633).
[16] Davenant, *Animadversions* (1641).
[17] Owen, *Two short catechismes* (1645); *Works* (1965), 1:463–94.
[18] Owen, *The duty of pastors and people distinguished* (1644); *Works* (1965), 13:1–49.
[19] Owen, *Eschol* (1647); *Works* (1965), 13:51–87.
[20] Owen, *The duty of pastors and people distinguished* (1644); *Works*, 13:1–49.
[21] Gribben, *John Owen and English Puritanism*, 61, 65. On Owen's ecclesiology, see James, 'The doctrine of the church in the theology of John Owen'; Lim, 'The Trinity, *adiaphora*, ecclesiology, and reformation', 281–300; Lee, 'All subjects of the kingdom of Christ'; Knapp, 'John Owen on schism and the nature of the church', 333–58; Cooper, *John Owen, Richard Baxter and the formation of Nonconformity*.
[22] Cf. Owen, *The duty of pastors and people distinguished* (1644), 8; *Works* (1965), 13:12, referencing Thorndike, *Of religious assemblies* (1642).
[23] Owen, *The duty of pastors and people distinguished* (1643), 18; *Works* (1965), 13:20.

to his later use of Hooker to justify his post-Restoration churchly sensibilities – and probably a reading of John Cotton. The treatise also reflects Owen's distress at the spiritual and educational 'estate' of the parish of Fordham, to which he had been appointed. Beyond the primary task of sound preaching, Owen signalled the importance of 'house-to house' catechizing, emphasizing proper participation in the sacraments.[24] In line with these concerns, Owen wrote his two early catechisms.

The *Greater catechism* reflects an early orthodox Reformed background to Owen's thought. He beings by asking, 'What is the Christian religion?' He answers, 'knowing God aright and living unto him', echoing the Perkinsian and Amesian definitions of theology and religion.[25] He then immediately considers the two principal topics of theology, Scripture and God. He echoes the covenantal developments of the era by defining original human duties in terms of a covenant with Adam equivalent to the eternal moral law of God, without however naming it as the 'covenant of works'. Among the emphases in the work is its extended Christological section in five chapters, dealing with the incarnation, the person of Christ, the threefold office and the two states. Owen does not lay out a historical or dispensational model of the covenant but reserves his definition of the covenant of grace as a 'new covenant' in Christ until his exposition of the priestly office.[26] If the organization of the catechism can be taken as evidence of emphases in Owen's thought, the document points towards a major interest in ecclesiology in its placement of ten chapters, including the order of salvation, into the framework of the church, prior to dealing with the 'Privileges of Believers'. Owen here is already defining the church as the body of the elect, even to the point of emphasizing the 'church militant' as the present generation of God's elect: the universal church is the 'communion of saints', and the visible church is defined in terms of particular congregations 'under officers of Christ's institution'.[27] There is no polemic against Episcopacy or Presbyterian government, but Owen, as of 1645, clearly affirmed a Congregational or Independent church order.

If *A display of Arminianisme* brought some notice and preferment, Owen's further forays in polemic were intended to establish his theological reputation against the backdrop of several invitations to preach before the Commons where, among other issues, he argued the need for continuing Reformation and pointedly addressed the Arminian threat to the English church with affirmations of the freedom of God's mercy and grace, the infinite value of

---

[24]Owen, *Two short catechismes* (1645), sig. A2v; *Works* (1965), 1:465.
[25]Owen, *Two short catechismes* (1645), 9; *Works* (1965), 1:470.
[26]Owen, *Two short catechismes* (1645), 36–7; *Works* (1965), 1:482.
[27]Owen, *Two short catechismes* (1645), 41–61; *Works* (1965), 1:484–93.

Christ's death, the indiscriminate preaching of the Gospel, but the salvation of the elect only.[28] Accordingly, the focus of anti-Arminian polemic shifted to a problem in the English church in Owen's *The death of death in the death of Christ* (1648), written at the time of the Westminster Assembly, specifically in response to Thomas Moore's universalism,[29] but also setting the problem of universalism into the broader context of Reformed works favouring hypothetical universalism and of continental Arminian arguments.[30] The treatise itself is directed towards a learned audience and intended to demonstrate its author's intellectual and theological prowess – Owen identifies his subject as 'of weight and concernment', handled 'in a great part scholasticall'[31] – and whether in detail, organization or length, it marks a major technical advance over *A display of Arminianisme*, as well as adumbrating Owen's developing Christological project against the Socinians.[32]

Whereas his sermons from this era reflect unabashed support of the victories of the parliamentary army, their published form in Owen's *Eben-ezer* (1648) added significant stress on religious toleration, probably representing a view that arose in his relation to the army, but that stood in opposition to the rising tide of a restrictive Presbyterianism in Parliament itself.[33] On the one hand, Owen could refer to the biblical 'accomplishment' of God's 'great worke of bringing his people into the promised land' as demonstrated in Fairfax's victories,[34] while on the other warn against 'dangerous encroaching' in matters of 'ordinances and Christ-purchased privileges'.[35] Here, as he would after the Restoration, Owen attempted to draw a firm line between the defeat of heresy and persecution in matters of church governance.

Owen's treatise *Of the death of Christ* (1650) continues the pattern established in *The death of death in the death of Christ* of addressing English opponents: it responds to Richard Baxter's critique of *The death of death in the death of Christ*,[36] but also briefly notes the publication of John Davenant's posthumous

---

[28]Owen, *A vision of unchangeable free mercy* (1646), 18–20, 28, 32; *Works* (1965), 8:19–20, 27, 31; cf. Gribben, *John Owen and English Puritanism*, 73–7.
[29]Moore, *The universality of God's free-grace* (1646).
[30]Note, for example, the references to the Reformed hypothetical universalists, Cameron, Testard, and Amyraut in Owen, *The death of death in the death of Christ* (1648), sig. A5r, 86, 95; *Works* (1965), 10:149, 222, 229–30; and to Arminius and Corvinus, in Owen, *The death of death in the death of Christ* (1648), 56, 93, 119, 196, 230; *Works*, 10:205, 228, 250, 317, 345.
[31]Owen, *The death of death in the death of Christ* (1648), last leaf; not included in *Works* (1965).
[32]Owen, *The death of death in the death of Christ* (1648), 166; *Works* (1965), 10:290.
[33]See Gribben, *John Owen and English Puritanism*, 93–6.
[34]Owen, *Eben-ezer* (1648), p. 14; *Works* (1965), 8:89.
[35]Owen, *Eben-ezer* (1648), p. 22; *Works* (1965), 8:96; and see Coffey, 'John Owen and the puritan toleration controversy, 1646–1659', 227–48.
[36]Baxter, *Aphorismes of justification* (1649), *appendix, ad fin.*, separate pagination, 9, 124–6, 137–45.

De morte Christi, a work sharing Owen's title,[37] with which he disagreed substantially, to the point of declaring it 'repugnant unto Truth itself', on the ground that it made the impossible claim that God has an unwilled intention to save 'millions' for whom Christ '*purchased* not one dram of saving Grace'.[38] As Gribben comments, Owen worked 'to settle the question of [his] orthodoxy by overwhelming Baxter with learning' and putting 'Baxter's arguments in the context of a wider textual culture',[39] which was, after all, Owen's chosen context for debate.

THE OXFORD YEARS: FORMULATION AND POLEMIC DURING THE COMMONWEALTH AND PROTECTORATE, 1651–60

Following 1651 Owen shifted the focus of his polemics and, as might be expected from one newly appointed as dean of Christ Church, Oxford, launched a series of works intended both to refute recognized opponents to orthodoxy and to display his erudition. English university theologians were not nearly as inclined as their continental counterparts to develop their lectures and the disputations over which they presided into detailed, technical systems of theology, although several notable works of divinity did appear from English pens in the seventeenth century (albeit not by university professors).[40] The English were far more likely to publish major topical treatises, whether positive or polemical, and Owen produced several of the most substantial, technical and lengthy treatises of the era.

Owen's academic appointment provided, arguably, the intellectual context that he had striven to establish for himself in his earlier theological polemics against Arminianism. It also positioned him to redress the situation that he had lamented during his student years at Oxford, namely the theological decline of the university as doctrinal allegiances drifted away from Reformed orthodoxy – although it needs to be kept in mind that Owen's approach to orthodoxy in the aftermath of the Synod of Dort was not at all of a piece with the understanding of the British delegation.[41] Owen was not of a mind to approve of the delegation's allowance for hypothetical universalism. There were several major fronts on which Owen's thought developed during his tenure at Oxford: his continued polemic against Arminianism and universalism, now directed primarily at

---

[37]Davenant, *Dissertationes duæ* (1650).
[38]Owen, *Of the death of Christ* (1650), A2r; *Works* (1965), 10:432.
[39]Gribben, *John Owen and English Puritanism*, 116.
[40]For example, Ussher, *A body of divinity* (1645); Leigh, *A systeme or body of divinity* (1654); Scrivener, *A course of divinity* (1674); Baxter, *Methodus theologiae christianae* (1681).
[41]On which, see Milton (ed.), *The British delegation and the Synod of Dort*.

English adversaries; his broadening anti-Socinian polemics, focused around the work of Christ, specifically the priesthood of Christ and the nature of Christ's satisfaction; the related arguments against Twisse and Rutherford on divine justice; and ecclesiology in his defence of Independency, primarily against the writings of Daniel Cawdrey.

In addressing the problem of English Arminianism, Owen turned to the refutation of Hoard, not by publishing his own response, but by penning a recommendatory preface to the posthumous printing of William Twisse's *Riches of Gods love* (1653).[42] The volume also contained a 'vindication' of Twisse from criticisms levelled by John Goodwin in his *Redemption redeemed* (1651).[43] Owen himself turned to the refutation of Goodwin in his massive account of *The doctrine of the saints perseverance* (1654). Owen's trajectory of dispute, then, evidences the rise of an English Arminian controversy, the implications of which were in a variety of ways different from the earlier English debates of the Laudian era as well as from the continental controversy.

Between 1653 and 1657, Owen devoted significant energy to countering the rise of a Socinian threat to orthodox trinitarianism and to Grotius's annotations on the Old Testament, which he took to be its exegetical enabler.[44] The initial stimulus to anti-Socinian polemic was the re-publication in early 1652 of the Latin text of the Socinian *Catechesis ecclesiarum quæ in regno Poloniæ, & magno ducatu Lithuaniæ*.[45] Shortly thereafter an English translation appeared, published in Amsterdam, titled *The Racovian catechisme*.[46] The appearance of these documents in close proximity to the release from prison of the notorious anti-trinitarian, John Biddle.[47] Owen's polemic looked in two directions – the immediate context of the Racovian Catechism and the works of Biddle and the broader context of Socinianism in Europe. Owen's later anti-Socinian writings evidence a detailed knowledge of the writings of the Socinians – based on the nine-volume *Bibliotheca fratrum Polonorum*, a copy of which he had in his library.[48]

---

[42]Twisse, *The riches of Gods love* (1653).
[43]Goodwin, *Apolytrosis apolytroseos, or, Redemption redeemed* (1651).
[44]Lloyd, 'The life and work of the Reverend John Owen D.D.'; also note Trueman, *The claims of truth*.
[45]*Catechesis ecclesiarum quae in regno Poloniae & magno ducatu Lithuaniae*. The catechism, as published in 1652, is dedicated to James I, a chronological curiosity explained by the earlier publication of the catechism, under the same title, dated from Racov, 1609, but thought to have been published in London by H. Lownes, *c.* 1614.
[46]*Racovian catechisme* (1652).
[47]On the political ramifications of the events, see Gribben, *John Owen and English Puritanism*, 137–8.
[48]Millington, *Bibliotheca Oweniana* (1684), 4, item 131.

Owen's *Diatriba de justitia divina* (1653), oddly placed by Goold in a volume of anti-Arminian polemic, is a further anti-Socinian work, also directed in part against the views of William Twisse and Samuel Rutherford.[49] In his prefatory remarks, Owen distinguishes between the major threat of Socinianism and the views of those 'very respectable theologians' whose argumentation fell short of fully supporting the necessity of Christ's satisfaction. As has been argued by several scholars, Owen changed his approach to divine justice, retracting the view expressed in his earlier work, *The death of death in the death of Christ*, where the necessity of Christ's satisfaction, argued against the Arminians, was defined as a necessary consequence of the divine decree and not an absolute necessity.[50] The Socinian threat induced Owen to take another direction on the subject, disagreeing not only with his earlier position but with the similar views of Twisse and Rutherford. Owen argued that the issue is not vindicatory justice as such, which is relational *ad extra*, but the essential justice of God and its egress: God's justice is essential to him and the *ad extra* egress of divine willing is necessary to the existence of creatures. The necessity of satisfaction for sin then rests not on the decree but on the free or unconstrained relationship of God to the world.[51]

The *Vindiciae evangelicae* (1655) is Owen's omnibus response to Biddle's catechism and the Racovian Catechism, with argumentation against what Owen took to be the Socinian inclinations of Grotius's *Annotationes*,[52] plus an appendix, 'Of the death of Christ, and of justification', responding to Baxter's hypothetical universalism.[53] Owen's preface to the reader offers a detailed documentary history of the rise of Socinianism and the ensuing debates in which Owen also registers his own view of the necessity of satisfaction in critical comments – here indicating that the view he adopted in 1653 had earlier been argued by the Basel theologian, Ludovicus Lucius.[54] The preface evidences the vast bibliographical context against which Owen framed his work.

The explicit inclusion of argument against Grotius's exegesis that Owen scattered throughout the assault on Biddle and the Racovian Catechism underlines his sense of the interconnected context of Socinian threat and problematic developments in exegesis. Of interest is Owen's sense of the

---

[49]Owen, *Diatriba de justitia divina* (1653); in translation, *A dissertation on divine justice*, Works (1965), 10:481–624, here 486. See also Trueman, 'John Owen's *Dissertation on divine justice*', 87–103; Schendel, 'A learned dispute among friends'.
[50]Owen, *The death of death in the death of Christ* (1648), 57; Works, 10:205; cf. Trueman, 'John Owen's *Dissertation*', 89.
[51]Cf. Trueman, 'John Owen's *Dissertation on Divine Justice*', 95–8.
[52]Grotius, *Annotata ad Vetus Testamentum* (1644).
[53]Owen, *Vindiciae evangelicae* (1655), Works, 12:1–590 (*Vindiciae*), 591–616 (appendix against Baxter).
[54]Lucius, *De satisfactione Christi, pro peccatis nostris* (1628).

distance between Grotius's earlier anti-Socinian *De satisfactio Christi*,[55] which he viewed as less than adequate but not specifically heretical work, and Grotius's later *Annotata*.[56] His *A review of the annotations of Hugo Grotius* (1656) continued the polemic of the preceding year with what Owen internally entitled 'A second consideration of the annotations of Hugo Grotius'.[57] Although focused on Christ's divinity and satisfaction, the work also serves as a prelude to the three treatises on Scripture and its interpretation, as Owen viewed the underlying problem of Grotius's work to be his text-critical exegesis. The treatise, then, points towards two contextual issues that Owen viewed as interrelated. Grotius's readings of Old Testament texts, notably the Messianic passages in Isaiah, as being rooted in ancient settings and as not being relevant to atonement theory, prompted Owen to view Grotius as sympathizing with the Socinians, both in their denials of Christ's satisfaction and in their literalistic approach to Old Testament texts that had traditionally been used to support the doctrines of the Trinity and the divinity of Christ.

Following his attack on Grotius, Owen wrote three treatises on the subject of the divinity and purity of the biblical text. The first of these, *Pro Sacris Scripturis*, was probably published in a separate edition in 1658 and was distinct from the other two in its address to the problem of Quakerism, specifically the emphasis on personal inspiration and inner light as having religious authority over Scripture.[58] It was also published as the final essay in a volume containing his *Of the divine originall, authority, self-evidencing light, and power of the Scriptures* and *Of the integrity and purity of the Hebrew and Greek texts of the Old and New Testament*.[59]

The occasion for the two treatises published under the main title *Of the divine originall* was the appearance of the great London Polyglot Bible edited by Brian Walton in 1653–7.[60] Owen's problem was not so much with the Polyglot text or, indeed, with the project of producing a polyglot Bible – as the catalogue of Owen's library indicates, he owned all eight volumes of the London Polyglot.[61]

---

[55] Grotius, *Defensio fidei catholicae de satisfactione Christi* (1617).
[56] Owen, *Vindiciae evangelicae* (1655), 24–5; *Works*, 12:27.
[57] Owen, *A review of the annotationes of Hugo Grotius* (1656), sig. A2r; *Works* (1965), 12:619.
[58] Owen, *Pro Sacris Scripturis* (1658); *Works* (1850), 16:423–76; translated by Stephen Westcott as *A defense of sacred Scripture against modern fanaticism*, in Owen, *Biblical theology*, 769–854.
[59] Owen, *Of the divine originall* (1659); *Works* (1965), 16:281–421; the treatise *Of the purity and integrity* appears as 145–349 in the 1659 printing and as *Works* (1965), 3:345–421; Owen, *Pro Sacris Scripturis*, although listed on the main title page is lacking from some of the 1659 editions. On Owen's doctrine of Scripture, see Leslie, *The light of grace*; on his exegetical method, see Knapp, 'Understanding the mind of God'; idem, 'John Owen's interpretation of Hebrews 6:4–6', 29–52.
[60] *Biblia sacra polyglotta, complectentia textus originales Hebraicum, cum Pentateucho Samaritano, Chaldaicum, Graecum*.
[61] Millington, *Bibliotheca Oweniana* (1684), 1, item 15.

It is also fairly clear that he used the Polyglot extensively in his exegesis of Hebrews, given his sense of the importance of the Syriac version. As Goold points out, there is no ground for claiming that Owen was antagonistic to the London Polyglot or that he devalued the textual work of its various editors and lexicographers.[62] Owen's problem with the Polyglot lay primarily with portions of the critical apparatus found in the prefatory or prolegomenal volume and with the seeming alliance of the editors of Polyglots, beginning with Ximénez's Complutensian Bible, to assume a text-critical approach that could argue for the late invention of the Hebrew vowel points and that might muddy the interpretive waters with 'innumerable various lections'.[63] In the hands of Roman Catholics, this method had been used to argue the normative value of the Vulgate and, given the seeming impossibility of reconciling all of the variants and the resulting view of the text of Scripture as corrupted, to claim the priority of church over Scripture in the determination of meaning and doctrine.[64] Owen also declaimed against the practice, advocated by some of the authors of the Polyglot's prolegomena, to edit or reconstruct the Hebrew and Greek text by a process of conjectural emendation based on ancient translations. In Owen's view, text-critical work was legitimate, as long as it respected the absolute priority of the original language of the text as found in surviving copies of the writings of the prophets and apostles.[65] Walton responded at length to Owen's charges, arguing for the legitimacy of the use of ancient versions and for the late origin of the vowel points, at the same time that he asserted his belief in the basic integrity of the biblical text.[66]

Owen's defence of Congregationalism or Independency in *Of schisme* (1657)[67] generated a heated controversy over ecclesiology, specifically over the nature of the visible church. The chief opponent of Owen was Daniel Cawdrey, a Presbyterian minister described by James Reid as 'a notable member of the assembly of divines at Westminster',[68] who pronounced schism to be a

---

[62] Goold, 'Prefatory note', in Owen, *Works* (1965), 16:345.
[63] Owen, *Of the divine originall* (1659), sig. *4v–A4v; *Works* (1965), 16:285–9; also Owen, *Of the integrity and purity of the Hebrew and Greek text* (1659), 145–61; *Works* (1965), 16:348–53. Note that *Of the integrity and purity* has a separate title page in the 1659 printing, but is paginated continuously after *Of the divine originall*.
[64] Owen, *Of the integrity and purity of the Hebrew and Greek text* (1659), 148–9; *Works* (1965), 16:348.
[65] Owen, *Of the integrity and purity of the Hebrew and Greek text* (1659), 159, 173–5; *Works* (1965), 16:352, 357.
[66] Walton, *The considerator considered* (1659). Also note, Todd, *Memoirs of the life and writings of the Right Rev. Brian Walton* (1821), the second volume of which contains an edition of *The considerator considered*.
[67] Owen, *Works* (1965), 13:89–206.
[68] Reid, *Memoirs of the lives and writings of those eminent divines* (1811–15), 1:217; and see Lee, 'All subjects of the kingdom of Christ', 167–8.

'heinous' crime that was so 'dangerous and *noxious* to the Church of God . . . that no *Invective* against the *evils* of it can wel *be* too great or high' – and who proceeded to identify Independency as schism and Owen as one of its chief advocates. Cawdrey added fuel to the fire by examining Owen's early *The duty of pastors and people distinguished* in order to demonstrate the inconsistency of Owen's views.[69] Owen responded with *A review of the true nature of schisme* (1657)[70] and, in a further response to a second polemical treatise by Cawdrey, with *An answer to a later treatise of Daniel Cawdrey about the nature of schisme* (1658).[71] *Of schisme* is a treatise of significant length, published without preface or introductory letter to the reader at a time when Owen was primarily occupied with responses to the threat of Socinianism. Apart from the ongoing debates over church polity between Presbyterians and Independents, and the background threats of episcopacy and Romanism, there is little in the treatise itself to indicate Owen's immediate reason for writing at such length other than deep distress over the fragmentation of the church and the inability of Protestants to come to an agreement. His definition of the visible catholic church as '*the Universality of men professing the Doctrine of the Gospell*, and obedience to God in Christ . . . throughout the World', bounded only by rules of faith and charity such as found in the New Testament, enabled him to detach catholicity from church polity and variations in confessionality and to argue that schism was in fact an intra-congregational matter.[72] Owen would maintain this view after the Restoration in debate with Edward Stillingfleet, the dean of St Paul's.[73]

In 1652, Owen served on a parliamentary committee that included Thomas Goodwin, Philip Nye and Sydrach Simpson (all of whom were Independents or Congregationalists), and in 1654 on another parliamentary committee that added Richard Vines, Thomas Manton, Francis Cheynell, Stephen Marshall and Richard Baxter (all of whom were Presbyterians). The committees produced two shorter, more generally accessible, confessions of faith that identified the basic beliefs that should be viewed as orthodox and that extended religious toleration to all who held them.[74] Both documents are notable for their clear trinitarianism and their focus on true believers and worship according to the revealed will of God, without any specific ecclesiological issues noted. The two documents coincide with Owen's views of catholicity, his sense of schism as not a matter of governance beyond the congregation, and the approach that he

---

[69]Cawdrey, *Independencie a great schism proved against Dr. Owen* (1657).
[70]Owen, *Works* (1965), 13:207–75.
[71]Owen, *Works* (1965), 13:277–302.
[72]Owen, *Of schisme* (1657), 112; *Works* (1965), 13:137.
[73]Owen, *A brief vindication of the non-conformists* (1680); *Works* (1965), 13:303–42.
[74]*Proposals for the furtherance and propagation of the Gospel in this nation* (1652).

would follow even after the Restoration in arguing for a unified Protestantism in England against the threat of Roman Catholicism.

Owen also produced a series of major theological treatises on largely positive theological topics, two of which belong to his tenure at Oxford and the rest to the post-Restoration phase of his career. The treatises *Of communion with God* (1657) and Θεολογουμενα παντοδαπα (1661) reflect the academic context of Oxford. The other works, the *Exposition of the epistle to the Hebrews* (1668–1687), Πνευματολογια (1674) and Χριστολογια (1679), were penned after the Restoration. Apart from their positive doctrinal, polemical or politico-ecclesial contexts, these were clearly designed as demonstrations of erudition, evidencing the scholastic context of Owen's major efforts and, with the exception of Θεολογουμενα παντοδαπα, they each evidence his central fascination with trinitarian and Christological formulation.

Of communion with God is the first of Owen's trinitarian expositions. Owen comments in his preface that he was 'brought under an engagement' to publish on the Trinity some six years prior to publication – which would place the beginning of his work on the treatise in 1651, when he assumed the position of dean of Christ Church. It was the strong practical focus of the treatise on communion with God that led Goold to view it as a product of meditations begun during Owen's earlier pastorate at Coggeshall, and it is certainly the case that the treatise lacks the scholastic density characteristic of most of his extended essays and that, despite its provenance, the treatise is remarkably free of reference to Socinianism.[75] It certainly reflects the Reformed and Puritan view of theology as at once practical and theoretical. Other works published by Owen during his Oxford tenure also evidence a deep concern for popular piety, notably *Of the mortification of sinne in believers* (1656)[76] and sermons like *God's presence with a people* (1656).[77] Perhaps the most remarkable, even speculative, aspect of Owen's *Of communion with God* is his tendency away from the usual assumption of an undivided trinitarian work *ad extra* to an emphasis not only on the *ad extra* appropriated works of the Son and Spirit, but to an extended representation of communion with God the Father as an *ad extra* work, when typically, the Father is understood as operative *ad extra*, if at all, in creation.[78] The context for this unique approach to the work of God the Father is certainly Owen's sense of the needs of piety in his time – but perhaps also the rising interest, characteristic of the 1650s, in the concept of

---

[75] Owen, *Works* (1965), 2:1–274, here, 2.
[76] Owen, *Works* (1965), 6:1–86.
[77] Owen, *Works* (1965), 8:427–52.
[78] Cf. Gribben, *John Owen and English Puritanism*, 172–3; with the discussion of *opera appropriata* in Muller, *Post-Reformation Reformed dogmatics*, 4:267–74.

a *pactum salutis* in which the Father eternally covenants with the Son for the accomplishment of redemption.[79]

Θεολογουμενα παντοδαπα stands in a category by itself among Owen's works. It was the result of lectures on theology and its history delivered at Oxford and developed following 1658 but finalized and published after the Restoration.[80] This work was also received on the continent, with Latin editions appearing from publishers in Bremen (1684) and Franeker (1700). It was also partially rendered in an English synopsis in the late seventeenth century by Lucy Hutchinson. Although her work was not published at the time, it demonstrates how a highly technical work like Owen's was of interest beyond its academic context.[81] Θεολογουμενα παντοδαπα is an academic tour de force illustrating Owen's vast grasp of sources and materials from the ancient classical and patristic eras to the early modernity, from philosophical, to lexical, to dogmatic works, and in his own time works from multiple confessionalities and of pan-European scholarship.[82]

More specifically, the work is a sui generis propaedeutic treatise that stands in a fairly clear relation to developments in the Reformed theological prolegomena and covenant theology, but is neither a prolegomenon to theology nor a 'biblical theology'.[83] Rather it presents understandings of theology both natural and supernatural through the stages of biblical history, beginning with a book examining theology in general and continuing with chapters on natural theology before and after the fall. Then, in a series of five books, Owen surveys the historical course of human theology as the reception and rejection of supernatural revelation after the fall in its post-lapsarian Adamic, post-diluvian Noahic, Abrahamic and Mosaic forms, concluding with a final book 'on evangelical theology properly so-called'. The definitions of theology as natural and supernatural, as well as the deployment of natural theology before and after the fall, reflect patterns of Reformed prolegomena beginning with Franciscus Junius.

Owen's approach to the division of biblical history reflects reception of the Reformed covenant theology of the era, perhaps Cocceius's *Summa de foedere* (1648), which Owen cites, although the historical divisions are closer in design

---

[79]See Muller, 'Toward the *pactum salutis*', 11–65.

[80]Owen, Θεολογουμενα παντοδαπα (1661); *Works* (1850), 17:1–480; cf. the description of the work and its context in Gribben, *John Owen and English Puritanism*, 213–6. On Owen's method, see Rehnman, *Divine discourse*.

[81]That is, the later portion 'on theology' in Hutchinson, *On the principles of the Christian religion* (1817); also note the periphrastic rendering, Owen, *Biblical theology*.

[82]Cf. the extended description in Gribben, *John Owen and English Puritanism*, 213–4.

[83]Cf. Muller, *Post-Reformation Reformed dogmatics*, 1:118; neither a prolegomenon to theology as indicated in McGraw, *John Owen: Trajectories in Reformed Orthodox theology*, 162, nor a 'biblical theology' as implied by the title of Owen, *Biblical theology*.

to Francis Roberts's massive *Mysterium & medulla Bibliorum* (1657).[84] Having patterned his work on the eras delineated in covenantal theology, Owen presents what amounts to a cultural history of the world based on classical sources, Jewish antiquities and patristic materials. His post-lapsarian chapters on natural theology offer a panorama of pagan philosophical and literary sources.

The work is also punctuated by eight major 'digressions' on the problem of universal grace, the antiquity of Hebrew letters, the origin of the Hebrew vowel points, the Septuagint, the origin of the Targums, Jewish religious rites in relation to Christian observance and on the mingling of philosophy with theology. Other portions of the work identified in Goold's *Index capitum* as digressions ('De philosophiae et scientiarum ortu' and 'De notis ecclesiae Romanae Bellarminiis') are portions of chapters not identified as digressions in the original. Taken as a group, these ten portions of the work offer the clearest sense of Owen's polemical contexts. By way of example, the lengthy digression on universal grace addresses a major controversy of the era that, by the time Owen wrote Θεολογούμενα παντοδαπα, included works by Amyraut, responses by Spanheim and initial debate between Owen and Baxter – although Owen, rather uncharacteristically, cited no sources in his digression. Owen also evidenced a certain degree of reserve in his digression on the vowel points. He maintained the canonical origin of the vowel points, disputing the conclusions of Elias Levita, noting the beginnings of Reformed debate between Buxtorff and Cappel, but not directly mentioning his problems with the London Polyglott and Brian Walton, even though he had disputed Walton's views in his *Of the divine originall* and was profoundly annoyed by Walton's response to his arguments.[85]

Work on the doctrine Trinity, including writings on Christ and the Holy Spirit, occupied Owen over three decades, beginning with a series of sermons preached at Oxford in 1651 that were eventually edited and published as *Of communion with God*,[86] and ending in three volumes of his posthumously published discourses.[87] The intellectual contexts, accordingly, were quite varied. His initial interest in trinitarian thought coincided with his encounter with Socinian literature. Still it took on a more profound positive focus as it progressed as well as encountering other contextual issues and obstacles –

---

[84] Roberts, *Mysterium & medulla Bibliorum* (1657). On Owen's covenantal thought, see Trueman, *John Owen*, 67–83.
[85] Owen, Θεολογούμενα παντοδαπα (1661), 388, 393; *Works* (1850), 17:350.
[86] On the date and location of the original sermons, see Owen, *Of communion with God*, sig. A2r; *Works* (1965), 2:2–3; and Gribben, *John Owen and English Puritanism*, 172.
[87] Owen's trinitarian thought is perhaps the most densely examined topic in recent scholarly studies of his work, albeit largely in a dogmatic to the exclusion of a historical manner; cf. the complaint in Gribben, *John Owen and English Puritanism*, 8, 10.

finally, in the last decade of Owen's life, engaging William Sherlock whose work would later itself become the centre of controversy, as we will see further.

AFTER THE RESTORATION, 1660–83

Owen was consistently sensitive to his political context. The Restoration of the monarchy and episcopal governance of the established church, coupled with persecution of dissent, led him to be wary of publishing works relating to ecclesiology and dissent under his own name. Between 1662, the year of the Great Ejection, and 1670, he published a series of anonymous tracts defending Nonconformity and the anti-Papal Protestant cause in general, among them *Animadversions on Fiat lux* (1662), *A discourse concerning liturgies* (1662), *Indulgence and toleration* (1667), *A peace-offering* (1667), *A brief instruction in the worship of God* (1667) and *Truth and innocence vindicated* (1669). Works published under Owen's name shortly after the Restoration, with the exception of *A vindication of the animadversions on Fiat lux* (1664), notably *Indwelling sin* (1668), *A practical exposition on the 130th Psalm* (1669), *A brief declaration and vindication of the doctrine of the Trinity* (1669) and *Sabbath* (1671), were all doctrinal works that supported piety and orthodoxy and that would not have led either to prosecution or persecution. In these later works, he identified himself as Doctor of Divinity and, in the cases of the *Vindication*, the *Practical exposition*, and the *Brief declaration*, was able to receive episcopal imprimatur for publication.

The two treatises addressed to John Vincent Cane,[88] the author of anonymously published *Fiat lux* and its defence, mark a new priority in Owen's ecclesiological argumentation. Not that anti-Roman lines of argument were absent from his earlier work – they were quite visible – but earlier church-political contexts had not motivated him to write major treatises on the subject. The Restoration, however, with its return to episcopacy and the prayer book, together with the Roman Catholic sympathies of the Crown, opened the way for the argument that Protestantism represented unresolved differences and dissents in religion, tumult and rebellion, whereas Romanism provided a stable and true religion. Owen's response played on Cane's claim that the 'moderation' of tumult could be achieved by 'embracement of Popery', arguing that moderation was a 'pretended' and Popery the genuine goal.[89] In the treatise, after attacking the method and motivation of Cane's work, Owen went

---

[88]Anon. [John Vincent Cane], *Fiat lux: or, A general conduct to a right understanding in the great combustions and broils about religion here in England* (1661); and, in response to Owen, *An epistle to the author of the Animadversions upon Fiat lux* (1662).
[89]Owen, *Animadversions on Fiat lux* (1662), sig. A4r; *Works* (1965), 14:3.

on to argue that Protestantism properly understood the relationship between Scripture and reason, and that Popery debased Scripture, claiming Scripture as its own property and put the church 'before the gospel'.[90] To Cane's charges concerning the excessive use of reason in Protestant denials of Roman thought and practice, Owen responded that 'if our author can persuade us first to throw away out Bibles, and then to lay aside the use of our reason, I suppose there is no doubt but we shall become Roman Catholics'.[91] The treatise displays both learning and rhetorical ability, the latter laden with sarcasm against such claims as the 'Pope . . . is a good man': Owen declares he is glad to know this, given the papal tactics of 'imprisoning, and torturing . . . Persons, and . . . burning their Bodies in fire'.[92] As to Cane's claims of the superiority of devotion among Romanists, Owen notes that it resembles nothing so much as the 'holier than thou' Pharisees of the New Testament.[93] Owen concluded with a series of chapters on 'popish contradictions', the mass, the Virgin, images, saints, purgatory and other issues in dispute. When Cane responded, Owen answered in his own name, in greater detail, and with an equal dose of venom.

During this time Owen was also probably preparing what would be his major exegetical effort, the massive *Exercitations on the Epistle to the Hebrews*, which may have had its beginnings during Owen's years of lecturing at Oxford, but was published over the course of more than a decade at the conclusion of his career.[94] Although a work published after the Restoration of the monarchy, the *Exercitations* reflect Owen's theological identity over the course of his whole career, embodying a wide range of echoes of earlier debates, notably with the Arminians, over Grotius's *Annotationes*, against Socinian theology, and on the issue of Judaism and its early modern Messianic theories.[95] Gribben is surely correct in noting that the theme of Christ's high priesthood was a central concern for Owen, beginning with his unpublished and presumably lost *Tractatus de sacerdotio Christi, contra Armin, Socin, et Papistas*.[96] Goold speculated that the unpublished work 'may have supplied part of the long and valuable exercitations on the priesthood of Christ prefixed to the Exposition

---

[90] Owen, *Animadversions on Fiat lux* (1662), 230–1; *Works* (1965), 14:88–9.
[91] Owen, *Animadversions on Fiat lux* (1662), 188; *Works* (1965), 14:73.
[92] Owen, *Animadversions on Fiat lux* (1662), 103; *Works* (1965), 14:42.
[93] Owen, *Animadversions on Fiat lux* (1662), 107; *Works* (1965), 14:43.
[94] See Gribben, *John Owen and English Puritanism*, 212, 235.
[95] See Gribben, *John Owen and English Puritanism*, 235–6.
[96] Cited in Owen, *The duty of pastors and people distinguished* (1644), 16, where in the context of commenting on the 'keys' to heaven and the way God executes his 'ordinances', Owen comments that he has discussed this subject 'elsewhere' and refers marginally to the title of the treatise as a work not yet edited; *Works* (1965), 13:18 n2; cf. Gribben, *John Owen and English Puritanism*, 42–3, 235–6.

of the Epistle to the Hebrews'.[97] In any case, the nature of Christ's priesthood remained central to Owen's anti-Arminian writings, his anti-Socinian polemics and his argumentation on divine justice against Twisse and Rutherford, and it is a focus not only of his exegesis of the text of Hebrews but also of the polemic in his *Exercitations*.

The commentary appeared in four volumes (1668, 1674, 1680 and 1687), the first two of which were divided between exercitations and commentary.[98] Standing in relation to the main commentary there is also the *Exercitations concerning . . . the original of the Sabbath*, published independently in 1671.[99] Volume one of the commentary contained twenty-four exercitations followed by a commentary on chapters one and two of the epistle. Volume two presented ten more exercitations and commentary on chapters three through five. The remaining two volumes contained commentary on chapters six through ten and eleven through thirteen, respectively.[100] The central theme of the epistle, 'the doctrine of the person and priesthood of Christ', had occupied Owen for much of his career.[101]

The exercitations are of interest inasmuch as they, perhaps more than any other portions of Owen's exposition, provide access to his interactions with the scholarly efforts of his era. By way of example, Owen took up at length the issues of the original language of the epistle, its occasion, canonicity and authorship, that had been debated in his own time as well as in the patristic era. The scholarly density of the exercitations is evident from Owen's lengthy exposition of the meaning of 'canon' and 'canonical' as derived via Greek from a Hebrew original. As to the authorship, Owen used patristic and textual evidence to argue for Pauline authorship, but at the same time he argued against the identification of authorship as being necessary to canonicity. He argued at length against patristic indications that the epistle had first been written in Hebrew and examined the style of the Greek text in detail to argue that it had originally been written in Greek. This argumentation did not, however, lead Owen away from his interest in Judaica, but rather led him into extended exercitations on how institutions of the 'Jewish church' were nonetheless referenced in the epistle – a study that brought to bear the fruits of early modern Protestant Hebraism.[102]

---

[97] Owen, *Works* (1965), 13:2.
[98] Owen, *Hebrews* (1668, 1674, 1680, 1684); *Works* (1965), volumes 17–23.
[99] Owen, *Sabbath*, in *Works*, 19:261–460, placed as a final exercitation in the commentary on Hebrews.
[100] See Tweeddale, 'John Owen's commentary on Hebrews in context', 49–63; also note Kapic, 'Typology, the messiah, and John Owen's theological reading of Hebrews', 135–54.
[101] Owen, *Hebrews* (1668), sig. (*)v; *Works* (1965), 18:6; and note Gribben, *John Owen and English Puritanism*, 236.
[102] Cf. Exercitations 1–4, 19–24 in Owen, *Hebrews* (1668); and *Works* (1965), 18.

Contemporaneously with this work on the epistle to the Hebrews, Owen penned two prefaces that, together with the Hebrews commentary, are noteworthy as indicators of his exegetical and interpretive preferences: the unsigned 'To the Christian Reader' in James Durham's *Clavis cantici* and the signed preface 'To the Christian Reader' in Henry Lukin's *An introduction to the Holy Scripture*.[103] Owen's praise for Lukin in particular highlighted his adherence to a traditional reading of the text that held to a 'rational understanding of the words and Propositions' in Scripture as providing 'saving understanding of the Mystery and Truths' contained in the text – as opposed to the new critical methods found in Grotius's *Annotations* and the London Polyglot,[104] this despite Owen's recognition of the value of the careful establishment of text and his recourse to ancient versions and Judaica. There are, then, several aspects of Owen's interpretive endeavours – all reflective of his intellectual context.

Owen's consistent appeal to ancient texts and versions in establishing and arguing the meaning of the epistle serves to evidence several of the contexts of his work. His appeal indicates a use of the Polyglot despite his critique of its prolegomena and, when taken together with his use of the Targums and his appeals to the Mishna and Talmud, it points towards his location in the scholarly milieu of contemporary biblical interpretation. Interest in the textual, lexical and contextual use of Judaica reflects not only a use of the Polyglot but also the work of exegetes like Henry Ainsworth, Christopher Cartwright and John Lightfoot.

In addition to this immersion in the exegetical models of his era, Owen viewed reliance on corrupt texts as a source of doctrinal error. In the case of Hebrews, with its focus on the priesthood of Christ, his multi-lingual textual work reflects the technical side of his polemic against the Socinians, where, given the Socinian approach to textual criticism, he had warned that one ought not to engage their arguments unless adept in the ancient languages.[105] At the same time, Owen polemicized against the early development of historical-critical work in favour of a more traditional analysis of the grammatical sense and the figures of the text as the foundation of his derivation of orthodox doctrine – evidence in particular by his advocacy of Lukin's work.

A brief declaration and vindication of the doctrine of the Trinity (1669)[106] is, by Owen's standards, a more popular work, no longer directed towards

---

[103]Durham, *Clavis cantici* (1668), two leaves, unmarked, *ad init.*; Lukin, *An introduction to the Holy Scripture* (1669), sig. A5r–(a)1v.
[104]Owen, 'To the Christian reader', in Lukin, *An introduction to the Holy Scripture* (1669), sig. A7r.
[105]Owen, *Vindiciae evangelicae* (1655), 65–6; *Works* (1965), 12:50; cf. Knapp, 'Understanding the mind of God', 118.
[106]Owen, *A brief declaration and vindication of the doctrine of the Trinity* (1669); *Works*, 2:365–454.

an erudite, university-trained readership, but towards a literate readership of Christian laity who might fall prey to the typical battery of Socinian errors. Given the address of the treatise to 'ordinary Christians', Owen added an appendix in which he offered a more detailed analysis of terms and arguments, notably an exegetical justification of the use of 'satisfaction' as the proper term describing Christ's atonement.[107] The work was published with the imprimatur of the bishop of London, as certified by Robert Grove, who was then the bishop's chaplain.

Owen's *Sabbath* (1671) could be classified as exegetical, doctrinal or ecclesiological, given its varied methodologies and the several contexts addressed by its arguments.[108] In addition to his detailed awareness of the English debates, and of earlier continental Reformed views, Owen evidences a clear grasp of the extended debates in the Netherlands over the question of the original institution of Sabbath worship, whether at Sinai (Gomarus) or in creation and later accommodated to the needs of Israel (Rivetus).[109] Owen's own conclusions concerning the origin of Sabbath observance in creation, its adaptation to Israel in the Decalogue and its observance by Christians also serve to situate his thought in the debates over covenant theology – where his argumentation has affinities with the covenantal theology of his friend Patrick Gillespie as well as evidencing knowledge of a wide swathe of earlier British and continental thought.[110]

Owen's *A vindication of some passages* (1674) was occasioned by a pointed critique of his *Of communion with God* by William Sherlock. Owen responded as if surprised by the criticism, coming some seventeen years after his book's publication. His response identified Sherlock's opinions as 'Wild, Uncouth, Extravagant, and contrary to the common Faith of Christians; being all of them traduced, and some of them transcribed, from the Writings of the *Socinians*'.[111] Sherlock, from a somewhat rationalist perspective, intended to critique nonconformist theology as overly mystical, immersed in an allegorical reading of the Song of Songs, and highly irrational in its appeal to 'an acquaintance with the Person of Christ' as the source of special discernment in religion.[112]

---

[107] Owen, *A brief declaration and vindication of the doctrine of the Trinity* (1669); *Works*, 2:441.
[108] Owen, *Sabbath* (1671); *Works* (1965), 18:261–459.
[109] On the Dutch debates, see Carmichael, *A Continental view*; Dieleman, *The battle for the Sabbath*, 110-30.
[110] See Trueman, *John Owen*, 67–99; Van Asselt, 'Covenant theology as relational theology: The contributions of Johannes Cocceius (1603–1669) and John Owen (1618–1683) to a living reformed theology', 65–84; and Bobick, 'Owen's razor: The role of Ramist logic in the covenant theology of John Owen (1616–1683)'.
[111] Owen, *A vindication of some passages* (1674), 8; *Works* (1965), 2:279.
[112] Sherlock, *A discourse concerning the knowledge of Jesus Christ* (1674), 37. Owen's work was also defended by his associate Robert Ferguson, *The interest of reason in religion* (1675); cf. Gribben,

Owen, albeit writing after the Restoration, would still identify his views as expressing 'the Doctrine of the Church of *England*', as well as the teachings of 'the Antient Church' – and in what must be seen as a political as well as theological rebuttal, he appealed to none other than Richard Hooker in his own defence.[113] Beyond the clash between a voice of the established church and an eminent nonconformist, the rationalistic Sherlock took the ground of a more literal approach to the text, whereas Owen, who had only four years earlier advocated James Durham's allegorical exegesis of the Song of Songs, followed the lines of traditional interpretation to argue for a Christological reading of the text.[114]

Like his other massive projects, Owen's work on the doctrine of the Holy Spirit, beginning with the Πνευματολογια (1674), followed by a series of further treatises, and concluding with the posthumous *Two discourses concerning the Holy Spirit* (1693),[115] reflects a wide background ranging from patristic to Reformation and post-Reformation era sources as well as the ecclesial and political contexts of dissent during the Restoration. The work, considered as part of Owen's trinitarian exposition, is the last portion of an enormous effort that began in 1657 with *Of communion with God* and would continue in Χριστολογια (1679) – and that would span four volumes in the Goold edition of his collected works.

Although the Πνευματολογια work is not polemical, Owen does offer several anti-Socinian arguments, notably against Schlichting's treatise on the Trinity and Crell's work on the Holy Spirit.[116] He also singled out Samuel Parker's 'opprobrious' claims that deep worries over personal sinfulness, including a sense of spiritual desertion or divine displeasure, were not the work of the Holy Spirit on the human heart, but 'melancholy reeks and vapours' to be explained in a 'mechanical account' of the workings of the human brain. Such claims, in Owen's view, undermined the doctrine of regeneration and thereby supported Pelagianism.[117] There are also scattered polemics against Rome and a vast array of patristic materials marshalled both to formulate doctrine and to demonstrate the catholicity of Owen's theology both against Roman Catholicism and in the face of criticisms of dissent.

John Owen and English Puritanism, 253.
[113]Owen, *A vindication of some passages* (1674), 13; *Works* (1965), 2:280.
[114]Owen, 'To the Christian reader', in Durham, *Clavis cantici* (1668), two leaves, unmarked, *ad init.*
[115]Owen, Πνευματολογια (1674); *Works* (1965), 3:1–651; 4:1–520.
[116]Schlichting, *De SS. Trinitate, de moralibus N.& V. Testamenti praeceptis* (1637); Crell, *Tractatus de Spiritu Sancto qui fidelibus datur* (1650); cited in Owen, Πνευματολογια (1674), 4, 34, 38, 47, 51, 54, 55, 57, 58, 61, 93, 141; *Works* (1965), 3:19, 54, 59, 68, 73, 77, 79, 81, 82, 85, 122, 173.
[117]Owen, Πνευματολογια (1674), 92, 177; *Works* (1965), 3:121, 213; responding to Parker, *A defence and continuation of the ecclesiastical politie* (1671), 339–42.

Prominent among the patristic authors cited are Didymus the Blind, Ambrose, Augustine and Cyprian, evidencing both Owen's sense of fundamental catholicity of Protestant doctrine and also a pattern or reception, typical of his era, according to which the church fathers were mined as a resource for formulation of doctrine, as distinct from a historical or critical analysis of patristic materials.[118] Given, among other issues, the interrelation of patristic thought in the East and West, which was evident, for example, in the reliance of Ambrose on Didymus, as well as in the dogmatic rather than historical use of the fathers in Owen's own work, Owen can be regarded as developing a genuinely catholic trinitarianism in response to the Socinians.[119]

The other treatises belonging to Owen's pneumatological work are *The reason of faith* (1677),[120] Σύνεσις πνευματική: *or, The causes, waies & means of understanding the mind of God* (1678),[121] *A discourse of the work of the Holy Spirit in prayer* (1682)[122] and *Two discourses concerning the Holy Spirit* (1693).[123] Of these the first two deserve comment inasmuch as they carry forward Owen's arguments on the inspiration, authority and interpretation of Scripture, including implicit polemic against an enthusiastic individualistic reading of the text, while at the same time arguing for the need for the inspiration of the Spirit together with knowledge of original languages, historical circumstances and the tradition of churchly interpretation. On the latter issue, Owen continues his polemic against Romanism but recognizes the usefulness of reading patristic works and the writings of the reformers as aids to understanding.[124] Unlike the initial Πνευματολογια, these are not highly technical works; they are more reflective of a popular churchly context and the need to identify Scripture as the sole norm of faith and practice, and as the primary basis for its own interpretation. So also, the two discourses on the work of the Spirit are of a practical nature.

Owen's Χριστολογια (1679),[125] if taken together with his other Christological essays, *Meditations and discourses on the glory of Christ* (1684),[126] and *Meditations and discourses concerning the glory of Christ* (1691),[127] constitutes

---

[118]See the general analysis and conclusions in Backus, 'The Fathers in Calvinist Orthodoxy', 839–66.
[119]On Owen's trinitarian thought, see Trueman, *John Owen*, 47–56; also note Letham, 'John Owen's doctrine of the Trinity', 190–6.
[120]Owen, *Works* (1965), 4:4–115.
[121]Owen, *Works* (1965), 4:118–234.
[122]Owen, *Works* (1965), 4:236–350.
[123]Owen, *Works* (1965), 4:351–419; 420–520.
[124]Owen, *The causes, waies & means of understanding the mind of God* (1678), 258–60; *Works* (1965), 4:228–9.
[125]Owen, *Works* (1965), 1:1–272.
[126]Owen, *Works* (1965), 1:273–415.
[127]Owen, *Works* (1965), 1:417–461.

a work more extensive than *Of communion with God* and is comparable in scope to the Πνευματολογια. Like most of Owen's other trinitarian works, the positive aspects of Χριστολογια reflect the context of an international scholastic orthodoxy, but its argumentation reflects, as did the other works, his deep concerns over heterodox and heretical views – evidenced in his historical account of opposition to a true doctrine of Christ's person from the early Gnostics to the Socinians of his own time. The treatise is also grounded on Peter's confession in Mt. 16.16, chosen clearly for the sake not only of identifying Christ as the foundation of the church but also with the intention of countering a Roman claim to the founding of the Papacy in the verses following: the text does not imply that the church was built on Peter as its foundation.[128] Still, the body of the treatise is not focused on polemics, nor does it adumbrate the major trinitarian controversies of the 1680s. If there is a central theme, it is a reflection of Owen's worries over the fate of Independency and Nonconformity in a fragmented church and a confused world, against which he posed 'the re-enthroning of the Person, Spirit, Grace, and Authority of Christ, in the hearts and consciences of men [as] the only way whereby an end may be put unto these woeful conflicts'.[129]

Discussion of Owen's intellectual contexts would be incomplete if it did not register the distinct turn in his polemics after the Restoration to concerted counter-attacks on the renewed threat of Roman Catholicism, beginning with *Animadversions on Fiat lux* (1662) and continuing with *A vindication of the animadversions on Fiat lux* (1664), *The testimony of the church* (1675), *The Church of Rome, no safe guide* (1679), *A brief and impartial account of the nature of the Protestant religion* (1682), *The chamber of imagery in the Church of Rome laid open* (1683), and with distinct overtones in *Some considerations about union among Protestants* (1680).

The short tract *Some considerations*, published anonymously in 1680, offers an important commentary on the state of the English church from the perspective of dissent and on the increased threat of Romanism during the reign of James II, as well as a restatement of Owen's views on catholicity and the non-schismatic character of Nonconformity. The true church in England, in Owen's view, was the entire 'body of Christian people in this nation', namely, all Protestants to whom the Gospel was preached 'and the sacraments duly administered', even 'under the rule of the king'.[130] In the name of Independency and peace in the English church, Owen continues by arguing against an 'Authoritative National

---

[128] Owen, Χριστολογια (1679), 4–10; *Works* (1965), 1:32–5.
[129] Owen, Χριστολογια (1679), sig. B2r; *Works* (1965), 1:5.
[130] Owen, *Some considerations about union among protestants* (1680), 3; *Works* (1965), 14:520.

Church', whether Papal, Episcopal or Presbyterian, as a barrier to Protestant union. He acknowledges that the Presbyterian form is the least problematic of those ecclesial options that he discusses, but he recognizes that it was still prone to the problem of interference from civil powers.[131] That Owen retained his assumptions concerning Independency or Congregationalism as the proper and biblical form of church governance is clear from the posthumous treatise, *The true nature of a Gospel church and its government* (1689).[132]

SOME CONCLUSIONS

John Owen's intellectual context was diverse, and it altered during the course of his career as minister, theologian, dean of Christ Church and nonconformist. Throughout his literary career he wrote as a defender of Reformed orthodoxy, initially looking to refute aspects of Arminian theology, later, as he perceived an altered context for debate, shifting his focus to address the threat of Socinianism, without losing sight of the Arminian problem. Arguably, throughout these polemics, Owen's primary interest was Christological, with an emphasis on the priesthood of Christ understood as satisfaction for sin. This emphasis on Christ's priesthood carried over into Owen's *Exposition of the epistle to the Hebrews*.

The broad Reformed orthodox context is evident in Owen's more positive formulations of doctrine, notably his extensive writings on the Trinity. Here, as in his polemical theology, Owen's intellectual context was both British and continental. He wrote as a proponent of the confessionality of the English church, but he also wrote with a view towards the continental Reformed, reflecting on the writings of Calvin, Vermigli, Beza, Zanchius, Junius, Polanus, Gomarus, Chamier, Hoornbeeck and Amyraut, among others.

A further general aspect of Owen's intellectual context was his chosen audience. Even in his sermons, like most Puritan preachers, Owen assumed not only a religiously devoted audience but also one that was theologically informed. His major treatises and his exposition of Hebrews were addressed to the academically trained theological community, written with an immersion in technical detail, and intended to display Owen's prodigious learning in a mastery of both sources and argument. Owen aimed at being definitive and unanswerable in the context of a massively educated international Protestant ecclesial and academic community.

---

[131] Owen, *Some considerations about union among protestants* (1680), 6–7; *Works* (1965), 14:522–3.
[132] Owen, *Works* (1965), 16:1–208.

As noted briefly at the outset of the chapter, Owen's grasp of the intellectual context of theological formulation in his era and of the relevant battery of materials that could be drawn into his argumentation placed him among the most learned and intellectually adept theologians of the seventeenth century. He ranks not only high on the list of British writers but also on a roster of Reformed thinkers that includes major continental writers as Johannes Cocceius, Gisbertus Voetius, Francis Turretin and Petrus van Mastricht.

CHAPTER 5

Owen and politics

CRAWFORD GRIBBEN

Dr: *Owens* Doctrine . . .
. . . heeds not well which way he *Goes* . . .
Now *here,* now *there,* this way, now *That,*
Now it is *One thing,* then *Another,*
And now and then nor t' *One* nor t' *Other.*
Somtimes it's *This, somtimes* it's *That,*
Somtimes its *This,* and *This,* and *That,*
Somtimes 'tis *either This,* or *That,*
Somtimes 'tis *neither This,* nor *That,*
Now *This,* not th' *Other,* anon its *Either,*
Then by and by both *Both,* and *Neither.*
One while it looks like *So,* not *No,*
Another while like *No,* not *So,*
One way it seems or *So,* or *No,*
Another way, nor *No,* nor *So,*
Some wayes it shewes both *So* and *No,*
So 'tis a meer endlesse *No,* and *So.*[1]

As Samuel Fisher's poem noted, John Owen had a marked capacity for changing his mind. This is not a feature of his work that has generated much discussion

---

[1] Fisher, *Rusticus ad academicos in exercitationibus expostulatoriis, apologeticis quatuor* (1660), 4.

in the growing body of Owen scholarship.[2] Yet this predilection for second thoughts was not something of which Owen was ashamed. 'He that can glory that . . . he hath not altered or improved in his conception of some things . . . shall not have me for his rivall', he explained in 1657.[3] Owen's critics recognized this mutability. They represented his work as being ambitious, inconsistent and pragmatic. They noted his chameleon-like character and ability to thrive during the revolution and survive in its aftermath, which they explained as a consequence of his being a 'trimmer' in politics and theology.[4] These criticisms came from individuals on both sides of the political division that developed during the civil wars and that endured in more complicated forms into and beyond the 1660s. In 1659, lamenting the failure of the revolution, an anonymous pamphleteer who styled himself as 'Thomas Truthsbye' accused Owen of being prepared to 'sordidly comply with every Government, pray and teach to each Faction, side with all Innovators', to pull down the government of 'timorous Richard', and to effect the 'dissolution' of the third Protectorate Parliament.[5] One decade later, the same charge came from the opposite side: a defender of the Church of England complained that Owen was a 'great a Weather-Cock in his principles about Government, Toleration and Liberty of Conscience', and that he 'could Sail with every Wind'.[6] Whatever their other differences, Owen's critics were remarkably consistent in recognizing, and condemning, his pragmatism.

In his political views, as in his theological views, England's most important high Calvinist theologian changed his mind on important, even defining, issues – although he mostly worked to conceal the fact.[7] Owen was a minor political theorist, whose contribution has been recognized in the scholarship on John Locke and in some of the most recent accounts of the rise of religious toleration: his overarching concentration on and evolving conclusions about the proper boundaries of religious freedom tracked his rise to and fall from political power, raising the question of whether his changing views did anything more than reflect his own self-interest.[8] Many of his contemporaries prepared

---

[2] Owen's habit of changing his mind is noted in Gribben, *John Owen and English Puritanism*.
[3] Owen, *A review of the true nature of schisme* (1657), 45; *Works* (1965), 13:227.
[4] *Moderation a vertue, or, A vindication of the principles and practices of the moderate divines and laity of the Church of England represented in some late immoderate discourses, under the nicknames of Grindalizers and Trimmers* (1683); Gribben, *John Owen and English Puritanism*, 210–11.
[5] 'Thomas Truthsbye', *A serious letter to Dr. John Owen, sent by a small friend of his* (1659), single sheet.
[6] *A letter to a friend concerning some of Dr. Owens principles and practices* (1670), 67, 70.
[7] Cooper, *John Owen, Richard Baxter and the formation of Nonconformity*; Gribben, *John Owen and English Puritanism*; Cowan, *John Owen and the civil war apocalypse*.
[8] Coffey, *Persecution and toleration in Protestant England, 1558–1689*; Coffey, 'John Owen and the Puritan toleration controversy, 1646–59', 227–48; VanDrunen, *Natural law and the two kingdoms*, 149–72; Wilken, *Liberty in the things of God*, 157–64. On Owen and Locke, see Woolhouse,

manifestos and carefully developed political theories. Owen engaged with some of these options: he preached in celebration of the defeat of the Leveller mutiny (1649) and engaged sympathetically with Thomas Hobbes's *Leviathan* (1651).[9] But Owen's own interests – at least as far as his published work attests – were more limited. The only political issue in which he took sustained interest and exercised any real influence was that of religious toleration.

Owen was a political actor who sat in the first Protectorate Parliament (1654), despite controversy about the eligibility of his election, and played an active role in devising the national church settlement during the republican period, sufficient for his inclusion within the History of Parliament project, alongside that of his much more politically active brother, Henry Owen, whose interventions stretched from his election to the second Protectorate Parliament (1656) at least until his participation in the Rye House plot (1683).[10] But, for all that Owen valued about the gains of the revolution, and wanted to establish its religious settlement, he was not much of a cheerleader for the Cromwellian government in its later conservative turn. For Owen was also a political conspirator, who identified with republican critics of the new administration during the first Protectorate Parliament (1654), and who defended the 'good old cause' by drafting the petition that army officers used to dissuade Oliver Cromwell from accepting the offer of the Crown (1657).[11] Owen could be politically inept: he appears to have worked with the officers who gathered in his congregation at Wallingford House to bring down the third Protectorate Parliament and Richard Cromwell's administration (1659), but he did not anticipate that these actions would lead to the vacuum of political power that in turn made possible the return of the king (1660).[12]

Owen could be politically unpredictable: he valorized Charles II in publications in the 1660s, the period in which he was breaking laws against the gathering of dissenting congregations and, apparently, hoarding the weapons that were confiscated from his house, and in 1670 took part in a scheme developed by London dissenters to lend £40,000 to the Crown. In later years he turned against the Caroline court, the sins of which he believed were bringing divine judgement on the nation.[13] For these and other activities, Owen remained politically suspect, and was monitored by spies. Their number

---

Locke, 31; Svensson, 'John Owen and John Locke', 302–16; Svensson, 'A dirty word? The Christian development of the traditional conception of toleration in Augustine, Aquinas, and John Owen', 43–60.
[9]Gribben, *John Owen and English Puritanism*, 107–8, 163–4.
[10]Gribben, *John Owen and English Puritanism*, 160–1, 260–1; *History of Parliament*, s.v., forthcoming.
[11]Gribben, *John Owen and English Puritanism*, 160–1, 169–70.
[12]Gribben, *John Owen and English Puritanism*, 200–7.
[13]Gribben, *John Owen and English Puritanism*, 212.

may have included Robert Ferguson, a Scottish Presbyterian minister who, in the early 1660s, was arrested for treasonable activities, was 'turned' against his English dissenting colleagues, and fed information on their activities to the secretary of state, Sir Joseph Williamson, all before working as Owen's assistant in the 1670s.[14] This surveillance continued until the end of Owen's life – and even as Owen was entertained in separate meetings with the Duke of York and Charles II.[15] In February 1682, government informers attended Owen's services and noted that he did not pray for the king.[16] They understood that plots were being hatched. And so, in spring 1683, Owen was arrested on suspicion of being involved in a conspiracy against the king's life, in which his brother Henry and Robert Ferguson were almost certainly involved.[17] But Owen was also politically influential: the theory of toleration that he elaborated over several decades eventually settled on arguments about religious liberty that would be taken up with the greatest consequence by his former student, John Locke, in the context of the Williamite revolution (1688–90).[18] For someone who wrote so little about the subject, Owen exercised significant impact on political theory and, through Locke, on the formation of classical liberalism.

This chapter will describe and analyse Owen's views of politics from the beginning of his publishing career in 1643 until his death in 1683. The growing body of scholarship on Owen's life and work, which focuses on reconstructing his theological arguments to the detriment of exploring his other achievements, has not paid a great deal of attention to his political opinions, although some debates have begun around such questions as Owen's commitment to republicanism.[19] Contrary to the work by Eric Nelson, who argues that in the mid-seventeenth century, republican authors begin to make the 'new and revolutionary argument' that monarchy is 'an illicit constitutional form', I argue for the contingency of political claims in Owen's imagination, and for his flexibility about particular constitutional orders.[20] Building on this work, this chapter will demonstrate that Owen was not an ideologue, and that in almost every respect his interventions in politics were pragmatic and defensive of his

---

[14]On Ferguson as a spy, see *ODNB*, s.v.; Turner, 'Williamson's spy book', 306; Zook, *Radical Whigs and conspiratorial politics in late Stuart England*, 96; Stevenson, 'Introduction', 300.
[15]Asty, 'Memoirs of the life of John Owen', xxix.
[16]*CSPD*, 1682, 104.
[17]Cook, 'A political biography of a religious Independent', 363–4, 374–88; Gribben, *John Owen and English Puritanism*, 260–2.
[18]Woolhouse, *Locke*, 31; Svensson, 'John Owen and John Locke', 302–16.
[19]Contrast the positions of Gribben, in *John Owen and English Puritanism*, 106, and Cowan, in *John Owen and the civil war apocalypse*, 104–9.
[20]Nelson, *The Hebrew Republic*, 3. For a wider discussion of Scripture, theology, and political forms, see McDowell, *The English radical imagination*; Tadmor, *The social universe of the English Bible*, 119–64; Killeen, *The political Bible in early modern England*.

own position in sometimes violently changing circumstances – in other words, that his defence of republicanism in the 1650s and his defence of monarchy in the 1660s and beyond were tactics consistent with his long-term goal of ensuring the toleration of Protestant dissenters.

THE REVOLUTION

Born as the Reformation entered its second century, Owen inherited several generations of Protestant thinking about Christianity and politics.[21] By the early seventeenth century, Reformed theologians had come to offer competing accounts of the relationship that ought to exist between church and state, the obligations of the civil magistrate to divine law, and the situations in which Christians could be permitted to take up arms in order to resist tyrannical rule. As he began his writing career in the context of an acute constitutional crisis, Owen's earliest publications reflected upon these debates as they juxtaposed political and theological arguments in the context of the first civil war (1642–6).

Owen began to publish his writing in the immediate aftermath of the abolition of the Star Chamber (1641), the consequent collapse of censorship and the move towards new forms of censorship under the Licensing Order (1643). His writing immediately engaged with the issues that made its publication possible. His first work, Θεομαχία αυτεξουσιαστική: or, *A display of Arminianisme* (1643), defended the Thirty-nine Articles by attacking the Arminian party that dominated the hierarchy of the Church of England, and was dedicated to the Committee for Religion, a group of MPs that oversaw the distribution of parish livings.[22] Owen's preface to this work offered a straightforward justification for the civil war that was then in its early stages. Owen identified the power of Parliament with the Calvinist doctrine of divine sovereignty and argued that the attempts made by Arminian theologians to undermine the sovereignty of God found their counterpart in attempts made by royalists to undermine the constitutional power of MPs. The civil war was in essence a war of religion, he claimed, a 'holy warre'.[23] Those who were 'robbing men of their privileges' had also 'nefariously attempted to spoil God of his providence'.[24] Owen's theological polemic drew upon English constitutional history to make its points. He complained that efforts made to introduce Arminian theology and practice into the English church were 'contrary to the express terms of the great charter [*Magna Carta*] of Heaven'.[25] Owen developed these themes in his

---

[21] A survey of these positions is provided in Beeke, *Duplex regnum Christi*.
[22] Gribben, *John Owen and English Puritanism*, 44–54.
[23] Owen, *A display of Arminianisme* (1643), sig. A^v; *Works* (1965), 10:7.
[24] Owen, *A display of Arminianisme* (1643), sig. 2^v; *Works* (1965), 10:5.
[25] Owen, *A display of Arminianisme* (1643), sig. 3^r; *Works* (1965), 10:5.

second book, *The duty of pastors and people distinguished* (1644), in which he turned his attention to ecclesiology, debates about which he continued to frame in political terms. If Satan had 'set up a shop on earth, to practice his trade in', he argued, 'it was our High Commission Court', the supreme ecclesiastical body that Parliament had abolished in 1641.[26] But Owen's view of the civil war was changing. If his earlier writing identified two positions in the civil war, *The duty of pastors and people distinguished* proposed the existence of a third party, which Owen located as being positioned between the 'Hierarchicall tyranny' of the bishops and the 'Democraticall confusion' of the new religious movements, whose almost anarchic form of church government he struggled to describe.[27] Owen identified this third party, which he represented as the *via media* between these two dangerous extremes, as Presbyterianism.[28] Having adopted this new identity, Owen continued to work as a parish minister in Fordham, Essex, far from the depredations of the conflict. In 1646, the forces of Parliament defeated those of the king, and civil war ceased. Presbyterians were buoyant, enthusiastic about the possibility of realizing their ambitions. But Owen was already an Independent.[29]

Owen's new ecclesiastical identity put him at a critical distance from the most obvious winners of the civil war. In April 1646, as discussions about the peace settlement continued, and in circumstances that are now difficult to reconstruct, Owen was invited to address MPs as part of series of sermons to Parliament.[30] Despite his youth, his lack of political connection and his inexperience in the recent conflict, Owen offered the politicians some clearly stated advice. He encouraged MPs to remember that the wars had been religious at the root. He worried that the rise of Arminianism within the English church had been made possible by the centralization of political power. Over the previous twenty years, he reminded his listeners, members of the Arminian party had advanced a political agenda that subverted the 'Civill' as well as the 'sacred state'.[31] Having 'centered in their bosoms an unfathomable depth of power, civil and ecclesiastical, to stamp their apostatical errors with authority', Arminians had pursued political power in order to impose their controversial religious reforms on the church. And they had succeeded in doing so. Puritans and Members of Parliament had discovered that they could not resist the introduction of these errors 'without the utmost danger of the Civil state'.[32] 'England's troubles'

---

[26]Owen, *The duty of pastors and people distinguished* (1644), 28; *Works* (1965), 13:28.
[27]Owen, *The duty of pastors and people distinguished* (1644), 10; *Works* (1965), 13:5.
[28]Owen, *The duty of pastors and people distinguished* (1644), 42; *Works* (1965), 13:39.
[29]Gribben, *John Owen and English Puritanism*, 65–6.
[30]Gribben, *John Owen and English Puritanism*, 73–9.
[31]Owen, *A vision of unchangeable free mercy* (1646), 29; *Works* (1965), 8:28.
[32]Owen, *A vision of unchangeable free mercy* (1646), 31; *Works* (1965), 8:29.

had been serious indeed, but, Owen insisted, Parliament had fought the war in order to secure religious freedom.[33] In Parliament's victory, the 'crown of all others mercies' had been the 'setting at liberty the truths of the Gospel'.[34] But Owen was worried that MPs might be pursuing a new agenda. He warned MPs against instrumentalizing the divine assistance that they had enjoyed in their struggle against the king: 'God will not have this Gospel made a stalking horse for carnall designes.'[35] The 'carnal designs' that Owen had in mind likely included the construction of a Presbyterian state, a constitutional form that the king was offering in order to buy the loyalty of the Scots and the more conservative English MPs, and which the latter group would attempt to realize in passing the Blasphemy Act (1648). Anticipating some of these moves, Owen appended to the published version of his sermon, *A vision of unchangeable free mercy* (1646), a 'country essay', in which he made further arguments in favour of religious toleration. No one should be put to death for their religious beliefs, he insisted. 'Hæresy is a canker, but a spirituall one', he explained, and it should be 'prevented by spirituall means'.[36] The state should support the work of the church by suppressing any doctrine that would disturb the civil peace, and those whose religious beliefs led them into immoral activities should be punished.[37]

Owen's defence of religious freedom intensified as he settled into his Independent convictions. His new ecclesiological preferences had been shaped by his reading of John Cotton's *The keyes of the kingdom of heaven* (1644), although the New England theologian had promoted a much narrower view of religious toleration than Owen was prepared to accept. In *Eschol* (1647), Owen repeated his argument that magistrates had a duty to provide for the material needs of ministers of the Gospel, in voluntary and parish congregations, though they had no responsibility to violently suppress heretical opinion.[38] But others disagreed. In May 1648, while the army was fighting a second civil war, the Presbyterian Blasphemy Act criminalized the public proclamation of any religious opinion that varied from that encoded in the Westminster Assembly's recently published confession of faith (1646). The terms of this act radically restricted public debate. Anyone convicted of atheism, or any denial of God's omnipresence, omniscience, omnipotence, holiness, eternity or any publicly expressed doubts about the Trinity, orthodox Christology, the Protestant canon as the word of God, resurrection or final judgement,

---

[33] Owen, *A vision of unchangeable free mercy* (1646), 15; *Works* (1965), 8:17.
[34] Owen, *A vision of unchangeable free mercy* (1646), 32; *Works* (1965), 8:30.
[35] Owen, *A vision of unchangeable free mercy* (1646), 34; *Works* (1965), 8:32.
[36] Owen, *A vision of unchangeable free mercy* (1646), 76; *Works* (1965), 8:64.
[37] Owen, *A vision of unchangeable free mercy* (1646), 75–6; *Works* (1965), 8:63.
[38] Owen, *Eschol* (1648), 18–19; *Works* (1965), 13:60.

would be punished by death. Anyone found guilty of promoting universalism, Arminianism, the use of images in worship, purgatory, mortalism, extraordinary revelation, antinomianism, opposition to infant baptism, anti-Sabbatarianism or opposition to Presbyterian church government would be imprisoned without maximum term and would be released only when two sureties guaranteed that the offense would not be repeated.[39] While Owen would not have had any difficulties with the theological demands of the new act, his convictions as an Independent would have put him in jeopardy with its ecclesiastical demands: as he later recognized, when he embraced Independent church government, 'I could expect nothing . . . but ruine in this world.'[40] The Blasphemy Act effectively criminalized the kinds of arguments that Owen had been making in favour of religious toleration, and, along with all others who protested against Presbyterian discipline, he could now be imprisoned without maximum term. The Blasphemy Act illustrated the serious divisions that now existed among the victors of the civil war.

Of course, many others shared Owen's concerns about the direction of the revolution. As the relationship between Parliament and its army deteriorated, he found allies among high-ranking officers. During the parliamentary army's siege of Colchester, which continued through the summer of 1648, Owen cultivated relationships with military leaders like Sir Thomas Fairfax and their allies in Parliament. In *Eben-ezer* (1648), a compilation of the two sermons that he preached before Fairfax after the relief of the city, Owen explained that the victories 'in the late tumults' had been given not to Parliament but to its army.[41] God had 'marched before' the armies of Parliament, and 'traced out their way from Kent to Essex, from Wales to the North'.[42] But Parliament had not recognized this, he feared, and the second civil war was viewed as punishment for the intransigence of those MPs who had denied the 'Liberties, Ordinances, Priviledges, Lives' of 'God's people'.[43] Of course, Owen was aware that soldiers were spreading religious error, sometimes of a serious kind.[44] But only in the most exceptional cases were legislators to prohibit religious discussion.[45] The revolution was to secure religious freedom.

Of course, the differences that existed among the opponents of the king made their cooperation unsustainable. Owen remained close to army leaders

---

[39]'An ordinance for the punishing of blasphemies and heresies, with the several penalties therein expressed', in *Acts and ordinances of the Interregnum, 1642–1660*, 1133–36.
[40]Owen, *A review of the true nature of schism* (1657), 36; *Works* (1965), 13:223.
[41]Owen, *Eben-ezer* (1648), 19; *Works* (1965), 8:93.
[42]Owen, *Eben-ezer* (1648), 24; *Works* (1965), 8:97.
[43]Owen, *Eben-ezer* (1648), 21; *Works* (1965), 8:95.
[44]Owen, *The death of death in the death of Christ* (1648), n.p.; *Works* (1965), 10:156.
[45]Owen, *Eben-ezer* (1648), 23; *Works* (1965), 8:96.

after some of their number mounted a coup against the Long Parliament, in December 1648, in which MPs who were suspected of sympathizing with the king were excluded from the House. The Blasphemy Act was quietly forgotten, pending a new religious settlement. Colonel Thomas Pride's 'purge' of Parliament allowed a radical faction of army leaders to put the king on trial on the charge of treason before an improvised High Court of Justice. Charles refused to recognize this unconstitutional court and would not plead before it. In a sequence of events that no one could have anticipated, he was found guilty, condemned to death and executed on 30 January 1649.[46] On the following day, Owen commemorated the regicide in his sermon to MPs, *Righteous zeal encouraged by divine protection* (1649) – the published title of which revealed his approbation of the execution. The sermon represented his first sustained discussion of forms of government. He recognized that Old Testament discussions of monarchy were often ambivalent: in a nod towards Hos. 13.10-11, he observed that 'to those that cry, Give me a King, God can give him in his anger; and from those, that cry, take him away, hee can take him away in his wrath'.[47] And, it seemed, this was the providential meaning of the regicide. God would stand against monarchy, in England and elsewhere, as long as 'superstition and persecution, will-worship and tyranny' continued to be its 'inseparable concomitants'.[48] 'When Kings command unrighteous things, and people suite them with willing complyance', he continued, 'none doubts, but the destruction of them both is just and righteous'.[49] On this most momentous of days, Owen offered no political counsel to politicians: 'waiting at the throne of Grace, that those whom God hath intrusted with, and enabled for the Transaction of these things, may be directed and supported in their employment, is the utmost of my undertaking', he claimed.[50]

Nevertheless, Owen did not want to miss this opportunity to influence policy. He appended to his published sermon a long discussion 'Of toleration, and the duty of the magistrate about religion'. Reflecting his sermon's concern about Presbyterian political objectives, Owen responded to a document produced by the Church of Scotland, which had argued against any form of religious

---

[46]Kelsey, 'The death of Charles I', 727–54; Kelsey, 'The trial of Charles I', 583–616; Holmes, 'The trial and execution of Charles I', 289–316; Kishlansky, 'Mission impossible', 844–74.

[47]Owen, *A sermon preached to the Honourable House of Commons, in Parliament assembled: on January 31* (1649), 3; *Works* (1965), 8:134–5.

[48]Owen, *A sermon preached to the Honourable House of Commons . . . on January 31* (1649), 6; *Works* (1965), 8:137.

[49]Owen, *A sermon preached to the Honourable House of Commons . . . on January 31* (1649), 5; *Works* (1965), 8:136.

[50]Owen, *A sermon preached to the Honourable House of Commons . . . on January 31* (1649), n.p.; *Works* (1965), 8:129.

toleration.[51] The Scottish Presbyterians wanted to have the sins that were listed in both tables of the Ten Commandments to be considered as crimes and to be punished accordingly.[52] Owen disagreed, arguing that the only sins that should become crimes were those that disturbed the public peace.[53] Of course, civil magistrates should 'take care that the truth of the Gospell be Preached to all the people of that Nation'.[54] Heretics should not be offered the same provision as the teachers of truth, but their lives should still be protected by law.[55] Owen offered no defence of heresy but argued that any violent suppression of religious opinion was the thin end of the wedge and a tactic that would eventually be used against the godly: 'the Devill durst not be so bold, as to imploy . . . his grand Agent in his Apprentiship against the saints: But he first suffers him, to exercise his hand against Hereticks, intending to make use of him afterward to another purpose'.[56]

Owen's arguments were not unassailable. The obvious Presbyterian response was that in defending the execution of the king and religious toleration, Owen was breaking the terms of the Solemn League and Covenant (1643), which during the first civil war had been the grounds of the alliance between the English Parliament and the Scots, and in the second civil war the justification for the Scots switching sides to support the king. While there is no record that Owen ever subscribed to the covenant, he would have been required to do so in order to move between his first two parishes.[57] In the late 1640s, Owen rejected the claim that the Solemn League and Covenant 'did tie us up absolutely to one formerly known way of church discipline' – an argument that he dismissed as being 'childish, ridiculous, selfish'.[58] But, his critics later observed, he did break the terms of the covenant, which included a promise to support the monarchy, when, as a member of the first Protectorate Parliament, he swore the engagement that renounced it.[59]

As discussions continued about how government should be Reformed, and as planning for an English republic continued, Owen preached again to the

---

[51]Owen, *A sermon preached to the Honourable House of Commons . . . on January 31* (1649), 40; *Works* (1965), 8:164.
[52]Gribben, 'Samuel Rutherford and liberty of conscience', 355–73.
[53]Owen, *A sermon preached to the Honourable House of Commons . . . on January 31* (1649), 41, *Works* (1965), 8:164.
[54]Owen, *A sermon preached to the Honourable House of Commons . . . on January 31* (1649), 72; *Works* (1965), 8:189.
[55]Owen, *A sermon preached to the Honourable House of Commons . . . on January 31* (1649), 78; *Works* (1965), 8:192.
[56]Owen, *A sermon preached to the Honourable House of Commons . . . on January 31* (1649), 67; *Works* (1965), 8:185.
[57]Gribben, *John Owen and English Puritanism*, 71.
[58]Owen, *A vision of unchangeable free mercy* (1646), 52; *Works* (1965), 8:46.
[59]*A letter to a friend concerning some of Dr. Owens principles and practices* (1670), 11–12.

House of Commons on 20 April 1649. This work, published as *The shaking and translation of heaven and earth* (1649), interpreted biblical descriptions of the 'shaking and translating of heaven and earth', as the subtitle put it, as accounts of dramatic changes in government. Owen was sure that these changes were necessary. 'For the present, the government of the nations . . . is purely framed for the interest of Antichrist', he explained. 'No kinde of Government in Europe, or line of Governors, [is] so ancient but that the Beast is as old as they.'[60] In fact, the influence of Antichrist was so embedded in the monarchical systems of Europe that 'no digging or mining, but an Earthquake, will cast up the foundation stones thereof'.[61] Owen understood the events of the English revolution in prophetic terms:

> The Lord Jesus Christ by his mighty Power, in these latter dais, as Antichristian Tyranny draws to it's period, will so farre shake and translate the politicall Heights, Governments, and strength of the Nations, as shall serve for the full bringing in of his own peaceable kingdom; the Nations so shaken, becoming thereby a quiet Habitation for the people of the most high.[62]

The kingdom of Jesus Christ would be established as the kingdoms of the earth were destroyed. He made the point more explicitly in early June 1649, preaching to commemorate the defeat of the Leveller mutiny: the 'breaking of the old monarchies and of papal power is a work meet for the Lord. And in this shall mainly consist the promised glory of the Church of Christ in after days'.[63] A revolution was required in which constitutions would be so transformed as to secure the freedoms of believers. Owen may not have had a political agenda, but he certainly had an agenda for politics.

THE REPUBLIC

As Owen might have anticipated, in May 1649, England became a republic. While Owen would have welcomed England's new constitutional arrangements, he grew concerned by their sustainability, for he was quickly disappointed with the government that he believed was predicted in the Bible. The new administration that was led by Oliver Cromwell soon fell short of Owen's ideals. He saw the workings of government at close hand during the invasions of Ireland (1649) and Scotland (1650) and in his efforts towards a national church

---

[60] Owen, *The shaking and translating of heaven and earth* (1649), 23; *Works* (1965), 8:264.
[61] Owen, *The shaking and translating of heaven and earth* (1649), 25; *Works* (1965), 8:266.
[62] Owen, *The shaking and translating of heaven and earth* (1649), 64; *Works* (1965), 8:260.
[63] Owen, 'Humane power defeated', in *A complete collection of the sermons of the Reverend and learned John Owen*, ed. Asty, 84; *Works* (1965), 9:206.

settlement in the early 1650s. While Owen was never a combatant, he appears to have taken an active role in both invasion campaigns by contributing to their printed propaganda. Austin Woolrych suggested that Owen had a hand in the writing of *A declaration of the Lord Lieutenant of Ireland, for the undeceiving of deluded and seduced people* (1650), which proposed limited toleration for the practice of Catholicism in Ireland.[64] The *Declaration* turned Owen's arguments into policy for the Cromwellian conquest. It began by emphasizing the value of political and religious freedom: men had 'begun to be weary' of 'arbitrary power . . . in Kings & Churchmen; their juggle between them, mutually to uphold Civill and Ecclesiasticall tyranny begins to be transparent'.[65] It continued by emphasizing that the Cromwellian administration would make Catholic public worship illegal, but that those who maintained their Catholic piety without attending mass, 'if they walke honestly and peaceably', would not 'in the least . . . suffer for the same'.[66] Owen may have made a similar contribution during the invasion of Scotland, as Scott Spurlock has suggested, crafting works of propaganda that attempted to persuade an even more homogenous society of the value of religious toleration.[67] Owen certainly included political ideas in his Scottish sermons. *The branch of the Lord, the beauty of Sion*, a compilation of material that he preached in Berwick and Edinburgh, was published in November 1650 and dedicated with proper deference to Cromwell. But Owen might already have been changing his view of Cromwell. Archibald Johnston of Wariston, the Scottish Covenanter leader, heard Owen preach in Berwick, but understood his oration as attacking Cromwell's pride.[68] The published version of Owen's sermon does not obviously comment upon Cromwell's pride, and so it is possible that Wariston had misunderstood Owen's intentions, or that he was commenting on a sermon that has not been preserved.[69] But Wariston may have been right to observe Owen's hesitation fully to endorse the new regime. In April 1652, in the published version of his sermon at the funeral of Henry Ireton, Owen noted that 'all forms of Government amongst men . . . so degenerate of themselves that they become directly opposite, or are so shattered by providential Revolutions as to become uselesse to their proper

---

[64]Woolrych, *Britain in revolution, 1625–1660*, 473.
[65]Cromwell, *A declaration of the Lord Lieutenant of Ireland, for the undeceiving of deluded and seduced people* (1649), 7.
[66]Cromwell, *A declaration of the Lord Lieutenant of Ireland, for the undeceiving of deluded and seduced people* (1649), 10–11.
[67]Spurlock, *Cromwell and Scotland*, 20–21; Gribben, 'Polemic and apocalyptic in the Cromwellian invasion of Scotland', 1–18.
[68]Johnston of Wariston, *Diary*, 2:16.
[69]Gribben, 'Polemic and apocalyptic in the Cromwellian invasion of Scotland', 1–18.

end, [and] may and ought to be changed'.[70] The English republic, Owen feared, would be no exception to this rule.

Six months later, in October 1652, Owen addressed the Rump Parliament on the theme of 'Christ's kingdom and the magistrate's power'. He was in a reflective mood. In all the affairs of Parliament since the 'beginning of the contests in this Nation', God had bound the cause of the Gospel with the liberties of Parliament, he argued: 'God secretly entwining the Interest of Christ with yours, wrapt up with you the whole Generation of the[m] that seek his face, & prospered your affairs on that accou[n]t.'[71] This homiletical flattery offered a rather more positive view of the Rump Parliament than that maintained among the army elite, who were increasingly frustrated by its hesitation and delay. Owen's rhetoric may also have concealed his frustration that MPs were not prepared to support the religious settlement for which he had been working.[72] Owen reminded MPs that the relationship of the church to state had still to be settled: 'Say some, the Magistrate must not support the Gospell; say others, the Gospell must subvert the Magistrate: say some, your rule is only for men, as men, you have nothing to doe with the interest of Christ and the Church: say others you have nothing to do to rule men, but on account of being Saints.'[73] But Owen insisted that magistrates did have a 'duty' to support the 'interest of the Church'.[74] 'If . . . you shall say, you have nothing to doe with Religion as Rulers of the Nation', he warned his listeners, 'God will quickly manifest that he hath nothing to doe with you as Rulers of the Nation'.[75] In other words, there should be no more parliamentary delay in approving the national church settlement that he had been preparing. But magistrates should not claim too much political power, he argued. While he recognized that there was 'something moral' in Old Testament discussions of government, 'which being uncloathed of their judaicall forme, [are] still binding . . . as to some Analogie and proportion', the history of the kings of Israel did not provide 'rules that should be obligatory unto all Magistrates now under the administration of the Gospell'.[76] It was true that God had intervened in the civil wars on behalf of the saints. God had rewarded the prayers of his people beyond their expectations: 'they little looked for the blood and banishment of Kings, change of Government, Alteration of Nations, such shakings of Heaven

---

[70] Owen, *The labouring saints dismission to rest* (1652), 7–8; *Works* (1965), 8:350.
[71] Owen, *A sermon preached to the Parliament, Octob. 13. 1652* (1652), 27; *Works* (1965), 8:381.
[72] Gribben, *John Owen and English Puritanism*, 137–40.
[73] Owen, *A sermon preached to the Parliament, Octob. 13. 1652* (1652), 20; *Works* (1965), 8:381.
[74] Owen, *A sermon preached to the Parliament, Octob. 13. 1652* (1652), 40; *Works* (1965), 8:387.
[75] Owen, *A sermon preached to the Parliament, Octob. 13. 1652* (1652), 36; *Works* (1965), 8:384.
[76] Owen, *A sermon preached to the Parliament, Octob. 13. 1652* (1652), 52; *Works* (1965), 8:394.

and Earth, as have insued'.⁷⁷ These blessings should cause the godly to continue to pray for political change, for 'all Nations . . . which in their present state and Government, have given their power to the Dragon and the Beast to oppose the Lord Christ . . . shall be shaken, broken, translated, and turned off their old foundations, and constitutions, into which the Antichristian interest hath been woven for a long season'.⁷⁸ But spiritual warfare was more important than physical arms, he continued: Christ's kingdom will advance 'with his Spirit and word', and so 'there is nothing more opposite to the spirit of the Gospell, then to suppose that Jesus Christ will take to himselfe a kingdome by the carnall sword and bow of the sonnes of men'.⁷⁹ This world revolution would begin with the conversion of the Jews and would end with the descent from heaven of the new Jerusalem.⁸⁰ The most lasting political changes would come through preaching, prayer and the work of the church.

Owen's political ascent continued as he continued this movement away from his earlier militarism. In June 1654, as vice-chancellor, Owen was instructed to oversee the election of a Member of Parliament to represent the University of Oxford.⁸¹ In circumstances that cannot now be reconstructed, Owen was 'chosen as a Parliament man', as he later put it.⁸² His election may have allowed him to present in person two new publications that offered Cromwell effusive praise, *Musarum Oxoniensium* (1654), an anthology of adulatory verse, and *The doctrine of the saints perseverance* (1654).⁸³ The latter text hinted at its author's concerns about the regime's direction of travel: arguing about elections in church government, Owen recognized that God had wanted the Israelites to 'come together to chuse' the man whom he had elected to be king, an appeal to popular sovereignty that was not adopted in the controversial transition from Commonwealth to Protectorate and in Cromwell's elevation as Lord Protector.⁸⁴ Owen's standing as an MP quickly became controversial. In November 1654, two months after taking his seat, his eligibility to sit as an MP was challenged under the terms of the Clerical Disabilities Act (1642), which precluded clergymen from accepting political office. It is not clear how long he continued to attend the House.⁸⁵ He was likely among the 300 MPs who gathered on Sunday, 3, and Monday, 4 September 1654, to listen to sermons

---

⁷⁷Owen, *A sermon preached to the Parliament, Octob. 13. 1652* (1652), 17; *Works* (1965), 8:379.
⁷⁸Owen, *A sermon preached to the Parliament, Octob. 13. 1652* (1652), 15; *Works* (1965), 8:374.
⁷⁹Owen, *A sermon preached to the Parliament, Octob. 13. 1652* (1652), 19; *Works* (1965), 8:376.
⁸⁰Owen, *A sermon preached to the Parliament, Octob. 13. 1652* (1652), 19; *Works* (1965), 8:375–6.
⁸¹Register of Convocation, 249, reprinted in *The correspondence of John Owen*, 70–1.
⁸²John Owen, *A defence of Mr John Cotton* (1658), 37; *Works* (1965), 13:287.
⁸³Ireland, *Momus elencticu* (1654), 1.
⁸⁴Owen, *The doctrine of the saints perseverance* (1654), n.p.; *Works* (1965), 11:38.
⁸⁵'The life of the late Reverend and learned John Owen', in *Seventeen sermons preach'd by the late Reverend and learning John Owen* (1720), xvi.

from Stephen Charnock and Thomas Goodwin to commemorate the opening of the Parliament.[86] And he would likely have participated in the vote on Thursday, 7 September, as to whether the government of the nation should be resolved into a single person and Parliament, a motion that was very narrowly passed, as well as the vote about the engagement that was devised one week later to enforce support for this new constitutional arrangement.[87]

The efforts to disbar Owen prompted some scurrilous table-talk in Oxford, in which Owen was supposed to have renounced his ordination and claimed the status of a layman.[88] Owen's Presbyterian antagonist Daniel Cawdrey reported a conversation in which he had not participated to Owen's discredit, suggesting that Owen's churchmanship was more radically informal than perhaps was the case. Owen replied in *An answer to a late treatise of Mr Cawdrey about the nature of schism* (1658), refuting the claim that he had belittled his ordination and that he had refused to present himself as a minister of the Gospel when he was 'chosen as a Parliament-man', but his defence was equivocal.[89] As Owen's status as MP became a matter of dispute, in mid-November, the convocation of the University of Oxford defended his election.[90] It is not clear what happened next. While Owen may have been disbarred from the House, he was not replaced as a Member of Parliament. He seems to have been associated in Parliament with critics of the new regime, including John Hildesley, MP for Winchester, and a group of republican activists that included Sir Arthur Hesilrige, Sir Henry Vane the senior and John Bradshaw, among whose company he was regarded by Archibald Johnston of Wariston as being 'of a contrary judgment to Cromwell'.[91] These critics likely preferred the earlier form of republican government to the newer form of Protectorate. But Owen certainly remained on good working terms with the administration. When the Council of State requested Owen to refute Socinian arguments, he wrote *Vindiciae evangelicae* (1655), which he dedicated to Cromwell and the council members. Even if Owen was not disbarred from the first Protectorate Parliament, he would have lost his seat when that body was dissolved, in January 1655, having failed to pass a single bill.[92]

---

[86]*Journal of the House of Commons*, vol. 7: *1651–1660*, 365–6; *The correspondence of John Owen*, 119–21.
[87]*Journal of the House of Commons*, vol. 7: *1651–1660*, 367–8.
[88]Nuttall, *Visible saints*, 89–90.
[89]Owen, *A defence of Mr John Cotton*, 37; *Works* (1965), 13:287.
[90]*Journal of the House of Commons*, vol. 7: *1651–1660*, 375; Bodl. OUA, NEP/supra/Reg. T., 254–5.
[91]Bodleian Tanner MS 69, f. 182; reprinted in *The correspondence of John Owen*, 74–5; *Calendar of the correspondence of Richard Baxter*, 1:158; *History of Parliament*, s.v.; Wariston, *Diary*, 2:287, 310.
[92]Smith, 'Oliver Cromwell and the Protectorate Parliaments', 14–31; Worden, 'Toleration and the Cromwellian Protectorate', 199–233.

Eighteen months later, on 17 September 1656, Owen attended the opening session of the second Protectorate Parliament, to which his brother Henry had been elected, to preach its opening sermon. By 1656, Owen's attitude to Cromwell was more obviously changing. He offered the Lord Protector some rather faint praise in the preface to *God's work in founding Zion* (1656), and there is also perhaps some evidence that he was no longer a committed republican. God had not worked to prosper the revolution in order to show his support for 'this, or that form of government, or civile administration of humane affairs . . . these, or those Governors, much less for the advantage of one or other sort of men: for the Enthroning of any one, or other perswasion', Owen insisted. Instead, God had been working for the 'generall interest of all the Sons and Daughters of Sion'.[93] He sounded annoyed, frustrated that the new administration was pushing for constitutional reforms without securing a national religious settlement. While the most important priorities remained unrealized, Owen still had to argue for first principles and against the dangers of sectional politics:

> I speak no more then I have sundry times since, sundry times complained of, to a Parliament of this Common-wealth. Every one, if not personally, yet in Association with them, of some peculiar perswasion with himselfe, would be the head; and because they are not, they conclude they are not of the body, nor will care for the body, but rather endeavour its ruine. Because their particular interest doth not raigne, the common interest shall be despised; and this hath been the temper or rather distemper, of the people of God in this Nation now for sundry years; and what it may yet produce I know not.[94]

He believed that he still had to combat Presbyterians, who argued that 'such a form of church government and discipline be established, such a rule of doctrine confirmed, and all men whatever compelled to submit unto them'. He believed that he still had to combat anti-formal radicals, who argued that 'discipline be eradicated, the ministers' provision destroyed, and the men of such a persuasion be enthroned, to rule all the rest at their pleasure; seeing that, notwithstanding all their pretended Reformation, they are yet antichristian'. He believed that he still had to combat Fifth Monarchists, who argued that 'a Kingdome and Rule be set up in our hands, to be exercised in the name and Authority of Jesus Christ, taking away all Law and Magistracy already established, to bring forth the Law of Righteousness conceived in our minds and therein to be preserved'.[95] Owen

---

[93] Owen, *God's work in founding Zion* (1656), 9; *Works* (1965), 8:405.
[94] Owen, *God's work in founding Zion* (1656), 30; *Works* (1965), 8:415–16.
[95] Owen, *God's work in founding Zion* (1656), 36; *Works* (1965), 8:418–19.

repeated his familiar claim that the great achievement of the revolution was religious freedom, and that the particular form of the government that enabled this freedom was of secondary importance:

> Because the founding of Sion, doth not consist in this or that form of the civile Administration of human affaires, there being nothing promised, nor designed concerning them, but that they be laid in an orderly subserviency, to the common interest of the Saints; which let men do what they will, yea what they can, all Governments shall at last be brought unto.[96]

Time was running out for the English revolution, Owen feared. He was glad that some MPs 'still speak with living affections to the old and common cause', and prayed that they would each become the 'preservers of the good old Cause of England'.[97] But, 'unless God end this frame, my expectations . . . of an happy issue of the great work of God amongst us, will wither day by day'.[98]

Owen's worry about the achievements of the English revolution can be tracked in his turn towards spiritual theology. But even in this genre he could not refrain from making a political comment. In *Of communion with God* (1657), he reminded his readers that God had established government to ensure 'prudence in the management of Civill affaires . . . nothing more useful for the common good of humane kind'.[99] The purpose of government was to 'keep the rationall world in bounds and order, to draw circles about the Sonnes of men, and to keep them from passing their allotted bounds and limits, to the mutual disturbance and destruction of each other'.[100] God had established this 'drawing of circles' for the benefit of the godly. For God

> disposeth of all Nations and their interest according as is for the good of Believers . . . in all the sifting of the nations, the eye of God is upon the house of Israell . . . Look into the world: the Nations in Generall are either blessed for their sakes, or destroyed on their account; preserved to try them, or rejected for their cruelty towards them: and will receive from Christ their finall doome according to their deportment towards these despised ones.[101]

Government could be made unstable by the religious indifference of governors. This was why, in *Of temptation* (1658), he worried about 'a visible declension

---

[96] Owen, *God's work in founding Zion* (1656), 40; *Works* (1965), 8:421.
[97] Owen, *God's work in founding Zion* (1656), 32, 47; *Works* (1965), 8:416, 425.
[98] Owen, *God's work in founding Zion* (1656), 30; *Works* (1965), 8:416.
[99] Owen, *Of communion with God* (1657), 129; *Works* (1965), 2:115.
[100] Owen, *Of communion with God* (1657), 129; *Works* (1965), 2:115.
[101] Owen, *Of communion with God* (1657), 154; *Works* (1965), 2:136.

from Reformation seizing upon the professing party of these nations, both as to personall holinesse, and zele for the interest of Christ . . . the Plague is begun'.[102] In the aftermath of the wedding celebrations in November 1657 of the Protector's daughters, which provided such lavish entertainments as dancing, masques, and orchestral music, Owen's criticism of the Cromwellian court was barely concealed:

> would any one have thought it possible, that such and such professors in our daies, should have fallen into waies of selfe, of flesh, of the world? to play at cards, dice, revell, dance? to neglect family, closet duties, to be proud, haughty, ambitious, worldly, covetous, oppressive? or that they should be turned away after foolish, vaine, ridiculous opinions, diserting the Gospell of Christ?[103]

After all, he continued, this declension had reached 'even the top boughs and branches of our profession'.[104] His fear was that the godly were now no more than a political party.[105]

Nevertheless, Owen did not give up on his ideals for government, which were coming to define the community of Independent churches. Late in 1658, the preface to the Savoy Declaration, which was composed by Thomas Goodwin and Philip Nye, reiterated familiar themes in Owen's writing.[106] Modifying the claims of the Westminster Confession, the Savoy Declaration argued for broad religious toleration: 'amongst all Christian States and Churches, there ought to be vouchsafed a forbearance and mutual indulgence of Saints of all perswasions, that keep unto, and hold fast the necessary foundations of faith and holiness, in all other matters extra fundamental, whether Faith or Order'.[107] The preface recognized that 'Christian clemency and indulgence in our Governors, hath been the foundation of that Freedom and Liberty, in the managing of Church-affairs, which our Brethren, as well as WE, that differ from them, do now, and have many years enjoyed'.[108] But the civil magistrate was also obliged to

---

[102] Owen, *Of temptation* (1658), n.p.; *Works* (1965), 6:90.
[103] Owen, *Of temptation* (1658), 64; *Works* (1965), 6:111; Holberton, *Poetry and the Cromwellian Protectorate*, 143–62.
[104] Owen, *Of temptation* (1658), 64; *Works* (1965), 6:112.
[105] Owen, *Of temptation* (1658), 116; *Works* (1965), 6:129.
[106] BL Add Ms 23622, fol. 132. I owe this reference to Tim Cooper.
[107] 'A preface' [Savoy Declaration], *A declaration of the faith and order owned and practised in the Congregational Churches in England*, n.p.
[108] 'A preface' [Savoy Declaration], *A declaration of the faith and order owned and practised in the Congregational Churches in England*, n.p.

incourage, promote, and protect the Professors and Profession of the Gospel, and to manage and order civil administrations in a due subserviency to the interest of Christ in the World, and to that end to take care that men of coroupt minds and conversations do not licentiously publish and divulge Blasphemy and Errors, in their own nature subverting the faith, and inevitably destroying the souls of them that receive them: Yet in such differences about the Doctrines of the Gospel, or ways of the worship of God, as may befal men exercising a good conscience, manifesting it in their conversation, and holding the foundation, not disturbing others in their ways or worship that differ from them; there is no warrant for the Magistrate under the Gospel to abridge them of their liberty.[109]

In the autumn of 1658, this was no longer a truism. With the death of Oliver Cromwell, and the installation of Richard as Lord Protector, the administration was moving back towards the Presbyterians as part of its long conservative turn. The leaders of the Independents were making a calculated risk in repeating demands for religious toleration while those in power were moving away from this ideal. As winter turned to spring, Owen and his circle of republican friends understood the revolution to be in danger. On 4 February 1659, Owen preached to MPs sitting in the third Protectorate Parliament at a private fast. In this sermon, which was published as *The glory and interest of nations professing the Gospel* (1659), he disclaimed any overtly political motives. Remembering 'our good old principles on which we first ingaged', he claimed that 'there is not any thing from the beginning to the ending of this short discourse that doth really interfer with any form of civil Government in the world, administred according to righteousness and equity'.[110] Nevertheless he understood what government was for: 'the end of all humane wisdom, in nations or the Rulers of them is, to preserve humane society in peace and quietness, within the several bonds and allotments that are given unto them by the providence of God'.[111] This did not mean that magistrates had to be believers: 'I shall not suspend my obedience whilst I inquire after my Lawful Governors conversion.'[112] But it did mean that believers should have lower expectations of those who were not among the godly: Owen admitted that he had 'no great expectation from them whom God loves not, delights not in'.[113] Lamenting sin among the ruling class,

---

[109][Savoy Declaration], *A declaration of the faith and order owned and practised in the Congregational Churches in England*, 18.
[110]Owen, *The glory and interest of nations professing the Gospel* (1659), n.p., 17–18; *Works* (1965), 8:455, 467.
[111]Owen, *The glory and interest of nations professing the Gospel* (1659), 7; *Works* (1965), 8:461.
[112]Owen, *The glory and interest of nations professing the Gospel* (1659), 16; *Works* (1965), 8:466.
[113]Owen, *The glory and interest of nations professing the Gospel* (1659), 16; *Works* (1965), 8:466.

Owen warned MPs of the 'evidences of the Lords departing from us'.[114] The gains of the revolution were slipping away. Owen lamented

> what woful divisions are there amongst this generation of professors? some are for one way, and some for another; some say one sort are the people of God, some another; some say the Prelatists are so, some the Presbiterians, some the Independents, some the Anabaptists; some the fifth Monarchy men, some others . . . But it is no party, but the party of Christ in the world . . . that I am pleading for.[115]

Divisions and backsliding represented a serious political danger: 'I pray God we loose not our ground faster then we won it.'[116]

Perhaps it was time for direct action. In early March 1659, Owen was appointed as minister of a new church that gathered in Wallingford House, in Whitehall, the home of Charles Fleetwood. The congregation was established in conventional ways. At Owen's installation, Philip Nye preached from 1 Tim. 3.1, and described the qualities of a teaching elder in fundamentally pastoral terms, and, according to notes taken by Smith Fleetwood, without any obvious political comment.[117] But many observers, including Richard Baxter, believed that the congregation had been established as a political project, as a vehicle through which Owen could influence Fleetwood, John Desborough and other officers to prevent the drift back towards a Presbyterian national church settlement by having Richard dissolve his government.[118] There was certainly evidence for this charge. On one visit to Fleetwood's house, Archibald Johnston of Wariston encountered Owen and William Sydenham, who, he believed, were plotting to 'maintain civil and spiritual liberties already obtained'.[119] Edmund Ludlow remembered that Owen asked him for a list of those Members of the Rump Parliament that were still alive, a list that he shared with his military friends as they wondered whether their Parliament could be reinstated.[120] A conspiracy was developing. By the end of April, the officers associated with the new fellowship had participated in another coup, bringing down Richard's government in an effort, among other things, to preserve religious liberty. The

---

[114]Owen, *The glory and interest of nations professing the Gospel* (1659), 17; *Works* (1965), 8:467.
[115]Owen, *The glory and interest of nations professing the Gospel* (1659), 21; *Works* (1965), 8:470.
[116]Owen, *The glory and interest of nations professing the Gospel* (1659), 17; *Works* (1965), 8:467.
[117]Edinburgh, New College, MS Comm 1, 'Mr Philip Nye upon Dr Owens setting downe with his Church at Wallingford House', 24–34. This notebook appears to have belonged to Charles Fleetwood's son, Smith Fleetwood.
[118]Toon, *God's statesman*, 109–10; 'General introduction', in Baxter, *Reliquiae Baxterianae*, vol. 1: *Introductions and Part 1*, 52–3, 90–1.
[119]Wariston, *Diary*, 3:106.
[120]*The memoirs of Edmund Ludlow*, 2:74.

Rump Parliament was reinstated on 6 May, and Owen appears to have been its first preacher. On 25 May, the Protector resigned.[121] It was time for a new constitutional order.

But, in the ensuing political vacuum, the conspirators lost control of London and the revolution began to unwind. In early August, royalist plotters led by Sir George Booth seized Chester and gained significant support among the capital's Presbyterian ministers.[122] In September 1659, and in a significant break with his previous positions, Owen signed *An essay towards settlement*, along with several Fifth Monarchists, which proposed a radical system of religious toleration, hoping that 'Rulers over men' might 'forebeare for ever to impose any nationall, parochiall Ministry, so as to inforce any forme of Worship suited to their interest, or compell men of one perswasion, to maintaine any man of another, in the Ministry'.[123] (It is possible that this was the publication that he later disclaimed.[124])

Owen was happier with broader religious liberty than with decisive moves towards Presbyterian uniformity. The instability continued as MPs and leaders of the radical army faction grew increasingly suspicious of each other. On 13 October, the officers ran out of patience with MPs, and locked them out of the chamber in another military coup.

With London in constitutional deadlock, General George Monck, commander of the army in Scotland, seized the initiative and began a public correspondence with leaders of the Independent churches. On 31 October, Owen and eighteen other ministers wrote to Monck, asking that he receive army officers Edmund Whalley and William Goffe and ministers Joseph Caryl and Matthew Barker as their representatives in a discussion about civil and ecclesiastical order. On 19 November, Owen wrote personally to Monck, pleading that he do what he could to prevent a third civil war. Monck's reply was equivocal and refused to engage with the issues. He was playing for time and seeing how events might unfold to his advantage.[125] Less than one week later, Monck wrote a second letter, emphasizing that only a freely elected Parliament could properly represent the will of the people. Owen and other ministers and officers replied on 13 December, rallying behind the army in London, and supporting its

---

[121]Gribben, *John Owen and English Puritanism*, 200–1. Owen's sermon to Rump mentioned in 'General introduction', in *Reliquiae Baxterianae*, 1:90.
[122]Gribben, *John Owen and English Puritanism*, 202.
[123]*An essay towards settlement* (1659), single sheet. I am grateful to Tim Cooper for this reference.
[124]Owen later complained that in 1658 his name was fixed to a paper that advanced political views that he did not share – but that they were shared by someone else of the same name; 'To the reader', Caryl, *The nature and principles of love*, n.p. (I owe this reference to Adam Quibell.) See also 'The life of the late Reverend and learned John Owen', xxiv.
[125]Gribben, *John Owen and English Puritanism*, 204–5.

political ambitions. Monck assembled his own troops and began to march south, with undeclared objectives.

With the government in flux, Owen and his colleagues continued to fight for religious freedom. In early December 1659, he continued to re-state his arguments, quoting the Savoy Declaration in his published letter, *Unto the questions sent me last night* (1659): 'there are many promises that in Gospel times Magistrates shall lay out their power, and exert their Authority, for the furtherance and preservation of the true Worship of God, the profession of the Faith, the Worshippers and Professors thereof, and therein the whole interest of Sion'.[126] Owen continued to argue that no one should be forced to subscribe to a confession of faith, and (quoting from the Savoy Declaration) that the publication of heretical ideas, either in print or in meetings of those other than family members, should be forbidden.[127]

Events were now moving too fast for the production of political theory. In late December 1659, as he prepared to cross the border into England, Monck wrote to Owen, Whalley and Goffe, warning them against the ambitions of army leaders in London. But they were undeterred. Lambert marched his regiments north to meet the threat from Scotland. As desertions increased, and the Corporation of London began its own rebellion, Fleetwood recalled the Rump. Monck called his bluff and continued to march south. Conflict seemed inevitable, until the southern army seemed to melt away. Nothing stood in the way of Monck's ambitions. Privately, Owen admitted that the revolution was over.[128] Monck and his army entered London in February 1660, and immediately restored the Long Parliament.[129] The Presbyterians were triumphant. Their newly conservative Parliament adopted the Westminster Confession and passed laws to ensure that the Solemn League and Covenant should be read in every parish church. On 29 May, on his thirtieth birthday, the king returned. Owen may not have enabled the construction of republican government, but he was one of a tiny handful of men who had brought it to an end. The conspiracy of Independents and republicans at Wallingford House had facilitated the return of the king and the construction of a Presbyterian state.

---

[126]Owen, *Two questions* (1659), 4; *Works* (1965), 13:511–12.
[127]Owen, *Two questions* (1659), 5–6; *Works* (1965), 13:514.
[128]Gribben, *John Owen and English Puritanism*, 205–7.
[129]Owen was not the first signature of *To his excellencie the Lord General Monck*, as I claimed in Gribben, *John Owen and English Puritanism*, 207. I am grateful to Richard Snoddy for identifying two versions of this document, in one of which the signature is that of Sir John Owen, the royalist commander.

THE RESTORATION

But Charles II had other plans. Within weeks of his return, some of those who had been closely identified with the death of his father were themselves being executed in front of baying crowds. Owen went into hiding, his former political achievements having become a serious liability, as he negotiated the reality of defeat. His movements during this period are hard to trace. He certainly found shelter with well-placed patrons, some of whom had strong royalist commitments.[130] But their support may have been unreliable. In 1663, spies reported that Owen was living in the fields near Moorgate, London, along with several other dissenting ministers.[131] In reduced circumstances, and at the mercy of the new government, he learned the rules of the new political game.

After the restoration, and as the Long Parliament's Presbyterian settlement gave way to an Episcopalian settlement under the Cavalier Parliament, Owen made some very cautious political interventions. In Θεολογουμενα παντοδαπα: Sive de natura, ortu, progressu, et studio veræ theologiæ (1661), a cultural history of theology that might have represented the content of his lectures to Oxford students, Owen recognized that governments used religion to promote social cohesion.[132] After the failure of the revolution – caused in such small part by religious politicking in a sequence of unsuccessful Parliaments – he recognized that 'our Churches have never been able to sufficiently disengage themselves from their involvement with peoples, states, nations, and the demands of politics with the resulting influence, morals, corruptions, and defilements of the world'.[133] The revolution had failed because the godly had been damaged by their ascent to political power.

But, even in defeat, Owen remained within the reach of major political actors. A 'person of honour', unnamed in the early biographies, asked Owen to prepare a response to *Fiat lux* (1661), an anti-Protestant invective by Vincent Cane that among other things cast doubt on Hyde's religious credentials.[134] Owen was at pains to pay his respects to this influential member of the court. His *Animadversions on a treatise called Fiat lux* (1662), which was published anonymously, lamented the 'late Miscarriages, and present Distempers of men about Religion'.[135] Owen, incognito, wrote in general terms to defend the cause of English Protestantism, and admitted that he had 'sundry reasons for not owning or avowing particularly any Party in this Discourse' – likely because his

---

[130] Gribben, *John Owen and English Puritanism*, 218.
[131] The National Archives, SP 9/26 fol. 107r; also available in 'Williamson's spy book', 253.
[132] Owen, Θεολογουμενα παντοδαπα (1661), 97–8; *Works* (1965), 17:110; *Biblical theology*, 129.
[133] Owen, Θεολογουμενα παντοδαπα (1661), 352–3; *Works* (1965), 17:318; *Biblical theology*, 440.
[134] Compare 'The life of the late Reverend and learned John Owen', xxv–xxvi, and Asty, 'Memoirs of the life of John Owen', 23, with Goold, 'Prefatory note', in Owen, *Works* (1965), 14:2.
[135] Owen, *Animadversions on Fiat lux* (1662), 1; *Works* (1965), 14:5.

own ecclesiastical position was, in the run-up to the 'great ejection', so much in jeopardy.[136] Turning the tables on Cane, Owen projected onto Catholics the blame for 'our late unhappy Troubles', explaining that 'our late Evils . . . began in Ireland, amongst . . . good Roman-Catholicks, who were blessed from Rome into Rebellion and Murder, somewhat before any drop of bloud was shed in England, or Scotland' – a statement that reflected a rather remarkable amnesia concerning the Bishops Wars and the Scottish invasion of England that seems to have inspired the Irish rebellion.[137] Owen fashioned himself as a defender of the king. 'Kingly authority in General is from God, and by his Providence was it established in this Land', he argued, describing Charles I as 'our late king, of glorious Memory'.[138] Owen argued that the government of the church should be monarchical, that the monarch should indeed be 'head of the church of England', and defended the orthodoxy of the English bishops, whose activities he had formerly spent so much time lamenting.[139] Owen still believed in toleration, but now offered more latitude than ever before: he could 'neither approve nor justifie' the persecution of Catholics, most likely because the best prospects for achieving the toleration of dissenters lay in broader arguments about the security of other religious minorities.[140]

Owen expanded upon his political ideas in *A discourse concerning liturgies* (1662), a short book that engaged immediately with the controversy surrounding the imposition of the prayer book and the ejection from the national church of those ministers who would not use it. 'All authority is originally in God', who delegates authority to 'Kings and Rulers of the Earth', he argued. But that did not mean that magistrates had to be obeyed in every circumstance, he reminded his fellow believers. The subject's duty to obey civil authorities 'doth not arise from the Authority vested in themselves, but from the immediate command of God, that in such things they ought to be obeyed'.[141] And so, Owen continued,

> we acknowledge the Power ordaining and imposing this Liturgy to be of God, to be good and lawful, to be obeyed to the utmost extent of that Obedience, which to man can be due, and that upon the account of the Institution and Command of God himself. But . . . in things which concern the Worship of God, the commanding Power is Christ; and his Command the adæquate Rule and Measure of our Obedience.[142]

---

[136] Owen, *Animadversions on Fiat lux* (1662), 11; *Works* (1965), 14:7.
[137] Owen, *Animadversions on Fiat lux* (1662), 14; *Works* (1965), 14:8.
[138] Owen, *Animadversions on Fiat lux* (1662), 274, 421; *Works* (1965), 14:108, 164.
[139] Owen, *Animadversions on Fiat lux* (1662), 271; *Works* (1965), 14:107.
[140] Owen, *Animadversions on Fiat lux* (1662), 303; *Works* (1965), 14:119.
[141] Owen, *A discourse concerning liturgies* (1662), 51; *Works* (1965), 15:43.
[142] Owen, *Animadversions on Fiat lux* (1662), 52–3; *Works* (1965), 15:44.

Kings and magistrates were legitimate rulers, but they were wrong to compel conscientious ministers to choose between 'sinning, or fore-going the publick exercise of their Ministry'.[143] This was a very different theory of resistance from that promoted by Owen in the later 1640s, when he had defended resistance against unlawful authority by force of arms. From this point on – until, perhaps, the early 1680s – he argued for passive resistance only.

This was a very significant change of heart, of course, and one that his critics could not fail to notice. By 1663, when Owen's responsibility for the *Animadversions* had become public knowledge, Vincent Cane responded by attacking Owen's character. It was a badly timed blow, for Owen was in straightened circumstances, living in the fields at Moorgate, London, along with a number of other dissenting ministers.[144] Somehow, in these unpromising circumstances, Owen completed *A vindication* of his earlier attack (1664). He wrote to defend himself from Cane's allegations that dissenters were inevitably rebels. Owen claimed never to have 'had a hand in, nor gave consent unto the raising of any War in these Nations, nor unto any politicall alternation in them, no nor to any one that was amongst us during our Revolutions'. Instead, he had lived as 'he thought his duty consisted, and challengeth all men to charge him with doing the least personall injury unto any, professing himself ready to give satisfaction to any one, that can justly claim it'. Owen claimed not only to accept the restoration, but to 'bless God and the King for the Act of Oblivion'.[145] Owen claimed that he 'ever did abhorre Swords and Guns and Crusadoes, in matters of Religion and Conscience, with all violence'.[146] He was a happy subject of Charles II, who was 'not only the greatest Protestant, but the greatest Potentate in Europe' – probably a nod to the king's efforts to secure religious toleration for Protestant dissenters against the wishes of his Parliament (although the king wanted to extend this toleration to Catholics).[147] Recognizing that his hopes for religious freedom now lay with the king, rather than with MPs, Owen's commitment to monarchical rule became so complete that he worked from presuppositions about the authority of the Crown to argue for ecclesiastical theory.[148] In *A vindication*, he attacked *Fiat lux* for undermining the king's power.[149] The king's 'supreme jurisdiction' in the Church of England was an 'inseparable Priviledge of his imperial Crown, exercised by his Royal Predecesssours, and asserted by them against the intrusions and usurpations of

---

[143] Owen, *Animadversions on Fiat lux* (1662), 65; *Works* (1965), 15:53.
[144] The National Archives, SP 9/26 fol. 107r; 'Williamson's spy book', 253.
[145] Owen, *A vindication of the animadversions on Fiat lux* (1664), 12; *Works* (1965), 14:190.
[146] Owen, *A vindication of the animadversions on Fiat lux* (1664), 16; *Works* (1965), 14:193.
[147] Owen, *A vindication of the animadversions on Fiat lux* (1664), 116; *Works* (1965), 14:254.
[148] Owen, *A vindication of the animadversions on Fiat lux* (1664), 171; *Works* (1965), 14:372.
[149] Owen, *A vindication of the animadversions on Fiat lux* (1664), 416–17; *Works* (1965), 14:389.

the Pope of Rome', in which, Owen insisted, Charles II laid claim to temporal rather than spiritual authority.[150] All Protestants

> do assert the King to be so Head of the Church within his own Realms and Dominions, as that he is by Gods appointment the sole fountain and spring amongst men of all Authority and Power to be exercised over the Persons of his subjects in matters of external cognizance and order . . . the only Protector under God of all his subjects, and the only Distributor of Justice in rewards and punishments unto them.[151]

While kings did not have 'any place in spiritual order' or any 'spiritual power', they were nevertheless entrusted with the 'Supreme place under Christ in external Government and Jurisdiction'.[152] 'Neither is this power granted unto our kings by the acts of Parliament', he claimed, for 'it was always inherent in them'.[153] This was quite an extraordinary ignoring of the role of Parliament – made all the more significant by the fact that less than one decade earlier Owen had been elected as a member of that institution. But, true to form, Owen was defending the form of government that promised to do most to secure the freedom of dissenters. Owen made a related point in *A brief instruction in the worship of God* (1667), which he addressed to his fellow Independents, reminding them of Old Testament kings who usurped their authority to develop innovations in divine worship, and warning them that 'now a more severe punishment is substituted against such transgressions'.[154] Whether responding to Catholic apologists or addressing his fellow Independents, Owen emphasized the king's temporal authority and its spiritual limitations. Throughout the 1640s, he had pled the rights of Parliament against the king in an effort to maximize religious liberty; but in the early and middle 1660s, and with the same end in mind, he was pleading the rights of the king against Parliament.

Towards the end of the decade, as Members of the Cavalier Parliament slowly warmed up to the king's aspiration for religious toleration and dissenters responded to the possibility of an indulgence, Owen began to publish interventions that were more explicitly political in character, developing arguments that would be taken up in the literary culture of the Whigs. In *A peace-offering* (1667), subtitled as 'an apology and humble plea for indulgence and liberty of conscience', Owen grounded his appeal for religious toleration in the self-interest of the state. Dissenters were 'mostly of that sort and condition

---

[150]Owen, *A vindication of the animadversions on Fiat lux* (1664), 397; *Works* (1965), 14:377.
[151]Owen, *A vindication of the animadversions on Fiat lux* (1664), 403; *Works* (1965), 14:381.
[152]Owen, *A vindication of the animadversions on Fiat lux* (1664), 411; *Works* (1965), 14:385.
[153]Owen, *A vindication of the animadversions on Fiat lux* (1664), 407; *Works* (1965), 14:383.
[154]Owen, *A brief instruction in the worship of God* (1667), 80; *Works* (1965), 15:476.

of men . . . upon whose industry and endeavours in their several ways and callings, the trade and wealth of the Nation do much depend', he noted.[155] But the penal laws and the system of espionage by which these laws were enforced were designed to push these tradesmen and merchants into financial ruin, with an obvious effect on the economy: those who informed on dissenters and testified to their breaking laws on public worship were being rewarded with their forfeited property.

Owen added to his arguments about economics some new arguments about citizenship. In an anonymous pamphlet, also published in 1667, he insisted that 'every English-man' was born with an interest 'in the Policy, Government, and Laws' of the nation, 'with the Benefits and Advantages of them, and the Obedience that is due unto them'.[156] He worried that the 'great multitudes' who had been penalized for not attending parish worship had been 'cast . . . into the condition of men out-Lawed and deprived of all priviledges of their birth-right as English-men', while others were 'cast into prisons, where they lye perishing (sundry being dead in that state already) whilst their families are starved or reduced to the utmost extremity of poverty, for want of those supplies which their industry formerly furnished them with all'. Ultimately, Owen argued, the state was the loser: 'hands . . . by this means are taken off from labour . . . stocks from imployment . . . minds from contrivances of industry', while 'poverty . . . is brought on Families'. The persecution of dissenters undermined the 'common good'.[157] After all, he reminded his critics, dissenters were not rebels. Whatever might have happened in the past, dissenters had 'no form of government, civil or ecclesiastical, to impose on the nation'. They laid 'no pretence unto power to be exercised on the persons of any of his majesty's subjects', and had 'no expectations from persons or nations, that might induce us to further or promote any sinister aims of other men'. They 'covet no men's silver or gold, their places or preferments'. They merely wanted to live quietly, worship freely, and see the nation prosper. 'The utmost of our aim is to pass the residue of our pilgrimage in peace, serving God in the way of our devotion', Owen explained. 'They are no great things which we desire for ourselves, the utmost of our aim being to pass the remainder of the few days of our Pilgrimage in the Land of our Nativity, serving the Lord according to what he hath been pleased to reveal of his mind and will unto us.'[158] But if persecution continued, and the godly found themselves 'scattered over the face of the earth, we shall pray for the prosperity of his Majesty and the Land of our Nativity, patiently bearing the indignation of

---

[155] Owen, *A peace-offering* (1667), 33; *Works* (1965), 13:571.
[156] Owen, *Indulgence and toleration* (1667), 19; *Works* (1965), 13:531–2.
[157] Owen, *Indulgence and toleration* (1667), 8; *Works* (1965), 13:523.
[158] Owen, *A peace-offering* (1667), 15; *Works* (1965), 13:555.

the Lord, against whom we have sinned, and waiting for his salvation'.[159] Until then, dissenters would remain steadfast. The state should tolerate religious variety because the 'harmony' that 'riseth from such differences' represents the 'chiefest glory and beauty of Civil Society'.[160] The state could control the external life of an individual, but the 'Empire of Conscience belonged unto GOD alone'.[161]

In the later 1660s, Owen's defence of religious toleration appealed to the 'law of nature' as much as to Scripture.[162] Owen's new emphasis on the 'law of nature' illustrated his realization that different kinds of audience required different kinds of argument. It might also suggest that he was moving towards a post-Constantinian, or perhaps even a Lutheran, view of the relationship between church and state, in which the church would be governed by Scripture while the light of nature should direct the 'common good'.[163] Yet even as he pushed the state to recognize the 'law of nature', he also asked it to be Christ-like: anyone who had 'read the Gospel . . . is a competent Judge whether External Force in these Things, do more answer the Spirit of Christ, or that from which he suffered', he believed, and 'it must needs seem strange that Men can perswade themselves that they do that for Christ which they cannot once think or imagine that He would do himself'.[164] Nevertheless, he exhorted the godly, even if dissenters continued to be persecuted, they were still responsible to 'live peacefully in subjection to the Government of the Nation, and usefully amongst their Neighbours', encouraging 'the mutual trust, confidence and assurance between all sorts of persons, which is the abiding foundation of publick peace and prosperity'.[165] Nevertheless, he remembered in *Indwelling sin* (1668), the 'greatest mercies and blessings that in this world we are made partakers of, next to them of the Gospel and Covenant of Grace', come by means of good government.[166] If bad government continued, God would 'cut off and destroy' the 'kings of the earth'. 'He can knock them on the head, or break out their teeth, or chain up their wrath, and who can oppose him?'[167] Perhaps, after all, Owen was still haunted by the regicide.

In 1670, when the prospect of an indulgence was renewed, London dissenters attempted to divide the interests of king and Parliament for their

---

[159] Owen, *A peace-offering* (1667), 8; *Works* (1965), 13:549.
[160] Owen, *A peace-offering* (1667), 16–17; *Works* (1965), 13:556–7.
[161] Owen, *A peace-offering* (1667), 27; *Works* (1965), 13:565.
[162] Owen, *A peace-offering* (1667), 27; *Works* (1965), 13:556.
[163] I made this case in Gribben, *An introduction to John Owen*, 95–104. For Owen's use of 'common good', see Owen, *Indulgence and toleration* (1667), 8; *Works* (1965), 13:523.
[164] Owen, *A peace-offering* (1667), 21; *Works* (1965), 13:560.
[165] Owen, *A peace-offering* (1667), 35–6; *Works* (1965), 13:572–3.
[166] Owen, *Indwelling sin* (1668), 204; *Works* (1965), 6:270.
[167] Owen, *Indwelling sin* (1668), 203; *Works* (1965), 6:269.

own strategic advantage. Their first tactic was financial. Charles had invited the city magistrates to loan him £60,000, but their efforts had managed to raise only one-third of this value. Identifying an opportunity, over 150 dissenters worked together to provide the Crown with the balance.[168] This investment of £40,000 in the crown represented an extraordinary commitment on the part of those whose livelihoods had been affected by the so-called Clarendon Code, and suggested that Owen's arguments about the goodwill of dissenters were much more than merely rhetoric. A number of individuals made very significant investments in the loan, including Owen, who contributed the sum of £1,000, while other members of his congregation made smaller investments in their own names, including Robert Mascall, a merchant, and William Staines, a physician, who each subscribed £200.[169] While working to gain this financial leverage, Owen continued to publish arguments in favour of the toleration that his investment underscored. He published *The case of present distresses of Nonconformists examined*, a short pamphlet complaining about the act against seditious conventicles (1670), which allowed convictions on the basis of the oaths of informers, who stood to gain from the estates of those against whom they informed – estates that the dissenting contributions to the loan to the Crown suggested could be quite substantial. Owen complained at this injustice, and pled for the application of English common law: 'every man is obliged unto, and is to be allowed the unblameable defence of himself and his own innocency, against evil and hurt from others'.[170] After all, government could only be respected when it was evident that 'not only the laws, but also the administration of them are for publick good'.[171] In the same circumstances, Owen appears to have written 'A word of advice to the citizens of London' (*c.* 1670), which John Asty found in his papers and published in 1721, and which complained of the injustice of securing convictions only on the basis of an oath-bound informer.[172] This appears to have been written around the same time as 'The state of the kingdom with respect to the present bill against conventicles' (*c.* 1670), a copy of which Asty also published. The work addressed the Conventicles Act, which was being renewed in 1670, and complained that dissenters, who shared the 'highest satisfaction in his majesty's government', were being faced with a choice between 'conformity, or . . . ruin'.[173] Dissenters had lived quietly during the plague (1665), fire (1666) and the second Dutch war (1665–7), when they could have fomented sedition, had that been their goal.

---

[168]De Krey, *London and the Restoration*, 125–7.
[169]De Krey, *London and the Restoration*, 408–10.
[170]*A complete collection of the sermons of . . . John Owen*, ed. Asty, 594; *Works* (1965), 13:579.
[171]*A complete collection of the sermons of . . . John Owen*, ed. Asty, 596; *Works* (1965), 13:581.
[172]*A complete collection of the sermons of . . . John Owen*, ed. Asty, 583–87; *Works* (1965), 13:587–92.
[173]*A complete collection of the sermons of . . . John Owen*, ed. Asty, 588; *Works* (1965), 13:583.

They had lived peaceably because they recognized that they were 'enjoying, under his majesty's government, the best condition they are capable of in this world, whilst they have liberty for their conscience in the things of God'.[174] Asty claimed that this paper had been placed for consideration before members of the House of Lords.[175] This may have been the incident that was noted by the anonymous author of *A letter to a friend concerning some of Dr Owens principles and practices* (1670), who noted Owen's subtlety in

> Politicks; For he so ordered his matters, that some Members of Parliament had his Books by unknown Hands laid in their lodgings, whilst they were busied in attending the concerns of their King and Country; thinking that if they would not be at the expense of so much money, as to purchase them of his Bookseller, yet they might venture the loss of so much time, as to give the Doctors Books a reading, when the Doctor was so kind to give them his Books.[176]

But Owen's direct appeal to politicians may not have been successful.

Owen's later writing more strictly divided his political and theological interests, but moments of crossover continued. In *Πνευματολογια: or, A discourse concerning the Holy Spirit* (1674), he noted, 'Government, or Supream Rule, is of great concernment unto the Glory of God in the World and of the highest usefulness unto Mankind. Without it the whole World would be filled with violence, and become a Stage for all Wickedness visibly and openly to act itself upon disorder and confusion.'[177] Owen argued that the help of the Holy Spirit was necessary for good government, for without such help 'men cannot chuse but either sink under the weight of it, or wretchedly miscarry in its Exercise and Management'.[178] But these spiritual gifts were not necessarily salvific: 'many on whom they are bestowed never consider the Author of them, but sacrifice to their own Nets and Drags, and look on themselves as the Springs of their own Wisdom and Ability'.[179] Those whom God 'raised up to do great and wonderful things, whereby God executeth his judgements' included Cyrus, who, 'by God's Designation . . . was utterly to ruine and destroy the Great, Ancient Babylonian Monarchy'.[180] Perhaps Owen was still thinking of the regicide. But he was not anticipating any taking up of arms, even though, as he argued in a

---

[174]*A complete collection of the sermons of . . . John Owen*, ed. Asty, 589; *Works* (1965), 13:584.
[175]Asty, 'Memoirs of the life of John Owen', xxvii; *Works* (1965), 13: 576.
[176]*A letter to a friend concerning some of Dr. Owens principles and practices* (1670), 66.
[177]Owen, *Πνευματολογια* (1674), 116; *Works* (1965), 3:147.
[178]Owen, *Πνευματολογια* (1674), 117; *Works* (1965), 3:149.
[179]Owen, *Πνευματολογια* (1674), 118; *Works* (1965), 3:149.
[180]Owen, *Πνευματολογια* (1674), 77; *Works* (1965), 3:103.

sermon in 1679, 'London is ruined and England fallen.'[181] In Χριστολογια: or, A declaration of the glorious mystery of the person of Christ, God and Man (1678), he made the familiar point that the 'pretended Defence of Truth with Arts and Arms of another kind, hath been the bane of Religion, and lost the Peace of Christians beyond recovery'.[182] Nevertheless, through Robert Ferguson, Owen and his congregation did have connections with the Scottish Covenanters, who had attempted their own armed rising, with disastrous consequences, in 1679.

Owen did not always put his name to his more controversial publications. *Some considerations about union among Protestants* (1680), which he published anonymously, complained that the rights secured for Englishmen in common law were being subverted in church courts, an 'Encroachment on the Civil Rights and Government of the Nation'.[183] Owen recognized that since the Reformation, 'sundry persons . . . interested in Honours, Dignities, Power, and wealth . . . have constantly made it their business to promote absolute Monarchical Power, without respect unto the true Constitution of the Government of this Nation, which in sundry Instances hath been disadvantageous to Kings themselves' – which might have been a rather nervous reference to the regicide.[184] These were the king's notorious 'evil counsellors', who 'contended for that absolute Power in the King, which he never owned, nor assumed to himself' – which was a fairly optimistic reading of the rather obvious ambition of Charles II to rule in the style of Louis XIV of France.[185] Owen framed his argument for religious liberty around the question of which kind of church settlement would do most to protect the king's liberties. He argued that Independent church government was most consistent with the supremacy of the Crown, that a Presbyterian national church would not be 'consistent with that Preheminence of the Crown, that Liberty of the Subjects, and freedom of the Consciences of Christians, which are their due', and that a strongly centralized Episcopalian system could accumulate so much power as eventually to undo the Protestant Reformation.[186] Owen proposed a remedy that resonated with that proposed in so many of his earlier publications: English Protestants should unite around opposition to Roman Catholicism; adopt a single confession of faith that drew upon the doctrinal articles of the Thirty-nine Articles; and ensure that

---

[181]Owen, *Works* (1965), 16:481 [BOT]. This sermon was printed for the first time in the Goold edition.
[182]Owen, Χριστολογια (1679), n.p.; *Works* (1965), 1:9.
[183]Owen, *Some considerations about union among Protestants* (1680), 4; *Works* (1965), 14:520–1.
[184]Owen, *Some considerations about union among Protestants* (1680), 5; *Works* (1965), 14:522.
[185]Owen, *Some considerations about union among Protestants* (1680), 6; *Works* (1965), 14:522.
[186]Owen, *Some considerations about union among Protestants* (1680), 6–7; *Works* (1965), 14: 523–4.

magistrates protect and encourage the church without intervening in its internal affairs.[187]

Then Owen's perspective began to change. In the summer of 1680, during the exclusion crisis, religious tempers were already running high, and, as he noted in a sermon in May 1680, 'half the talk of the world is upon the subject'.[188] In *A brief vindication of the non-conformists from the charge of schisme* (1680), he responded to a sermon by Edward Stillingfleet, the dean of St Paul's, which argued that those who recognized the established church as a true church but dissented from it were guilty of schism. Owen replied, worried about the 'present danger of this Nation . . . from Popery', and the 'common danger' facing all Protestants.[189] It was an embarrassing moment for Owen, for Stillingfleet had drawn attention to two of his earlier publications, *Unto the questions sent me last night* (1659) and *A discourse concerning evangelical love* (1672), arguing that Owen had changed his mind on the question of toleration.[190] Owen responded by drawing attention to the statement on the civil magistrate contained in the Savoy Declaration, which he claimed continued to represent the convictions of the Independent churches.[191] Again, Stillingfleet invoked the Westminster Confession, arguing for the inconsistency of those who proscribed religious toleration in one decade only to appeal for it in another.[192] Owen emphasized to his dissenting readers that only the king was willing to defend them.[193] He repeated these themes in *An account of the grounds and reasons on which Protestant dissenters desire their liberty* (dated 1680 on EEBO), a short statement of opposition to Catholic claims: 'We own and acknowledge the power of the king or supreme magistrate in this nation, as it is declared in the thirty-seventh article of religion; and are ready to defend and assist in the administration of the government in all causes, according to the law of the land, with all other good Protestant subjects of the kingdom.'[194] This was to be a very contingent loyalty. It might have been during this period that Owen met the Duke of York while they were drinking the waters at Tunbridge Wells, and that Owen met Charles II upon his return to London. Their two-hour conversation about religious toleration led to the king providing Owen with one thousand guineas to ease suffering dissenters. Asty, who provides the earliest account of these meetings, did not date them but indicated that they occurred before the

---

[187] Owen, *Some considerations about union among Protestants* (1680), 8; *Works* (1965), 14:526.
[188] Owen, *Thirteen sermons preached on various occasions* (1756), 126; *Works* (1965), 9:505.
[189] Owen, *A brief vindication of the non-conformists* (1680), 1–2; *Works* (1965), 13:305–6.
[190] Owen, *A brief vindication of the non-conformists* (1680), 14, 34; *Works* (1965), 13:314, 327.
[191] Owen, *A brief vindication of the non-conformists* (1680), 14; *Works* (1965), 13:314.
[192] Owen, *A brief vindication of the non-conformists* (1680), 26–7; *Works* (1965), 13:338.
[193] Owen, *A brief vindication of the non-conformists* (1680), 53–4; *Works* (1965), 13:341.
[194] Owen, *An account of the grounds and reasons on which Protestant dissenters desire their liberty* (1680), 1; *Works* (1965), 13:578.

publication of *An enquiry into the original, nature, institution, power, order and communion of evangelical churches* (1681), in which Owen defended himself from allegations that he had taken part in discussions about the toleration of Catholicism.[195]

For, in the context of the exclusion crisis, as Whig politicians did what they could to stave off the accession of a Catholic king, Owen's views were growing more radical. For several years, he had been warning his congregation of 'an approaching calamitous time', but now these fears took on new forms.[196] Owen began to re-think his commitment to passive resistance. In 1680, he was being associated with a group of republicans who were plotting to overturn the monarchy, the number of whom included members of his congregation. Owen himself, as the 'patriarch of the sectaries', was reported as being 'at the bottom' of the plot.[197] In May 1680, he encouraged his congregants to remember that 'the destruction of this cursed antichristian state (of the head of it) will be brought about by none of these means we see or know of; but . . . the strong Lord God shall break in upon her and destroy her by ways unknown . . . it may be tomorrow; it may be not these hundred years'.[198] *An humble testimony unto the goodness and severity of God in his dealing with sinful churches and nations* (1681) had its origins in a series of sermons that he delivered to a private meeting of believers.[199] It marked a sharpening of tone, and a much more critical view of government. Owen announced his intention as being to 'confront the wisdom of politicians' by promoting the national, ecclesiastical and individual Reformation that only would prevent divine judgement.[200] Those involved in the nation's government were now part of the problem – 'profane Swearers, or Scoffers at the Power of Religion, or Drunkards, or unclean Persons, or covetous Oppressors'.[201] Owen's criticism of the government reached its peak after the failure of these attempts to exclude the openly Catholic brother of the king, James, Duke of York, from the line of succession. In the aftermath of the exclusion crisis, Owen recognized that the English Reformation was effectively over. In a sermon in December 1681, he directly attacked the 'provoking sins' of 'the throne' and 'the court',[202] describing the evidence provided by Titus Oates of a 'popish plot' as evidence that God had not yet forsaken England.[203] In *A brief and impartial account of the nature of the Protestant religion* (1682),

---

[195] Asty, 'Memoirs of the life of John Owen', xxix.
[196] Owen, *Thirteen sermons*, 108; *Works* (1965), 9:491.
[197] Scott, *Algernon Sidney and the restoration crisis, 1677–1683*, 122.
[198] Owen, *Thirteen sermons*, 130; *Works* (1965), 9:508.
[199] Owen, *An humble testimony* (1681), n.p.; *Works* (1965), 8:595.
[200] Owen, *An humble testimony* (1681), n.p.; *Works* (1965), 8:595.
[201] Owen, *An humble testimony* (1681), 86; *Works* (1965), 8:631.
[202] Owen, *Seasonable words for English Protestants* (1690), 15–16; *Works* (1965), 9:10.
[203] Owen, *Seasonable words for English Protestants* (1690), 21; *Works* (1965), 9:13.

he recognized that 'Designs' for the 'utter Extirpation' of the Protestant religion were being 'managed with policy and power'. Some who were involved in 'public affairs' had done what they could to forestall the return of Catholicism – including his old friend, Shaftesbury.[204] But Owen recognized that the 'Protestant interest' in politics was now 'beyond hopes of a revival'.[205] The political forces that were ranged against true religion were simply too great to be resisted by constitutional means. But, he continued, 'where the Protestant Religion is received, publickly professed, and established by Law, it cannot be changed without the extream Havock and Ruine of the greatest and best part of their Subjects, in all their Temporal concerns'.[206] Facing the prospect of a return to Catholic rule, Owen expected constitutional upheavals that would lead to 'rage and fury'.[207] He began to consider possibilities that he had long dismissed. Cautiously, he raised the possibility of armed resistance to any return to Catholic rule. His suggestions were oblique, but obvious. He could think of 'no instance' of any 'defending themselves in the Profession of the Protestant Religion by arms, but where together with their Religion their Enemies did design and endeavour to destroy those Rights, Liberties, and Priviledges, which not only the Light of Nature, but the Laws and Customs of their several Countreys did secure unto them as part of their Birthright Inheritance'.[208] In this resort to arms, the godly would need to be prepared to 'suffer . . . even unto death' in defence of their faith.[209] In other words, Owen was hinting, now that politics had failed to secure the English Reformation, the time might have come for another war.

Owen's comments lend some credence to claims that in the early 1680s he did, in fact, become involved in an attempt to defend the cause of English Protestantism by force of arms. During the winter of 1682–3, a large number of dissenters and their supporters among the Whigs banded together in a plot to assassinate Charles and his brother, the Duke of York, in order to install on the throne the king's reliably Protestant but illegitimate son, the Duke of Monmouth. While most of Owen's biographers have dismissed the possibility

---

[204]Owen, *A brief and impartial account of the nature of the Protestant religion* (1682), 3; *Works* (1965), 14:531.
[205]Owen, *A brief and impartial account of the nature of the Protestant religion* (1682), 16; *Works* (1965), 14:540.
[206]Owen, *A brief and impartial account of the nature of the Protestant religion* (1682), 39; *Works* (1965), 14:554.
[207]Owen, *A brief and impartial account of the nature of the Protestant religion* (1682), 39; *Works* (1965), 14:554.
[208]Owen, *A brief and impartial account of the nature of the Protestant religion* (1682), 12; *Works* (1965), 14:537.
[209]Owen, *A brief and impartial account of the nature of the Protestant religion* (1682), 40; *Works* (1965), 14:555.

that he was involved in the Rye House plot, Sarah Gibbard Cook has brought together some very suggestive lines of enquiry, noting the testimony of informers, the close connections between Owen and several conspirators, his behaviour in the period around the assassination attempt, and the plausibility of his involvement given what we know about his thinking about religion and politics. Taken together with his comments in *A brief and impartial account of the nature of the Protestant religion*, which to the best of my knowledge have never been read in this context, the evidence suggests that Owen might at the very least have approved of the conspiracy. The plot was discovered in June 1683, several months after it had failed. Appearing before the king, Owen swore under oath not to have known about the plot.[210] This did not alleviate all suspicions. The Duke of Monmouth himself testified that Owen had approved of the conspiracy.[211] This confirmed the claim of Owen's former pastoral assistant, Robert Ferguson – who was now being spied upon – who told an informer that Owen believed that the assassination of the king was 'both lawful and necessary'.[212] Bridget Ireton Bendish, a former member of Owen's church, may also have supported the plot, and certainly helped her brother when his involvement was discovered.[213] The son of another member, John Desborough, was also incriminated.[214] Owen's brother, Henry, appears to have conspired with Robert Ferguson at their meetings in Owen's house on Leadenhall Street, London.[215] The plot had involved Owen's brother, his pastoral assistant and several of the younger members of his church. Owen had at least validated their objectives and their methods. But his actual involvement in the plot remains unknown.[216] Owen died, on 24 August 1683, as investigations continued, and before another round of executions began.

CONCLUSION

Owen's political opinions certainly changed over the course of his life. His critics repeatedly accused him of being a 'trimmer', of being prepared to 'sordidly comply with every Government, pray and teach to each Faction, side with all Innovators', or of being a 'great a Weather-Cock in his principles

---

[210] Cook, 'A political biography of a religious Independent', 375.
[211] Ferguson, *Robert Ferguson, 'the plotter'*, 191.
[212] Ferguson, *Robert Ferguson, 'the plotter'*, 136–7.
[213] *ODNB*, s.v. Crippen, 'Dr. Watts's church-book'.
[214] *CSPD*, 1683a, 368, as quoted by Cook, 'A political biography of a religious Independent', 377.
[215] *CSPD*, 1684–5, 258.
[216] Cook, 'A political biography of a religious Independent', 385.

about Government, Toleration and Liberty of Conscience'.[217] They were right. Owen did change his mind on key issues. In the 'country essay' he argued against the toleration of heresy, and argued that the state should put down any teaching that disturbed the peace.[218] Two years later, in the appendix on toleration that was published along with his sermon on the regicide, he made the opposite cause, arguing that 'error has as much right to a forcible defence as Truth'.[219] By October 1652, he had changed his mind again, and in a sermon to Parliament urged MPs to take seriously their responsibility to 'thresh, break, destroy, burthen, fire, consume and slay' the enemies of the Gospel.[220] In the chaos that followed upon the downfall of Richard Cromwell's administration, he hoped that 'Rulers over men' might 'forebeare for ever to impose any nationall, parochiall Ministry, so as to inforce any forme of Worship suited to their interest, or compell men of one perswasion, to maintaine any man of another, in the Ministry'.[221] And after the restoration, he defended the rights of English monarchs to be recognized as 'head' of the established church, but began to suggest the need for armed resistance to government when he faced the prospect of a return to Catholic rule. Owen certainly changed his mind. But he did not change his mind on the underlying commitment that made sense of these opinions in rapidly changing circumstances. Fundamentally, Owen had one political goal, for which he worked during the civil war, the republic and after the restoration. He defended broader or narrower varieties of religious freedom, government by republic or monarchy, as well as passive and active resistance, in order to make the best case he could in changing circumstances for the toleration of orthodox Protestants. Those critics who pointed to Owen's political instability did not recognize his underlying consistency, and could not understand his argument that forms of government were much less important than what those forms of government provided for the godly. Owen had to negotiate the changing fortunes of the period's political revolutions. In the 1640s, as a newly minted Independent, he depended upon being tolerated by the mainly Presbyterian government. In the 1660s, he depended upon being tolerated by the mainly Anglican government. In between, he tried to fashion a national church settlement that would offer some of the period's most generous religious liberties.

Owen was remembered for his accomplishments. Over one century after his death, and in the very different circumstances of the new American

---

[217]*A serious letter to Dr John Owen, sent by a small friend of his* (1659), single sheet; *A letter to a friend concerning some of Dr. Owens principles and practices* (1670), 67.
[218]*A letter to a friend concerning some of Dr. Owens principles and practices* (1670), 67–8.
[219]*A letter to a friend concerning some of Dr. Owens principles and practices* (1670), 69.
[220]*A letter to a friend concerning some of Dr. Owens principles and practices* (1670), 71.
[221]*An essay towards settlement* (1659), single sheet. I am grateful to Tim Cooper for this reference.

republic, Benjamin Rush and Thomas Jefferson were debating the best ways to 'keep religion and government independant [sic] of each Other'. Rush was particularly concerned to emphasize the spiritual rather than the political nature of primitive Christianity. St Paul, he believed, would rebuke those clergy who were engaging themselves in the affairs of the world: 'Read my Epistles', he imagined the apostle arguing. 'In no part of them will you perceive me aiming to depose a pagan Emperor, or to place a Christian upon a throne. Christianity disdains to receive Support from human Governments.' Rush reinforced the point by referring to an eminent 'disciple of St Paul', a 'minister of the Gospel among the dissenters in England, & a sincere friend to liberty', 'a certain Dr Owen'. This man, Rush reported, was

> once complained of by one of Cromwell's time serving priests, – that he did not preach to the *times*. 'My business and duty . . . is to preach – to *Eternity* – not to the *times*.' He has left many Volumes of Sermons behind him, that are so wholly religious, that no One from reading them, could tell, in what country, – or age they were preached.[222]

Rush's use of this anecdote was telling. More often used with reference to Robert Leighton, whose saintly reputation certainly justified this otherworldly spirituality, the anecdote presented Owen as a preacher with no interest in politics. Nothing, of course, could have been further from the truth. Owen's attempt to work out the relationship between church and state laid the foundation for American political culture and classical liberal theory. For, however else he changed, throughout his long and active life, Owen remained relentlessly political.

---

[222] To Thomas Jefferson from Benjamin Rush, 6 October 1800, https://founders.archives.gov/documents/Jefferson/01-32-02-0120, accessed 26 August 2019.

CHAPTER 6

Owen the preacher

MARTYN C. COWAN

John Owen preached across five turbulent decades and in a wide variety of contexts: as pastor of congregations in rural Essex during the English Civil Wars, before Members of Parliament at Westminster, on foreign soil while accompanying occupying armies in Ireland and Scotland, to the University of Oxford and while ministering to dissenters after the Restoration. Theologically, Owen shared with the Reformed orthodox a high view of preaching, particularly its instrumentality in salvation. His sermon style was typical of later English Puritan preaching, with its threefold division into doctrine, reason and use. The most fruitful approach to analysing his extant sermons is a contextual one that seeks to recover the sermon as an event. Close examination of these texts allows a number of previously undated sermons, or treatises whose first form was sermonic, to be linked to specific moments in his career. Furthermore, careful contextualized reading reveals how biblical tropes were employed to make sometimes oblique references to contemporary events.

By way of an overall assessment, Owen's preaching is best described as 'prophetic'.[1] His understanding of providence and eschatology led him to believe that he and his hearers had experienced unique and undeserved divine blessings, which placed upon them the obligation to respond by embracing godly Reformation individually, corporately and nationally. Frequently, Owen's sermons lament what he perceived to be consistently negligent responses to his prophetic call. Consequently, throughout his ministry, he issued ominous

---

[1] Cowan, *John Owen and the civil war apocalypse*.

warnings concerning providential signs of coming divine judgement. Such a portrait may, at first, seem far removed from the impression that many have of Owen as a rather austere scholastic theologian. However, it reminds us that much of his literary work had its genesis in his pulpit ministry. As we shall see, this consideration of Owen as preacher will help us better understand his opinions on religious, political and intellectual life during the Laudian, civil war, Interregnum and Restoration eras.

OWEN'S THEOLOGY AND METHOD OF PREACHING

From his first published work, Owen expressed his conviction that the preaching of the gospel occasioned a 'great shaking' of the earth.[2] He articulated his high view of preaching in a sermon preached at an ordination service in September 1682 on the text, 'And I will give you pastors according to my heart, which shall feed you with knowledge and understanding' (Jer. 3.15). Owen explained that the 'first and principal duty' of a pastor was to feed the flock by means of 'diligent preaching'. Furthermore, pastors were to preach with a powerful 'unction' that came from prayerful dependence upon the Spirit of God. Owen's pulpit rhetoric is discernible in his discussion of this experiential dimension of preaching: 'I think, truly, that no man preaches that sermon well to others that doth not first preach it to his own heart'; and '[i]t is an easier thing to bring our heads to preach than our hearts to preach'.[3] Owen expressed his opinion that 'many' of the 20–30,000 men in holy orders in England lacked this power, and instead delivered nothing more than 'quaint orations'. In contrast, he believed that the true preaching of the Gospel 'is accompanied by a powerful persuasive efficacy'.[4]

Owen laid out the most significant theological foundation for this high view of preaching in Πνευματολογία (1674). Owen called all preachers to 'acquaint themselves thoroughly' with the doctrine of regeneration in order 'to comply with the will of God and grace of the Spirit in the effecting and accomplishment of it upon the souls of them unto whom they dispense the word'. For Owen, it would be scandalous if those who had been 'appointed by God' to be 'instruments' in the regeneration of their hearers would neglect to inquire into the nature of that work and the 'means whereby it is wrought'. He provides a sophisticated account of the instrumentality of preaching in regeneration, a mysterious work that is 'discoverable' through a study of its causes. Although

---

[2]Owen, *A display of Arminianisme* (1643), 'Epistle dedicatorie'; *Works* (1965), 10:6.
[3]Owen, *Thirteen sermons preached on various occasions* (1756), 99–100, 103–6; *Works* (1965), 9:453, 455–6.
[4]Van den Belt, '*Vocatio* as regeneration', 153.

regeneration was a work of the Spirit, it did not occur to the exclusion of the Word's instrumental agency. Preachers were 'used and employed' by the Spirit, who made them 'instrumental for the effecting of this new birth and life'.[5] This was, of course, something that Owen himself had experienced when sermon gadding in London in 1642, when he received assurance of salvation through the 'plain familiar discourse' of an otherwise unknown country preacher.[6]

Owen's monergistic doctrine of regeneration was just one part of the high Calvinist conception of divine sovereignty in salvation that was also reflected in his doctrine of limited atonement. Despite Arminian objections, Owen did not believe that his doctrine of particular redemption was incompatible with the well-meant offer of the Gospel. He articulated his understanding of the compatibility of his soteriology with unrestricted and sincere Gospel preaching in *Salus electorum, sanguis Jesu: or, The death of death in the death of Christ* (1648), as he answered the objection that the Gospel may not be preached to those for whom Christ did not die. For Owen, the basis for the general and unrestricted offer of the Gospel was the hiddenness of God's sovereign purposes of election; the preacher did not know who among their hearers was of the elect. He reminded his readers that the preacher is 'unacquainted with God's distinguishing counsels' in the hidden divine decree, and so was 'not to make inquiry after, nor to trouble himself about, those secrets of the eternal mind of God'.[7] Rather, preachers are to 'command and invite all to repent and believe' with an 'external offer' in the preaching of the Gospel, which 'is not declarative to any in particular, neither of what God hath done nor what he will do in reference to him, but of what he ought to do'. Such unrestricted preaching was to be done with an awareness of the divinely ordained two-fold purpose of preaching: in this purpose, God would 'bring his own home to himself . . . by exhortations, entreaties, promises, and the like means', while also effecting 'conviction, restraint, hardening, [and] inexcusableness' in others. Thus, the Gospel call was, for Owen, not 'absolutely universal' but rather 'indefinite, without respect to outward differences'.[8] As Van den Belt explains, while Owen did not restrict the free call of the Gospel, he did seem to 'restrict the promise of the Gospel exclusively to those who truly repent'. In other words, the preacher was only to offer Christ in the Gospel to repentant sinners who were under conviction.[9] MacLean observes that for Owen the exegetical basis for upholding the free offer was 'more limited' than it was for some other

---

[5] Owen, Πνευματολογία (1674), 177, 188, 189; *Works* (1965), 3:213, 227, 236.
[6] Asty, 'Memoirs of the life of John Owen', 5.
[7] Owen, *The death of death in the death of Christ* (1648), 178; *Works* (1965), 10:299–300.
[8] Owen, *The death of death in the death of Christ* (1648), 192; *Works* (1965), 10:314.
[9] Van den Belt, '*Vocatio* as regeneration', 158.

contemporary divines.[10] Nonetheless, in his preaching Owen urged all, even unrepentant sinners, to come and to 'close' with Christ, 'rolling' upon him as he was 'tendered' or 'proffered' in the Gospel.[11]

For Owen, this exalted view of the preacher as an ambassador of Christ was not incompatible with lay preaching. In the 1640s he outlined how he believed the English church to be under threat from preachers who were, at best, 'dumb, sleeping dogs', or, even worse, 'devouring wolves'. In such circumstances he was prepared to allow gifted laymen to preach.[12] His first parliamentary sermon placed great emphasis upon the 'variety' of means employed in the propagation of the Gospel and, while lamenting the dearth of godly preaching in parts of England, Wales and Ireland, announced that he would 'rejoice' if Christ would be preached even 'with some defects in some circumstances'.[13] Thus, as he set out during his early ministry, he would cautiously accept lay preaching.[14]

In terms of method, Owen's sermons bear the hallmark of what Morrissey has termed the generic 'English Reformed' homiletic method, in which sermons were structured according to the tripartite model of text, doctrine and use.[15] A methodology akin to Owen's was clearly laid out by John Wilkins in his preaching manual *Ecclesiastes* (1646).[16] Wilkins, who was a contemporary of Owen's both at Edward Sylvester's school and in the Cromwellian University of Oxford, argued that 'the chief parts of a Sermon' are 'Explication. Confirmation. Application'.[17] Although, in practice, this structure is sometimes blurred in Owen's sermons, we generally find him 'opening' the text by carefully exegeting its context, grammar and vocabulary. He then 'divides' the text, a process in which keywords and phrases are identified and from which he derives or 'raises' the doctrine(s) to be expounded. Owen then concisely states a doctrinal thesis before establishing it by recourse to multiple scriptural proof texts and supporting argumentative heads that are termed 'reasons'. In this part of his exposition, Owen frequently resolves possible objections to the doctrine by way of confirmation. The third element involves him applying the doctrine under consideration according to certain observations of its use(s). This methodology, as practised by Owen, was ridiculed by some detractors. For example, Samuel Parker lampooned Owen's detailed comments in *Eben-ezer*

---

[10]MacLean, *James Durham (1622–1658)*, 135. See also Foord, 'John Owen's Gospel offer', 295.
[11]Owen, *A practical exposition on the 130th Psalm* (1669), 259–262; *Works* (1965), 6:528–30; Owen, *The death of death in the death of Christ* (1648), 304; *Works* (1965), 10:407.
[12]Owen, *The duty of pastors and people distinguished* (1644), 15, 39; *Works* (1965), 13:18, 37.
[13]Owen, *A vision of unchangeable free mercy* (1646), 44–5; *Works* (1965), 8:40–1.
[14]Owen, *Eshcol* (1648), 58; *Works* (1965), 13:70.
[15]Morrissey, 'Scripture, style and persuasion in seventeenth-century English theories of preaching', 687, 693.
[16]Shapiro, *John Wilkins, 1614–1672*, 5, 86–8.
[17]Wilkins, *Ecclesiastes* (1647), 5.

(1648) about the nature of a song 'upon Shigionoth' (Hab. 3.1), jesting that Owen was 'able to raise Edification out of a pair of Bagpipes'.[18] The eighteenth-century dissenter, Robert Robinson, also condemned the method employed in that sermon as 'abstruse', since Owen resorted to 'almost one hundred and fifty observations, uses, reasons, &c'.[19] Despite these criticisms, the formal structure of his sermons provided both Owen and his hearers with a shared set of expectations.

RECONSTRUCTING THE SERMON AS AN 'EVENT'

There is, of course, an important distinction between the study of preaching and the study of sermons. As Morrissey notes, an 'ineliminable element of uncertainty' is involved in any 'consideration of the relationship between the performance as an event and the textual witnesses it leaves'.[20] The challenge is only increased because, according to an early biographer, Owen did not tend to use notes in the pulpit.[21] It is almost impossible to reconstruct Owen's preaching, since there are only occasional accounts of how he behaved in the pulpit, and even these are difficult to assess. For example, preaching at St Mary's, Oxford, in July 1660, Robert South, a far from unbiased source, taunted the 'whimsical cant' and 'Jargon' of 'one J.O. a great leader and oracle in these times', and mocked the *'saving Way of Preaching'* that used to be heard from that pulpit.[22] However, Anthony Wood, another writer with his own agenda, remembered Owen's preaching somewhat differently:

> [H]e had a very graceful behaviour in the Pulpit, an eloquent Elocution, a winning and insinuating deportment, and could by the persuasion of his oratory, in conjunction with some other outward advantages, move and wind the affections of his admiring Auditory almost as he pleased.[23]

These comments serve as helpful reminders that Owen's sermons stand as textual artefacts that bear the marks of the times in which he preached and wrote. On occasion, modern scholarly engagement with Owen's sermons has fallen prey to the type of 'source-mining' approach that quarries texts for little more than historical footnotes. A more appropriate contextual approach involves the 'opening up of texts to their historic meaning, not the crude

---

[18]Parker, *A defence and continuation of the ecclesiastical politie* (1671), 604.
[19]See Robinson's notes, in John Claude, *An essay on the composition of a sermon* (1779), 458.
[20]Morrissey, 'Sermon-notes and seventeenth-century manuscript communities', 295.
[21]Asty, 'Memoirs of the life of John Owen', xxxv.
[22]Simon, *Three Restoration divines*, 247–8.
[23]Wood, *Athenæ Oxonienses*, 2:741.

locating of texts in the past'.²⁴ The most illuminating studies of early modern sermons are those in which the texts are assessed 'in the context and evaluative terms of the culture that produced them', and are treated as events, as dynamic encounters between the preacher and his auditors.²⁵ A carefully contextualized reading will be one that is aware that Scripture presented the preacher with a 'nuanced and adaptable language' from which listeners and readers could draw their own conclusions.²⁶ This allowed for the 'oblique discourse' in which criticism of contemporary political events could be voiced by its being couched in Scriptural metaphor. Preachers employed this code of communication 'partly to protect themselves from hostile and hence dangerous readings of their work, partly in order to say what they had to publicly without directly provoking or confronting the authorities'.²⁷ In the early modern sermon, 'the biblical idiom was its own and sufficient political comment: a measured, subtle, and precise medium of criticism and a vocabulary of political exordium'.²⁸ Owen's sermons, therefore, provide significant insight not only into his thought but also the details of his life.

The corpus of Owen's sermonic material is diverse. It includes a number of stand-alone public sermons that Owen prepared for publication, usually in response to an invitation to publish. Most of the sermon genre works that Owen prepared for the press were delivered between 1646 and 1659, although one notable later exception is *An humble testimony* (1681). However, large amounts of his sermonic material emerged in other forms. From the early days of his ministry, he was adapting his preaching for publication in the form of treatises. For example, *The duty of pastors and people distinguished* (1644) was 'resolved from the ordinary pulpit method into its own principles'.²⁹ This was a habit which he would continue throughout his life. For example, well-known works such as *Of the mortification of sinne in believers* (1656) and *Of communion with God* (1657) found their origin in his pulpit ministry in Oxford. The latter work took a number of years, and some persuasion from others, to find its way into print. The former work came about because Owen's preaching on mortification had enjoyed 'some comfortable success', and he published the material 'with such additions and alterations as I should judge necessary'.³⁰ Gribben has detected the 'strategies of the pulpit' in Owen's 'pithy

---

²⁴Ferrell, *Government by polemic*, 17.
²⁵Ferrell and McCullough, 'Revising the study of the English sermon', 9.
²⁶Killeen, 'Chastising with scorpions', 493.
²⁷Patterson, *Censorship and interpretation*, 10–11, 21.
²⁸Killeen, 'Veiled speech', 387–8.
²⁹Owen, *The duty of pastors and people distinguished* (1644), A2r; *Works* (1965), 13:3.
³⁰Owen, *Of the mortification of sinne in believers* (1656), A3r; *Works* (1965), 6:3.

soundbites' in that volume.[31] His *A practical exposition on the 130th Psalm* (1669) has obvious links to his preaching from the later part of the decade. Likewise, his massive commentary on Hebrews most likely provided fodder for Owen's preaching, since during its composition he preached multiple sermons from the epistle. Even at the end of his life, there are numerous connections between his sermons on death, delivered in autumn 1680, and the preface to his *Meditations and discourses on the glory of Christ* (1684).[32] Consequently, it is important to recognize that the genesis of much of Owen's work lay in a pastoral context in which he was engaged in the time-consuming labour of preaching. Scholarly work on Owen should therefore take care not to divorce his work as preacher from his work as a Reformed scholastic divine.

Other sermons by Owen have come down to us in different ways. Although some of Owen's posthumously published sermons arose from his copy of the text, most have been drawn from notes taken by auditors.[33] Morrissey highlights the general incompleteness of 'hearers' notes'. For example, 'most hearers could not copy down every word and so they concentrated on getting a summary of the sermon's main argument.' Despite this, she recognizes, the 'success rate of many early modern hearers is impressive'.[34] As Sullivan has shown, that was certainly the case in Cromwellian Oxford – which was where Thomas Aldersey, a student at Brasenose, recorded notes of Owen's sermons.[35] During the Restoration, 'note-taking was common in Owen's congregation'.[36] From the mid-1660s, Sir John Hartopp took shorthand notes that he later wrote out in notebooks, producing a record that Gribben describes as often being 'detailed and compelling'.[37] In 1673, Lucy Hutchinson also took notes of Owen's preaching. Gibson suggests that from the differences in the writing style it is possible that she 'took the volume along to Owen's sermons, writing in her notes on the spot'.[38] Her theological notebook also contains some unattributed sermons that may well record other instances of Owen's preaching in 1673.[39] Considered together, these auditors' notes are important because they provide a record of Owen's thought on matters that he might have been unlikely to put into print.

---

[31]Gribben, *John Owen and English Puritanism*, 165.
[32]MacPhail, 'This peculiar constitution of our nature', 10–11.
[33]Owen, *A complete collection of the sermons* (1721), preface.
[34]Morrissey, 'Sermon-notes and seventeenth-century manuscript communities', 302.
[35]Oxford, Bodleian Library: MSS. Don. f. 38–41, 75v–77v (versos only, on 1 John 1:3) and 115v–117v (versos only, on John 21:20–21).
[36]Norbrook, 'Introduction', 27.
[37]Gribben, *John Owen and English Puritanism*, 239.
[38]Gibson, 'Textual introduction', 57.
[39]Norbrook, 'Introduction', 29.

The extant corpus of Owen's sermons contains well over 100 sermon texts and, in addition, an extensive body of literature that had its genesis in his preaching.[40] A contextualized reading of these texts which seeks to recover the sermon as event will enable us to understand much more of Owen, not only as a preacher but also as an individual who is still regarded as somewhat 'elusive', and to see the priority that he placed upon preaching in his vision for further church reform.[41]

A CONTEXTUALIZED SURVEY OF OWEN, THE PREACHER

In his ministry in rural Essex, Owen thought his hearers to be largely ignorant of spiritual things, and he criticized those who had condemned conventicles.[42] He hoped his preaching would bring conversion, but he was all too aware that 'a pastor's life should be vocal; sermons must be practised as well as preached'.[43]

Owen's move to Coggeshall would have involved an appearance before the Westminster Assembly, a body 'obsessed with pulpit reform', in order to preach a trial sermon.[44] In this new parish, Owen was preaching to, perhaps, some 2,000 people at public worship.[45] He sought assistance by appointing John Sams as a teaching elder, something that was 'entirely consistent' with his views on lay preaching.[46] During this time, Owen was called to preach his first Parliamentary sermon (April 1646). Subsequently, his involvement with the Parliamentary forces during the siege of Colchester resulted in him preaching the thanksgiving services published as *Eben-ezer* (1648). His circle of influence was widening, and he would soon become the 'unofficial preacher-in-chief' of the revolutionary regime.[47] In the days after Pride's Purge, in early December 1648, Bulstrode Whitelock heard Owen preach 'two excellent sermons', noting that he 'seemed much to favour' the cause of the army.[48] Weeks later, Owen preached his most (in)famous sermon on the day after the regicide. Gribben claims that the sermon 'pulls its punches', especially in comparison to the other

---

[40]The fullest record has been catalogued by Mark Burden as 'John Owen, learned Puritan' on the Oxford University Centre for Early Modern Studies website, accessed 8 June 2020, https://earlymodern.web.ox.ac.uk/john-owen-learned-Puritan.
[41]Toon, *God's statesman*, 176.
[42]Owen, *The duty of pastors and people distinguished* (1644), 11; *Works* (1965), 13:47.
[43]Owen, *Eshcol* (1648), 9; *Works* (1965), 13:57.
[44]Halcomb, 'The examination of ministers', 1:217–26; Van Dixhoorn, *God's ambassadors*, xv.
[45]Cooper, *John Owen, Richard Baxter and the formation of Nonconformity*, 40.
[46]Gribben, 'John Owen and congregational life in England', 126.
[47]Hill, *Experience of defeat*, 165.
[48]Whitelocke, *Diary*, 227.

sermon delivered that day by John Cardell.⁴⁹ However, Owen implicitly likened Charles to King Manasseh, the very worst of the Judean kings (2 Kings 21), and contemporaries felt the sermon sufficiently pointed to have it burned in Oxford in 1683.⁵⁰ Several months after the regicide, in June 1649, Owen delivered a 'fiery' sermon at a celebration of the defeat of the Levellers in which, as a 'prophet of a new world order', he constructed an ideological justification of the forthcoming Cromwellian conquest of Ireland.⁵¹ Although Owen was invited to print what the establishment regarded as a very satisfactory sermon, he chose not to, and the sermon would only be published posthumously.

When Owen was in Dublin as part of the Cromwellian expeditionary force, he preached at a chapel on Wood Street where, as Gribben points out, we find the earliest evidence that his preaching resulted in conversions.⁵² For example, one sympathetic hearer recounted how Owen made him 'see *my misery* in the *want* of *Christ*', and another spoke of how she became 'sensible' of her spiritual condition through his ministry.⁵³

Soon after he returned to England, Owen preached a Parliamentary fast sermon that was published as Ουρανων ουρανια: *The shaking and translating of heaven and earth* (1649). The monthly fasts were now becoming something of a liability and were discontinued.⁵⁴ Nonetheless, Owen's role as a spokesman for the regime was made evident in his being appointed to preach every Sunday to the Council of State, and in the invitation that he deliver another sermon to Parliament that June, the text of which is not extant.⁵⁵ After the invasion of Scotland, in summer 1650, Cromwell appears to have requested that Owen be sent north, so that he might 'receive comfort' by his 'prayers and preaching'.⁵⁶ In Scotland, Owen participated in a 'vigorous culture of preaching', to which it appears that un-ordained officers, including Cromwell, also contributed.⁵⁷ Owen's sermons played a significant role in the propaganda campaign that was designed to help define the rationale for invasion and to persuade the Scots to accept it. For example, Cromwell's press in Leith printed one of Owen's sermons, and the officer and regicide Robert Lilburne wrote to Cromwell asking for copies of Owen's sermons for distribution.⁵⁸

---

⁴⁹Gribben, *John Owen and English Puritanism*, 98; Wilson, *Pulpit in Parliament*, 95.
⁵⁰Owen, *A discourse about toleration* (1649), 4–6; *Works* (1965), 8:135–7.
⁵¹Gribben, *John Owen and English Puritanism*, 104.
⁵²Gribben, *John Owen and English Puritanism*, 112.
⁵³Rogers, *Ohel or Bethshemesh*, 412; Gribben, *God's Irishmen*, 26.
⁵⁴Worden, *The Rump Parliament 1648–53*, 80–3.
⁵⁵Gribben, *John Owen and English Puritanism*, 115.
⁵⁶Wood, *Athenæ Oxonienses*, 2:376.
⁵⁷Reece, *The army in Cromwellian England, 1649–1660*, 119.
⁵⁸Spurlock, *Cromwell and Scotland*, 45–6.

Owen was back preaching to the Rump in March 1651. According to one report, 'Mr. Owen did preach very excellently', the purpose of his sermon being the 'vindication of the present government'.[59] The next day Owen was offered the deanery of Christ Church, and with this position, a new sphere of preaching ministry. Some of his earliest preaching in Oxford were the sermons that would become *Of communion with God* (1657). Alongside this work, he continued to preach some high-profile sermons in London. He preached in celebration of the defeat of the Scots at Worcester on 3 September and another Parliamentary sermon on 24 October 1651. The published versions of both sermons indicate Owen's sense of the 'messianic quality of the political and military executive of the English Revolution'.[60] The following February, Owen preached at Henry Ireton's funeral, and in October he delivered his final sermon before the Rump. On both occasions, he selected texts from the book of Daniel, perhaps a shrewd move as that Old Testament figure could be taken as an ideal non-monarchical civil magistrate. He also preached to the Nominated Assembly in August 1653, but no known copy of the text is extant.[61] In the wake of this body's failure, Owen was involved in significant discussions about the religious settlement that resulted in two Protectoral Ordinances which demonstrated the priority of the national preaching ministry for further reformation.[62] The first of these ordinances established the Commission for the Approbation of Public Preachers. On this central committee, Owen and thirty-seven other 'triers' would vet and approve new candidates for parish ministry as well as existing ministers seeking new positions. The second ordinance established county lay commissions for the ejection of 'ignorant, scandalous, insufficient or negligent' ministers. Owen, who was appointed to assist the Oxfordshire 'ejectors', shared the hope that this activity would purge and purify the pulpits of the land and reform the English church through the agency of godly preachers.[63]

Owen's quest for a national reformation in preachers and preaching was also a significant part of his vision for reform in Oxford. As well as preaching at Christ Church and delivering his fortnightly Sunday afternoon sermons at St Mary's, he was involved in other measures to reform the pulpits of Oxford. In 1651, the Christ Church chapter asked suitably qualified ministers to preach in neighbouring vacant pulpits, and required all scholars to repeat the sermons that they heard to their tutors. In 1653, in his role as vice-chancellor of the university, Owen required other College heads to report on the quality

---

[59] *Perfect account* (12–19 March 1651), 77.
[60] Gribben, *John Owen and English Puritanism*, 133.
[61] Toon, *God's statesman*, 88.
[62] Cooper, *John Owen, Richard Baxter and the formation of Nonconformity*, 171; Gaunt, 'To create a little world out of chaos', 105–26.
[63] Hughes, 'The public profession of these nations', 97–9.

of preaching for which their staff were responsible.[64] This reform was given architectural expression when, *c.* 1655, a new wooden pulpit was installed in St Mary's on the old stone pedestal.[65] Owen's discontent with responses to what was regarded as his 'new-fangled' form of preaching is discernible in a series of sermons that could very well have been delivered in Cromwellian Oxford: 'Walking humbly with God.' Owen lamented how many, 'running after sermons', were concerned only with 'novelty, or the ability of the preacher'.[66] For Owen, many preached only 'fopperies' and were 'mere moral men', self-righteous and 'utter strangers to a new spiritual life'. There are good reasons to believe that Owen was denouncing the preaching of John Wilkins and his circle (Aldersey's notebook contains notes from sermons by Owen and Wilkins).[67] He believed such preachers were 'ignorant of God and themselves' and failed to press people about 'this business of a new life'.[68]

In September 1656, Owen preached an 'adulatory sermon' at the opening of the second Protectorate Parliament.[69] He preached again to MPs that October. These sermons were printed as *God's work in founding Zion* (1656) and *God's presence with a people* (1656). However, with the reorientation of the Protectorate, Owen's relationship with the Cromwellian establishment deteriorated. In Oxford, he found himself removed from preaching at St Mary's and responded by setting up a rival lecture at St Peter's in the East.[70] On the basis of internal evidence it is possible that a series of undated sermons titled 'Providential changes, an argument for universal holiness' were preached the following year, most likely in the first half of 1657.[71] Similarly, the sermons on 'Spiritual barrenness' may, tentatively, be dated to 1658.[72] As we shall see, this often-overlooked material may provide an important window into Owen's thinking as he grew increasingly disillusioned with the Cromwellian regime.

Owen preached a fast sermon to the third Protectorate Parliament on 4 February 1659. It was reported that Owen preached 'very seriously'.[73] There was some controversy over whether the sermon should be printed, but it appeared as *The glory and interest of nations* (1659). In March 1659, Owen gathered a church at Charles Fleetwood's residence, Wallingford House,

---

[64]*The register of the visitors of the University of Oxford*, 335–6, 358–60.
[65]Jackson, *The Church of St Mary the Virgin, Oxford*, 180–1.
[66]Owen, *A complete collection of the sermons* (1721), 25, 30; *Works* (1965), 9:93, 100.
[67]Owen, *A complete collection of the sermons* (1721), 24; *Works* (1965), 9:90–1, 130; Cowan, *John Owen and the civil war apocalypse*, 84–5.
[68]Owen, *A complete collection of the sermons* (1721), 25, 30; *Works* (1965), 9:92–3, 100.
[69]Woolrych, *Britain in revolution*, 646.
[70]Cooper, *John Owen, Richard Baxter and the Formation of Nonconformity*, 122–3.
[71]Cowan, *John Owen and the civil war apocalypse*, 105–6.
[72]Cowan, *John Owen and the civil war apocalypse*, 161–2.
[73]*The correspondence of Henry Cromwell*, 449.

London, of which many discontented officers were members. When the Council of Officers took the decision to recall the Rump Parliament, Owen was invited to preach to its members.[74] It was reported that 'Doctor Owen entertained them with a comfortable Sermon'.[75] According to a Quaker source, Owen 'calledst them dry Bones breathed into', thus invoking a prophetic trope to speak of Parliament being divinely resurrected (Ezekiel 37).[76] The Council of State requested that Owen preach at Whitehall each Sunday in October and November: Gribben suggests the Council was 'keeping its friends close, and its enemies even closer'.[77] In the chaos which ensued, as the regime began its collapse, Richard Baxter levelled significant blame on Owen and his preaching, arguing that 'one mans Pride' had brought 'the nation into utter confusion', pondering, 'O *what* may *Pride* do in men th*at* can preach ag*ainst* it as much as others'.[78] This perspective on the instrumental role of Owen's preaching was shared by the parody funeral sermon printed in January 1660, in which Owen was represented as preaching at the interment of the revolution.[79]

In the Restoration, Owen preached to a variety of dissenting groups. In the early 1660s, he gathered a church in his own home in Stadhampton, which was kept under observation by the authorities.[80] He was also preaching for Lady Abney, the daughter of Joseph Caryl, in her houses at Theobalds in Hertfordshire and in London.[81] In 1664, Owen joined the household of Sir Charles Fleetwood in Stoke Newington, Middlesex, where many of his former associates had formed a small congregation; in the following year, he was found preaching to a congregation of around thirty.[82] In 1669, the year the first Conventicle Act expired, there were reports of Owen preaching in White's Alley and at a weekday lecture in Hackney.[83] One wonders how Owen managed to sustain his work of preaching and writing at this time, so it is perhaps unsurprising that during a sermon he admitted that he was unable to finish it because 'my strength is gone'.[84] The issue of preaching was one that occupied Owen and Baxter during their negotiations about reconciliation between Presbyterians and Congregationalists. One of the questions in their correspondence concerned *'what words to use in preaching'*, and whether

---

[74]Toon, *God's statesman*, 113.
[75]*The weekly intelligencer of the common-wealth* (3–10 May 1659), 8.
[76]*The correspondence of John Owen*, 118.
[77]Gribben, *John Owen and English Puritanism*, 202.
[78]*Reliquiæ Baxterianæ*, ed. Keeble et al, 1:444, 447.
[79]*Bradshaws ultimum vale* (1660), 10, 12.
[80]Gribben, *John Owen and English Puritanism*, 29, 181.
[81]*The correspondence of John Owen*, 131.
[82]Gribben, *John Owen and English Puritanism*, 226–8.
[83]Greaves, *John Bunyan and English Nonconformity*, 160.
[84]Owen, *Works* (1965), 16:439.

Baxter intended the reading of 'homelys'.[85] Owen had already made it clear in *A discourse concerning liturgies* (1662) that 'Christ equips his pastors with gifts, not liturgies'.[86] This continued to be a theme in his preaching, which he expounded, among many other instances, in an ordination sermon in 1678.[87]

The various notebooks containing Owen's sermons from this season reveal how central preaching was to religious experience in dissenting communities. Owen was preaching several times a week, and often delivered extended series of sermons on particular texts.[88] His preaching continued despite his own weakness and the government clampdown with the new Conventicle Act in spring 1670. In 1672, the year of the king's declaration of indulgence, a weekly preaching lecture on Tuesday mornings was established at Pinners' Hall on Old Broad Street, and Owen was one of the divines who delivered these Merchants' Lectures.[89]

In June 1673, Owen's smaller congregation merged with a larger church that had been pastored by Joseph Caryl. The new church became 'one of the most aristocratic of the London Nonconformist congregations'.[90] As Gribben notes, from this time Owen appears to move away from longer series of sermons to preaching on a variety of texts.[91] This was a time of heightened tension because of the failure of the declaration of indulgence in March. Notes by Hutchinson of a sermon delivered in April on Rev. 14.13 may be those from a sermon preached by Owen which was 'aymd for yᵉ saints in time of persecution by yᵉ Antichristian Rome' and which therefore was 'applicable to our times'.[92] This represents Owen's attempt to locate the dissenting community in the cosmic context of the apocalypse. The passing of the first Test Act required, among other things, all officer-holders under the crown to take communion in the Church of England, and by September action was being taken against Fleetwood, Hartopp and other members of Owen's congregation for their Nonconformity.[93]

There are other glimpses of Owen's preaching ministry during this period. The Huguenot Lewis Du Moulin spoke highly of him and his congregation.[94] The merchant and antiquarian Ralph Thoresby, who listened to various London

---

[85] *Reliquiæ Baxterianæ*, eds Keeble et al., 4:53, 57.
[86] Gribben, *John Owen and English Puritanism*, 217.
[87] Owen, *Thirteen sermons* (1756), 74–5; *Works* (1965), 9:442, 485.
[88] Norbrook, 'Introduction', 2:28.
[89] Wilson, *The history and antiquities of dissenting churches and meeting houses, in London, Westminster, and Southwark*, 2:252–3.
[90] Whiting, *Studies in English Puritanism*, 78.
[91] Gribben, *John Owen and English Puritanism*, 251.
[92] Norbrook, 'Introduction', 29.
[93] Cliffe, *The Puritan gentry besieged, 1650–1700*, 84.
[94] Nuttall, 'Milton's churchmanship in 1659', 229.

preachers and then gathered with friends to 'repeat' the sermons, heard Owen twice in September 1677. On the first occasion, he recorded that 'Dr Owen preached very well on the power of Christ; but was sore thronged, that I could neither write nor hear very well'.[95]

Owen found himself preaching in an increasingly hostile environment. Early in 1676, the government began a concerted crackdown on dissent, and in February, an informer reported that Owen's congregation was 'praying and preaching to the decrying of the present power and all authority to them contrary'.[96] By now Owen was weary, and becoming convinced of his own failure, telling his congregation: 'I have now been very long, though very unprofitable, in the ministration of the word. . . . I am ready to faint, and give over, and to beg of the church they would think of some other person to conduct them in my room.'[97] His preaching around this time became 'quieter and more reflective' as he 'adopts the role of a dying man speaking to dying people', conscious that his was a 'dying time, especially among good ministers, one or another [dying] almost every day'.[98] In autumn 1681, magistrates were again ordered to clamp down on conventicles, and by the end of November Owen was included on a list of dissenting ministers.[99] In February 1682, the authorities were watching Owen's conventicle, and by this stage much of the preaching was being undertaken by his assistant.[100] As the year went on, coercion escalated, and, by the autumn, the notorious Hilton gang claimed to have a network of more than fifty men searching for conventicles in and around London.[101] Soon, as his preaching ministry drew to a quiet and rather sombre close, Owen himself would again be fined and indicted for preaching at conventicles.[102]

OWEN'S PROPHETIC PREACHING

Owen's sermons are best described as a form of prophetic preaching. Taking the voices and assuming tropes of the biblical prophets, Owen offered an explanation of the days in which the church found itself and urged his hearers and readers to make a proper response. Collinson very helpfully summarizes

---

[95]Sangha, 'Ralph Thoresby and individual devotion in late seventeenth- and early eighteenth-century England', 139–59.
[96]Greaves, *Enemies under his feet*, 128.
[97]Owen, *A complete collection of the sermons* (1721), 571; *Works* (1965), 9:405.
[98]MacPhail, 'This peculiar constitution of our nature', 5–6.
[99]Gribben, *John Owen and English Puritanism*, 258–9.
[100]*The correspondence of John Owen*, 170–2.
[101]Goldie, 'The Hilton gang and the purge of London in the 1680s', 48.
[102]Greaves, *Glimpses of glory*, 459.

the message of this genre as 'always the same: most favoured, more obligated, most negligent'.[103] This pattern is certainly evident in Owen's preaching as he drew attention to the undeserved blessings of apocalyptic significance that the nation had experienced, set forth the obligations incumbent upon it to respond appropriately to this unique providential moment, while lamenting the nation's failures to do so, and warning of the consequent threat of divine judgement. In what follows, we will explore how these four elements are discernible right across the nearly four decades of preaching which have been surveyed.

Preaching to those uniquely blessed

Throughout his public ministry, Owen believed that he was preaching in days of unique significance. The events of the mid-seventeenth century crisis were to him nothing less than an undeserved divine visitation of apocalyptic significance. In a rare autobiographical note in the 1670s, he revealed that 'it is now towards forty years since God enabled me to observe . . . that God had a controversy with the nation'.[104] He believed that this arose from the widespread influence of Antichrist during the eleven-year tyranny of King Charles's reign and in the policies that were pursued by Archbishop Laud.[105] Owen bemoaned how these influences had been particularly evident in the implementation of liturgical ceremonialism and the rise of doctrinal anti-Calvinism. He was deeply troubled by the ongoing and widespread effect that Laudianism had on the preaching of the English church, as a consequence of which 'shepherds may be turned into dumb, sleeping dogs and devouring wolves; the watchmen may be turned smiters, her prophets to prophesy falsely'.[106] A 'strict canon' had outlawed conventicles, and bishops had oppressed 'true' ministers of the Gospel. Employing the language of 1 Cor. 2.4, he accused the Laudian regime of endeavouring to 'silence, destroy and banish' those whose preaching was 'in demonstration of the Spirit and of Power'.[107] In their place, 'false prophets' preached 'altar-worship, Arminianism, Popery, [and] superstition', seducing people with 'cobweb homilies'.[108] Consequently, Owen believed that the land stood under divine judgement, and he feared that the nation had so 'abused' and 'forsaken' the Gospel that it might have forfeited it altogether. Employing a prophetic trope from Ezekiel, he announced that the glory of God stood poised

---

[103] Collinson, 'Biblical rhetoric', 27–8; Morrissey, 'Elect nations and prophetic preaching', 43–58.
[104] Owen, *A complete collection of the sermons* (1721), 544; *Works* (1965), 9:366.
[105] Owen, *The advantage of the kingdome of Christ* (1651), 12–13; *Works* (1965), 8:323.
[106] Owen, *The duty of pastors and people distinguished* (1644), 11, 15, 39; *Works* (1965), 13:15, 18, 37.
[107] Owen, *Of communion with God* (1657), 297; *Works* (1965), 2:255.
[108] Owen, *The duty of pastors and people distinguished* (1644), 43, 45; *Works* (1965), 13:40, 42.

to depart from the people because of their idolatry and corrupt government (Ezek. 8.1–11.25).[109]

From Owen's perspective, things changed dramatically with the English revolution. In 1646, he proclaimed that 'this is the day of England's visitation', suggesting that because of God's 'unchangeable free mercy', the 'house of England' was under 'as full a dispensation of mercy and grace, as ever Nation in the world enjoyed'. He believed that God had broken the Laudian 'snare', and he claimed that God had set the Gospel 'at liberty in England' in an unprecedented manner.[110]

Owen confidently identified the *digitus Dei* in the works of providence.[111] His sermons are replete with references to providentially significant events: the reforms of 1641;[112] the decisive battles of Naseby and Marston Moor; the conclusion of the Second Civil War;[113] the trial and execution of the king; the conquest of Ireland;[114] the suppression of the Levellers;[115] the victories at Dunbar and Worcester;[116] and even the capture of Spanish cargo in 1656.[117] Owen offered an interpretation of such events by placing them within his very particular eschatological framework.[118] He used several biblical images and motifs to provide rich rhetorical texture to his explanation: the vengeance of the temple (Jeremiah 50 and 51), the measuring of the temple and the restoration of true worship (Revelation 11 and 22), a period of transitional shaking (Hebrews 12) and dissolutions that usher in a new heaven and earth (2 Peter 3).[119] This rhetorical texture is vividly captured in a sermon from April 1649, which was subsequently published as Ουρανων ουρανια: *The shaking and translating of heaven and earth* (1649). Owen's eschatology led him to believe that the fifth vial of divine wrath (Rev. 16.10) was being poured out on all forms of Episcopalianism.[120]

---

[109] Owen, *A vision of unchangeable free mercy* (1646), 32–4; *Works* (1965), 8:31–2.
[110] Owen, *A vision of unchangeable free mercy* (1646), 2, 31, 41, 44–5; *Works* (1965), 8:6, 30, 38, 40.
[111] Owen, *Eben-ezer* (1648), 31; *Works* (1965), 8:104; *A complete collection of sermons* (1721), 63, 82; *Works* (1965), 9:153, 203; *Works* (1965), 16:487.
[112] Owen, *God's work in founding Zion* (1656), 22; *Works* (1965), 8:411.
[113] Owen, *Eben-ezer* (1648), 13; *Works* (1965), 8:88.
[114] Owen, *The steadfastness of promises, and the sinfulness of staggering* (1650), 34; *Works* (1965), 8:230.
[115] Owen, *A complete collection of sermons* (1721), 82–3, 88–9; *Works* (1965), 9:203–4, 213–14.
[116] Owen, *The branch of the Lord, the beauty of Sion* (1650), 10–11, 31–2; *Works* (1965), 8:290–1, 302–3; *The advantage of the kingdome of Christ* (1651), 15; *Works* (1965), 8:325; *A sermon preached to the Parliament, Octob. 13. 1652* (1652), 24–5; *Works* (1965), 8:379.
[117] Owen, *God's presence with a people* (1656), 1–2; *Works* (1965), 8:431.
[118] Cowan, *John Owen and the civil war apocalypse*, 47–60.
[119] For the latter see Duff, *A knot worth unloosing*, 53–60.
[120] Owen, *A vision of unchangeable free mercy* (1646), 31; *Works* (1965), 8:30; *A sermon preached to the Parliament, Octob. 13. 1652* (1652), 13; *Works* (1965), 8:373.

For Owen, these military, civil and ecclesiastical providences were evidence that the English republic was receiving unprecedented and undeserved divine blessings of end-times significance. As he confidently informed members of the Rump Parliament, 'from the days of old', there had never been a time when God's 'presence, power and providence' had been seen as clearly. As Owen surveyed all the providences of the English revolution from his study in Christ Church, he announced that the nation was now under the greatest 'outward dispensation' of mercy as had been heard of in 2,000 years.[121]

Preaching to those obligated to respond

For Owen, the favour shown to the nation placed great obligation upon the people to respond appropriately. His preaching was a prophetic call for the nation to understand the times and to 'improve' these mercies by comprehensive godly reformation.

Preaching to Parliament at the end of the First Civil War, Owen told MPs that it would be the height of rebellion to despise the mercies England now enjoyed by being barren and unfruitful in their response. The English 'vineyard' had received such care, culture and watering that great fruit was to be expected.[122] Subsequently, on the day after the regicide, he summoned his hearers to fervent action in light of what God had done. In *The steadfastness of the promises* (1650), Owen called the saints to follow Abraham, setting out in faith, even if they were unsure of exactly where their journey might lead. Then, at Ireton's funeral, Owen's highlighted how his friend had offered a heroic role model of one who responded to God's 'providential voice' by serving God 'in his Generation'.[123] As he would later explain, the providential 'alterations and dissolutions' were to be improved by listening to their 'special call'.[124] Owen likened himself to an Old Testament prophet advising the people how to answer that call and make such a fitting improvement.[125]

The general response that Owen's preaching required could be summed up as 'universal holiness'. Owen made clear that this was far beyond the general call to ordinary holiness: this was to be a holiness suitable for those who were living in the dispensation during which Christ had come to destroy his Antichristian enemies (Rev. 19.11-12).[126] Owen argued that those who understood the nature of God's work among them would appreciate that such holiness entailed

---

[121]Owen, *The advantage of the kingdome of Christ* (1651), A2v; *Works* (1965), 8:313–14.
[122]Owen, *A vision of unchangeable free mercy* (1646), 37, 42–3; *Works* (1965), 8:27, 39.
[123]Owen, *The labouring saints dismission to rest* (1652), 5; *Works* (1965), 8:348.
[124]Owen, *A complete collection of the sermons* (1721), 53; *Works* (1965), 9:137.
[125]Owen, *God's presence with a people* (1656), 3–4; *Works* (1965), 8:432.
[126]See, for example, Owen, *A complete collection of sermons* (1721), 49–78; *Works* (1965), 9:141, 159–60.

reformation and separation. In 1658, he explained that one of the works in which Christ was 'peculiarly engaged in our days and seasons' was the 'owning' of his people 'in a distinguishing manner, putting a difference between the precious and the vile'.[127] This entailed gathering churches of true saints and abandoning all forms of worship which Owen believed to be idolatrous. Although it is not possible to establish a firm dating of Owen's sermons 'Gospel Worship', they undoubtedly resonate with the liturgical debates of the 1650s.[128]

Owen and his associates were 'Magisterial Congregationalists' who believed that the civil magistrate had an instrumental role in national reformation.[129] In his preaching we hear his call to those in civil power to implement godly reform in two specific areas. The first was legal reform, and, in this regard, Owen commended the measures suggested by William Sheppard. A second area was that provision be made for the poor, widows and orphans.[130] For Owen, the successful implementation of such reforms would have been a fitting response to the divine visitation he believed England to have experienced.

The magistrate also had a role in the search for a church settlement. Owen's first Parliamentary sermon was nothing short of a 'Macedonian call' (Acts 16.9). He urged MPs to take upon themselves the task of sending out godly ministers 'acknowledged, owned, and maintained by the supreme magistrate', especially to Wales and the north of England.[131] Similarly, in 1649, he insisted that it was the government's responsibility to ensure that the Gospel be declared to the whole nation.[132] When Owen returned from Ireland he took the opportunity to challenge MPs to 'do your utmost for the preaching of the Gospel in Ireland', calling them to send 'one Gospel preacher for every walled town in the English possession', and suggested that a committee might be appointed to consider such proposals.[133] At Ireton's funeral, Owen pressed those with authority to use their 'industry and wisdom' to determine how 'places destitute of the Gospel ... might be furnished and supplied'.[134] One week later, Owen and his colleagues

---

[127]Owen, *Of temptation* (1658), 175; *Works* (1965), 6:148.
[128]Owen, *A complete collection of sermons* (1721), 3–12; *Works*, 9:57–71; Durston, 'By the book or with the Spirit', 50–73.
[129]Collins, *The allegiance of Thomas Hobbes*, 102–14.
[130]Owen, *A sermon preached* (1649), 20; *Works* (1965), 8:148; *The advantage of the kingdome of Christ* (1651), 28; *Works*, 8:334–5; *The labouring saints dismission to rest* (1652), 14; *Works* (1965), 8:355; *A sermon preached to the Parliament, Octob. 13. 1652* (1652), 50–4; *Works* (1965), 8:392–4; *God's work in founding Zion* (1656), 36–8; *Works* (1965), 8:452; Matthews, *William Sheppard, Cromwell's law Reformer*, 58, 144–86.
[131]Owen, *A vision of unchangeable free mercy* (1646), 3–4, 31, 44–5; *Works* (1965), 8:7, 30, 40–1; Hill, 'Puritans and the "dark corners of the land"', 77–102.
[132]Owen, *Of toleration* (1649), 72–3, 79; *Works* (1965), 8:189, 194.
[133]Owen, *The steadfastness of promises, and the sinfulness of staggering* (1650), 42–7; *Works* (1965), 8:235–7; Worden, *The Rump Parliament, 1648–1652*, 120, 234–5.
[134]Owen, *The labouring saints dismission to rest* (1652),14–15; *Works* (1965), 8:355–6.

submitted a blueprint for a church settlement to the committee. In a sermon from 1652 dealing expressly with the magistrate's power in matters of religion, Owen spoke of how it was incumbent upon MPs that 'the faith', and 'all the necessary concernments of it', be 'protected, preserved, propagated'.[135] Owen would have been delighted when the Rump Parliament appeared to respond to his plea by reviving the Committee for the Propagation of the Gospel.[136]

Owen's sermons reveal that the response he called for was not wedded to one particular political form. His preaching adapted 'interest theory' into his political theology to argue that government should be ordered according to 'the interest of Christ'.[137] Despite Owen's proximity to those involved in the revolutionary experiment in the republican government, Owen was no doctrinaire republican.[138] For Owen, the government's ability to pursue the interest of Christ and the godliness of those in power mattered more than the exact form of government. Indeed, in his sermons the obligation which he placed upon those in government involved a remarkable degree of political flexibility towards various constitutional settlements and even at times justified the use of irregular means and extraordinary power.[139]

This call for individuals, churches, government and the nation to 'improve' divine blessings by fruitful faith and obedient holiness was a consistent theme throughout Owen's sermons. In the Restoration this took the form of what Gribben describes as Owen's 'most enduring challenge: calling upon his congregants to embrace, rather than deny, a Dissenting identity'.[140] Alongside it, and with ever-increasing force, there is another characteristic of Owen's prophetic preaching, namely, that his hearers and readers forgot God's mercies and were lax and remiss in their response.

Preaching to those consistently negligent

Like the biblical prophets of old, Owen believed that the nation had persistently failed to respond to God's work, and he decried what he saw as both individual and national ingratitude, infidelity and negligence. In this, Owen was not alone in perceiving a disconnection between 'the profusion of preaching' and the 'paucity of individual and social transformation'.[141]

---

[135] Owen, *The kingdome of Christ, and the power of the civile magistrate* (1652), 38; *Works* (1965), 8:386.
[136] Powell, 'Promote, protect, prosecute', 226–8.
[137] See discussion in Cowan, *John Owen and the civil war apocalypse*, 98–9.
[138] See Gribben's chapter in this volume.
[139] Cowan, *John Owen and the civil war apocalypse*, 104–12.
[140] Gribben, 'John Owen and congregational life in England', 121.
[141] Craig, 'Sermon reception', 180.

Even from his days of parish ministry in Essex, Owen was troubled by his people's lack of response to his preaching.[142] This was only highlighted by the much more positive reception that his preaching received in Ireland.[143] Writing from Dublin Castle in December 1649, Owen described how he was constantly preaching to 'a numerous multitude of as thirsting a people after the Gospel as ever yet I conversed withal'. Indeed, there is evidence that a number of people were converted through his ministry in Ireland.[144]

Some of those that Owen believed to be most spiritually negligent were those who had been entrusted with political power. For Owen, the twin temptations of unbelief and pride had caused many of the leaders of the new administration to backslide from implementing godly reform. The temptation of unbelief received particular attention from Owen in his sermon from February 1650 when he warned MPs that they were failing to make progress because of their lack of faith.[145] Similarly, two years later, at Ireton's funeral Owen portrayed him as an exemplary and heroic magistrate precisely because he 'staggered not' but was 'steadfast in faith'. This provided him with the opportunity to make an implicit criticism of the government by cautioning his hearers to be 'diligent' and not to let the work of reformation 'too long hang upon your hands'.[146] The second major temptation for those in authority was pride. Owen was horrified that pride was, from his perspective, so often cloaked in religion. For example, he believed that those who were doggedly committed to the Solemn League and Covenant were actually motivated by simple pride.[147]

Owen's posthumously published sermons collected as 'Walking humbly with God' are undated, but they may, tentatively, on the basis of internal and external evidence be assigned to the period of his preaching at Oxford, sometime in or after 1653.[148] Owen reveals his thoughts about the state of his congregation, claiming that among its number were 'empty professors', the 'profligate', and 'bitter scoffers, neglecters of ordinances, haters of the power of godliness and the purity of religion'.[149]

Owen's awareness of negligence among his hearers was only to increase. In his sermons to the second Protectorate Parliament in the autumn of 1656 he

---

[142] Owen, *Two short catechismes* (1645), A2r; *Works* (1965), 1:465.
[143] Owen, *The shaking and translating of heaven and earth* (1649), A2v; *Works* (1965), 8:245.
[144] Owen, *Of the death of Christ* (1650), 97; *Works* (1965), 10:479; Gribben, *God's Irishmen*, 26.
[145] Owen, *The steadfastness of promises, and the sinfulness of staggering* (1650), 12–15, 49–50; *Works* (1965), 8:218–19, 239.
[146] Owen, *The labouring saints dismission to rest* (1652), 9, 14–15, 19–20; *Works* (1965), 8:351, 355–6, 359–60.
[147] See for example Owen, *The advantage of the kingdome of Christ* (1651), 20; *Works* (1965), 8:328.
[148] Cowan, *John Owen and the civil war apocalypse*, 84–6.
[149] Owen, *A complete collection of sermons* (1721), 48; *Works* (1965), 9:130.

identified as enemies of 'real reformation' those who were 'zealous for the traditions of their fathers', turning back to the 'old road'.[150] Owen's fall from power occurred rapidly after this sermon had been delivered.[151] Further insight into his disillusionment with the regime is gained by considering the sermons titled 'Providential changes, an argument for universal holiness', which can by careful contextualization be plausibly dated to 1657 and the events surrounding the Sindercombe plot.[152] Owen believed that he was addressing a sinfully negligent nation, guilty of a litany of sins. For instance, in only a few lines of the sermon he inveighed against 'unbelief, worldliness, atheism, and contempt of the Gospel', denounced 'swearers, drunkards, and other vicious people' and finally castigated the 'abominable pride, folly, vanity, luxury' of the city. According to Owen, the 'peculiar controversy' that Christ had with the saints was their 'inordinate cleaving unto the shaken, passing things of the world'. Set within the context of the kingship debate, Owen's description of men desiring, 'in things of a public tendency', that some 'fleshly imagination' be 'enthroned' is striking.[153]

Owen's famous work *Of temptation* (1658) is based on sermons that he delivered in Oxford while he was losing influence both in the university and at Westminster. Owen emphasized that these sermons were particularly 'suited to the times that pass over us' in which 'providential dispensations, in reference to the public concernments of these nations' had seen all things 'shaken'.[154] It is important to note that Owen was not dealing with temptation in a general sense: he was providing a probing analysis of the 'hour of temptation', which comes to 'try them that dwell upon the earth' (Rev. 3.10). He spoke of a time of 'backsliding' in which 'thousands' had apostatized 'within a few years'. Now increasingly alienated, he highlighted how 'the prevailing party of these nations, many of those in rule, power [and] favour' had formerly been regarded as lowly 'Puritans', but their attitudes had changed once they had been 'translated by a high hand to the mountains they now possess'. Owen lamented: 'how soon they have forgot the customs, manners, ways, of their own old people, and are cast into the mould of them that went before them.'[155] He specifically referred to those 'in high places' who were particularly tempted to pursue 'crowns, glories, thrones, pleasures, [and] profits of the world'. Owen's litany of sins resonated with the temptations which he believed accompanied the monarchical drift of

---

[150]Owen, *God's work in founding Zion* (1656), 46; *Works* (1656), 8:424–425; *God's presence with a people* (1656), 37; *Works* (1965), 8:452.
[151]Gribben, *John Owen and English Puritanism*, 169.
[152]Cowan, *John Owen and the civil war apocalypse*, 105–6.
[153]Owen, *A complete collection of sermons* (1721), 57–9, 66, 68; *Works* (1965), 9:143–6, 158, 162.
[154]Owen, *Of temptation* (1658), A2v-r; *Works* (1965), 6:89.
[155]Owen, *Of temptation* (1658), 66–7; *Works* (1965), 6:112.

the Protectorate.[156] The subversive tenor of his pulpit ministry helps explain why he was replaced at St Mary's. In November 1659, John Locke mocked the dispirited preaching about the state of the nation that he regularly heard from Owen's pulpit in Christ Church.[157]

Owen saw still more evidence of spiritual declension after the Restoration. He complained that the 'course and lives' of most necessitated that he compile a series of sermons for publications as *The nature, power, deceit and prevalency of the remainders of indwelling sin* (1668).[158] Throughout the following year, Owen was well aware that he had spoken persistently about spiritual decay, but he was frustrated that his hearers left 'shaking their heads, and striking on their breasts' but bore no lasting spiritual fruit.[159] Owen began a long series of sermons on Heb. 12.14 in November 1681. In these he allowed for no compromise as he called believers to strive for 'holiness, without which no man shall see the Lord'.

In March 1674, Owen reminded his church of what was entailed by their 'vow and covenant' of membership, recalling how in the past separation had resulted in God carrying 'many of his people out of this nation into the wilderness, and . . . hid them for a season'. This is a reference to the flight of the godly to the continent and the new world as a result of Laudian persecution. However, at this point, Owen opined: 'I see no ground for that now.'[160]

In 1676 Owen attributed much of this 'general plague' of 'apostasy' to the prevalence of a style of preaching that simply dealt with 'virtue and vice'.[161] In contrast, he resolved to preach 'plainly and familiarly' about the present 'infirmities' of the church in order to discharge his duties as a watchman (Ezekiel 33). He was concerned that the 'efficacy of the truth' was beginning to 'decay', particularly with respect to the doctrines of election and justification. As he struggled both in pulpit and press to persuade people of Reformed orthodoxy, he urged his hearers not to be 'half Arminian and half Socinian, half Papist and half I know not what'.[162]

In the years that followed, he continued to despair over the lack of fruit, the 'decay of love', and the 'withering' of spiritual life.[163] In May 1680, his assessment of the 'general declension in religion' was that it was prevalent

---

[156]Owen, *Of temptation* (1658), 157, 174; *Works* (1965), 6:143, 148–9.
[157]*The correspondence of John Locke*, 1:83–4.
[158]Owen, *Indwelling sin* (1668), A3r; *Works* (1965), 6:155.
[159]Owen, *Works* (1965), 16:519; *A practical exposition on the 130th Psalm* (1669), 91; *Works* (1965), 6:396.
[160]Owen, *A complete collection of sermons* (1721), 169–70; *Works* (1965), 9:293, 295.
[161]Owen, *A complete collection of sermons* (1721), 546; *Works* (1965), 9:368–9.
[162]Owen, *A complete collection of sermons* (1721), 110, 114–116; *Works* (1965), 9:320, 326–7, 329.
[163]Owen, *Works* (1965), 16:479.

across England and neighbouring nations.[164] After contemplating his own death during an illness, he published the thoughts that he had shared with a 'private congregation' as Φρόνεμα του πνεύματου: *The grace and duty of being spiritually-minded* (1681). This work revealed his concern about a 'worldly frame of spirit in many who make profession of religion'.[165] In 1681, he issued 'the substance of sundry sermons preached in a private congregation'.[166] As Gribben puts it, the 'prophetic impulse' is clearly discernible in these sermons, and this was 'one of the few occasions in which his providential analysis of his private sermons was reflected in the culture of print'.[167] Owen was concerned about the deep divisions within society as well as external threats to the nation's security, and went on to advocate repentance and 'universal Reformation' as the only response.[168]

In the early months of 1682, Owen's sermons evinced his reaction to the growing persecution.[169] In March he spoke of how 'Sin hath broken forth' in 'the Persecution of the Upright Faithfull Ministers and Christians in a Violent and extreame manner' and in May he told the congregation that suffering should be regarded as commonplace.[170] At the end of the year, he urged his followers not to yield to the temptations offered by occasional conformity, arguing that it would only make matters worse for other dissenters and mar the godly reputation of those who had suffered in the past for Nonconformity.[171]

Preaching to those warned by judgement

Owen's sermons warned a sinfully negligent nation and its government about the threat of divine judgement. By means of the 'Israelite paradigm', Owen applied the warnings of the Old Testament prophets to the nation. It has been noted that such preaching during the civil war and Interregnum was the 'climax' of a century of English jeremiads.[172] For Owen, England was like Israel because she was a chosen land that had witnessed many glorious providences and yet, despite these unparalleled blessings, had failed to respond appropriately.

Owen frequently portrayed England's position as particularly precarious. In 1646, he outlined how England had historically been spiritually unfruitful.

---

[164]Owen, *Thirteen sermons* (1756), 228; *Works* (1965), 9:510–1.
[165]Owen, *The grace and duty of being spiritually-minded* (1681), 'Preface'; *Works* (1965), 7:264.
[166]Owen, *Humble testimony* (1681), A3r; *Works* (1965), 8:595.
[167]Gribben, *John Owen and English Puritanism*, 254.
[168]Owen, *Humble testimony* (1681), A5r, 117–18; *Works* (1965), 8:596, 643
[169]Dr Williams's Library (DWL), MS L6/3 sermons preached on 10 February 1682 and 10 March 1682.
[170]DWL, MS L6/3 sermons preached on 10 March 1682 (fol. 127r) and 5 May 1682 (fol. 143r).
[171]DWL, MS L6/4 sermon preached on 23 December 1682 (fol. 45r).
[172]Collinson, 'Biblical rhetoric', 27–8.

Using the biblical motif of the vineyard, Owen spoke of occasions during the sixth century and in the period before the Reformation during which a divine visitation had found only 'wild grapes' and because of which the land had forfeited the Gospel. Owen cautioned that since every provision had now been made for the plant to produce fruit, if upon a third visitation it was found to be fruitless, it would be cut down and burned. He implored his hearers to 'mend or end'.[173]

At the end of the Second Civil War, Owen was left pondering 'what will be the issue of the visitations of the last years', remembering how history had revealed that when God intends the destruction of a people he often weakens them with previous judgements such as those they had just experienced.[174] Months later, he claimed that the nation had been 'eminently sick of the folly of backsliding' for the past three years – in effect since the fracturing of the Parliamentary cause in the early months of 1646. Ominously, he asserted that England had now fallen three times and thus, without renewal, it was inevitable that, as an 'empty vine', the nation was destined for the flames.[175]

At the parliamentary fast of April 1649, Owen outlined the 'dangerous and pernicious consequence of backsliding', telling MPs to 'search your hearts' because the nation was about to enter 'the most purging, trying furnace that ever the Lord set up on the earth'.[176] A year later, he warned Parliament to repent of fleshly reasoning and carnal contrivances 'before it be too late'.[177] At Ireton's funeral, Owen drew attention to how the death of the godly should be viewed as a warning, since God often removed significant individuals (often ministers or magistrates) before a coming judgement.[178] Months later, in October 1652, he urged the implementation of reform, telling MPs that they had 'certainly backslidden'. Charging them to 'renew your old frame', he told them starkly: 'The rejection of the Gospel by any people or nation to whom it is tendered is always attended with the certain and inevitable destruction of that people or nation.'[179]

The frequency with which he sounded these alarms would only increase. In 'Providential Changes', Owen continued to lament the 'general backsliding of most, if not of all, professors'. Such provocations were, he believed, enough for God 'to forsake the work on the wheel'. This refers to Jeremiah's description of

---

[173] Owen, *A vision of unchangeable free mercy* (1646), 26–7, 33; *Works* (1965), 8:26, 31.
[174] Owen, *Eben-ezer* (1648), 17; *Works* (1965), 8:92.
[175] Owen, *Of toleration* (1649), 18; *Works* (1965), 8:146.
[176] Owen, *The shaking and translating of heaven and earth* (1649), 4, 42; *Works* (1965), 8:249, 279.
[177] Owen, *The steadfastness of promises, and the sinfulness of staggering* (1650), 52–3; *Works* (1965), 8:240–1.
[178] Owen, *The labouring saints dismission to rest* (1652), 15; *Works* (1965), 8:356.
[179] Owen, *The kingdome of Christ, and the power of the civile magistrate* (1652), 48; *Works* (1965), 8:391.

a potter refusing to rework the vessel as symbolizing a nation being prepared for destruction (Jer. 18.4, 10).[180] Those who heard the allusion would remember that in the following chapter Jeremiah shattered a clay flask as a sign of coming national judgement (Jer. 19.1, 10).

The series of sermons titled 'Spiritual barrenness' resonate with the events of 1658. Owen's prognosis was that ominous in this 'special season' in which 'providential calls do join in with, and further, Gospel calls'. In his lament, Owen pondered over what would be the outcome of 'England's enjoying the Gospel so long as it hath done', given the high-handed provocation and spiritual backsliding that he observed. Like Ezekiel, he identified signs or 'tokens' of God's wrath against the nation, including sickness, conflict and extreme weather (Ezek. 38.22). The healing streams of the preaching of the Gospel had, like the waters from Ezekiel's temple, flowed over the land for an allotted 'season of healing'. He warned that if repeatedly rejected, these 'waters of the sanctuary' would dry up, leaving only 'barrenness and everlasting ruin' (Ezek. 47.11).[181]

In his February 1659 fast sermon to the third Protectoral Parliament, Owen insisted that, despite the 'outward peace' that the nation enjoyed, danger lay ahead. In what must be seen as an indictment of the current policy, Owen described a return to 'old forms and ways', which he regarded as a 'badge of apostasy' from the 'good old principles on which we first engaged'. Employing motifs from the Old Testament prophets, he was fearful that bloodshed and ruin were approaching (Hos. 7.9; Amos 4.1-13).[182]

With the Restoration, these themes of providentialism and apocalypticism less frequently appeared in Owen's printed work. However, we know from his posthumously published and unpublished sermons that Owen's preaching continued in the same prophetic mould. In what Gribben has described as one of his 'strategies for survival', Owen was increasingly 'distinguishing the private voice of the prophet from the public voice of the scribe'.[183] For example, in 'The furnace of divine wrath', Owen lamented people's unresponsiveness not only to his preaching with its 'entreaties, beggings, exhortations' but also to the providential warnings that were represented by the great comet, the plague and the fire of London (1664–6). Consequently, as he had been warning 'for some years', they were all 'going into the same furnace'.[184] Gribben notes how this sermon affords a 'privileged glimpse into the ideological formation of

---

[180] Owen, *A complete collection of sermons* (1721), 69, 77–8; *Works* (1965), 9:164, 176, 178.
[181] Owen, *A complete collection of sermons* (1721), 92–3, 101; *Works* (1965), 9:181–2, 195.
[182] Owen, *The glory and interest of nations professing the Gospel* (1659), 15–18; *Works* (1965), 8:466–8.
[183] Gribben, *John Owen and English Puritanism*, 238.
[184] Owen, 'The furnace of divine wrath', *Works* (1965), 16:425, 428.

Owen's church community' with preaching that Owen 'could not dare commit to print' because in it he continued to 'enunciate the prophetic analysis that had dominated in his public preaching in earlier decades'.[185]

Owen's continued his efforts to instil in his congregation a sense of the need for an urgent response to God's claims. In a sermon delivered in July 1673, he prayed that his church might be 'awakened to a diligent watchfulness' because of the 'signs and tokens of an approaching dissolution' that had included the portentous events of the previous decade.[186] In March 1674, he was fearful that the national sins that had reigned 'for a long season' might be followed by the nation's reversion to the Roman Catholic Church.[187] The following year he declared that God might withdraw his presence to correct a church that had refused to heed the forthright warnings not only of the plague and fire but also of 'inundations'.[188]

At a fast on New Year's Day 1676, Owen described God as hiding his face, and attributed this to the nation's 'non-compliance with the calls of providence'.[189] At another day of fasting in November, he lamented that his preaching had made little impact, describing it as 'poor', 'weak' and 'quickly forgotten'. He offered little comfort as he solemnly informed his listeners that none of them could have any confidence of escaping God's 'outward judgements'. Reminding them again of the catastrophes of the previous decade, Owen explained that what he was prophesying was not 'a great way off' but was already upon them.[190] In October 1677, as the campaign to suppress conventicles was intensifying, Owen was again anticipating a period of major persecution, which was 'neere at hand'.[191] The following year he pondered whether the men and women 'in the Assemblye of Gods People, be Fitt to meet the Lord in the Way of his Judgmente'.[192]

In early 1679, public opinion was still dominated by allegations of a 'popish plot' and, in time for the first so-called Exclusion Parliament, Owen issued two of his sermons under the title *The Church of Rome, no safe guide* (1679).[193] On 11 April, a nationwide day of humiliation, Owen expounded Isa. 3.8-9 to a 'ruined' and 'dying nation' in the sermons collected as 'National Sins and

---

[185]Gribben, *John Owen and English Puritanism*, 238–9.
[186]Owen, 'Holiness urged from the liability of all things to dissolution', *Works* (1965), 16:462.
[187]Owen, *A complete collection of sermons* (1721), 169; *Works* (1965), 9:294.
[188]Owen, *A complete collection of sermons* (1721), 102, 105; *Works* (1965), 9:296, 299.
[189]Owen, 'A fast sermon: Christian duty under the hidings of God's face', *Works* (1965), 16:525.
[190]Owen, *A complete collection of sermons* (1721), 112–14, 117; *Works* (1965), 9:323, 325, 327, 332.
[191]DWL, MS L6/3 sermon preached on 18 October 1677 (fol. 4v).
[192]DWL, MS L6/3 sermon preached 13 March 1678 (fol. 41v).
[193]Owen, *The Church of Rome, no safe guide* (1679), A2r; *Works* (1965), 14:481. See Miller, *Popery and politics in England, 1660–1688*, 174.

National Judgments'. Sir John Hartopp, his most consistent notetaker, arrived late and recorded Owen calling the congregation to remember the warnings of 'signs in the heavens above' and the death of godly men, as well as the plague and fire, predicting that 'London will be undone and England will fall'.[194] This 'sense of failure' continued to dominate Owen's later sermons.[195] At a church meeting in December 1679, Owen spoke starkly of a day of 'great Triall, of great Temptations, of great Dangers', and so recommended (unsuccessfully) that the congregation renew its church covenant. Early in January 1680, Owen once again preached about renewing the church covenant, telling his congregation that all the ministers with whom he was conversing thought that God was about to impose a period of darkness on England, disagreeing only on its length.[196]

During April and May 1680, Owen preached four expositions on 'The use of faith' from Hab. 2.4, and in them surveyed the possibility of a return of Roman Catholicism. His pessimism was obvious as he synthesized many of the issues that he had been addressing for over a decade.[197] Owen's fast day sermon from Jer. 51.5 was preached during the second Exclusion Parliament (December 1680). Owen asked what the 'greatest aggravations' were to 'national sins'. For him the answer was 'plain' – those sins that were committed 'against all sorts of warnings and against all sorts of mercies'. Owen was still preoccupied with the plague and the fire but was also remembering the second Dutch war and the more recent 'prodigious appearances in heaven above'.[198] Here the urgency of Owen's point is heightened by this reference to the great comet that appeared in November 1680 and stayed in the sky until the end of March.[199] And yet, Owen believed that there was still time to heed these warnings, believing that the discovery of the alleged 'popish plot' was a token of divine mercy, indicating that 'England is not yet . . . utterly forsaken of the Lord'. Owen was confident that his hearers knew his mind on the matter because for the last three years he had taken every opportunity to warn of the meaning of these providences.[200]

In March 1682, Owen again predicted that public calamities would befall the church.[201] The plight of dissenters worsened after London elections in the summer, and in September Owen pondered, 'Where is the man of Wisdome now to save the Citty?'[202] As his preaching ministry drew to a close, his prophetic hope remained strong. In the year before his death, he pointedly warned that

---

[194]Owen, 'National sins and national judgments', *Works* (1965), 16:482.
[195]Gribben, *John Owen and English Puritanism*, 256.
[196]DWL, MS L6/4 sermon preached 8 January 1680 (fol. 26v).
[197]Owen, *Thirteen sermons* (1756), 183, 201–3, 216–17; *Works* (1965), 9:491, 499, 505.
[198]Owen, *Seasonable words for English Protestants* (1690), 17; *Works* (1965), 9:10–11.
[199]Forbes, 'The comet of 1680–1681', 312–23.
[200]Owen, *Seasonable words for English Protestants* (1690), 16–17, 21; *Works* (1965), 9:10, 13.
[201]DWL, MS L6/3 sermons preached 10 and 31 March 1682 (fol. 124r-141r).
[202]DWL, MS L6/3 sermon preached 22 September 1682 (fol. 93r).

'princes' who reconciled with Rome would 'bring Bondage on themselves and their subjects'. However, he concluded this treatise with the confident assertion that 'Antichrist shall not be a final gainer in this contest; his success herein will be a forerunner of his utter destruction. . . . Religion shall again be restored in a more refined profession.'[203]

CONCLUSION

Owen's prophetic preaching was, in a sense, authenticated rather than challenged by his changing experiences. For a generation, he had warned of the possibility of a purging judgement if the English church failed to make a fruitful response to unprecedented divine blessing, and he sounded this alarm with every increasing frequency throughout his ministry. In a sermon from 1672, he described a minister as a 'prophet', a man who had been called to interpret God's 'special design' in the 'calamities' and 'devastations' brought upon the church and nation.[204] This analysis of Owen as a preacher demonstrates that he ought not to be regarded merely as an abstracted academic theologian. Indeed, much of his scholarly writing found its origins in his preaching. The pulpit stood centre-stage in his vision for the church and the nation, and, in his estimation, the nation's response to godly preaching determined its success or failure. While many of his sermons, particularly those recorded in unpublished auditors' notes from the Restoration era, have received very little scholarly attention, a recovery of the sermon as an 'event' promises to open many new avenues into Owen studies.

---

[203] Owen, *A brief and impartial account of the nature of the Protestant religion* (1682), 19, 40; *Works* (1965), 14:549, 555.
[204] Owen, *Works* (1965), 16:440, 443.

CHAPTER 7

Owen and education

ERIC NEWTON

In January 1651, shortly after Oliver Cromwell became chancellor of the University of Oxford, Parliament appointed one of his younger army chaplains as dean of Christ Church. The following year Cromwell appointed this dean and fellow Independent to become the university's vice-chancellor, an educational position unsurpassed in England.[1] As senior administrator from 1652 to 1657, John Owen stands out as one of the Interregnum's most prominent figures, not only due to his meteoric rise to national prominence but also because of his distinctive view of education.

JOHN OWEN'S EDUCATIONAL CONTEXT

Owen served in academic posts in a university that was long on heritage and, after the chaos of the civil wars, longing for stability.[2] During the 1640s, conflict between the armies of the king and Parliament left Oxford divided politically

---

[1] A series of vice-chancellors served at Cambridge during the years of Owen's stint at Oxford: Richard Minshall (1652), Lazarus Seaman (1653), John Lightfoot (1654), Theophilus Dillingham (1655–6) and John Worthington (1657); Carter, *The history of the University of Cambridge, from its original, to the year 1753*, 412–13.

[2] Theobald of Etampes arrived as Oxford's first schoolmaster sometime before 1100. Record of theological lectures dates to the arrival of Robert Pullen in Oxford in 1133; Southern, 'From schools to university', 5–6.

and depleted economically.[3] This elite but beleaguered academic environment prided itself on tradition and boasted a diverse group of intellectuals. In 1651, Owen returned to his *alma mater* to lead the spiritual reform that Cromwell believed would unite Oxford and help position England for success as a nation of the godly.[4]

The University of Oxford in the seventeenth century

In the seventeenth century, an Oxford education was thoroughly religious. Student attendance at college sermons and catechetical lectures was compulsory, the study of Hebrew and Greek was emphasized, teaching gave consideration to the religious questions raised by philosophy, tutors provided 'moral and religious' guidance and the university contributed to many religious debates. At Oxford, 'theology remained the "queen of sciences" in an academic sense, and a career in the ministry still the single most likely post for a university graduate'.[5]

The primacy of theology within the university provided the context for its ministerial training.[6] While wary of the potential harm such an education entailed, many Puritans chose Cambridge or Oxford in pursuit of a 'learned ministry'. The characteristic pathway to such a ministry involved traditional learning viewed through the lens of Scripture and interwoven with a fervent pursuit of godliness.[7] However, what 'inspired seventeenth-century academics' at Oxford was not necessarily ministerial zeal, but a 'commitment to the ideal of the general scholar'.[8] In other words, the many future ministers attending university participated not only in the religious aspects but also the common

---

[3]Gribben, *John Owen and English Puritanism*, 124. Oxford had served as headquarters for Charles I during the first civil war. Worden observes that while 'royalism had mostly kept its head down in Cromwellian Oxford, it had never disappeared'; Worden, *God's Instruments*, 140.
[4]Worden, *God's instruments*, 123.
[5]Morgan, *Godly learning*, 229.
[6]John Morgan observes that 'by the seventeenth century there was a common expectation that a new minister would hold a degree. This change was fostered by pressure from the administration, rising standards of lay education, and the increasingly professional nature of the universities themselves'; Morgan, *Godly learning*, 220.
[7]The English Reformation had demonstrated the need for well-educated ministers; Hall, *The Puritans*, 44. Puritans were attached to higher education in order to provide ministers to lead congregations, to challenge the possibility of Roman Catholic superiority in learning, to align with the objectivity of scriptural authority over against the subjectivity of Protestant radicals, and to employ sanctified casuistry to aid saints in their Christian perseverance; Morgan, *Godly learning*, 95–8.
[8]Feingold, 'The humanities', 227.

features of an Oxford education: respect for tradition, study of the humanities and the 'inculcation of an almost intemperate love of the classics'.[9]

Although in the early decades of the seventeenth century the number of graduates in vocations other than ministry was growing, even as the consensus on church governance and the relationship of ministry to the state was disintegrating, mid-century debates regarding higher education still revolved around the subject of ministerial ordination.[10] Consequently, to suggest changes in university curriculum or method, as many radicals did, was to foment the political and religious instability that boiled over during the Interregnum.

Agendas for educational reform

Owen's interest in education developed in a context of multiple and competing proposals to revamp the university curriculum. In the late sixteenth century, the separatists Robert Browne and Henry Barrow had launched deeper critiques of university education than had yet been levelled by Puritans. Barrow condemned the curriculum's traditional reliance on pagan philosophers and poets, as well as the classical subjects of rhetoric and logic. Additionally, he opposed ministerial reliance on Cambridge and Oxford, worried that theology had become 'professionaliz[ed]' so that ministry had become confined to those thus trained – the same reasons that Puritans deemed the universities to be essential.[11] In fact, Barrow objected to the university environment itself, contending that the education of ministers should be conducted 'in an established church (I meane in such places where the saintes live together in the faith, order, obedience and communion with Christ) and not in such monkish idolatrous, confused, idle, profane colledges and fellowships as theirs are'.[12]

After the Long Parliament eliminated the Star Chamber in 1641, educational philosophy flowed freely, thanks in part to Samuel Hartlib, whom Parliament funded to trade stock in ideas. Hartlib influenced John Milton, who criticized universities in his tract, *Of education* (1644).[13] Milton asserted that learning should serve the spiritual ends of regaining the true knowledge of God that Adam and Eve had lost in the Garden of Eden, a knowledge displayed in love

---

[9]Feingold, 'The humanities', 229. Feingold explains that 'students developed an emotional commitment to antiquity and its repository of useful knowledge, which illuminated the human condition and guided behaviour. Not that the study of Cicero or Horace or Terence was thought capable of turning students into wise and virtuous citizens all at once. But the cumulative effect of reading the classics over time was believed to ensure the formation of their character and make them upright and judicious'; also see Trueman, *John Owen*, 15.
[10]Morgan, *Godly learning*, 230; Greaves, *The Puritan revolution and educational thought*, 25.
[11]Morgan, *Godly learning*, 242.
[12]Barrow, *A brief discoverie of the false church* (1590), 178.
[13]For an explanation of Milton's relationship to Jan Amos Comenius, Samuel Hartlib and the Hartlib circle, see Lewalksi, *The life of John Milton*, 172–4. Also see Hall, *The Puritans*, 276.

for and virtuous likeness to God.[14] But education also served political ends, as Milton applied the 'classical principle that the state is an extension of the ethical qualities of its citizens'.[15] These objectives necessitated an approach less enmeshed in logic and metaphysics and more aligned with a 'Baconian emphasis on "useful" knowledge'.[16]

From within the Barebone's Parliament in 1653 came drastic proposals to cut the government's financial support to the church and universities.[17] This radical critique took aim at traditions such as the conferral of divinity degrees and the use of academic regalia – an assessment with which Owen had some sympathy.[18] Nevertheless, Owen viewed the ultimate failure of these parliamentary schemes to be a clear sign of a sovereign God's intervention to protect these venerable institutions.[19] The traditional scholastic curriculum at both Cambridge and Oxford weathered the assault of those who accused it of being unfit for training pious ministers.[20]

Fundamental to these radical propositions concerning education was an exaltation of Spirit over reason. This propensity grabbed hold of the typical

---

[14]Milton argued that the 'end then of Learning is to repair the ruines of our first Parents by regaining to know God aright, and out of that knowledge to love him, to imitate him, to be like him, as we may the neerest by possessing our souls of true vertue, which being united to the heavenly grace of faith makes up the highest perfection'; Milton, *Of education* (1644), 2.

[15]Worden, *God's instruments*, 363.

[16]Lewalksi, *The life of John Milton*, 174. The themes of virtue and practical knowledge were transposed when John Owen's most recognizable Christ Church student, John Locke, published one of the century's most influential educational philosophies, *Some thoughts concerning education* (1693). His essay extolled forming habits of the mind early. Axtell, *The educational writings of John Locke*, 52, 54, 64.

[17]Peter Toon explains that, in 1653, there were 'moves to abolish the Universities within the Barebones Parliament. Most of the radicals were against the support of the Church and the Universities by tithes; most of them also were opposed to the reading of pagan poets and philosophers by those who were supposedly training for the Christian ministry. In 1654 the Quakers first visited Oxford and Ludowicke Muggleton and John Reeve had been in the city in 1652–3'; in Owen, *The Oxford orations*, 18.

[18]Toon, *God's statesman*, 70–3; Greaves, *The Puritan revolution and educational thought*, 135–6. Owen's reform agenda met stiff resistance from John Wilkins and other university delegates, deeming the sweeping nature of Owen's proposals concerning university statutes as the 'subversion of all our charters', probably due to worries about governance more than opposition to the revisions themselves; Worden, *God's instruments*, 137–8.

[19]Owen provided this analysis in his speech at Convocation on 9 October 1657, at the end of his vice-chancellorship; Owen, *The Oxford orations*, 41.

[20]The debate over the appropriateness of university education for training ministers waxed warmly at Cambridge in a series of sermons between proponents such as Sydrach Simpson, master of Pembroke Hall, and Joseph Sedgwick, fellow of Christ's College, and a vocal opponent, William Dell, master of Gonville and Caius, in 1652–3. The irony of Dell's opposition to university training though himself a 'minister of the Gospel' serving as a Cambridge master was not lost on Sedgwick; Sedgwick, *A sermon*, 39. See a full discussion of the controversy between Dell and Sedgwick in Maitland, *Three Puritan attitudes toward learning*, 167–94.

Puritan's 'distrust of reason' and 'pushed [it] to its logical extreme'.[21] Whereas most Puritans taught that human rationality enabled someone who believes to understand what the Holy Spirit reveals in Scripture, radicals such as the Quakers disavowed this supposed balance, accentuating the primacy of faith by suggesting that the Spirit could immediately impart knowledge.[22] This radical agenda for educational reform emphasized that preparation for ministry should concentrate on spirituality and experience over the traditional curricula. Human reasoning may have its place in other fields of study, but not in the field of divinity.

Owen had some sympathy for the radical critique of the link between university education and Christian ministry. Not insignificantly, he argued for the validity of the preaching of those who were not trained expositors, even writing an introductory commendation for the publication of Francis Osborne's *The private Christians non ultra, or, A plea for the lay-man's interpreting the Scriptures* (1656).[23] But Owen's senior administrative posts at Oxford testify to his agreement with most Puritans, who regarded university education to be a 'prerequisite for the ministry'.[24] In other words, while the Holy Spirit was confessed to be every Christian's teacher, a university education developed a future minister's ability to help congregants understand the scriptural revelation that God ordained to rule not only their thoughts but also their emotions and behaviour.[25] In Owen's final year as dean (1660), Henry Thurman, a Christ Church student, published a defence of classical learning's role in ministerial training. Thurman observed that the university's own statutes established the importance of such a study, though 'in subordination to divinity'.[26]

---

[21]Greaves, *The Puritan revolution and educational thought*, 116. Greaves notes the comments of a Puritan known as E.F., who counselled his readers not to renounce reason but to subjugate it to faith, 'to long more to feel communion with God than to be able to dispute of the genus or species of any question, either human or divine'; citing Fisher, *The marrow of modern divinity*, ed. C. G. McCrie, 226; cf. Fisher, *The marrow of modern divinity* (1646), 241.

[22]Greaves, *The Puritan revolution and educational thought*, 117. Greaves illustrates this radical outlook from the writings of John Webster, William Dell and Edward Burrough, among others.

[23]Osborne, *The private Christians non ultra, or, A plea for the lay-man's interpreting the Scriptures* (1656); cited in Greaves, *The Puritan revolution and educational thought*, 126. Owen also befriended the famously uneducated John Bunyan and possibly even helped the Baptist tinker publish *The Pilgrim's Progress* (1678); Gribben, *John Owen and English Puritanism*, 250, 255.

[24]Greaves, *The Puritan revolution and educational thought*, 126.

[25]Greaves, *The Puritan revolution and educational thought*, 128. Greaves summarizes: 'A basic difference between the Puritans and many sectaries was the Puritan idea that what enabled a man to be a Christian did not at the same time enable him to be a minister'; ibid, 127.

[26]Thurman, *A defence of humane learning in the ministry* (1660), 57. Thurman proceeded to declare, 'To put downe Universities, or Nurseries of learning, is contrary to Gods holy will, for whose service they were erected, and so ought to be continued'; ibid.

A Puritan administration

Owen's appointment as dean of Christ Church, on 9 May 1651, brought him back to his *alma mater*. He had studied at Queen's College under the tutelage of Thomas Barlow, who served as librarian of Oxford's Bodleian Library from 1642 to 1660.[27] Though Owen had shown considerable promise as a scholar, his studies ended abruptly because of his principled unwillingness to remain under the growing influence of an Arminianism that had entrenched its influence with the revision and publication of William Laud's university statutes in 1636. Owen left Oxford the following year as a matter of conscience.[28]

On 26 September 1652, in his first oration before Convocation as vice-chancellor, Owen attempted to lower the expectations of his audience, admitting that 'unskilful in the government of a University I am come here'.[29] Nevertheless, he understood the crucial role that an Oxford education played in shaping the church and nation and, therefore, took his stewardship seriously as dean and vice-chancellor during a pivotal period.[30] And he was willing to make personal sacrifice to meet the demands of his academic responsibilities: 'If I should be able to offer the services of a contrite spirit to those who dwell on the boundaries and the border territory of virtue, I must not perhaps regret the loss of peace, fame and studies – things which I sacrifice knowing fully what their loss will mean to me.' But he rested his confidence in God's 'eternal fountain of succour in Christ who furnishes "seasonable help" to every pious endeavour'.[31]

Owen reflected a traditional Puritan outlook on education in his focus on Reformed doctrine and godly practice. His role involved administrative discipline. In his inaugural oration as vice-chancellor, he linked problems in student behaviour to the perilous times of the previous few years.[32] These

---

[27]Gribben, *John Owen and English Puritanism*, 158. Another significant theological influence during Owen's student days was the Regius Professor of Divinity, John Prideaux; Rehnman, *Divine discourse*, 20.

[28]Gribben, *John Owen and English Puritanism*, 36.

[29]Owen, *The Oxford orations*, 6. Owen's Oxford speeches, lectures and writings focus on higher education, but he had already demonstrated a high regard for primary education in the catechism he produced for children, *The primer* (1652).

[30]Though Owen could not have easily anticipated their future significance, Joseph Alleine, Philip Henry, Thomas Ken, John Locke, William Penn, Henry Stubbe, Daniel Whitby and Christopher Wren attended Oxford as undergraduates during his administration; Thomson, 'Life of Dr Owen', *Works* (1965), 1:lxv–lxvi.

[31]Owen, *The Oxford orations*, 6–7.

[32]Owen, *The Oxford orations*, 7. Of this occasion, Toon observes that the 'oration was delivered before Convocation on 26 September 1652. It was traditional for a newly elected Vice-Chancellor to deliver such a Latin speech, with suitable quotations from Greek and Roman writers'; ibid., 8. Those who did not identify with Puritanism, such as John Wilkins and Seth Ward, expressed similar sentiments concerning the moral laxity of Cromwellian Oxford; Worden, *God's Instruments*, 172.

comments echoed the common practice of incoming vice-chancellors to 'warn scholars of the firmness with which [they] would enforce discipline and learning'.³³ Owen desired students who were 'pious, sober and modest', so his administrative proposals did not focus exclusively on academic reform. Instead, he attempted to curb traditions and activities, such as the annual Act, that drew the hearts of students away from spiritually improving thoughts.³⁴ He insisted on discipline as a vital component of education.³⁵ Against such moral discipline stood not only teenage students' natural mischief but also enticements in the broader community.³⁶ The vice-chancellor asked his students to 'consider . . . that you are exceedingly prone to the corrupting practices of the evil and the indolent'.³⁷ He had good reason for concern: Christ Church scholars, in particular, were renowned for their dissolute deportment.³⁸

Of course, Owen was not alone in pursuing this godly reform. Cromwell's academicians intended that universities should 'become nurseries not of heresy and profanity but of orthodoxy and sobriety'.³⁹ The Visitors appointed by Parliament, whose number included Owen and his fellow Independent Thomas Goodwin, deemed godly living at Oxford their utmost concern, as indicated by the entry in *The register of the Visitors* on 14 November 1653:

---

³³Feingold, 'The humanities', 230. Nor was enforcement of ethical and educational regulations the provenance of vice-chancellors alone. While head of Exeter College, John Conant, who would succeed Owen as vice-chancellor of Oxford in 1657, 'habitually attended lectures and disputations and frequently entered the students' rooms to observe what books they read and "reprove them if he found them turning over any modern authors", sending them instead to Cicero for language'; ibid., 233, citing Stride, *Exeter College*, 61–2.

³⁴Owen, *The Oxford orations*, 32. See Toon, *God's statesman*, 79. Gribben states, 'Owen, who was tasked with controlling [student] behavior, settled into his new role, not by engaging in destructive and polemical faction, but by promoting a Calvinistic piety that transcended the political and cultural division of the university'; Gribben, *John Owen and English Puritanism*, 129–30. Thomas Norton's *Devices for a godly realm* (1582) provides an earlier precedent for this Puritan perspective on education; Morgan, *Godly learning*, 239–40. Also see Worden, 'Cromwellian Oxford', 753.

³⁵For example, see 'From the visitors to the University of Oxford', 8 November 1653, in Owen, *The correspondence of John Owen*, 63.

³⁶In his speech at the Act in 1657 Owen pinned blame for students' ungodly behaviour on immoral influences outside the university: 'If on this occasion anything appears to occur beyond what is meet, let the blame lie on the shoulders of those who have endeavored with all their might that the allurements and opportunities for sinful acts should not perish; the things which are now taking place in public outside these walls, I should scarcely call our own affairs; we appeal to the peaceful times of studies and to the retreats of the students'; Owen, *The Oxford orations*, 35–6.

³⁷Owen, *The Oxford orations*, 27.

³⁸Worden, *God's instruments*, 104–5.

³⁹Worden, 'Cromwellian Oxford', 740. In a letter dated 2 July 1651, the commissioners in Ireland solicited Owen's advice for implementing their Puritan vision at Trinity College Dublin: 'Wherein we desire that the educating of youth in the knowledge of God and principles of piety may be in the first place promoted, experience having taught that where learning is attained before the work of grace upon the heart, it serves only to make a sharper opposition against the power of godliness'; Owen, *The correspondence of John Owen*, 51.

Upon consideration that the one maine end of the University is to traine up men as well in Divine as Humane Learning that they may be able (when the providence of God shall call them) to publish the Gospell of Christ to the conversion and building up of soules to eternal life, and that exercise in the things of God doth much increase knowledge and savour therein.[40]

By the end of his tenure as vice-chancellor, Owen counted among his accomplishments the encouragement of piety, along with respect for time-honoured educational principles, innovation in certain disciplines and the publishing of 'literature either checked or suppressed or drawing sustenance from other sources'.[41] Philip Henry, who attended Christ Church from 1647 to 1653, often reflected on his time at Oxford with gratitude not only for the academic training he received but also for what he learned of true religion, observing that 'serious godliness was in reputation'.[42]

Yet, the emphasis on practical piety was rooted in orthodox theology. The Puritan agenda for higher education focused on instruction in orthodoxy and the development of exemplary Christian character in educators and students, accompanied by a chastened attitude towards reason. What Owen attempted to accomplish was quite different from what eventuated at Oxford in the following decades. If Puritan doctrines regarding faith and reason had prevailed, 'their suggestions would have carried the intellectual thrust of England in seriously different directions from those which dominated by the end of the seventeenth century'.[43]

JOHN OWEN'S VIEW OF EDUCATION

While Owen's career as vice-chancellor reflected his Puritanism, his educational outlook had an even more fine-tuned prescription. This lens becomes apparent through several writings during his administrative tenure and culminates in his most well-known statement related to theological education, Θεολογουμενα παντοδαπα (1661), which he published shortly after leaving Oxford. Owen's polemic treatise *Vindiciae evangelicae* (1655) and his three devotional publications of 1656–8 serve as precursors to an important interpretive grid for

---

[40]*The register of the Visitors of the University of Oxford, from A.D. 1647 to A.D. 1658*, 327.
[41]Owen, *The Oxford orations*, 42–3. Midway through his administration, Owen declared in his speech at the Act of July 1655 that the university had never 'nourished a greater number of innocent and saintly souls than it now does'. Owen, *The Oxford orations*, 24.
[42]Henry, *An account of the life and death of Mr. Philip Henry* (1698), 25. Philip Henry apparently excelled academically, being selected 'to be junior of the act' from among the Master of Arts students in 1653 and *Magister Replicans* in 1654; ibid., 26.
[43]Morgan, *Godly learning*, 2.

the complex perspectives that Owen offered in Θεολογουμενα παντοδαπα. The intertextual relationship between Owen's devotional treatises of the late 1650s and this redemptive-historical account of religion is apparent. For example, in *Of communion with God* (1657), Owen anticipated the argument against arid knowledge of classical literature that he would develop in Θεολογουμενα παντοδαπα: 'He that has attained to the greatest height of literature, yet if he has nothing else, – if he have not Christ, – is as much under the curse of blindness, ignorance, stupidity, dullness, as the poorest, silliest soul in the world. The curse is only removed in him who was made a curse for us.'[44]

Like the late-sixteenth-century separatists, Owen targeted classical philosophers and poets as problematic educational resources. Much the same as John Milton, Owen understood the importance of a student's personal character for the nation's good. In agreement with the radicals, Owen disclaimed some of academia's accoutrements and opposed the exaltation of reason.[45] However, Owen's viewpoint markedly differed from each of these proposals. His critique of classical literature, his appreciation of moral character, his interrelating of faith and reason and his scriptural hermeneutic point to a deeper issue. These and other elements of Owen's writing coalesce in a Christological vision expressed in redeemed affection for the triune God.[46]

Vindiciae evangelicae (1655): An affective polemic

Owen described Θεολογουμενα παντοδαπα as the 'fruits of my study and reflection on theological truth', but he had already penned advice to scholars during his time at Oxford.[47] In 1655, Owen dedicated *Vindiciae evangelicae*, a polemical work against Socinianism, to the 'right worship, his reverend, learned, and worthy friends and brethren, the heads and governors of the colleges and halls, with all other students in divinity, or of the truth which is after godliness, in the famous University of Oxford'.[48] The subject matter was of grave concern, not only for reasons doctrinal (John Biddle was promulgating Polish Socinianism in England) and political (the Council of State commissioned

---

[44]Owen, *Of communion with God* (1657), 128; *Works* (1965), 2:114.

[45]In the following decade, Owen clearly expressed his view that Scripture can be rationally understood only by the gracious illumination of the Holy Spirit; Owen, Πνευματολογια (1674), 3; *Works* (1965), 3:6; cf. Haigh, 'The Church of England, the nonconformists and reason', 551.

[46]Ryan McGraw rightly argues that in Θεολογουμενα παντοδαπα, Owen 'implied that the most effective way to reform (and to justify) theological education was to displace philosophy as a foundation for truth, in order to reshape theological education in a way that made communion with Christ indispensable'; McGraw, '*Quid est?*', in *John Owen*, 165. This chapter aims to further substantiate and develop McGraw's claim.

[47]'Cogitata mea de theologiæ natura et studio'; Owen, Θεολογουμενα παντοδαπα (1661), 'Ad Lectorem Epistola'; *Works* (1850), 17:23; cf. *Biblical theology*, xlviii.

[48]Owen, *Vindiciae evangelicae* (1655), 'The epistle dedicatory'; *Works* (1965), 12:6.

Owen in 1654 to rebut Socinianism) but also academic (Biddle proudly claimed the MA that he had been awarded by Oxford in 1641).[49] In 'The preface to the reader', Owen articulated his concern to 'boldly acquaint the younger students in these weighty points of the religion of Jesus Christ', arguing that a sound explanation of the necessity of punishment for sin to satisfy divine justice will 'securely carry them through all the sophisms of the adversaries'.[50]

In his advice to divinity students concerning Socinianism, Owen interwove the necessities of sound doctrine and personal appropriation of the truth. He counselled students to 'take heed of the snare of Satan in affecting eminency by singularity', which he proceeded to explain in terms of growing dissatisfied with the commonness of sound orthodoxy and pursuing attention and prominence through theological innovations.[51] Instead, scholars should strive 'for a diligent endeavour to have the power of the truths professed and contended for abiding upon our hearts, that we may not contend for notions, but [for] what we have a practical acquaintance with in our own souls'.[52] As one of his cautions Owen brought forward the theme of communion with God:

> when we have communion with God in the doctrine we contend for, – then shall we be garrisoned, by the grace of God, against all the assaults of men. And without this all our contending is, as to ourselves, of no value. What am I the better if I can dispute that Christ is God, but have no sense of sweetness in my heart from hence that he is a God in covenant with my soul?[53]

Owen clearly eschewed the wrong appropriation of and dependence on reason, as his studied battle against Socinianism demonstrates. It was a deadly error against which Owen did not mince words: 'The evil is at the door; there is not a city, a town, scarce a village, in England, wherein some of this poison is not poured forth.'[54] Owen also recognized that a firm grasp of Hebrew and Greek was necessary for the defence of orthodoxy.[55] But even a studied explanation of Scripture would be insufficient armament against error apart from a heart affected and drawn to worship by true theology – after all, 'theology is wisdom with a practical aim in transforming man'.[56] Owen exhorted scholars not to

---

[49]Owen, *Vindiciae evangelicae* (1655), 'The epistle dedicatory'; *Works* (1965), 12:7.
[50]Owen, *Vindiciae evangelicae* (1655), 26; *Works* (1965), 12:28.
[51]Owen, *Vindiciae evangelicae* (1655), 64; *Works* (1965), 12:49.
[52]Owen, *Vindiciae evangelicae* (1655), 68; *Works* (1965), 12:52.
[53]Owen, *Vindiciae evangelicae* (1655), 69; *Works* (1965), 12:52. Owen used the term 'communion' twenty-eight times in *Vindiciae evangelicae*, half of which refer to communion with persons of the triune God.
[54]Owen, *Vindiciae evangelicae* (1655), 69; *Works* (1965), 12:52.
[55]Owen, *Vindiciae evangelicae* (1655), 65; *Works* (1965), 12:50.
[56]Rehnman, *Divine discourse*, 182.

think that we are any thing the better for our conviction of the truths of the great doctrines of the Gospel, for which we contend with these men, unless we find the power of the truths abiding in our own hearts, and have a continual experience of their necessity and excellency in our standing before God and our communion with him.[57]

Only those who commune with the triune God are true theologians.[58]

Three devotional treatises

While the preface to *Vindiciae evangelicae* provides a glimpse of Owen's concern for university students, his publications in the following three years get at its heart. For Owen, sound education entailed both academy and church.[59] The Sunday sermons he preached in St Mary's Church positively reinforced his worldview by appealing for the heart piety necessary to true education. In other words, Owen's writings in the late 1650s apply his Puritan perspective on the Christian life to a holistic understanding of godly education that integrates intellect and devotion.

Amid many pressing obligations, Owen published in quick succession *Of the mortification of sinne in believers* (1656), *Of communion with God* (1657) and *Of temptation* (1658). But chronological proximity is only one reason to consider these writings together. Owen interweaves common themes among the three books.[60] Perhaps most significantly, each of these books began as sermons he delivered on Sunday afternoons at St Mary's. What Owen taught in a church context 'outlined the qualities of that Calvinistic piety', targeting the gap in education between theological knowledge and a vibrant spiritual relationship with the triune God.[61] Students such as Thomas Aldersey not only gathered to hear the vice-chancellor exposit sanctification in union with Christ but also took careful notes to rehearse and apply Owen's practical divinity.[62]

---

[57] Owen, *Vindiciae evangelicae* (1655), 69; *Works* (1965), 12:52.
[58] Ryan McGraw emphasizes the trinitarian shape of true theology and theologians according to Owen: 'Just as the primary end of theology was not the glory of God generically considered but God as triune, so the subordinate end of theology involved the salvation of the theologian who enjoyed communion with the Father through the Son, by the Spirit'; McGraw, '*Quid est?*', 187.
[59] 'Sometimes the benefit of historical theology is not discovering answers to the questions we currently have, but discovering the questions that we should be asking. If Owen teaches a contemporary audience anything about the Trinity, then it likely lies in furnishing the church with a model for wedding the precision of the academy to the devotion of the pew'; McGraw, 'John Owen's trinitarian theology and piety', 200.
[60] For example, there are twenty-one references in *Of the mortification of sinne in believers* (1656) to a Christian's communion with God, as well as nine references in *Of temptation* (1658).
[61] Gribben, *John Owen and English Puritanism*, 130, 173.
[62] See Gribben, *An introduction to John Owen*, 79–81.

In particular, the first two works show how Owen's educational perspective had a Christological and affective core. Owen understood the goal of his academic leadership to be holiness for God's glory and the medium of preaching a primary means.[63] In the preface to *Of the mortification of sinne in believers*, he explained:

> I hope I may own in sincerity, that my heart's desire unto God, and the chief design of my life in the station wherein the good providence of God hath placed me, are, that mortification and universal holiness may be promoted in my own and in the hearts and ways of others, to the glory of God; that so the Gospel of our Lord and Saviour Jesus Christ may be adorned in all things.[64]

In *Of the mortification of sinne in believers*, his counsel for students – many of them teenagers – was uncompromising: 'Do you mortify; do you make it your daily work; be always at it while you live; cease not a day from this work; be killing sin or it will be killing you.'[65] But this was no bootstrap self-improvement plan. In his directions for putting sin to death, Owen appealed to the believer's relationship with the triune God.

> Those who are Christ's, and are acted in their obedience upon Gospel principles, have the death of Christ, the love of God, the detestable nature of sin, the preciousness of communion with God, a deep-grounded abhorrency of sin as sin, to oppose to any seduction of sin, to all the workings, strivings, rightings of lust in their hearts.[66]

---

[63] Blair Worden captures the essential significance of Owen's proclaimed doctrine: 'True doctrine needed to be defined and defended in print. Yet it was in sermons that it could best be made vivid and be stamped on the university's young imaginations'; Worden, *God's Instruments*, 160. Kelly Kapic similarly remarks, 'Young students were most likely the bulk of his original audience – Owen had entered Queen's College Oxford as a student at the age of twelve, which was not uncommon for the time. One consequence of addressing this youthful audience seems to be that his reflections tend toward the concrete and practical, emphasizing the particular rather than lingering too long on the abstract. Here were young people who were beginning to experience the complexity of sin and self, and Owen was compelled to help'; Kapic, 'Introduction: Worshiping the Triune God', 25.
[64] Owen, *Of the mortification of sinne in believers* (1656), sig. A4; *Works* (1965), 6:4. Also see Owen, *The Oxford orations*, 12. As he explained in the preface, dated 10 July 1657, Owen had preached on the subject of communion with God six years earlier. Although 'sundry noble and worthy Christian friends' had awaited the publication of his doctrine of 'peace and communion with God', Owen offered his work on mortification 'as interest for their forbearance'; Owen, *Of the mortification of sinne in believers* (1656), sig. A3; *Works* (1965), 6:3.
[65] Owen, *Of the mortification of sinne in believers* (1656), 14; *Works* (1965), 6:9.
[66] Owen, *Of the mortification of sinne in believers* (1656), 134; *Works* (1965), 6:47; cf. Owen, *Of temptation* (1658), 131–2, 161–3; *Works* (1965), 6:134, 144–5. *Of temptation* expresses similar emphases, though Owen's concerns were heightened in a year marked by Oliver Cromwell's death and signs of increasing political and religious trouble. Only those whose hearts were tuned to

Most of Owen's counsel concerning mortification articulates principles of its necessity and descriptions of its nature. From the outset Owen endeavoured to differentiate his viewpoint from a moralistic mortification, a distinction most clearly seen in the final section of his work.[67] At the beginning of the closing chapter, Owen clarified that the foregoing counsel was 'preparatory to the work aimed at than such as will effect it'.[68] The means by which mortification is accomplished directly relate to a believer's communion with Christ. The believer must actively mortify his sin in the power of the Holy Spirit. But mortification cannot be accomplished except by faith in Christ as experienced through the 'graces and ordinances' whereby Christ is 'wont to communicate himself to the soul'.[69]

Owen's concern for his students' devotion to God bursts forth in *Of communion with God*, an exposition of the fellowship that believers have with the triune God. Each person of the Trinity – Father, Son and Holy Spirit – gives saving benefits to Christians and should receive grateful worship from Christians in response to those particular benefits. Such communion with the 'infinitely holy God is an astonishing dispensation'.[70] Owen's profound insight is that 'God's ultimate purpose in revealing himself as triune is therefore to deepen his communion with his people by affecting their hearts with what he has done on their behalf'.[71] A believer fellowships with each member of the Trinity personally, not just God generally.[72]

This trinitarian theology manifests a Christological orientation, for the Son makes the Father known and the Holy Spirit draws attention to Christ.[73] Owen asserted that 'our communion . . . with God consisteth in his communication

---

glorify God could escape the snares everywhere present. See Owen, *Of temptation* (1658), 16, 87; *Works* (1965), 6:96, 119.

[67] Owen, *Of the mortification of sinne in believers* (1656), sig. A3, 7; *Works* (1965), 6:3, 7.

[68] Owen, *Of the mortification of sinne in believers* (1656), 232; *Works* (1965), 6:78.

[69] Owen, *Of the mortification of sinne in believers* (1656), 247; *Works* (1965), 6:83.

[70] Owen, *Of communion with God* (1657), 3; *Works* (1965), 2:7. Owen stated, 'There is no grace whereby our souls go forth unto God, no act of divine worship yielded unto him, no duty or obedience performed, but they are distinctly directed unto Father, Son, and Spirit'; Owen, *Of communion with God* (1657), 12; *Works* (1965), 2:14.

[71] Kay, *Trinitarian spirituality*, 102; cf. Owen, Πνευματολογια, 126–127; *Works* (1965), 3:158.

[72] Owen clarified, however, that the 'divine nature is the reason and cause of all worship; so that it is impossible to worship any one person, and not worship the whole Trinity'; Owen, *Of communion with God* (1657), 313; *Works* (1965), 2:268.

[73] Owen, *Of communion with God* (1657), 277; *Works* (1965), 2:239. As Kelly Kapic has noted, the number of pages in *Of communion of God* dedicated to communion with the Son (183 pp.) by comparison with communion with the Father (17 pp.) and the Holy Spirit (53 pp.) reveals Owen's Christological focus. Kapic, 'Introduction: Worshiping the Triune God', 20 n. 10. Owen affirms that the Father does not need persuasion to love His children; yet the 'design of [His love's] accomplishment is only in Christ'; Owen, *Of communion with God* (1657), 277; *Works* (1965), 2:27.

of himself unto us, with our returnal unto him of that which he requireth and accepteth, flowing from that union which in Jesus Christ we have with him'.[74] Alan Spence writes of Owen's view of the centrality of Christ in divine revelation: 'It is through [Jesus Christ], that is through the historical reality of his person as the representative of the divine nature and will, that we have a basis or ground for our knowledge of and response to God.'[75] True knowledge has three components: knowledge of God, knowledge of ourselves and the 'skill to walk in communion with God'.[76] God demonstrates His perfections most clearly and benevolently in Christ.[77] Mankind pursues learning in response to the 'soul's struggling with the curse for sin' and attempts to gain 'prudence in the management of civil affairs'. But the darkness of human erudition and folly of human conduct testify that the 'crown of wisdom' belongs to Christ alone.[78] In Owen's view, the fundamental problem with scholastic knowledge was its failure to address the heart.

The vice-chancellor's message to Oxford students was penetrating yet rapturous. Owen taught that 'union with Christ is not the end but the beginning of the Christian life'.[79] To walk in fellowship with the triune God entails six necessities, all of which are found in Christ alone: agreement (reconciliation), acquaintance (revelation), a way (access), strength, boldness and joint purpose (God's glory).[80] Just as in *Of the mortification of sinne in believers*, Owen

---

[74]Owen, *Of communion with God* (1657), 26; *Works* (1965), 2:8–9. The triune God communicates grace to his people as follows: the Father 'by the way of original authority'; the Son 'by the way of making out a purchased treasury'; and the Holy Spirit 'by the way of immediate efficacy'; Owen, *Of communion with God* (1657), 14; *Works* (1965), 2:16–17.

[75]Spence, *Incarnation and inspiration*, 33. Andrew Leslie concurs: Owen's *Meditations and discourses on the glory of Christ* (1684) is 'chiefly designed to fan into flame that christological vision each believer receives in their spiritual unction, by exhorting them to meditate on Christ's mediatorial love as showcased throughout biblical history in all its kaleidoscopic variety. . . . Indeed, in Owen's mind, a person's actual conformity to Christ is directly correlated to their actual view of Christ'; Leslie, *The light of grace*, 244.

[76]Gribben points out that the third component is an addition to Calvin's classic articulation of the first two; Gribben, *John Owen and English Puritanism*, 173. To argue that we know God's attributes by looking to Christ is unsurprising. What may be less typical is Owen's subsequent assertion that we know ourselves by knowing Christ; Owen, *Of communion with God* (1657), 104–19; *Works*, 2:94–106. See Kapic, 'Introduction: Worshiping the Triune God', 33.

[77]Owen, *Of communion with God* (1657), 101; *Works* (1965), 2:91. In 1733, Jonathan Edwards made a similar case for the Christological revelation of divine attributes in his series of sermons from Eph. 3.10; Edwards, 'The wisdom of God, displayed in the way of salvation', 181–4.

[78]Owen, *Of communion with God* (1657), 125–32; *Works* (1965), 2:112–17. See also Gribben, *An introduction to John Owen*, 77–8.

[79]Kay, *Trinitarian spirituality*, 119.

[80]Owen, *Of communion with God* (1657), 119; *Works* (1965), 2:106. 'The programmatic center, at least, of Owen's encouragement toward mental communion with Christ through sanctification hangs upon the power of Christ's blood – shed in his act of passive obedience – as a cleanser of the mind and will'; Kay, *Trinitarian Spirituality*, 158–9.

correlated the work of waging war against one's own sinfulness with spiritual communion:

> [Believers'] daily work is, to get their hearts crucified to the world and the things of it, and the world to their hearts; that they may not have living affections to dying things . . . and if at any times they have been entangled with creatures and inferior contentment, and have lost their better joys, they cry out to Christ, 'O restore to us the joys of thy Spirit!'[81]

Doctrine must reach down into one's soul, and it does so through meditation – gazing on Christ, rather than merely observing Him.[82] 'One moment's communion with Christ by faith herein is more effectual to the purging of the soul, to the increasing of grace, than the utmost self-endeavours of a thousand ages.'[83]

Θεολογούμενα παντοδαπά (1661): Reflections of a displaced academic

Among the eight million words in the John Owen corpus, there are no essays explicitly dedicated to educational philosophy. However, in 1661 Owen published Θεολογούμενα παντοδαπά, which provides insight into his views on education soon after his time at Oxford. The research involved is likely the fruit of his 'wilderness year' of 1658–9, when he still served as dean of Christ Church and had access to the riches of Bodleian Library but was no longer vice-chancellor nor in a favoured position politically.[84] Θεολογούμενα παντοδαπά apparently incorporated Owen's lectures on theology to Oxford students, though now in retrospect.[85]

The former dean took some solace in his newfound distance from academic life, remarking, 'I hate the din of the universities and the hubbub of their

---

[81]Owen, *Of communion with God* (1657), 169; *Works* (1965), 2:150; cf. Owen, *Of communion with God* (1657), 216; *Works* (1965), 2:188. See also Oh, *Beholding the glory of God in Christ*, 262–91.
[82]Kay, *Trinitarian spirituality*, 133.
[83]Owen, *Of communion with God* (1657) 234; *Works* (1965), 2:204.
[84]Westcott, 'Editor's notes to the English version', in *Biblical theology*, 725. As Ryan McGraw argues, the first subtitle of Westcott's translation, 'The history of theology from Adam to Christ', confuses modern readers as to the nature of Θεολογούμενα παντοδαπά. The second subtitle reproduces Owen's Latin subtitle and situates this work as theological prolegomena; '*Quid est?*', 167–9.
[85]Rehnman, *Divine discourse*, 18; cf. Gribben, *John Owen and English Puritanism*, 213–14. Stephen Westcott proposes, 'His work on reforming the University and its curriculum from mediaeval scholasticism towards Biblical lines had been abruptly curtailed. His materials, so painstakingly gathered for that end, lay about him unused'; Westcott, 'Editor's notes to the English version', in *Biblical theology*, 725.

endless sophistries. By God's grace, I live at home and am my own man.'[86] Yet he sustained a keen interest in education.[87] With the threads of his Bodleian research, administrative experience and Puritan proclivities, Owen engaged a wide swath of learning to weave a tapestry of theological reflection set in the frame of federal theology.[88] Θεολογουμενα παντοδαπα is Owen's redemptive-historical argument for true theology. Gribben explains:

> [Θεολογουμενα παντοδαπα] is in fact an almost encyclopaedic historical account of the history of ideas associated within Owen's doctrine of revelation: the book offers an expansive account of the history of language, literature, and culture to support its argument that the original knowledge of God given to Adam and Eve slowly dissipated, except among the descendants of Abraham, among whom it was gradually corrupted.[89]

Owen's critique of classical literature and human philosophy

Owen opened a window into his literary purpose with an 'Epistle to the Reader'. He roundly objected to the vices baldly described in classical literature and took aim at human philosophy, bolstering his argument with a theme he had preached and published while at Oxford, that the only true source of wisdom is 'communion with God'.[90] Owen levelled this criticism because, instead of seeking God, philosophers have attempted to make sense of the remnants of natural theology on their own. In other words, 'philosophy is an off-shoot from the true inborn theology of our first ancestor before the fall, amplified by the revelation proclaimed by the words of God'.[91] But even seemingly profound attempts to explain and motivate ethical conduct fall short because, at best,

---

[86]'Odi scholarum strepitus et sophisticam. Domi, Deo ita gratiose disponente, et apud me ipsum vivo'; Owen, Θεολογουμενα παντοδαπα (1661), 6.9.5; *Works* (1850), 17:470; cf. *Biblical theology*, 687.

[87]Owen, Θεολογουμενα παντοδαπα (1661), 'Ad lectorem epistola'; *Works* (1850), 17:23; cf. *Biblical theology*, xlviii.

[88]Rehnman, *Divine discourse*, 156. Rehnman distinguishes Owen's use of federal theology in Θεολογουμενα παντοδαπα from a more typical employment of covenant as a 'means of explaining the dispensation of divine grace'; ibid., 165. See also Tweeddale, *John Owen and Hebrews*, 59–63.

[89]Gribben, *John Owen and English Puritanism*, 213.

[90]'cum Deo communion'; Owen, Θεολογουμενα παντοδαπα (1661), 'Ad lectorem epistola'; *Works* (1850), 17:19; cf. *Biblical theology*, xxxix. English translations of Θεολογουμενα παντοδαπα are taken from Westcott (1994).

[91]'Residuæ illius theologiæ, quam in statu naturæ integræ primus homo congenitam habuit, revelatione prædictâ per opera Dei ampliatæ, effectum, inquam, et quasi surculus est, *philosophia*'; Owen, Θεολογουμενα παντοδαπα (1661), 1.7.3; *Works* (1850), 17:79; cf. *Biblical theology*, 85. Owen avowed, 'I have no hesitation in declaring that not one true virtue is certainly and correctly taught in all of the pages of Aristotle's *Nicomachean Ethics*.' 'Ausim dicere, non unam veram virtutem vere et certe doceri, in omnibus Aristotelicis libris ad Nicomachum.' Owen, Θεολογουμενα παντοδαπα (1661), 1.7.19; *Works* (1850), 17:85; cf. *Biblical theology*, 92.

philosophical ethics 'can point only to the covenant of works'.⁹² The apparent virtues extolled in classical writings were not truly honourable because their authors neither relied on God in their philosophy nor demonstrated a true knowledge of God through righteous living to his glory.⁹³

Owen qualified his strong sentiment regarding Greek moral philosophy, acknowledging that it 'offered a sincere education according [to] the best rules of virtue then known'.⁹⁴ It had become commonplace by the 1650s for tutors to provide second-year students with instruction in moral philosophy, often starting with a manual the tutors themselves had written and continuing with independent study from works suggested by tutors. Tutors 'invariably assigned Aristotle', though sometimes his writings were refracted through modern writers.⁹⁵ However, as Owen's time as an Oxford administrator had proven, sinful human nature requires a remedy greater than the principles of moral philosophy. The classical education of his day inclined fallen people to trust in the reasoning of other fallen people.⁹⁶

Although not dismissing classical literature as entirely vacuous, Owen suggested that it evidenced not only the remnants of original revelation but also the demonic origin of sinful culture. The poets wrongfully introduced impressionable minds to wickedness that was nearly irradicable. 'How frequently are diseases more powerful than remedies.'⁹⁷ Owen's explanation picks up themes from the argument he made five years earlier, in *Of the mortification of sinne in believers*: 'The man who would deny that his inborn vanity must daily be held in check from the temptations of pleasures and lusts is not worthy of the name of a Christian.'⁹⁸ These problems warranted tremendous caution.⁹⁹

In addition to the pitfalls of philosophy and classical literature, Owen observed that students also faced the challenges of their own fallen human nature.

---

⁹²'ethica hæc pertinet ad fœdus operum'; Owen, Θεολογουμενα παντοδαπα (1661), 1.7.18; *Works* (1850), 17:84; cf. *Biblical theology*, 91.
⁹³Owen, Θεολογουμενα παντοδαπα (1661), 'Ad lectorem epistola', 1.7.5–7; *Works* (1850), 17:19, 80–1; cf. *Biblical theology*, xl, 86.
⁹⁴'Philosophia moralis Gentilium practica erat in honestate morum et gravis institutio, secundùm optimas quas scirent virtutis regulas'; Owen, Θεολογουμενα παντοδαπα (1661), 'Ad lectorem epistola'; *Works* (1850), 17:20; cf. *Biblical theology*, xli.
⁹⁵Feingold, 'The humanities', 321–22.
⁹⁶Owen, Θεολογουμενα παντοδαπα (1661), 'Ad lectorem epistola'; *Works* (1850), 17:22; cf. *Biblical theology*, xliii.
⁹⁷'Certa magis est malorum, quàm remediorum efficacia'; Owen, Θεολογουμενα παντοδαπα (1661), 'Ad lectorem epistola'; *Works* (1850), 17:17; cf. *Biblical theology*, xxxvi.
⁹⁸'Qui innatam ejus vanitatem ab omnibus voluptatum et libidinum incentivis omni modo cohibendam negaret, Christiano nomine prorsus esset indignus'; Owen, Θεολογουμενα παντοδαπα (1661), 'Ad lectorem epistola'; *Works* (1850), 17:17; cf. *Biblical theology*, xxxvii.
⁹⁹Owen, Θεολογουμενα παντοδαπα (1661), 'Ad lectorem epistola'; *Works* (1850), 17:18; cf. *Biblical theology*, xxxvii.

Central to his concerns was students' propensity for intellectual arrogance,[100] but laziness, faintheartedness, carnal habits and lack of discernment commonly surfaced as well. Many students also succumbed to the pressures of theological ideas that diverged from orthodoxy.[101] In *Of temptation*, Owen had lamented, 'Go to our several colleges, inquire for such and such young men; what is the answer in respect of many? "Ah! such a one was very hopeful for a season; but he fell into ill company, and he is quite lost".'[102]

Owen's critical appraisal of the value of established curricula was not novel. In 1530, the Oxford-educated William Tyndale complained that 'in the universities they have ordained no man shall look on the Scripture, until he be noselled in heathen learning eight or nine years, and armed with false principles; with which he is clean shut out of the understanding of Scripture'.[103] Owen's critique of classical learning and literature fit the general Puritan suspicion, present since the 1560s, concerning the reigning viewpoint that sought common ground between faith and philosophy.[104] Furthermore, Owen's negative stance on classical literature, especially poetry, ran parallel to other critiques made at Oxford in the mid-seventeenth century. For example, Robert Boyle disputed the teaching of ethics from secular texts.[105] Owen's opinion even echoed the arguments of those advocating radical reformation of the universities during the Interregnum. As Feingold relates, 'in a sermon he delivered at St Mary's Church in 1654 the fiery Peter French admonished the students that 'the search after true wisdom' was to be found in scriptures, not in "the books of philosophers".'[106]

Owen's Christological hermeneutic

Various factors could help explain the stance on classical literature and philosophy that Owen articulated in Θεολογουμενα παντοδαπα. Owen may

---

[100]For example, see Owen, Θεολογουμενα παντοδαπα (1661), 5.14.2; *Works* (1850), 17:376; cf. *Biblical theology*, 538. Matthew Henry wrote of his father, Philip, that 'coming from *Westminster* School, his attainments in School-learning were beyond what generally others had that came from other Schools, so that he was tempred to think there was no need for him to study much, because it was so easie to him to keep pace with others'; Henry, *An account of the life and death of Mr. Philip Henry* (1698), 22; Feingold, 'The humanities', 284.
[101]Owen, Θεολογουμενα παντοδαπα (1661), 'Ad lectorem epistola'; *Works* (1850), 17:14; cf. *Biblical theology*, xxx.
[102]Owen, *Of temptation* (1658), 180; *Works* (1965), 6:150.
[103]Tyndale, *The practice of prelates* (1530), in *The works of William Tyndale*, 291.
[104]For example, see Preston, *The doctrine of the saints infirmities* (1637), 59–60. Morgan, *Godly learning*, 48–55; Feingold, 'The humanities', 312.
[105]Feingold notes, 'Echoing Hobbes and anticipating Locke, Boyle proceeded, in about 1660, to chastise those who wrangled "about the titles and precedencies of the parts of ethical philosophy, and things extrinsical enough to vice and virtue" and who spent "more time in asserting their method, than the prerogatives of virtue above vice"'; Feingold, 'The humanities', 308.
[106]Feingold, 'The humanities', 310.

have anticipated that natural theology would serve as a key philosophical and theological foundation of the restored regime and national church.¹⁰⁷ His critique of traditional education may also have been encouraged by self-doubt concerning the success of his own university labours in the previous decade, especially in preparing ministers.¹⁰⁸ But Owen's appraisal cannot be relegated to an apprehensive prospect or a bitter retrospect. His vision was higher.

Near the end of Θεολογούμενα παντοδαπά, Owen explained that true theology is the 'disciplined efforts of the student's intellect (directed according to the rule of Scripture) to enhance and improve those inner spiritual gifts and saving light which constitute true, heavenly wisdom'.¹⁰⁹ Because the fall corrupted the *imago Dei* and the knowledge of God inherent to it, transformation into the image of Christ is crucial to the renewal of theology.¹¹⁰ Scriptural revelation is supernatural in both its 'origin' and its 'method of delivery';¹¹¹ therefore, true learning also occurs supernaturally and is impossible apart from union with Christ. The 'theology of Christ' is 'not just the teaching of the Gospel but the disposition of mind which alone can embrace it'.¹¹² By exalting Christ as the focus of theology, Owen argued that the New Testament fulfils what the Old Testament promised. At the point when human learning had reached its apex in the Greeks and Romans, in the fullness of time God the Son became incarnate.¹¹³

After unfolding in the first five books the revelation of theology and its ultimate rejection through successive eras of redemptive history, Owen arrived at his point in Book VI. God the Son authored 'evangelical theology',¹¹⁴ and one

---

¹⁰⁷Gribben, *John Owen and English Puritanism*, 213. Rehnman suggests that Owen had become wary of the rationalizing direction of Reformed orthodoxy that eventuated in the form of Cambridge Platonism and other variations of enlightened Protestantism in the late seventeenth and early eighteenth centuries; Rehnman, *Divine discourse*, 125–6.

¹⁰⁸Owen, Θεολογούμενα παντοδαπά (1661), 'Ad lectorem epistola'; *Works* (1850), 17:23; cf. *Biblical theology*, xlvii.

¹⁰⁹'Studium itaque theologiæ nihil aliud est, quàm promovendi lumen salutare, et dona spiritualia, quibus sapientia hæc coelestis consistit in mente theologi conatus, ad normam verbi divini institutus'; Owen, Θεολογούμενα παντοδαπά (1661), 6.9.9; *Works* (1850), 17:471; cf. *Biblical theology*, 688.

¹¹⁰Owen, Θεολογούμενα παντοδαπά (1661), 1.7.29; *Works* (1850), 17:89; cf. *Biblical theology*, 99.

¹¹¹Rehnman, *Divine discourse*, 160–1.

¹¹²'Nec doctrina evangelica, sed is mentis nostræ habitus, quo eam amplectimur'; Owen, Θεολογούμενα παντοδαπά (1661), 6.1.1; *Works* (1850), 17:409–10; cf. *Biblical theology*, 591.

¹¹³Owen, Θεολογούμενα παντοδαπά (1661), 6.1.6–7; *Works* (1850), 17:412–13; cf. *Biblical theology*, 595–6.

¹¹⁴'Auctor ideo theologiæ evangelicæ immediatus est ipse Jesus Christus, Filius Dei unigenitus'; Owen, Θεολογούμενα παντοδαπά (1661), 6.1.2; *Works* (1850), 411; cf. *Biblical theology*, 593. 'At the centre [of Owen's understanding of theology] stands the category of the *theologia Mediatoris*, which both makes true knowledge of the infinite divine theology possible and regulates the character of human theology as a practical wisdom in the pilgrimage'; Rehnman, *Divine discourse*, 71.

of its chief ends is the 'cultivation of a most holy and sweet communion with God, wherein lies the true happiness of mankind. . . . Evangelical theology has been instituted by God in order that sinners may once again enjoy communion with God Himself, the All-Holy One'.[115] Owen called communion with the triune God 'this most deep and mysterious doctrine [which] is the very essence of evangelical theology'.[116] Delighting in and worshipping God brings together the theoretical and practical aspects of theology, so that 'saving truths' become experiential knowledge.[117] The active presence and communion of Christ in a regenerated heart 'is what gives perception, feeling, and taste for matters evangelical'.[118]

Scholars ponder what Owen's diatribe against philosophy really means. Though he rejected the value of scandalous ancient poets, he clearly did not spurn classical learning in every sense.[119] The former vice-chancellor took a common Puritan stance by acknowledging the educational benefits of grammar (especially of Hebrew and Greek), logic and rhetoric.[120] He did not advocate eliminating moral philosophy but warned against its two dangers: its corruption

---

[115]'Deinde communio sanctissima suavissimaque cum Deo colenda, quæ initialis est hominis beatitas, finis alius est theologiæ . . . Ut peccatores iterum communionem cum Deo Sanctissimo assequerentur, instituta ab ipso est hæc nova theologia'; Owen, Θεολογουμενα παντοδαπα (1661), 6.4.8; Works (1850), 427; cf. Biblical theology, 618.

[116]'Hæc, inquam, doctrina μυστηριώδης objectum est theologiæ evangelicæ'; Owen, Θεολογουμενα παντοδαπα (1661), 6.6.12; Works (1850), 443; cf. Biblical theology, 643.

[117]'veritatum salutarium'; Owen, Θεολογουμενα παντοδαπα (1661), 6.9.3; Works (1850), 469; cf. Biblical theology, 686. The dual-pronged focus on theology as both theoretical and practical owes its widespread use in seventeenth-century Reformed theology, in part, to the influence of Peter Ramus; Muller, Prolegomena to theology, 182. McGraw explains, 'Knowledge or belief could be "practical," in the sense of leading to practice, without involving communion with God at all'; McGraw, 'Quid est?', 186. Consequently, communion with God does not set aside theoretical knowledge but rather captures its essence.

[118]'sensus et gustus spiritualis ipsarum rerum evangelicarum'; Owen, Θεολογουμενα παντοδαπα (1661), 6.6.13; Works (1850), 444; cf. Biblical theology, 644.

[119]Rehnman explains, 'Owen did, of course, dismiss Greek philosophers as opposed to Scripture, but in reality this relationship was more complex and he, for short, adhered to the traditional Christian assimilation of classical philosophy'; Rehnman, 'John Owen: A Reformed scholastic at Oxford', 195–6. Cf. Owen, Works (1965), 2:8, 2:343.

[120]Owen, Θεολογουμενα παντοδαπα (1661), 6.9.12; Works (1850), 17:472; cf. Biblical theology, 690. See Morgan, Godly learning, 232, 235. Owen's perspective in Θεολογουμενα παντοδαπα has precedent in statements during his days of authority at Oxford, such as his oration at the Comitia in July 1654: 'I call to witness theology, the queen and mistress of the other branches of learning, and it is almost our especial task to see that these are ready handmaids to it . . . [This is true] theology that daily blossoms forth using all the supports of true philosophy and the other branches of knowledge which can serve to help or adorn it'; Owen, The Oxford orations, 15. Though affirming the subordinate role of 'other branches of learning', Owen distinguished true theology from 'confused theology drawn from the ditches of the scholastics, nor the theology that is merely common and teachable material handed down in a variety of manuals by scores of quite worthy and not inadequate men'; ibid.

of youths' perspective on the purity and simplicity of the Gospel and its infiltration into many aspects of theology.[121]

Owen explained his purpose in the final chapter of Θεολογουμενα παντοδαπα. His relentless critique of philosophy and classical literature may seem to drive towards a drastic overhaul of pedagogical method and curriculum.[122] Instead, he offered an understanding of education even more radical. Θεολογουμενα παντοδαπα critiques a merely traditional view of knowledge and proposes a Christological hermeneutic grounded in 'saving grace'. What students ultimately need is a true knowledge of Christ that introduces them to relational communion with the triune God.[123]

JOHN OWEN'S EDUCATIONAL LEGACY

Though his Nonconformity ensured he would never resume administration at Oxford, and his writing found other foci, Owen's educational legacy persisted beyond 1661. Θεολογουμενα παντοδαπα influenced a massive work published the following decade by one of Owen's students, Theophilus Gale, who graduated from Oxford with his MA in 1652.[124] Gale's *The court of the Gentiles* reflects an organic development of theology, like that articulated in Θεολογουμενα

---

[121]Owen, Θεολογουμενα παντοδαπα (1661), 1.7.22; *Works* (1850), 17:86; cf. *Biblical theology*, 94.

[122]Ryan McGraw observes, 'The fact that [Owen] criticized aspects of the method that he had studied at Oxford does not mean that he wanted to sever himself from the methodology of the schools. If anything, he sought to modify it by closing the gap between academic and practical theology'; McGraw, *A heavenly directory*, 38–9. References in Owen's other writings to scholasticism and the Scholastics vary in their emphases. Perhaps the following statement captures the tension: '[Linguistic study and scholastic accuracy] are great in themselves, but go for nothing when they are alone'; Owen, *The causes, waies & means of understanding the mind of God*, 150–1; *Works* (1965), 4:182.

[123]'nisi per gratiam Christi salutarem'; Owen, Θεολογουμενα παντοδαπα (1661), 6.9.14; *Works* (1850), 17:474; cf. *Biblical theology*, 693. Owen's assertion of the centrality of Christ to all wisdom and learning is not unique among English Puritan divines. For example, in one of his posthumously published sermons expositing the Westminster Shorter Catechism, Thomas Watson declared, 'Christ is the great Luminary. In him are hid *all Treasures of Knowledge,* Col. 2.3. . . . We are apt to admire the Learning of *Aristotle* and *Plato*; alas! what is this poor Spark of Light to that which is in Christ, from whose infinite Wisdom both Men and Angels light their Lamp'; Watson, *A body of practical divinity* (1692), 98.

[124]Gale drew from Owen in arguing that any truth found in pagan philosophy is derived from the Jews and their Scriptures. '*Owen* in his learned Discourse of *Gentile Theologie* (which I must confess, has given me much light, and confirmation herein) does frequently assert the same Conclusion'; Gale, *The court of the Gentiles* (1670), part II, 90. Dewey Wallace summarizes, 'Gale imbibed Puritan spirituality and scholastic Calvinist theology in the Oxford of John Owen and spent time in the 1660s in the company of Hugenot scholars in France'; Wallace, *Shapers of English Calvinism, 1660–1714*, 243.

παντοδαπα, as well as the viewpoint that pagan philosophy expresses remnants of true theology that are skewed and can find coherence only in Christ.[125]

In response to conformist requirements for entry into Oxford and Cambridge, dissenting academies sprang up in the aftermath of the Restoration. Some of these academies became 'ministerial seminaries' in the 1670s.[126] Several students from Owen's Oxford days served as tutors of these academies, including Theophilus Gale, Philip Henry, Thomas Vincent and Edward Veal. Owen exerted influence on some in the dissenting academy circles in London, including Samuel Wesley, who later penned a scathing critique of the nonconformist approach to education. However, Wesley admitted that he had been 'received very civilly by [Owen], encouraged in the prosecution of my Studies, and advised to have a particular regard to Critical Learning'.[127] Wesley's comment helps to confirm that Owen had not repudiated traditional curricula as much as scholastic pedantry and pride. Wesley was particularly critical of dissenters' opinion that Oxford and Cambridge 'were debauched so scandalously'. But this was their opinion: Owen and fellow nonconformists denounced the state of Oxford and Cambridge as environments ill-suited for healthy doctrine and godly living.[128] Consequently, the dissenting academies sought to maintain a balance of 'learning and religious observance'.[129]

On 25 December 1666, Thomas Vincent convened the pupils of his dissenting academy to impart words of advice, a practice he would repeat exactly one year later. In these addresses to the 'youth of the city of London', the nonconformist minister exhorted his students with words reminiscent of his former college dean, John Owen. What Vincent longed for most in these teenagers was not

---

[125]Mark Burden, *A biographical dictionary of tutors at the dissenters' private academies, 1660–1729*, 216. Also, see Feingold, 'The humanities', 268. McGraw suggests, 'The purpose, both of book three [of Θεολογούμενα παντοδαπα] and of Gale's work [*The court of the Gentiles*], was to argue that extra-biblical religion and philosophy marked a gradual apostasy from the true religion and that the presence of elements resembling truth were actually distortions of what the nations once did and should have known'; McGraw, '*Quid est?*', 174.
[126]Burden, *A biographical dictionary of tutors at the dissenters' private academies, 1660–1729*, 15.
[127]Wesley, *A letter from a country divine* (1703), 5.
[128]Wesley, *A letter from a country divine* (1703), 11. Wesley was not alone in his denunciation of the academies. The authors of *Sphinx Lvgdvno-Genevensis, sive, Reformator proteus* laid the blame for the academies on the ongoing influence of Owen through displaced university tutors from the 1650s. *Sphinx Lvgdvno-Genevensis, sive, reformator proteus* (1683), 2. Also see Shaw, *No reformation of the established reformation* (1685), 195.
[129]Burden, *A biographical dictionary of tutors at the dissenters' private academies, 1660–1729*, 26. The nonconforming Puritans were not uniform in their view of the universities or, therefore, the dissenting academies. In contrast with his estimation of Owen's group, Wesley judges Richard Baxter to have been 'inclined to the Universities, and did not much approve our private academies'; Wesley, *A letter from a country divine* (1703), 15.

academic diligence or acumen, but true love for God (his first text was Prov. 8.17) and obedience to God's word (his second text was Ps. 119.9).[130]

Admittedly, not all of Owen's scholars embraced this viewpoint – as the career of John Locke demonstrates. Though he shared with Owen an interest in education and misgiving about aspects of scholastic curriculum, Locke did not follow his former dean's Christological worldview. A notable feature of Locke's *Some thoughts concerning education* (1693) is the complete absence of reference to Jesus Christ. Locke considers the 'great Principle and Foundation of all Vertue and Worth . . . that a Man is able to deny himself his own Desires, cross his own Inclinations, and purely follow what Reason directs as best, tho' the appetite lean the other way'.[131] However, some of Owen's students, like Philip Henry, Thomas Aldersey, Theophilus Gale, Thomas Vincent and Joseph Alleine, caught the vision of their former teacher, and in Owen's writings it lives on.[132]

In 1651, Owen began his work at the University of Oxford with high expectations of cultivating godly, learned ministers and challenging all students to abide in Christ. The obstacles were real. He was confronted by delicate politics and numerous administrative challenges. His agenda for reform competed with many more radical proposals for revision of curriculum or abolition of the university itself. Within the walls of the university, human philosophy pulled impressionable minds towards pride and rationalism. Matthew Henry relates his father's struggle to associate with other students at Oxford who would influence him rightly:

> But there were others that were of the old Spirit and way, Enemies to the Parliament, and the Reformation they made; and these were the better *Scholars,* but generally not the better *Men.* With them for a while he struck in because of their Learning, and conversed most with them, but

---

[130]Vincent, *Words of advice to young men* (1668).

[131]Locke, *Some thoughts concerning education* (1693), 33; cf. Feingold, 'The humanities', 319. Locke does recommend that a child learn by memory 'the Lord's Prayer, the Creeds, and Ten Commandments'; Locke, *Some thoughts concerning education*, 185. The relationship between the Christ Church dean and his temperamental scholar is highly intriguing. Owen probably contributed to Locke's understanding of toleration, although direct influence is difficult to pinpoint. What is clearer is that Locke's 'doctrinal minimalism' is in contrast with his former dean's 'robust confessionalism', as is Locke's affinity for viewpoints promoted by Latitudinarians and Cambridge Platonists; Svensson, 'John Owen and John Locke', 306–10; Nathan Guy, *Finding Locke's God*, 63–73. For a positive construal of Owen's influence on Locke's understanding of toleration, see Toon, *God's statesman*, 62; Guy, *Finding Locke's God*, 54; Gribben, *An introduction to John Owen*, 95–6, 147–9.

[132]Joseph Alleine is best known for his posthumous publication, *An alarme to unconverted sinners* (1675). For a study on Alleine's significance among nonconformists, see Wallace, *Shapers of English Calvinism*, 121–66.

he soon found it a snare to him, and that it took him off from the Life of Religion, and Communion with God.[133]

Outside its walls, Oxford enticements allured teenage desires. And every scholar's worst enemy – the flesh – was a constant companion.

Amid these sobering realities Owen pinned his hopes not on curriculum or policy but on a Christological worldview that integrated biblical revelation, redemptive history, spiritual union and devotion. He recognized that one filters what he studies through the grid of what he loves. Human learning bears the remnants of an original theology given so that mankind could know and worship the triune God. But because sin has deeply affected human knowledge, only Gospel theology revealed through a divine mediator opens the way to commune with God. Spiritual life, as experienced in fellowship with Father, Son and Spirit, inclines the soul to battle against fleshly lusts and to rightly interpret human knowledge. For Owen, true education flows from the wisdom of Christ revealed in Scripture and experienced affectively in worshipful devotion.[134]

---

[133]Henry, *An account of the life and death of Mr. Philip Henry* (1698), 22. Matthew Henry also remarks that, 'for many years' after the Act of Uniformity (1662), his father recommended that fathers send their sons to study at Oxford. However, when Matthew's time for university arrived, Philip Henry trained him at home: 'But long experience altered his mind herein, and he chose rather to keep *his own Son* at home with him, and to give him what help he could there, in his Education, than venture him into the Snares and Temptations of the *University*'; ibid., 132–3. The elder Henry's choice for his son provides evidence that Owen's vision had not prevailed at Oxford.
[134]Owen developed the theme of Christ's supremacy throughout his writings, including the work published shortly after his death, *Meditations and discourses on the glory of Christ*. In its preface Owen declared, 'The revelation made of Christ in the blessed Gospel is far more excellent, more glorious, and more filled with rays of divine wisdom and goodness, than the whole creation and the just comprehension of it, if attainable, can contain or afford. Without the knowledge hereof, the mind of man, however priding itself in other inventions and discoveries, is wrapped up in darkness and confusion'; Owen, *Meditations and discourses on the glory of Christ* (1684), sig. A4; *Works* (1965), 1:275.

CHAPTER 8

Owen and the Church of England

LEE GATISS

In a recent book on church polity and politics in the seventeenth century, Elliot Vernon sums up the Reformation Church of England thus: 'The church settlement of England's Elizabeth I, combining an Episcopalian structure, a traditional liturgy, Reformed confessional theology and magisterial supremacy would become a cherished institution for many Christians throughout the British Atlantic world.' On the other hand, however, 'to others, the worship and polity of the Church of England continued to remain "but half-reformed" and unfit for the evangelical mission of Protestantism'.[1] These four aspects of the Tudor legacy, it might be said, constituted the main pillars of Anglican ecclesiology: episcopacy, liturgy, Reformed theology, and royal supremacy over both church and state. The son of a clergyman, John Owen was born into this church, and was ordained into it himself, becoming not just a parish minister but a cathedral dean. Yet he died outside this church, having spent a great deal of time and effort trying to undermine two of the pillars upon which it had been built, while pleading throughout his career for a policy of ecclesiastical toleration.

Perhaps unexpectedly, Owen's dream of toleration was in seventeenth-century England only achievable with all four pillars in place and with a

---

[1] Vernon, 'Introduction: Church polity and politics in the British Atlantic world, c. 1635–66', 4–5.

Stuart on the throne. Neither the Presbyterians, with their Directory of Worship, nor Congregationalists, with their rejection of all imposed liturgies, could provide a sufficiently strong umbrella for various groups of Reformed Christians to flourish together in that febrile political atmosphere. What Owen argued for – toleration – was not possible under the system that he advocated (Independency, no set liturgy, Reformed theology and republican magisterial supremacy); and neither could the Presbyterians whom he disliked so much provide a meaningful toleration, whether with the king or without. In England, after the 1689 Act of Toleration under William and Mary, it proved possible for Congregationalists, Presbyterians, Particular Baptists and Episcopalians to co-exist in a stable, peaceful toleration under Anglicanism. Yet Owen's consistent advocacy of the theology of the Thirty-nine Articles of Religion was one of the factors contributing to the success of that magisterial Act, the benefits of which he never lived to see or enjoy.

ANGLICANISM

As John Coffey has written, 'Historians used to trace the ecclesiastical divide to a fundamental theological rift between "Anglicans" and "Puritans". Increasingly, however, scholars have emphasized the doctrinal common ground shared by Calvinist conformists and Puritans.'[2] It has also been clear, at least since the work of Patrick Collinson, that the Puritans usually were Anglicans, in the sense that they were not normally separatists working outside the national established Church of England but a movement working for reform from within. As Collinson so helpfully concluded, 'That our modern conception of Anglicanism commonly excludes Puritanism is both a distortion of a part of our religious history and a memorial to one of its more regrettable episodes.'[3] Importantly, Anglicanism was first defined, as a word, in the year that John Owen was born. *Ecclesia Anglicana* had long been the Latin designation for the Church of England, of course, and both 'Anglican' and 'Anglical' were used in the seventeenth century to describe religion in that green and pleasant land.[4] The more abstract concept, however, did not gain its '-ism' in English until 1616. For it was then that the Roman Catholic polemicist Thomas Harrab published a scurrilous pamphlet called *Tessaradelphus, or The four brothers*, in which he sought to lay out the main points of what he called 'the four Principal Sects, which are either allowed, or permitted in some countries

---

[2]Coffey, 'The Bible and theology', 389.
[3]Collinson, *The Elizabethan Puritan movement*, 467.
[4]For both terms, for example, see Heylyn, *Theologia veterum: or, The summe of Christian theologie* (1654), where 'Anglican' appears on the third page of 'To the Reader' and on 368, and 'Anglical' appears in the Syllabus Capitum for Book 3 Chapter 6 (around 514).

here in Europe'.⁵ He sought to undermine the claims of these 'sects' to be fundamentally agreed on matters of faith against the 'Catholike and universall Church of Christendome', in order to tarnish Protestantism with a reputation for encouraging 'the multitude of petite sects'. The 'religions' that Harrab targeted were Lutheranism, Calvinism, Anabaptism and 'Anglianism' – the last admittedly without the more common 'middle "c"'. 'I call the religion of England Anglianism', Harrab declared, 'because it among the rest hath no one especial Author, but is set forth by the Prince, and Parliament'. It was the religion, he said, not just of England but also of Scotland and Ireland, since the king of England was now king of those other kingdoms too. Harrab claims that while Henry VIII did not really change religion 'but in a few points', his son adopted a mixture of Lutheranism and Calvinism. Elizabeth I, he asserts, disliked both Luther and Calvin, but kept some semblance of the old order in the way things were done. Harrab's main concern is with outward aesthetics: vestments, ceremonies, liturgical calendar, systems of church governance and so on. He concludes that observing these, one may plainly see 'the religion of England, is composed of Catholike Religion, of Lutheranisme, and Calvinisme, and yet approveth no one of them, but differeth much from every one, singled out by themselves'. In his view, the English church was a most unholy mixture.

Thomas Harrab was thus the first person to define 'Anglianism', in print, as a distinctive, mediating form of the Protestant heresy. But was he right to do so? Some Church of England clergy would themselves see a certain moderation in ceremonial aspects as one of the great strengths of the established religion. In his poem 'The British Church', for example, the country parson George Herbert (1593–1633) exults: 'I Joy, deare Mother, when I view / Thy perfect lineaments, and hue / Both sweet and bright.' His mother church is 'Neither too mean, nor yet too gay' in her outward appearance; neither wantonly painted like Rome, nor too shyly modest like Geneva. The Church of England, and she alone, was 'double-moated' with God's grace, avoiding both extremes.⁶ Later in the seventeenth century, others would take up this thought and give it a decidedly doctrinal twist. The Laudian propagandist Peter Heylyn (1599–1662), for example, spoke of 'the Anglican Church' as a distinctive entity, separate from the Reformed churches of Europe, and played up its links with second-generation Lutheranism in order to oppose the Calvinian understanding of the Church of England's foundations.⁷ One popular Arminian ploy (borrowed

---

⁵Harrab, *Tessaradelphus* (1616), A.ii and E.iv.
⁶Herbert, *The temple* (1633), 102. This was published by Philemon Stephens, who also published Owen's first book, *A display of Arminianisme* (1643).
⁷Heylyn, *Ecclesias restaurata*, I, 193. See Gatiss, *The true profession of the gospel*, 21–3, on Heylyn's polemic and the link with Lutheranism as an evasion of Anglicanism's Reformed confessional theology.

from Romanist polemics) that he also pressed into service was to intimate that Reformed theology was an insidiously 'foreign' influence upon the Church of England, emanating particularly from Switzerland but also from the foreign wives of early reformers such as Archbishop Cranmer, Bishop Hooper and the famous Bible translator Myles Coverdale.[8] On the other hand, the Spanish Jesuit Francisco Suarez (1547–1617) simply thought that the English had been more or less Calvinist since Queen Elizabeth, and that 'the Anglican sect, which is Calvinist, whether pure or mixed with other errors, is a heresy, and all those who obstinately follow it are heretics'.[9] In the nineteenth century, J. H. Newman was perhaps the most prominent advocate of the so-called *via media* approach to Anglican identity. Some have even said that it was he, and the Oxford Movement, that invented the idea of 'Anglicanism' (especially since the *Oxford English Dictionary* does not seem to have yet noticed Harrab's far earlier use of the term). So it has become popular to describe the Anglican religious ethos as a middle way between Rome and Geneva, a *tertium quid*, or a careful balancing act. Ironically, however, it was this very conception that pushed Newman himself into becoming a Roman Catholic, as he rejected such attempts at 'balance' or compromise during theological crises (such as semi-Arianism and semi-Pelagianism) as fatally flawed both doctrinally and historically.[10]

Some historians speak of the post-Restoration eclipse or 'overthrow of Calvinism'.[11] J. I. Packer says that after 1662, 'Calvinism had the status only of an oddity maintained by Nonconformists'.[12] Yet, as Stephen Hampton and others have demonstrated, while after 1662 the Reformed may not have been in the majority, they remained an extremely significant group within the church.[13] Conscious of standing within a much wider European Reformed tradition, they were also keen to demonstrate that they were the heirs of a respectable home-grown branch of that movement. Many of these men taught what Hampton describes as 'Reformed divinity, but with Restoration curlicues',

---

[8] MacCulloch, *The boy king*, 167, 170–2.
[9] 'Posteà verò tempore Elizabethæ Caluinismus introductus est, idemque usque in hunc diem, vel omniuò, vel maiori ex parte perseuerat . . . ergò dubitari non potest sectam Anglicanam, quæ Caluiniana est, siue pura, siue mista ex alijs erroribus, hæresim esse, omnesque illam pertinaciter sequentes, hæreticos esse.' Suarez, *Defensio fidei Catholicae et Apostolicae adversus Anglicanae sectae errores* (1614), 128 (1.22.9).
[10] See for example Newman, *Apologia pro Vita Sua*, 144: 'I saw clearly, that in the history of Arianism, the pure Arians were the Protestants, the semi-Arians were the Anglicans, and that Rome now was what it was then. The truth lay, not with the *Via Media*, but with what was called "the extreme party"'.
[11] See, for example, Cragg, *From Puritanism to the age of reason*, 13.
[12] Packer, 'Arminianisms', 289.
[13] See Hampton, *Anti-Arminians*, 269; cf. Griesel, 'John Edwards of Cambridge (1637–1716)'.

that is, ornamental twists associated with the neo-Laudian agenda, such as a devotion to episcopacy as of the *esse* of the church (rather than simply for its *bene esse*, its well-being), the suppression of Nonconformity, and use of high-church stage props like robes, candles, elaborate church architecture and furnishings. This makes some of the Reformed Anglicanism of this period a somewhat peculiar and eccentric phenomenon within the wider intellectual movement, but still recognizably Reformed in terms of its soteriology and other major doctrinal commitments.

What is often missed in this debate about the essence of Anglicanism, however, is the fundamental position of the Thirty-nine Articles of Religion and the official confessional formularies of the Church of England. Let us return to what Thomas Harrab said in 1616: 'I call the religion of England Anglianism, because it among the rest hath no one especial Author, but is set forth by the Prince, and Parliament.' What was it that prince and Parliament had established? Not the codified religion of a single visionary – which some sectarian spirits have in the past used as the basis for their denominations and cults. No, Anglicanism has 'no one especial Author' and was not merely the eccentric dream of one man. Rather, the established church followed a collectively defined and corporately decided path, as Protestant and Reformed. This church did so by accepting a Reformed confession of faith, the Thirty-nine Articles.

THE PURITANS AND THE THIRTY-NINE ARTICLES

Puritans in the English church were not entirely unhappy that the Articles were enshrined in the Elizabethan settlement. Parliamentary debates in 1571 show MPs concerned for the doctrinal soundness and Protestant orthodoxy of ministers, and asking for a confession like their Reformed counterparts on the Continent. However, an *Act to reform certain disorders touching Ministers of the Church* (13 Eliz. c.12) prescribed assent 'to all the Artycles of Religion, which onely concerne the Confession of the true Christian Faithe and the Doctrine of the Sacraments'.[14] As William Haugaard notes, 'The "onely" was to permit Puritans of tender conscience to subscribe the doctrinal articles but not such "disciplinary" articles as those on the traditions of the church and the consecration of bishops.'[15] In the House of Commons, William Strickland

---

[14]See Strype, *Annals of the Reformation and establishment of religion,* volume 2, part 1, 104–5. Strype conjectures that the limitation of subscription to those major doctrinal and sacramental articles was for the sake of those who wanted to have a new confession drawn up, but it was the Articles that were accepted as that confession.
[15]Haugaard, *Elizabeth and the English Reformation,* 257.

(d. 1598) pleaded for liberty of conscience and some amendments in these traditional and ceremonial matters, claiming that,

> although the Book of Common Prayer is (God be praised) drawn very near to the sincerity of the truth, yet are there some things inserted more superstitious, than in so high matters be tolerable; as namely, in the Administration of the Sacrament of Baptism, the sign of the Cross to be made with some Ceremonies, and such other Errors, all which, he said, might well be changed, without note of chopping or changing of Religion, whereby the Enemies might slander us; it being a Reformation not contrariant, but directly pursuant to our Profession, that is, to have all things brought to the purity of the Primitive Church, and institution of Christ.[16]

The bishops, however, decided to insist not only on conformity to the doctrinal and sacramental articles (Articles 1–18, 25–31) but to all of them, via canon law. The articles, they said, 'in all points agree with the heavenly doctrine' contained in the Bible, and both the Book of Common Prayer and the ordinal by which archbishops, bishops, ministers (*presbyterorum*) and deacons are consecrated 'contain nothing repugnant to the same doctrine'. Therefore all preachers must 'not only in their preaching but also by subscription confirm the authority and truth of those articles', and that on pain of excommunication.[17] This is why, at the Hampton Court Conference in 1604, Puritans renewed their request that clergy be made to subscribe only 'according to the statutes of the realm': they were happy to be held to Reformed orthodoxy on the major doctrines of the faith (including those which differentiated the Anglican Church from the Lutheran) but wished to be permitted some leeway with regards to holding alternative views on episcopacy and the disputed ceremonies. King James was not minded to allow this.[18] Neither were the bishops. The Canons of 1603 (1604) were even more explicit in prohibiting dissension regarding ceremonies and episcopal government.[19]

After a protracted campaign to undermine the already fragile settlement by Archbishop Laud and his co-religionists, many Puritans felt they had

---

[16] d'Ewes, 'Journal of the House of Commons: April 1571', 155–180. Strickland spoke of the English as 'men not sufficiently instructed what is truth, or so that we think it not convenient to publish and profess it openly, and that all reproachful Speeches of the slanderous might be stopped, the draw-backs brought forward, and the Over-runners, such as over-run, and exceed the rule of the Law, reduced to a certainty, he thought it *Operæ pretium*, to be occupied therein; for which purpose he said, the Professors of the Gospel in other Nations, had writ and published to the World the Confession of their Faith, as did those of *Strasburgh* and *Franckford*, &c'.
[17] From the Canons of 1571, in *The Anglican canons*, 198–9.
[18] See Hampton, 'Confessional identity', 219–20.
[19] *The Anglican canons*, 272–7 (Canons 6–8 of 1603/04).

had enough. The Root and Branch Petition was presented to the House of Commons in 1640, demanding the overthrow of 'prelacy', that is, the episcopal system of church governance: it claimed that 'the said government is found by woeful experience to be a main cause and occasion of may foul evils, pressures and grievances of a very high nature'.[20] Sometime later, both Houses of Parliament declared that 'they intend a due and necessary reformation of the government and liturgy of the Church, and to take away nothing in the one or the other but what shall be evil and justly offensive, or at the least, unnecessary and burdensome'.[21] In 1643, the Solemn League and Covenant bound its signatories to the 'reformed religion' and especially in England to the 'reformation of religion in the kingdoms of England and Ireland, in doctrine, worship, discipline and government, according to the Word of God, and the example of the best reformed Churches'. It particularly engaged them to 'endeavour the extirpation of Popery, prelacy (that is, Church government by Archbishops, Bishops, their Chancellors and Commissaries, Deans, Deans and Chapters, Archdeacons, and all other ecclesiastical officers depending on that hierarchy)'.[22] The Westminster Assembly of Divines was called initially to amend the Thirty-nine Articles of Religion, not because they were not Reformed, but to make them less susceptible to Laudian spin: 'to free and vindicate the Doctrine of them from all aspersions and false interpretations'.[23] The divines broke off from this task before it was completed, having made some light revisions to the Articles, because they were asked to consider church government instead and, eventually, to prepare a new confession and catechisms. This is vital context for understanding Owen's attitude towards the English church, its confession of faith, its worship and its governance. His peculiar emphases on doctrinal Anglicanism and on toleration make sense as part of this long-running story.

NO 'MERE CHRISTIAN'

After the civil wars and the rise of Oliver Cromwell, the Instrument of Government (1653) made provision for a new settlement of religion: the Christian religion was to be recognized as 'the public profession of these nations', and ministry was to be provided for out of public income (tithes), but with liberty and freedom from restraint 'provided this liberty be not extended to Popery or Prelacy'.[24] A similar proviso was contained in the Humble Petition

---

[20]*The constitutional documents of the Puritan revolution*, 137.
[21]*The constitutional documents of the Puritan revolution*, 247 (8 April 1642).
[22]*The constitutional documents of the Puritan revolution*, 268–9 (September 1643).
[23]See *The proceedings of the Assembly of Divines upon the Thirty-nine Articles of the Church of England*; *The minutes and papers of the Westminster Assembly*, 1:20–1.
[24]*The constitutional documents of the Puritan revolution*, 416 (December 1653).

and Advice (1657), which allowed for a new confession of faith to be drawn up for those ministers that were to be publicly supported, but which prevented the re-establishment of archbishops and bishops.[25] Charged with overseeing these developments, Owen and his fellow committee members presented their *Humble proposals* (1652, 1654) and *A new confession of the faith* (1654). At only a couple of pages in length, these were nowhere near as detailed as the Westminster Confession, but they were still clearly Reformed and Protestant in content and form.[26] The *Humble proposals* clearly envisaged the magistrate enforcing church attendance and clerical testing, and may have been deliberately circumspect enough to enable Arminian Puritans such as John Goodwin to sign up.[27] The *New confession* was a little sharper on original sin, and so may have been harder for such people to subscribe, as well as being even more of an anathema to Socinians. Indeed, Parliament explicitly voted to add the words 'Reformed, Protestant' to the statement 'That the True Reformed, Protestant, Christian Religion, as it is contained in the Holy Scriptures of the Old and New Testament, and no other, shall be asserted and maintained, as the publick Profession of these Nations'. It also specified that compulsory tithes should continue to support ministers: 'until some better Provision be made by the Parliament, for the Encouragement and Maintenance of able, godly and painful Ministers, and publick Preachers of the Gospel, for instructing the People, and for Discovery and Confutation of Errors, Heresy, and whatsoever is contrary to sound Doctrine, the present publick Maintenance shall not be taken away, nor impeached'.[28] Neither of these attempts at Cromwellian-era confessions, however, prescribes anything about liturgy, sacraments or church governance.

This effort to create a Cromwellian confession was supported by Sir William Strickland (1596–1673), the grandson of the Strickland who had led the Puritans in the Commons in 1571, and a Protectorate MP. Owen, however, close to the action, was the 'great doer of all that worded the Articles' in these confessions, and was careful to avoid and exclude what he saw as dangerous doctrinal heresies.[29] As with the Westminster Assembly, calling together a group

---

[25] *The constitutional documents of the Puritan revolution*, 455–6 (May 1657).
[26] Dennison, *Reformed confessions of the 16th and 17th centuries in English translation*, 4:423–31, for the text of *The humble proposals of Mr. Owen, Mr. Tho. Goodwin, Mr. Nye, Mr Sympson, and other ministers . . . for the furtherance and propagation of the Gospel in this nation* (1652) and *The principles of faith* (1654), a practically identical re-issue; and *A new confession of faith, or the first principles of the Christian religion* (1654).
[27] See Coffey, *John Goodwin and the Puritan revolution*, 234–5.
[28] *Journal of the House of Commons*, 7:397 (7 December 1654).
[29] Baxter, *Reliquiae Baxterianae* (1696), 2:198–9. Major-General John Lambert, the author of the *Instrument of government*, was later a member of one of Owen's gathered congregations, and may have been a close associate of his at this point too; see Farr, *John Lambert, Parliamentary soldier and Cromwellian Major-General, 1619–1684*, 188.

of theologians to discuss a settlement for the church exposed various fissures and factions among them, and their different approaches to achieving the peace of the church. Owen wanted a clear confession of doctrine to be at the heart of the settlement of religion, yet he found influential Puritan voices raised against this, however minimalistic the confession might be. Sarah Mortimer claims that Owen's accusation that Richard Baxter was promoting Socinianism in 1654 can only be understood in the light of these disputes about the Interregnum church settlement.[30] It was, however, part of Owen's far wider and longer-lasting defence of orthodoxy against that anti-trinitarian impulse.[31] But it is certainly the case that Baxter's approach to making a settlement was criticized for being too open to the Socinians, as was that of John Goodwin.[32]

Baxter remembered the discussions of 1654. 'I would have had the Brethren to have offered the Parliament the Creed, Lord's Prayer, and Decalogue alone as our Essentials or Fundamentals', he explained:

> which at least contain all that is necessary to Salvation, and hath been by all the Ancient Churches taken for the Sum of their Religion. And whereas they still said, [a Socinian or a Papist will Subscribe all this] I answered them, So much the better, and so much the fitter it is to be the Matter of our Concord.[33]

Although he himself was a trinitarian,[34] it is clear that he often spoke in such a way that Socinians themselves considered him to be sympathetic to their ways of thinking, and he confesses that they did at one time attempt secretly to recruit him.[35] Far from being a merely short-term political issue in 1654, it would continue to divide Owen and Baxter after the Restoration: in 1668, Baxter resisted Owen's suggestion for explicit exclusion of Socinian errors in a formula of concord between dissenters.[36]

The problem of perception on this issue of subscription to confessions was a difficult one for Baxter. He liked to call himself a 'meer Christian' and tried

---

[30] Mortimer, *Reason and religion in the English revolution*, 223.
[31] See Gatiss, 'Socinianism and John Owen', 43–62.
[32] *Faces about, or, A recrimination charged upon Mr. John Goodwin* (1644), 12. Goodwin wrote the 'Epistle to the Reader' for an edition of Acontius's *Satans strategems*, which contained a list of 'fundamentals' that 'even Socinians could endorse', according to Coffey, *John Goodwin and the Puritan revolution*, 160. Baxter defended Goodwin from the charge of Socinianism; see Cooper, *John Owen, Richard Baxter and the formation of Nonconformity*, 52 n111, 81.
[33] Baxter, *Reliquiae Baxterianae* (1696), 2:198.
[34] For example, see Baxter, *The reasons of the Christian religion*, 377: 'I unfeignedly account the doctrine of the Trinity, the very summ and kernel of the Christian Religion.'
[35] Baxter, *Reliquiae Baxterianae* (1696), 2:205–6.
[36] See their letters in Baxter, *Reliquiae Baxterianae* (1696), 3:63–5.

to promote the Bible and the Apostles' Creed as sufficient tests for orthodoxy (sometimes adding the Lord's Prayer and Ten Commandments as additional touchstones).[37] As early as 1659, he used the term 'meer Christians'[38] to describe those who took his view, and this became one of his regular slogans in later years, so that in 1680 he could write:

> I am a CHRISTIAN, a MEER CHRISTIAN, of no other Religion; and the Church that I am of is the Christian Church. . . . I am against all Sects and dividing Parties: But if any will call Meer Christians by the name of a Party, because they take up with Meer Christianity, Creed, and Scripture, and will not be of any dividing or contentious Sect, I am of that Party which is so against Parties.[39]

Indeed, one might say of Baxter's 'autobiography' that 'his attraction to "meer Christianity" functions as an organising principle throughout his narrative and colours the way he sees and describes events'.[40]

Baxter held this slogan and this approach to ecclesiology in common with some other groups, including anti-trinitarians.[41] Most prominently, John Biddle had claimed on the title page that his *A twofold catechism* (1654) was 'composed for their sakes that would fain be meer Christians, and not of this or that sect'. This claim was assailed one year later by the London Provincial Assembly, which complained, 'How blasphemously have some disputed against the infinite merit, yea, and Deity of our Saviour. . . . Thus pretending to make their disciples meere Christians, they have taken a faire course, to leave them meere Atheists.'[42] Owen also mocked Biddle's self-designation as a 'mere Christian' in *Vindiciae evangelicae* (1655), insinuating that his 'mere Christian'

---

[37] Cf. Baxter, *The Christian religion* (1660).
[38] Baxter, *Five disputations of church-government and worship* (1659), 137.
[39] Baxter, *Church-history of the government of bishops and their councils* (1680), in the section entitled, 'What history is Credible?' See the use of 'meer Christian/Christianity' in Baxter, *Christian directory* (1673), 31; Baxter, *Which is the true church?* (1679), 125; Baxter, *An apology for the nonconformists ministry* (1681), 131 (mostly written 1668-9); Baxter, *A paraphrase on the New Testament* (1685), on Rev. 13.18.
[40] Gatiss, 'The autobiography of a "meer Christian"', 169.
[41] William Chillingworth desired to see 'plain and honest Christians' who tolerated others in the name of Christ instead of fighting over party labels; Chillingworth, *The religion of Protestants a safe way to salvation* (1638), 180. The Cambridge Platonist Henry More spoke highly of 'a meer man, a true man, a Christian', as opposed to sectaries; More, *The second lash of Alazonomastix, laid on in mercie upon that stubborn youth Eugenius Philalethes* (1651), 15. The Roman Catholic author J. Lewgar, in *The only way to rest of soule in religion here, in heaven hereafter* (1657), 108–10, contrasts the 'meer Christian' to the Catholick. The Quaker author Robert Barclay, in *Universal love considered and established upon its right foundation* (1677), 30, 31, 34, praises the 'meer Christian'.
[42] [London Provincial Assembly], *An exhortation to catechizing* (1655), 3–4.

doctrine was more Islamic than Christian.⁴³ He also added an appendix to this, his major work against Socinianism, specifically aimed at Richard Baxter, an intimation of association that did not go unnoticed.⁴⁴ The Polish Socinian writer Jonas Schlichting (1592–1661) sought in his *Confessio fidei* (1642) to promote Socinian views by 'insisting on the sufficiency of the Apostles' Creed as an adequate and sufficient summary of Scripture'.⁴⁵ It was, he said, 'a full and genuine mark of Christianity'.⁴⁶ Anglicans like Jeremy Taylor (1613–67) had long been happy with this uniting approach to various sects.⁴⁷ This meant that in the mid-seventeenth century a 'meer Christian' who claimed to stand on Scripture and the Apostles' Creed alone could actually be, if pressed further, a Quaker, a Roman Catholic, an Episcopalian or a Socinian. In such a context, it was no wonder, then, that Owen and other Reformed divines not only opposed such a loose definition of essential articles of faith but could also attack Baxter's method as both sounding like and ultimately sponsoring Socinianism. Socinians did indeed promote and benefit from such tolerationism which, as Paul Lim puts it, Owen saw as a 'recipe for Socinian proliferation'.⁴⁸

It was in 1657 that Owen first gave the world a glimpse into his journey from episcopal ordination to Congregationalism. Back in 1643, as a young minister in the first year of his ministry, he explained, he had not really understood the great debates between Presbyterians and Congregationalists. Of the two, he had only known people of the former persuasion, and was convinced against episcopacy, ceremonies and 'democratical confusion' (indeed, he was still against this). He surveyed the literature and chose one book to work through methodically: John Cotton's *The keyes of the kingdom* (1644). This book persuaded him of Congregationalism, 'contrary to my expectation, at a time, and season wherein I could expect nothing on that account but *ruine* in this world'.⁴⁹ As Oliver Cromwell approached his end, and with the Presbyterians once more in the ascendent, Owen and his fellow Independents tweaked the Westminster Confession of Faith in their Savoy Declaration (1658). This had some eccentricities of its own, but was purposely framed with a view to achieving a workable compromise with the Presbyterians by demonstrating their doctrinal

---

⁴³Owen, *Vindiciae evangelicae* (1655), 32; *Works* (1965), 12:76 (see his censure of 'mere Christian' in *Works*, 12:70).
⁴⁴Baxter, *Reliquiae Baxterianae* (1696), 1:111.
⁴⁵Williams, *The Polish Brethren*, 2:386. Williams claims this approach dates back at least to Hilary and was shared by Erasmus.
⁴⁶Williams, *The Polish Brethren*, 2:391.
⁴⁷Taylor, ΘΕΟΛΟΓΙΑ ΕΚΛΕΚΤΙΚΗ (1647), 32–3, suggests that Papists, the Greek church, Lutherans, Zwinglians, Calvinists, Socinians, Anabaptists and Ethiopian (Nestorian) churches could all unite around the Apostles' Creed.
⁴⁸Lim, *Mystery unveiled*, 251.
⁴⁹Owen, *A review of the true nature of schism* (1657), 36; *Works* (1965), 13:223.

accord on the vast majority of issues.[50] Naturally, the Savoy divines also added a Congregationalist postscript on church government, which made it clear that, in their view, 'besides these particular churches, there is not instituted by Christ any church more extensive or catholic entrusted with power for the administration of His ordinances, or the execution of any authority in His name'.[51] There ought still to be 'public maintenance' of preachers according to this declaration on church order, but the power of censure or excommunication should not be given to either magistrates or trans-local synods.[52]

If a doctrinal consensus could have been reached on the basis of something like the Westminster Confession, there might have been scope for a toleration that still permitted Congregationalists to peacefully co-exist. This would have fulfilled a hope that had been expressed in Parliament back in 1644, to consider differences about church governance in order 'to endeavour a union if it be possible' and, if not, to find some way of tolerating tender consciences 'as may stand with the publique peace'.[53] As Ryan Kelly has argued, by saying this, the Independents were 'making a subtle-yet-persistent case for the past *legality* of Nonconformity alongside a Presbyterian State church'.[54] At the same time, they were conscious that one ought not to compel people to subscribe to such a confession of faith: 'Whatever is of force or constraint in matters of this nature causeth them to degenerate from the *name* and *nature* of *Confessions*, and turns them from being *Confessions of Faith*, into *exactions* and *impositions of Faith*.'[55] Owen did think that the state had a duty to stop anti-trinitarians infiltrating the church, and to silence those who rejected justification by faith alone; indeed it was against the light and law of nature, he said, for supreme magistrates not to exert their authority to support, preserve and further the cause of the Gospel

---

[50]See Woolrych, *Britain in revolution*, 717, though note also the caution about Woolrych's sources in Kelly, 'Reformed or reforming?', 14.
[51]Dennison, *Reformed confessions*, 4:490 (§VI).
[52]See Dennison, *Reformed confessions*, 4:492–3 (§XVI, §XXII).
[53]See the 'Preface' in [Savoy Declaration], *A declaration of the faith and order owned and practised in the Congregational churches in England* (1658); *The Savoy Declaration of faith and order, 1658*, ed. Matthews, 70, which quotes this remit of a Parliamentary committee verbatim from the House of Commons Journal of 13 September 1644. Cf. Kelly, 'Reformed or reforming?', 22.
[54]Kelly, 'Reformed or reforming?', 24. [Savoy Declaration], *A declaration of the faith and order owned and practised in the Congregational churches in England* (1658) states that 'this Christian clemency and indulgence in our Governors, hath been the foundation of that *Freedom and Liberty*, in the managing of Church-affairs, which *our Brethren* as well as *WE*, that differ from them, do now, and have many years enjoyed'.
[55]*A declaration of the faith and order owned and practised in the Congregational churches in England* (1658), 'Preface' (this is usually considered to have been written by Owen, although Increase Mather identified Thomas Goodwin and Philip Nye as its 'penmen'; BL Add Ms 23622, fol. 132); [Savoy Declaration], *The Savoy Declaration*, ed. Matthews, 51–2. Cf. Owen, *Two questions* (1659), 6–7; *Works* (1965), 13:514.

and forbid, coerce and restrain false teaching.[56] John Milton even wrote some nasty things about him because of this: in a famous poem that hailed Oliver Cromwell as 'our chief of men', Milton warned that 'new Foes arise / Threatning to bind our Souls in secular Chains', and appealed to the revolutionary hero to 'save Free Conscience from the paw / Of Hireling Wolves, whose Gospel is their Maw'.[57] Yet the Independents also recognized that there ought to be an indulgence for all who 'hold fast the necessary foundations of faith and holiness', even if they disagree on 'other matters extrafundamental'. 'This to have been our constant principle, we are not ashamed to confess to the whole Christian world.'[58] They also claimed, via a footnote to *English Puritanisme* (1641), to be in a direct line of descent on these issues with 'the *old Puritan non-Conformists*'.[59]

So Owen was somewhat flexible on the issue of confessions. When Baxter was pushing for mere minimalism, Owen was worried about Socinianism but did in fact get behind a fairly minimal approach to doctrinal confession, in the *Humble proposals* and the *New confession of faith* – both far shorter and less detailed than the Westminster Confession but still clearly and carefully trinitarian and Reformed. When the political turn of the tide made a deal with the Presbyterians a more likely path to peace, he was able to use the Westminster Confession as a basis for the Savoy Declaration, to show how much common ground they had, but without neglecting to spell out his preferred form of church governance. After all, as John Cotton (who had originally persuaded Owen of Congregationalism) wrote, 'error in Judgment about Discipline is not a Heresie against the Foundation of Christian Religion'.[60] Owen could even complain to the secretary of the Council of State about worthy men such as Edward Pococke being persecuted on the basis of what Owen described as 'slight and trivial pretences', that is, for their continued (and illegal) use of the Book of Common Prayer. As Gribben comments, 'Even for pious prayer

---

[56]For example, Owen, *Two questions* (1659), 1–6; *Works* (1965), 13:509–13.
[57]Milton, *Letters of state written by Mr. John Milton* (1694), xlv.
[58][Savoy Declaration], *A declaration of the faith and order owned and practised in the Congregational churches in England* (1658), 'Preface'; *The Savoy Declaration*, ed. Matthews, 56. Regarding the consistency, see Lechford, *Plain Dealing*, 9–10, who speaks about John Cotton's willingness to be flexible on some issues of church governance, but not on the twelve articles of doctrine that he considered to form 'the foundation of religion'; and see the similar phrase and idea in Owen, *A brief vindication of the non-conformists* (1680), 23; *Works* (1965), 13:320.
[59][Savoy Declaration], *A declaration of the faith and order owned and practiced in the Congregational churches in England* (1658), 'Preface'; *The Savoy Declaration*, ed. Matthews, 72. Bradshaw, *English Puritanisme*, is a collection of Puritan opinions on various issues by Fox, Deering, Greenham, Cartwright, Perkins and others translated from a 1610 publication, *Puritanismus Anglicanus*, said to have been written by William Ames (1575–1633).
[60]Cotton, *Certain queries tending to an accommodation and communion of Presbyteriall and congregational churches* (1654), 8.

book Anglicans, Owen could be a formidable ally.'[61] The important thing for 'magisterial Congregationalists' such as Owen was to try to unite 'the Reformed centre ground', as Hunter Powell puts it.[62] At the same time, Owen continued to push the idea that the state ought to exert its power and authority 'for the supportment, preservation and furtherance of the worship of God, and to coerce and restrain that which would ruine it'.[63]

EJECTED BUT STILL CONFESSING

Following the instability of the later years of the Protectorate came a restoration of monarchy and prelacy in 1660. Initially, some parties entertained hopes for some kind of compromise system of ecclesiastical polity and a reformation of liturgy. As some earlier proposals were republished, including Archbishop James Ussher's plan for 'Reduced episcopacy',[64] Owen fought back against plans to re-impose a set liturgy. The Cavalier Parliament's Act of Uniformity (1662) put an end to such hopes, though various changes were made to the Book of Common Prayer (few of which were comfortable for the Puritans). There followed a period of persecution for Protestant dissenters under the so-called Clarendon Code.[65]

Throughout this period, Owen wrote against the imposition of liturgies per se, seeing this as contradictory to the gifting given to pastors by the ascended Christ, as mentioned in Eph. 4.11.[66] He had no argument particularly with those who thought liturgies were the best way of discharging their ministerial duty, he explained: 'It is onely about its Imposition, and the Necessity of its Observance by vertue of that Imposition, that we Discourse.'[67] He may have overstated his case, however, because it led him to assert that the Lord's Prayer, 'which the Lord Jesus prescribed unto his disciples, for their present practice in the worship of God, seems to have belonged unto the economy of the Old Testament'. One cannot argue from the use of the Lord's Prayer under the old covenant that New Testament Christians also require such prescribed forms of prayer, he continued, because that would be 'to deny that Christ is ascended on high, and to have given spiritual Gifts unto men, eminently distinct from, and

---

[61]Gribben, *John Owen and English Puritanism*, 153.
[62]Powell, 'Promote, protect, prosecute', 227.
[63]Owen, *Two questions* (1659), 2; *Works* (1965), 13:510.
[64]Ussher, *The reduction of episcopacie* (1660). Richard Baxter was keen on this proposal.
[65]See Gatiss, *The tragedy of 1662*.
[66]Owen, *A discourse concerning liturgies* (1662), 12, 57, 60, 61; *Works* (1965), 15:10–11, 47, 50, 51, for his use of Eph. 4.7-13 in this argument.
[67]Owen, *A discourse concerning liturgies* (1662), 40; *Works* (1965), 15:34. Cf. page 24; *Works* (1965), 15:21.

above those given out by him under the Judaical Pedagogy'.[68] He had earlier written against the use of the Lord's Prayer as a form, per se, in *Vindiciae evangelicae* (1655), adding that there was no evidence that the apostles had ever used or prescribed it as such.[69] Later, in 1670, he did seem to backtrack from what some called his 'blaspheming the Lord's Prayer'. Rumours had circulated that he wore his hat when the Lord's Prayer was being said, a sign that he did not esteem it, and he had previously published a refutation of that rumour in 1655. But after Méric Casaubon (1599–1671) published a defence against their 'ungrounded zeal who are so strict for the observation of the Lord's Day and make so light of the Lord's Prayer',[70] Owen insisted in a letter:

> I do, and ever did, believe it the most perfect form of prayer that ever was composed, and the words of it so disposed by the divine wisdom of our blessed Saviour that it comprehends the substance of all the matter of prayer to God. I do, and did always, believe that it ought to be continually meditated on, that we may learn from thence both what we ought to pray for and in what manner.

However, he stuck to his guns in saying, 'I judge not that our Lord Jesus Christ, in the giving of this prayer unto his disciples, did prescribe unto them the precise use or repetition of those words, but only taught them what to pray for or how.' Yet, at the same time, he admitted, 'it is true, I have said that there were manifold abuses in the rehearsal of it amongst people ignorant and superstitious; and I did deliver my thoughts, it may be, too freely and severely, against some kind of repetition of it'.[71] He also corrected what he claimed was a false impression about his view of Anglicans who were happy to use the Book of Common Prayer. Someone, he explained, had poisonously concluded that

> I judge, that all who in the worship of God make use of the *Common prayer*, are not loyal to Christ, nor have communion with God, nor can promote the interest of the Gospel; all which are notoriously false, never thought, never spoken, never written by me. And I do believe, that many that have used that book in the publick administrations, have been as loyal to Christ, had as

---

[68] Owen, *A discourse concerning liturgies* (1662), 16; *Works* (1965), 15:14.
[69] Owen, *Vindiciae evangelicae* (1655), 667–9; *Works* (1965), 12:577–9.
[70] Casaubon, *A vindication of the Lords prayer* (1660).
[71] Owen, 'Reflections on a slanderous libel against Dr. Owen, in a letter to Sir Thomas Overbury' (1670), in *A complete collection of the sermons of the reverend and learned John Owen*, ed. Asty, 618–20; *Works* (1965), 16:276–8.

much communion with God, and been as zealous to promote the interest of the Gospel, as any who have lived in the world this thousand years.[72]

To invent and lay down liturgies was a new way of excluding people from the church, Owen explained, which the apostles never considered in their day. However, he did concede that 'Confessions of Faith, or acknowledged Forms of wholesome Words, with the care of the Disciples of Christ, or his Churches, which are enabled by him to judge and discern of Truth and Error, are the preservations against the danger intimated, that the Gospel hath provided'.[73] In 1663, however, he would complain that since people do not have the same measure of understanding in the things of God, 'to frame for them all, in rigid confessions, or systems of supposed credible propositions, a Procrustes' bed to stretch them upon, or crop them unto the size of, so to reduce them to the same opinion in all things, is a vain and fruitless attempt, that men have for many generations wearied themselves about, and yet continue so to do'. There should be no 'anathemas upon *propositions* arbitrarily composed and expressed, *philosophical conclusions, rules of faith* of a mere human composure', though it may be permissible to 'testify the voluntary consent of men's minds in expressing to their own satisfaction the things which they do believe', which would bring the church 'nearer unto quietness than most men imagine'. In other words, it was still pointless to try and compel people to agree to a confession that they did not really own for themselves. There should not be exactions or impositions, as he had argued a few years previously.

> When Christians had any unity in the world, the *Bible* alone was thought to contain their Religion, and every one endeavoured to *learn* the mind of God out of it, both by their *own endeavours*, and as they were instructed therein by their *guides*. . . . Nor will there ever, I fear, be again any *Unity* among them, untill things are reduced to the *same state* and condition.[74]

This being said, it was permissible, 'for the more open declaration and proposition of the truths of the Gospel which they profess, and for the vindication both of the truth, and themselves, from false charges and imputations', for churches to pen confessions of faith as a *'form of sound words'*.[75] In 1667, Owen defended the confession that had been agreed upon by the Independent divines at the Savoy. First, he claimed, its contents were consonant with 'the judgment of *the*

---

[72]Owen, 'Reflections on a slanderous libel', 618; *Works* (1965), 16:275–6. See Hyde, 'John Owen on public prayer', 238–54.
[73]Owen, *A discourse concerning liturgies* (1662), 33; *Works* (1965), 15:28.
[74]Owen, *A vindication of the animadversions on Fiat lux* (1664), 210–11; *Works* (1965), 14:314.
[75]Owen, *A brief instruction in the worship of God* (1667), 199–200; *Works* (1965), 15:530.

primitive church': 'the first four general councils, as to what was determined in them in matters of faith, are confirmed by law in this nation; which is all that from antiquity hath any peculiar stamp of authority put upon it amongst us: this also we willingly admit of, and fully assert in our confession'. Second, he continued, when it was compared to 'the confessions of the reformed churches', the Savoy Declaration was 'in all material points the same with them'. Third, among those Reformed confessions, the Thirty-nine Articles had a special place, and he was content to subscribe to their doctrinal content. 'That which amongst them is of most special regard and consideration unto us, is that of the *Church of England*, declared in the *Articles of Religion*: and herein, in particular, what is purely *Doctrinal*, we fully embrace, and constantly adhere unto.' Thus, he repeated the standard Puritan line. He also felt he ought to defend the way in which Savoy had expanded on the Articles in the light of later developments:

> It is true indeed, there are some *Enlargements* in our Confession of the things delivered in the Thirty Nine Articles, some Additions of things not expressly contained in them, which we were necessitated unto, for the full declaration of our Minds, and to obviate that *obloquy* which otherwise we might have been exposed unto, as reserving our Judgement in matters that had received great publick debate since the composure of those Articles: But yet we are fully perswaded, that there is not any proposition in our whole Confession, which is repugnant unto any thing contained in the Articles, or is not by just consequence deducible from them. Neither were we the *Authors* of the Explanations or Enlargements mentioned; there being nothing contained in them, but what we *have learned* and been instructed in from the Writings of the most famous *Divines* of this Nation, *Bishops* and *Others*, ever since the Reformation; which being published by *Legal Authority*, have been always esteemed, both at home and abroad, faithfully to represent the Doctrine of the *Church of England*. We have *no new faith to declare, no new doctrine to teach, no private opinions to divulge*; no Point or Truth do we Profess, *no not one*, which hath not been declared, taught, divulged, and esteemed as the common Doctrine of *the Church of England*, ever since the Reformation.[76]

The political purpose of this confessional situating was to defend his post-Restoration Nonconformity to the Church of England. It seemed strange to him and others that dissenters should be treated as severely as those who utterly renounced 'that doctrine which is here publickly avowed, and confirmed by Law'. Why, since they did not seek to challenge or upset 'public tranquility', should orthodox dissenters not be left unmolested to enjoy their 'Publique Rights

---

[76]Owen, *A peace-offering* (1667), 12–13; *Works* (1965), 13:551–2.

as *English Men*, and benefit of their private Estates'?[77] His small congregation managed to survive amid the persecution of the age by 'staying under the radar' of the authorities as much as possible, but also perhaps by judicious use of their wealth.[78] It would be better, however, if it could have a more stable and legally recognizable foundation.

OWEN AND THE GLORIOUS REVOLUTION

The end of the 'Long Reformation', and what proved to be a more stable system, came with the Toleration Act of 1689.[79] This enabled Protestant dissenters to co-exist alongside the established church, such that Congregationalists, Presbyterians and even Baptists could publicly assemble in a legal way, though it was still some time before they enjoyed the same level of civil liberties as those in the established church. It was not, however, an ecclesiastical free-for-all. Section 6 of the Toleration Act enjoined toleration of certain nonconforming, dissenting churches on the basis that their ministers subscribe to the Thirty-nine Articles with the exception of article 34 ('On the traditions of the church'), article 35 ('Of homilies'), article 36 ('Of consecration of bishops and ministers') and the first sentence of article 20 ('The church hath power to decree rites and ceremonies, and authority in controversies of faith'). This, essentially, is what the Puritans had tried to achieve in 1571, although the toleration of Baptists was surely something more than they could have imagined.[80] Had James I granted by grace what William and Mary were able to allow only after the tumultuous middle years of the century, might England have been spared civil war and ecclesiastical strife?

What would Owen, who died in 1683, have thought about this 'glorious revolution', had he lived to see it? Some have tried to claim Owen for the Baptist cause of late, because of what I have argued is a misreading of his covenant theology.[81] I have shown elsewhere that Owen was a consistent

---

[77] Owen, *A peace-offering* (1667), 13; *Works* (1965), 13:552–3.
[78] Owen's wealth is suggested by the impressive contribution of £1,000 that was made in his name to the 1670 dissenters' loan to the crown. Other members of his congregation made smaller contributions. See De Krey, *London and the Restoration, 1659–1683*, 127, 409.
[79] 1 William III and Mary II, c.18.
[80] In 1648, Parliament had declared that those who held to 'a difference about a circumstance of time in the administration of an ordinance' could still be considered orthodox; see *A declaration of the Lords and Commons assembled in Parliament concerning the papers of the Scots Commissioners* (1648), 50–1. The Act for confirming and restoring of ministers (1660) removed what few Baptists there were from the ministry of the public church. Matthews, *Calamy revised*, xv, notes that under the indulgence of 1672, just over 200 ministers were licenced as Baptists, but of them only 5 were among the officially ejected of 1660–2.
[81] See, for example, Denault, *The distinctiveness of Baptist covenant theology*, which, perhaps jokingly, refers to 'John Owen the Baptist'.

advocate for infant baptism throughout his life, and that according to him, his covenant theology supported, promoted and demanded the practice.[82] However, he did not, like some Presbyterians, want to criminalize Baptists.[83] In 1657, he compared Baptists to Donatists, but said it would be difficult to label them schismatics for their errant doctrine of baptism alone.[84] And while he refused in 1669 to defend their opinions and practices, saying 'you know our judgment and practice to be contrary unto theirs . . . wherein (God assisting) we shall continue to the end', he did write to the governor of Massachusetts that it was not 'indispensably necessary' to be quite so rigorous in physically punishing Baptists in the new world.[85] Others have tried to claim Owen for Presbyterianism.[86] Yet if we examine Owen's own writings, we can see that in many ways – important ways – he was far more Anglican than anything else. This is true despite the fact that Owen was, from 1662 onwards, excluded from the established church by the iniquitous Act of Uniformity. As we will see, both before and after that moment of defeat and dejection, Owen claimed (quite sincerely and with a straight face) to be in line with the doctrine of what Thomas Harrab had called 'Anglianism'. At the same time, he was a pertinacious advocate for toleration, under a Reformed Protestant umbrella, of various different groups.

For Owen, the *Ecclesia Anglicana* went back to the very earliest days of Christianity. In print at least, he was convinced that the Gospel had been brought to England in the first century by Joseph of Arimathea, whose feet had walked upon England's 'mountains green'.[87] Like Thomas Harrab, Owen also recognized that at the Reformation, the Church of England did not follow any particular individual, but that her glory consisted in the very fact that she

---

[82]See the much-expanded version of an earlier paper in Gatiss, '*Cornerstones of Salvation*', 159–201.
[83]See *An ordinance for the punishing of blasphemies and heresies*, in *Acts and ordinances of the Interregnum, 1642–1660*, 1133–6, which would have criminalized those who taught that 'the baptizing of Infants is unlawfull, or such Baptism is void, and that such persons ought to be baptized again, and in pursuance thereof shall baptize any person formerly baptized'.
[84]Owen, *Of schisme* (1657), 226; *Works* (1965), 13:184.
[85]*The correspondence of John Owen*, 145–6. This letter is addressed from Owen and other Independent ministers.
[86]See Lee, *John Owen represbyterianized*, as well as the comments of Owen's nineteenth-century editor in *Works* (1965), 16:2. Goold's edition routinely drops the capital letters in Church (of England) and Articles (of Religion), which can obscure Owen's meaning and relationship to the established church.
[87]Owen, *Animadversions on a treatise intituled Fiat lux* (1662), 42, 248; *Works* (1965), 14:19, 95, and *A vindication of the animadversions on Fiat lux* (1664), 38, 425; *Works* (1965), 14:206, 394. These are strange books, with the feel of being position papers written on someone else's behalf. I have often wondered, just as Francis Walsingham commissioned the controversial Presbyterian Thomas Cartwright to confute the Rheims New Testament, in the hope of sapping his potentially divisive scholarly energies by directing them towards anti-Roman polemics, whether the earl of Clarendon had the same thought regarding Owen, and that these *Animadversions* are the result.

corporately adopted a more biblical confession. 'It was not *Luther*, nor *Calvin*, but the Word of God, and the practise of the primitive church, that *England* proposed for her rule and pattern in her Reformation', he explained; and 'where any of the *Reformers* forsook them, she counted it her duty, without reflexions on them, or their wayes, to walk in that safe one, she had chosen out for herself'.[88] This word of God even made it clear that Henry VIII and his successors ought to be head of the church; this meant, said Owen,

> no more, but that there was no other person in the world, from whom any Jurisdiction to be exercised in this Church over his Subjects might be derived, the Supreme Authority for all exterior Government being vested in him alone. That this should be so, the Word of God, the nature of the Kingly Office, and the antient Laws of this Realm, do require.[89]

So as far as 'the Practical Truths of the Gospel' are concerned, 'they are maintained, and asserted in the Church of *England*'.[90]

Yes, Owen was a Puritan, but he had been ordained as an Anglican minister (a deacon in 1632 at the very early and uncanonical age of sixteen; and a presbyter or priest in 1638) by the bishop of Oxford – though he later claimed that he had never taken the oath of canonical obedience in doing so.[91] He served for several years as the vicar (in succession) of two parish churches in Essex, before becoming the dean of the Cathedral Church of Christ in Oxford. Indeed, it is often not mentioned, but almost all the great Puritans celebrated these days were episcopally ordained Anglican ministers: William Perkins, Richard Sibbes, Edmund Calamy, Edward Reynolds, Richard Baxter, William Gouge, Thomas Manton, Samuel Bolton, Ralph Venning, Stephen Charnock and Thomas Goodwin. The Westminster Confession was written mostly by men ordained into the Anglican Church.[92] Puritanism was, for most of its history, a strong and vibrant force within the Church of England, even under 'prelacy'. After the 1662 Ejection, many Puritans still attended their parish churches, and not all Puritan ministers were ejected or remained forever outside the national church.

---

[88] For example, Owen, *Animadversions on Fiat lux* (1662), 275; *Works* (1965), 14:109. See also *Works* (1965), 14:19, 95–6, 206, 331–2, 394.
[89] Owen, *Animadversions on Fiat lux* (1662), 271; *Works* (1965), 14:107.
[90] Owen, *Animadversions on Fiat lux* (1662), 167; *Works* (1965), 14:65.
[91] Owen, 'Reflections on a slanderous libel', 618; *Works*, 16:276. In *A discourse concerning evangelical love* (1672), 208, 214; *Works* (1965), 15:161, 164, Owen declares this oath to be unscriptural and 'contrary to the Liberty, and unworthy of the Office of a Minister of the Gospel', particularly since no exceptions were permitted to be expressed.
[92] None of the Scottish commissioners is among the twelve most frequent contributors in the Westminster Assembly. See *The minutes and papers of the Westminster Assembly*, 1:212–13.

His old tutor from Queen's College, Thomas Barlow, observed in January 1669 that Owen had kissed the king's hand, and there were rumours that he or Richard Baxter would receive the next vacant bishopric.[93] This indicates Owen's continuing prominence, although, just as Baxter had refused Hereford when offered it in 1660, he would surely have refused any other see had such a position actually been offered to him. Like his father, whom he described as a Nonconformist, Owen identified as a Puritan because he was not in favour of some aspects of the church's governance and ceremonies. In 1657, in a rare personal comment that tied together his public and private lives, Owen revealed that he had been 'bred up from my infancy under the care of my father, who was a Nonconformist all his days, and a painful labourer in the vineyard of the Lord', and 'so ever since I came to have any distinct knowledge of the things belonging to the worship of God, I have been fixed in judgment against that which I am calumniated withal', that is, episcopacy and 'ceremonies'.[94] Owen's father was a parish minister in Oxfordshire, whose 'Nonconformity' did not equate to separatism from the national church but merely dissent from various aspects of prayer book worship, such as kneeling to receive the Lord's Supper, making the sign of the cross on a child's forehead in baptism, wearing the surplice in church services or objecting to wedding rings (though Owen does not explain exactly how this Nonconformity was expressed). Yet doctrinally, Owen always claimed to be entirely in accord with the confessional basis of Anglicanism, as it had been corporately established by prince and Parliament.

As Gribben explains, 'it is unlikely that Owen had any difficulty with the doctrinal content of the articles: his publications in the 1640s would enthusiastically endorse the Thirty-nine Articles as being entirely opposed to the new Arminian menace'.[95] Indeed, in his first published work, Θεομαχία αυτεξουσιαστικη: or, A display of Arminianisme (1643), Owen considered the popish-Arminian errors of Belgic semi-Pelagians to be 'a doctrine so opposite to *that truth our Chruch* [sic] hath quietly enjoyed, ever since the first reformation'.[96] He spoke about the doctrine of predestination 'with special reference to the seventeenth Article of our Church, where it is cleerly avowed',[97] and of the 'grosse *Pelagianisme*' of Episcopius on faith and free will as being

---

[93]Greaves, 'Owen, John (1616–1683)'. See also Toon, *God's statesman*, 129, on a report that an offer was actually made.
[94]Owen, *A review of the true nature of schisme* (1657), 38; *Works* (1965), 13:224. We must note here that at this stage the term 'Nonconformist' usually referred to a clergyman who dissented from some of the official positions of the Church of England (often related to ecclesiology) but remained within her bounds. After 1662, however, it would come to refer to those dissenters who were ejected from or unable to join the established church.
[95]Gribben, *John Owen and English Puritanism*, 35.
[96]Owen, *A display of Arminianisme* (1643), 'The Epistle Dedicatory', A; *Works* (1965), 10:6.
[97]Owen, *A display of Arminianisme* (1643), 50; *Works* (1965), 10:53.

contrary to the doctrine of the Church of England, citing article 10.[98] Indeed, even in 1669 he could write that 'the chief glory of the *English Reformation* consisted in the purity of its Doctrine, then first restored to the nation. This, as it is expressed in the Articles of Religion, and in the publickly authorized Writings of the Bishops and chief Divines of the Church of *England*, is, as was said, the glory of the English Reformation'.[99] Rather than focusing on aesthetics or adiaphora, if we ask what Owen believed in terms of basic doctrine, we can point to the articles of religion. As he himself says of those articles, 'what is purely *Doctrinal*, we fully embrace, and constantly adhere unto'.[100] Even after 1662, he was happy to say, 'I embrace the Doctrine of the Church of *England*, as declared in the *29 Articles* [sic], and other approved publick writings, of the most famous Bishops and other Divines thereof.'[101] That is tighter than the current form of subscription required of ministers in the Church of England; and note again the corporate nature of the doctrine he aligned himself with.

It is, of course, true that during this period of persecution Owen would have had a political motive in affirming that he still held to the Reformed consensus of the church. He no doubt meant to shame those in the post-Restoration church who did not hold sincerely to those articles (and who were at that time actively persecuting dissenters). He could also imply that though they were now excluded and penalized by the Conventicle Act (1664) and the Five Mile Act (1665), he and other Nonconformists had not moved away from the teaching that had been officially confessed by the Church of England for over a century. Indeed, from his first book in the 1640s onwards, he was perfectly capable of attacking the established church while simultaneously defending its constitution, highlighting (as Gribben puts it) 'that prominent individuals in the English hierarchy, including the archbishop of Canterbury, were insufficiently Anglican'.[102] Owen was not forced to embrace and publicly affirm this as he did; but it remained his consistent doctrinal stance, for he always refused to cede legitimacy to those theological cuckoos who had invaded the Church of England's nest. This was politically expedient for him, as it highlighted the iniquity of his forced alienation from the national church, which was in some respects abandoning its own foundational formularies. Later, this could also serve as a rallying cry for all Protestants against the resurgent Roman Catholicism that was being sponsored by James, Duke of York, the future James II.

What was this Anglican confessional doctrine to which Owen adhered? He would not, of course, have approved of Laudianism. He was implacably

---

[98] Owen, *A display of Arminianisme* (1643), 132–3; *Works* (1965), 10:122–3.
[99] Owen, *Truth and innocence vindicated* (1669), 33–4; *Works* (1965), 13:354.
[100] Owen, *A peace-offering* (1667), 12; *Works* (1965), 13:551.
[101] Owen, *A vindication of the animadversions on Fiat lux* (1664), 21; *Works* (1965), 14:196.
[102] Gribben, *John Owen and English Puritanism*, 48.

opposed to the 'Antichrist' and his religion, believing the Church of Rome to have committed heresy, schism, apostasy and idolatry.[103] And as for high-church stage props and the sumptuous outward aesthetic beloved of that movement, he declared: 'In worship, their paintings, crossings, crucifixes, bowings, cringings, Altars, Tapers, Wafers, Organs, Anthems, Letany [Litany], Rails, Images, Copes, vestments; what were they, but *Roman vernish* [varnish], an *Italian* dresse for our devotion, to draw on *conformity* with that enemy of the Lord Jesus?'[104] However, on the Trinity, on Scripture, on predestination, free will, the role of the law and the sacraments, Owen was as Reformed as were the Articles. He also affirmed that on the subject of justification by faith and the imputation of the righteousness of Christ, he was entirely on the side of the Church of England's authentic writings, 'that is', he said, 'the *Articles of Religion*, and *Books of Homilies*, and other Writings publickly authorized'. In his 1677 book on justification, which expounds and defends the 'comfortable doctrine' of justification by faith alone, he added, 'I shall not in the least depart from the *ancient Doctrine of the Church of England*; yea, I have no design but to declare and vindicate it, as God shall enable.'[105] This is why in 1670 he pleaded for liberty for Protestant dissenters, even offering to subscribe to the Articles as a condition of doing so:

> We do therefore humbly desire, *First*, That we may have an exemption from all laws and penalties, civil or ecclesiastical, for our dissent in some things from the Church of *England*, as at present established in the rule of it; and a liberty to worship God peaceably in our own assemblies; upon our renunciation of Popery, by law prescribed, and the subscription of our ministers, or publick teachers, unto the *articles* of religion, as before expressed.[106]

In 1672, Owen thanked the king for his declaration of indulgence, but it was not long until he was before him again to complain about the treatment of Nonconformists.[107] Moreover, a certain Dr Goodman, an Anglican rector, published *An inquiry into the causes of the present separation from the Church of England* (1674) in order to attack Nonconformists for preferring what he

---

[103] Owen, *Animadversions on Fiat lux* (1662), 70–1; *Works* (1965), 14:29–30.
[104] Owen, *A vision of unchangeable free mercy* (1646), 29; *Works* (1965), 8:28.
[105] Owen, *The doctrine of justification by faith* (1677), 229–30; *Works* (1965), 5:164.
[106] Owen, *An account of the grounds and reasons on which Protestant dissenters desire their liberty* (1670), in Asty (ed.), *A complete collection*, 593; *Works* (1965), 13:578. It is likely that Owen meant to exclude such articles as concerned 'church order, rule, and worship', as in the immediate passage he mentioned differing from the Church of England in those principles.
[107] *CSPD*, 28 March 1672; *CSPD*, 15 January 1675 (Yarmouth).

regarded as the terrible and desperately foreign Synod of Dort to Anglican doctrine. Owen included an aside against Goodman in his work on the nature of apostasy two years later:

> It is but a pretence, that those whom he reflects upon do dislike *the Doctrine of the Church of England*. For look upon it as it is contained in the *Articles of Religion*, the *Books of Homelies*, and declared in the Authenticated Writings of all the Learned Prelates and others for *Sixty years* after the Reformation, wherein the Doctrine taught, approved, and confirmed in this Church, was testified unto all the world; and the generality of those reflected on by him do sacredly adhere unto it.[108]

What Nonconformists disliked, he said, was beneficed clergymen such as Goodman defecting from that established doctrine themselves, while praising the work of Curcellæus (1586–1659) or Limborch (1633–1712), from the Remonstrant Seminary in Amsterdam – an action that could by no means be reconciled with the Thirty-nine Articles on 'the most weighty points of Religion'. If only the Church of England would adhere to its own doctrine, 'established at the first Reformation, as explained and declared in the Writings of the principal Persons who presided, lived and died in the Communion of this Church, which are the Measure of it in the judgement of all other Churches in the World', then, Owen insisted, there would be 'neither difference nor complaint in this Matter'.[109]

There were some in the seventeenth century who attacked orthodox Nonconformists, but who left all manner of heretics alone merely because they conformed. This was scandalous to Owen: 'it is somewhat strange to me', he wrote, that

> whilst one writes against *Original Sin*, another preaches up *Justification by Works*, and scoffs at the *Imputation of the Righteousness of Christ* to them that believe; yea, whilst some can openly dispute against *the Doctrine of the Trinity*, the *Deity of Christ*, and *the Holy Ghost*; whilst Instances may be collected of some mens impeaching all the *Articles* almost throughout, there should be no Reflection in the least on these things; only those who dissent from some outward Methods of Worship must be made the Object of all this wrath and indignation.[110]

---

[108] Owen, *The nature of apostasie* (1676), 157; *Works* (1965), 7:74.
[109] Owen, *The nature of apostasie* (1676), 157–8; *Works* (1965), 7:74–5.
[110] Owen, *Truth and innocence vindicated* (1669), 34; *Works* (1965), 13:354–5.

This was his consistent complaint. In his first published book, well before all the unhappy troubles that were to come in the civil war, Owen gave some instances of people 'opposing the received doctrine of *the Church of England*, contained in divers of the 39 Articles'. We are living in iniquitous times, he said, because 'had a *poor Puritan* offended against half so many *Canons* as they opposed *Articles*, he had forfeited his livelihood, if not endangered his life'. It was acceptable to many to oppose the doctrine of the Articles of Religion but not to break the outward minutiae of canon law; indeed, even many senior church leaders 'were so zealous for the discipline, and so negligent of the Doctrine of the Church'.[111] Owen considered this an outrage, because he was deeply attached to the Reformed doctrine of the Church of England.

In 1680, after many difficult years for Nonconformists, Owen was still pleading for toleration, but within a magisterial, Reformed framework. 'Let there be one solemn stated *Confession of the* Christian Protestant Faith, such as is the Doctrine of the Articles of the Church of *England*', he advised in *Some considerations about union among Protestants* (1680), 'especially as explained in the publick authorized writings of the Church in the Days of *Queen Elizabeth and King James*, before the Inroad of Novel Opinions among us; to be subscribed by all enjoying a publick Ministry'.[112] At the same time,

> let the magistrate assume unto himself the exercise of his just power, in the preservation of the public peace in all instances; in the encouragement and protection of the professors of the Protestant religion . . . leaving only things purely spiritual and evangelical to the care and power of the churches . . . and a great progress will be made towards order and peace amongst us.

So Protestantism ought to be established: 'Let the *King and Parliament* secure the Protestant Religion, as it is the publick Interest of the Nation, against all Attempts of the Papacy for its Destruction, with proper Laws, and their due execution', while at the same time 'Provision be made for the sedulous Preaching of the Gospel in all Parts and Places of the Land, or all *Parochial* Churches, the care whereof is incumbent on the Magistrates'.[113] Yet all the while, he continued to be watched by Government informers, who attended his church to observe and hear him at close quarters.[114] He was even charged under the so-called Clarendon Code legislation, and liable to huge fines.[115]

---

[111]Owen, *A display of Arminianisme* (1643), 'To the Christian Reader'; *Works* (1965), 10:9.
[112]Owen, *Some considerations about union among Protestants* (1680), 11; *Works* (1965), 14:526.
[113]Owen, *Some considerations about union among Protestants*, 12; *Works* (1965), 14:526.
[114]*CSPD*, 19 February and 1 March 1682. See Greaves, *John Bunyan and English Nonconformity*, 160, and Greaves, *Secrets of the kingdom*, 93.
[115]See Gribben, *John Owen and English Puritanism*, 259.

THE TRUE PROFESSION OF THE GOSPEL

At the end of this turbulent period, in 1689, the coronation oath for King William and Queen Mary was specifically written to bind the new monarchs to the established religion of their kingdoms. What did Scottish Presbyterians with their Westminster Confession have in common with their Episcopal English neighbours and their Thirty-nine Articles? Like the Dutch Calvinism of the new king, both were, in essence, considered different manifestations of 'the true profession of the gospel . . . the Protestant Reformed religion'. Kings had sworn to uphold the 'true profession of the gospel' before, but only now was this more carefully defined. In the Parliamentary debate about the coronation oath, it was initially suggested that the king should be asked to maintain the 'Protestant religion', without any additional qualifier. Perhaps some at this stage may have used 'Reformed' merely as a synonym for non-Catholic. Yet there was a recognition in the debate that there might be other forms of Protestant religion besides 'Reformed', and that the (Lutheran) Augsburg Confession did not correspond as closely to it as might be imagined. It also seems to have been presupposed that adding 'Reformed' narrowed the doctrinal emphasis while still denoting a doctrinal stance that could have varying manifestations in terms of church discipline, polity and practice – just as in 1654, when 'Reformed, Protestant' was added to the Protectorate's definition of the public faith. Some Anabaptists called themselves 'Reformed' too, MPs noted in 1689, and provided they demonstrate this by signing up to the doctrinal parts of the Thirty-nine Articles, their meetings would be granted toleration.[116]

Hunter Powell argues that the 'solution to the attempt simultaneously to tolerate and to restrict was a tension that perhaps could only have been resolved in the person of Oliver Cromwell'.[117] However, this tension was in fact resolved in William and Mary, and the 1689 Act of Toleration, which restricted the national establishment to those in favour of episcopacy and liturgy, but extended toleration to others if they submitted to the role of the magistrate and signed up for the common confessional Reformed theology of the Articles. So, as Gribben puts it, 'the result of this protracted debate was that the religious settlement of the Glorious Revolution was essentially the settlement for which Owen had been arguing for the previous forty years.'[118] It could have ended differently. Michael Winship has written that in England 'only relatively small numbers of Puritans adopted Congregationalism . . . while other Puritans no less intensely opposed it. The wound Congregationalism created in English Puritanism would never heal, and it helped ensure that Puritan efforts to bring

---

[116]See *Debates of the House of Commons, from the year 1667 to the year 1694*, 9:190–8.
[117]Powell, 'Promote, protect, prosecute', 237.
[118]Gribben, *An introduction to John Owen*, 149.

about reformation in England failed.'[119] The Congregationalism of people such as Owen was, he says 'a bitter, divisive disappointment', which led to 'the failure and collapse of the Puritan reformation'.[120] However, if we see Owen's achievement as helping to maintain and defend 'the true profession of the gospel . . . the Protestant Reformed religion established by law', through a period when other definitions of religion could have risen to supremacy and the protection of the law could have been removed from this Gospel altogether, then it does not have to be seen as such a disappointment. He may have died 'in the wilderness', as he told Charles Fleetwood he feared he might;[121] but he would surely have seen the post-1689 religious scene as a recognizable form of the promised land that he had been seeking on earth.

'We still confesse our selves members of the *Church of England*', said Owen in 1657. '[W]e owne our selves to have been, and to be *Children of the Church of England*.'[122] This aspect of his thinking is rarely noted.[123] Owen was astute, changing his approach to promoting the Protestant Reformed religion depending on the prevailing political circumstances of the time. When under episcopacy, leaning on the Articles, but feeling his way towards a distinctive ecclesiology; when having to compromise with 'meer Christians', taking a more minimalist but still firmly Reformed approach; when attempting rapprochement with Presbyterians, adapting their Confession but without failing to take an Independent negotiating stance; when once again under episcopacy, returning to reliance on the Thirty-nine Articles. He was consistently in favour of an established, magisterial Reformed Protestant church, an 'Anglianism' established by prince and Parliament (or Protector and Parliament) of a Calvinistic flavour, such as Suarez or Harrab would recognize from the outside as the distinctive Anglican heresy. He fought for further reformation of this system throughout his ministry, wanting to purge it of Arminians, Socinians, Grotians and the scandalously unqualified. He wished for more liberty from set forms of prayer, and more independence in church government, but his stance towards the Thirty-nine Articles throughout his career is not strange and inexplicable when seen against the backdrop of the century as a whole and the long-term goals of the Puritan sensibility since at least 1571. As David Clarkson said in his funeral sermon, Owen 'did not affect Singularity, especially in vindicating those Truths that were transmitted to us by our first Reformers, and were owned by the best Divines of the Church of *England*'.[124]

---

[119]See Winship, *Hot Protestants*, 4.
[120]Winship, *Hot Protestants*, 145–6.
[121]*The correspondence of John Owen*, 159 (from 1674).
[122]Owen, *Of schisme* (1657), 225–6; *Works* (1965), 13:184.
[123]I made some of these points in Gatiss, 'Adoring the fullness of the Scriptures in John Owen's commentary on Hebrews', 194, noting that it is often simply assumed that Owen looked to the Westminster Confession or Savoy Declaration as his confessional standard.
[124]Clarkson, 'A funeral sermon of the much lamented death of the late reverend and learned divine John Owen, D.D.', 1:lxxiv.

CHAPTER 9

Owen the polemicist

PAUL C.-H. LIM

In *A Dialogue between the pope and the devil, about Owen and Baxter* (1681), a broadside with an improbable title, the pope fulminated against the 'evils' brought by 'Scribbling Fellows' whose penchant to 'write for ever' produced a 'a Heap of *Quarto's;* and another of *Folio's'*. The character was concerned about the steady demand for works by Baxter and Owen from readers who 'Dote on their Labours'. The dire consequence of their literary success meant the loss of foothold of the Jesuit encroachment upon the souls of England: 'a MASS-BOOK, a Crucifix, or such like things cannot so much as oblige them to cast one Courteous Eye towards them'. The pope denounced those who 'Ridicule and Laugh at my Pictures', and those who refuse to fall 'down to my Breaden-GOD, that the Villains despise it as they do the Organs in the Church!' Consequently, he dispatched the Devil to concoct a diabolical plan to 'lessen their increasing Number', likely referring to the 'hotter sort of Protestants', a phrase popularized by Patrick Collinson, who were devouring publications by Owen and Baxter.[1] Written at the height of the Exclusion Crisis – when the conversion to Catholicism of James, Duke of York (1633–1701), was the cause of rebuff he suffered at the hands of such subjects of his brother Charles II as Anthony Cooper, Earl of Shaftesbury (1621–83) and James Scott, Duke of Monmouth (1649–85) – one can read this pamphlet as a clear indicator of

---

[1]*A dialogue between the pope and the devil, about Owen and Baxter* (1681), 1; Collinson, *The Elizabethan Puritan movement*, 27.

the ferocity of the religious conflict afoot and the role that was being played by these two dissenters.[2]

In what follows, we shall highlight a few salient aspects of the literary career of John Owen, focusing on his engagement as a polemicist, illuminating his contribution to intra-Protestant and inter-confessional polemical exchanges. Owen's theology was formed in response to the constant ebbs and flows of polemical and political situations in seventeenth-century England. They were, inter alia: the civil wars; the regicide of Charles I; the Interregnum, Commonwealth and Protectorate, under the rule of Oliver Cromwell; the restoration of monarchy and episcopacy in 1660; the experiences of dissent and defeat; and the rise and fall of Calvinist orthodoxy, Arminian ascendency, anti-trinitarian heresy, and the meteoric rise of Quakerism and other vagaries of theo-political dramas in England's 'Long Reformation'.

As a young student at Oxford under the tutelage of Thomas Barlow, the Bodleian librarian and an intellectual gadfly, Owen's intellectual *habitus* was formed by the influence of Greek philosophy (both Aristotle and Plato), patristic theology and medieval scholasticism. Seen throughout his polemical treatises is Owen's own Renaissance self-fashioning by copious citations from and engagement with figures such as Aristotle, Cicero and Gregory Nazianzen, often in Greek, and less frequently without specific citations, as a display of his erudition that may have been intended to cow his opponents into intellectual submission.[3]

Keenly aware of the multifarious theological controversies raging in Europe as well as in Britain, both as a chief theological architect during the Protectorate and as vice-chancellor of one of Europe's leading centres of learning, the University of Oxford, between 1652 and 1657, Owen assiduously thrust himself – and was thrust upon by the desires of both his supporters as well as his pugilists – in most major polemical controversies of the day. Owen was deeply connected with the continental 'Republic of Letters', thus abetting his library acquisitions as well as intelligence gathering of the spread of 'dangerous ideas' that would unsettle the Reformed orthodoxy that, to him, was synonymous with true Christianity. Consequently, while it is possible to deal with nearly all aspects of his controversial engagement with what he perceived to be threats to

---

[2]On the exclusion crisis, see Knights, *Politics and opinion in crisis, 1678–81*; Harris, *London crowds in the reign of Charles II*, esp. chap. 5; Glassey, 'Shaftesbury and the exclusion crisis', 207–31; Clarke, 'Re-reading the exclusion crisis', 141–59. For religious milieu of this period, see Spurr, 'Religion in restoration England', 90–124; De Krey, 'London radicals and revolutionary politics, 1675–1683', 133–62.
[3]For a fascinating look at Owen's personal library collection, see Gribben, 'John Owen, renaissance man? The evidence of Edward Millington's *Bibliotheca Oweniana*', 321–32. See also Trueman, *John Owen*.

Reformed orthodoxy, we shall delimit the scope of our investigation, analysis and interpretation to the following three aspects of Owen's role as a polemicist. They are Arminianism, trinitarianism, and Christology.

ARMINIANISM

Owen's first foray into publication focused on the perceived threat of Arminianism to English Christianity. His 'anti-Arminian' rebuttal had a couple of significant predecessors. William Perkins, often heralded as the key figure in Elizabethan Puritanism, defended an Augustinian view of predestination, especially in *De praedestinationis modo et ordine* (1598), as a way out of the 'predestinarian labyrinth' in which many Christians were trapped. While reading this treatise by Perkins, Jacob Arminius, then a pastor in Amsterdam, unleashed his moral outrage and theological horror by responding to Perkins in order to restore the legacy of Calvin.[4] Arminius's response to England's most celebrated theologian was arguably the precipitating cause of the Arminian revolt, namely the Calvinistic determinism, which allegedly made God the author of sin, thereby exacerbating the problem of theodicy, at the metaphysical level, and its implications for pastoral theology and practical divinity. The second Anglo-Dutch theological war happened in 1618 when the British delegates were dispatched by James I to settle the ecclesiastical-cum-political mayhem caused by the Arminian Remonstrants at the Synod of Dort. As Anthony Milton, Nicholas Tyacke, Margo Todd and W. B. Patterson have persuasively demonstrated, the British delegates were seen as moderating Calvinistic voices, offering a genuine Reformed alternative to the hyper-leaning Calvinism of Francis Gomarus and Johannes Maccovius.[5]

Here are two interesting, though not altogether surprising, factoids about the Synod of Dort and its connection with Owen's sustained attack on Arminianism. First, whereas Owen's polemical archnemesis, Richard Baxter, never tired of extolling John Davenant (1572–1641), one of the leading British delegates of Dort, who had been a beloved Jacobean theologian-cum-bishop, both Lady Margaret Professor of Divinity at Cambridge and bishop of Salisbury

---

[4]Perkins's *De praedestinationis mode et ordine* is discussed in Patterson, *William Perkins and the making of a Protestant England*, 80–9. On Jacobus Arminius, the remaining classic is Bangs, *Arminius*. See also Muller, *God, creation, and providence in the thought of Jacob Arminius*; Muller, 'The Christological problem in the thought of Jacobus Arminius', 145–63; Stanglin, *Arminius on the assurance of salvation*; Stanglin and McCall, *Jacob Arminius*; and van Leeuwen, Stanglin and Tolsma (eds), *Arminius, Arminianism, and Europe*.
[5]Milton (ed.), *The British delegation and the Synod of Dort (1618–19)*; Milton, *Catholic and reformed: The Roman and Protestant churches in English Protestant thought 1600–1640*, 418–35; Tyacke, *Anti-Calvinists*, 87–180; Todd, 'Justifying God', 272–90; Patterson, *King James VI and I and the reunion of Christendom*, 260–92.

from 1621 until his death, which was likely to have been James's gift to the erudite ecclesiastical 'diplomat', Owen went after his posthumous reputation. The fact that Owen would mark the boundaries of Reformed orthodoxy so as to exclude the deeply revered theologian whose Calvinistic bona fides had never been seriously questioned prompted Baxter to declare war on Owen.[6] The second factoid concerns the figure of Hugo Grotius. He had been tried and imprisoned between 1618 and 1621 as a consequence of the Synod of Dort, which deemed Grotius to be one of the major culprits for stirring the otherwise tranquil pot of Dutch Reformed theology.[7] In most of Owen's treatises dealing with justification and Socinianism, particularly *Of the death of Christ, the price he paid, the purchase he made* (1650) and *Vindiciae evangelicae, or The mystery of the Gospel vindicated, and Socinianism examined* (1655), Grotius is mentioned as the ultimate bête noire 43 and 134 times, respectively. To be more precise, the overwhelming majority of Owen's citations of Grotius sought to render the Dutch jurist singularly responsible for vitiating the belief on Christ's satisfaction of divine justice and averting of God's wrath.

Crawford Gribben noted that Θεομαχία αυτεξουσιαστική: or, A display of Arminianisme (1643) was a well-calibrated effort on Owen's part to launch his ecclesiastical career by sycophancy, since it 'evidenced its author's obvious intention to bring himself to the attention of those best placed to advance his career, and it was advertised as being dedicated to the lords and gentlemen of the parliamentary Committee for Religion'.[8] Employing a slippery slope argument, a mode of polemic *au courant* among some heresy-hunters such as Thomas Edwards and Ephraim Pagitt who were – as contemporaries of Owen – equally deeply troubled by the proliferation of the gangrene (per Edwards's memorable title of his heresiography: *Grangræna* [1646]), Owen noted even from the title page that Arminians were Pelagians *redivivus*. Before we set off in a detailed look at the specifics of Owen's polemic, it behoves us to ask this question: 'What was Owen afraid of?' Put differently: 'Why was Owen reacting so virulently against that particular articulation of doctrine espoused by so and so?' In that vein of polemical engagement, Owen averred that Arminians were 'hewing at the *very root* of Christianity' in their denial of the 'fundamental Article of *Original sin*'. If that were so, then the *reductio ad absurdum* of Arminian theology was that there was no need for Christ himself, since '*our nature be not guilty, depraved, corrupted*'.[9] Owen puts it epigrammatically: no church true to its orthodox roots can be so capacious and charitable as to

---

[6]See Owen, 'To the reader', in *Of the death of Christ* (1650), sigs. A1v-A2r; *Works* (1965), 10:432.
[7]On Grotius's trial and imprisonment as a result of the Synod of Dort, see Butler, *The life of Hugo Grotius*, 97–123.
[8]Gribben, *John Owen and English Puritanism*, 46.
[9]Owen, *A display of Arminanisme* (1643), sig. A1v; *Works* (1965), 10:7.

include '*Austin* and *Pelagius*; *Calvine*, and *Arminius*'.[10] Furthermore, he called Arminians Satan's 'Emissaries' who were superlative in 'skill and diligence' whose feigned 'pretence of furthering Piety' was a mere prevarication against the 'very *grounds of Christianitie*'.[11]

Owen saw his task in *A display of Arminianisme* as the defender of divine sovereignty, since the Arminians were the 'modern blinded Patrons of humane selfe-sufficiencie' who were eagerly 'erecting this Babel'. Their ultimate aim was twofold: 'First, to exempt themselves from Gods jurisdiction, to free themselves from . . . all-ruling providence', and instead to 'have an absolute independent power' independently of God, grounding their sufficiency on nothing but 'chance, contingencie, and their owne wils', which Owen called out as a most 'nefarious, sacrilegious attempt'. To achieve this end of the emancipation of human subjection from the concatenating bondage of divine sovereignty, Owen thundered, Arminians denied the 'eternitie and unchangeablenesse of Gods decrees', opting instead for 'temporary and changeable' decrees that were dependent upon the 'several mutations he sees in' human actions. In other words, for the Arminian, predestination was not anchored immutably on God's own decree and covenant of redemption, as Calvin, Gomarus, Maccovius and now Owen had fastidiously averred. The second part of the twofold folly and heterodoxy of the Arminians was their jettisoning of the 'præscience, or foreknowledge of God'. The claim was predicated on this rationale. If God foreknows all contingent events before they come to being, then it 'seems to cast an infallibilitie of event upon all their actions' which will inexorably encroach upon a sacrosanct realm of 'their new goddesse': contingency. Owen summed up the tragic upshot of this anthropocentric revision of God-human modality:

> They depose the all-governing providence of this King of Nations, denying its energeticall, effectuall power, in turning the hearts, ruling the thoughts, determining the wils, and disposing the actions of men, by granting nothing unto it, but a *generall power*, and influence, and used, according to the inclination, and will of every particular agent: so *making Almighty God a desirer*, that many things, were otherwise, then they are, and *an idle spectator of most things* that are done in the world.[12]

Owen closes his first chapter of attacking Arminianism by encapsulating its *telos* as divided spoils between God and humans: '*neo Deo, nec libero Arbitrie,*

---

[10] Owen, *A display of Arminianisme* (1643), sig. A1v; *Works* (1965), 10:7.
[11] Owen, *A display of Arminianisme* (1643), sig. A3v; *Works* (1965), 10:8.
[12] Owen, *A display of Arminianisme* (1643), 3; *Works* (1965), 10:12.

sed dividatur: not all to God, nor all to Free-will, but let the Sacrifice of praise, for all good things, be divided between them'.[13]

As Christopher Cleveland judiciously noted, Owen displays a great deal of indebtedness to Aquinas, thereby making *A display of Arminianisme* a 'most Thomistic' work, refracted through the perspectives of Protestant scholasticism as well as Suarez's metaphysical commitments.[14] Either way, Owen would argue, Arminianism was an aberration of the grossest sort. Owen also seems to be offering a harbinger-like perspective of the rise of Enlightenment rationalism when he argues that the Arminian efforts to carve out some epistemic 'elbow room' for human beings to prepare for divine grace, as well as the notion that God's predestinating grace was predicated on the foreseen knowledge of human response to God, would inexorably lead to an emancipation of humanity from the concatenating bondage of God's predestinating and all-willing knowledge. For Owen, this Arminian slippage was a highway to hell, whereas for Arminians and their modern descendants – as secularists or Enlightenment *philosophes* – to leave nothing to human participation was but a continuation of 'self-incurred immaturity' under the thumb of the predestinarian God of Calvin. It is arguably the case that the deity against whom many Enlightenment thinkers revolted and repudiated was the God of Calvin, the God of double-predestination, which ended up disenchanting the mystery of divine sovereignty and human responsibility, as Roy Porter noted that the 'displacement of Calvinism by a confidence in cosmic benevolism blessed the pursuit of happiness'.[15] For the Arminians, then, this immaturity was nothing, as Immanuel Kant would later put it, but an 'inability to make use one's own understanding without direction from another'.[16] To be sure, the fraught enterprise of any intellectual 'genealogical accounts' emerges here in that no matter how 'modernistic' Arminius was, it would be preposterous to conclude that he was attempting to rob God's glory by dividing up the praiseworthy good between humankind and God, which would inexorably lead to atheism. Quite the opposite: Arminius was indefatigably seeking to restore the beauty of the Gospel of God's grace by removing the thorn of God being the potential author of sin.[17] For Owen,

---

[13] Owen, *A display of Arminianisme* (1643), 5; *Works* (1965), 10:14.
[14] Cleveland, *Thomism in John Owen*.
[15] Porter, *The creation of the modern world*, 15; Clark, 'Providence, predestination and progress: Or, did the Enlightenment fail?', 559–89. On the changing contours of Calvinism in England and its Arminian challenges which presaged a more robust repudiation of predestinarian Calvinism among the Deists and Enlightenment thinkers, see Harrison, *'Religion' and the religions in the English Enlightenment*, 19–28.
[16] Kant, 'An answer to the question: What is enlightenment?' (1784) in *Practical Philosophy*, ed. Mary J. Gregor. *The Cambridge edition of the works of Immanuel Kant* (Cambridge: Cambridge University Press, 1996), 11.
[17] On Arminius as a theologian of grace rather than human declaration of independence, see the convincing account by Stanglin and McCall, *Jacob Arminius*, especially chaps. 3 and 4.

however, the Arminian revisionism of the immutability of divine decrees was tantamount to 'transcendent Atheism, in the highest decree'.[18]

Quoting directly from Johannes Arnoldi Corvinus, Jacobus Arminius and Nicolaas Grevinchovius (here from Grevinchovius's polemical exchange with William Ames, who had served as a professor at the University of Franeker in Friesland), Owen's point was that all Arminians tended to understand the divine decrees as being based upon foreseen human actions: 'God willeth many things, which he neither would, nor justly could will, and purpose, did not some action of the creature precede.'[19] By weaving together his exegesis of Rom. 9.11 and Eph. 1.4, Owen pungently excoriated Arminian perspectives – as seen in Simon Episcopius and Jacobus Arminius, and the Jesuits – which inexcusably end up handcuffing God, so much so that God ends up being a

> debtor to the *Arminians*, theeves give, what they do not take, having robbed God of his power, they will yet leave him so much goodnesse, as that he shall not be troubled at it, though he be sometimes compelled to, what he is very loath to do: how doe they and their fellows the Jesuits, exclaime upon poore *Calvin*, for sometimes using the harsh words of compulsion, describing the effectuall, powerfull working of the providence of God, in the actions of men, but they, can fasten the same terme, on the will of God, and no harme done: surely, God will one day plead his own cause against them: but yet blame them not, *si violandum est ius, regnandi causa violandum est*: it is to make themselves absolute, that they thus cast off the yoke of the Almightie.[20]

For Owen, defending an Augustinian–Calvinian view of divine sovereignty in election had great pastoral implications: anchoring one's soul in the voyage seeking assurance of salvation. Owen criticized the Arminian conviction regarding the 'alterable' nature of God's decrees precisely because then those 'which are damned, as *Pharaoh, Judas, &c.* might have been saved, and those which are saved, as the blessed Virgin, *Peter, John,* might have been damned, which must needs reflect with a strong charge of mutability on Almightie God'.

---

[18]Owen, *A display of Arminianisme* (1643), 6; *Works* (1965), 10:14.

[19]Owen, *A display of Arminianisme* (1643), 6; *Works* (1965), 10:14. Grevinchovius had rendered it as vis-à-vis Ames's commitment to anchor all divine actions within divine decrees, and not based upon future contingent actions of creatures: 'Multa tamen arbitror Deum velle, quæ non vellet, adeòque nec justè velle posset, nisi aliqua creaturæ action præcederet.' He continued: 'Et sic actio creaturæ evadit in causam sine qua non, quâ ablatâ auferatur & voluntas seu potiùs volition Dei.' See Grevinchovius, *Dissertatio theologica de duabus quaestionibus hoc tempore controversis* (1617), 24.

[20]Owen, *A display of Arminianisme* (1643), 7–8, 11; *Works* (1965), 10:16. The Latin quote is from Cicero, *De officiis*, lib. III, cap. 21, p. 168. 'Nam si violandum est jus, regnandi gratia Violandum est: aliis rebus pietatem colas.'

Assigning mutability to God was to leave nothing in the world as unchanging and constant. Furthermore, precisely because Owen knew well the fickle and frail nature of humankind, following the theological footsteps of Augustine, Bradwardine and Calvin, he sought to assign immutability to God. Applying the doctrine of divine immutability, Owen noted that the 'decree of election' was the 'fountaine of all spirituall blessings,, offering the believers a 'saving sense, and assurance thereof', which had often proven so elusive. Whether it was Nehemiah Wallington, Elizabeth Isham, John Bunyan or innumerable other Puritans, attaining one's sense of assurance of faith was both a theological quagmire and a pastoral labyrinth.[21] Judging from the fact that this sense of experiencing the love of God as being constant and the call of God irrevocable so often addressed by Anglicans and Puritans from the pulpit shows the significance of this phenomenon as a spiritual dilemma of national proportions.[22] For Owen, the fact that God is '*actus simplex,* & purely free from all composition' meant that believers can rest assured concerning the immutability of his decree of predestination for them, since the 'certaine and infallible execution' of God's pleasure was 'extended to particular contingent events', including the perseverance of the saints and their eschatological justification.[23] Just as Owen defended unconditional predestination for pastoral purposes, Arminians were convinced that by espousing the possibility of losing one's salvation unless one persevered to the end, they, too, were defending the honour of God and rescuing the believers from the sin of presumption. Baxter had attacked Owen because he feared antinomianism to be the theological *cul-de-sac* of Calvinism. Baxter's anti-antinomianism was nothing if not pastorally motivated and morally grounded. To have human wills thwart the eternal decrees of God for predestination was tantamount to setting up 'impotency against omnipotency, and arme the clay, against the Potter'. As ludicrous as that must have sounded to all readers, argued Owen, so was the Arminian theological anthropology that exalted the power of human will to deny the will of God.[24]

---

[21]Seaver, *Wallington's world*; Stephens, *The gentlewoman's remembrance*; on Bunyan, see his own account in *Grace abounding to the chief of sinners* (1666). Noteworthy in the lengthy subtitle of *Grace abounding* is Bunyan's use of expressions such as 'his Dreadful Temptations', 'how he despaired of Gods mercy, and how the Lord did deliver him from all the guilt and terrour that lay upon him' as well as his authorial intention as 'now published for the support of the weak and tempted People of God'. See also Davies, *Graceful reading*, esp. chaps. 1, 2. On assurance of faith, see Winship, 'Weak Christians, backsliders, and carnal gospelers', 462–81; Zachman, *The assurance of faith*.
[22]Lake, *Anglican and Puritans?*
[23]Owen, *A display of Arminianisme* (1643), 11; *Works* (1965), 10:20.
[24]Owen, *A display of Arminianisme* (1643), 12; *Works* (1965), 10:20. On Baxter's anti-antinomian tendencies in most of his polemical and practical divinity, see Lim, *In pursuit of purity, unity, and liberty*; Cooper, *Fear and polemic in seventeenth-century England*. On antinomianism's influence

Owen produced two contrasting columns of perspectives, one of which represented 'S.S.' ('Sacred Scripture', viz., the Calvinist view), and the other 'Lib. Arbit.' ('freedom of the will'). In essence, this was reminiscent of the bondage versus freedom of the will diatribe between Luther and Erasmus, which had occurred nearly 120 years prior to Owen's publication of *A display of Arminianisme*. Weaving together biblical texts such as Eph. 1.4, 2 Tim. 1.9, Acts 15.18, Isa. 46.10, Rom. 9.11, 2 Tim. 2.19, Ps. 3312 and Mal. 3.6, Owen taught that God's will and decretal purposes can never be ultimately opposed; that God does not change; that God knows those who are his; that God's election was not predicated on foreseen human actions; thus God's predestination was established through the covenant of redemption 'before the foundation of the world' (Eph. 1.4). In contradistinction to those 'self-evident' biblical texts were texts from the *Apologia* of the Remonstrants, Arminius, Corvinus, Grevinchovius and Simon Episcopius. Their views converged on the adaptability/mutability of divine will in response to human actions, summarized in Arminius's perspective: 'God would have all men to be saved, but compelled with the stubborne malice of some; hee changeth his purpose, and will have them to perish.'[25]

Owen accused the Arminians of denying 'præscience, or foreknowledge of God' (chap. 3);[26] of exalting their 'Idol of Free-will' as more pre-eminent than the providence of God (chap. 4);[27] of making God's purposes to be liable to resistance, frustration and ultimate repudiation (chap. 5);[28] of truncating the doctrine of original sin beyond recognition;[29] of reducing the efficacy of the merits of Christ resulting from this death;[30] and of catapulting the 'power of Free-will' sufficient to prepare the unbeliever for conversion.[31] Throughout *A display of Arminianisme*, Owen's primary fear was that this devolution of God's power of foreknowledge and predestination would inescapably have secondary and tertiary effects on the overall plan of salvation. In particular, he was concerned that an Arminian anthropology would – however unintentionally – vitiate the fabric of Christology that fully embraced the accomplishment of Christ's satisfaction through his death and resurrection. For instance, the fourth and final part of his *Salus electorum, sanguis Jesu: or The death of death in the death of Christ* was devoted to correcting the errors of Arminians whose logical

---

on Puritan divinity and Calvinist theology, see Bozeman, *The precisianist strain*; Como, *Blown by the Spirit*.
[25] Owen, *A display of Arminianisme* (1643), 14; *Works* (1965), 10:22.
[26] Owen, *A display of Arminianisme* (1643), 14–23; *Works* (1965), 10:22–30.
[27] Owen, *A display of Arminianisme* (1643), 23–39; *Works* (1965), 10:30–43.
[28] Owen, *A display of Arminianisme* (1643), 39–49; *Works* (1965), 10:43–52.
[29] Owen, *A display of Arminianisme* (1643), 68–84; *Works* (1965), 10:68–82.
[30] Owen, *A display of Arminianisme* (1643), 91–106; *Works* (1965), 10:87–100.
[31] Owen, *A display of Arminianisme* (1643), 133–40; *Works* (1965), 10:114–23.

consequence of their theology led, Owen argued, to an espousal of universal redemption.[32] Why was Owen so bent on ensuring that Arminianism did not establish a stronghold among English Christians? To use Owen's own words, it was because they were teaching a 'non-necessity of satisfaction by Christ'. Then he offered up an established pedigree of orthodox theologians and 'doctors of the church' who solemnly engaged in a battle against '*Pelagian* hereticks'. Thus Augustine is cited as a foundational figure, followed by Calvin (from his *Institutes*, Bk. 2, chap. 16), and Thomas Aquinas is adduced as a direct influence upon Calvin and the Reformed tradition in this regard. Owen cites from *Summa theologiae,* Pars III, Q. 49, Art. 4: 'Whether we were thereby reconciled through Christ's Passion?'[33]

Owen's Parthian shot in *The death of death in the death of Christ* encapsulates what he believed to be the ultimate edifice of the Pelagian-cum-Arminian Tower of Babel:

> The sum and meaning of the whole Assertion is, that there is an universality of sufficient grace granted to all, even of grace subjective, enabling them to obedience, which receives addition, increase, degrees, and augmentation, according as they who have it, do make use of what they presently enjoy: which is a position so contradictory to innumerable places of Scripture, so derogatory to the free grace of God, so destructive to the efficacy of it, such a clear exaltation, of the old Idol free-will, into the throne of God, as any thing, that the decaying estate of Christianity hath invented and broached. So far is it from being plain and clear in Scripture, that it is universally repugnant to the whole dispensation of the new Covenant.[34]

This attack on divine freedom and sovereignty and the excellency of the satisfaction accomplished by Christ – as perfectly divine and completely human, *à la* the Chalcedonian creedal formulation – would also have crucial consequences on trinitarian and Christological doctrines, to which we now turn.

TRINITARIANISM

As recent scholarship has amply demonstrated, challenges to the doctrine of the Trinity since the beginnings of the Protestant Reformation provide contextual backgrounds to better situate Owen's efforts to defend the identity and

---

[32]Owen, *The death of death in the death of Christ* (1648), 86, emphasis added; *Works* 10:294.
[33]Owen, *The death of death in the death of Christ* (1648), 148; *Works* 10:275.
[34]Owen, *The death of death in the death of Christ* (1648), 272; *Works* 10:381–2.

economy of the triune God.[35] Although Owen's commitment to the doctrine of the Trinity permeates all of his writings, we will focus on the two which were explicitly focused on the threats posed to Nicene formulations of the Trinity: *Vindiciae evangelicae* (1655), published at the height of the challenge of English Socinianism during the Interregnum, and *A brief declaration and vindication of the doctrine of the Trinity* (1669), which sought to shore up orthodoxy by emphasizing both the ontology of Christ (his essential equality with the Father and Spirit) and his economic role (particularly his satisfaction for sin). For Owen and his Puritan co-religionists, there was a porous membrane between 'polemical' and 'practical' divinity. Therefore, while exposing anti-trinitarian errors, Owen extols the superlative grace of the incarnation of Jesus, thereby excoriating the coldness of his own heart: an amalgamation of theological strands rarely seen in contemporary systemic theology texts. This is what Geoffrey F. Nuttall referred to as an Augustinian '*theologia pectoris*'.[36] Owen urges the learned readership of *Vindiciae evangelicae* towards

> a *diligent endeavour* to have the *power of the truths professed* and *contended* for, abiding upon our *hearts*, that we may not *contend* for *notions*; but what we have a *practical acquaintance* within our own souls. . . . What am I the better if I can *dispute* that *Christ* is God, but have no *sense* or *sweetness* in my heart from hence, that he is a *God in Covenant* with my *soul*, what will it *avail* me to evince by *Testimonies* and *Arguments,* that he hath made *satisfaction* for sin, If through my *unbelief* the *wrath of God abides on me*, and I have no experience of my own being made the *Righteousness of God in him*. . . . It is the *power of Truth* in the *heart* alone, that will *make* us *cleave* unto it indeed, in an hour of temptation.[37]

It was entirely *apropos* that Owen would be tasked by the first Protectorate Parliament to provide a clear repudiation of John Biddle's anti-trinitarian catechism, and that for three reasons. First, when Biddle's *A twofold catechism* (1654) was published, Owen was the vice-chancellor of the University of Oxford. Second, Biddle had been a student at Oxford. Thus, it fell upon Owen to remove the thorns of anti-trinitarian heresy that had sprouted in his institutional home. Third, as the Protectorate government was producing fundamental articles of religion in their quest for a religious settlement, Owen feared that the final language of the Instrument of Government was too capacious and could

---

[35]Lim, *Mystery unveiled*; Mortimer, *Reason and religion in the English revolution*; Smith, 'And if God was one of us', 160–84; Lucci, 'Ante-Nicene authority and the Trinity in seventeenth-century England', 101–24.
[36]Nuttall, *The Holy Spirit in Puritan faith and experience*, 7.
[37]Owen, 'The preface to the reader', in *Vindiciae evangelicae* (1655), 68–9; *Works* 12:52.

accommodate Biddle and his anti-trinitarian co-religionists. Article XXXVII, for example, was not explicitly trinitarian, although it did stipulate that 'Popery and Prelacy' would not be beneficiaries of the tolerationist approach of the Cromwellian Parliament: those who 'profess faith in God by Jesus Christ (though differing in judgment from the doctrine, worship or discipline publicly held forth) shall not be restrained from, but shall be protected in, the professor of the faith and exercise of their religion'.[38] Owen, rightly or wrongly, blamed Richard Baxter for this theological obfuscation which left a hole in the dragnet that would allow Socinians to pass through with ease. Baxter returned the favour by condemning the 'over-Orthodox Doctors, Owen and Cheynell' for the inordinately strict boundaries of Christian orthodoxy in Cromwellian England.[39]

Returning, then, to Owen's critique of Biddle's *A twofold catechism*, arguably the *locus classicus* of anti-trinitarian argument, whether English, Polish or otherwise, Owen rightly saw the connection between Biddle, *The Racovian catechism* – published originally in Polish in 1605 in Racow – and Valentine Smalcius and Jonas Schlinctingius, two leading anti-trinitarians on the Continent.[40] Biddle's main critique can be expressed aphoristically: '*ante*-Nicene writers were unequivocally *anti*-Nicene', especially when it came to the deity of Christ and the doctrine of the Trinity. Or as Owen summarizes his position: 'the Confessions of Faith which the first *Generall Councells* . . . during the space of 400 years and upward, Composed and put forth, were framed according to the *fancies* and *interests* of men, *besides the word*', and 'confirmed by the Civil Magistrate . . . without any regard to the Scripture'.[41] One of the key anti-trinitarian shibboleths was that Nicene and other trinitarian doctrinal formulations were deviations from scriptural orthodoxy because they employed terms nowhere to be found in Scriptures themselves. Owen's riposte included references to Calvin's *Institutes* Bk. 1, chap. 13, and he expressly repudiated the Socinian/anti-trinitarian perspective: 'if any word or phrase, do expressly

---

[38]*The instrument of government* (16 December 1653), in *The commonwealth of England*, ed. Blitzer, 162.

[39]On this fascinating sub-committee convened to hammer out workable theological solution for the British Commonwealth and its ultimate *denouement*, see Gribben, *John Owen and English Puritanism*,151–4; Coffey, 'A ticklish business', 108–36; Lim, *In pursuit of purity, unity, and liberty,* chap. 6.

[40]Owen, 'The preface of Mr. Biddle to his catechism examined', in *Vindiciae evangelicae* (1655), 5; Works (1965), 12:59. Owen is referring to Schlictingius, *Confessio fidei Christianae edita nominee Ecclesiarum quae in Polonia* (1651).

[41]On Biddle and his equating of ante-Nicene writers with anti-Nicene perspectives, see Lim, *Mystery unveiled,* 38–60. Owen, 'Preface of Mr. Biddle', in *Vindiciae evangelicae* (1655), 6, 7; Works (1965), 12:60. On Biddle, see Wilbur's older, yet not outdated, account in *A history of Unitarianism in Transylvania, England, and America*, 193–208.

signify any Doctrine, or matter, contained in the Scripture, though the Word or Phrase it selfe, be not in so many letters found in the Scripture, that such words or phrases may not be used for the explication of the mind of God' was a matter 'not easily be proved'. Predictably, here Owen cites the appropriation of ὁμοούσιας, which was used by the first Nicene Council in 325 CE 'to express the unity of Essence and Being that is in the Father and Son' in order to 'obviate *Arius* and his followers', who also used non-biblical expressions to 'destroy the true and Eternal Deity of the Son of God'.[42] With this mode of argumentation, we can see a pro-trinitarian lineage that connects Augustine, Hilary of Poitiers, Aquinas, Calvin and now Owen in their defence of the usage of non-biblical terms to articulate the tri-unity of God.

Another key polemical divergence between Biddle and Owen was on how the incarnation of Jesus was to be interpreted. It turned out to be an exegetical departure. For Owen and his pro-trinitarian colleagues, passages such as Jn 1.1-18 (the Johannine Prologue), 1 Tim. 3.16 ('that *God was manifest in the flesh*'), Heb. 2.14 ('that *Christ took part of Flesh and Blood*'), Gal. 4.4 ('that he was *made of a Woman*'), Rom. 8.3 ('*sent forth in the likeness of sinful flesh*') and Heb. 2.17 ('*made like unto us in all things*') would be tautological nonsense unless the fact of the incarnation was more than a mere appearance of a mortal man, however exalted he might have been in office and economy, if not on ontology. For Biddle, however, these texts clearly demarcated the ontological distinction between God the Father and Christ the servant of God, thus inferior to God the One and Only. The '*Hypostaticall Union*' between the humanity and divinity of Jesus – as Owen uses Rom. 9.5 ('*God . . . blessed forever, over all*') – was another holdover from the patristic period that Biddle and the antitrinitarians rejected.[43] Biddle joined other anti-trinitarians who saw the early modern proponents of the Trinity as those who were fastidiously holding onto things that were clearly out of step with 'true biblical' Christianity, namely, Protestant faith: Trinity, tradition and transubstantiation.[44] Equally pernicious to Owen – thus his fear that Arminians and Socinians were basically heretical cousins – was the outright rejection of the doctrine of original sin and the necessity of satisfaction by the death of Christ, both of which Biddle rejected. For Owen, denial of the Trinity by Biddle and others was but one step towards the denial of the nature of humanity, the nature of salvation, indeed the nature of Christianity. His summary of Biddle's religion is pungent as well as powerful:

> The *Nature* of God being abased, the *Deity* & *Grace* of Christ denied, the sin of our *Natures*, and their renovation by Grace in Christ rejected: M. B[iddle]'s

---

[42]Owen, 'Preface of Mr. Biddle', in *Vindiciae evangelicae* (1655), 18; *Works* (1965), 12:67.
[43]Owen, 'Preface of Mr. Biddle', in *Vindiciae evangelicae* (1655), 29; *Works* (1965), 12:74–5.
[44]On the 'Three T's' of anti-trinitarian mantra, see Lim, *Mystery unveiled*, 'Introduction'.

remaining Religion, will be found scarce worth the inquiry after, by those whom he undertakes to instruct: there being scarcely any thing left by him, from whence we are peculiarly denominated Christians: nor any thing that should support the weight of a sinful soul, which approaches God for life and Salvation.[45]

In this clearly laid out theo-logic, Owen argued that the categorical mistake committed by Biddle was to ascribe to an infinite God the same qualities and qualifications as would be true for humans. Owen's main thrust was that distinction of persons between Father and Son did not in any way 'prove difference of Essence' between them because God was of an '*Infinite* substance', thereby having to be classified differently from mere mortals. Just because Christ as 'Mediator' was distinct from the Father in terms of personhood did not naturally lead to the conclusion that Christ was 'not partaker of the same nature with him'. To argue that there can be 'but one person' per 'one Essence' is true only when the 'Substance is *Finite*, and limited', but could not be referred to 'that which is *infinite*'. Similarly, the 'distinction and inequality in respect of *office*' in Christ did not naturally lead to an ontological inferiority of the Son in relation to the Father.[46]

A key polemical strategy for Owen was to go after Hugo Grotius, a leading Dutch jurist whose infamy in the realm of theology was that his tolerationist and inclusivist approach towards the Remonstrants had led to his own incarceration in the States of Holland after the Synod of Dort in 1619. Regardless of his contribution to international law, philology and humanistic learning, in the eyes of Owen and his fellow high Calvinists, Grotius was the ultimate bête noire. In *Vindiciae evangelicae*, Owen mentions and cites from Grotius over 130 times, more than any other author, ancient or contemporary, and in none of these instances did Owen praise him. In other words, the connection between Arminianism and Socinianism was all too obvious for Owen, so much so that 'Grotius, Episcopius, Curcaellaeus' were listed together as espousing a '*middle way* to accommodate the *Socinians*'.[47]

In his post-Restoration writings, Owen continued his defence of the Trinity for orthodoxy and orthopraxy. *A brief declaration and vindication of the doctrine*

---

[45]Owen, 'Preface of Mr. Biddle', in *Vindiciae evangelicae* (1655), 30; *Works* (1965), 12:75. By linking Biddle with the Ebionites and Cerinthians, Paul of Samosata and Arius (denial of the deity of Christ), Audaeus and the Anthropomorphites (denial of the simplicity and spirituality of divine essence), Pelagius (denial of original sin), Peter Abelard (denial of the satisfaction of Christ), Socinus, Smalcius and Crellius (denial of *all the foregoing*!), Owen pointed out that Biddle's religion was hardly novel, but has a long heterodox pedigree. 'Preface of Mr. Biddle', in *Vindiciae evangelicae* (1655), 40–1; *Works* (1965), 12:82.
[46]Owen, *Vindiciae evangelicae* (1655), 149–50; *Works* (1965), 12:171.
[47]Owen, 'Preface of Mr. Biddle', in *Vindiciae evangelicae* (1655), 64; *Works* 12:49.

of the Trinity was published in 1669, and reprinted in 1676, underscoring its popularity and the urgency of defence of trinitarian doctrine. Owen noted on the title page of *A brief declaration* that his writings were 'accommodated to the capacity' of those who 'may be in danger to be seduced' by heretical notions of the identity of the triune God. Furthermore, Owen established that his trinitarianism was predicated on the ontology of the Son of God ('of the Person') and the economy of all three persons of the Trinity in redemption ('Satisfaction of Christ').[48] Here, we note an interesting piece of evidence that Owen was seeking to recruit Richard Baxter into his own cause. After a litany of luminaries who had written against Socinianism, 'Paraeus, Piscator, Lubbertus, Voetius, Amiraldus, Placaeus, Rivetus . . . Turretin . . . Aquinas, Durandus, Biel', Owen included 'Baxter, *with many others*'. In the list were figures such as Amiraldus and Rivetus who were not necessarily champions of high Calvinism. Baxter was of similar theological orientation. Writing in 1669, Owen was seeking to establish a more broad-based support for the defence of trinitarian orthodoxy.[49]

After affirming the oneness of God – with which Jews, Muslims and anti-trinitarians would agree – Owen moved to the second affirmation, namely, '*that the Father is God*', which, again, would brook little opposition.[50] The formidable theological hurdle for those who had little difficulty in affirming propositions one and two was this: '*Jesus Christ is God; the Eternal Son of God*', thus worthy to be 'served, worshipped, believed in, obeyed as God' on account of his 'own *Divine excellencies*', and though as human, it was confessed and declared by the early Church that he was '*God also*', he existed before his incarnation. Owen's interesting exegetical confluence – though in no way unique among the patristic, medieval and early modern orthodox theologians – was to see Ps. 45.6 ('Thy Throne O God is for ever and ever') as applied to and fulfilled in Christ, as in Heb. 1.8 ('But unto thy Son he saith, thy Throne O God is for ever and ever'). Owen made a similar hermeneutical move with Ps. 110.1 ('The Lord said unto my Lord, sit thou at my right hand') and Mt. 22.44, where Christ applied that text unto himself. The third and final example was the vision of Isaiah in chapter 6.1-3 ('I saw also the Lord sitting upon a Throne, high and lifted up') which was 'applied unto the Son' in Jn 12.41 ('These things said Esaias, when he saw Jesus' glory and spake of him').[51] For ten pages in the

---

[48] Owen, *A brief declaration and vindication of the doctrine of the Trinity* (1669), t.p.; *Works* 2:365.
[49] Owen, 'To the reader', in *A brief declaration and vindication of the doctrine of the Trinity* (1669), sigs. A11v, A12r; *Works* (1965), 2:369.
[50] Owen, *A brief declaration and vindication of the doctrine of the Trinity* (1669), 37–8; *Works* (1965), 2:379.
[51] Owen, *A brief declaration and vindication of the doctrine of the Trinity* (1669), 42–3, 45; *Works* (1965), 2:382–4.

first chapter of *A brief declaration . . . of the Trinity*, Owen adduced Scripture proof texts to buttress lay readers' confidence in the trustworthiness of the Trinity doctrine from Scripture itself, which, for Protestants, was a sine qua non authority for faith and praxis. For Owen, there was a subtle-yet-substantial distinction between affirming Christ to be 'God by *Office*' and affirming him to be 'God by nature'. The former affirmation would inevitably lead to the conclusion that Christ is 'God, but he is not the *most high God*'. In so doing, Owen lamented that this was leading so many astray by creating an ontological ranking (Christ is an inferior and secondary deity) after making an economic ranking (the Father sending the Son; the Father and Son together sending the Spirit, thereby ranking the Father as first, Son as second and Spirit as third-ranked deity). For Owen, this would lead to a liturgical and practical deviation, if not a 'new abomination', since to ascribe worship to someone who was '*not God by nature*, is Idolatry'. And as such, this Christ was the kind of false god against whom Jeremiah excoriates in his prophecy in Jer. 10.11.[52] Owen also made an amiable attempt to express in common parlance the mystery of the *communicatio idiomatum*: '[t]he Scriptures asserting the *Humanity* of Christ with the concernments thereof, as his birth, life, and death, do no more thereby deny his *Deity*, than by asserting his Deity with the essential properties thereof, they deny his humanity'.[53]

As a former vice-chancellor of Oxford in the turbulent era of the 1650s, Owen was keenly aware of the exegetical and theological perspectives employed by both anti-trinitarians and their antagonists. The Johannine prologue (Jn 1.1-18) was a key site of exegetical and philological battle, from Augustine's *In evangelium Joannis tractatus* and Thomas Aquinas's defence of the prologue as a key proof text of the deity of Jesus. It was now Owen's turn to defend the same. For Owen, *pace* the anti-trinitarians, Jn 1.1-3 was unequivocally a reference to the One who would become en-fleshed. The marvellous mystery was this: How can – or better yet, why would – the 'Eternal Word and wisdom of the Father' come into the world (Jn 1.10), be rejected by his own (1.11), be made flesh and dwell among us (1.14)? The pre-existence of the Word, as indicated in Jn 1.1 ('In the beginning was the Word, and the Word was with God') could only lead to the conclusion that the ontological matrix of the Word must have the '*nature* of God, which is *eternal*', unless one were to assume the existence of a '*creature* before the Creation of any'.[54] For Owen,

---

[52]Owen, *A brief declaration and vindication of the doctrine of the Trinity* (1669), 58; *Works* (1965), 2:388.
[53]Owen, *A brief declaration and vindication of the doctrine of the Trinity* (1669), 60; *Works* (1965), 2:389.
[54]Owen, *A brief declaration and vindication of the doctrine of the Trinity* (1669), 61-3, 69-83; *Works* (1965), 2:390-1, 392-9 (for an extended theological exegesis of the Johannine Prologue

both Prov. 8.23 ('I was set up from everlasting before the beginning, or ever the earth was') and Jn 17.5 ('Glorifie thou me with thine own self, with the glory which I had with thee before the world was') undeniably testified to the '*Eternal preexistence* of Christ the Son of God'.[55] It is important to note that for patristic authors, ranging from Origen to Athanasius, Augustine to John Chrysostom, Proverbs 8 was a key text to support the eternal nature of God's wisdom that became incarnate in Jesus, which is precisely what Owen does in *A brief declaration . . .of the Trinity*.[56] Owen further wove together biblical texts ranging from Gen. 1.1 to Prov. 8.23, from Mk 1.1 to Heb. 1.10, all of which talked about 'in the beginning', as intertextual clues to further buttress the pre-existence of the Son of God. In addition to the pre-existence of the Son as a clue to build towards the deity of Christ, Owen also elaborated on the fact that the Son's being the creator of all things, seen and unseen, provided further support for the deity of Jesus.[57]

One of the more intriguing aspects of Socinian theological exegesis was the emphasis on the '*Rapture* of the humane Nature of Christ'. Owen excoriated Biddle and the continental Socinians for their forced exegesis, which arose from their refusal to acknowledge the two-nature doctrine of Christ, and their correlative doctrine of the Trinity. Owen averred that the '*imaginary* Rapture' was anchored on the Socinian conviction that 'the LORD Christ in his *whole Person* was no more than a meer man'.[58] Owen had exposed the 'indefensible' claim of the 'pre-ascension ascension of Christ' in his *Vindiciae evangelicae* and continued on the same vein of polemical attack in his Hebrews commentary, published after the Restoration and his loss of power and prominence.[59] Owen was more dependent on Hebrews than on any other New Testament book (with the possible exception of the Gospel of John), so that in this instance, too, he argued from Heb. 9.12: 'Christ entered *once into the Holy Place*' after he had obtained eternal redemption for the people of God.[60] The *locus classicus* for the Socinian claim regarding the pre-ascension ascension of Christ was Jn 3.13, and

---

here). For the significance of the Gospel of John in post-Reformation England, see Lim, *Mystery unveiled*, 172–216; Cefalu, *The Johannine Renaissance in early modern English literature and theology*.

[55] Owen, *A brief declaration and vindication of the doctrine of the Trinity* (1669), 63, 65; *Works* (1965), 2:390–1.

[56] Beeley, *The unity of Christ*, 18, 82, 143, 154–9; Bradshaw, 'The Logoi of beings in Greek Patristic thought', 9–22; van Loon, *The Dyophysite Christology of Cyril of Alexandria*, 171, 182, 297.

[57] See McDonough, *Christ as creator*; Gathercole, *The preexistent son*.

[58] Owen, *Hebrews* (1668), 16 (comm. Heb. 1:1, 2); *Works* (1965), 19:29.

[59] Owen, *Vindiciae evangelicae* (1655), 377, 381; *Works* (1965), 12:355, 358. On this Socinian doctrinal predilection, see Gomes, 'The rapture of the Christ', 75–99.

[60] Owen, *Vindiciae evangelicae* (1655), 377, 381; *Works* (1965), 12:355, 358. On this Socinian doctrinal predilection, see Gomes, 'The rapture of the Christ', 75–99.

Owen called it a '*Mahumetan* fancy' to believe that Jesus 'before his *entrance* of his publick Ministry, was *locally* taken up into *Heaven*, and there instructed in the mysterie of the Gospel'.[61] Continuing his anti-Socinian polemic, Owen argued that to deny Christ's 'sufferings were *poenal*, or that he died to make satisfaction for sin; but only that he did so, to confirm the Doctrine that he had taught' or to 'set us an example to suffer for the truth', was to remove the Christological core from the work of Christ, in his substitutionary, penal satisfaction.[62]

In addition to the Socinians, the other pugilists against whom Owen saw himself fighting were the Quakers. Owen felt that the Quaker 'threat' to orthodoxy came from the other end of the theological spectrum. Whereas most Socinians were guilty of inordinate rationalism in their theological method and exegesis, Quakers were guilty of maintaining an over-realized eschatology, of harbouring a 'misguided certitude' regarding the '*light within them*, or an infallible *afflatus*'.[63] Elsewhere he identified these two groups for mis-identifying the glory of Christ, thereby missing the mark on the identity of the triune God:

> Men may talk what they please of the *Light within them*, or of the Power of Reason, to conduct them unto that Knowledge of God. . . . But . . . if they did not boast *themselves* of that Light, which hath its Foundation and Original in Divine Revelation alone, they would not excel them, who, in the best Management of their own Reasonings, *knew not God*, but waxed vain in their Imaginations.[64]

Thus, for Owen, a robust defence of the Trinity required a two-pronged critique of Socinian rationalism and Quaker enthusiasm. His conclusion was as pithy as was poignant: 'The sum of this Revelation is, that the Holy Spirit is an eternally divine existing substance, the Author of Divine operations, and the Object of Divine and Religious Worship; that is *over all God Blessed for ever*; as the ensuing testimonies evince. Gen. 1.2 *The spirit of God moved upon the face of the waters.*'[65] In other words, misguided confidence in the human ability to know God – whether through the light within (the Quakers' source of certitude), or through human reason alone *sans* recognition of the limits of

---

[61]Owen, *Hebrews* (1668), 16 (comm. Heb. 1:1, 2); *Works* (1965), 19:29.
[62]Owen, *Hebrews* (1668), 242 (comm. Heb. 2:10); *Works* (1965), 19:402.
[63]Owen, *A brief declaration and vindication of the doctrine of the Trinity* (1669), 89–91; *Works* 2:399.
[64]Owen, *Meditations and discourses concerning the glory of Christ* (1691), 19; *Works* (1965), 1:297.
[65]Owen, *A brief declaration and vindication of the doctrine of the Trinity* (1669), 90; *Works* (1965), 2:399–400.

theo-logical faculty (the Socinians' reason for certitude) – would lead people away from the confession and worship of the triune God.

The foregoing shows the contextual contours of Owen's polemical exchange with those who intentionally or inadvertently denied the received doctrine of the Trinity, whether Socinians or Quakers, and it leads to the final part of our chapter: delving into Owen's Christology as a way of seeing his contribution as a theological polemicist in early modern England.

CHRISTOLOGY

Christology was the central hub of Christian theology and piety for Owen, as it was, quite naturally, for Augustine, Aquinas and Calvin: three key sources and influences for Owen's mature theology. There are a number of Christological texts in Owen's *œuvre*, and for our purposes we will look at the following treatises: Χριστολογια, *or, A declaration of the glorious mystery of the person of Christ, God and man* (1679), and *Meditations and discourses on the glory of Christ* (1684). In Χριστολογια, Owen delves further into an 'apophatic Christology' rather than toning it down in order to satisfy the desires of the 'cultured despisers' among Restoration Anglicans. This mystical and trinitarian Christology continued on in his *Meditations*. Owen's Christology was formally trinitarian, soteriologically anchored on the satisfaction of Christ, devotionally affective and philosophically apophatic.

By the time Owen came to write Χριστολογια, much of the ecclesiastical landscape in England had changed, and he and his fellow Congregationalists were being pummelled in experiences of defeat. Punitive legislation such as Conventicle Act (1664) and the Five Mile Act (1665), as part of the Clarendon Code – passed between 1661 and 1665 – penalized anyone who would not acknowledge prayer book religion and the Church of England as the only legitimate modus vivendi.[66] The bare-knuckle strategy of demanding ecclesio-political submission did not always work, thereby necessitating a more accommodationist approach from Charles II, as in his declaration of indulgence in 1672. Having lost an earthly, albeit republican, government, Owen's theological reflections turned to the kingdom of Christ, which was both *already* here but *not* consummated *yet*.

The collusion between 'Emperor and *Ekklesia*', which was entirely warranted in and guaranteed by Henry VIII's Act of Supremacy (1534), and reaffirmed by the Elizabethan Act of Supremacy (1559), meant that Owen's perspective on the precedents set by Constantine and the Councils of Nicaea was unmitigatedly

---

[66]See Hill, *The experience of defeat*, for a fascinating look at the fate of Milton and other proponents of republican regime, including Owen.

critical. Then the trick was how to preserve the theological legacies of Nicaea, namely, keep the doctrine of the Trinity, without castigating it as merely a political chicanery of bishops behaving in an un-Christian manner. Therefore, we can see Owen employing a polemical strategy that excoriates the political ambitions of both emperor and bishops while giving credence to the work of divine providence in keeping the trinitarian and Christological orthodoxies of Nicaea and Chalcedon unsullied. In other words, Owen sought to extol the theological formulations while expressing deep aversion to the political corruption that accompanied them. It was a rhetorical tight rope, yet one that had to be walked. Owen writes:

> For men began much to forego the Primitive ways of opposing Errors, and extinguishing Heresies, betaking themselves unto their Interest, the number of their Party, and prevalency with the present Emperors. And although it so fell out, as in that at *Constantinople,* the first at *Ephesus,* and that at *Chalcedon,* that the Truth for the substance of it did prevail, (for in many others it happened quite otherwise) yet did they always give occasions unto new divisions, animosities, and even mutual hatreds, among the principal Leaders of the Christian People.[67]

Put differently, Owen dared not to criticize the eventual trinitarian and Christological doctrines that emerged while lamenting the 'occasions unto new divisions, animosities' and implacable hatred that festered among 'the principal Leaders', which was a clear jab at bishops then and now. Owen faced a bit of a quandary regarding which to affirm: Tradition, or tradition? Or as Heiko Oberman had devised a schema of reformers' understanding of Tradition as Tradition 1 and Tradition 2?[68] On the one hand, Owen does insist that Councils often erred, and yet he was also quite dependent upon patristic authorities for building up his theological case. As Jean-Louis Quantin had demonstrated, for many Anglicans of the period, Christian antiquity and patristic theology were seamlessly connected, and conciliar authorities demonstrated and buttressed the ecclesiastical authority of the Church of England since it, *pace* Catholic presumptions and arrogance, alone was apostolic.[69]

In chapter IX of Χριστολογια, Owen continued on the theme that he had developed in *Of communion with God* (1657) as a trinitarian spirituality text. Here Owen demonstrated that his Christology was firmly trinitarian. The title

---

[67]Owen, 'The preface', in Χριστολογια (1679), sig. C2r; *Works* (1965), 1:11. On this, see Lim, *Mystery unveiled*, 217–70.
[68]Oberman, 'Quo Vadis? Tradition from Irenaeus to Humani Generis', 225–55; Booty, 'Tradition and traditions', 453–66.
[69]Quantin, *The Church of England and Christian antiquity*.

of the chapter was self-explanatory: 'Honour due to the Person of Christ; the Nature and Causes of it.' Owen started with the assumption that God absolutely loathed idolatry, whether of the golden calf or any other variety, for it was an act of adoration and worship of anything other than God. Yet, in the New Testament, Owen insisted, there are repeated references to Christ being a worthy object of worship, not just in the Epistles but also in the Gospels, especially in the Gospel of John. John 5.23 was cited by Owen: *'That all men should honour the Son, even as they honour the Father: He that honoureth not the Son, honoureth not the Father that sent him.'* It was the whole person of Christ in his role as mediator of revelation and redemption that was being honoured, for all 'Power, Authority, and Judgment' had been committed unto the Son.[70]

One of the neglected aspects of Owen's Christology is the influence upon his ideas of the Western mystical tradition of Augustine and Aquinas: with its proper emphasis on the limits of human fallible-yet-redeemed reason to understand the *ousia* of God's triune Being, thereby correspondingly proper apophatic Christology. Recently, Hans Boersma's *Seeing God: The beatific vision in Christian tradition* has offered a supplementary depiction of Owen's Christology as being more than just a product of Protestant scholasticism.[71] Thomas Aquinas's Christology in his *Summa Theologiae* and biblical commentaries – especially on the Gospel of John – had a robust simultaneity of medieval scholasticism *and* apophatic, mystical tone. We see the same trend in Owen. It appears in Χριστολογια with great clarity and frequency. Owen interpreted the gradual transformation of the believer in 2 Cor. 3.18 ('Beholding as in a glass the glory of the Lord, we are changed into the same Image from glory to glory'). For Owen, this glory was none other than the 'glory of the Face of God in Jesus Christ'. Then he opened up the vista of the trajectory of human transformation:

> That which shall at last perfectly effect our utmost conformity to God, and therein our eternal Blessedness, is *Vision,* or sight. *We shall be like him, for we shall see him as he is,* 1 *John* 3.2. Here Faith begins what Sight shall perfect hereafter. But yet *we walk by Faith, and not by sight,* 2 *Cor.* 5.7. And although the life of Faith and Vision differ in degrees, or as some think in kind, yet have they both the same Object, and the same Operations; and there is a great cognation between them. The Object of *Vision* is the whole Mystery of the Divine Existence and Will; and its Operation, is a perfect

---

[70]Owen, Χριστολογια (1679), 114; *Works* (1965), 1:105.
[71]Boersma, *Seeing God*. See also McDonald, 'Beholding the glory of God in the face of Jesus Christ', 141–58.

conformity unto God, a likeness unto him, wherein our blessedness shall consist.[72]

Note here that the 'Object' of the beatific vision was 'the whole Mystery of the Divine Existence and Will', and its operation was a 'perfect conformity unto God', which would manifest itself in the believer's *theosis*, or divinization. Owen does not explicitly state it but comes quite close. For Owen, it was not merely an intellectual vision but he pushes the theological envelope for something beyond an intellectualist approach. Judging from the fact that Χριστολογια was published in 1679, merely five years after the virulent attack from William Sherlock for Owen's putative Quaker-like enthusiasm, belief in the reality of the beatific vision must have formed a core Christological commitment for Owen. Anticipating the turn-of-phrase that would be popularized by Jonathan Edwards, Owen argued that this exercise of faith in the perfecting work of God's Spirit disposes the believer unto 'holy heavenly . . . affections'. Then he expounded on the type and trajectory of our conformity unto God further: 'To be *nigh unto God,* and to be *like unto him,* are the same. To be always with him, and perfectly like him according to the capacity of our Nature, is to be eternally blessed.' While contemplations of God's glory in 'Nature, in the works of Creation and Providence' do have their place and 'deserve their just commendation', Owen insists that to 'abide' in such things was to miss the entire point of divine desires for human transformation, since 'we are made like unto God'.[73] Then Owen reiterated his point regarding the true worthiness of entities that are beyond reason, thus his *apophatic turn*: 'those who are *inconversant* with' or 'are not delighted in . . . things incomprehensible, such as is the constitution of the Person of Christ', would reduce all things to 'the measure of their own understandings, or else willfully live in the neglect of what they cannot comprehend'.[74] For those rationalistic seventeenth-century versions of '*Pneumatomachi*' (lit. fighters against the Spirit, as was the case of the Eunomians, against whom Gregory Nyssa wrote in *Against Eunomius*), to acknowledge anything of faith beyond what was acceptable to human reason was guilty of fideism and abdication of human *ratio*.[75]

In his exegesis of Prov. 8.22-23, Owen spoke of the Son as the eternal and as the 'Essential Wisdom' of God who was 'and is always in the bosom of the Father, in the mutual ineffable Love of the Father and Son, in the eternal

---

[72]Owen, Χριστολογια (1679), 34; *Works* (1965), 1:51.
[73]Owen, Χριστολογια (1679), 35; *Works* (1965), 1:52.
[74]Owen, Χριστολογια (1679), 35; *Works* (1965), 1:52.
[75]See Gregory of Nyssa, *Gregory of Nyssa: Contra Eunomium I*, especially Giulio Maspero, 'Trinitarian theology in Gregory of Nyssa's *Contra Eunomium* I: The interplay between ontology and Scripture', 441–93.

Bond of the Spirit', thereby forming the triune circle of love and perichoretic indwelling.[76] This was another hotly contested text from the Old Testament between anti- and pro-trinitarians, particularly over the identity of 'Wisdom'. For most pro-trinitarians, this verse referred to the *'eternal Personal Existence of the Son of God'*, whereas for most anti-trinitarians, the fact that the Lord – as God *simpliciter* – possessed him in the beginning of his ways could only lead to the conclusion of the superiority and priority of the Lord, as divine wisdom. Trinitarian exegesis would lead to a conclusion that divine wisdom was an essential attribute of God, who would appear in time as full human being.[77] For the anti-trinitarians, since they were a priori convinced of the impossibility of God taking on human flesh and identity, to read Prov. 8.22-23 as a foreshadowing of the incarnation of the Son of God was simply preposterous and unwarrantedly forced exegesis.

Similar to Calvin, we see that Owen demonstrated little interest in scholastic divinity per se, or in peering into divine ontology for the sake of disputations, whether at Oxford or elsewhere. He was emphatic in asserting that we can 'have no apprehension of the Interest of *other Properties* of the Divine Nature' of infinite wisdom, glory and love without considering the *'state and consideration of our own'*. This is precisely how the Nicene Creed of 325 CE renders the reason for the incarnation: 'for us and for our salvation [the Son] came down and became incarnate and became man'. Owen employed similar verbiage: 'this great work of the *Incarnation of his Son*' was for the 'Redemption of Mankind, or the recovery and salvation of the Church'. Thus, Owen argued, to delve into metaphysical discussions of God's being and act, without a biblical understanding of human depravity and redemption, was mere *'curiosity'* and 'presumptuous folly'.[78]

Even in this treatise, published in the late 1670s, Owen was deeply concerned about the vitiation of trinitarian orthodoxy through the subtle encroachment of Socinianism. Due to the Socinian's denial of original sin and the satisfaction of Christ, Owen was convinced, revealed religion could soon become indistinguishable from natural religion. Revealed religion included a robust and high Christology, which acknowledged the hypostatic union of divine and human natures in one Christ: 'To deny the Person of Christ to fall under this double consideration, of a Divine Person absolutely, wherein he is *over all God blessed for ever*, and as *manifested in the flesh*, exercising the Office of Mediator between God and Man, is to renounce the Gospel.'[79] This truth was crucial,

---

[76]Owen, Χριστολογια (1679), 39; *Works* (1965), 1:54.
[77]Owen, Χριστολογια (1679), 38; *Works* (1965), 1:53.
[78]Owen, Χριστολογια (1679), 229; *Works* (1965), 1:180.
[79]Owen, Χριστολογια (1679), 155; *Works* (1965), 1:133.

not merely for theological orthodoxy, but far more importantly for the comfort of believers, thereby illustrating the inseparable connection for Owen and his Puritan co-religionists between polemical divinity and practical divinity. The most non-negotiable aspect of the office of Christ was his *'Sacerdotal Office'*, in that it was the administration of his role as the priest as well as the lamb chosen for the sacrifice that offers truly 'comfortable refreshing thoughts of God' and inestimable 'Boldness' in access unto God. Thus, if one were to deny that the role of Christ as High Priest 'be not the principle whereby the whole is animated and guided, *Christianity* is renounced, and the vain cloud of natural Religion embraced' in its stead.[80] Here, Owen explicitly mentioned Socinians who were endeavouring to 'set forth and adorn a *natural Religion*, as if it were sufficient unto all ends of our living unto God', and the reason for the erecting of natural religion – as opposed to revealed religion – proceeded from a 'dislike of the Mediation of Christ'. Then how to solve it? Here Owen the polemicist becomes Owen the pastoral guide. If in our journey we are never 'affected with Supernatural Revelations, with the Mystery of the Gospel, beyond the owning of some Notions of Truth, who never had experience of its Power in the Life of God', then we are far more likely to adopt natural religion, or be given to religious despair. For Owen, polemical exchange was never the end. In fact, with Owen, there was a 'teleological suspension of the polemical', since polemics would not be the final end of all human wayfaring and warfaring. The end was delight, the goal of union and communion, and the destiny was experiencing the glory of God in ways that all earthly experiences of God were but broken arrows and veiled rays.

In the posthumous publication, *Meditations and discourses on the glory of Christ* – published in 1684, 1691 and 1696, thereby underscoring its popular demand – Owen continued his trinitarian Christological reflections on the necessity of desiring communion with Christ in heaven, by faith and in love. Owen was concerned that those with deficient or insufficient understanding of and desire for the glory of Christ have 'filled their Divine Worship with *Images*, *Pictures* and *Musick*'. Here, rather than going after the Quakers, Arminians or Socinians, the triumvirate of his polemical objects, Owen offered a lacerating rebuke on Episcopal worship, and insisted that adherence to prayer book religion was proof that adherents of the established church had no experience of the transformative power of the glory and love of Christ in themselves, nor had they tasted its 'Goodness by any of its First-fruits in their own minds'.[81] This was no small indictment on Owen's part. We had

---

[80]Owen, Χριστολογια (1679), 157; *Works* (1965), 1:134.
[81]Owen, *Meditations and discourses concerning the glory of Christ* (1691), 9; *Works* (1965), 1:290–1.

always known that, *pace* Baxter, Owen had much less tolerance for prayer book religion, as it had been restored since the restoration of both monarchy and episcopacy with the accession of Charles II in 1660. Owen was acutely aware of the fact that the failure to comprehend fully the glory of Christ was not entirely owing to deficiency in ecclesial identity. While it was true that those in the Restoration Church of England were missing out on the 'transforming power' to change the believer increasingly into the image of Christ the Son who perfectly images the Father (2 Cor. 3.18), Owen also knew that dissenters – whether Congregationalists, Baptists or Presbyterians – struggled with a 'Multitude of perplexed Thoughts, Fears, Cares, Dangers, Distressed, Passions, and Lusts', which filled them with 'Disorder, Darkness, and Confusion'. Thus a 'Defect herein makes many of us Strangers unto an Heavenly Life' to cause them to 'live beneath the Spiritual Refreshments and Satisfactions' offered by the glory of the beatific vision of God in Christ.[82] For Owen, as Suzanne McDonald persuasively argued, beholding God in God's glory in heaven could only be actualized through Christological mediation. Just as Christ 'on earth' was the mediator *nonpareil*, Christ 'in heaven' in his perfected humanity and eternal divinity was the mediator for all saints beholding the glory of the triune God. In other words, according to Owen's theo-logic, the deficiency of understanding Christ's mediatorial office on earth, as espoused by those who denied the necessity of Christ's satisfaction (including Grotius) and by those who denied the ontological equality of the Son in relation to the Father (Socinians, of both English and continental types), would inexorably lead to a deficiency of appropriating the glory of the beatific vision. Recognizing the Calvinistic maxim, *finitum non capax infiniti* and the ontological conundrum that it represented, Owen sought a Christological pathway to cut through this philosophical Gordian knot: 'For nothing can perfectly comprehend that which is infinite, but what is itself Infinite. Wherefore the Blessed and *Blessing Sight* which we shall have of God, will be *always in the Face of Jesus Christ.*' Yet, here is also Owen's apophatic *caveat lector*: 'These things we here admire, but cannot comprehend.' Nonetheless, Owen's mystical rejoinder is truly noteworthy:

> We know not well what we say, when we speak of them: yet . . . [t]here enters sometimes by the Word and Spirit into their hearts such a sense of the *uncreated Glory* of God, shining forth in Christ, as Affects and Satiates their Souls with ineffable Joy . . . *Christ in Believers the Hope of Glory,* gives them to taste of the First fruits of it; yea, sometimes to bathe their Souls in the *Fountain of Life,* and to *drink of the Rivers of Pleasure* that are at his Right hand. . . . These Enjoyments indeed are rare, and for the most part of

---

[82] Owen, *Meditations and discourses concerning the glory of Christ* (1691), 11–12; *Works* (1965), 1:292.

short Continuance. *Rara hora, brevis mora*. But it is from our own Sloth and Darkness that we do not enjoy more *Visits* of this Grace; and that the Dawnings of Glory do not more shine on our Souls.[83]

For Owen, all the polemical exchanges, indeed all wrangling about words to produce a more precise theology, could be, at best, misguided and, at worst, exercise in idolatrous exaltation of self. It is perhaps apropos to listen to Owen's last paragraph in *Meditations and discourses on the glory of Christ*. Perhaps this is redolent of Thomas Aquinas's own experience, as reported to his secretary, Reginald. While celebrating Mass sometime around St Nicholas's day (6 December 1273), Aquinas had an epiphanous mystical experience, compared to which, he believed, 'all his writings were as straw'.[84] Owen wrote similarly of the lexical and logical inadequacy and impossibility of encapsulating the glory of the beatific vision in Christ:

> There is nothing farther for us to do herein but that now and always we shut up all our Meditations concerning it, with the *deepest Self-abasement* out of a Sense of our Unworthiness and Insufficiency to comprehend those things, *Admiration* of that excellent Glory which we cannot comprehend, and *vehement Longings* for that Season when he shall *see him as he is,* be *ever with him,* and know him, even as we are known.[85]

The final destination of all our longings and writings – polemical, pastoral or both – was perfection of our union and communion with the triune God in the person of Jesus Christ.

---

[83]Owen, *Meditations and discourses concerning the glory of Christ* (1691), 13; *Works* (1965), 1:293.
[84]Nichols, *Discovering Aquinas*, 51.
[85]Owen, *Meditations and discourses concerning the glory of Christ* (1691), 200; *Works* (1965), 1:415.

CHAPTER 10

Owen and scientific reform

KATHERINE CALLOWAY

Dr. Owen . . . besides that his profession was Divinity, not Philosophy or Mathematicks, neither is nor ever was of our Society.

Robert Boyle, 1662[1]

I hope [the Royal Society] are upon some serious consultations for the benefit of mankind, how a hen may sit on her eggs and addle none, how oysters may be so geometrically layd that instead of 200 or 300, an oyster wench may lay 8 or 900 in her basket at once and sell them all without tearing her throat or tyring her head . . . besides many other devices for the promoting of trade, the preventing the Dutch, and the ruine of Gayland and all which are under deliberation.

John Owen, 1663[2]

On view in these two quotations is a certain antipathy between John Owen and the Royal Society, the pioneering scientific institution chartered in the early 1660s 'to the glory of God . . . and the advantage of the human race'. With a sentence worthy of Jonathan Swift, Owen suggests that the 'glory of

---

[1] Boyle, *New experiments physico-mechanical* (1662), 72.
[2] John Owen to John Thornton, n.d., *The correspondence of John Owen*, 132.

God' is nowhere in sight for the society's members and questions whether their activities really benefit mankind either. In turn, Robert Boyle, a founding member of that society, disclaims Owen. And yet, it appears that Boyle had more books by Owen under his roof than by any other author besides himself;[3] moreover, Boyle's stark declaration that Owen 'neither is nor ever was of our Society' raises the question of why this needed to be pointed out. And Boyle was not the last to do so.[4] Why does the subject keep coming up? One reason surely lies in Owen's political position and social connections during a time of great scientific as well as political and religious upheaval. Another, related to the first, is a general correlation between religious and scientific reform that has been evident (if not easily characterized or explained) to scholars since the first half of the twentieth century.

In this chapter, I explore Owen's complicated relationship to scientific reform. Owen's attitude towards scientific reform was not merely one of hostility: he had positive relationships with some scientific reformers, aligned aspects of his thought with empirical science, and acknowledged that natural science might serve worthy ends. These points of harmony have yet to be studied. Here I will lay out some general definitions and questions surrounding the 'Scientific Revolution' in seventeenth-century England before considering Owen's particular relationships with various figures associated with scientific reform. Finally, I will turn from reformers to reform itself, asking what an understanding of Owen might contribute to the scholarly conversation about the historical relationship between Protestantism and modern natural science that has unfolded over the past century.

SCIENTIFIC REFORM AND PROTESTANTISM IN SEVENTEENTH-CENTURY ENGLAND

For several decades of the twentieth century, historians debated whether there was a correlation between Puritanism and the rise of modern science, and why any such correlation might exist; this controversy had reached such a state by 1969 that Owen's biographer Richard L. Greaves set out to 'anatomize' it, to 'examine the possible ways in which Puritanism might have aided in the acceptance and development of scientific thought'.[5] Owen was to his mind not a good example of such cooperation: in his entry on Owen in the *Oxford*

---

[3]Wintraub, 'Looking glass of facts', 219, explains the difficulty of identifying which books on the booklist supplied in Harwood's *Early essays and ethics of Robert Boyle* actually belonged to Boyle, but concludes that the list 'remains a valuable source of evidence for understanding the intellectual milieu within which Boyle lived and worked'.
[4]Greaves, 'John Owen (1616–1683)', *ODNB*.
[5]Greaves, 'Puritanism and science', 346.

Dictionary of National Biography, Greaves went out of his way to point out that 'unlike his friend John Wilkins [Owen] displayed little interest in curricular reform, especially the new science' during his years as vice-chancellor of the University of Oxford. Given changes in how we understand the 'new science', however, now is a good time to reassess this claim.

Intellectual historians now use scare quotes and other strategies to avoid giving the impression that the 'scientific revolution' was a simple or straightforward affair. Nevertheless, it is clear that some kind of scientific reform was afoot in seventeenth-century England.[6] This reform had a number of recognizable tendencies, including (1) suspicion or rejection of Aristotelianism; (2) atomic or corpuscularian theories of matter (associated with the revival of interest in Epicureanism, especially as presented in Lucretius's *De rerum natura* and championed by Hobbes); (3) an emphasis on observation, experimentation and collaboration as the best method for advancing knowledge (set forth, e.g. in Bacon's *Advancement of learning*); and (4) an aim of marshalling natural knowledge for the glory of God and the benefit of mankind, as in the charter of the Royal Society of London.[7] If Owen saw the Royal Society as spiritually bankrupt, he may not have dismissed every aspect of the broader reform; certainly he had friends who were interested in or promoted these things.

What is more, Owen was a Protestant as well as a Puritan, and affinities do exist between Protestantism and modern natural science. There is still a strong case to be made, for instance, that the theological voluntarism associated with Calvin and his followers has affinities with empirical method. As John Henry puts it:

> The voluntarist emphasis upon God's freedom of operation is associated with a belief in the radical contingency of the natural world and the concomitant belief that we can only understand God's creation *a posteriori*, by examining it and drawing empirically based conclusions as to what he actually did, or as to what kind of world he created.[8]

To this long-standing thesis about science and Protestantism we may add what has been dubbed 'Harrison's hypothesis'. This argument, developed by Peter

---

[6] In this chapter I use 'science' and 'scientific' in the broad older sense of 'pertaining to natural knowledge'. 'Science' in the modern sense of empirical observation and experimentation corresponds most closely to the early modern category of 'natural philosophy', though the two are not synonymous. When I refer to 'scientific reform', I mean along the lines described here, and particularly the reforms inspired by Bacon.
[7] For an overview of scientific developments in early modern Europe, see Henry, *The scientific revolution and the origins of modern science*, and Shapin, *The scientific revolution*.
[8] Henry, 'Voluntarist theology at the origins of modern science', 81. For a counter argument, see van der Meer, 'European Calvinists and the study of nature', 129–30.

Harrison first in 1998 and further clarified and defended in a number of places, holds that the 'Protestant Reformation effected a dramatic contraction of the realm of the sacred, through its constriction of sacramental practices, its incipient iconoclasm and, crucially, its emphasis on the word and literal sense of Scripture'. These and other features of Protestantism helped scientific reform to thrive, Harrison argues, and such factors 'were particularly significant in seventeenth-century England'.[9] One of these features has since received book-length treatment by Harrison: the belief of many English Protestants that the purpose of learning should be, as John Milton put it, 'to repair the ruins of our first parents', or reverse the effects of the fall as far as possible.[10] Many felt this endeavour must be partly intellectual rather than only moral or spiritual, for Adam had clearly been a consummate natural philosopher if he could have named all the animals as he was described as doing in Genesis 2.[11] Owen too viewed Adam and Eve as possessing prodigious God-given knowledge that gradually dissipated after the fall.[12]

The idea that a *telos* of human learning might be to reverse the effects of the fall raises the larger question, much on the minds of scientific reformers, of the ultimate *telos* of human learning or, put in terms from the Westminster Assembly's Shorter Catechism, its 'chief end'.[13] Proponents of scientific reform sought to show how the new philosophy would glorify God, and one of the ways it might do this is by giving new weight, direction and scope to natural theology.[14] Predicated on the biblical idea that God's glory is evident in nature as well as the Bible, Christian natural theology was to give rise in seventeenth-century England to physico-theology, the practice of inferring God's existence and attributes from the observation of design

---

[9] Harrison, 'Religion and the early Royal Society', 13. Harrison first put forward this argument in *The Bible, Protestantism, and the rise of modern science*. Objections to aspects of Harrison's hypothesis have been raised in van der Meer and Oosterhoff, 'God, Scripture, and the rise of modern science (1200–1700)'; Mandelbrote, 'Early modern Biblical interpretation and the emergence of science'; and Serjeantson, 'Francis Bacon and the "interpretation of nature" in the late Renaissance'. Harrison's hypothesis remains highly influential, however: Henry, for instance, concludes that the 'voluntarism and science thesis should stand shoulder to shoulder alongside Harrison's thesis'; 'Voluntarist theology at the origins of modern science', 103.

[10] Milton, *Of education* (1644), 2; *The complete poetry and essential prose of John Milton*, eds Kerrigan et al, 971.

[11] Harrison, *The fall of man and the foundations of modern science*. See also Poole, *Milton and the idea of the fall*, and Picciotto, *Labors of innocence in early modern England*.

[12] Gribben, *John Owen and English Puritanism*, 213, points out that this is the argument of Owen's Θεολογούμενα παντοδαπά (1661).

[13] [Westminster Assembly], *The humble advice of the assembly of divines . . . concerning a shorter catechism* (1648), p. 5.

[14] Harrison, 'Religion, the Royal Society, and the rise of science'.

in the physical world.[15] But seventeenth-century English natural theology included other things as well. Well before physico-theology began to gain ground, Calvin legitimatized natural theology in the opening chapters of the *Institutes*, drawing on the claim in Rom. 1.19-20 that God's divinity and power are evident in creation; Calvin even asserted that those with training in 'astronomy, medicine, and all natural science' can 'penetrate with their aid far more deeply into the secrets of divine wisdom' than those without such training.[16] Robert Boyle agreed with this and was arguably the most important patron of English natural theology: at his death, he endowed the famous Boyle Lectures, which became a vehicle for the proliferation of physico-theology over the ensuing century. But Boyle was also interested in another natural–theological practice: the 'occasional meditation'. These theological meditations need not be 'occasioned' by phenomena uncovered through the new sciences, but they could be, Boyle recognized, and they might be the better for it.[17] This understudied genre is an important avenue for reconsidering Owen's relationship to scientific reform, for Owen too saw value in occasional meditation.

In this brief survey of scientific reform and Protestantism in seventeenth-century England, a few such avenues suggest themselves, not all of which there is space to consider here. For instance, both Owen and scientific reformers were reexamining the roles of both Scripture and nature in the life of faith – how these 'two books' of divine revelation should be read, and by whom – and in many cases they were in harmony against the Catholic answers to these questions. Another enemy Owen shared with a number of scientific reformers was the threat of atheism that was increasingly viewed as an important reason to undertake natural theology: Owen was particularly concerned by Thomas Hobbes's philosophy, for instance, even though Hobbes's view of church and state accorded in many ways with his own.[18] Owen's theological voluntarism, too, positioned him to see the benefits of sensory observation as a means of learning – and he did give a measure of credence to experience and observation in spite of his scholastic formation. Finally, Owen had a stake in evolving ideas about natural theology. At a time when physico-theology began to dominate conversations about science and religion – with disastrous consequences for Christianity, many would now say – Owen was already opposed to the thinking

---

[15] Calloway, *Natural theology in the scientific revolution*, 1–19. See also Blair and von Greyerz (eds), *Physico-theology*.
[16] Calvin, *Institutes of the Christian religion*, 1.5.1. See also Calloway, 'A "metaphorical God" and the book of nature', 129–32.
[17] Boyle, *Occasional reflections*, 17–19.
[18] Gribben, *John Owen and English Puritanism*, 163–4.

underlying physico-theology. He was, however, interested in other ways that knowledge of the natural world might conduce to the 'chief end of man'.

OWEN AMONG THE SCIENTIFIC REFORMERS

Both as an influential theologian and as an important figure in English politics, Owen had many connections, positive and negative, with people involved with scientific reform; these people of course also interacted with each other. Out of this social network I trace here a few important interactions, many of which saw important development during Owen's years as the 'manager of a galaxy of Oxford stars': when he served as dean of Christ Church (1651–60) and vice-chancellor of the University of Oxford (1652–7).[19] Among those 'stars' were champions of scientific reform who would later inaugurate the Royal Society: John Wilkins, Robert Boyle, John Wallis, Seth Ward, Henry Oldenburg, Christopher Wren, a young Robert Hooke and Thomas Sprat. As their efforts gained ground and sponsorship, these 'virtuosi' would be criticized not only by Owen but also by Hobbes and Henry Stubbe.[20] On the other side, there were also ideologues, such as John Webster and William Dell, who wanted yet more stringent academic reform and a total break with traditional curricula.[21] At the Restoration, the virtuosi of the Royal Society lost much of their motivation for engaging with Owen, but he had reason to maintain connections with them. Among the topics taken up by these scientific reformers at Oxford and beyond was the controversy over atomism, a philosophy championed in England by Walter Charleton and Thomas Hobbes and entertained by Owen's friend Lucy Hutchinson through her translation of the first-century Latin poet Lucretius. Finally, in his last decade of life, Owen opposed in print such 'latitudinarians' as Joseph Glanvill and Edward Stillingfleet, who promoted both natural science and natural theology. Paradoxically, this conflict highlighted the harmony between Owen's views and those of Robert Boyle, a harmony which had been under the surface all along.

Scientific reform at Oxford

As Richard Greaves pointed out, Owen seems to have been uninterested in implementing scientific reform during the years when he had a fair amount of power to do so at Oxford, preferring instead reforms along theological and practical lines. This was in contrast with his fellow university administrator John Wilkins (1612–72). A conciliatory soul, Wilkins would manage to become

---

[19] Gribben, *John Owen and English Puritanism*, 268.
[20] Harrison, 'Religion, the Royal Society, and the rise of science', 255–62.
[21] Toon, *God's statesman*, 70–2; Mandelbrote, 'Uses of natural theology', 452–60.

both Cromwell's brother-in-law and a bishop in the Restoration church. He also stood at the social centre of English scientific reform in the 1650s and 1660s. His interest in the new philosophy was evident from at least 1638, when he published his *The discovery of a new world, or, A discourse tending to prove, that ('tis probable) there may be another habitable world in the moon*. As warden of Wadham College from 1648 until 1659, he attracted a number of the scientific virtuosi who had been meeting in London and Oxford and encouraged their continued meetings during the Interregnum.[22] He was also a lifelong friend of Owen: as boys, Wilkins and Owen had attended a private school in Oxford under the direction of Edward Sylvester, and both of them continued to attend annual dinners in Sylvester's honour until his death in 1653.[23] In 1652, Cromwell appointed both Owen and Wilkins to a committee with the authority to carry out many of his own duties as chancellor of Oxford.[24] In their administrative capacities, Owen and Wilkins could work well together, as was the case in 1654 when they campaigned (along with John Wallis and Seth Ward) against the removal of the orientalist Edward Pococke, already ejected from the university, from his parish church.[25] The same year, in fact, a correspondent complained to Richard Baxter that Owen was 'so intimate' with Wilkins as to ensure Wilkins's protection from accountability for alleged mismanagement of Wadham.[26]

If Owen could demonstrate restraint in ejecting prayer book-users, Wilkins and the other virtuosi seem to have shown restraint regarding reform of university curricula. As Toon observes in his biography of Owen,

> To the scientific society, which met at Wadham and which developed into the Royal Society, science was a subject to be studied outside the normal curriculum by mature students. . . . Simpson, Sedgwick, Wilkins and Ward, together with others who defended traditional learning, had the full support of Owen.[27]

This complaisance to Aristotle, possibly aided by the continuing influence of Owen's former tutor Thomas Barlow, provoked strident criticism by ideologues

---

[22]Henry, 'Wilkins, John', *ODNB*, s.v.
[23]Gribben, *John Owen and English Puritanism*, 29–30. Owen was two years younger than Wilkins, but the two would have been at Oxford at the same time, as Wilkins left in 1627 and Owen in 1628; *ODNB*, s.v.
[24]*The correspondence of John Owen*, 53–4.
[25]Toon, *God's statesman*, 93; Gribben, *John Owen and English Puritanism*, 153.
[26]Baxter, *Correspondence*, 1:152.
[27]Toon, *God's statesman*, 72. See also Greaves, *The Puritan revolution and educational thought*, 35: 'It is probable that those Puritans who actively supported the new educational thought, with its emphasis on utilitarianism and experimental science, were a minority.'

such as William Dell, of Caius College at Cambridge, and John Webster, a former army chaplain with radical religious leanings. Dell's contention, in brief, was that 'human learning mingled with divinity, or the Gospel of Christ understood according to Aristotle, hath begun, continued, and perfected the Mysterie of Iniquity in the outward Church'; England thus needed to begin again with schools in all cities and towns, free from Aristotle and emphasizing relevant practical disciplines.[28] Webster similarly asserted the complete 'groundlessness, ruinousness, and ill composure of the Scholastic Fabrick of learning', and urged that the schools rebuild – not, as he said the Presbyterians and Independents had done, by simply occupying the power vacuum left by the established clergy, but with a thorough overhaul of university curricula along Baconian lines.[29]

Against such criticism Owen stood allied with future Royal Society members in defence of England's two ancient universities. At his most congenial, in fact, he was willing to praise those at Oxford who were then 'widening the boundaries of the sciences'. Using Baconian language, Owen applauds in his jubilant fourth Oxford oration (1657) those who were learning 'new, marvellous, astonishing things, extracted from the very entrails of nature, unknown to their predecessors, to be admired by their successors, not without glory and fame both to themselves and the University'.[30] To be sure, in these orations Owen still gives the university's theologians prime importance, the other sciences being valuable to the extent that they serve the 'queen of the sciences'. Still, they are a testament to Owen's capacity to see good in the advancement of learning underway at Wilkins's Wadham College.

Though often willing to cooperate, Owen and Wilkins could also differ politically, most spectacularly in 1655, when Wilkins headed up a committee protesting actions taken by Owen and his fellow university reformer Thomas Goodwin that overstepped their authority.[31] Owen slighted the committee's protests, and Wilkins took the matter to London. At this point, however, Wilkins's powerful friends in London assured him that he had been right, and both Owen and Wilkins let the matter drop. The two college heads' interests nonetheless remained somewhat opposed, and this as Owen's power in both Oxford and London waned. Wilkins's influence did not wane: in 1656, he married Oliver Cromwell's youngest sister and became a close advisor to Richard Cromwell. At the Restoration, Wilkins had made so many friends at the university that he landed quickly and safely in the re-established church

---

[28]Dell, *The tryal of spirits* (1653), 72.
[29]Webster, *Academiarum examen* (1654), 96, dedication.
[30]*The Oxford orations*, 15, 34. Toon glosses these passages as referring to the 'Oxford science club' at Wadham College.
[31]Worden, 'Politics, piety, and learning', 130–3; Cooper, *John Owen, Richard Baxter and the formation of Nonconformity*, 108–11; Gribben, *John Owen and English Puritanism*, 161–2.

and from there rose to the position of Bishop of Chester by 1668.[32] Less safely, in the same period, Owen made a corresponding rise to prominence among Nonconformists. By 1670 Owen and Wilkins had reconfigured their relationship to the point where George Vernon could describe Wilkins as one of Owen's 'friends among the bishops'.[33]

John Wallis, Savilian professor of geometry at Oxford, was likewise part of the group that would become the Royal Society, and he likewise could find common cause with Owen, as the Pococke episode illustrates. On the other hand, despite acting as secretary to the Westminster Assembly, Wallis opposed the execution of Charles I and tolerated rather than embraced the circumstances of the Interregnum. On 10 October 1655, Wallis dedicated to Owen his *Elenchus Geometriae Hobbianae*, a refutation of Hobbes's *Leviathan* (1651) on geometrical grounds. The dedication is formal and lacking in warmth – Wallis omits to spin out praises of Owen on the grounds that people, like theorems, stand or fall based on 'proofs' and not praise – but Wallis could be sure that Owen too found the theological implications of Hobbes's work reprehensible.[34] Wallis recognized a need to explain his decision to refute Hobbes's geometry, 'leaving out Theology and other Philosophies, when there are other things in which he has made far more dangerous errors'.[35] The reason, Wallis explains, is that people might otherwise believe that Hobbes's geometry is unassailable, when in fact it is very shoddy; Wallis has the competency to expose this. There are many others who can and will attack Hobbes on other grounds, Wallis is sure.[36] It is unclear what Owen thought of this letter, but there was another matter on which Owen's position was much closer to the position of Hobbes than Wallis: church Independency.[37]

A year after Wallis dedicated his refutation of Hobbes to Owen, Owen asked Henry Stubbe, the young deputy keeper of the Bodleian Library, to write a refutation of Wallis, who 'hath put out some theses against a branch of independency'.[38] Like Owen, Stubbe was a defender of 'independency';

---

[32] Henry, 'Wilkins, John', *ODNB*, s.v.
[33] Cooper, *John Owen, Richard Baxter, and the formation of Nonconformity*, 272.
[34] John Wallis, 'To the worthy gentleman John Owen, doctor of sacred theology, dean of Christ Church, Oxford, vice chancellor of the university', 10 October 1655, *The correspondence of John Owen*, 86. On Owen's engagement with Hobbes's atomism and materialism in particular, see below.
[35] Wallis, 'To the worthy gentleman John Owen', *The correspondence of John Owen*, 86.
[36] Wallis, 'To the worthy gentleman John Owen', *The correspondence of John Owen*, 86–8.
[37] Collins, *The allegiance of Thomas Hobbes*, 224–5, paints a picture of Stubbe as encouraging Hobbes to see the extent of his 'crucial intellectual affinity' with Owen and against Wallis; Hobbes appears to have 'endorsed' Owen's *On schisme*. See also Feingold, 'Stubbe, Henry', *ODNB*, s.v., and Gribben, *John Owen and English Puritanism*, 164.
[38] Jacob, *Henry Stubbe, radical Protestantism and the early Enlightenment*, 18.

unlike Owen, Stubbe was very taken with Hobbes's philosophy as a whole and did what he could to promote it. In his subordination to Owen, he could not do much: he undertook to translate *Leviathan* into Latin but had to give that up, largely due to pressure from Owen. As he worked to promote Hobbes's thought, Stubbe also tried to enlist Hobbes in the project of refuting Wallis, which Hobbes did to a limited extent.[39] In sum, during the 1650s Owen, Hobbes and Stubbe found themselves on one side of the ecclesial controversy and Wallis on another; on the theological controversy, by contrast, Owen and Wallis had common cause against Hobbes and (unbeknownst to Owen) Stubbe. Further complicating this web of ecclesiastical and philosophical commitments was Hobbes's and Stubbe's opposition to experimentalism. While Hobbes was a notorious proponent of the newly fashionable atomistic philosophy, he was no friend of experimentalism; nor was Stubbe. In his *Campanella revived* (1670), Stubbe would disparage the virtuosi as 'very great Impostors' whose neglect of studies was not conducive to 'that Moral discipline which instructs us in the nature of virtue and vice',[40] and in 1680 Hobbes would likewise complain about the experimentalists, insisting that 'not every one that brings from beyond seas a new gin, or other jaunty device, is therefore a philosopher'.[41] Wallis of course was a steady promoter of the virtuosi in the 1650s and then a founding member of the Royal Society, so Hobbes and Stubbe appear to have opposed him at every turn.

Where was Owen in all of this? In the epigraph to this chapter, Owen expresses views that were similar in tone and content to those of Hobbes, suggesting that the two men were unlikely bedfellows on the issue of experimentalism no less than with regards to Erastianism. In these cases the picture that begins to emerge of Owen's interactions with scientific reformers during his time in power at Oxford is one of toleration, possibly even approbation at times, but only within strict theological and ecclesial bounds. At the Restoration he would have, in turn, to fight for toleration for himself and other dissenters, and his relationships to various scientific reformers likewise shifted.

Scientific reform beyond Oxford

Owen's complaint that the Royal Society members were wasting their time with hens and oysters certainly reflects a conviction on his part that such activities were useless – but it also reflects frustration particular to that moment. Owen

---

[39]Jacob, *Henry Stubbe, radical Protestantism and the early Enlightenment*, 18–24. See also Shapin and Schaffer, *Leviathan and the air pump*, 308–9.
[40]Stubbe, *Campanella revived*, preface, 14.
[41]Hobbes, *Considerations upon the reputation, loyalty, manners, & religion of Thomas Hobbes*, 53–4. See also Harrison, 'Religion, the Royal Society, and the rise of science', 260–1.

had committed some 'papers' to Henry Oldenburg, FRS, and a former Oxford colleague, apparently in the hopes of some kind of support. Oldenburg failed to provide this support, provoking Owen to explain to John Thornton that 'my papers are as you said with Mr Oldeburgh who pretends his relation to the virtuosi to increase so much worke upon his hands, that he must leave my papers untoucht'.[42] Then follows Owen's scathing critique of the virtuosi as woefully misdirecting their intellectual resources. No longer in a position to help or hinder the experimentalists' projects, Owen now chafed at being passed over for these unworthy pursuits. On the other hand, the fact that Owen's papers found their way to Oldenburg in the first place testifies that channels of communication were still open between himself and members of the Royal Society, and that he had some reason to hope for Oldenburg's support.

Owen's voice also echoed into the debate between the virtuosi and Hobbes in the 1660s: in his *Dialogus physicus* (1661), Hobbes named Owen as promoting an unfair *odium Hobbii* that prevented his ideas from receiving due consideration on their own merits. Ever since Hobbes 'had very freely written the truth about Academies', he complained, 'angry mathematicians and physicists have publicly declared that they would not accept any truth that came from [me]: "Whatever be Hobbes's doctrine, we will not accept it", said Owen, vice-chancellor of Oxford.'[43] If Hobbes had been willing to acknowledge his political common ground with Owen in the 1650s, he now de-emphasized that common ground and described himself as a critic of 'the academies', while also implying that Owen's views were representative of mathematicians and physicists at the university. It was this accusation that occasioned Boyle's retort, in his *Examen of the greatest part of Mr. Hobbs's Dialogus Physicus* (1662), that Hobbes,

> to prove that our Naturalists and Mathematicians professed they would not receive Truth coming from him ... alledges only a saying (whether true or no I examine not) of Dr. Owen, who, besides that his profession was Divinity, not Philosophy or Mathematicks, neither is nor ever was of our Society.[44]

In this instance, in the early 1660s, then, Owen was a hot potato that no natural philosopher wanted to touch, though Boyle does leave open the possibility of Owen's being falsely accused by Hobbes. Owen's profession was divinity, Boyle flatly states; in the new order, he has no profession.

---

[42] John Owen to John Thorton, n.d., *The correspondence of John Owen*, 132.
[43] Shapin and Schaffer, *Leviathan and the air pump*, 309, 379.
[44] Boyle, *New experiments physico-mechanical* (1662), 72.

While the Restoration drove a social and political wedge between Owen and the members of the Royal Society as well as Hobbes, it was this period that brought his story together with that of Lucy Hutchinson, a fellow Calvinist and Republican who could share his grief at the demise of the 'Good Old Cause'. By 1673, Hutchinson was attending Owen's sermons in London; around this time she also translated parts of his Θεολογούμενα παντοδαπά (1661) into English. This effort illustrates a notable redirection of her translating energies, for she had previously undertaken to translate Lucretius's *De rerum natura* – the first complete surviving translation of this notorious philosophical poem into English.[45] While Hutchinson was not a scientific reformer in the sense of promoting or practising experimentalism, she thus played a role in the dissemination of scientific ideas that were then gaining ground. She did not publish her Lucretius translation, but an unauthorized manuscript was circulated, prompting her to make a new copy in 1675. This she dedicated to Arthur Annesley, earl of Anglesey, a defender and friend of Owen as well as Hutchinson.

The Epicurean philosophy espoused in this poem, which mushroomed in popularity in early modern Europe, was in many ways consonant with that of Hobbes and opposed to Reformed and even Christian theology.[46] Besides asserting (against the more traditional 'plenist' view) that nature is basically constituted by atoms and void, *De rerum natura* describes the universe as infinite in time and space, rather than created, and denies the existence of the supernatural. The 'gods', though material, are too rarefied to meddle with human affairs: the best way for humans to live, therefore, is without reference to them, maximizing pleasure and minimizing pain – though in a more holistic and long-sighted way than Owen had in mind when he lamented that university students behaved with a 'licentiousness nearly Epicurean'.[47] Hutchinson was aware of these heresies and responded to them in various ways in her translation as well as the dedication and marginalia she later attached to it. Indeed, her engagement with Owen likely played a role in her changing attitude towards her own translation of Lucretius.[48]

A final movement in Owen's engagement with scientific reformers occurred in the 1670s and early 1680s, as he crossed swords with two 'latitude-

---

[45] It is not known for certain when Hutchinson translated *DRN*, but Barbour et al. point out that 'setting the translation in the context of Hutchinson's world in the 1650s, rather than the very different circumstances of the Restoration, helps to make more sense of her life'; 'Introduction', xv–xvii.

[46] On the relationship between Lucretius and Hobbes, see Norbrook, 'Atheists and republicans', 225–7.

[47] Owen, *The Oxford orations*, 5. See Englert, 'Introduction', xiii–xvi.

[48] Barbour et al., 'Introduction', cviii–cix.

men': Joseph Glanvill and Edward Stillingfleet. While categories such as 'latitudinarian' can obscure important differences between individual thinkers, this can nonetheless be a helpful label to apply to churchmen who, as Scott Mandelbrote summarizes, were characterized by a

> preference for the use of reason, rather than coercion, to convert theological opponents and a willingness to make compromises in ecclesiology, if not in matters of doctrine, in order to live in charity within a single church and alongside as broad a group of Christians as possible.[49]

It was the commitment to a 'single church' that put this group conspicuously at odds with Owen, but the question of reason versus 'coercion' was equally divisive. From another angle, this is the question of the theological use and limits of natural knowledge. Glanvill's *Defense of reason in the affairs of religion* was published first in 1670 and appended to his defence of the experimental philosophy of the Royal Society in 1671. Owen took issue with Glanvill's thoroughgoing assertion of the reasonableness of Christianity in these works, countering that Christianity contains many things above reason, in his *The nature of apostasie* (1676).[50] Stillingfleet's *Mischief of separation* (1680) set off a pamphlet battle with Owen over ecclesiastical polity, but Stillingfleet's view of reason was similar to Glanvill's and similarly at odds with Owen's: he had published an ambitious and popular work of natural theology, *Origines sacrae*, in 1662 and would after Owen's death publish *A discourse concerning the nature and grounds of the certainty of faith* (1688).

Perhaps the most interesting aspect of Owen's conflict with the latitudinarians is the harmony that it highlighted between himself and Robert Boyle on the matter of reason and faith. Although Boyle avoided Owen even during the Interregnum and disclaimed association with him in 1662, the two men had been circling each other since Boyle's youth.[51] In the 1640s they were already connected indirectly through Robert Rich, the second earl of Warwick: Rich was both a patron of Owen's and father-in-law to Boyle's older sister, Mary. It is likely that Boyle read Owen's Θεομαχία αυτεξουσιαστική: or, *A display of Arminianisme* (1643); in any case, Boyle was keenly interested in the theological discourse around free will and predestination, despite the fact that the lecture

---

[49]Mandelbrote, 'The uses of natural theology in seventeenth-century England', 457.
[50]Wojcik, 'The theological context of Boyle's *Things above reason*', 146–7.
[51]Hunter, *Boyle*, 103–4, cites Sir Peter Pett's account that Boyle refused to associate with Owen in the 1650s to avoid 'all guilt and scandal' by not showing the slightest approval of 'Cromwell's Usurpation'.

series bearing his name aimed to avoid meddling in sectarian controversies.[52] Boyle even participated in this discourse himself, and – despite his deep commitment to natural theology – he positioned himself against Glanvill, arguing in his *Discourse of things above reason* (1681) that there are things above reason, inconsistencies viewed from a human perspective that only God can resolve. Michael Hunter observes that 'this work, more than any other, signals Boyle's position as a "voluntarist" in the theological and philosophical debates of the day'.[53] Against the latitudinarians' ambitious project of proving Christianity conclusively, then, both Boyle and Owen asserted the limits of human reason in divine things. Just as importantly, however, all of these men stood arrayed against a (Baconian) line of thought holding that reason should stay out of divine things.

OWEN AND NATURAL SCIENCE

Francis Bacon did not entirely proscribe natural theology, but he would have been happy to see the enterprise halted in preference for natural philosophy and natural history. In his *Advancement of learning* (1605), he argued that there was already an 'excess' of natural theology and that this branch of learning had 'been excellently handled by diverse'. What is more, Bacon argued, there was a great danger of enquiring minds pridefully overstepping bounds:

> Out of the contemplation of Nature, or ground of humane knowledges to induce any veritie, or perswasion concerning the points of Faith, is in my judgement, not safe: *Da fidei, quae fidei sunt* . . . *Men and Gods were not able to draw Jupiter down to Earth, but contrariwise, Jupiter was able to draw them up to Heaven*. So as wee ought not to attempt to drawe downe or submit the Mysteries of GOD to our Reason: but contrariwise, to raise and advance our Reason to the Divine Truthe.[54]

Owen would agree that humans should give to faith what belongs to faith; what he would oppose is the subsequent call to 'raise and advance our Reason to Divine Truthe', by which Bacon means to engage in a rigorous collaborative programme of observation and experimentation towards the eventual god-like mastery of nature for the benefit of mankind. In Owen's view, those who

---

[52]Harwood, *The early essays and ethics of Robert Boyle*, xviii, xxviii, 272; Wojcik, 'The theological context of Boyle's *Things above reason*'. On the Boyle Lectures see n. below. Owen's *The reason of faith* (1677) was also among the ten books by Owen that were probably kept at Boyle's home.
[53]Hunter, *Boyle*, 200–1.
[54]Bacon, *The works of Francis Bacon*, 4:78–9. There is a Calvinist element in Bacon's thought; Gascoigne, 'Religious thought of Francis Bacon'.

devoted themselves to natural knowledge in this way, keeping 'their Thoughts in continual Exercise about the Things of this World, as unto the Advantages and Emoluments which they expect from them', would inevitably be 'transformed into the Image of the World, becoming earthly, carnal and vain'.[55]

Having ruled out the intellectual plot devoted to a continual focus on earthly things, we still may ask what kinds of natural reasoning and attention to the natural world might, in Owen's view, be licit or even productive. If he opposed a sweeping redirection of intellectual resources towards observation and experimentation, did he also reject sensory evidence and reason altogether in preference for faith? A closer look at Owen's treatment of sensory evidence reveals harmony with the scientific reformers' emphasis on induction, insofar as these methods can reveal the 'blindness' of Catholicism or (atomistic) materialism. This bounded respect for sensory evidence corresponds to Owen's growing esteem for natural knowledge in general, as he came to realize that reason was a useful and necessary weapon against theological opponents.[56] Still, there is always the danger that natural science will be raised too high, in which case it makes people 'carnal', unresponsive to the Gospel, and inattentive to theological matters of far greater importance than the 'things of this world'.

THE DANGERS OF NATURAL SCIENCE

Owen's relative suspicion of natural science is especially visible when his censure of the Royal Society – particularly their sustained attention to empirical observation at the expense of other things – is compared with Calvin's comments on natural science (*physica scientia*) one century prior, before Bacon's 'great instauration'. On the one hand, Calvin stressed that natural science cannot benefit the unregenerate in any way, and that unschooled people are perfectly capable of seeing God's wisdom in creation.[57] On the other hand, Calvin insists,

> there is a need of art and of more exacting toil in order to investigate the motion of the stars, to determine their assigned stations, to measure their intervals, to note their properties. As God's providence shows itself more

---

[55]Owen, *Meditations and discourses on the glory of Christ* (1684), 51–2; *Works* (1965), 12:399. There may be a conflation here of two biblical senses of 'world' (κοσμος): the created order that God loves and seeks to redeem, as in Jn 3.16, and humans' use of that order to try to live without reference to God, as in 1 Jn 2.15-17.
[56]Mortimer, *Reason and religion in the English revolution*, 209–10.
[57]Calvin, *Institutes*, 1.5.11: 'But although the Lord represents both himself and his everlasting Kingdom in the mirror of his works with very great clarity, such is our stupidity that we grow increasingly dull towards so manifest testimonies, and they flow away without profiting us.'

explicitly when one observes these, so the mind must rise to a somewhat higher level to look upon his glory.[58]

Calvin has in view a direct positive correlation between growth in natural knowledge and apprehension of God's glory. In Owen's own time, this idea was rehearsed more expansively by Richard Baxter:

> If we had a sight of all the Orbs, both fixed Starrs and Planets, and of their matter, and form, and order, and relation to each other, and their communications and influences on each other, and the cause of all their wonderous motions: If we saw not only the nature of the Elements, especially the active Element, Fire; but also the constitution, magnitude, and use, of all those thousand Suns, and lesser Worlds, which constitute the universal World: And, if they be inhabited, if we knew the Inhabitants of each: Did we know all the Intelligences, blessed Angels, and holy Spirits, which possess the nobler parts of Nature; and the unhappy degenerate Spirits, that have departed from light and joy, into darkness and horrour, by departing from God; yea, if we could see all these comprehensively, at one view; what thoughts should we have of the wisdom of the Creator?[59]

Owen's answer to Baxter's final rhetorical question would be that we might well have forgotten the Creator completely in searching after all these things (only some of which would ultimately be ruled within the Royal Society's remit). Passages such as these are conspicuously absent from Owen's oeuvre, suggesting that to his mind there was no necessary correlation between empirically gained natural knowledge and godliness. What is more, this might be a zero-sum game in which time spent acquiring one detracted from the other, as was the case when Henry Oldenburg did not have time to read Owen's papers because of his own scientific work. This zero-sum thinking ran both ways: while most Royal Society members agreed that growth in godliness was the ultimate end of learning, they largely disagreed that this goal would be achieved by arguing about what they considered to be fruitless sectarian disputes. Rather than 'meddling' in these things, they held, it was better to re-affirm central truths of Christianity and to enlarge our understanding of God's wisdom and providence as evident in the beauty and order of the natural world.[60]

---

[58]Calvin, *Institutes*, 1.5.2.
[59]Baxter, *The reasons of the Christian religion* (1667), 23.
[60]For a helpful discussion of Thomas Sprat's claim that 'the *Royal Society* is abundantly cautious not to intermeddle in *Spiritual things*', see Harrison, 'Religion and the Early Royal Society', 3–4. The famous Boyle Lectures were endowed to 'prove the Christian religion against notorious infidels . . .

Because of Owen's conviction that empirical science was generally a waste of time, there is in his works a dearth of engagement with specific scientific topics. An instance of Owen's wilful non-engagement with science, for example, may be in view in John Bunyan's poem introducing his 1682 allegory *The Holy War*. Bunyan writes:

Count me not then with them that to amaze
The people, set them on the stars to gaze,
Insinuating with much confidence,
That each of them is now the residence
Of some brave Creatures; yea, a world they will
Have in each Star, though it be past their skill
To make it manifest to any man,
That reason hath, or tell his fingers can. (7–14)

Here Bunyan presents one of the scientific topics Baxter had listed as conducing to thoughts of God's wisdom: knowledge of 'all those thousand Suns, and lesser Worlds, which constitute the universal World: And, if they be inhabited, . . . the Inhabitants of each'. Bunyan's twentieth-century editors paused here to consider how Bunyan came to be aware of contemporary works imagining extra-terrestrial life, suggesting that 'Bunyan may have heard at second hand through Owen of the speculations of John Wilkins'.[61] As mentioned earlier, Wilkins had published works about the possibility of space travel and life on other planets; it is unlikely that his lifelong friend Owen was unaware of these.[62] It is also likely that Owen would have approved of Bunyan's desire to discipline his imagination away from such unprofitable and unverifiable speculations, towards the more spiritually edifying allegory that followed these lines.

Owen does break his silence on specific aspects of the new science in the case of atomism. We have seen that this particular topic was raised not only among Royal Society members but also by Lucy Hutchinson, and Calvin before her: public awareness of atomism was growing due to the rediscovery and dissemination of Lucretius's *De rerum natura* throughout Europe. It was because of Lucretius's practical atheism that Calvin had called him a 'filthy dog' who made 'a shadow deity to drive away the true God', a moniker that Hutchinson would pick up in her 1675 dedication of her translation to

---

not descending to any Controversies that are among Christians themselves'; Bentley, *The folly and unreasonableness of atheism* (1693), Dedication.
[61]Bunyan, *The holy war*, 5.
[62]To his *Discovery of a world in the moone* (1638), Wilkins added *Discourse concerning a new planet* (1640). Another space-travel work dating to this period was Francis Godwin's *The man in the moone* (1638).

Anglesey.[63] However, Lucretius's atomistic philosophy could also be suspect in itself, because he linked atomism to a reductive naturalistic explanation of human origins. Calvin taunts, 'let Epicurus answer what concourse of atoms . . . begets such industry in the several members [of the human body] to carry out their tasks, as if so many souls ruled one body by common counsel!'[64] The perceived threat of atomism was ratcheted up in England by Hobbes, who espoused not only atomism but also Lucretius's irreligious view that the world is nothing but matter in motion.[65] *Pace* Calvin's summary dismissal of Lucretius, but in line with his contention that a 'concourse of atoms' could not possibly produce or maintain our world, a number of efforts were made to divorce atomism from Lucretius's heretical claims.[66] For instance, Bacon wrote in his essay 'Of atheism' (1612) that

> it is a thousand times more Credible, that foure Mutable Elements, and one Immuable Fift Essence, duly and Eternally placed, need no God; then that an Army, of Infinite small Portions, or Seedes unplaced, should have produced this Order, and Beauty, without a Divine Marshall.[67]

Hutchinson herself demonstrates a canny ability to make common cause with Lucretius even as she recognized that many of his beliefs were 'impious' and later came to describe her translation of *De rerum natura* as an act of youthful folly.[68]

Owen committed no such act of folly, preferring (like Calvin) summarily to scoff at Epicurean doctrine. As was the case in Calvin's *Institutes*, however, Owen explicitly condemns not atomism itself but a reductive materialist account of the origin and preservation of the world. He mentions atomism in *A vision of unchangeable free mercy* (1646), his first published sermon. As the title suggests, the sermon stresses God's absolute freedom to order human events. One aspect of God's sovereignty is that he is free to act in a variety of ways, as evidenced by the events of the English revolution that was then in process:

---

[63] Calvin, *Institutes*, 1.5.5; Hutchinson, *Works*, 1:13 and note.
[64] Calvin, *Institutes*, 1.5.4.
[65] Fallon, *Milton among the philosophers*, 60–1.
[66] Notable works in this vein were Pierre Gassendi's Latin *Animadversiones* (1649), which was followed in England by Walter Charleton's *Physiologia epicuro-gassendo-Charletoniana* (1654). Ralph Cudworth, head of two Cambridge colleges during the Interregnum and co-signer with Owen of a letter 'To the evangelical churches of Europe', insisted in his *True intellectual system* (1678), 12, that atomism 'if rightly understood . . . is the most effectual Engin against Atheism that can be'.
[67] Bacon, *Works*, 51.
[68] Barbour et al, 'Introduction'; Hutchinson, *Works*, 1:7–9, Dedication.

> Now, is all this variety, think you, to be ascribed unto chance, as the Philosopher thought the world was made by a casuall concurrence of atomes? Or hath the Idol free-will, with the new goddesse contingency, ruled in these dispensations? Truly neither the one nor the other, no more then the fly raised the dust, by sitting on the chariot wheel; but all these things have come to passe, according to a certain unerring rule, given them by Gods determinate purpose and counsell.[69]

The 'casual' nature of Lucretius's cosmos was the problem for Owen, particularly at a moment when it appeared that God was determinately reforming England after its long slide into darkness. Owen reiterates this notion in passing in *Of schisme* (1657), his contribution to the defence of church Independency against John Wallis and others. In an attack on apostolic succession, Owen avers that there is 'nothing at all being pleaded to ground this succession . . . but only it is so fallen out, as the world was composed by a casuall concurrence of Atomes'.[70] Here Owen uses the absurdity of the fortuitous composition of the world by errant atoms to figure the equally absurd idea that 'the bishop of Rome succeeds Peter'. In so doing he signals the distance between himself and Hobbes, even as he aligns himself with Hobbes's own position on Erastianism so well that Hobbes commended the work.[71]

An interesting final instance of Owen on atomism arises in *Of the divine originall* (1659), a work asserting the divine authorship of Scripture. Considering the highly rule-bound nature of 'points, or vowels and Accents' in the Hebrew Bible, Owen proclaims that 'things are not thus come to pass by chance; nor was this *world* [i.e. the Bible] created by a casuall concurrence of these *Atomes* [i.e. points, vowels, and accents]'. Here again Owen uses atomism metaphorically, now to underscore the impossibility that the Bible, any more than the natural world, could have been composed 'casually'. With this line of thought Owen taps into the venerable tradition of God's 'two books': like the book of Scripture, this tradition holds, the book of nature was authored by God and is therefore significant in the most capacious sense of the word. The idea that vowels and points are analogous to atoms, moreover, is strikingly similar to the analogy of an *alphabetum naturae* used by the atomists themselves and, later, in English physico-theology. Just as a book is composed of words made from a finite set of basic letters, so too is the world composed of a finite set of corpuscles or atoms, ingeniously arranged by the author.[72] Did Owen, like

---

[69]Owen, *A vision of unchangeable free mercy* (1646), 10; *Works* (1965), 8:12.
[70]Owen, *Of schisme* (1657), 181; *Works* (1965), 13:165.
[71]Collins, *Allegiance of Thomas Hobbes*, 231.
[72]Hudson, *Writing and European thought, 1600–1850*, 38–9; Calloway, *Natural theology in the scientific revolution*, 134. On the corpuscular versus atomic hypotheses, see Henry, *Scientific*

the atomists, see atomism therefore as an effective 'engine against atheism' that also accurately described reality? Or was he committed to the Aristotelian elements, as he was to the scholastic method, yoking atomism together with materialism as clearly false beliefs? Perhaps he considered the question a matter indifferent, unimportant relative to the pressing need to stem the tide of heresy and apostasy.

More relevant to this goal was the need to counter the reductive materialism of Lucretius and Hobbes, which Owen linked to an idolization of the senses. Sensory evidence, the key source of knowledge in Bacon's inductive method, was to Owen's (Restoration) mind often placed too high, with disastrous spiritual consequences. This is the case, for instance, when spiritual guilt over sin is reductively explained by atheists as mere 'Melancholy reeks and vapours' in the brain.[73] It is also the case when nominal Christians replace the real Christ with 'false Representations' of his human person 'by the help of their outward senses', leading to carnal and corrupt affections.[74] The Catholic Church is a primary offender in this way, for they set about 'entertaining . . . outward senses' of worshippers so as to gratify their inward superstition.[75] In sum, Owen is generally suspicious of the outward senses because of their 'serviceableness . . . unto Sin and Folly, if not watched against'.[76] In these cases, however, it is worth noting that he opposes the outward senses, not to deductive reason but to faith. It remains an open possibility that, for Owen, sensory evidence should indeed be given more credence relative to cogitation and deduction than had been the case in foregoing centuries.

Productive possibilities

For the senses could also be a helpful check against obviously wrong notions. Owen recognized 'external senses' as the first among 'three ways whereby we come to know anything', ordained by God to help humans move from ignorance to truth.[77] Humans should therefore be wary of

> Men that have so great a confidence of their own Abilities, and such a contempt of the World, as to undertake to dispute them out of conclusions from their natural senses, about their proper Objects, in what they see, feele,

---

revolution, 68–84.

[73]Owen, Πνευματολογια (1674), 92–3; *Works* (1965), 3:121.

[74]Owen, Χριστολογια (1679), 196; *Works* (1965), 1:159.

[75]Owen, *Discourse of the work of the Holy Spirit in prayer* (1682), preface; *Works* (1965), 4:245.

[76]Owen, *The grace and duty of being spiritually-minded* (1681), 319; *Works* (1965), 7:487.

[77]Owen, Πνευματολογια (1674), 106; *Works* (1965), 3:135; see also *The causes, waies & means of understanding the mind of God* (1678), 75; *Works* (1965), 4:151.

and handle, and will not be satisfied, that they have not proved there is no motion, whilst a man walks for a conviction under their eye.[78]

If the outward senses, and 'the World', can be held in too high an esteem, they can also be held too low. Owen is careful to emphasize that the natural senses have their 'proper objects'. Within proper bounds, though, the senses should be believed over disputations. Nor did Owen's confidence in sensory observation disappear after the Restoration, when he became more apt to question the senses: he continued to insist that our natural senses could help in the fight against the 'blind Idolatry' of the Church of Rome, which tries to demand that we 'renounce the use of our senses, the exercise of our Reason, and actings of Faith on Divine Revelations, all things whereby we are either Men or Christians'.[79] Here sense, reason and faith act in tandem rather than opposing each other. Indeed, in his last published work, Owen meditates on the redemption of bodily senses at the resurrection: 'while we know not here what power and spirituality there will be in the acts of our glorified bodies', he writes, we can be sure that the 'body as glorified, with its senses, shall have its use and place' in eternity.[80]

Like his attitude towards sensory observation, Owen's attitude towards nonhuman creation was likewise one of carefully bounded appreciation. His early sermon, *A vision of unchangeable free mercy*, advertises a tension in his thought between such appreciation and the *contemptus mundi* he would malign himself in *Of schisme*. Opening the sermon with the idea that the 'Kingdom of Jesus Christ is frequently in the Scripture compared to growing things' – a nod, one might think, to the goodness and beauty of creation – Owen then insists that this positive use of natural imagery is 'in direct opposition to the combined power of this whole creation, as fallen, and in subjection to the god of this world'. Even in this early sermon, however, Owen recognized that there is a lot of the book of nature in the book of Scripture, listing a litany of natural phenomena that figure the kingdom of Christ (a mountain, a vine, a cedar, a mustard tree) followed by those figuring Christ himself (a tender plant, a root, a lily, a sheep, a turtle dove).[81] Such references to the natural world

---

[78] Owen, *Of schisme* (1657), 101; *Works* (1965), 13:132. Owen's (Aristotelian) conviction that various faculties had their proper objects and types of certainty was shared by John Wilkins and is on view in the opening chapters of Wilkins's *Principles and duties of natural religion* (1667).
[79] Owen, *The Church of Rome, no safe guide* (1679), 31; *Works* (1965), 14:505. Similarly, Owen places 'naturally significant' phenomena, such as smoke as signifying fire, above the artificially significant rites and ceremonies of the Catholic church; see Owen, *Truth and innocence vindicated* (1669), 278–9; *Works* (1965), 13:451.
[80] Owen, *Meditations and discourses concerning the glory of Christ* (1691), 152; *Works* (1965), 1:383.
[81] Owen, *Vision of unchangeable free mercy* (1646), 1–2; *Works* (1965), 8:5.

bookend Owen's writing career. In his posthumous *Meditations and discourses concerning the glory of Christ* (1691), he praises the 'Infinite Condescension of Divine Wisdom in [the Bible's] way of Instruction, Representing unto us the Power of Things Spiritual, in what we naturally discern'. He adds:

> Instances of this kind in calling the Lord Christ by the Names of those Creatures which unto our senses represent that Excellency which is spiritually in him, are innumerable. So is he called the Rose . . . the Lilly . . . the Pearl . . . the Vine . . . the Lion . . . the Lamb, with other things of the like kind almost innumerable.[82]

In accommodating itself to human understanding in this way, the Bible sanctioned and perhaps even required the practice of natural theology, as Calvin had averred. It was this biblical conviction that grounded Owen's most constructive engagements with natural science and non-human creation.

OWEN AND NATURAL THEOLOGY

If natural science is at its worst for Owen when it eclipses spiritual things, it is at its best when it illuminates them. Although the 'works of creation and providence' are dimmed to the point of 'no Glory' next to Christ, it is nonetheless a work both worthy and suitable for people to meditate on them. Owen states,

> SOME of more refined parts and notional Minds, do arise unto a sedulous Meditation on the Works of Creation and Providence. Hence many excellent Discourses on that Subject, adorned with Eloquence, are published among us. And a Work this is worthy of our Nature, and suited unto our rational Capacities; yea, the first end of our natural Endowment with them. But in all these things there is *no Glory* in comparison of what is proposed unto us in the mysterious Constitution of the Person of Christ.[83]

It is clear from this passage, moreover, that Owen has read such natural-theological meditations penned by others and found them 'excellent'. On the other hand, as we have seen, Owen viewed the natural theology of the latitudinarians as pridefully attempting to bring the things of faith into the sphere of reason. The pamphlet battles with Glanvill and Stillingfleet in

---

[82] Owen, *Meditations and discourses concerning the glory of Christ* (1691), 103–4; *Works* (1965), 1:352.
[83] Owen, *Meditations and discourses concerning the glory of Christ* (1691), 44; *Works* (1965), 1:313.

the final years of Owen's life were just one instance of a broader Calvinist war on 'natural theology' that was waged by Owen, Hutchinson and others, and in which figures such as Boyle, Baxter and Wilkins occupied a middle ground.[84] Clearly, there is some need to define 'natural theology' in asking what, to Owen's mind, were the appropriate uses and limits of natural knowledge in the pursuit of theological insight.

In 1605, Bacon had defined natural theology as 'that knowledge or Rudiment of knowledge concerning GOD, which may be obtained by the contemplation of his Creatures'; by 1991, William P. Alston would define it as 'the enterprise of providing support for religious beliefs by starting from premises that neither are nor presuppose any religious beliefs'.[85] What I want to point out in this concluding section is that even someone as Reformed as Owen could applaud activities encompassed by this older and broader definition while being part of a large-scale assault on the newer and narrower one. Crucially, the older definition encompasses 'post-fideal' natural theology, a kind practised within a context of faith.[86] This is what Calvin had in mind when he wrote that scientific study would allow the mind to 'rise to a somewhat higher level to look upon [God's] glory'. By the time Owen was writing, there was in England a growing interest in 'pre-fideal' natural theology, geared towards combating atheists on their own ground and increasingly relying on the logic of physico-theology; this type would come to dominate the natural–theological landscape.[87] It was this enterprise that Owen viewed as bankrupt. Post-fideal natural theology, by contrast, he recognized as a worthy pursuit and even a Christian duty.

The limits of natural theology

The limits Owen sets on natural theology stand out when we compare his views with those of his Puritan 'frenemy' Richard Baxter. Baxter engaged with contemporary philosophy more readily than Owen, and Baxter correspondingly thought that natural theology could accomplish more than Owen was willing to concede.[88] The most obvious evidence for this is that Baxter wrote multiple works of natural theology while Owen did not. Baxter even recognized, moreover, that his method in these works was similar to Stillingfleet's, and he thought it might be possible for them to benefit 'unbelieving readers', although

---

[84]Barbour et al., 'Introduction', cix–cxxii.
[85]Bacon, *Works of Francis Bacon*, 78; Alston, *Perceiving God*, 289. This latter definition has now been roundly challenged as historically and philosophically inaccurate; see Brooke et al., 'Introduction'.
[86]Woolford, 'Natural theology and natural philosophy in the late Renaissance', 13–14.
[87]I have argued (based on John Ray) that physico-theology need not be pre-fideal; nonetheless, there is much historical overlap of these two subsets; Calloway, 'Rather theological than philosophical'.
[88]On Baxter and contemporary philosophy, see Sytsma, *Richard Baxter and the mechanical philosophers*.

he was not nearly as sanguine about this prospect as were the latitudinarians.[89] In his most influential work of natural theology, *Reasons of the Christian religion* (1667), Baxter pauses to attack 'over-wise and over-doing Divines, who will tell their followers in private, where there is none to contradict them, that the method of this Treatise is perverse, as appealing too much to natural light, and over-valuing humane reason'. He concludes that

> these over-wise men, who need themselves no reason for their Religion, and judge accordingly of others, and think that those men who rest not in the authority of Jesus Christ, should rest in theirs, are many of them so well acquainted with me, as not to expect that I should trouble them in their way, or reason against them, who speak against reason; even in the greatest matters which our reason is given us for.[90]

If Baxter had Owen in mind when he wrote this, he was being unfair.[91] Nevertheless, Baxter recognized that his time and energy were limited, and made explicit his decision to pass over the 'abundance of hot and vehement Disputes, and tedious or Critical discourses about many small lesse needful things' in favour of equipping people 'with Sense and Reason [to] defend their Christianity against an Infidel'. In so doing he passed tacit judgement on Owen's rather different authorial choices.

Although Owen never wrote a work of natural theology, he did outline his position on reason and faith at length in *The reason of faith* (1677). Owen had elsewhere already denied purely 'natural' knowledge of God, placing such knowledge, however gained, 'under the general head of Revelation'.[92] With that caveat in place, Owen affirms that God does reveal himself to people through both 'inbred principles of natural light' and the external created world. Sense, reason and faith will all agree on such things as the existence of a deity, and doctrines plainly contrary to sense and reason (such as transubstantiation)

---

[89]On Baxter's natural theology, see Calloway, *Natural theology in the scientific revolution*, 49–70. Baxter credits Stillingfleet in the preface to *Reasons of the Christian religion*.
[90]Baxter, *Reasons of the Christian religion*, 491–2.
[91]See Rehnmann, 'John Owen on faith and reason'. I am grateful to J. I. Packer for pointing this out to me, strenuously, in a phone conversation in 2011.
[92]Owen, *Truth and innocence vindicated* (1669), 311; *Works* (1965), 13:465. Both ἐνδιάθετος (knowledge residing in the mind) and προφορικός (knowledge gained by divine utterance) are species of revelation. The editors of the Geneva Bible do much the same thing in glossing the 'candle of the Lord' in Prov. 20.27 as 'the word of God' rather than as human conscience. Owen uses the image of a candle to figure supernatural revelation in pre-biblical times rather than natural knowledge. See Greene, 'Whichcote, the candle of the Lord, and synderesis', 621, and Owen, *The duty of pastors and people distinguished* (1644), 10–11; *Works* (1965), 13:13–14, and Owen, *The reason of faith* (1677), 5–6; *Works* (1965), 4:9–10.

should be rejected. However, some Christian doctrines, such as the Trinity, are not contrary to reason but rather higher than reason; in this case, it is the Christian's duty to believe those things. Pagans who think carefully about these matters will arrive close to knowledge of God, but this is of no spiritual use. Faith is by definition supernatural, so it is for Owen categorically impossible to bring any person into faith by natural means, even when natural knowledge is understood as a subspecies of divine revelation. In his words, 'The Evidence which we have of Things *scientifical* is Speculative, and affects the Mind only; but the Evidence which we have by Faith effectually worketh on the Will also.'[93]

Baxter, by contrast, was not willing to foreclose the possibility that 'Things scientifical' could interact with the will: in his 'Letter to the Christian reader' prefacing *Reasons*, he avers that if people would 'seriously Believe as Christians, they would not live as the Enemies of Christianity!' He therefore takes it 'to be the surest and most expeditious Cure of the security, presumption, pride, perfidiousnesse, sensuality, and wickednesse of these Hypocrites, to convince them that there is a God, and a Life to come, and that the Gospel is true'. This plan, by Owen's lights, did indeed overvalue human reason.

The uses of natural theology

While Owen eschewed the pre-fideal application of natural theology, he approved its post-fideal application, both in principle and in practice. In principle, Owen recognized that the Bible itself proclaimed in Psalm 19 that 'the heavens declare the glory of God', and he repeated this proclamation multiple times throughout his writings.[94] Owen insists that 'it was to express himself, that God made any thing without himself', further explaining that 'He made the Heavens and the Earth to express his Being, Goodness and Power'.[95] What is more, humans need to exercise their reason to appreciate God's self-expression in nature, for God's works of creation 'do not thus declare, evidence and reveal the Glory of God . . . without the actual exercise of Reason'. Instead, he continues, 'A rational Consideration of them, their Greatness, Order, Beauty, and Use, is required unto that Testimony and Evidence which God gives in them and by them unto Himself.'[96] In other words, it is worth spending significant mental effort on natural theology, and quite probably worth committing those efforts to print.

---

[93] Owen, *The reason of faith* (1677), 164; *Works* (1965), 4:101.
[94] For example Owen, *Of the divine originall* (1659), 40–1; *Works* (1965), 16:309; Owen, *Sabbath* (1671), 127–8; *Works* (1991), 18:334; Owen, *The reason of faith* (1677), 135; *Works* (1965), 4:84; and Owen, Χριστολογια (1679), 58; *Works* (1965), 1:182.
[95] Owen, Χριστολογια (1679), 174; *Works* (1965), 1:145.
[96] Owen, *Reason of faith* (1677), 134–5; *Works* (1965), 4:84.

If not a physico-theological attack on atheists, what should such an effort look like in practice? Owen mentions 'sedulous Meditation on the Works of Creation and Providence' as the content of 'many excellent Discourses' already published in England.[97] He may have had in mind Wilkins's *Discourse concerning the beauty of providence* (1644), a less rationalistic precursor to his highly influential *Principles and duties of natural religion* (1675).[98] He almost certainly had in mind the genre of 'occasional meditation'. Influentially defined in Joseph Hall's 1606 *The arte of divine meditation* as a 'bending of the mind upon some spirituall obiect, . . . occasioned by outward occurrences offred to the mind', the occasional meditation was viewed by English Protestants as an excellent way to redeem time, not letting any mental energy go to waste.[99] Both Robert Boyle and Mary Boyle Rich, whose father-in-law had been Owen's patron, contributed to this genre. Though written 'several years ago, under an Usurping government', Boyle's *Occasional reflections upon several subjects* appeared in 1665 and was warmly praised by Baxter.[100] Even Bunyan would take up this practice, though after Owen's death, in the second part of *Pilgrim's Progress* (1684) as well as his *Book for boys and girls* (1688). This was a kind of natural theology that people at the Reformed end of the theological spectrum could get behind.

While occasions for divine meditation did not need to be natural but only 'outward' – one might, for example, meditate on 'the sight of a Looking-glass, with a rich Frame' – Boyle urged that the natural world be placed foremost as a source for such meditation. An early working title for his *Occasional reflections*, accordingly, was 'Of the study of the book of nature'.[101] In the 'Discourse touching occasional meditations' published with the finished work, Boyle writes,

> 'Twas doubtless a very great pleasure to *Aesop,* that by his ingenious Fictions he could, in a manner, lend Reason and Speech to Lions, Foxes, Crows, and other Animals, to whom Nature had deni'd both; and I know not why it should be less delightful, by Occasional Reflections, to turn not onely Birds and Beasts, but all kinds of Creatures in the world, as well mute and inanimate, as irrational, not onely into Teachers of Ethicks, but oftentimes into Doctors of Divinity, and by compelling senseless Creatures to reveal Truths to us.[102]

---

[97]Owen, *Meditations and discourses concerning the glory of Christ* (1691), 44; *Works* (1965), 1:313.
[98]Calloway, *Natural theology in the scientific revolution*, 77–86.
[99]Hall, *The arte of divine meditation* (1606), 7.
[100]Coolahan, 'Redeeming parcels of time', 124–5, 129–30.
[101]Hunter, *Boyle*, 74.
[102]Boyle, *Occasional reflections* (1665), 19. The looking-glass appears on 251.

Pleasurable as it might be to draw lessons from 'fictions' authored by humans, Boyle proclaims, it is yet more delightful to draw truth from works authored by God himself. This 'truth' was not the conclusion of physico-theology, namely, that God exists and creation evinces God's wisdom and power; these things were already assumed. Instead, all sorts of insights about God's attributes and the life of faith were gathered from the observation of nature. Unlike in old fables, this was Nature as she really was, uncovered by the new sciences. This genre fell out of favour after the seventeenth century, though Swift knew Boyle's *Occasional reflections* well enough to lampoon the work with his *Meditation upon a broomstick* (1701).

Unlike Swift, Owen heartily approved of occasional meditations, including those drawing on scientific observation. We know this, first, because of his praise of recently published 'sedulous meditations' on God's works of creation and his recognition of the 'Infinite Condescension' of the Bible itself in appealing to the natural world to reveal spiritual truth. Second, Owen licenced just such a work when he was vice-chancellor at the University of Oxford. In 1653, a horticulturist named Ralph Austen published *A treatise of fruit-trees*, a work of pomonology along explicitly Baconian lines, to which he added some spiritual reflections. Austen then expanded these reflections for publication on their own, as *The spirituall use of an orchard*, in 1657. While working on these revisions, Austen wrote to Samuel Hartlib that he had

> manifold encouragements here about [the book], not only from the acceptance of the worke in generall, but also from some spetiall hands: Mr Owen, Vice Chancellor having been pleased to take much paines in perusing of it (in order to lycence the Printing) & giving me great encouragements in it.[103]

The book does bear Owen's imprimatur, dated 1656. This was not a privilege Owen exercised often, raising the question of why Austen should approach him (or vice versa) with this book in particular.[104] In any case, the imprimatur is a testament to Owen's approval of this strand of natural theology, which Austen defines and promotes enthusiastically in his preface to the reader. There

---

[103] Ralph Austen to Samuel Hartlib, 8 July 1653, The Hartlib Papers, 41/1/38A-39B: 38B, 39A, https://www.dhi.ac.uk/hartlib/view?docset=main&docname=41A_01_038&term0=transtext_owen#highlight, accessed 1 January 2020.

[104] Of the 216 books turned up on EEBO as bearing an 'imprimatur' and published between 1652 and 1657, only this work and Humphry Chambers's answer to William Dell appear to have been licenced by Owen. Orme, *Memoirs*, 210, says that Kendall's *Vindication of the doctrine commonly received in Reformed churches* has Owen's imprimatur, though this endorsement does not appear on the copies that are available on EEBO.

he brings together numerous biblical references to the natural world and its testimony to spiritual things, including Psalm 19, with a quotation by 'the Lord *Bacon*', who says, 'God hath two great Books which we ought to study, his Word, and his Works: the one discovers his Will, the other his power'. Unlike Bacon, however, Austen does not limit the book of nature to commenting only on God's power; instead, 'the creatures of God are to be studied as Books, for in them we may read the Attributes of God and observe some small resemblances, and darke shadowes of his infinite Excellencies'.[105] Although he preferred to spend his own writing energy on the book of Scripture, Owen agreed with this and promoted Austen's study of the book of nature because it was so clearly directed at theological insight and conducted within a context of faith.

Increasingly, this would cease to be the case in English natural theology. As Peter Harrison summarizes, 'No longer a meditative process, the scientific study of nature was regarded as yielding a set of premises upon which rational arguments for God's existence could be constructed.'[106] Long before problems with physico-theological 'rational arguments for God's existence' would become clear to David Hume and others, Owen vociferously opposed this way of thinking as prideful and out of bounds. If scientific reform really could be brought into the service of the chief end of man, however, Owen would cheer it on.

---

[105]On this limitation in Bacon, see Calloway, 'A "metaphorical God" and the book of nature', 132–7, and Serjeantson, 'Francis Bacon and the "interpretation of nature"'.
[106]Harrison, 'Religion, the Royal Society, and the rise of science', 267.

CHAPTER 11

Owen and philosophy

PAUL HELM[1]

John Owen was educated at Queen's College, Oxford, to become a minister in the Church of England. His father was a minister, as was his brother William. His education for pastoral ministry involved the study of scholastic philosophy, which was a version of late Roman Catholic scholasticism, a field of study that was 'reformed', but not abandoned, as part of the wider Reformation. At the Reformation, many Reformed theologians sought to purify Roman Catholicism of its extremes, and Owen contributed to this goal even as, over the course of his lifetime, the influence of Protestant scholasticism waned, and he moved ever further from the scholastic method.

Common with other exponents of Reformed orthodoxy, Owen held a positive view of nature, one version of the nature/grace outlook. Nature as God's creation is regularly endorsed in Scripture, such as in the nature Psalms and throughout the New Testament – for example, in Christ's invitation to Thomas to see and feel his wounds. The earth is accessible to the senses and intelligence, allowing for human fallibility. Natural theology is endorsed in Paul's preaching to the Gentiles in Lystra (Acts 14.15), and in his statements in Romans (1.18-20; 2.14-15), as well in his recognizing the ability of pagans to speak the truth: see, for example, his citation of Aratus of Sicyon (315 BC–24 BC) in Acts 17.28; his citation of Epimenides of Cnossos (a semi-mythical seventh- or sixth-century BC Greek seer and philosopher-poet, author of the *Phaenomena*) in Acts 17.33 and Tit. 1.12; and his citation of Menander (342–

---

[1] In memory of Peter Toon (1939–2009).

290 BC) in 1 Cor. 15.33. Owen was well acquainted with this literature. His library contained numerous classical works and writings of the Fathers and medieval theologians, including Augustine and Aquinas, which were augmented by writings of later catholic scholastics and important Renaissance thinkers, as well as Reformed works on philosophy and natural theology, by authors such as Amandus Polanus (1561–1610) and Franciscus Junius (1545–1602).[2]

During Owen's lifetime, Christian theology was socially and politically significant, and was characterized by rival methods of understanding its structure and content. In a Puritan household such as Owen's, Reformed theology would have been considered in its scholastic dressing, contrasting in this post-Tridentine era with the Roman Catholic alternative. But scholasticism was evolving through this period. As the seventeenth century progressed, innovations in Protestant theology, notably Arminianism and Socinianism, were indebted to scholasticism in varying degrees, while Reformed scholastics continued to borrow from Aquinas (1225–74) and later from Roman Catholic scholastics such as Diego Alvarez (1555–1625) and Francisco Suarez (1548–1617). To understand why this occurred, we must understand what these methodological resources were.

Besides requiring mastery (in Latin) of Greek and Latin authors, university students in early modern England were expected to participate in instruction in scholastic philosophy. Scholastic philosophy was (and is) a derivation of the philosophy of Aristotle, whose writings were translated by Arabic scholars in the twelfth century, and adopted by Albert the Great (d. 1280) and his star pupil, Thomas Aquinas. In their hands, this philosophy presented batteries of questions on the meaning and implications of the propositions thrown up by Christian doctrine. Developing this approach, philosophers learned to make distinctions such as that between theoretical and practical reason. The question of whether Christian theology was a development of the 'theoretical' or 'practical' reason was widely discussed. The 'practical' reason had to do with the goals of an agent and the means to their using four different causes (efficient, material, formal and final) to find different answers to the question, 'Why?' The 'theoretical' reason had the aim of establishing what is true. It provided a set of analytic tools in studying both Christian anthropology (the doctrine of mankind) and theology (the doctrine of God). In the doctrine of justification by faith, for example, the role of faith was none of the usual four causes, but was said by the Reformed to be an 'instrumental' cause of the imputation of righteousness. Owen goes this way in *The doctrine of justification by faith* (1677).[3] Education in scholasticism provided practice in

---

[2] For more information on Owen's education and his library, see Rehnman, *Divine discourse*.
[3] Owen, *The doctrine of justification by faith* (1677); *Works* (1965), vol. 5.

deploying these distinctions in composing *disputationes* on the aptness of the senses of 'by' in asserting justification 'by' faith. Owen came to be critical of the tendency, particularly but not only of Roman Catholic theologians, to show their mastery or their ingenuity by multiplying distinctions.

Owen was educated in such scholasticism, but, as he grew older, he became less satisfied that it represented the proper place of philosophy in the work of theology. He was aware, for example, that among earlier Reformed thinkers, John Calvin held the view that God could have pardoned sinners by a word.[4] And, in the early decades of the seventeenth century, Samuel Rutherford (1600–61) and William Twisse (1578–1646) had, independently, arrived at that same view, fearing that any other claim would compromise God's sovereignty. But, by the middle of the seventeenth century, such a view of God's will was a cornerstone of Socinianism. The proposal that was being defended by Twisse and Rutherford could play into the hands of Socinian apologists. In the early 1650s, Owen, who had defended this claim in print, quickly backtracked from it.[5] This movement reflected his attitude to theology more generally, which involves not only the doctrine of God in the abstract but the insistence that

> theology is the 'wisdom that is from above,' a habit of grace and spiritual gifts, the manifestation of the Spirit. . . . It is not a science to be learned from the precepts of man, or from the rules of arts, or methods of other sciences, as those represent it who also claim that a 'natural man' may attain all that artificial and methodical theology, even though, in the matters of God and mysteries of the Gospel, he be blinder than a mole. What a distinguished theologian must he be 'who receiveth not the things of the Spirit of God!'[6]

As this example suggests, Owen shared the general Reformed suspicion of using scholastic tools for speculative purposes. Reformed theologians saw a general deterioration from Aquinas, whose work they generally followed, into later scholasticism. The method encouraged speculation, they feared, and was more suited to Roman Catholic doctrine than that of the Reformed. Besides this, Owen gradually shifted in his own method in the immense body of work on which he expended so much effort. He certainly moved away from a uniform treatment of each topic of theology, following the scholastic organization of material. This was especially obvious in his pneumatology. He regarded the great hole in the church's theology as the lack of interest in the theological

---

[4] Helm, *Calvin at the centre*, ch. 6.
[5] See discussion in Trueman, 'John Owen's *Dissertation on divine justice*', 87–103.
[6] Owen, *Diatriba de justitia divina* (1653), n.p.; *Works* (1965), 10:488.

development of the work of the Holy Spirit. This he noted in the preface to his Latin scholastic work, *Diatriba de justitia divina* (1653), a translation of which is included in volume 10 of Goold's edition of Owen's works. Owen feared that the ability to make distinctions, the activity at the heart of the scholastic mind-set, engendered a lust to out-think one's fellow scholastics. This encouraged Owen to move away from doctrinal theology towards the 'experimental' theology of the 'godly', and to take theology in the direction of narrative.

Scholastic philosophy gave one a teleological outlook on reality. The catena of causes that we have mentioned was intrinsic to that. This is God's creation, the Gospel being his eternal will to culminate in the reign of Christ with the redeemed. This outlook was chiefly concerned with God and human nature, with the external world and its occupants, and the souls of men and women, the data of which included introspection, memory and conscience. Its anthropology has since often been regarded as naïve and simplistic when compared to the modern world's emphasis on the unconscious and the effects of culture on the human self and its actions. This verdict is somewhat unjust in the case of Owen's anthropology, for he had a strong conviction of the human capacity for self-deceit and how it manifests itself, as we shall see. Scholastics insisted that the external world has creatures whose changes are to do with movement that is the result of forces, powers which partly or wholly fulfil goals, practical and theoretical. There is a hierarchy between spirits, angels and human beings having the power of intelligence, intellect or understanding, and will (choice) being closely connected in human action, and in animate and inanimate forces. In this literature, human beings are treated in a way that is unfamiliar to us, who routinely think of the distinction between body and soul. For the Reformed scholastics, by contrast, the soul is not exclusively spiritual nor is the body exclusively physical. Rather, the soul is said to be the 'form' of the body, as Aristotle and Genesis 1 were understood to have taught. Puritan anthropology embraces all the appetites of body and soul, and so regards the human being as a psychophysical unity. This made for a difficult consequence: what is the intermediate state between bodily death and bodily resurrection? Scholastics, including Owen, met this problem by stressing the unnaturalness of bodily death, and the incompleteness of the intermediate state.

Owen was not a philosopher, and he was certainly not an out-and-out scholastic, but nonetheless he was thoroughly acquainted with philosophy as an adjunct of his theological education. In Oxford he was taught by someone who certainly was a philosopher, Thomas Barlow (1608/9–1691) – a man who was to become the Bishop of Lincoln in the restored Church of England. But Owen came to critique and eventually substantially modify the influence of philosophy on theology.

APPROACHING OWEN'S THEOLOGY

The massive, unwieldy corpus of Owen's writings – 14,000 pages in the Goold edition, and almost eighty publications created over forty tumultuous years – looks to be insurmountable as far as coming to an estimate of his philosophy is concerned. Contemporary writing on Owen's writings stress his reliance on Aquinas's writings, and its being scholastic in character.[7] I shall not attempt to discuss Owen's eschatology, nor his sermons, nor his ecclesiology, nor his massive commentary on Hebrews. But I shall range over the theological productions of his other writings, to try to estimate his relation of philosophy to theology. It seems clear that Owen's insatiable appetite for writing was not one of orderly development. In his corpus, later works are anticipated, and earlier themes are repeated. To identify Owen's philosophy, if that is achievable, it is necessary to track developments in his theological writings. In what follows, I shall discuss his career in terms of its theological development in anthropology, in the doctrine of the Holy Spirit and theological methodology. I shall then offer a reading of Owen's philosophy, recognizing that others may come to different conclusions by emphasizing other features of his immense output.

Throughout his life Owen maintained a regular, scholastic view of God's being. So in *Vindiciae evangelicae* (1655), to take an example from his mid-career, Owen maintained what has come to be called 'classical theism', stressing God's eternity, ubiquity and omnipresence.[8] God is 'present to all by and in his infinite essence and being, exerting his power variously, in any or all places, as he pleaseth, revealing and manifesting his glory more or less, as it seemeth good to him'.[9] 'God is absolutely perfect; whatever is of perfection is to be ascribed to him: otherwise he could neither be absolutely self-sufficient, all-sufficient, nor eternally blessed in himself.'[10] And (expressed with more difficulty), he is impassible: 'He who is blessed in himself is all-sufficient for himself. If God wants or desires anything for himself, he is neither perfect nor blessed. To ascribe, then, affections to God properly . . . is to deprive him of his perfection and blessedness.'[11]

Owen developed these convictions – which were Greek in origin – in many writings in which he respected the biblical revelation and its boundaries, and allowed that much of its language of God, as revealed, was anthropomorphic or anthropopathic. God cannot be said to be tired, but he is said to be angry and to possess ears, for example. As we briefly saw in the case of Owen's anthropology,

---

[7]Trueman, *The claims of truth*; Rehnman, *Divine discourse*; and Cleveland, *Thomism in John Owen*.
[8]Owen, *Vindiciae evangelicae* (1655), 52–3; *Works* (1965), 12:91.
[9]Owen, *Vindiciae evangelicae* (1655), 54; *Works* (1965), 12:92.
[10]Owen, *Vindiciae evangelicae* (1655), 57; *Works* (1965), 12:95.
[11]Owen, *Vindiciae evangelicae* (1655), 74; *Works* (1965), 12:109.

Reformed theologians of the period were scholastic in general, but not as speculative in their views as were Roman Catholic scholastic theologians. As we shall see, Owen was typical of these Reformed theologians, though he was able to differ from some of their number, such as Rutherford and Twisse, who were inclined to be more speculative in temperament. From this doctrine of God, classical theism, he never deviated. So in the doctrine of God he remained a scholastic.

ANTHROPOLOGY AND SOTERIOLOGY

As noted, Owen had a considerable output in Christian theological anthropology, the doctrine of created human nature, particularly stressing the impact of the fall on the human race, and in soteriology, including *Of the mortification of sinne in believers* (second edition, 1658), *Of temptation* (1658) and *The nature, power, deceit and prevalency of the remainders of indwelling sin in believers* (1658).[12] The significant intellectual changes in Owen's career largely concern anthropology and soteriology.

In this set of studies on the effect of sin of human nature, Owen adopted the prevalent faculty theology, in which the powers of the soul are understood to be the intellect or reason or understanding, the will and the affections, and their influence on the conscience and memory. Owen shows his mastery of these topics. His work on indwelling sin, for example, is characterized by a stress on self-deception, on the phenomenology of deception, and its role in temptation, as a consequence of the knowledge of ourselves. This stress seems unique to Owen, and comes into its own as an aspect of his experimental theology. I will consider more of this later in the chapter.

The evidence of Owen's employment of scholasticism produced by his earlier writings is somewhat mixed. His first book, Θεομαχία αυτεξουσιαστικη: or, A display of Arminianisme (1643), which was published when he was twenty-six, was a short work prepared for a lay audience, and to display his theological orthodoxy, as a strictly doctrinal effort in his polemic against Arminianism.[13] To demonstrate his orthodoxy, Owen occasionally cites schoolmen and their distinctions. We shall look at his treatment of free will as an example. In his treatment of the 'great deity of free will', he recognizes that the Reformed were not opposed to free will in every sense. Owen understands that

> we grant man, in this substance of all his actions, as much power, liberty, and freedom as a mere created nature is capable of. We grant him to be free in

---

[12]Owen, *Of the mortification of sinne in believers* (1656); Owen, *Of temptation* (1658); and Owen, *Indwelling sin* (1668); *Works* (1965), vol. 6
[13]Owen, *A display of Arminianisme* (1643), 123; *Works* (1965), 10:114.

his choice from all outward coaction, or inward natural necessity, to work according to election and deliberation, spontaneously embracing. But we are not properly free until the Son makes us free.[14]

Behind the claims of Arminianism was an altogether stronger sense of human choice. Arminius 'consisteth the liberty of the will, that all things required to enable it to will anything being accomplished, it still remains indifferent to will or not'.[15] For the Arminians, fallen man has a residual power of indeterminate indifference. By contrast, for Owen, people are free from compulsion and inward necessity, as by such a necessity – for example, as sheep eat grass. But in respect of spiritual matters, which are 'supernatural', people require a supernatural cause in order to overcome impotence and enmity to spiritual things. As Owen states, 'All spiritual acts well-pleasing unto God, as faith, repentance, obedience, are supernatural; flesh and blood revealeth not these things . . . Now, to the performance of any supernatural acts it is required that the productive power thereof be also supernatural; for nothing hath an activity in causing above its own sphere.'[16]

Owen developed these themes in *Salus electorum, sanguis Jesu: or, The death of death in the death of Christ*, which he published in 1648, and which has a thoroughly scholastic framework.[17] This work represented the work of Christ as teleological, as the provision of means to the end of redemption and reconciliation through its being the satisfaction of the divine 'practical' reason, in terms of the vocabulary previously discussed, the redemption of the elect. This is a work of doctrinal exactness, a sustained polemic against universal redemption, and of any deviation from it, such as hypothetical universalism, which was upheld by the Reformed bishop of Salisbury, John Davenant (1572–1642), for example. *The death of death in the death of Christ* was a public display of Owen's considerable learning and skill, combining scholastic distinctions, biblical exegesis and Christological reflection. Its author tells his readers of the nature, consequences and end of the work of Christ. It is not disparaging to these books to observe that their approach and style is predominately doctrinal, and exclusively polemical, showing the errors of Arminianism, and deviant positions on the extent of Christ's work. No doubt these works had the effect of bolstering Owen's name as an orthodox and learned divine. But in terms of Puritan publications, they were standard fare.

---

[14]Owen, *A display of Arminianisme* (1643), 125; *Works* (1965), 10:116.
[15]Owen, *A display of Arminianisme* (1643), 126; *Works* (1965), 10:117.
[16]Owen, *A display of Arminianisme* (1643), 131–2; *Works* (1965), 10:122.
[17]Owen, *The death of death in the death of Christ* (1648); *Works*, (1965), 10:139–428.

Owen expanded upon these early discussions in Πνευματολογια (1674), in which he discusses the effect of regeneration not only on the bound will but on all the powers of the soul. The freed will of believers consists in a 'gracious freedom and ability to choose, will, and do that which is spiritually good, in opposition to the bondage and slavery unto sin wherein we were before detained'.[18] The sanctified will does not consist in indifference: 'I say, then, that by the habit of grace and holiness by the Spirit of sanctification, the will is freed, enlarged, and enabled to answer the commands of God for obedience, according to the tenor of the new covenant.'[19] Besides the powers or faculties of the soul, such as the will and its freedom, the scholastic view of the relation of the soul and the body emphasized the human being as a psychophysical unity, borrowing from the hylomorphism of Aristotle via Aquinas. In scholastic terms, the soul is the 'form' of the body. Owen showed himself a thorough scholastic in his incidental remarks on what a living soul is. The fact that regeneration was the infusing of new spiritual life, a new creation, leads him to spend time reflecting on what life is:

> These are the *acts of this life itself*; and they are of two sorts – (1) Such as flow from life as *life*. (2) Such as proceed from it as such a life, from the principle of a rational soul. Those of the first sort are natural and necessary, as are all the actings and energies of the senses, and of the locomotive faculty, as also what belongs to the receiving and improving of nutriment. These are acts of life as life, inseparable from it; and their end is, to preserve the union of the whole between the quickening and quickened principles. (2) There are such acts of life as proceed from the especial nature of this quickening principle. Such are all the elicit and imperate acts of our understandings and will; all acts that are voluntary, rational, and peculiarly human.[20]

The acts of our understanding and will are divided into two sorts, the 'elicit' and 'imperate' acts of willing:

> [A]s are all the actings and energies of the senses, and of the locomotive faculty, as also what belongs to the receiving and improving of nutriment. . . . These are acts of life as life, inseparable from it; and their end is, to preserve the union of the whole between the quickening and quickened principles. (2.) There are such acts of life as proceed from the especial nature of this quickening principle. Such are all the elicit and imperate acts of our

---

[18] Owen, Πνευματολογια (1674), 434; *Works* (1965), 3:495.
[19] Owen, Πνευματολογια (1674), 435; *Works* (1965), 3:496.
[20] Owen, Πνευματολογια (1674), 239–40; *Works* (1965), 3:284.

understandings and wills; all actions that are voluntary, rational, and peculiarly human. These proceed from that special kind of life which is given by the especial quickening principle of a rational soul.[21]

Owen believes, as I have explained elsewhere, that there are aspects of life that are 'reflexive and automatic, those to do with eating, walking, and growing, which do not arise from particular volitions'.[22] These acts are what Owen calls 'elicit'. Besides, there are acts of will 'that are brought about in a characteristically human way, by the understanding and the will'.[23] These are what Owen calls the 'imperate' acts of willing. And what happens in bodily death? 'Death is or involves the separation of the soul from the body. The infusing of the body for all that it does, the whole range of actions, ceases. For it is a principle of life only insofar as it is united to the body.'[24] Owen states,

> As a consequent of these [ceasings], there is in the body an impotency for and an ineptitude unto all vital operations. Not only do all operations of life actually cease, but the body is no more able to effect them. There remains in it [the dead body], indeed, 'potentia obedientialis,' a 'passive power' to receive life again if communicate unto by an external efficient cause, – so the body of Lazarus being dead had the receptive power of a living soul – but an active power to dispose itself or vital actions it hath not.[25]

Here we see Owen accepting the detail of Aristotelian and scholastic states of affairs regarding the will and the 'passive powers', the latter developed by Aquinas to cope with the reception of a resurrected body, which was unknown to Aristotle. There is in the dead body an 'aptness' for resurrection, for this body to be reunited to this soul. It is important to notice Owen's distance from the arguments of his contemporary, René Descartes (1596–1650), whose body-soul 'dualism', a consequence of his scepticism, seems to have had little or no influence on English Reformed thinkers at this time, though it influenced some Dutch Reformed theologians. Certainly, it had no influence on Owen. That position was soon to change as body-soul 'dualism' become dominant. But it is also important to notice that Owen's position is far from being 'rationalistic', as has been charged by some of his modern students: Carl Trueman and others have recognized that Alan C. Clifford is mistaken in characterizing Owen as

---

[21] Owen, Πνευματολογια (1674), 240; *Works* (1965), 3:284.
[22] Helm, *Human nature from Calvin to Edwards*, 75.
[23] Helm, *Human nature from Calvin to Edwards*, 75.
[24] Helm, *Human nature from Calvin to Edwards*, 75.
[25] Owen, Πνευματολογια (1674), 240; *Works* (1965), 3:284.

'rationalistic' in his teleological outlook on the work of Christ.[26] A rationalistic outlook has one or more principles which are non-biblical to which the theological theses must be subordinate.

EXPERIENTIAL THEOLOGY

We come now to the significance of Owen's lifelong development of experiential (or 'experimental') theology. I do not doubt that others may make other choices of the place of philosophy in Owen's theology. But in his experiential theology are undeniably mainstream topics in Owen's theological output, topics in which we find him exercised in philosophy and its influence on the needs and methods of Christian theology, about which he wrote extensively throughout his life.

In reconstructing Owen's experiential theology, it is important to notice the autobiographical remarks that are supplied in the prefaces to his publications. And this is so, I believe, with the first book he published in Latin, *Diatriba de justitia divina* (1653), which is translated under the title *A dissertation of justice* in the Goold edition.[27] This book provides early evidence for how Owen himself came to view his work as a theologian. It was published during his career as dean of Christ Church and vice-chancellor of the University of Oxford. In the preface, he refers to lecturing for 'an hour on the topic', and suggests that he agreed to publish the work

> after the scruples of several had been removed by a fuller consideration of our opinion . . . namely, that they clearly saw this doctrine conduced to the establishment to the necessity of the satisfaction of Jesus Christ, a precious truth, which these worthy and good men, partakers of the grace and gift of righteousness through means of the blood of Christ not only warmly favoured, but dearly venerated, as the most honourable treasure of the church. . . . I was greatly encouraged in the conferences with these gentlemen to take a deeper view of the subject, and to examine it more closely, for the benefit of mankind. . . . *[T]he great difficulty of the subject* itself, which, among the more abstruse points of truth, is by no means the least abstruse.[28]

Owen feared that the position of his opponents on divine justice could be used as a weapon by the Socinians. This was evidence in his discussion of the reading that lay behind the *Diatriba*. To start with, he admits that he would

---

[26]For example, Trueman, *The claims of truth*, 85 and 'Appendix one: The role of Aristotelian teleology in Owen's doctrine of atonement' (233–40); cf. for example, Clifford, *Atonement and justification*, ch. 6.
[27]Owen, *Diatriba de justitia divina* (1655); *Works* (1965), 10:481–624.
[28]Owen, *Diatriba de justitia divina* (1653), n.p.; *Works* (1965), 10:486–7.

not have written on the topic had he not known that while the 'mighty names' of Augustine, Calvin, Musculus, Twisse and Vossius maintained the position he attacked, 'other very learned theologians, Paraeus, Piscator, Molinaeus, Rivetus, Cameron, Maccovius, Junius, the professors at Saumur, and others', held the position that he defended.[29] He would prefer, he tells us, to develop straightforward doctrinal theology, 'subjects unencumbered by the thickets of scholastic terms and distinctions, unembarrassed by the impediments and sophisms of an enslaving philosophy or false knowledge'. This would be more in keeping with his place in life as a preacher of God's grace, 'whose genius is by no means quick, and who have even forgot, in some measure, the portion of polite learning that he might have formerly acquired', and who had hoped that the 'goodness of God, in giving me leisure, and retirement, and strength for study, the deficiency of genius and penetration might be made up by industry and diligence, was now so circumstanced that the career of my studies must be interrupted by more and greater impediments than ever before'.[30] He has matters of more importance to acknowledge about his plans for the future:

> [H]ow sparingly, for instance, yea, how obscurely, how confusedly, is the whole economy of the Spirit towards believers (one of the greatest mysteries of our religion – a most invaluable treasure of the salvation brought about for us by Christ) described by divines in general! or rather, by the most, is it not altogether neglected? In their catechisms, common-place books, public and private theses, systems, theses, compends, etc., even in their commentaries, harmonies, and expositions, concerning the indwelling, sealing testimony, unction, and consolation of the Spirit, – Good God! Concerning this inestimable fruit of the death and resurrection of Jesus Christ, this invaluable treasure of the godly, though copiously revealed and explained in the Scriptures there is almost a total silence; and with regard to union and communion with Christ, and with his Father, and our Father, and some other doctrines respecting his person, as the husband and head of the church, the same observation holds good.[31]

These sentiments stayed with Owen through the years, slowly (and as opportunities allowed) generating his development of 'experimental' religion. He believed that theological work on the Holy Spirit needed to be done, and that he could be the man to do it. This invites an inspection of his later books on the Holy Spirit and on Christian spirituality. These, together with his books

---

[29] Owen, *Diatriba de justitia divina* (1653), n.p.; *Works* (1965), 10:488.
[30] Owen, *Diatriba de justitia divina* (1653), n.p.; *Works* (1965), 10:492.
[31] Owen, *Diatriba de justitia divina* (1653), n.p.; *Works* (1965), 10:490.

on Independent (Congregational) ecclesiology, provide the reader with work that was not that of a thoroughgoing scholastic, but perhaps with a modified philosophical method, which would offer evidence of a different philosophical methodology than scholasticism – something more distinctly 'experiential'.

PHILOSOPHY AND THE SHAPE OF CHRISTIAN THEOLOGY

In the preface to the reader in Πνευματολογια: or, A discourse concerning the Holy Spirit (1674), the foundation work of his treatment of the Holy Spirit, Owen takes up the spirit of *Diatriba*, stating the novelty of its contents: 'I know not any who ever went before me in this design of representing the whole economy of the Holy Spirit, with all his adjuncts, operations and effects, whereof this is the first part.'[32] It seems that in the closing of the book, in the extensive treatment of evangelical holiness, that Owen thinks that he was also making a new theological work. He is sensitive to the dangers of irrationality and the need of our minds to be made teachable.[33] The focus in Πνευματολογια on the Spirit's regeneration and sanctification of the elect required Owen to modify the scholastic treatments of virtue to encompass what he has made of the change in human faculties in the development of holiness, and when dealing with the 'positive work of the Spirit in the sanctification of believers'.[34] He would make a further application of this idea in his repeated contrast between morality and holiness, and in critiquing Roman Catholic scholastics and some theologians of the Restoration, such as Samuel Parker.[35] Writing of holiness, Owen explains:

> This, therefore, is that which I intend – a virtue, a power, a principle of spiritual life and grace, wrought, created, infused into our souls, and inlaid in all the faculties of them, constantly abiding and unchangeably residing in them, which is antecedent unto, and the next cause of, all acts of true holiness whatever. . . . Habits that are acquired by many actions have a natural efficacy to preserve themselves, until some opposition that is too hard for them prevail against them; which is frequently (though not easily) done. But this is preserved in us by the constant powerful actings and influence of the Holy Ghost. He which works in us doth also preserve it in

---

[32] Owen, Πνευματολογια (1674), n.p.; *Works* (1965), 3:7.
[33] Owen, Πνευματολογια (1674), n.p.; *Works* (1965), 3:10–12.
[34] Owen, Πνευματολογια (1674), 410; *Works* (1965), 3:436.
[35] Owen, Πνευματολογια (1674), 327, 393, 414–15, 460; *Works* (1965), 3:373, 449, 473, 525. Samuel Parker (1640–88) was an English churchman, and eventually Bishop of Oxford, of strong Erastian views and a fierce opponent of dissenters.

us. And the reason hereof is, because the spring of it is in our head, Jesus Christ, it being only an emanation of virtue and power from him unto us by the Holy Ghost.[36]

Owen's contribution would reflect the fact that the work of the Holy Spirit in regeneration and sanctification is an immediate work on the soul, a case of divine power, creating states of human experience, with moral and spiritual changes in the understanding, the will and affections, along with what Owen calls 'physical' changes, changes in the nature of these human traits.[37] The Spirit is a divine agent, God himself, who exerts causal powers on those individuals that benefit from his regenerative activity in the development of new habits. These may be known by the subjects in introspective self-knowledge. These processes have a new start, the new birth, and a new 'spiritual experience', a relatively new term for Owen.[38] In this passage, which is typical of many others in the book, Owen employed routine scholastic terms such as 'habit', 'power', 'immediate', 'form' and 'matter', because he knew no other. But his arguments took a different shape than might have been the case in scholasticism. For he uses a narrative of human states in various regenerated phases. His focus on such spiritual states might be said to be a case of 'supernaturalism'. In his own mind, Owen must have made an earlier start to this project, for he footnotes *Of the mortification of sinne in believers* (1656), which had been the fruit of his lecturing and preaching in Oxford, more than once in the book. Owen had followed this book with *Of temptation* (1658), *Indwelling sin* (1668) and in the following year, *A practical exposition on the 130th Psalm* (1669). Each of these works has an experiential dimension. The scope of this body of work in his middle years was focused on the work of the Holy Spirit in the human heart, as the fruit of the death and resurrection of Christ, including the change of the heart's self-knowledge, as found particularly in the Pauline letters. His outlook may be called 'supernaturalism', a term that I will take up later on.

So I am arguing that Πνευματολογια is the foundational realization of the project first set out twenty or so years earlier in the preface to *Diatriba de justitia divina*. It is a rambling and, it must be said, a repetitive treatment of the theology of the Spirit, and on the needs and plight and phases of the experience of its human recipients. This also reflects the fact that, in his later years, Owen centred on developing a theology and an attitude to Christian doctrine that he calls 'wholly revelational' in content, following of the contours of the New

---

[36] Owen, Πνευματολογια, 417; *Works* (1965), 3:475.
[37] Variously, Owen, Πνευματολογια, 269, 349+394, 433–4, 435–6; *Works* (1965), 3: 316, 399+450, 494, 496, 498.
[38] Owen, Πνευματολογια (1674), 254, 372; *Works* (1965), 3:299, 425.

Testament in these issues. In an age that had a place for religious fanaticism, Owen had things to say on the place of reason, and he develops the contrast between morality and holiness which is so important to him, which in a sense is distinctive of the project. It requires some sophistication. For example, writing of sanctification as a progressive work, he writes:

> This, then, is to be fixed that all this increase of holiness is immediately the work of the Holy Ghost, who therein gradually carries on his design of sanctifying us throughout, in our whole spirits, souls and bodies. There is in our regeneration and habitual grace received a nature bestowed on us capable of growth and increase, and that is all; if it be left unto itself it will not thrive, it will decay and die. The actual supplies of the Spirit are the waterings that are the immediate cause of its increase. It wholly depends on continual influences from God. He cherisheth and improves the work he hath begun with new and fresh supplies of grace every moment: Isa xxvii.3, 'I the Lord will water it every moment.' And it is the Spirit which is this water, as the Scripture everywhere declares. God the Father is the head, fountain, and treasure of all actual supplies; and the Spirit is the *efficient cause*, communicating them unto us from him. From hence it is that any grace in us is kept alive one moment, that it is ever acted in one single duty, that ever it receives the least measure of increase or strengthening. With respect unto all these it is that our apostle saith, 'Nevertheless, I live, yet not I, but Christ liveth in me,' Gal. II.20. Spiritual life and living by it, in all the acts of it, are immediately from Christ.[39]

Behind all this account of the production of holiness is but the real but mysterious act of regeneration. Philosophically, the work of the Spirit in regeneration is a metaphysical change. God the Spirit is the immediate author and cause of this work of regeneration:

> And here again, as I suppose, we have in general, the consent of all. . . . Our sole inquiry, must be after the manner and nature of this work; for the nature of it depends on the working of the Spirit of God herein. . . . I shall, therefore, in general, refer the whole of the work of the Spirit of God with respect unto the regeneration of sinners unto two heads, That which is *preparatory* for it, and, secondly, That which is *effective* of it. . . . Our principle inquiry in the present design is the work itself, or the nature and manner of the working of the Spirit of God on the souls of men in their regeneration.[40]

---

[39] Owen, Πνευματολογια (1674), 344; *Works* (1965), 3:393.
[40] Owen, Πνευματολογια (1674), 254; *Works* (1965), 3:299–301.

Owen goes on to assert that the work of the Spirit is not on suasion only. 'By *suasion* we intend to such a persuasion as may or may not be effectual; so absolutely we call that only *persuasion* whereby is actually persuaded.'[41] The means of persuasion are the instructions, precepts, promises and threatenings of it.[42] And as mortification of sin is part of the Spirit's work in regeneration, he contrasts his approach with how Roman Catholics understood mortification.[43]

> We may look into the *Papacy*, and take a view of the great appearance of this duty which is therein, and we shall find it all disappointed; because they are not led unto or taught the duties whereby it might be brought about by the Spirit of God. They have, by the light of Scripture, a far clearer discovery of the nature and power of sin than had the philosophers of old. The commandment, also, being variously brought and applied unto their consciences, they may be, and doubtless are and have been, many of them, deeply sensible of the actings and tendency of indwelling sin. Hereon ensues a terror of death and eternal judgment. Things being as stated, persons who were not profligate nor had their consciences seared could not refrain from contriving ways and means how sin might be mortified and destroyed. But whereas they had lost a true apprehension of why this might be effected, they betook themselves into innumerable false ones of their own. His was the spring of all the austerities, disciplines, fastings, self-macerations, and the like, which are effected or in use among them: for although they are now in practice turned mostly to the benefit of the priests, and an indulgence unto sin in the penitents, yet they were invented and set on foot at first with a design to use them as engines for the mortification of sin; and they have as great appearance in the flesh unto that end and purpose. But yet, when all was done, they found by experience that they were insufficient hereunto: sin was not destroyed, nor conscience pacified, by them. This made them betake themselves to purgatory.[44]

So what Owen is doing, theologically speaking, is tightening up the contemporary understanding of his theme. There may be traces of scholastic terminology here, used by habit, but spiritual mortification is something that Thomas Aquinas did not have a place for.[45] But Owen argues that holy virtues are not the same as moral virtues, which are developed as the result of repetition and practice. In

---

[41] Owen, *Πνευματολογια* (1674), 256; *Works* (1965), 3:301.
[42] Owen, *Πνευματολογια* (1674), 257; *Works* (1965), 3:302.
[43] Owen, *Πνευματολογια* (1674), 468–70; *Works* (1965), 3:533–5.
[44] Owen, *Πνευματολογια* (1674), 487–8; *Works* (1965), 3:555–6.
[45] Owen, *Πνευματολογια* (1674), 106; *Works* (1965), 3:135.

a regenerate person, 'there is a real *physical work* of the Spirit'.⁴⁶ By this Owen means a direct immediate work of the Spirit:

> If the Holy Spirit work no otherwise on men, in their regeneration or conversion, but by proposing unto them and urging upon them *reasons*, *arguments* and *motives* to that purpose, then after his whole work, and notwithstanding it, the will of man remains absolutely indifferent whether it will admit them or no, or whether it will *convert itself* unto God upon them or no, for the *whole* of this consists in proposing objects unto the will, with respect whereunto it is left *undetermined* whether it will close with them or no. And, indeed, this is that which some plead for. . . . What this grace is, or whence men have this power and ability, by some is not declared. Neither is it much to be doubted but that many do imagine that it is purely natural; only they will allow it to be called grace, because it is from God who made us . . . the act, therefore itself of willing in our conversion is of God's operation; and although we will ourselves, yet it is he who causeth us to will, by working in us to do.⁴⁷

There is no root and branch change in his method, insofar as he is dealing with a long-neglected theme. But there is some evidence that this data, if he is to work thoroughly on it, calls for a modification of scholasticism when it concerns the life of God in the souls of men and women. While modifying scholasticism in his work on the experience of the Spirit in the believer, he also vents his disenchantment with scholasticism in other writings of the same time, notably in *The doctrine of justification by faith* (1677).⁴⁸

OWEN'S DISENCHANTMENT WITH SCHOLASTICISM

In this experiential turn, Owen appears to tire of scholasticism. In *Diatriba de justitia divina* (1653), he had already complained of the 'thickets of scholastic terms and distinctions . . . the impediments and sophisms of an enslaving philosophy or false knowledge'.⁴⁹ In such moods, Owen draws attention to the fact that analytical and subtle distinctions have their place, but that they carry their own dangers, and are often subordinate in value to other ways of description that can be used in theology. In his introduction to *The doctrine of justification by faith* he claims that there were in circulation in his day 'twenty

---

⁴⁶Owen, Πνευματολογια (1674), 261; *Works* (1965), 3:307.
⁴⁷Owen, Πνευματολογια (1674), 261–2; *Works* (1965), 3:303–5.
⁴⁸Owen, *The doctrine of justification by faith* (1677); *Works* (1965), vol. 5.
⁴⁹Owen, *Diatriba de justitia divina* (1653), n.p.; *Works* (1965), 10:490.

several opinions among Protestants' about the place of faith in justification.[50] Scholasticism was going to seed. Perhaps it was dawning on Owen that, whatever its merits, scholastic theology was an application of a pagan philosophy to the Christian mysteries. Calvin had stressed that the pagans had no conception of the fall and its consequences, particularly in their ethics, and, in seventeenth-century scholasticism, this limitation was working itself out in terms of method.[51]

Owen states in *The doctrine of justification by faith* that it is

> the direction, satisfaction, and peace of the consciences of men, and not the curiosity of notions or subtilty of disputations which it is our duty to design. And therefore, I shall, as much as I possibly may, avoid all those *philosophical* terms and distinctions wherewith this *evangelical* doctrine hath been perplexed rather than illustrated; for more weight is to be put on the steady guidance of the mind and conscience about the foundation of his peace and acceptance with God, than on the confutation of ten wrangling disputers.[52]

Owen is gesturing here to the stress on the inward self in the mind and conscience that he would develop in his work on the Spirit. The scholastics have a different project:

> When men are once advanced into that field of disputation [that is, scholasticism], which is all overgrown with thorns of subtilties, perplexed notions, and futilious [futile] terms of art, they, the scholastics teachers consider principally how they may entangle others in it, scarce at all how they may get out of it themselves. And in this posture they oftentimes utterly forget the business they are about, especially in this matter of justification, – namely, how a guilty sinner may come to obtain favour and acceptance with God. And not only so, but I doubt they oftentimes dispute themselves beyond what they can well abide by, when they return home unto a sedate meditation of the state of things between God and their souls.[53]

So what was Owen to do? In Πνευματολογια, his response to the understanding of the work of the Spirit in regeneration and sanctification of the elect was not to make even finer scholastic distinctions but to offer descriptions – descriptions of what causes men to become aware of themselves as regenerated and justified.

---

[50] Owen, *The doctrine of justification by faith* (1677), 6; *Works* (1965), 5:11.
[51] For example, Calvin, *Institutes*, 1.15.8; 2.2.18.
[52] Owen, *The doctrine of justification by faith* (1677), 3; *Works* (1965), 5:8, see also 68f.
[53] Owen, *The doctrine of justification by faith* (1677), 6; *Works* (1965), 5:11.

So, he advises his readers not to adopt the doctrine wrought in scholastic terms, but to affirm it in its biblical terms and its personal consequences:

> [E]very true believer, who is *taught of God*, knows how to put his whole trust in Christ alone, and the grace of God by him, for mercy, righteousness and glory, and not at all concern himself with those loads of thorns and briers, which, under the names of definitions, distinctions, accurate notions, in a number of exotic pedagogical and philosophical terms, some pretend to accommodate them withal.[54]

Owen here provides a brief experiential commentary of the topic of justification by faith. He goes on to argue that

> It is, therefore, to no purpose to handle the mysteries of the Gospel as if Holcot and Bricot, Thomas and Gabriel, with all their Sententiarists, Summists and Quodlibertarians of the old Roman peripatetical [Aristotelian] school, were to be raked out of their graves to be our guides. Especially will they be of no use unto this doctrine of justification. For whereas they pertinaciously adhered unto the philosophy of Aristotle, who knew nothing of any righteousness but what is a habit inherent in ourselves, and the acts of it, they wrested the whole doctrine of justification unto a compliance therewithal.[55]

Owen refers to Thomas Aquinas, Gabriel and later scholastics such as Robert Holcot (1290–1349) and Thomas Bricot (1490–1516). A 'Summist' is the writer of a *Summa*, and a 'Quodlibertarian' is a pedantic reasoner. This is a significant passage, in which Owen appeals to those who are 'taught of God' – that is, those who are regenerate over those who are taught by the scholastic method. This is a kind of experiential teaching and learning different from that promoted by scholasticism, which confines its appeal to the powers of human reason. Owen is not using scholastic language, but the language of experiential religion, and of the prophets and apostles.

So, Owen observes prominently, in the first chapter of his book, that the causes and objects of faith have to do with their grounds and their effects, in their different degrees in the life of the true believer. Faith may produce great effects in the minds, affections and lives of people.[56] The responsibility of the

---

[54] Owen, *The doctrine of justification by faith* (1677), 7; *Works* (1965), 5:12.
[55] Owen, *The doctrine of justification by faith* (1677), 8; *Works* (1965), 5:12.
[56] Owen, *The doctrine of justification by faith* (1677), 94; *Works* (1965), 5:72–3.

theologian is to describe these experiences by appealing to special revelation or by drawing inferences from that revelation.

THE THEOLOGY OF THE HOLY SPIRIT

We return to look in more detail at Owen's programme for the doctrine of the Holy Spirit, as expressed originally in the preface of his own scholastic work on the vindicatory justice of God. Of his early books, we have mentioned Owen's writings on Arminianism and the death of Christ, but he also prepared other publications, such as *The doctrine of the saints perseverance* (1654), a vast, learned tome, which occupies over 600 pages in Goold's edition. It is another production of a work on theological anthropology.[57] This was a distinctively Calvinistic work, upholding one of the central tenets of the Synod of Dort (1618–19) and of the Westminster Confession (1647). Owen is concerned to show that perseverance was a patristic doctrine, not a Reformed novelty. Judged by the development of Owen's thought, the book is a hybrid between a standard scholastic treatment and the style that he adopted when he came later to develop the work of the Holy Spirit in the believer. In *The doctrine of the saints perseverance*, Owen provides an elaborate treatment of 'evangelical perseverance', the 'certain permanency' that the saints have in their endurance with Christ to the end.

In that work, Owen argued that grace is a habit, the product of the Holy Spirit, and that there are two ways of losing the Spirit, efficiently and meritoriously. Believers, indwelt by the Spirit, have an inherent holiness.[58] The Spirit's work is to strengthen weak believers.[59] Perseverance is based on the divine immutability of his purposes, particularly the covenant of grace, so this is an explicit example of covenant theology, which is worthy of note.[60] For, during this period, covenant theology was undergoing its own crisis of method. In Holland, in the mid-seventeenth century, the methodological development of covenant theology by Johannes Cocceius (1603–69) and Herman Witsius (1636–1708) challenged the strict scholasticism of those such as Gisbertus Voetius (1589–1676) at Utrecht. In scholasticism, what was uppermost was a doctrine, and its elaboration and connection with other doctrines. The work of Cocceius and Witsius – which ought to have been a complementary theological approach to scholasticism – was instead regarded as a dangerous assault on orthodoxy. Structuring the study of Christian theology had the merit

---

[57] Owen, *The doctrine of the saints perseverance* (1654); *Works* (1965), vol. 11.
[58] Owen, *The doctrine of the saints perseverance* (1654), 31; *Works* (1965), 11:119.
[59] Owen, *The doctrine of the saints perseverance* (1654), 26–7; *Works* (1965), 11:112–13.
[60] Owen, *The doctrine of the saints perseverance* (1654), 32; *Works* (1965), 11:120.

of focusing on the sequence of Bible history, on the relations between the Old and New Testaments. What Owen saw in covenant theology was that Scripture was to be understood in narrative terms – a mode that he developed in his experiential theology.

This mode was especially evident in Owen's later writing. By the publication of Πνευματολογια (1674), Owen had placed his account of the Spirit's indwelling within a covenant theology framework. This is anticipated on the central topic of communion with Christ – which he described as a 'doctrine of pure revelation'. His direct, continuous appeal to the Bible is not a case of 'Biblicism' but gives pre-eminence to the contours of anthropological theology that is missed by scholastic treatments of the work of the Spirit. For example, writing of sanctification as a progressive work, he explained that

> all this increase of holiness is immediately the work of the Holy Ghost, who therein gradually carries on his design of sanctifying us throughout, in our whole spirits, souls and bodies. There is in our regeneration and habitual grace received a nature bestowed on us capable of growth and increase, and that is all; if it be left unto itself it will not thrive, it will decay and die. The actual supplies of the Spirit are the waterings that are the immediate cause of its increase. It wholly depends on continual influences from God. He cherisheth and improves the work he hath begun with new and fresh supplies of grace every moment: Isa xxvii.3, the Lord will water it every moment. And it is the Spirit which is this water, as the Scripture everywhere declares. God the Father is the head, fountain, and treasure of all actual supplies; and the Spirit is the *efficient cause*, communicating them unto us from him. From hence it is that any grace in us is kept alive one moment, that it is ever acted in one single duty, that ever it receives the least measure of increase or strengthening. With respect unto all these it is that our apostle saith, 'Nevertheless, I live, yet not I, but Christ liveth in me' (Gal. II.20). Spiritual life and living by it, in all the acts of it, are immediately from Christ.[61]

In an age that had a place for religious fanaticism, and with the ever-present danger of 'enthusiasm', Owen had steadying things to say on the place of reason, which required some sophistication.

THE PLACE OF REASON

As this chapter has demonstrated, the claim that Owen continued as a scholastic theologian to the end of his life requires some qualification, for he increasingly

---

[61] Owen, Πνευματολογια (1674), 344; *Works* (1965), 3:393.

feared that the behaviour and spiritual temper of some scholastics turned the method into a vehicle for defending non-Protestant positions. After all, where in the New Testament was such a theological project warranted? We have noted Owen's expression of a sort of weariness and exasperation with the making of distinctions for their own sake, and for the importance of personal experience as a test of proper understanding. This last point is characteristic of the experiential aspect of Owen's anthropology, an aspect of his understanding of how Christian doctrine should be assented to and obeyed, but in the way its recipient should develop his assent and obedience. This is a characteristic of Owen's view of his own duty as a Christian theologian.

For Owen, the means of satisfaction in regeneration and sanctification were the Scriptures only. But how do they gain their authority over us? How do we believe the Scriptures to be the word of God? Owen's answer is that these questions addressed the work of the Holy Ghost. He revisits what Calvin had written in his *Institutes*. In *The reason of faith* (1677), unusually, if not uniquely, Owen quotes the *Institutes* at 1.3.5.[62] There are external arguments for the divinity of the Scriptures, which at best yields moral certainty, the sort of certainty that we need to get us through the business of a day. But moral certainty is not good enough for reliance on what purports to be God's revelation. So, the chief argument is an internal argument, the fact that the Scripture presents itself as the word of God. It shines by its own light.

In this short book, Owen shows himself to be a competent philosopher. He begins with 'our reason singly', noting that without 'divine grace and illumination', it is weak and limited, depraved and corrupted.[63] But if the mind is illuminated by the Holy Spirit, what kind of certainty does it provide?

[The Holy Ghost] gives unto believers a spiritual sense of the power and reality of the things believed, hereby their faith is greatly established; and although the divine witness, whereunto our faith is ultimately resolved, doth not consist herein, is the greatest corroborating testimony whereof we are capable. This is that which brings us unto the 'riches of the full assurance of understanding,' Col ii.2; as also I Thess.1.5. And on the account of this spiritual experience is our perception of spiritual things so often expressed in acts of sense, as tasting, seeing, feeling and the like means of assurance in things natural. And when believers have attained hereunto, they do find the divine wisdom, goodness, and authority of God so present unto them as that they need neither argument, nor motive, nor anything else, to persuade them or confirm them in believing. And whereas this spiritual experience, which

---

[62] Owen, *The reason of faith* (1677), 108; *Works* (1965), 4:69.
[63] Owen, *The reason of faith* (1677), 83; *Works* (1965), 4:54.

believers obtain through the Holy Ghost, is such as cannot be rationally be contended about seeing those who have received it cannot fully express it, and those who have nor received it cannot understand it, nor the efficacy which it hath to secure and establish the mind, it is left to be determined on by them alone who have their 'senses exercised to discern good and evil.' And this belongs unto the internal subjective testimony of the Holy Ghost.[64]

THE LAST PHASE: OWEN'S INDEPENDENT MINISTRY IN RESTORATION ENGLAND

The Restoration radically changed Owen's circumstances. An explosion of printing and publishing in English took Owen further away from the circle of a Latin-dominated style. Yet his memory must have returned to the preface of the *Diatriba*, and the need for theologians to turn their attention to the person and work of the Holy Spirit – and how fruitful that proved to be. Owen's style in the prefaces to his later works is in strong contrast to his earlier efforts at wordy, learned, cumbersome English, in which scholastic words and phrases had jostled with the vernacular. He wrestles with the problem of how the work of the Spirit on the deep things of God can be constructed to be communicated, given that the Spirit's work is immediate to the soul, and how readily it is ridiculed. In this period, Owen's English style may be said to be not scholastic, but *congregational*.

In this chapter, I have suggested that in his later anthropology Owen was a 'supernaturalist', or a 'revelationist', and in the eyes of some no doubt also a 'fideist'. The foundations of his thought were the result of the immediate workings of the Holy Spirit to the elect to which Scripture was witness. Yet in *The reason of faith* he uses terms in epistemology that later philosophers would recognize even though that usage might have repelled them. Paradoxically, this 'supernaturalism' was defended at the very time when the variety of rationalism known as 'deism' was about to emerge.

Owen was nothing if not a many-sided theologian. His answer to the question, 'How is theology helped by scholasticism?' is very mixed, as I hope we have seen. Owen's philosophy always follows his theology. His emphasis on the work of the Holy Spirit in the hearts and lives of God's elect was in any case new territory, yet the evidence of scholasticism was still apparent in the habits of Owen's English prose. I have argued that Owen's life led him not to a total repudiation of scholasticism, but into a more narratival direction, in which it was in his interests to describe the inner life of the hearts and spirits of the elect.

---

[64]Owen, *The reason of faith* (1677), 100; *Works* (1965), 4:64.

PART II
Owen's writings

CHAPTER 12

Θεομαχία αυτεξουσιαστικη

or, A display of Arminianisme (1643)

CHRISTOPHER CLEVELAND

John Owen began his writing career with the publication of *Θεομαχία αυτεξουσιαστικη: or, A display of Arminianisme* in 1643. In this book, Owen outlines the beliefs of the Arminian theology of his day, and compares them to the teachings of Scripture. Throughout the work, Owen deploys scholastic argumentation and distinctions in his defence of Calvinistic orthodoxy. He also demonstrates great familiarity with contemporary debates, including both the Remonstrant controversy and the *congregatio de auxiliis* of the Roman Catholic Church.

This chapter will explain the background and content of *A display of Arminianisme*. First, it will explain the historical context of the book, looking at the controversies and issues relevant to its composition. Second, it will examine Owen's references, noting the origin of his sources and the background of the arguments that he utilizes. Third, the chapter will summarize the argument of the book, analysing Owen's critique of Arminian ideas and his defence of Reformed orthodoxy. Fourth, it will assess the strengths and weaknesses of Owen's argumentation, and conclude with a defence of his thought.

HISTORICAL CONTEXT: THE CONTROVERSIES OF GRACE

Owen inherited a distinct theological tradition, as an heir to over 1,600 years of Christian theological debate and discussion. He possessed a profound knowledge of the history of the debates concerning grace in the Christian church, from the earliest times until his own era. Many of his arguments follow in the patterns laid down in those controversies. Much of Owen's argumentation is focused upon demonstrating that the views of his opponents are either novel or associated with a strain of theology that has already been identified as heretical. As these controversies were vital to Owen's thought, it is necessary to examine the most important of these conflicts concerning grace in the Christian church, and their impact upon Owen's work.

Augustine and the Pelagian controversy

The Christian church began to debate issues regarding grace, predestination and election in earnest during the Pelagian controversy of the fifth century. A British monk, Pelagius (354–418), argued that man was essentially good. What God required of man was absolute duty and perfect obedience. Pelagius had been scandalized by the teaching of Augustine of Hippo (354–430) in a prayer in his *Confessions*: 'Give what Thou commandest, and commandest what Thou wilt.'[1] Peter Brown describes the theology of Pelagius and his followers:

> The basic conviction of Pelagius and his followers was that man's nature was certain and fundamentally unchanging. Originally created good by God, the powers of human nature had, admittedly, been constricted by the weight of past habits and by the corruption of society. But such constriction was purely superficial. The 'remission of sins' in baptism, could mean for the Christian, the immediate recovery of a full freedom of action, that had merely been kept in abeyance by ignorance and convention.[2]

To put it another way, Pelagianism taught that man was fundamentally good, and capable of not sinning. To be sinless and perfect was within man's natural powers and abilities. He was no more 'fallen' than Adam had been before he ate the forbidden fruit.

Augustine responded to these claims by arguing that after Adam had sinned, sin had infected the entirety of the human race. Men were thus hopelessly corrupted, and stood in need of grace to do any good whatsoever. It was necessary for men to receive the grace of predestination in order to be lifted up to communion with God. As Matthew Levering describes Augustine's thought on predestination,

---

[1] Augustine, *Confessions*, 10.29 (NPNF 1/1:153).
[2] Brown, *Augustine of Hippo*, 367.

the order of salvation depends on God's decision from eternity with respect to whether to give grace to particular persons. In emphasizing the radical priority of the grace of the Holy Spirit, Augustine focuses the debate away from the difficulties caused by the fact that God does not predestine all persons – although Augustine readily acknowledges these difficulties – and toward the praise of God for curing our pride by his gift of love and thereby enabling our intimate participation in the trinitarian life.[3]

This background is important for Owen in *A display of Arminianisme*, as he saw himself in the tradition of Augustine, and his opponents in the tradition of Pelagius. The very title of the work makes the point that *A display of Arminianisme* was also a *Discovery of the old Pelagian idol free-will, with the new goddess contingency*. Owen thus frames the debate as a new version of the old debate between biblical Augustinianism and satanic Pelagianism. He argues that 'these are not things "in quibus possimus dissentire salvâ pace ac charitate," as Austin speaks, – "about which we may differ without loss of peace or charity." One church cannot wrap in her communion Austin and Pelagius, Calvin and Arminius'.[4] This in Owen's mind is the distinction between the two sides: there is Augustinianism and Calvinism on one side, and Pelagianism and Arminianism on the other.

Moreover, as this argument suggests, Owen's greatest theological influence was Augustine. As Carl Trueman has noted,

> it is worth noting that, above all, we find Owen interacting extensively with, and positively using at every opportunity, the writings of Augustine, who is quoted by him more than any other single author. This is not surprising, as the Reformation itself was, on one level, a struggle over how Augustine was to be interpreted, a battle 'over who owned Augustine.'[5]

Augustine was a major influence upon Owen's thought in general, and Owen finds him to be particularly useful in his theological critique of Arminian thought.

Congregatio de auxiliis

The Pelagian controversy was not the only one to influence Owen's thought on the subject of grace. Owen was also heavily influenced by a more recent

---

[3]Levering, *The theology of Augustine*, 71.
[4]Owen, *A display of Arminianisme* (1643), Epistle Dedicatory; *Works* (1965), 10:7.
[5]Trueman, *John Owen*, 11–12. Truman is reflecting on Warfield's well-known statement that the Reformation was the 'triumph of Augustine's doctrine of the grace over Augustine's doctrine of the church'. Warfield, *Studies in Tertullian and Augustine*, 130.

Roman Catholic controversy regarding grace and predestination, known as *de auxiliis*.[6] The controversy *de auxiliis* was a series of conflicts within the Roman Catholic Church after the Council of Trent. These were conflicts focused upon the nature of grace, free will and predestination. On the one side were the Jesuits, whose beliefs were largely represented by the thought of Luis de Molina (1535–1600). Molina had developed the idea of middle knowledge, in which God foresees how a creature will react among multiple future contingencies and different situations, and then predestines the creature according to their foreseen action. On the other side of the conflict were the Dominicans, who were led in the controversy by Domingo Bañez (1528–1604) and Diego Alvarez (1555–1635). Following in the Thomist tradition, the Dominicans emphasized the primacy of divine movement in the work of grace. Bañez had argued for a conception of physical premotion, in which God physically premoves the creature to a certain action. That is to say, God predetermines how the creature will act, and then moves them accordingly.[7] Bañez and the Dominicans had argued that the Molinist account was Pelagian. Molina and the Jesuits argued that the Dominican teaching was too Protestant and Calvinist.

Owen was clearly interested in the controversy *de auxiliis*. He came down decisively on the side of the Dominican Thomists. Owen references Diego Alvarez on several occasions, and deploys his arguments extensively against the Arminians. Alvarez is referenced alongside Augustine in support of the teaching that God does not will anything that does not occur.[8] Owen also references Alvarez in support of his teaching on original sin: 'original sin is a defect of nature, and not of this or that particular person: whereon Alvarez grounds this difference of actual and original sin – that the one is always committed by the proper will of the sinner; to the other is required only the will of our first parent, who was the head of human nature'.[9] Owen also references Alvarez in discussing the importance of an actual movement of the creature as opposed to a mere moral persuasion.[10] These arguments would help Owen in his case against the Arminians.

---

[6]For a full account of the controversy, see Matava, *Divine causality and human free choice*; 'A sketch of the controversy *de auxiliis*'; Serry, *Historia Congregationum de auxiliis* (1700); Eleutherius, *Historia controversarium de divinæ gratiæ auxiliis* (1742); Bañez, *Scholastica commentaria in primam partem Summae Theologiae* (1584); Molina, *Liberi arbrbitrii cum gratiae donis* (1588); Alvarez and Bañez, *Disputationes theologicæ in primam secundæ S. Thomæ* (1617).
[7]'Physical' is contrasted with 'moral'. God actually moves the creature to act rather than simply persuading it to act in a certain manner.
[8]Owen, *A display of Arminianisme* (1643), 49; *Works* (1965), 10:52.
[9]Owen, *A display of Arminianisme* (1643), 74; *Works* (1965), 10:73.
[10]Owen, *A display of Arminianisme* (1643), 142; *Works* (1965), 10:131.

Socinianism

One of the great theological foils of Owen's life was Socinianism. Socinianism began with the work of two Italian thinkers: Laelius Socinus (1525–62) and his nephew, Faustus Socinus (1539–1604). Laelius had been well acquainted with the reformers, even corresponding with John Calvin.[11] His thought was continued after his death in the work of his nephew, who began a career in law. Inspired by the writings of his uncle, Faustus developed a system of thought that would be known as Socinianism.

The heart of Socinianism was the belief that men should ultimately rely upon their reason above all.[12] The way that Socinus worked this out was to develop startingly novel and heretical understandings of nearly every major Christian doctrine. Socinus denied the Trinity, claiming that it was irrational and unbiblical. He denied the deity of Christ. He stated that men were saved by following Christ's teaching, which they were perfectly capable of doing. The whole system was a type of proto-Enlightenment project, in which Scripture was placed into the procrustean bed of human rationality. Socinus's teachings were explicitly contradictory to those of every Christian communion in Europe, and so he fled to Poland, where his ideas were tolerated. The Polish community of Socinians disseminated his writings throughout Europe, thus leading to controversy over the course of the next century.[13]

The spectre of Socinianism soon began to loom over every major theological controversy in the seventeenth century. Socinianism began to be a growing threat to Christian orthodoxy. As Socinianism was so clearly heretical from a confessional standpoint, Socinian ties or suggestions immediately cast doubt upon the orthodoxy of the individual who possessed them. This became quite evident in the controversy with the Remonstrants and the Arminians. Nevertheless, Socinian ideas were still dispersed throughout the continent. Many were drawn to Socinian thought, including Remonstrants and Arminians, who appreciated the appeal to action and the right use of free will in Socinian writings. One student claimed that Jacobus Arminius (1560–1609) himself had recommended Socinus in his classes.[14] Reckoning with the Socinian objection, Simon Episcopius (1583–1643), one of the leading Remonstrants, would struggle with the idea of divine foreknowledge, before consenting to the belief.[15] Thus Socinianism and Arminianism were tied together in a loose fashion, as many of the Remonstrant thinkers were influenced by Socinian ideas.

---

[11] Mortimer, *Reason and religion in the English revolution*, 14.
[12] Mortimer, *Reason and religion in the English revolution*, 15; Dixon, *Nice and hot disputes*, 40.
[13] Dixon, *Nice and hot disputes*, 40.
[14] Mortimer, *Reason and religion in the English revolution*, 25.
[15] Bac, *Perfect will theology*, 169.

Owen does not reference Socinianism often in *A display of Arminianisme* but the shadow of this innovative theology is present throughout the work. The argument of chapter three, on divine foreknowledge, is predicated upon the fact that Arminianism came dangerously close to denying this doctrine in the way that Socinianism did. This charge is not without reason, as was demonstrated by Episcopius's difficulties with the doctrine. Owen states that the Remonstrants 'vindicate themselves so coldly in their Apology, that some learned men do from hence conclude, that certainly, in their most secret judgments, all the Arminians do consent with Socinus in ascribing unto God only a conjectural foreknowledge'.[16] This charge is perhaps unfair, as it is certainly not a charitable assessment of the Arminian approach to foreknowledge.[17] Nevertheless, Owen is able to make this claim because both the Socinian and the Arminian accounts deny a foreordained future, thus leaving the possibility of divine foreknowledge upon unclear rational grounding.

It could be argued that the references to Socinianism in *A display of Arminianisme* may be merely 'poisoning the well' by negative association, but Owen nevertheless saw a very real connection between Arminian teachings and the Socinian denial of classic confessional Christianity. As Trueman notes, 'in Owen's mind, Socinianism and Arminianism were intimately related. This arose from the fact that he understood both as arguing for doctrinal positions which granted human beings a level of autonomy and self-sufficiency which he regarded as unbiblical'.[18] Owen saw a logical connection in many areas between the Arminian diminishing of grace and the Socinian denial of its necessity.

The Remonstrant controversy and the origins of Arminianism

Of course, Owen's chief theological target in *A display of Arminianisme* was the theology that arose out of the Remonstrant controversy in Holland. The Remonstrant controversy began in 1603, when Arminius was appointed to the theology faculty at the university in Leiden.[19] Arminius was opposed by both his fellow faculty member Franciscus Gomarus (1563–1641) and the Reformed churches, who in June 1605 sent five synod members to confront him concerning his teaching. The resulting conflict resulted in a national synod, which caused followers of Arminius to produce a Remonstrance, or written protest. The five points of the Remonstrance affirmed a general atonement,

---

[16]Owen, *A display of Arminianisme* (1643), 19; *Works* (1965), 10:27.
[17]For Arminius's doctrine of foreknowledge, see his *Disputationes privatae*, in *Opera theologica* (1629), IV.xliv (p. 223). For analysis, see Muller, *God, creation, and providence in the thought of Jacob Arminius*, 152–5; Stanglin and McCall, *Jacob Arminius*, 63–9.
[18]Trueman, *The claims of truth*, 23.
[19]For a summary of the Remonstrant controversy, see Rohls, 'Calvinism, Arminianism, and Socinianism in the Netherlands until the Synod of Dort'.

in which God predestined that those who believed would be saved and those who did not would be damned. They also affirmed that Christ died for all equally, but that only those who believed would actually receive salvation. They affirmed that grace was necessary, but was not irresistible. Finally, they posited the possibility of a true believer falling away.[20] These articles of Remonstrance were answered in the Synod of Dort in 1618–19.

The Arminians and the Remonstrants are the chief targets of Owen's first published work. In this text, Owen makes twenty-two references to Arminius. Simon Episcopius, the leader of the Remonstrants after Arminius's death, is referenced eleven times. Nicolaas Grevinchovius (d. 1632) is referenced eight times, and Johannes Arnoldi Corvinus (1582–1650) twenty. Owen demonstrates extensive knowledge of the work of the Remonstrants, which he utilizes to argue against their teaching. At the end of every chapter, Owen placed quotations from the Arminians and Remonstrant leaders alongside passages of Scripture to contrast them negatively.

English Arminianism

While these events were unfolding in the Netherlands, a slowly growing movement of those who were opposed to Calvinist principles was gaining steam in England. King Charles I had been raised with Arminian preachers, through the machinations of Lancelot Andrewes. When Charles came to the throne in 1625, the Arminians found in him a strong ally to their cause.[21] In 1626, the king proclaimed that disputants 'are forbidden either "by writing, preaching, printing, conferences or otherwise, [to] raise any doubts, or publish or maintain any new inventions, or opinions, concerning religion than such as [are] clearly grounded and warranted by the doctrine and discipline of the church of England"'.[22] This was interpreted as an attack upon traditional English Calvinism, and opened the way for Arminianism to be taught and propagated.[23] This was advanced further by an additional royal declaration in 1628, appended to a reissue of the Thirty-nine Articles, which ordered that the disputes over predestination be 'shut up in God's promises, as they be generally set forth to us in the holy scriptures'.[24] This in one sense placed the royal *imprimatur* upon the Arminian interpretation of the confessional standards of the Church of England. The Calvinist cause received a further setback when

---

[20]Schaff, *The Evangelical Protestant creeds*, 545–50.
[21]MacCulloch, *The Reformation*, 516–17; Patterson, *William Perkins and the making of a Protestant England*, 211.
[22]Tyacke, *Anti-Calvinists*, 48–9.
[23]Tyacke, *Anti-Calvinists*, 49.
[24]Tyacke, *Anti-Calvinists*, 50.

Parliament was dissolved, in 1629, leading to the 'personal rule' of the king. Most MPs were Calvinists, and had in fact taken action to remove Arminians from the universities.[25] With these moves, the Arminian cause was emboldened, and in 1633, William Laud, a devout Arminian, was appointed as archbishop of Canterbury. When another Parliament was convened, in 1640, MPs had Laud arrested and imprisoned in the Tower of London in 1641.[26]

It was in this context that Owen wrote *A display of Arminianisme*. He dedicates the work to the 'Lords and Gentlemen of the Committee for Religion', a parliamentary committee appointed by the House of Lords to 'examine all religious innovations introduced since the reformation'. Gribben notes that the book displayed an 'intention to bring himself to the attention of those best placed to advance his career'.[27] With this work, Owen entered into the fray of English public theological conversation, intending to present traditional English Reformed theology against the innovations of the Arminians.

Owen references very few English writers. As Gribben notes, the political situation was too volatile for him to reference many of them.[28] Nevertheless, Owen does mention a select few. He references Thomas Jackson (1579–1640), president of Corpus Christi College, who wrote *A treatise of the divine essence and attributes* (1628–9).[29] Owen observes Jackson arguing that 'it is a dream ... to thinke of Gods decrees, concerning things to come, as of acts, irrevocably finished, which would hinder that which Welsingius laies down for a truth, to wit, that the elect, may become reprobates, and the reprobates, elect'.[30] Here Owen takes issue with Jackson's objection to the idea that the divine decrees are permanent and complete. This ties in with Owen's critique of the Arminian understanding of the decrees as being temporal in nature.

Perhaps the most vitriolic comment in the entire work, however, is reserved for a book titled *God's love to mankind*, which was published in 1633 by Samuel Hoard (1599–1658). Owen describes this book as being

> full of palpable ignorance, gross sophistry, and abominable blasphemy, whose author seems to have proposed nothing unto himself but to rake all the dunghills of a few of the most invective Arminians, and to collect the most filthy scum and pollution of their railings to cast upon the truth of God; and, under I know not what self-coined pretences, belch out odious blasphemies against his holy name. The sum, saith he, of all these speeches

---

[25] Tyacke, *Anti-Calvinists*, 51.
[26] Tyacke, *Anti-Calvinists*, 243; MacCulloch, *The Reformation*, 522.
[27] Gribben, *John Owen and English Puritanism*, 46.
[28] Gribben, *John Owen and English Puritanism*, 47.
[29] Gribben, *John Owen and English Puritanism*, 47.
[30] Owen, *A display of Arminianisme* (1643), 8; *Works* (1965), 10:17.

(he cited to his purpose) is, 'That there is no decree of saving men but what is built on God's foreknowledge of the good actions of men.' No decree? No, not that whereby God determineth to give some unto Christ, to ingraft them in him by faith, and bring them by him unto glory.[31]

Owen's strong words may be understood to reflect his political situation, in which the conflict between Arminians and Calvinist forces had caused upheaval. They may also be driven by Hoard's unfair characterization of Calvinist orthodoxy itself. Hoard reduces the entirety of predestinarian thought, the works of Calvin, Beza, Zanchius, Piscator and Gomarus, as well as the teaching of the Synod of Dort, to a focus on the decree of reprobation.[32] This one-sided and imbalanced presentation of the Reformed faith certainly would have incensed Owen, leading to his strong language. Nevertheless, despite Owen's strong words, he does present a core argument: that the denial of the divine decree is a denial of salvation itself. The divine decree of salvation is not simply a cold act of God determining some human beings for heaven and others for hell, but encompasses every element of salvation in the love of Christ, from eternity, to the temporal reality of the believer, unto glory.

Owen's familiarity with controversies both recent and ancient provides support to his argument for Reformed predestinarianism. Owen is clearly able to categorize both his own thought and that of his opponents with respect to traditional controversies and parties. In addition to sources dealing with controversies, Owen also references a wide array of sources in the formulation of his argument.

REFERENCES IN *A DISPLAY OF ARMINIANISME*

As *A display of Arminianisme* was Owen's first published work, he sought to employ his capabilities to the fullest to demonstrate his acumen. He therefore quotes from a wide variety of sources in the work. Owen refers to classical

---

[31] Owen, *A display of Arminianisme* (1643), 59–60; *Works* (1965), 10:61.
[32] Hoard, *God's love to mankind* (1633), 3–4. Tim Cooper takes issue with Owen's wrathful response and characterization of the work: 'Rather than engaging with Hoard's thesis, Owen heaped abuse and then distorted it. Hoard's main argument did not concern an obscure point about God's foreknowledge. Instead, as the title made very clear, it was an objection to the idea that God hated most men and women from eternity. Owen would have been well capable of deflecting the criticism but, curiously, he never even tried'; Cooper, *John Owen, Richard Baxter, and the formation of Nonconformity*, 69–70. Despite Cooper's frustration with Owen on this point, one can argue that Owen felt a similar frustration with Hoard's work, and a failure of it to interact with Reformed theology on a fair level. In no way could classic Reformed orthodoxy be accurately summarized as 'God hating most men and women from eternity'. This perhaps explains some of Owen's hasty dismissal of the work.

authors, patristic and medieval authors, and interacts with contemporary authors, in order to more fully explain his thought and deal with Arminian errors.³³

Classical references

Owen references a wide array of classical sources. He mostly places the classical references at the beginning of each chapter, in order to explain how the Arminians are waging war against God. Owen references Homer in multiple places. In chapter three he observes that

> Christians hitherto, yea, and heathens, in all things of this nature, have usually, upon their event, reflected on God as one whose determination was passed on them from eternity, and who knew them long before; as the killing of men by the fall of a house, who might, in respect of the freedom of their own wills, have not been there. Or if a man fall into the hands of thieves, we presently conclude it was the will of God. It must be so; he knew it before.³⁴

In referencing the 'heathen', Owen quotes Homer's Διός δ' ετελείετο βουλή: 'God's will was done.' He references the Trojan war, in his reference to the 'Helen for whose enjoyment, these thrice ten years, they have maintained warfare with the hosts of the living God'.³⁵ Likewise, he references the tragedy of the death of Sarpedon in *The Iliad*:

> Now, let any good-natured man, who hath been a little troubled for poor Jupiter in Homer, mourning for the death of his son Sarpedon, which he could not prevent, or hath been grieved for the sorrow of a distressed father, not able to remove the wickedness and inevitable ruin of an only son, drop one tear for the restrained condition of the God of heaven, who, when he would have all and every man in the world to come to heaven . . . yet, being not in himself alone able to save one.³⁶

---

³³Some caution should be taken when assessing Owen's use of sources. Throughout the work, he clearly used citations to serve his polemical purposes. Richard Snoddy has argued that Owen 'was heavily reliant on the compendia of Festus Hommius and Johannes Peltius for his presentation of Arminianism' and may have relied on similar sourcebooks for other material in the book. See Snoddy, 'A Display of Learning? Citations and Shortcuts in John Owen's *Display of Arminianisme* (1643)', 332.
³⁴Owen, *A display of Arminianisme* (1643), 15; *Works* (1965), 10:22.
³⁵Owen, *A display of Arminianisme* (1643), 32; *Works* (1965), 10:38.
³⁶Owen, *A display of Arminianisme* (1643), 47; *Works* (1965), 10:50.

Owen also references Latin authors, including Virgil (70–19 BC), author of *The Aeneid*. In arguing that the Arminians join together their idol free will with divine providence, Owen observes that 'they must be tied together with the same ligament "quo ille mortua jungebat corpora vivis," – wherewith the tyrant tied dead bodies to living men'.[37] This is a quotation from *The Aeneid* (book VIII, line 485), which Owen slightly amends from *Mortua quin etiam iungebat corpora vivis*. He also references *The Metamorphoses* (book III, lines 136–7), by Ovid (43 BC–AD 17): 'As the poet thought none happy, so they think no man to be elected, or a reprobate, before his death.'[38] Here Owen's reference from Ovid reads, *Dicique beatus – ante Obitum nemo*: 'None are called happy before death.' Owen also references Cicero (106 BC–43 BC) to negatively compare the Arminians to the heathen:

> The sum of them all you may find in Cicero, his third book De Natura Deorum. 'Every one,' saith he, 'obtaineth virtue for himself; never any wise man thanked God for that: for our virtue we are praised; in virtue we glory, which might not be were it a gift of God.' And truly this, in softer terms, is the sum of the Remonstrants' arguments in this particular.[39]

As Owen sees it, the Remonstrants agree with pagan authors that we should never thank God for the good that we do and for the virtue that we possess.

In addition to specific authors quoted and referenced, Owen also makes several classical references in passing. He refers to Oedipus and the riddle of the Sphinx: 'In a word, that there should be a purpose of God to bring men unto glory, standing inviolable, though never any one attained the purposed end, is such a riddle as no Oedipus can unfold. Now, such an election, such a predestination, have the Arminians substituted in the place of God's everlasting decree.'[40] The Arminian separation of the divine purpose from actual election is a paradox that rivals the riddle of the Sphinx. He also references the tale of Leto or Latona, the mother of Apollo and Artemis:

> This . . . was heretofore unknown to the more refined Paganism. As these of contingency, so they, with a better error, made a goddess of providence, because, as they feigned, she helped Latona to bring forth in the isle of Delos; intimating that Latona, or nature, though big and great with sundry sorts of effects, could yet produce nothing without the interceding help of

---

[37] Owen, *A display of Arminianisme* (1643), 23; *Works* (1965), 10:30.
[38] Owen, *A display of Arminianisme* (1643), 9; *Works* (1965), 10:18.
[39] Owen, *A display of Arminianisme* (1643), 113; *Works* (1965), 10:104.
[40] Owen, *A display of Arminianisme* (1643), 55; *Works* (1965), 10:57.

divine providence: which mythology of theirs seems to contain a sweeter gust of divine truth than any we can expect from their towering fancies.[41]

He calls the idea that we should depend upon free will rather than divine Providence an 'opinion fitter for a hog of the Epicurus herd than for a scholar in the school of Christ'.[42] And in one humorous example, he compares the Arminians in their discovery of free will to Archimedes yelling 'Eureka!' at his discovery: 'presently, with no less joy than did the mathematician at the discovery of a new geometrical proportion, exclaim, "We have found it! we have found it!"'[43]

Patristic and medieval authors

Owen brings forth a number of patristic and medieval authors in defence of his theology of grace. 'If any would know how considerable this article concerning original sin hath ever been accounted in the church of Christ', he observes, 'let him but consult the writings of St Augustine, Prosper, Hilary, Fulgentius, any of those learned fathers whom God stirred up to resist, and enabled to overcome, the spreading Pelagian heresy'.[44] The use of the fathers enables Owen to claim the mantle of tradition, and charge his opponents with heretical novelty.

Drawing upon this medieval scholarship, Owen chiefly uses Western authors, likely because they were less susceptible to Pelagianism than were those of the East. As noted earlier, Owen references Augustine more often than any other patristic or medieval author. Augustine is such a profound authority that Owen often uses him as a standard by which to judge other patristic authors. With reference to John of Damascus (675–749), Owen writes that

> St Augustine judged Cicero worthy of special blame, even among the heathens, for so attempting to make men free that he made them sacrilegious, by denying them to be subject to an overruling providence: which gross error was directly maintained by Damascen, a learned Christian, teaching, 'Things whereof we have any power, not to depend on providence, but on our own free will.'[45]

Likewise, he notes that Jerome (347–419/20) was

> injurious to [God's] providence, and cast a blemish on his absolute perfection, whilst he thought to have cleared his majesty from being defiled with the

---

[41]Owen, *A display of Arminianisme* (1643), 22–3; *Works* (1965), 10:31.
[42]Owen, *A display of Arminianisme* (1643), 30; *Works* (1965), 10:36.
[43]Owen, *A display of Arminianisme* (1643), 124; *Works* (1965), 10:115–16.
[44]Owen, *A display of Arminianisme* (1643), 69; *Works* (1965), 10:69.
[45]Owen, *A display of Arminianisme* (1643), 30; *Works* (1965), 10:36.

knowledge and care of the smallest reptiles and vermin every moment; and St Austin is express to the contrary: 'Who,' saith he, 'hath disposed the several members of the flea and gnat, that hath given unto them order, life, and motion?'[46]

After Augustine, Owen also makes several references to Prosper of Aquitaine (390–463), a protégé of Augustine: 'St Prosper, in his treatise against Cassianus the semi-Pelagian, affirmeth it to be a foolish complaint of proud men "that free-will is destroyed, if the beginning, progress, and continuance in good be said to be the gifts of God".'[47] Prosper also is utilized in support of the idea that salvation could be found in Christ before His incarnation: 'So Prosper, also, "We must believe that never any man was justified by any other faith, either before the law or under the law, than by faith in Christ coming to save that which was lost".'[48] Owen also uses Prosper to define free will: 'I shall be content to call it with Prosper, a "spontaneous appetite of what seemeth good unto it," free from all compulsion, but subservient to the providence of God.'[49] Owen also references Prosper's account of Pelagius, without mentioning him by name.[50]

Owen makes a positive reference to Jerome. In speaking of God's possession of foreknowledge, he writes, 'But yet that he doth so in respect of things free and contingent is much questioned by the Arminians in express terms, and denied by consequence, notwithstanding St Jerome affirmeth that so to do is destructive to the very essence of the Deity.'[51] Owen also alludes to Jerome's account of Origen's devotion to free will.[52] Owen references Gregory the Great (540–604): 'On this ground Gregory affirmeth, "That many fulfill the will of God" (that is, his intentions) "when they think to change it" (by transgressing his precepts); "and by resisting imprudently, obey God's purpose".'[53]

While Owen pays most attention to the Western fathers, he also references those from the eastern church. In speaking of how Christ was believed upon in the Old Testament, he remembers that 'holy Ignatius called Abel "A martyr of Christ"; he died for his faith in the promised Seed. And in another place, "All the saints were saved by Christ; hoping in him, and waiting on him, they obtained salvation by him."'[54] And shortly thereafter, Owen references

---

[46]Owen, *A display of Arminianisme* (1643), 27; *Works* (1965), 10:33.
[47]Owen, *A display of Arminianisme* (1643), 114; *Works* (1965), 10:107.
[48]Owen, *A display of Arminianisme* (1643), 120; *Works* (1965), 10:112.
[49]Owen, *A display of Arminianisme* (1643), 129; *Works* (1965), 10:119.
[50]Owen, *A display of Arminianisme* (1643), 123; *Works* (1965) 10:115.
[51]Owen, *A display of Arminianisme* (1643), 17; *Works* (1965), 10:24.
[52]Owen, *A display of Arminianisme* (1643), 123; *Works* (1965), 10:114.
[53]Owen, *A display of Arminianisme* (1643), 45; *Works* (1965), 10:48.
[54]Owen, *A display of Arminianisme* (1643), 120; *Works* (1965), 10:112.

Eusebius of Caesarea (265–339), who 'contendeth that all the old patriarchs might properly be called Christians; they all ate of the same spiritual meat, and all drank of the same spiritual drink, even of the rock that followed them, which rock was Christ'.[55]

Among medieval authors, Owen takes particular interest in Thomas Aquinas (1225–74).[56] Owen references Thomas numerous times throughout the work. He makes a great deal of use of Thomistic logic, especially his understanding of divine causality in his argumentation. As Trueman notes, 'The kind of causal scheme envisaged here is the same as that used by Thomas in the Five Ways, each of which famously ends with a self-caused cause, an αυτο ον, which Thomas declares by common consent to be a god.'[57] Moreover, the work displays the same Thomistic logic of *exitus-reditus*, whereby creatures come from God, and return to Him by grace.[58] Owen also references Durandus (1275–1334) with respect to the commands of God, and Bernard of Clairvaux (1090–1153).[59] In speaking of the necessity of faith in Christ for salvation, Owen quotes Bernard to the effect that 'many laboring to make Plato a Christian, do prove themselves to be heathens'.[60]

Reformed authors

As a theologian in the Reformed tradition, Owen naturally uses authors from the Reformation. On the very first page of his book, he references *On the bondage of the will* (1525), by Martin Luther (1483–1546).[61] Owen positively mentions Calvin (1509–64), though he does not reference his work explicitly.[62] Owen also references Martin Bucer (1491–1551), the Strasbourg reformer who influenced Calvin, to the effect that the moral goodness of every action comes from God.[63] He references Samuel Rutherford (1600–61) and also William Twisse (1578–1646) in affirmation of his explanation of the divine knowledge.[64] He also references Edward Reynolds (1599–1676), whom he

---

[55] Owen, *A display of Arminianisme* (1643), 120; *Works* (1965), 10:112.
[56] Cleveland, *Thomism in John Owen*, 33–46.
[57] Trueman, *John Owen*, 29.
[58] Chenu and Bremner, 'The plan of St. Thomas' *Summa Theologiae*', 67–79.
[59] Owen, *A display of Arminianisme* (1643), 42; *Works* (1965), 10:46.
[60] Owen, *A display of Arminianisme* (1643), 118; *Works* (1965), 10:111.
[61] Owen, *A display of Arminianisme* (1643), 1; *Works* (1965), 10:11.
[62] Owen, *A display of Arminianisme* (1643), 7; *Works* (1965), 10:16. 'How do they and their fellows, the Jesuits, exclaim upon poor Calvin, for sometimes using the hard word of compulsion, describing the effectual, powerful working of the providence of God', and in the dedicatory note: 'One church cannot wrap in her communion Austin and Pelagius, Calvin and Arminius'; *Works* (1965), 10:7.
[63] Owen, *A display of Arminianisme* (1643), 37; *Works* (1965), 10:42.
[64] Owen, *A display of Arminianisme* (1643), 15; *Works* (1965), 10:23.

feels has thoroughly refuted the Arminian doctrine of original sin.[65] One of the Protestants whom he references the most, however, is Jerome Zanchius (1516–90), arguably the most Thomistic of Reformed Protestants in the sixteenth and seventeenth centuries.[66] Zanchius is referenced with respect to the simple intelligence and knowledge of vision, and divine foreknowledge, as well as the Thomistic understanding of divine causality. Zanchius is referenced alongside Thomas Aquinas in the use of Thomistic categories. Zanchius is also referenced as the source of a conspiracy theory about Jesuits supporting Lutherans against the Calvinists.[67] Owen also uses the Thirty-nine Articles of the Church of England to make his case. As the Westminster Assembly had only just begun its great work relatively recently, these comprised the confessional standard by which the Reformed English church was bound.

Owen's references, both to controversies and beyond, demonstrate an impressive array of resources marshalled in defence of Reformed predestinarianism. They aid in giving weight to his argument that Arminianism is outside the fold of historic Augustinian and Reformed orthodoxy. Ultimately, however, it is Owen's argument itself that provides the real strength of the book.

THE ARGUMENT OF THE BOOK

Owen begins *A display of Arminianisme* with the statement of the question: 'Whether the first, and chiefest part, in disposing of things in this world, ought to be ascribed to God or man?'[68] Owen's answer is that it should belong to God, and to God alone. In order to make this case, he divides the work into two parts: Arminian errors concerning God, and Arminian errors concerning man. As Owen puts it, the Arminian goal was, 'first, To exempt themselves from God's jurisdiction, to free themselves from the supreme dominion of his all-ruling providence; not to live and move in him, but to have an absolute independent power in all their actions'.[69] These would be the errors concerning God. Furthermore,

---

[65]Owen, *A display of Arminianisme* (1643), 77; *Works* (1965), 10:76. 'I shall not shew their opposition unto the truth in many more particulars, concerning this Article of Originall sinne: having beene long agoe most excellently prevented even in this very method, by the way of Antithesis to the Scripture, and the Orthodoxe doctrine of our Church, by the famously learned Master Reynolds, in his excellent Treatise Of the sinfulnesse of sinne: where he hath discovered their errours, fully answered their sophisticall objections, and invincibly confirmed the truth from the word of God.'
[66]'He is the best example of Calvinist Thomism'; Donnelly, *Calvinist Thomism*, 444.
[67]Owen, *A display of Arminianisme* (1643), epistle dedicatory; *Works* (1965), 10:7.
[68]Owen, *A display of Arminianisme* (1643), 2; *Works* (1965), 10:11.
[69]Owen, *A display of Arminianisme* (1643), 2; *Works* (1965), 10:12.

the second end at which the new doctrine of the Arminians aimeth is, to clear human nature from the heavy imputation of being sinful, corrupted, wise to do evil but unable to do good; and so to vindicate unto themselves a power and ability of doing all that good which God can justly require to be done by them in the state wherein they are . . . that so the first and chiefest part in the work of their salvation may be ascribed unto themselves.[70]

These would be errors concerning man.

Owen begins with the divine decree. In this section, he presents the core of his argument. His primary argument against the Arminians is that God has sovereignly decreed all that shall occur before anything was created. That decree is the unalterable, immutable act of the divine persons in ordaining whatsoever should come to pass. To look at it another way, the decree may be simply seen as the way by which God plans whatever will happen in history before the creature is even created.

Owen notes several particular aspects of the decree with which the Arminians have a problem. First, it is important that the divine decree be properly understood as immutable. It cannot be changed. Owen argues in the opening of the second chapter that

> it hath been always believed among Christians, and that upon infallible grounds, as I shall show hereafter, that all the decrees of God, as they are internal, so they are eternal, acts of his will; and therefore unchangeable and irrevocable. Mutable decrees and occasional resolutions are most contrary to the pure nature of Almighty God.[71]

The divine decree should be understood to be immutable and unchangeable because God himself is immutable and unchangeable. The decree is an internal act of his will, and thus reflects his nature. This point is essential for Owen because the denial of it is at the heart of the Arminian error. Any attempt to say that human beings can change or affect reality apart from the divine will is a reflection of this error. The decree establishes God's absolute dominion over all of reality, for in it, God has determined what shall be, and the course of temporal history.

Second, Owen notes that this decree must be eternal. That is to say, it must precede the creation of the temporal realm, as it is an act of God, who is eternal. This is important because there is nothing that the creature can do to alter the decree, as it precedes the creation of the creature. Like immutability, eternality

---

[70]Owen, *A display of Arminianisme* (1643), 3; *Works* (1965), 10:13.
[71]Owen, *A display of Arminianisme* (1643), 5; *Works* (1965), 10:14.

is an attribute of God, and reflects his nature.[72] The decree must be eternal as God does not act in a reactive way to his creation. Rather, he is Lord over it, and it must reflect his complete and absolute dominion. If the decree were not eternal, then God would be in a reactive and interactive relationship with his creation, rather than one of complete dominion and lordship.

Third, Owen emphasizes the irresistibility of the divine decree.[73] While he will develop this argument, this is an important underlying presupposition. It is of no purpose if the eternal and immutable divine decrees may be opposed and resisted by creatures. This would mean, ultimately, that the decrees were mutable, and capable of change and alteration.

The Arminian objections which Owen highlights reflect objections to one of these points. Owen takes issue with the Arminian order of the decrees which would make some temporal, and follow the actions of the creature. Owen here references Corvinus, Grevinchovius and Arminius himself to the effect that certain decrees may follow the actions of the creature.[74] Owen also takes issue with the idea of temporary decrees: 'As they affirm them to be temporary and to have had a beginning, so also to expire and have an ending, to be subject to change and variableness. "Some acts of God's will do cease at a certain time," saith Episcopius.'[75] Owen takes particular issue with the Arminian distinction between 'peremptory' and 'not-peremptory' decrees, meaning decrees which are final and absolute, and those which are open to change and alteration, depending upon the actions of free creatures. Owen argues that 'their distinction of them into peremptory and not peremptory . . . is not, as by them applied, compatible with the unchangeableness of God's eternal purposes'.[76]

Owen's argument at its heart ties the decree to the divine nature itself. Due to divine simplicity, the divine decrees are inseparable from God in himself. As Owen notes, they are 'internal, eternal acts of His will'. This is significant because what it means is that the decree is not an arbitrary action upon God's part. Rather, predestination and providence are placed within the nature of God himself, and thus centred on his essence. This makes the argument less about the free will of man, and more about the nature of almighty God, whose decrees determine all things.

It is important to note that the decree is not a 'central dogma' to Owen's theology, or a single doctrine from which all other doctrines are derived.[77]

---

[72] Owen, *A display of Arminianisme* (1643), 11; *Works* (1965), 10:19.
[73] 'An eternal purpose, proceeding from such a will as to which none can resist'; Owen, *A display of Arminianisme* (1643), 11; *Works* (1965), 10:19.
[74] Owen, *A display of Arminianisme* (1643), 6; *Works* (1965), 10:15.
[75] Owen, *A display of Arminianisme* (1643), 7; *Works* (1965), 10:16.
[76] Owen, *A display of Arminianisme* (1643), 8; *Works* (1965), 10:17.
[77] For a critique of 'central dogma' theories, see Muller, *Post-Reformation Reformed dogmatics*, vol. 1: *Prolegomena*, 38–9.

Rather, it is an important touchstone that helps Owen to demonstrate the nature of divine dominion over creation. The role of the decree in the doctrine of predestination and providence reflects a traditional English Calvinism. Owen's understanding of the divine decree reflects that of the Lambeth Articles of the Church of England (1595) and that of William Perkins, in his *Golden chaine* (1600).[78] In this sense, Owen's work is well within the mainstream of Reformed tradition.[79]

With the doctrine of the decree settled, Owen then proceeds to examine the connected doctrines which are under attack by the Arminians. In chapter four, he argues that

> three things concerning his providence are considerable: 1. His decree or purpose, whereby he hath disposed of all things in order, and appointed them for certain ends, which he hath foreordained. 2. His prescience, whereby he certainly fore-knoweth all things that shall come to pass. 3. His temporal operation, or working in time . . . whereby he actually executeth all his good pleasure.[80]

Thus as the decree is first, next is divine foreknowledge. This on one level is a strange choice, as the Arminians affirmed divine foreknowledge. Yet on another level, this makes sense. As the Arminians did not believe in an immutable and eternal decree, the foundation for divine foreknowledge was removed. Owen observes that the 'prescience or foreknowledge of God hath not hitherto, in express terms, been denied by the Arminians, but only questioned and overthrown by consequence, inasmuch as they deny the certainty and unchangeableness of his decrees, on which it is founded'.[81] This is the centre of his argument in the chapter: the Arminians have no real place to affirm divine foreknowledge, as they have removed the foundation of it by removing the eternal decree.

Owen argues for the classic Thomistic understanding of divine foreknowledge categorized into simple intelligence, and knowledge of vision. Simple intelligence is God's perfect knowledge of all that is possible, and which he could bring about if he so chose. Knowledge of vision is God's knowledge of what he will sovereignly choose to occur. Owen uses Thomistic categories extensively to make this claim, noting that God has ordained some things to occur necessarily, others contingently, according to the order of their operation. This means that

---

[78]Patterson, *William Perkins and the making of a Protestant England*, 64–89.
[79]For an understanding of the role of the decree in Reformed thought, see Muller, *Christ and the decree*.
[80]Owen, *A display of Arminianisme* (1643), 24; *Works* (1965), 10:31.
[81]Owen, *A display of Arminianisme* (1643), 14; *Works* (1965), 10:22.

some things he ordains to occur by their very nature, such as the sun shining. This is necessary. Other things he ordains to occur contingently, meaning as a consequence of the action of a free creature. As he notes, 'God hath determined it, both for the matter and manner, even so as is agreeable to their causes, some necessarily, some freely, some casually or contingently, yet also, as having a certain futurition from his decree, he infallibly foreseeth that they shall so come to pass.'[82]

This leads Owen to the doctrine of providence, or the execution of the divine decree in time. Owen defines providence as being an 'ineffable act or work of Almighty God, whereby he cherisheth, sustaineth, and governeth the world, or all things by him created, moving them, agreeably to those natures which he endowed them withal in the beginning, unto those ends which he hath proposed'.[83] Owen's point here is that God's providence extends to all that exists. God governs it and brings it to its appointed end. This governance does not exempt the wicked, but extends even to them.[84]

And this divine providence is ordered through the divine sustenance of all things. Owen insists that God's 'sustentation or upholding of all things is his powerful continuing of their being, natural strength, and faculties, bestowed on them at their creation'. God upholds all things by his divine power, giving them existence and animation. This, Owen notes, is not to remove from them all agency of their own, 'so that he doth neither work all himself in them, without any co-operation of theirs, which would not only turn all things into stocks, yea, and take from stocks their own proper nature'.[85] Humans are not mere puppets, but God works in and through them, upholding their secondary causality.

This sovereign divine operation works in all things, so that contingent things which he has purposed to occur in a certain way do so, 'making them in some sort necessary, inasmuch as they are certainly disposed of to some proposed ends'.[86] This providential guidance upholds the freedom of the creature in their choices and actions as they 'are inclined and disposed to do this or that, according to their proper manner of working, that is, most freely'.[87]

It is thus clear that for Owen, God works providentially in guiding men in their free acts to those ends which he has foreordained in the decree. Those actions are inevitable and infallible, and yet performed with absolute freedom. As he will express so clearly towards the end of the book, 'it is no more necessary

---

[82]Owen, *A display of Arminianisme* (1643), 16–17; *Works* (1965), 10:24.
[83]Owen, *A display of Arminianisme* (1643), 24–5; *Works* (1965), 10:31.
[84]Owen, *A display of Arminianisme* (1643), 26–7; *Works* (1965), 10:33.
[85]Owen, *A display of Arminianisme* (1643), 28; *Works* (1965), 10:34.
[86]Owen, *A display of Arminianisme* (1643), 29; *Works* (1965), 10:35.
[87]Owen, *A display of Arminianisme* (1643), 30; *Works* (1965), 10:36.

to the nature of a free cause, from whence a free action must proceed, that it be the first beginning of it, than it is necessary to the nature of a cause that it be the first cause'.[88] God moves the creature to a specific action, which it freely chooses.

This leads Owen to the question of whether the will and purpose of God may be resisted. Here Owen makes a key argument, placing once again the purposes and will of God into the divine essence:

> 'Divinum velle est ejus esse,' say the schoolmen, 'The will of God is nothing but God willing'; not differing from his essence 'secundum rem,' in the thing itself, but only 'secundum rationem,' in that it importeth a relation to the thing willed. The essence of God, then, being a most absolute, pure, simple act or substance, his will consequently can be but simply one; whereof we ought to make neither division nor distinction.[89]

Thus the will of God is inseparable from the divine essence. As God is pure simple act, he possesses no parts, and so his will cannot be separated from his nature. Once again, Owen is locating the divine purposes within God himself, the divine essence, which means that the divine will is not arbitrary or random, but is united to the immutable, holy, wise nature of God.

In order to more properly explain this, Owen brings forth the 'vulgar distinction' of the secret and revealed will of God: 'The secret will of God is his eternal, unchangeable purpose concerning all things which he hath made, to be brought by certain means to their appointed ends.'[90] This is the divine sovereign purpose for all things, which he is working out through his providential governance. In contrast, 'the revealed will of God containeth not his purpose and decree, but our duty, not what he will do according to his good pleasure, but what we should do if we will please him; and this, consisting in his word, his precepts and promises'.[91] The one concerns the eternal purpose of God for all that occurs, while the other concerns what we are commanded to do as his creatures. This helpful distinction explains why the will of God may be said to be frustrated in some aspects, but not in others. With respect to the first, the will of God is always done, without fail. As Paul enquires, 'who resists His will?' (Rom. 9.19). With respect to the second, God's will may be said not to be done, as men disobey the divine commandments. Owen's problem with the Arminian objections is that they

---

[88]Owen, *A display of Arminianisme* (1643), 130; *Works* (1965), 10:120.
[89]Owen, *A display of Arminianisme* (1643), 39–40; *Works* (1965), 10:44.
[90]Owen, *A display of Arminianisme* (1643), 40–1; *Works* (1965), 10:45.
[91]Owen, *A display of Arminianisme* (1643), 41; *Works* (1965), 10:45.

do not see this distinction, and often argue that the immutable divine purposes may be resisted and frustrated.

Owen's objection to the Arminian position frequently comes down to the fact that it does not affirm that God has immutably and sovereignly ordained all that occurs. Rather, Arminians believe that God ordains some things, while leaving others up to the determination of free creatures, which are outside of the purview of divine providence. This leads Owen to explain how the whole doctrine of predestination is corrupted by the Arminians. Predestination itself, Owen explains, is the 'counsel, decree, or purpose of Almighty God concerning the last and supernatural end of his rational creatures, to be accomplished for the praise of his glory'.[92] Here Owen returns once again to the divine decree, noting that it is the foundation of the doctrine of election and predestination. At this point, Owen uses the seventeenth of the Thirty-nine Articles of the Church of England to explain predestination.[93]

First, Owen notes that the article states that predestination is an 'eternal decree, made before the foundations of the world were laid'.[94] This goes along with all that he has said about the decree before this point: it is eternal and it is unchangeable. Second, Owen notes that predestination is 'constant, that is, one immutable decree; agreeably also to the Scriptures, teaching but one purpose, but one foreknowledge, one good pleasure, one decree of God, concerning the infallible ordination of his elect unto glory'.[95] This, Owen emphasizes, is against the Arminian idea of different types of election, such as peremptory or non-peremptory. There is one divine act of election, which is unalterable, and cannot be resisted or changed. Third, Owen notes that the 'object of this predestination is some particular men chosen out of mankind; that is, it is such an act of God as concerneth some men in particular'.[96] God chooses particular men to redeem. His predestination is not a general act, in which he merely gives salvation to any man who chooses to believe. This is in opposition to the Arminian idea of a general election. Fourth, Owen notes that 'there is no other cause of our election but God's own counsel. It recounteth no motives in us, nothing impelling the will of God to choose some out of mankind, rejecting others, but his own decree, that is, his absolute will and good pleasure'.[97] This is in contrast to the Arminian understanding of predestination that is based upon the foreseen merits or foreseen faith. To this end, Owen quotes the Remonstrants to the effect that 'faith in the consideration of God choosing

---

[92] Owen, *A display of Arminianisme* (1643), 51; *Works* (1965), 10:53.
[93] Owen, *A display of Arminianisme* (1643), 51–3; *Works* (1965), 10:54.
[94] Owen, *A display of Arminianisme* (1643), 52; *Works* (1965), 10:54.
[95] Owen, *A display of Arminianisme* (1643), 53; *Works* (1965), 10:55.
[96] Owen, *A display of Arminianisme* (1643), 54; *Works* (1965), 10:57.
[97] Owen, *A display of Arminianisme* (1643), 57; *Works* (1965), 10:60.

us unto salvation, doth precede, and not follow as a fruit of election'.[98] This, Owen notes, is illogical, as the cause cannot follow the effect, and faith is the effect of election.[99]

This brings Owen to the second part of the treatise, where he deals specifically with Arminian errors concerning man. There are three major points to this section of the work. First, Owen explains the nature of human corruption and fallenness. Second, he explains the work of Christ in the atonement, and the necessity thereof. Finally, he finishes the work explaining the true nature of created agency.

Owen begins in chapter seven by explaining the corruption of mankind due to original sin. This sin was committed by Adam, and is transmitted to all of his posterity, thus bringing both an internal corruption and a legal state of condemnation. Arminian theories had sought to lessen this impact of sin upon the human race, in order to retain human powers with respect to salvation. Like the previous chapter, Owen uses the ninth article of the Thirty-nine Articles of the Church of England to argue his case regarding original sin:

> In the ninth article of our church, which is concerning original sin, I observe especially four things: First, That it is an inherent evil, the fault and corruption of the nature of every man. Secondly, That it is a thing not subject or conformable to the law of God, but hath in itself, even after baptism, the nature of sin. Thirdly, That by it we are averse from God, and inclined to all manner of evil. Fourthly, That it deserveth God's wrath and damnation.[100]

This is important for Owen because original sin limits human action in such a way that the human being cannot merit favour before God. Every action which he commits is sinful and corrupt. Even the greatest of human actions is tainted by sin. Moreover, even one sin merits the wrath of God, which means that even the greatest of sinful humans is in need of a Saviour.

Owen then briefly touches upon original righteousness. The Arminians had sought to affirm that man possessed an inclination to sin as he was created, though not quite so great as he was afterwards. Owen responds that man was created perfectly upright, without sin, and that the fall introduced sinful corruption into his soul. The reason why this is significant is because if humanity remains in a similar or identical state to that wherein it was created, then the way by which humanity relates to God is similar to the way it was as created. If man could work his way to virtue and righteousness before the fall, then he

---

[98] Owen, *A display of Arminianisme* (1643), 58–9; *Works* (1965), 10:60.
[99] Owen, *A display of Arminianisme* (1643), 64; *Works* (1965), 10:65.
[100] Owen, *A display of Arminianisme* (1643), 69–70; *Works* (1965), 10:70.

can do the same now. If he was capable of faith in his own powers before, then he is capable of it now. Owen notes the distinction between these two states, before the fall and after, in order to highlight the need for divine action in the human heart.

Owen then comes to the second major point of this section, which is the death of Christ. Owen in this section seeks to demonstrate that Christ's work is perfectly efficacious. His death upon the cross needs nothing added to it, but it brings redemption for those for whom it is wrought. Owen notes that there are two aspects of this question: first, for whom did Christ die? Second, what did Christ obtain or merit for those for whom He died?[101] Owen argues that Christ died for a specific and particular group of individuals, to merit for them a perfect salvation. Owen argues that

> the proper counsel and intention of God in sending his Son into the world to die was, that thereby he might confirm and ratify the new covenant to his elect, and purchase for them all the good things which are contained in the tenure of that covenant, to wit, grace and glory; that by his death he might bring many (yet some certain) children to glory, obtaining for them that were given unto him by his Father (that is, his whole church) reconciliation with God, remission of sins, faith, righteousness, sanctification, and life eternal.[102]

To put it another way, Christ died for the chosen elect, to bring them every benefit of salvation. He did not die for all equally, for all do not receive the benefits of salvation. He died for his people, to bring them salvation without fail. This, in Owen's mind, marks the logic of salvation: the divine purposes of the decree are united to the action of Christ in redemption, and brought to fruition in the work of the Holy Spirit. Those purposed for salvation in eternity have their sins paid for by Christ, and brought to a living faith by the Spirit. This is a holistic view of salvation, wherein the elect receive every benefit purchased for them by Christ. Owen also notes that the work of Christ the High Priest cannot be partitioned. As he intercedes only for his people, so also does he sacrifice only for his people: 'seeing he doth not intercede and pray for every one, he did not die for every one'.[103]

Against these arguments, Owen contrasts the Arminian position, which posits not an actual but a merely hypothetical redemption. He references Corvinus to the effect that what Christ's death obtains is a 'potential, conditionate

---

[101] Owen, *A display of Arminianisme* (1643), 91; *Works* (1965), 10:88.
[102] Owen, *A display of Arminianisme* (1643), 94; *Works* (1965), 10:90.
[103] Owen, *A display of Arminianisme* (1643), 96; *Works* (1965), 10:92.

reconciliation, not actual and absolute'.[104] The Arminian position argues that Christ's death produces the opportunity or possibility of redemption, not the actual redemption itself. The strength of Owen's contrast here is to point out that he argues for a work of redemption that is actual and real, while that argued by the Arminians is merely hypothetical and potential. It is these arguments which he will develop more fully in his later work *Salus electorum, sanguis Jesu: or, The death of death in the death of Christ* (1648).

Owen then begins the final movement of the work, which is to explain the true nature of created agency. He begins by examining the cause of faith, grace and righteousness. For Owen, this is nothing other than the Holy Spirit, applying the merits of Christ to the believer. He argues that the 'death of Christ is their meritorious cause; the Spirit of God and his effectual grace their efficient, working instrumentally with power by the word and ordinances'.[105] The argument of the Arminians was that 'that ought not to be commanded which is wrought in us; and that cannot be wrought in us which is commanded. He foolishly commandeth that to be done of others who will work in them what he commandeth'.[106] To put it another way, there is a separation between that which is required as a duty, and that which is given by God as a gift. The Arminians argued that the two could not overlap. Owen's response was to note that there is no other source of these gifts. If God required faith, it would have to come from Him. Everything good which we possess comes from God.

This leads Owen to examine the nature of free will itself, and the ability of human creatures to act of their own power. Owen's chief argument in this section is exactly what was noted earlier: that the will of men is subject to the foreordination and causal priority of God. Owen argues that

> we do not absolutely oppose free-will, as if it were 'nomen inane', a mere figment, when there is no such thing in the world, but only in that sense the Pelagians and Arminians do assert it. About words we will not contend. We grant man, in the substance of all his actions, as much power, liberty, and freedom as a mere created nature is capable of.[107]

Owen did not deny free will. Rather, he placed it in its context as a created faculty, subject to divine working. The problem is that the Arminians and Remonstrants argued for an independency of free will, such that it was unmoved by divine action. This, Owen notes, is impossible for any created thing. He observes that

---

[104] Owen, *A display of Arminianisme* (1643), 99; *Works* (1965), 10:94.
[105] Owen, *A display of Arminianisme* (1643), 106; *Works* (1965), 10:100.
[106] Owen, *A display of Arminianisme* (1643), 109; *Works* (1965), 10:103.
[107] Owen, *A display of Arminianisme* (1643), 125; *Works* (1965), 10:116.

everything that is independent of any else in operation is purely active, and so consequently a god; for nothing but a divine will can be a pure act, possessing such a liberty by virtue of its own essence. Every created will must have a liberty by participation, which includeth such an imperfect potentiality as cannot be brought into act without some premotion (as I may so say) of a superior agent.[108]

This is the heart of Owen's argument regarding free will and human causality: human beings are mixed creatures of act and passive potency, receiving the ability to act only from God himself. They are dependent upon the physical premotion of God to act in any way. This does not hinder the liberty of the will, as it is given the power, freedom and ability to act in a certain fashion, rather than being compelled in some way. This is an argument derived from the Dominicans in the controversy *de auxiliis*, particularly from Diego Alvarez.[109]

This leads Owen to discuss the way in which the Arminians argue for the power of free will in preparing for conversion. As Owen has already discussed faith as the gift of God, and free will, he brings them both together. The Arminians argued that men should 'make themselves differ from others' and 'dispose themselves for such a blessing'.[110] In response, Owen notes that human beings are dead in their trespasses and sins (echoing Ephesians 2), and have 'not only an impotency but an enmity in corrupted nature to anything spiritually good'.[111] There is no spiritual good in the human being apart from the work of the Spirit in regeneration. They cannot thus dispose themselves in any way in preparation for conversion.

Owen then addresses the act of conversion itself. The Arminians argued that there was in free will 'first, A power of co-operation and working with grace, to make it at all effectual; secondly, A power of resisting its operation, and making it altogether ineffectual'.[112] There was for the Arminians a power of working for or against the grace of God. Against this, Owen argues for a very careful explanation of grace which changes the faculties and wills of men so that they are irresistibly drawn to God. He writes that

the effectual grace which God useth in the great work of our conversion, by reason of its own nature, being also the instrument of and God's intention for that purpose, doth surely produce the effect intended, without successful

---

[108] Owen, *A display of Arminianisme* (1643), 129; *Works* (1965), 10:119.
[109] Cleveland, *Thomism in John Owen*, 41–6.
[110] Owen, *A display of Arminianisme* (1643), 134–5; *Works* (1965), 10:124–5.
[111] Owen, *A display of Arminianisme* (1643), 137; *Works* (1965), 10:127.
[112] Owen, *A display of Arminianisme* (1643), 141; *Works* (1965), 10:130.

resistance, and solely, without any considerable co-operation of our own wills, until they are prepared and changed by that very grace.[113]

There is a radical transformation of the will, so that it is effectually drawn to God, without resistance, over and above its own power. This is the infusion or creation of a new spiritual principle in the soul of man, a habit of grace which produces faith, love and holiness. Thus, this divine act of grace produces a 'new birth', whereby man is now made capable of living rightly unto God, and dwelling in holiness.[114] Owen thus is arguing for the necessity of the work of the Holy Spirit in renovating the human soul, and changing it by grace, such that it is no longer in a state of spiritual enmity against God, but is now in a state of love unto Him.

This is Owen's argument: that God is the beginning and ending of all that occurs, working all things to the counsel of his will. He physically premoves all things so that creatures may act freely according to the workings of divine causality. God particularly works to bring his elect unto salvation, for whom Christ has died, and to whom God the Holy Spirit applies the merits won by Christ. God gives the creature grace to act and faith to believe, and infuses within their souls a new, vital, spiritual principle, or habit of grace, such that they are now a new creature, capable of living unto God.

ASSESSMENT AND CRITIQUE

Despite traces of immaturity, Owen presents a fundamentally sound argument. Shorn of its rhetorical excesses, *A display of Arminianisme* presents a clear and logical argument for the priority of divine action in the 'disposing of things in this world'. The strength of Owen's argumentation lies in the logical order and rigour of his argument. Beginning with the divine decree, this logic leads him to subsequent corollaries regarding foreknowledge, providence and predestination. With respect to humanity, Owen begins with human corruption and total depravity. This logic leads him to the complete necessity of divine grace in the work of salvation and human action. This allows him to develop a strong argument regarding the nature of divine and human relations in the world.

Fundamentally, Owen and his Arminian opponents represent two opposing systems of thought regarding divine and human action in the world. Owen's thought represents the idea that all things come from God and return back to

---

[113]Owen, *A display of Arminianisme* (1643), 145; *Works* (1965), 10:133.
[114]Owen, *A display of Arminianisme* (1643), 147–50; *Works* (1965), 10:135–7.

God, which is in many ways a Thomistic argument of *exitus-reditus*.[115] The creature is created by God and is in need of divine grace to return to him in holiness and glory. In contrast, the Arminian system sees God and the creature in a state of synergy and semi-dependency upon one another. God gives the creature free will, and cannot interfere in the free choices of the creature. This in one sense leads to a type of co-creation of the state of events of the world, and of history.

Owen's argument is further aided by fine Thomistic and Augustinian distinctions which present a clear and subtle framework by which divine and human action may be understood. His reliance upon Thomistic causality finely tunes Owen's argument to demonstrate that his opponents' arguments are either illogical or idolatrous. His reliance upon Augustinian thought militates an emphasis upon the grace of God, and demonstrates his opponents' diminution of it. United with his Reformed heritage, these influences converge in the development of a fully orbed theology of divine sovereignty and human creaturely action.

The only real weakness of *A display of Arminianisme* are Owen's rhetorical flourishes, which occasionally come across as immature or as mere rants. These can belie the serious argumentation that Owen puts into each chapter, thus diminishing the impact of the work. One could argue that he does not always present his opponents with accuracy, particularly in the tables at the end of most of the chapters, in which their quotations are laid next to opposing quotes from Scripture and the fathers.[116] This criticism, however, is largely overstated. The purpose of *A display of Arminianisme* is actually to present a cogent positive argument for the nature of divine and human relations. Owen's dealings with Arminian arguments are largely attempts to remove what he sees as irritating errors and to set up biblical truth in their place. Owen's positive argument is quite strong, and clearly his focus in the work.

CONCLUSION

Despite some immaturity and rhetorical excess, *A display of Arminianisme* is a strong work of high Calvinist rigour, utilizing an array of classical and ecclesiastical resources in the development of an argument for Reformed predestinarianism. Owen's arguments will return with greater precision in later works, particularly *The doctrine of the saints perseverance* (1654), written against the Arminian Independent theologian, John Goodwin, *Vindiciae evangelicae*

---

[115]Chenu and Bremner, 'The plan of St. Thomas' *Summa Theologiae*', 67–79.
[116]Cooper, *John Owen, Richard Baxter, and the formation of Nonconformity*, 69–72; Gribben, *John Owen and English Puritanism*, 48.

(1655), written against the Socinian apologist John Biddle, and his masterpiece, *The death of death in the death of Christ*, in defence of definite atonement. In *A display of Arminianisme*, Owen laid the groundwork for arguments that he would develop further to become an integral part of the Reformed tradition.

A display of Arminianisme was Owen's first written work, but in content, if not in form, it became characteristic of his work as a whole. Nearly all of Owen's writings would display the same characteristic logical rigour, classical learning and rootedness in the larger Western catholic tradition. In this work, Owen laid down a standard for which he would become known. The work reveals a learned, deeply catholic Reformed theology, sensitive to the major issues of the day. In that sense, it remains a thoroughly helpful and valuable work for those seeking to know and understand the Reformed tradition.

CHAPTER 13

Salus electorum, sanguis Jesu

or, The death of death in the death of Christ (1648)

TIMOTHY ROBERT BAYLOR

Of John Owen's many works, *Salus electorum, sanguis Jesu: or, The death of death in the death of Christ* (1648) is without question his most famous – or infamous, depending on your perspective. Nearly 400 years after its publication, it is still widely regarded as the best defence of a doctrine so controversial it has to go by aliases: 'definite atonement' or 'particular redemption' among the Reformed, 'limited atonement' everywhere else. In essence, the doctrine holds that the mission of the Son in his saving work intended to redeem the church – not humankind in general but the saints in particular, those who are elect and chosen by God for salvation from all eternity. It is opposed to a theology of 'general' or 'universal redemption', which maintains the work of Christ to have a universal applicability because it was intended to redeem not particular persons but the whole of humankind as a class.

For better or worse, Owen's name has become synonymous with particular redemption. And it can hardly be doubted that the polarizing nature of the doctrine has impacted Owen's legacy. Among dyed-in-the-wool Calvinists, Owen is positively iconic. He is regarded as one of the greatest theologians (if not *the* greatest) ever to write in the English language, with *The death of death* ranking among his chief literary achievements. Outside of these circles, though, Owen is a more marginal, sometimes alienating figure, remembered as an advocate for an especially inflexible form of Calvinism. It is not hard to see why this is the case. Particular redemption is a doctrine that appeals to insiders. It sets out a vision of God and God's works in the world that places the church directly at its centre. Even within the church, such claims can be uncomfortable. It appears to contradict the plain reading of several biblical texts, and can easily (if perhaps superficially) be presented as a constriction of God's generosity. But setting aside its exegetical and theological disputability, the greatest challenge to the doctrine may be its ability to pass the sniff-test. The notion that God gave his Son, not indiscriminately for all, but only for the persons of the elect runs counter to some very deeply held cultural sensibilities in liberal Western societies. It seems to violate a basic sense of fairness, and in a time highly alert to the abuse of religious authority, it can appear self-indulgent or even dangerous if used to support a kind of institutional exceptionalism in the church.

And yet, for all those challenges, *The death of death* has proven to be a work of remarkable durability and persuasiveness. Much of that is due to Owen's own skill as a dialectician and controversialist. While forceful, the argument of the book is patient and deliberate. It builds its case slowly, proceeding from common axioms of the Christian faith to its more contestable judgements. Its exegesis is both credible and creative. And though Owen does not have much of a reputation as a stylist, there is little doubt that the rhetorical focus of the work has contributed a great deal to its success. Rather than centring the argument on the doctrine of election or the church, from the very first, the focus is firmly on the efficiency of God's saving work and the conclusive reality of that reconciliation that God has effected through Christ. This Christo-centric focus roots the work in a deeply ecumenical interest and prevents it from devolving into a narrow sort of sophistry. Indeed, read from this vantage point, *The death of death* addresses themes of fundamental significance to theology and Christian faith more generally.

When the New Testament sets forward the death of Christ as the culminating event of our salvation – when it speaks of Christ being broken for our sins, or when it speaks of us as being crucified together with him – in what sense does it envision this as an event that is decisive for us? What transpires in that moment, so distant from our own in time, that is really determinative of me? And how does it come to pass that an event of history might be of such definitive significance for my identity that it might truly be said to put my own death behind me? In other words, what is the relation between Christ's identity and our own? *The death of death* is Owen's attempt – or rather, his first attempt – to answer these questions.

THEOLOGICAL BACKGROUND TO *THE DEATH OF DEATH*

The death of death presents itself as a work of polemical theology – a response to Thomas Moore, the weaver-turned-theologian whose *Universality of God's free grace to mankind in Christ proclaimed and displayed* (1646) argued for an Arminian theology of universal redemption. Though written early in Owen's career, it fits a definite pattern. Nearly a decade earlier, Owen's academic ambitions in Oxford had been cut short, the casualty (as he understood it) of an aggressive high-church Arminianism increasing on the back of reforms instituted by William Laud, who was then Bishop of Oxford. Owen's first work, Θεομαχία αυτεξουσιαστικη: or, *A display of Arminianisme* (1643), was published a few years thereafter as an exposé of errors in Arminian theology.

Much of *A display of Arminianisme* focused on how the innovative doctrine of free will and the 'new goddess contingency' tampered with various aspects of Christian doctrine. Among complaints about its effects on divine immutability, foreknowledge and providence, Owen also took issue with the Arminian theology of atonement. Their error, he claimed, could be reduced to two, interrelated issues: 'the object of [Christ's] merit, or whom he died for', and 'the efficacie and end of his death'. 'In resolution of the first, they affirme, that he died for all, and every one; of the second, that he died for no one man at all; in that sense, Christians have hitherto believed.'[1] The object and efficacy of Christ's death are joined with one another. Because if Christ died for all, then the fruit of Christ's death must be suspended upon some other condition to render that work effective for sinners. In Arminian theology, this condition is supplied by the free and spontaneous decision of the human will. But, Owen argues, if the movement of the human will is finally contingent, and not effectually converted by the grace of Christ, then Arminians could not guarantee that Christ's work will save anyone at all. He cites a dialogue of the Remonstrant Apology to this effect: 'Why then the efficacie of the death of Christ depends wholly on us: true? it cannot otherwise be.'[2]

The error here, Owen believed, was that Arminians allowed a condition to intervene between Christ's work and its effect on his people. This emphasis upon the freedom of the will displaced the cross of Christ as the definitive cause of our salvation, 'denying the effectuall operation of his death'.[3] 'It seems to me', Owen continued, 'a strange extenuation of the merit of Christ, to teach,

---

[1] Owen, *A display of Arminianisme* (1643), 91; *Works* (1965), 10:88.
[2] Owen, *A display of Arminianisme* (1643), 106; *Works* (1965), 10:100.
[3] Owen, *A display of Arminianisme* (1643), 97–8; *Works* (1965), 10:93. Further, see van den Brink, 'Impetration and application in John Owen's theology', 85–96.

that no good at all by his death doth redound to divers of them for whom he died'.[4] The remedy that he proposed was a recovery of the biblical emphasis on the efficiency of Christ's work as that event which 'procured for us remission of all our sinnes, an actuall reconciliation with God, faith, and obedience'. Such doctrine 'stabs at the very heart of the Idol' of free will. 'What remaineth for him to doe, if all things in this great worke of our salvation must be thus ascribed unto Christ, and the merit of his death?'[5]

The death of death continues and expands this earlier line of argument, this time directing it more broadly against accounts of 'universal redemption'. While the Arminians were the principal target of Owen's polemic, we should note that universal redemption was not an exclusively Arminian doctrine. A number of Reformed theologians also argued for a universal redemption, but unlike the Arminians, maintained election to be an unconditional gift of grace. This position has often been depicted as an outlier in Reformed theology, but it enlisted several very notable advocates. These included Richard Hooker, one of the leading churchmen and theologians of his day; John Davenant, the senior delegate of the Church of England to the Synod of Dort; and, as we will see a little later, Richard Baxter, one of Owen's chief opponents.

These 'hypothetical universalists',[6] as they are sometimes called, followed a medieval tradition originating with Lombard, and repeated at the Synod of Dort, which distinguished Christ's work as being 'for all with regard to the sufficiency of the price, but only for the elect with regard to its efficiency'.[7] In essence, they argued that, out of his love for sinners and a desire to alleviate their misery, God sent Christ to satisfy divine justice and to redeem God's creatures from the curse of the law. Christ truly died for all and his work was really sufficient to save all. However, the enjoyment of Christ's benefits is conditional upon faith – only those that believe enjoy the promises of the covenant (Rom. 10.14). And while Scripture teaches that God wills that none should perish (Ezek. 33.11), and that all might believe and be saved (1 Tim. 2.4), God nonetheless grants the effectual grace necessary to believe only to his elect. So, while Christ's death is thus sufficient for all, its benefits are made efficient in the elect alone.

As the title of Moore's work implies, his argument went considerably further than the claims of the hypothetical universalists. Moore claimed that Christ's death had actually secured a grace that was universally extended to all. This grace

---

[4] Owen, *A display of Arminianisme* (1643), 91; *Works* (1965), 10:88.
[5] Owen, *A display of Arminianisme* (1643), 98; *Works* (1965), 10:93.
[6] For a concise and helpful summary of this stream of the Reformed tradition, see Lynch, 'Richard Hooker and the development of English hypothetical universalism'. See also Lynch, *John Davenant's hypothetical universalism*; Snoddy, *The soteriology of James Ussher*, 40–92; Muller, *Calvin and the Reformed tradition*, 126–60; Moore, *English hypothetical universalism*.
[7] Lombard, *Sentences*, III.xx.5.

communicated a power of believing upon all humankind so that, in the event that individuals heard the Gospel, they might be able to receive it and so be converted. This was the real tell-tale sign of Arminian theology. Reformed theologians of this period typically reserved the term 'grace' for saving grace, understanding by this an effectual divine act which indomitably causes the sinner's conversion.[8] The effectual character of this grace was crucial here because it maintained the character of God's election as unconditional. Were God's grace not the efficient cause of the sinner's faith, then the enjoyment of Christ's benefits would ultimately be caused by some spontaneous act of the sinner, making election conditional upon a foreseen, but contingent, human response. We might say that, by extending grace to all persons, Arminians 'democratized' Christ's benefits. But this came at the expense of the *efficacy* of these benefits. For if all possessed grace equally, the grace of God is not the specific difference between belief and unbelief. Grace, then, becomes cooperative in nature, making the enjoyment of Christ's benefits contingent on the free action of the sinner.

The principle aim of *The death of death* was to close this gap, eliminating any room for a condition to intervene between the accomplishment and application of Christ's work. To that end, Owen argued that in the work of Christ, God intended not merely to make reconciliation possible but to render it actual in the persons of the church. Christ himself is that saving grace which God gives to sinners, and this gift is given to the church so absolutely that participation in Christ is the cause and not the effect of the Christian's faith. Though Owen acknowledged the differences between the views of Arminians and hypothetical universalists, he believed that any theology of the atonement that placed conditions on participation in Christ unavoidably weakens the definitiveness of Christ's work. In that respect, both of these views were guilty of abusing the distinction between redemption and its application in ways that ultimately undermined the consolation of the sinner. To Owen's mind, a general ransom of any kind was 'an uncomfortable doctrine, cutting all the nerves and sinews of that strong consolation which God is so abundantly willing that we should receive'.[9]

THE ARGUMENT AND STRUCTURE OF *THE DEATH OF DEATH*

Trinity and economy

The death of death is laid out in four books. The first two books are largely positive, developing the core of the argument; the final two are largely

---

[8] The concept of 'common grace', now so familiar to Reformed theologians, was a later development.
[9] Owen, *The death of death in the death of Christ* (1648), 34; *Works* (1965), 10:186.

polemical, levelling critiques against universal redemption and clearing the argument of any objections. The central task of Book I is to locate the death of Christ within the wider economy of God's works in an attempt to identify its intended end. All parties conceded God to be capable of accomplishing all that he intends by Christ's work. The real dispute, however, concerned 'that which [Christ's] Father, and himselfe intended *in* it; and, secondly, that which was effectually fulfilled and accomplished by it'.[10] Owen stresses that Christ's death is the focus here, not to the exclusion of his life, but only as it represents in Scripture the culmination and fulfilment of his whole redeeming work.

Of course, supplying an answer to what was intended and effected in the death of Christ is a complex affair. It requires close attention to Scripture, and a method of reading open to discerning the signs of God's intention in the sending of the Son. Owen found these signs in a range of biblical expressions, including Christ's own statements of purpose, metaphors used by the apostles to express the benefit of Christ's life and death, and Old Testament prophecy read as divine promises made to Christ. Owen argues that, in various ways, these different forms of speech refer us to the inner life of God, and particularly to the works of the Trinity within eternity. It is only against this background that the intended end of Christ's death can be understood, because it is here that the work of redemption is conceived, and we can identify the end of Christ's death only if we can grasp the effect for the sake of which it exists as a means.

It is indeed a strange thing to think of any death as a means – particularly in the intention of the one dying. And yet, as Owen points out, if ends and means are 'mutually causes one of another', then to make this claim is simply to name an intelligible relation between the death of Christ on the one hand and its redemptive effects on the other.[11] An end, after all, is simply the 'moving cause' of any means, just as a means is a fitting 'procuring cause' of any end. There is, in other words, a discernible parity between the death of Christ and its effects. Some means are good in themselves, but serve higher goods, the way study serves the higher good of understanding. Other means are not things good in themselves, but might become good by virtue of their relation to their effects. For example, cutting off an arm is itself an evil. But in certain situations, it can serve the good of survival. The death of Christ is a means of this second sort. It is an evil thing in itself – the slaying of an innocent life, and one of unparalleled dignity at that. But in the wisdom of God which confounds the wise, even this act comes to serve a good end. How does it do so?

---

[10]Owen, *The death of death in the death of Christ* (1648), 1; *Works* (1965), 10:157; cf. Aquinas, *ST* IIIa, q. 46, a. 1.
[11]Owen, *The death of death in the death of Christ* (1648), 5; *Works* (1965), 10:160.

Owen claims that some means bring about their end naturally. Their 'fruit and product' is the result of a kind of efficient causality, in the way that driving a nail is the 'fruit and product' of a hammer's motion. Other means, however, bring about their ends morally – they act by means of 'some morall rule, or Law prescribed to the Agent' through which they come to deserve or merit some result.[12] Here, the effect is not the necessary consequence of the action. It works by way of a legal mechanism. Which is to say that its effect depends on justice: that the right which this action secures will be honoured by others. In that respect, it requires another, outside actor to render it effective. Owen regarded the death of Christ as bringing about its end morally, by means of a law to which the Son consents within the internal councils of the Trinity.

'The *end* of any thing, is that which the Agent intendeth to accomplish.'[13] To speak of Christ's death as having an 'end', therefore, is to identify it as the intentional act of a rational agent. We should not rush past this point. In contrast with the Socinians, who regarded the death of Christ as a pure contingency, an accident of history both unnecessary and unintended, Owen sees reason in the death of Christ – indeed, divine reason. Of course, this stems from the fact that Owen, unlike the Socinians, affirmed the deity of Christ and consequently understood the whole of Christ's history, including his death, as a willing and intentional act of divine self-giving: 'I lay down my life. . . . No one takes it from me, but I lay it down of my own accord. I have power to lay it down, and I have power to take it up again' (Jn 10.17-18, NRSV). The agent here, in other words, is God – 'the whole Blessed Trinity'. Naming the Trinity as the agent of this work is crucial, both because it identifies the life and death of Christ as a divine act but also because it locates that history as a central event within the wider economy of God's works. To identify this event as the work of the Son of God, and yet to fail to observe its unity with the other works of God, would invariably skew our judgement about the intended end of Christ's death. The mission of the Son cannot be divided from the work of the Father and the Spirit, for the works of the Trinity *ad extra* are 'undevided [sic], & belong equally to each person; their distinct manner of subsistence and order being observed'.[14]

The works of the Trinity in redemption

There are, according to Owen, two 'peculiar acts' which belong to the Father in the work of our redemption. The first consists in the Father's sending of the Son. This is, of course, a prominent theme in the Gospel of John, and in

---

[12] Owen, *The death of death in the death of Christ* (1648), 6; *Works* (1965), 10:161.
[13] Owen, *The death of death in the death of Christ* (1648), 5; *Works* (1965), 10:160.
[14] Owen, *The death of death in the death of Christ* (1648), 8; *Works* (1965), 10:163.

the New Testament more generally: 'when the fullness of time had come, God sent his Son, born of a woman, born under the law, in order to redeem those who were under the law' (Gal. 4.4-5, NRSV). Though this 'sending' is a pre-temporal act, one 'eternally established in the minde and will of God', it is nonetheless a work of the Father because it is a free and contingent act that the Father undertakes for the benefit of creatures.[15] Owen argues that this sending includes three things:

(1) The Father's 'Authoritative imposition of the office of Mediator', to which Christ willingly consents, humbling himself to become 'obedient unto death' (Phil. 2.6-8, KJV).[16]

(2) The Father's filling of the Son with 'all guifts and graces . . . requisite for the office he was to undertake'.[17]

(3) The Father's 'entering into Covenant, and compact with his Son concerning the work to be undertaken'.[18]

Though no mention is made of this covenant in *A display of Arminianisme*, from *The death of death* onward, Owen explicitly roots the saving mission of the Son in a pre-temporal 'treaty . . . about the redemption of man' – that is, in the covenant of redemption.[19] Using the theme of covenant to frame the work of redemption has a number of material benefits for Owen, as we shall see. Given its importance to his argument, one might expect some extensive exegesis to establish the claim. Owen provides nothing as extensive as his treatments of the theme in *Vindiciae evangelicae* (1655) or in his Hebrews commentary.[20] Instead, he simply cites a series of biblical texts, each of them referring to some promise of God to Christ. Importantly, Owen takes these texts to signify an inner-trinitarian act – a solemn promise of the Father tendered to the Son before the world began. These promises were of two sorts: those relating to Christ's person and the Father's promise to 'protect and assist him', and those pertaining to the 'good issue' or promised reward of Christ's labour.[21] For the

---

[15]Owen, *The death of death in the death of Christ* (1648), 10; *Works* (1965), 10:163.
[16]Owen, *The death of death in the death of Christ* (1648), 9; *Works* (1965), 10:164.
[17]Owen, *The death of death in the death of Christ* (1648), 12; *Works* (1965), 10:166.
[18]Owen, *The death of death in the death of Christ* (1648), 14; *Works* (1965), 10:168. Owen here presents this as a 'third act' of the Father, which logically follows the inauguration of the Son into the office of the mediator. In his Hebrews commentary, the Son's assumption of the office of mediator takes place within the context of the covenant; cf. Owen, *Hebrews* (1674), 49; *Works* (1850), 19:77.
[19]Owen, *The death of death in the death of Christ* (1648), 15; *Works* (1965), 10:169.
[20]Owen, *Vindiciae evangelicae* (1655), 568–82; *Works*, 12:496–508; 19:77–97. For a discussion of Owen's theology of the *pactum salutis*, see Cleveland, 'The covenant of redemption in the trinitarian theology of John Owen'.
[21]Owen, *The death of death in the death of Christ* (1648), 14–15; *Works* (1965), 10:168–71.

latter, Owen points to a number of texts, including Isa. 49.6-12, 53.10-12; John 17; and Heb. 2.10, which envision the effect of Christ's work in terms of the gathering of a people:

> This then our Saviour certainely aimed at, as being the promise upon which he undertooke the worke, the gathering of the sonnes of God together, their bringing unto God, and passing to eternal salvation; which being well considered, it will utterly overthrow the generall ransome, or universall redemption.[22]

The sending of the Son thus has a *covenantal* form which explicitly includes the promise that Christ would 'gather to himself a glorious Church of beleevers'.[23] This is important because it frames the application of Christ's benefits to the church as something due to Christ in justice.

The second work of the Father is that of 'laying upon [Christ] the punishment of sinnes'.[24] Owen cites a number of texts in which the suffering of Christ is said to have been at the will of God (e.g. Isa. 53.4, 10; Mt. 26.31; Acts 4.27-28), as well as other texts that speak of Christ dying for us and in our place (e.g. Isa. 53.6; Gal. 3.13; 2 Cor. 5.21). As with the Father's 'authoritative imposition' of the office of the mediator, Owen sees this as a work of supreme sovereignty and authority.[25] The reason for this is that the law requires the death of the sinner. To institute a mediator and allow him to bear the punishment of sinners in their place thus requires an exception, or as Owen puts it, 'a relaxation of the Law, in respect of the persons suffering'.[26] In other words, this is an extra-legal act – one which the Father undertakes in his office as Sovereign and Ruler.

Owen figures the Son as an agent of redemption and his mission as having its ground in his 'concurring' with that eternal covenant proposed by the Father. By his 'willing undertaking' of the office of the mediator, the Son sets himself entirely to the fulfilment of the Father's will.[27] This is a hallmark of Jesus's self-understanding. The whole of his life is consecrated to the obedience of the Father: 'I glorified you on earth by finishing the work that you gave me to do' (Jn 17.4). Owen suggests that this work consisted in three parts, each of integral importance to his redemptive mission. The first is that of incarnation –

---

[22] Owen, *The death of death in the death of Christ* (1648), 16; *Works* (1965), 10:170.
[23] Owen, *The death of death in the death of Christ* (1648), 16; *Works* (1965), 10:170.
[24] Owen, *The death of death in the death of Christ* (1648), 17; *Works* (1965), 10:171.
[25] More on the significance of this in the following.
[26] Owen, *The death of death in the death of Christ* (1648), 19; *Works* (1965), 10:173.
[27] Owen, *The death of death in the death of Christ* (1648), 20; *Works* (1965), 10:174. The free and voluntary character of the Son's will in assuming this obligation is important for Owen's theology of grace as a whole. On this point, see Baylor, 'He humbled himself', 165–94.

the Son's assumption of flesh 'into personal union with himself', an act that formed the 'common foundation' for the Son's other redemptive works.[28] According to Heb. 2.13, this was necessitated by the fact that 'the children are partakers of flesh and blood':

> It was the *children* that he considered. . . . Their participation in flesh and blood, moved him to partake of the same: not because all the world, all the posterity of *Adam*, but because the children were in that condition, for their sakes he sanctified himself.[29]

The second work of the Son is that of his oblation, the offering of himself to God on behalf of sinners.[30] Once again, Scripture often associates Christ's self-offering with his suffering and death because these are acts which most fully reveal the work of Christ to be for us (e.g. Heb. 9.14). But Owen was quick to point out that the whole of Christ's work is included in his oblation – not just his suffering and death, but his active obedience to God as well. In fact, he argues that, in an important sense, it is Christ's obedience for us that is the principal matter here, even in Christ's death: 'for if the will of Christ had not been in it, it could never have purged our sins'. The whole virtue of Christ's sacrificial death derives from it being a voluntary act of the Son of God. Were it not *his*, had he not lowered himself to perform this task, the sacrifice and oblation of Christ 'would not have been of any value'.[31] For that reason, Owen argued that Christ's oblation consisted in 'the whole oeconomy and dispensation of God manifested in the flesh . . . with all those things which he performed in the dayes of his flesh . . . untill he had fully by himself purged our sins, and sate down on the right hand of the majesty on high' (Heb. 1:3)'.[32]

The final work of the Son for our redemption consists in his 'intercession, For all & every one of those, for whom he gave himselfe for an oblation'.[33] Christ began this work on earth (as recorded in John 17), and continues it in heaven, following his ascension and exaltation to the right hand of God. By his prayers, Christ seeks the application of those benefits obtained by his oblation. And his prayers are efficacious: 'We know the Father always heareth the Son . . . so to grant his request.'[34] Why? Because his prayers are principled upon

---

[28]Owen, *The death of death in the death of Christ* (1648), 21; *Works* (1965), 10:174.
[29]Owen, *The death of death in the death of Christ* (1648), 21; *Works* (1965), 10:175. Unless otherwise stated, emphasis is original.
[30]From the Latin *oblatio*, 'an offering'.
[31]Owen, *The death of death in the death of Christ* (1648), 22; *Works* (1965), 10:175.
[32]Owen, *The death of death in the death of Christ* (1648), 22; *Works* (1965), 10:176.
[33]Owen, *The death of death in the death of Christ* (1648), 23; *Works* (1965), 10:176.
[34]Owen here echoing John 11:42: 'I knew that you always hear me'.

the promise of God. Owen cites Ps. 2.8 for support: 'Ask of me and I will give thee the nations for thine inheritance, and the uttermost parts of the earth for thy possession.' The New Testament authors frequently read this Psalm as Messianic prophecy, understanding it as the Father's direct address to the Son (cf. Heb. 1.5).[35] Owen reads the passage as an intra-trinitarian dialogue – the promise of the Father to the Son within the covenant of redemption, a pact which constitutes the moral principle underwriting Christ's intercession.

Finally, Owen argues that, together with the Father and the Son, the Spirit also concurs in the covenant to the various works of his temporal mission. Later, in Πνευματολογια (1674), Owen would articulate the Spirit's redemptive missions more fully. There he would distinguish between those works that have the person of Christ as their immediate object, and those that are directed toward others on Christ's behalf, in Christ's capacity as the head of the church.[36] The latter are certainly relevant, since Owen understood these to be effects of Christ's heavenly intercession. Here, however, Owen focuses primarily on the former as the matter under consideration principally concerns the procurement of redemption.[37] These works of the Spirit are, again, threefold in nature, corresponding to the threefold work of Christ.

With respect to the incarnation, Owen continues, the Spirit is the agent of that new creation in Mary's womb – the human nature of Christ – which she is said to have conceived 'from the Holy Spirit' (Mt. 1.18). This as a creative work, analogous to the formation of heaven and earth in Genesis 1. Second, with respect to Christ's oblation, Owen understands the teaching of Heb. 9.14 ('through the eternal Spirit offered himself without blemish to God') to be a reference to the ministry of the Holy Spirit. In Christ's great sorrow and distress, it was the Spirit's gracious influence that enabled his 'willing offering [of] himselfe' to God. In this sense, the Spirit is the 'eternall fire under this sacrifice, which made it acceptable unto God'. Finally, it belongs to the Spirit to be the 'quickening' agent – both in the resurrection of Christ and in the new life created by Christ within the church (citing Rom. 8.11).[38]

The unity of Christ's oblation and intercession

As the redemptive works of the Father, Son and Holy Spirit are all rooted in the one will of God, and formalized within the covenant of redemption, so they are unified in their intention and execution. But the central question at issue here concerns the intended end of Christ's death. Now, one might conceive of Christ's death and

---

[35]See Bates, *The birth of the Trinity*, 62–80.
[36]Owen, Πνευματολογια (1674), 128–9; *Works* (1965), 3:160.
[37]Owen, *The death of death in the death of Christ* (1648), 25; *Works* (1965), 10:179.
[38]Owen, *The death of death in the death of Christ* (1648), 25; *Works* (1965), 10:178.

oblation as standing in a disjunctive relation to his intercession, so that they have distinct objects and ends. The hypothetical universalists argued something similar, allowing them to introduce a condition on participation in Christ's benefits. For them, Christ's oblation makes satisfaction to the justice of God on behalf of humankind as a whole, but he intercedes on behalf of those elect to whom God wills to grant the gift of faith. Alternatively, one might think of Christ's death and intercession as being a single means, so that the object and end of each are strictly co-extensive with one another. Owen argued in favour of the latter.

Oblation and intercession are often linked in Scripture (Isa. 53.11-12; Rom. 4.25), and both are depicted as functions of the priestly office of Christ (Heb. 9.11-13; 1 Jn 2.1-2). Moreover, Owen observes that the two themes exist in an 'inseparable conjunction' with one another. For Christ's intercession in heaven is nothing other than the 'demonstration of his sacred body, wherein for us he suffered', that his oblation might have 'perpetual efficacy, untill the many sons given unto him are brought to glory'.[39] This was already a theme in *A display of Arminianisme*. There Owen described Christ's intercessory ministry as consisting in

> a presentation of himself, and his merits, accompanied with the prayers of his Mediatour-ship before God: that he would be pleased to grant, and effectually to apply, the good things, he hath by them obtained, to all for whom he hath obtained them: his intercession in heaven, is nothing but a continued oblation of himselfe.[40]

Identifying Christ's intercession as the simple act of his self-presentation refers the efficacy of this act to the right secured by his oblation. On the one hand, this move consolidates Owen's emphasis on the definitive nature of the atonement. On the other, it excludes any intervening condition that might be thought necessary to merit or activate the saving virtue of Christ's sacrifice.[41] It is Christ's self-offering, and this alone, that is the 'procuring cause' of our redemption.[42]

Though Owen had included the unity of Christ's intercession and oblation as a theme in his earlier writings, his introduction of the concept of the covenant of redemption in *The death of death* offered a means of explaining this unity.

---

[39] Owen, *The death of death in the death of Christ* (1648), 32; *Works* (1965), 10:184.
[40] Owen, *A display of Arminianisme* (1643), 94; *Works*, 10:90.
[41] Cf. Owen, *The death of death in the death of Christ* (1648), 43; *Works* (1965), 10:194, where Owen denies that there could be any condition, either on the part of sinners (as the Arminians argued) or even on the part of the divine will (as the hypothetical universalists maintained), which could render Christ's intercession uncertain or ineffectual.
[42] Owen, *The death of death in the death of Christ* (1648), 6; *Works* (1965), 10:94.

'[F]or the proof of this supposal', Owen argued, 'we must remember that which we delivered before concerning the compact and agreement that was between the Father and the Son.' It was in this pact that the Son voluntarily assumed the work of the mediator. But this also included promises and obligations assumed by the Father toward the Son. So, Owen inquired, 'what is the ground and foundation of our Saviour's intercession?' 'Must it not rest upon some promise made unto him? . . . Is it not apparent that the intercession of Christ doth rest on such a promise as Psal. 2:8. *Ask of me, and I will give thee the heathen for thine inheritance*, &c.?'[43]

By grounding Christ's intercession on the promise of the Father in the covenant of redemption, Owen could frame the communication of Christ's benefits to the saints as something due to the Son for the obligation he assumed to the work of the mediator. Having fulfilled the conditions of the covenant, the benefits of Christ's sacrifice now accrue to all for whom he died:

> The intercession of Christ then, being founded on promises made unto him, and these promises being nothing but an engagement to bestow, and actually collate upon them for whom he suffered, all those good things which his death and Oblation did merit, and purchase, it cannot be but that he intercedeth for all, for whom he dyed, that his death procured all and every thing, which upon his *Intercession* is bestowed, and untill they are bestowed, it hath not its full fruits and effects.[44]

The covenantal framework here invests the language of 'merit', 'purchase', 'procured' and 'bestowed' with a distinctly legal character. These benefits are due as a matter of justice. As such, Christ's intercession is not 'an humble, dejected supplication'. It is 'authoritative'.[45] It is certain and effectual, being founded upon God's own faithfulness to his promise. And since Christ's intercession seeks only the conferral of those benefits merited by his oblation, Owen concludes that both the oblation and intercession of Christ are 'means tending to one and the same end'.[46]

THE END(S) OF THE WORK OF CHRIST

Having explored the works of the Trinity, as the agent of redemption, and the works of Christ's oblation and intercession, as the means, Book II of *The death of*

---

[43] Owen, *The death of death in the death of Christ* (1648), 33; *Works* (1965), 10:185.
[44] Owen, *The death of death in the death of Christ* (1648), 33–4; *Works* (1965), 10:185.
[45] Owen, *The death of death in the death of Christ* (1648), 24; *Works* (1965), 10:177.
[46] Owen, *The death of death in the death of Christ* (1648), 33; *Works* (1965), 10:185.

death sets forward Owen's account of the end of Christ's work. In this section, Owen distinguishes between ultimate and intermediate ends.[47] The ultimate end of Christ's work, as with all divine works *ad extra*, is the manifestation of God's glory. As God is the greatest good, it belongs to him to act for the highest end, which is the communication of himself in all things. The work of Christ serves this ultimate end by means of an intermediate end, which Owen identifies as 'the bringing of us unto God' with a 'real[,] effectuall and infallible bestowing, and applying' of every grace necessary for our salvation.[48]

Specifying the real and effectual deliverance of sinners as the immediate end of Christ's work is crucial for Owen's argument. In the first instance, this allows him to push back on Arminian and hypothetical universalist accounts of redemption which made the efficiency of Christ's death conditional upon the sinner's belief. The sinner's belief might be understood, as it was by the hypothetical universalists, as the fruit of an unconditionally free gift, grounded in the absolute dominion of God exercised in predestination. Or, it might be regarded as the spontaneous effect of the creature's cooperation with prevenient grace, as the Arminians understood it. Yet, in either case, the only *immediate* effect of Christ's work is the satisfaction of divine justice so as to secure in God 'a right and liberty . . . of pardoning sinne upon what condition he pleased'.[49]

Owen opposes this argument for several reasons. In the first instance, he thinks it introduces an imperfection into God's inner life. If Christ's work secures a power in God to pardon, then it seems that it is God, rather than sinners, that needs the incarnation – as though God might be 'enlarged from that estate, wherein it was impossible for him to do that which he desired, and which his nature enclined him to'.[50] Owen would eventually reverse his opinion on this in his *Diatriba de justitia divina* (1653). But at this stage, he thinks it absurd to argue that God's power was constrained by his justice, such that God 'could not have mercy on mankind unless satisfaction were made by his Son'. God does indeed will that Christ should make satisfaction for sin, but antecedent to this determination, God is absolutely free. The suggestion that God must make satisfaction for sin by a necessity of his nature is an 'unwritten tradition, the Scripture affirming no such thing'.[51] The death of Christ cannot therefore be thought to acquire any right or power in God to pardon.

More directly to the point here, however, Owen thinks that suspending the efficiency of Christ's work upon a condition 'utterly overthrows all the merit of the death of Christ towards us'. For it is in the nature of merit that it confers

---

[47] Owen, *The death of death in the death of Christ* (1648), 51; *Works* (1965), 10:201.
[48] Owen, *The death of death in the death of Christ* (1648), 54; *Works* (1965), 10:202–3.
[49] Owen, *The death of death in the death of Christ* (1648), 56; *Works* (1965), 10:205.
[50] Owen, *The death of death in the death of Christ* (1648), 57; *Works* (1965), 10:206.
[51] Owen, *The death of death in the death of Christ* (1648), 57; *Works* (1965), 10:205.

a 'real right' to some thing – 'that which is truly meritorious indeed, deserves that the thing merited or procured and obtained by it, shall be done, or ought to be bestowed, and not that it may be done'.[52] Owen cites Rom. 4.4 to establish the point: 'To him that worketh is the reward not reckoned of grace, but of debt.' The uniform teaching of the New Testament is that Christ has merited eternal life on our behalf. How, then, can Christ truly be said to have 'merited' anything at all, if in fact all his benefits remain conditional upon our belief? In that instance, would it not be more proper to say that we procure these benefits by our belief?

This, Owen thinks, is the error underlying Arminian theologies of salvation. If the grace of Christ is not fully effectual in drawing sinners to himself, then our faith becomes a kind of meritorious cause of the benefits of redemption. Indeed, it is the definitive one, since without our faith, it would be 'possible that not one soul might be saved', Christ's death for sinners notwithstanding.[53] In addition to undermining the consolation of the Gospel, Owen thinks that placing such a condition on Christ's work is impious: 'This pride is inbred; it is a part of our corruption to defend it.'[54] The whole doctrine is in fact nothing other than 'a sacred orgie to the long-bewailed manes of St Pelagius'.[55]

Of course, the hypothetical universalists would ardently insist that they neither attended nor had any interest in attending such an 'orgie'. For though participation in Christ's benefits is conditional, the condition is itself a gift supplied of God's absolute dominion and grace. It is therefore no more dependent on our merit than our own election is – which is to say, not at all.[56] To Owen's mind, however, if the benefits of redemption remain conditional, even upon an act of divine dominion, then it remains possible that Christ might be left without reward:

> for suppose the Father would not bestow it, as hee is by no engagement according to this perswasion bound to do, he had a right to do it, it is true; but that which is any ones right he may use, or not use at his pleasure: againe, suppose he had prescribed a condition of workes which it had been impossible for them to fulfill, the death of Christ might have had its full end, and yet not one beene saved.[57]

---

[52]Owen, *The death of death in the death of Christ* (1648), 58; *Works* (1965), 10:206.
[53]Owen, *The death of death in the death of Christ* (1648), 58; *Works* (1965), 10:207.
[54]Owen, *The death of death in the death of Christ* (1648), n.p.; *Works* (1965), 10:153.
[55]Owen, *The death of death in the death of Christ* (1648), n.p.; *Works* (1965), 10:150.
[56]See Davenant's response to this criticism in his *A dissertation on the death of Christ* in *An exposition of the epistle of St. Paul to the Colossians*, 2:389f.
[57]Owen, *The death of death in the death of Christ* (1648), 58–9; *Works* (1965), 10:207.

Owen's explanation here is very peculiar. It is true, of course, that if Christ died conditionally for all, then Christ's benefits are not strictly due to any. But why should we think that this means that these benefits might not be granted? A person might have an intention to give a gift even if they do not have an obligation to do so. And it would be absurd, even on an Arminian theology of the divine decrees, to imagine that the Father, having sent his Son to die for the whole of humankind, would withhold his right and not bestow its benefits on any. After all, the works of the Trinity *ad extra* are indivisible, so it is surely unthinkable that the work of one person of the Trinity would render the work of another fruitless.

Owen's line of reasoning here may simply be a bit of failed polemic, or may indicate that, at this stage at least, he has a fairly abstract notion of divine dominion, which he attempts to correct by appeal to legal categories. In either case, however, it does effectively underscore his aversion to thinking of the benefits of redemption apart from the election of Christ as our representative within the covenant of redemption. Christ's whole being has its basis and ground in this work – he is entirely *pro nobis*.[58] It is not that Christ has made the divine gift possible: Christ himself is the gift. It is not that Christ's death procures the new covenant: 'Christ himselfe, with his death and passion, is the chiefe promise of the new Covenant.'[59]

This identification of Christ with the gift of salvation is, for Owen, the only way to make sense of the biblical idiom which so consistently ties the sinner's deliverance to the person of Christ himself. For example,

(1) Scripture expressly states that this was Christ's own intention in his mission. Christ came into the world in order 'to seek and to save that which was lost' (Lk. 19.10). Similarly, the apostle says that Christ 'loved the church, and gave himself for it'. Why? '[T]hat he might sanctify and cleanse it with the washing of water by the word that he might present it to himself a glorious church' (Eph. 5.25). This idiom suggests to Owen that Christ's work was not undertaken to obtain a power or right in God, but to set captives free.

(2) When Scripture speaks of the effects of Christ's work, it does so in terms of the concrete benefits that it delivers to sinners. In Colossians, for example, we who were enemies of God are said to have been 'reconciled in the body of his flesh through death' (Col. 1.21-22; cf.

---

[58]See Owen, *The death of death in the death of Christ* (1648), 54–6; *Works* (1965), 10:203–5, where Owen argues, in contrast to much of the scholastic tradition, that Christ does not merit for himself, but only for us. Further on this point in the Reformed tradition, see Baylor, 'With him in heavenly realms', 152–75.

[59]Owen, *The death of death in the death of Christ* (1648), 59; *Works* (1965), 10:207.

Eph. 2.13-16). In this way, the apostle sees the cross as establishing an 'actuall peace by the removal of all enmity'.[60] Again, in the book of Hebrews, Christ is said to have 'obtained eternal redemption', 'purge[d] [our] conscience of dead works' (9.12-14), and 'put away sin by the sacrifice of himself' (9.26). Owen claims that this refers to 'that justification with God', which is 'the immediate product of that blood, by which he entred into the holy place'.[61] In other words, the death of Christ has inaugurated a new reality, one which definitively alters the state of the sinner, placing her in a new relation to God.

(3) Finally, Scripture also speaks of Christ's work as though it were for a definite population of people. Owen is thinking chiefly of texts like Mt. 26.28 which speaks of the death of Christ as 'the blood of the New Testament . . . shed for many, for the remission of sins'. Though the 'many' in view here might seem ambiguous, Owen thinks it to refer to the persons of the elect, those who had been 'given' to Christ by his Father (Jn 17.2, 6, 9, 11). Elsewhere, these are called Christ's 'sheep': 'I lay down my life for the sheep' (Jn 10.15). These are those to whom Christ says, 'I give unto them eternal life, that they might never perish' (10.28). Christ came not to deliver a nameless, faceless multitude, but the individual members of his body.

In all of these ways, Scripture binds the person of Christ to the salvation of the church. For that reason, Owen insists, any distinction between Christ and his gifts, or between the 'impetration'[62] and 'application' of redemption, must be policed very closely.[63] Is there a difference between Christ's 'meritorious purchase' of the benefits of the covenant and our 'actual enjoyment of those good things upon our believing'? Yes, of course. But Owen thinks the two of these are so closely conjoined that the former includes and is the cause of the latter. Because if Christ truly *merits* these benefits, then they are due in justice to those for whom he has been appointed a representative:

The very sence of the word, whether you call it *Merit, Impetration, Purchase, Acquisition,* or *Obtaining,* doth bespeak a right in them, for whose good the merit is effected, and the purchase made: can that be said to be obtained for me which is no wayes mine?[64]

---

[60]Owen, *The death of death in the death of Christ* (1648), 65; *Works* (1965), 10:212.
[61]Owen, *The death of death in the death of Christ* (1648), 64; *Works* (1965), 10:211–12.
[62]From the Latin *impetrare*, 'to obtain'.
[63]Owen, *The death of death in the death of Christ* (1648), 86f.; *Works* (1965), 10:222f.
[64]Owen, *The death of death in the death of Christ* (1648), 87; *Works* (1965), 10:225.

In other words, Christ's merit confers an *ius ad rem* – a right to the benefits of redemption – upon all he represents. The elect are entitled to them. Only an act of injustice could deny them their rightful share in these benefits. In that sense, Owen says, Christ's merit is less like 'medicine in a box, laid up for all that shall come to have any of it', and more like 'a ransom . . . paid for captives', in that it confers a right to 'be made free' on those for whom it is given.[65]

Of course, the church comes to enjoy Christ's benefits only on the occassion of its believing: 'Actually a man cannot be in Christ untill he be.'[66] But this does nothing to obviate the fact that Christ has really obtained a right to these benefits and, in a sense, earmarked them for the persons of his elect. Furthermore, Owen insists, faith is not a separate condition that intervenes between Christ and the church, because faith is in no way a meritorious cause of our salvation. As Paul teaches, we are granted all spiritual blessings in Christ (Eph. 1.3), and among those blessings is faith itself: 'unto you it is given on the behalf of Christ . . . to believe on him' (Phil. 1.29). The very faith by which we come to enjoy Christ's benefits is itself a benefit of Christ. Christ would only be 'a half mediator' if by his death he had not merited this, 'the chiefest grace', on our behalf.[67] So even the means by which we receive Christ's benefits is itself procured by him. The definitiveness and efficiency of his work are therefore beyond question because 'the application of the good things procured, be the end why they are procured'.[68]

This emphasis on the efficiency of Christ's work as a single means devoted to the 'bringing of those many sons to glory' leads Owen to see Christ not as 'a public person in the room of all mankind', but as the great sign of God's electing love – the sponsor and representative of the church.[69] The redemptive mission of Christ thus has its 'fountain and cause' from within God's 'eternal love to his Elect, and to them alone'.[70] By virtue of this electing love, Christ is, in a real sense, already theirs. There is no qualification in the bestowal of this gift.[71] It is unconditional, depending only and entirely on 'God's free grace'.[72] To place a condition on the sending of the Son would separate Christ from his people, compromising the given-ness of this gift, and by extension, the consolation that it offers.

---

[65] Owen, *The death of death in the death of Christ* (1648), 100; *Works* (1965), 10:233.
[66] Owen, *The death of death in the death of Christ* (1648), 153; *Works* (1965), 10:279.
[67] Owen, *The death of death in the death of Christ* (1648), 101; *Works* (1965), 10:234–5.
[68] Owen, *The death of death in the death of Christ* (1648), 88; *Works* (1965), 10:224.
[69] Owen, *The death of death in the death of Christ* (1648), 96; *Works* (1965), 10:230.
[70] Owen, *The death of death in the death of Christ* (1648), 97; *Works* (1965), 10:231.
[71] Owen, *The death of death in the death of Christ* (1648), 88; *Works* (1965), 10:223.
[72] Owen, *The death of death in the death of Christ* (1648), n.p.; *Works* (1965), 10:154.

This is ultimately why Owen rejects arguments that attempt to ground the saving mission of the Son in the 'universal love' of God for his creatures. Not all are saved.[73] And therefore, if God's universal love were the real moving cause of Christ's saving mission, then God has clearly failed to achieve his aim. Hypothetical universalists typically distinguished the divine intention here by appealing to God's 'antecedent' and 'consequent' wills. God's antecedent will concerns the willing of some providential order, while God's consequent will concerns his willing of some event that may (or may not) deviate from that order. The acts of election and predestination were commonly related using this distinction. In his antecedent will, God desires the flourishing of his creatures and thus destines the whole human race to the end of communion with himself. It is from this love that God is said to desire the salvation of all (1 Tim. 2.4). But in his consequent will, God wills the salvation only of those to whom, by predestination, he grants the means necessary to attain their end. Owen, however, regards this distinction as a kind of sophistry. For while it upholds the supreme efficiency of God's power, it introduces a grammar of the divine will that allows some divine intentions to go unfulfilled:

> a naturall affection in God to the good and salvation of all, being never completed nor perfected, carrieth along with it a great deal of imperfection and weakness; and not only so, but it must also needs be exceedingly prejudicial to the absolute blessedness and happiness of Almighty God. . . . If the Lord hath such a naturall affection to all, as to love them so farre, as to send his Sonne to dye for them; whence is it that this affection of his doth not receive accomplishment?[74]

In other words, if we believe in the absolute efficiency of God's purposes, Owen does not see any point in affirming some intention in God that never comes to pass.

To some extent, this criticism reflects the anti-speculative character of Owen's theology. He generally sees little reason to engage in speculation about the logical ordering of the divine decrees, or the significance that this order might carry for an understanding of God's government of creatures. But additionally, Owen maintains that, because all divine acts *ad extra* are absolutely contingent and grounded in God's own freedom and right, there could be no natural or necessary 'velleity' in God toward creatures:[75]

---

[73]Owen never really countenances the possibility of universalism, believing it to be clearly excluded on exegetical grounds.
[74]Owen, *The death of death in the death of Christ* (1648), 115; *Works* (1965), 10:322.
[75]Owen, *The death of death in the death of Christ* (1648), 93; *Works* (1965), 10:228.

> That God hath any naturall or necessary inclination by his goodnesse, or any other property to doe good to us, or any of his creatures, we do deny: every thing that concernes us is an act of his free will, and good pleasure, and not a naturall necessary act of his Deity.[76]

This appeal to divine freedom resists attempts to ground the logic of God's saving work immediately within the Creator–creature relation. In that respect, it treats redemption as a super-eminent work of God – one that transcends the purposes and ends of the natural order itself. As we noted earlier, Owen would eventually come to think that certain divine acts *ad extra* could be considered natural and necessary. But importantly, he will maintain this only in relation to divine justice, not in relation to divine goodness or mercy. The reason for this is that Owen wishes to assert, in the strongest possible terms, that the gift of redemption in Christ is absolute and unconditional. The best way to do this, he believes, is to firmly root it in the free grace of election. From the first to the last, the work of redemption is intent on bringing sinners home.

THE SATISFACTION OF CHRIST

Book III of *The death of death* includes a series of arguments, sixteen in all, each levelling a critique against general redemption. The most important of these is probably the argument found in chapter VII, which concerns the satisfaction of Christ. This was a crucially strategic topic for Owen. If he could demonstrate that Christ made satisfaction for particular persons, then he could argue that placing any further conditions on their salvation would be unjust – the equivalent of forcing a payment of the same debt twice. The themes of this chapter have dominated reception of *The death of death*. Not only would they occupy Owen in controversy for more than a decade, but they have also come to define his thought on the atonement – particularly among those who find in his work an overly 'pecuniary' account of sin and satisfaction. Literature on Owen has frequently taken this chapter as a definitive statement of his views. This is unfortunate since Owen wrote *The death of death* fairly early in his career, and his thought developed considerably in the years following its publication. His *Diatriba de justitia divina* (1653) revises central elements of his argument here, and yet these rarely qualify critiques of his atonement theology. Still, the argument of this chapter is at least of historical interest, and while some of his judgements on this matter would change, the concepts and questions involved remain crucial to his thought throughout his career.

---

[76]Owen, *The death of death in the death of Christ* (1648), 92; *Works* (1965), 10:227.

Satisfaction in early modern theology

In early modern theology, the term 'satisfaction' had a technical meaning that has been largely lost over time. Today, the word often carries heavily psychological connotations. It signifies a state of contentment which follows one's desires being fulfilled. But in the late medieval and early modern world, 'satisfaction' was primarily moral and legal concept. The Latin *satisfactio* was originally a financial term referring to the discharge of a debt. On the strength of the analogy between financial and moral obligations, the term was, in Owen's words, 'translated to things personall'.[77] That is, it came to refer to the discharge of moral duties more generally. Moral obligations, like financial ones, are responsibilities that we hold toward others, and to which we are bound by justice. In this way, the concept of 'debt' (*debitum*), financial or otherwise, is regulated by the logic of justice and right. One has a debt to do anything that one is obligated in justice to perform. And when one discharges that obligation, the debt is said to be 'satisfied'.

To speak of Christ making 'satisfaction', then, is to address the manner in which Christ's work frees us from some debt or obligation that we owe to God under the law. Christians in the early modern period were widely in agreement that Christ did in fact make satisfaction for sin. Of course, this is attributable in part to the success of Anselm's *Cur Deus Homo*, which argued that the necessity of the incarnation is most apparent if understood as a type of restitution. Since it is from God that creatures derive their very being, they are unavoidably subject to God's government and to the laws that God institutes to serve his government. It is not merely to their benefit to serve God, it is also just and right that they do so. But by sin, creatures turn from God as their highest good, and in doing so deny him what is his due. They thus become liable to the sanctions of the law and incur a 'debt' (or obligation) to punishment. It was to make satisfaction of this debt, Anselm argued, that Christ became a man. For as it is humankind which owes this debt, so by assuming their nature, Christ may render on their behalf that honour which creatures rightly owe to God. Sinners are thus freed from punishment through an act of restitution – the Son's own love and service of the Father.[78]

For all the critiques of Anselm's theory of satisfaction, the argument was widely influential in medieval and early modern theology, in large part because it illuminated so many texts of the New Testament. Scripture may not use the language of 'satisfaction' directly, but it does make fairly substantial use of commercial analogies. For example, it describes sinners as debtors (Mt.

---

[77] Owen, *The death of death in the death of Christ* (1648), 137; *Works* (1965), 10:265.
[78] Note, however, that for Anselm, Christ's satisfaction does not include, but is an alternative to, punishment. See *Cur Deus homo*, I.8–10; II.18.

18.24), and sin as a 'debt' (Mt. 6.12). It speaks of Christ's life as a 'ransom' (Mt. 20.28), of his death as the cause of our 'redemption' (Eph. 1.7), and of his work as the 'price' (τιμῆς) of our redemption (1 Cor. 6.20). The language of 'price' here was seen as particularly significant since a price is by definition a thing given in exchange for some other good. Peter makes the analogy directly when he describes the saints as being 'ransomed from the futile ways inherited from your ancestors, not with perishable things like silver or gold, but with the precious blood of Christ' (1 Pet. 1.18-19, NRSV). One need not take this commercial language literally to see in it some reference to Christ's death as a satisfaction. Even as metaphors, they clearly intend some causal relation between the death of Christ on the one hand and the salvation of the church on the other. They may depict this relation in terms of a commercial exchange, but a similar relation might be adduced from passages which make no appeal to commercial analogies, but still speak of Christ's death as being 'for us' (Rom. 5.6; 1 Pet. 3.18).

Even more crucially though, in some passages, the nature and effect of Christ's work for us is expressed in terms of the fulfilment of the law and its requirements. So, for example, Peter says that Christ 'bore our sins in his own body on the tree' (1 Pet. 2.24), while Paul claims Christ was 'made sin' for us (2 Cor. 5.21), and that he 'redeemed us from the curse of the law, being made a curse for us' (Gal. 3.13). Minimally, expressions like these indicate a benefit which accrues to the church from Christ's self-offering and death. That benefit is understood in terms of the removal of some requirement of the law. And the very nature of a satisfaction is that it dissolves an obligation by the giving of that which the law requires. As Owen puts it, to make satisfaction is simply the 'lawful breaking of [an] obligation, by making it null and void'.[79] So while Catholics and Protestants often disagreed on the extent of Christ's merit – whether it excluded the need for further satisfactions to be offered by the church through acts of contrition or penance – they were in fundamental agreement that Christ did really make satisfaction for sinners by fulfilling obligations that were rightly theirs under the law of God.[80]

Socinians were conspicuous in their rejection of this point, challenging both the necessity and the possibility of Christ's satisfaction. Socinus had denied that Christ could serve as a substitute in any obligation that the moral law required of us, either with regard to merit or punishment. For the nature of the moral law is that it governs us as individual persons. It is impossible that one person might stand in the place of another without altogether destroying the nature of this law. Each person must merit for himself, just as he must bear the punishment

---

[79] Owen, *The death of death in the death of Christ* (1648), 137; *Works* (1965), 10:265.
[80] For a summary of this point, see Turretin, *Institutes of elenctic theology*, XIV.XII.

due to his sins.⁸¹ Therefore, Christ can neither suffer nor merit in our stead. At the same time, the Socinians also rejected the argument that satisfaction for sin was in any way necessary. For punishment is ultimately the right and prerogative of God alone. As the supreme Lord of all, God has an absolute right of ownership over all his creatures, so that he may do as he pleases with his own. Just as it is within the right and power of any creditor to cancel a debt, so too God has the right and power to pardon sinners, cancelling their debt, and remitting their punishment without any satisfaction to his justice. In fact, Socinus argued that, strictly speaking, satisfaction and pardon are contrary to one another. For the same debt cannot be both paid and remitted at the same time.⁸² In order that he may freely pardon sinners, therefore, God does not require satisfaction for sin.⁸³

In an appendix to *The death of death*, Owen notes that his chapters on the satisfaction of Christ primarily target Socinian teaching, attempting to show the 'inconsistency of [satisfaction] with a general ransome'.⁸⁴ In order to do this, Owen draws on a distinction outlined in Grotius's *De satisfactione* between two different types of satisfaction.⁸⁵ The first he identifies as a *solutio ejusdem*, because it is a payment (*solutio*) of the 'very thing' (*ejusdem*) due in the obligation. This payment may be made 'either by himself that is bound, or by some other in his stead'. Imagine a person who owes twenty pounds to a creditor but discovers that his friend had paid the debt for him. Though the debtor may not pay the debt himself, because his friend offers the very thing owed, payment cannot be refused. The payment thus satisfies the debt and the debtor's obligation to the creditor is dissolved ipso facto.⁸⁶ The second kind of satisfaction Owen identifies as a *solutio tantidem,* because it is a payment of 'so much' (*tantidem*) which, while perhaps proportionate to the thing owed, is ultimately 'another kind, not the same that is in the obligation'. This would be like one person owing twenty pounds to another but, rather than paying the debt in cash, offers to mow the lawn or paint the kitchen instead. In this case, 'the creditor's acceptation' is required to amend the obligation so that a different form of payment may be received 'in lieu' of the original thing owed.

---

⁸¹Socinus, *De Jesu Christo servatore* (1594), III.V, 278. See also Gomes's translation of Part III of this work, 'Faustus Socinus' *De Jesu Christo Servatore*, Part III: Historical introduction, translation, and critical notes'.
⁸²Socinus, *De Jesu Christo servatore* (1594), III.V, 242.
⁸³For a summary of Socinus's views on Christ's satisfaction, see Gomes, '*De Jesu Christo servatore*', 209–31.
⁸⁴Owen, *The death of death in the death of Christ* (1648), 327; *Works* (1965), 10:425.
⁸⁵*Defensio fidei Catholicae de satisfactione Christi* (1617), c. VI, §VI. See the English translation, *A defence of the Catholick faith concerning the satisfaction of Christ* (1692). Grotius draws this distinction from Justinian's *Institutes*, Book III:XXIX.
⁸⁶Owen, *The death of death in the death of Christ* (1648), 136; *Works* (1965), 10:265.

Unlike the *solutio ejusdem*, then, freedom from the obligation does not follow ipso facto on the payment offered but depends upon an 'act of favour' by the creditor to accept an alternative form of payment.[87]

Grotius used this distinction to refute the claim of Socinus that satisfaction and remission are mutually exclusive, arguing that this is only true if one supposes the satisfaction of Christ to be a *solutio ejusdem*. But, according to Grotius, this is not possible. For if Christ's satisfaction had been a *solutio ejusdem*, then actual freedom from the obligation to punishment would follow immediately on the death of Christ. But Scripture teaches that, prior to conversion, the saints are 'children of wrath, like everyone else' (Eph. 2.3, NRSV), which suggests that freedom from the debt becomes actual only in conversion. More basically, though, Grotius maintained that Christ's satisfaction was not a payment of the very thing owed by the sinner. In the first instance, punishment is not restitution of a debt but instruction in paying one's debts.[88] And where one has a debt to *punishment* in particular, the punishment of the *offender* is itself part of the obligation.[89] The satisfaction of Christ, then, is not merely the same payment from another person, but the payment of another thing entirely.[90] God's admitting Christ as our substitute is an act of remission in that it entails an alteration to the essence of our obligation to him. God must therefore be considered here in his capacity as a Ruler and Governor, exercising sovereignty over his law. In that way, remission and satisfaction might be seen as complementary acts in the work of redemption. But the efficacy of Christ's work is unavoidably dependent upon a sovereign act of God to accept it, because it is not the very thing due.

Satisfaction in The death of death

Owen's account of Christ's satisfaction agrees in some respects with that of Grotius. But because he wants to uphold the unconditionally given character of Christ's work and affirm that his satisfaction frees us ipso facto from an obligation to the law, Owen classifies Christ's death as a *solutio ejusdem*. Defending this point is important because it entitles Owen to some powerful claims. If Christ has made satisfaction of the very thing which sinners owe

---

[87]Owen, *The death of death in the death of Christ* (1648), 137; *Works* (1965), 10:265.
[88]Cf. *Jure Belli*, II.xx.v; xxi.xi–xii.
[89]'*Est enim in obligatione afflictio ipsius, qui deliquit: unde dici solet, noxam caput sequi*' (*De Satisfactione*, c. VI, § VIII).
[90]Grotius here seems to reflect Aquinas's distinction between punishment simply considered, which properly refers to a penalty of suffering inflicted on a person against his will, from a satisfactory punishment. According to Aquinas, the latter removes, to some degree, the proper nature of punishment. For though it is against the will absolutely, for the purpose of making satisfaction for sin, it is elected voluntarily (*ST* IaIIae, q. 87, a. 6). Further, see Peterson, 'Paving the way?', 265–83.

to God, then no requirements of the law remain unfulfilled, and eternal life belongs to the elect by right. This same logic also funds Owen's 'double-payment' argument, which levels a critique of universal redemption on the grounds that it implicates God in injustice. For if Christ died for all but not all are saved, then God requires some for whom Christ has made satisfaction to be punished for their own sins, effectively requiring satisfaction of the same debt twice.

But while classifying Christ's death as a *solutio ejusdem* carries some definite advantages, it also leads Owen here to treat sin and punishment within a strictly commercial relation. He thus defines satisfaction as 'a full compensation of the Creditour from the Debtor', and argues that God ought to be considered as a *creditor* in this matter.[91] God, according to Owen, accepts the punishment of Christ 'as a creditor accepteth of his due Debt'.[92] Owen has often been criticized for his over-dependence on commercial themes and his 'pecuniary' understanding of sin as a debt to be paid.[93] And it needs to be said that, as a reading of *The death of death*, the criticism is a fair one. For while Owen acknowledges sin and punishment may come under considerations other than that of debt and restitution, the account of divine dominion that he articulates here excludes any other consideration as irrelevant. Owen in fact raises the critiques of Grotius to his argument: (1) that punishment does not admit of a creditor because punishment is not owed to any individual person but to the common good; and (2) that God cannot be considered a creditor in this matter because a creditor exercises his right for his own sake, and the right of punishment is not a private but a public right, exercised for the good of the community. Formally, Owen concedes both of these points, holding that the right of punishment is properly a public rather than a private right: '*Delicta puniri publicè interest.*'[94] But he denies that any distinction between public and private rights can properly apply to God. For since all things exist for God's sake, and God acts for no other end than his own glory, 'the good of the community is the glory of God, and that only'.[95]

Reducing God's relation to the sinner to that of a creditor essentially collapses the distinction between punishment and restitution, which poses a serious problem. Not only does it encourage an overly literal reading of the commercial language in Scripture, and occasionally lead Owen to crudely proportional ways of thinking about the dishonour of sin and the sufferings

---

[91] Owen, *The death of death in the death of Christ* (1648), 137; *Works* (1965), 10:265.
[92] Owen, *The death of death in the death of Christ* (1648), 143; *Works* (1965), 10:270.
[93] For example, Clifford, *Atonement and justification*, 127; Bavinck, *Reformed dogmatics*, 3:401.
[94] Owen, *The death of death in the death of Christ* (1648), 143; *Works* (1965), 10:270.
[95] Owen, *The death of death in the death of Christ* (1648), 144; *Works* (1965), 10:271.

of Christ.⁹⁶ It also implies that punishment is somehow equivalent to the gift given – the gift of life. But, of course, it is not equivalent. There is an infinite qualitative distinction here. Eternal punishment may be an ending, but sinners that undergo eternal punishment most definitely do not attain their *telos*. For rational creatures are ordained to the end of communion with God and that only. If Owen's judgement here were left uncorrected, it could seriously confound the ends of God's government and compromise the character of divine providence as a life-giving movement. Thankfully, in exchanges following the publication of *The death of death*, Owen comes to see the insufficiency of this line of argument. His *Diatriba de justitia divina* reframes the basis of Christ's satisfaction rooting it not in a commercial relation but in the natural dependence of creatures upon God's government. Divine punishment is not properly an attempt to exact the payment of a debt, but to uphold the good of the creature.

Still, identifying God as a creditor here does have a rhetorical advantage. It allows Owen to keep the focus on the way that Christ occupies our place, making satisfaction for the very thing we owe to God. That Christ does occupy our place appears evident to Owen from a number of places in Scripture. He regularly appeals to the teaching of Heb. 7.22 to make this point. There Christ is described as the 'surety' (ἔγγυος) of the new covenant. Owen takes ἔγγυος to be a technical term designating Christ's legal status as a *fidejussor* – one who legally assumes responsibility to fulfil an obligation held by another.⁹⁷ In this case, it indicates the special obligation he holds as a mediator within the covenant of redemption to make satisfaction and to vouchsafe the benefits of that covenant to us.⁹⁸ It is in virtue of this office that Christ's death is said to have 'condemned sin in the flesh' (Rom. 8.3), and 'blotted out the handwriting of ordinances that was against us' (Col. 2.14). Owen also points to texts where the union between Christ and the persons of the church are the basis of a common identification, such as when the persons of the church are spoken of

---

⁹⁶Carl Trueman has denied that this emphasis leads Owen to 'thinking in crudely quantitative terms' about Christ's suffering: 'It is not that Christ has to pile up a heap of suffering to match the offence human beings have given to God' (in 'Atonement and the covenant of redemption', 211). But there are texts where Owen clearly does insist on a proportionality between Christ's suffering and the offence of sin. In *Of communion with God*, for instance, Owen stated: 'Some of the Popish deviationists tell us that one drop, the least, of the blood of Christ, was abundantly enough to redeeme all the World; but they err not knowing the desert of sinne, nor the severity of the Justice of God. If one drop, lesse then was shed, one pang, lesse then was laid on, would have done it; those other dropps had not been shed, nor those other pangs laid on. God did not cruciate the dearly Beloved of his soule for nought'; Owen, *Of communion with God* (1657), 107–8; *Works* (1965), 2:97.
⁹⁷Owen, *Hebrews* (1680), 220–1; *Works* (1850), 22:501. Again, the concept has roots in the law of Justinian (*Institutes*, III.XX).
⁹⁸Owen, *The death of death in the death of Christ* (1648), 246; *Works* (1965), 10:358.

as members of Christ's own body (1 Cor. 6.17; Eph. 5.30),[99] or when they are said to have died and risen together with Christ (Rom. 6.4-5; Eph. 2.5-6).[100]

But the most crucial and determinative are those passages, mentioned previously, that suggest the communication of some legal or moral qualities between Christ and the church. So, for example, although Christ is said to be 'without blemish and without spot' (1 Pet. 1.19), Peter says that he bore 'our sins in his own body on the tree' (2.24). Paul says that Christ was 'made sin' (2 Cor. 5.21) and became 'a curse' for us (Gal. 3.13). Conversely, we are said to have been made 'the righteousness of God in him' (2 Cor. 5.21).[101] Each of these texts presents the union of Christ and the church as the occasion for some exchange in legal status. Taken collectively, Owen thinks that they indicate 'a change or commutation of persons, one being accepted in the roome of the other'.[102] As the law that bound us had a twofold character, both commanding our obedience and stipulating punishment for our disobedience, so too does the work of Christ. By his obedience and love, Christ renders that service to God through which we are reckoned righteous and obtain the promise of eternal life; and by his humbling and death, Christ bears our guilt and the punishments due to our sin, satisfying the sanctions of the law that stood against us. In this way, Christ's work makes full and complete satisfaction of our obligations under the law.

Against Grotius, then, Owen insists that Christ's work being a *solutio ejusdem* is not irreconcilable with the free pardon of God, which is so consistently celebrated in Scripture. On the contrary, 'Gods gracious pardoning of sinne comprizeth the whole dispensation of grace towards us in Christ.'[103] For as we have seen already, Owen argues that Christ's mission has its ground in 'a free compact and covenant' between the Father and the Son.[104] There are thus two distinct acts of God presupposed in Christ's satisfaction. The first is an act of 'severe justice', in which God wills to require sinners to make satisfaction of their debt to punishment. But the second act is one 'of sovereignty or supreme dominion, in translating the punishment from the principal debtor to the surety'. God must therefore be considered in a twofold relation here. In relation to sinners, God is a creditor – the one who has been injured by sin, and the one to whom restitution is due. In relation to Christ, however, God

---

[99]This is an important theme for Owen's theology of union with Christ. See Owen, *The duty of people and pastors distinguished* (1644), 20–1; *Works* (1965), 13:22. Further on this point see Baylor, 'One with him in Spirit', 427–52.
[100]Owen, *The death of death in the death of Christ* (1648), 144; *Works* (1965), 10:268.
[101]Owen, *The death of death in the death of Christ* (1648), 144–5; *Works* (1965), 10:269–70.
[102]Owen, *The death of death in the death of Christ* (1648), 114; *Works* (1965), 10:246.
[103]Owen, *The death of death in the death of Christ* (1648), 141; *Works* (1965), 10:268–9.
[104]Owen, *The death of death in the death of Christ* (1648), 141; *Works* (1965), 10:269.

is considered as 'the supreme Lord and Governor of all, the only Lawgiver'. For the appointment of Christ as a sponsor of the elect requires the act of a Sovereign 'to relax his own law as to have the name of a surety put into the obligation, which before was not there, and then to require the whole debt of that surety'.[105]

The institution of the mediator is thus an act in which God interposes the person of Christ into the obligations of the persons of the elect. And not just any obligations but obligations which are constitutive of the persons of the elect as *persons*, namely, to obey God or to bear the punishment of their sins. In that respect, the union between Christ and the elect is of a wholly unique sort. Christ not only represents a definite population of people. To use a seventeenth-century term, we might say that Christ 'personates' the elect.[106] That is, the persons of the elect are so united to him in the covenant of redemption that, as far as God's justice is concerned, his action is their own. He has done all in their place. No obligation is left unfilled. No condition unsatisfied. In every way that matters, Christ is the living, breathing incorporation of the persons of the elect. In this way, the 'remission[,] grace and pardon, which is in God for sinners, is not opposed to Christs merits, but ours'.[107]

But one might reasonably push back on Owen at this point, insisting that God's law is not merely an aggregation of abstract moral duties. Its purpose is to govern – to facilitate that necessary confrontation between justice and the actions of real persons. We cannot speak casually about the transfer of a legal status or obligation, for the same reason that we cannot speak casually about the freedoms and responsibilities of individual persons. But if this is the case, then in what sense can Christ's oblation be considered an offering of the very thing due, since it is a different person that makes satisfaction? Does this not imply a sovereign contravention of the law in a manner that fundamentally alters the obligation itself? Owen argues that it does not. Drawing a distinction here between the essence and accidents of the debt due, he claims that Christ's satisfaction was 'essentially the same in weight and pressure, though not in all accidents of duration and the like'. In other words, the person paying the debt is accidental to its substance. It is sufficient that Christ undergoes 'the same punishment . . . [sinners] themselves were bound to undergo'.[108] Just so, Owen concludes that God 'pardons all to us; but he spared not his only Son, he bated him not one farthing'.[109]

---

[105] Owen, *The death of death in the death of Christ* (1648), 143; *Works* (1965), 10:270.
[106] Cf. Owen, 'Christ's pastoral care', in *Works* (1965), 9:276.
[107] Owen, *The death of death in the death of Christ* (1648), 141; *Works* (1965), 10:269.
[108] Owen, *The death of death in the death of Christ* (1648), 144; *Works* (1965), 10:269.
[109] Owen, *The death of death in the death of Christ* (1648), 141; *Works* (1965), 10:269.

If indeed Christ has made satisfaction of the very thing due in the obligation, then the blood of Christ cannot be shed in vain, unless God would be shown to be unjust and unfaithful to his promise. For 'the Lord who is a just creditor, ought in all equity to cancel the bond . . . full payment being made unto him for the Debt'.[110] It would in fact be unjust for God to require punishment at the hands of any for whom Christ died, Christ having made full satisfaction for sin. Many of Christ's elect still await the full enjoyment of this freedom in their conscience. For, as Scripture teaches, prior to believing, the elect and the un-elect are all alike 'guilty before God' (Rom. 3.19) and living under the effects of God's judgement as 'children of wrath' (Eph. 2.3).[111] But by virtue of their incorporation into Christ within the covenant of redemption, the elect truly obtain a right and title to eternal life from his work. Owen thus likens the persons of the elect to prisoners whose ransom has been paid and whose right to freedom has been secured, but who 'cannot enjoy it until such time as tidings of it are brought unto him'.[112]

RECEPTION OF *THE DEATH OF DEATH*

Almost immediately after its publication, *The death of death* drew a strong reaction from Richard Baxter. In an appendix to his *Aphorismes of justification* (1649),[113] Baxter took issue with Owen's account of the satisfaction of Christ, initiating a dispute that would extend over the better part of two decades and run to several hundred pages.[114] The central matter of the dispute picked up the question of whether Christ's satisfaction was equivalent or identical to the obligation owed by the elect. While Baxter could grant that there was a material identity between Christ's satisfaction and the obligation of the creature, he denied that there was any formal identity between them.[115] 'If the same thing in the Obligation is paid, then the law be executed; but if executed (fully and properly) then not relaxed.'[116] But the law was relaxed to admit Christ in place of the sinner, as Owen himself conceded. Moreover Owen's analogy, comparing the elect to a prisoner whose ransom had been paid and thus had a right to freedom even before conversion, suggested to Baxter that

---

[110]Owen, *The death of death in the death of Christ* (1648), 145; *Works* (1965), 10:272.
[111]Owen, *The death of death in the death of Christ* (1648), 149; *Works* (1965), 10:276.
[112]Owen, *The death of death in the death of Christ* (1648), 141; *Works* (1965), 10:268.
[113]Baxter, *Aphorismes of justification* (1649).
[114]For summaries, see Boersma, *A hot peppercorn*, 219–56; Cooper, *John Owen, Richard Baxter and the formation of Nonconformity*, 55–86; Tay, *The priesthood of Christ*, 136–50; Trueman, *The claims of truth*, 206–26.
[115]Boersma, *A hot pepper corn*, 245–54.
[116]Baxter, *Aphorismes of justification* (1649), 145.

Owen believed justification to precede faith.[117] He thus suspected Owen of harbouring antinomian sympathies that would minimize the necessity of human response to the Gospel.

In May of the following year, while introducing reforms to Trinity College Dublin at the behest of Oliver Cromwell, Owen published *Of the death of Christ, the price he paid, and the purchase he made* (1650), responding to Baxter's critiques, which he felt were more a matter of 'Words, then Things; Expressions, then Oppinions, wayes of Delivering things, then the Doctrines themselves'.[118] As we have noted already, Owen had acknowledged in *The death of death* that not all the benefits of Christ's satisfaction accrue to the elect immediately and automatically upon Christ's death. In *Of the death of Christ*, Owen again insisted that Christ's satisfaction is formally identical with the obligation, thus endowing the church with a right to freedom from the law. But he clarified here that the right which the saints acquire through Christ's satisfaction includes a stipulation *sub termino* – that is, it is a right to enjoy some privilege at a specified time. We might think here of the way that a child may possess a right to enjoy an endowment or inheritance which is held in trust for him until the time when he comes of age.[119] Though he does not yet actively have a right over the thing (*ius in re*) promised, he does truly have a right to that thing (*ius ad rem*).[120]

Owen denies that this *ius ad rem* amounts to a full justification of the sinner prior to her believing. The benefits of Christ are enacted across time, such that the state of the sinner is no different because of her election. Of the elect prior to conversion, Owen writes: 'I leave them as before, not Justified, not Sanctified, not entred into Covenant.'[121] It is only in saving faith that the elect person experiences that 'pardoning mercy on the part of God which is to be terminated and completed in the conscience of the sinner'. At the same time, though, Owen does insist that a real 'absolution from the guilt of sin and obligation unto death' must precede our act of believing. This absolution is not apprehended and understood by the conscience. It is an immanent act within God himself, existing solely in the divine will, and is the immediate effect of the imputation of Christ's work to our account. Owen believed that such a

---

[117]Baxter, *Aphorismes of justification* (1649), 154–9.
[118]Owen, *Of the death of Christ* (1650), 2; *Works* (1965), 10:435.
[119]Owen, *Of the death of Christ* (1650), 70; *Works* (1965), 10:466.
[120]Owen elsewhere draws on Grotius's distinction between a 'faculty' and an 'aptitude', as different ways of holding a subjective right. Prior to their conversion, the elect do not hold their right to eternal life as 'faculty', making active use of it; rather, they hold it only *passively*, as an 'aptitude'. See Owen, *Vindiciae evangelicae* (1655), 31–5; *Works* (1965), 12:609–11; cf. Grotius, *Jure belli*, I.i.4. Further on these terms in the history of subjective rights as a concept, see Tuck, *Natural rights theories*.
[121]Owen, *Of the death of Christ* (1650), 69; *Works* (1965), 10:465.

divine absolution must really precede our believing because 'a discharge from the effects of [God's] anger naturally precedes all collation of any fruits of [his] love, such as is faith'. In other words, justification is not complete until, in the act of believing, we feel the 'Soul freeing discharge' of our conscience by the knowledge of the forgiveness of our sins. Still, the gift of effectual calling and faith is itself a sign of God's propitiation toward us, and as such is definitive evidence of the efficacy of Christ's satisfaction on our behalf.[122]

This answer did not allay Baxter's concern, and he reopened the controversy again in 1655 with the publication of his *Confession of faith*, in which he flatly charged Owen with antinomianism. The suggestion that absolution might precede justification seemed an absurdity to Baxter. For if absolution includes the remission of guilt and punishment, what remains left to justification but the subjective appropriation of this fact – a justification *in foro conscientiæ*, not *in foro Dei*. Moreover, if Christ has made complete satisfaction of the very obligation contained in the law, then is not the moral dependence of creatures upon God entirely overturned?

Baxter's concern here is sometimes depicted as a kind of incipient moralism, but as he saw it, the matter concerned a fundamental issue of meta-ethics. Creatures do not merely owe God obedience or punishment in the abstract. They owe God their very selves. The law, in that respect, is concretely personal – it enjoins us to a particular form of life, yes, but it does so for the sake of offering our lives as a living sacrifice to God. To have a right to freedom through the satisfaction of the law's obligation, then, requires an inherent justice of life: 'I take *Ius*, Right in a person, in our case, to be that which answers *Debitum* in this thing.'[123] But the church is a company of sinners. And for that reason, Baxter thinks, it cannot possibly have a *right* to its freedom because it has not made satisfaction for *itself*: 'It could not be ourselves Legally, because it was not ourselves Naturally.'[124]

The right of which the church lives is not its own, but Christ's. Baxter also denied the possibility of a proper covenant between the persons of the Trinity: 'It is spoken improperly, after the manner of men, that God makes a Covenant with God, the Father with the second person of the Trinity.'[125] For being an immanent act of God, the election of Christ as the mediator cannot differ in any way from a decree, which is an act of absolute dominion. As such, it imparts no new right to any. The elect receive a share in Christ's benefits, then, as a gift given, not of a legal obligation, but of God's free dominion and grace. Positing

---

[122]Owen, *Of the death of Christ* (1650), 80; *Works* (1965), 10:470.
[123]Baxter, *R. Baxter's Confession of his faith* (1655), 256.
[124]Baxter, *R. Baxter's Confession of his faith* (1655), 290.
[125]Baxter, *R. Baxter's Confession of his faith* (1655), 259.

a formal identity between our obligation under the law and the satisfaction of Christ only confuses this, allowing Christ's self-offering to so displace the persons of the church that it turns Christ's benefits into entitlements, and nullifies the gift which the saints themselves are called to return to God.

Owen responded in the same year with *Of the death of Christ, and of justification* (1655), a treatise dripping with sarcasm and irritation, which he appended to his *Vindiciæ evangelicæ*. To the charge of antinomianism, he insists that absolution precedes faith only logically; temporally, it is simultaneous with the act of believing.[126] On the more sticky issue of the law and its relation to particular persons, Owen denies that the obligation of the law formally requires the obedience or punishment of each individual person. It is enough, he believes, that the duty itself is performed:

> It is personal punishment that the law originally requires; but he that undergoes the punishment (though he be not personally disobedient) which the law judgeth to him that was personally disobedient, undergoes the *idem* that the law requires. The *idem* is *supplicium delinquenti debitum* by whomsoever it be undergone, not *supplicium ipsius delinquentis* only.[127]

Baxter would have seen this as question-begging, but this distinction between person and obligation is a position from which Owen never really moved. In fact, it became a fixture of the moral theology that developed in Owen's later works, which regards the moral law as taking different forms under distinct covenants. It is the covenant that defines the law's relation to particular persons. And unlike the covenant of works in which we had to merit for ourselves, the hallmark of the covenant of grace is the introduction of a mediator whose person is the principle and basis of our merit.[128] The foundation for this administration is laid in the covenant of redemption, through which God innovates the obligation of the elect to interpose Christ as their sponsor. As a result, 'A man may be accounted to do a thing legally by a sponsor, though he do it not in his own person.'[129] The law has thus been fully satisfied and a right to freedom unconditionally secured through the self-offering of Christ.

---

[126]See Owen, *Vindiciae evangelicae* (1655), 20; *Works* (1965), 12:602.
[127]See Owen, *Vindiciae evangelicae* (1655), 38; *Works* (1965), 12:613.
[128]Owen, *Πνευματολογια* (1674), 534; *Works* (1965), 3:606–7; cf. Owen, *Sabbath* (1671), 258–63; *Works* (1850), 19:405–7.
[129]See Owen, *Vindiciae evangelicae* (1655), 40; *Works* (1965), 12:614.

CONCLUSION

As we have seen in the foregoing, for Owen, the intention of God in sending Christ was not simply to make people saveable, but to save them. Christ's work must effect a definitive alteration in the status of his people. Though some of the central concepts Owen treats here may be unfamiliar, the questions in this work are hardly remote. They are in fact of perennial interest to Christian theology. In that respect, we might read it against that wider conversation in Protestant thought seeking the proper relation between Christ and the believer, justification and sanctification, faith and works. *The death of death* represents the side of the dialectic, of which Barth is a more recent example, that sees the life of Jesus as a corporate event, a history in which the persons of the church are really taken up and determined. Baxter's critique of Owen, like Pannenberg's critique of Barth, reflects the other side of the dialectic: that the work of Christ should not displace the agency of the believer, but orient and activate it. To be sure, this is a matter of tremendous significance to Christian faith. But there can be no question in Owen's mind which side of this dialectic must have priority. For the cross of Christ is not merely a sign of hope, it is the only cause for boasting – an absolute and unconditional gift, the provision of which is utterly full and complete. Christian acts of faith and obedience cannot render this more actual or real. They can merely prove its abundance again, and again, and again.

CHAPTER 14

Of the mortification of sinne in believers (1656)

JOEL R. BEEKE

John Owen published numerous books in the 1650s. These were some of his most productive years. In 1651, Owen became dean of Christ Church, Oxford, where he regularly lectured and preached. He was promoted to the position of vice-chancellor of the university some eighteen months later. Throughout much of this period, on alternate Sundays, he shared the pulpit at St Mary's with his Independent colleague, Thomas Goodwin. Owen's publications during this time include theological works on the Gospel, such as works on the perseverance of the saints and communion with the triune God. He also published a practical work on schism and an apologetic defence of Scripture's authority.[1] These works champion Reformed theology through careful exegesis and nuanced theological reasoning. Indisputably, the writings of this 'prince of the English divines' abundantly testify to Owen's accolade as a theologian. But no publication of his has received the amount of attention or been esteemed so highly as *Of the mortification of sinne in believers* (1656; hereafter, *Mortification*). In this work, Owen the theologian shines as Owen the pastor. He weaves together the theological acumen of the scholastic Reformed tradition with the practical orientation towards holistic piety so characteristic of the Puritan movement.

---

[1] Beeke and Pederson, *Meet the Puritans*, 458–9.

Mortification is the substance of a series of sermons that Owen preached to university students.² *Mortification* addressed the student body with plain teaching about indwelling sin, explaining how sinful desires prevail in Christian experience, while providing instruction about how to overcome sin. The broader seventeenth-century context conditioned the points that Owen would make as well as the emphases that he would place upon those points. Owen contrasted the evangelical nature of Reformed teaching on sanctification with the legal nature of Roman Catholic approaches. Against the Unitarianism of the Socinianians, Owen stressed the trinitarian nature of Christian spirituality, highlighting the Spirit's hypostatic distinction as the very personal power behind all success in mortification. Contrary to Arminianism, Owen taught the unbreakable unity of the Trinity in God's plan to save and sanctify his people. And in refutation of antinomianism, strands of which taught that the duty of mortifying sin was non-essential, he insisted on the necessity, urgency and personal responsibility of every believer with respect to killing sin.³ Though he does not call out these groups by name in this treatise, he does make numerous allusions to their arguments, demonstrating that correcting their perceived errors was not far from his view. The polemical nature of his treatment makes for some fine-tuned theology brought into high definition (if for no other reason) through apologetic elencticism – though the elencticism is rather implicit. It seems that Owen's primary purpose was to provide a training manual for mortifying sin, a work of which the primary goal was the edification of believers. The burden was, in Owen's words, that 'mortification and universal holiness may be promoted in my own and in the hearts and ways of others, to the glory of God; that so the Gospel of our Lord and Saviour Jesus Christ may be adorned in all things'.⁴ In what follows, I will critically summarize Owen's teaching in *Mortification*. Other works will be consulted as they illuminate this subject, but our primary focus will remain on this treatise.

THE FOUNDATIONAL PRINCIPLES: MORTIFICATION BY GRACE

Among the chief errors to avoid when addressing mortification, Owen argued, was the assumption that it was a work that an individual could perform without the special grace of God.⁵ Mortification involves human effort, but it is not

---

²Toon, *God's statesman*, 56.
³For background on Owen's theological and polemical context, see Trueman, *John Owen*, 17–33 (on Roman Catholicism, Arminianism, and Socinianism); and Craig, *The bond of grace and duty*, 184–96 (on antinomianism).
⁴Owen, *Of the mortification of sinne in believers* (1656), A3v sig.–A4r sig.; *Works* (1965), 6:4.
⁵In this chapter, I will often use 'mortification' as shorthand for 'the mortification of sin'.

accomplished by human effort alone, nor is it mere opposition to sin based on the resolute or determinate purpose of human will. It is based on a number of foundational principles and is conceptualized in Owen's theology with regard to its relatedness to these principles, which root this duty in the redeeming grace of God. These principles include concepts such as Christ's atoning satisfaction, the Holy Spirit's necessary work and the evangelical nature of sanctification.

The atonement: The meritorious ground of sanctification

The grace-based nature of Owen's doctrine of mortification stems from its rootedness in the blood of Jesus Christ, shed vicariously for sinners. At the outset of *Mortification*, Owen speaks of a 'meritorious mortification' whereby 'all and every sin' of the believer is forensically absolved by Christ's death.[6] This includes indwelling sin, which is 'meritoriously, and by way of example, utterly mortified and slain by the cross of Christ'.[7] The believer's sin is judicially and exhaustively eradicated with regard to his or her positional standing before God's judgement seat. What Owen calls the believer's 'personal righteousness' ('personal', in this case, because it is inherently characteristic of one's person by grace) is only possible on the juridical basis of one's antecedent justification 'in the sight of God'.[8] No sin could be actually mortified unless the basis had been established by which the person engaging in mortification had already been justified. Not only does progressive sanctification come subsequent to the inception of personal justification but all sanctification – whether initial, ongoing or perfected – rests on the forensic and covenantal foundation of Christ's atoning death.[9] Sanctification is not to be confused with justification, nor is the latter in any way dependent upon the former. How sin is permanently put away in justification differs from how it is to be continually 'mortified' in sanctification. We must keep these categories distinct, or we will be confused by Owen's overlapping terminology.

Paul connects sanctification with the purchase effected by the cross when he writes that Christ 'gave himself for us, that he might redeem us from all iniquity, and purify unto himself a peculiar people, zealous of good works', and teaches that Christ gave his life to sanctify his bride (Tit. 2.14; Eph. 5.25-26). Owen asserts, 'the blood of Jesus Christ doth *wash, purge, cleanse*, and *sanctify* them for whom it was shed', and, he insists, it is 'effectual' for that purpose.[10]

---

[6] Owen, *Of the mortification of sinne in believers* (1656), 25; *Works* (1965), 6:14.
[7] Owen, *Of the mortification of sinne in believers* (1656), 10; *Works* (1965), 6:8.
[8] Owen, *The doctrine of justification by faith* (1677), 217; *Works* (1965), 5:156.
[9] Owen, *The death of death in the death of Christ* (1648), 119; *Works* (1965), 10:250; cf. Owen, *The doctrine of justification by faith* (1677), 399; *Works* (1965), 5:277.
[10] Owen, *The death of death in the death of Christ* (1648), 119; *Works* (1965), 10:250.

Christ has secured for his elect with infallible certainty 'every spiritual blessing' (Eph. 1.3), including sanctification, and bestows these blessings upon them, so that 'he procured for us remission of all our sins, an actual reconciliation with God, faith, and obedience'.[11] There is no room for a hypothetical atonement in Owen's theology. The cross does not merely make salvation possible – it actually saves God's people, because it is the meritorious basis for all the particular salvific blessings of which salvation (as a whole) consists.[12]

Mortification as an expression of obedience is carried out by faith in Christ's death.[13] This faith is the gift of God, secured by Christ's work of impetration (what the twentieth-century Reformed theologian John Murray called 'redemption accomplished'), and bestowed by the Spirit's work of application, according to the indivisible bond of intra-trinitarian harmony that unites the work of the Spirit with the work of the Son.[14] Being secured, faith and mortification are effectively imparted in due time. Owen argues that 'mortification of sin is peculiarly from the death of Christ. It is one peculiar, yea, eminent end of the death of Christ, which shall assuredly be accomplished by it'.[15]

Since mortification has Christ's vicarious righteousness as its meritorious basis, does this mean that the believer is absolved from its duty? Owen repudiates such an idea. The death of Christ does not excuse negligence in mortification; rather, it secures and enables successful mortification. Moreover, the procurement of the grace of justification does not excuse any from the duty of mortification but heightens their responsibility in it. The cross also motivates mortification, and is far from providing a licence to countenance the practice of sin. Owen reminds his readers of the 'blood of Christ, which is given to *cleanse us*, 1 John 1:7, Tit. 2:14; the exaltation of Christ, which is to give us *repentance*, Acts 5:31; the doctrine of grace, which teaches us to *deny all ungodliness*, Tit. 2:11, 12, to countenance sin, is a rebellion that in the issue [outcome] will break the bones' (see Ps. 51.8).[16] He cautions that to attempt to abuse the atonement in such a way may be a slippery slope to apostasy, an irreversible fall from the faith that would betray the fact that one was never truly among the number of God's elect.[17] The true believer does not trample

---

[11]Owen, *A display of Arminianisme* (1643), 98; *Works* (1965), 10:93.
[12]Trueman notes how prominent in Owen's thinking 'is the notion that merit is covenantally determined' and makes the whole system of soteriology depend on the *pactum salutis* and Christ's cross; 'Atonement and the covenant of redemption', in Gibson and Gibson (eds), *From heaven he came and sought her*, 215.
[13]Owen, *Of the mortification of sinne in believers* (1656), 212–13; *Works* (1965), 6:83–4.
[14]Owen, *The death of death in the death of Christ* (1648), 101–2; *Works* (1965), 10:235. See Murray, *Redemption accomplished and applied*.
[15]Owen, *Of the mortification of sinne in believers* (1656), 212; *Works* (1965), 6:83.
[16]Owen, *Of the mortification of sinne in believers* (1656), 28; *Works* (1965), 6:15.
[17]Owen, *Of the mortification of sinne in believers* (1656), 28; *Works* (1965), 6:15.

on Christ's blood but esteems it as precious for its twofold cure in saving from wrath and making one pure (as Augustus Toplady would later put it in his well-known hymn, 'Rock of Ages').[18]

The Spirit's necessary work

For Owen, the Gospel reflects the Godhead, because the Gospel is structured by the trinitarian nature of the God who is its author. The mission of God the Son gives way to the mission of God the Spirit who proceeds from the Father and the Son (Jn 15.26), because the 'order of the dispensation of the divine persons towards us ariseth from the order of their own subsistence' in the Godhead.[19] Suzanne McDonald observes that 'it is a rigorously applied axiom throughout Owen's theology that the economic acts of God express the being of God'. She adds: 'Inner-trinitarian relations are therefore', for Owen, a 'touchstone for the right understanding of all doctrines'.[20] Owen affirms this when he writes that the Spirit 'is the *immediate, peculiar, efficient cause* of all external divine operations'.[21] This is true in creation, providence and most clearly in redemption. Carl Trueman notes how in Owen's theology, 'the Spirit's activity does indeed proceed from the Godhead in relation to both Father and Son. The emphasis on the processional order . . . is evident again in the structure of the economy of salvation, and, indeed, is essential to it'.[22] The economical works of the Trinity are not the ontological Trinity but they are more than a little suggestive of it.

All of Christ's gifts come to the elect through the Spirit of Christ, who takes what is Christ's and communicates it to his people.[23] Owen stands in the Western stream of Catholic theology by affirming the *filioque*, and he adapts it to the Protestant and Reformed Gospel so that the redemptive outworking of God's sovereign plan is revelatory of the truth of the internal divine processions.[24] Commentating on Jn 15.26, long held to be the *locus classicus* of the *filioque* doctrine, Owen describes the nature of the ἐκπόρευσις, or 'procession'. He says

---

[18]Calvin's *duplex gratia* in relation to union with Christ finds general agreement in Owen, but Owen's theology is more elaborate and articulate. For a comparison, see Gleason, *John Calvin and John Owen on mortification*.
[19]Owen, Πνευματολογια (1674), 39; *Works* (1965), 3:61.
[20]McDonald, 'The pneumatology of the "lost" image in John Owen', 326.
[21]Owen, Πνευματολογια (1674), 130; *Works* (1965), 3:161.
[22]Trueman, *The claims of truth*, 146.
[23]Owen, *Of the mortification of sinne in believers* (1656), 36–7; *Works* (1965), 6:19.
[24]Trueman, *The claims of truth*, 146; Kapic, 'The Spirit as gift: Explorations in John Owen's pneumatology', 113. Of course, this revelation is accommodated to humanity. Owen would agree with Thomas Aquinas that God's revelation of himself is analogical and not univocal. It cannot be any other way, because God is infinite and incomprehensible.

the procession as an external act of the Trinity is a 'voluntary act' of God's will involving both the Father and the Son.

> And he is said thus to proceed from the Father, because he goeth forth or proceedeth in the pursuit of the counsels and purposes of the Father, and, as sent by him, to put them into execution, or to make them effectual. And in like manner he proceedeth from the Son, sent by him for the application of his grace unto the souls of his elect, John 15:26.[25]

The Spirit is breathed forth in salvation history to fulfil the purpose of the Father's eternal counsel and to manifest Christ's grace to his people (Ps. 33.6; Job 33.4; Jn 20.22).

Not least among the Spirit's graces is his empowerment of the Christian to kill sin. Sanctification by the Spirit is central to the will of the Father and to the Son's purpose in dying (1 Pet. 1.2; 1 Thess. 4.3; Eph. 5.25-26). Sinclair Ferguson comments that 'mortification is a gift of the Crucified, Risen, Ascended Christ, and is mediated through the Spirit'.[26] The Spirit does more than help his people to mortify sin; he is the necessary source of the vital energy by which it is accomplished. Owen writes that in the experience of God's elect, the Spirit is the 'great sovereign cause' of mortification, the only one 'sufficient for this work', and the 'great efficient of it' (i.e. the efficient cause).[27] Because of the power of indwelling sin and its degenerating influence on human nature, mortification requires the Spirit's supernatural agency. As Owen puts it, 'an almighty energy is necessary for its accomplishment'.[28] Sanctification is not in believers' own power, for it is 'a work of God in them and upon them'.[29] Since mortification is a particular soteriological subset of Gospel sanctification, the priority of the Spirit's agency applies to both.

The prominence of the Spirit in mortification can be seen in the foundational text of *Mortification*: 'If ye through the Spirit do mortify the deeds of the body, ye shall live' (Rom. 8.13). There are three general ways the Spirit works in mortification. First, he causes our hearts to abound in grace and in the fruits of the Spirit that are contrary to the works of the flesh (Gal. 5.19-23).[30] Second, he works 'by a *real physical efficiency* on the root and habit of sin, for the weakening, destroying, and taking it away'.[31] The Spirit's role, in other words,

---

[25] Owen, Πνευματολογια (1674), 89; Works (1965), 3:117.
[26] Ferguson, *John Owen on the Christian life*, 147.
[27] Owen, *Of the mortification of sinne in believers* (1656), 31; Works (1965), 6:16.
[28] Owen, *Of the mortification of sinne in believers* (1656), 36; Works (1965), 6:18.
[29] Owen, Πνευματολογια (1674), 322; Works (1965), 3:367.
[30] Owen, *Of the mortification of sinne in believers* (1656), 38; Works (1965), 6:19.
[31] Owen, *Of the mortification of sinne in believers* (1656), 39; Works (1965), 6:19.

goes beyond moral influence, beyond illuminating, convincing and instructing; it includes the operation of his cleansing power on the depths of our fallen-yet-redeemed humanity, which brings into further expression the principle, or 'habit of grace', that is infused into the soul at regeneration.[32] Third, the Spirit 'brings the *cross of Christ* into the heart of a sinner by faith, and gives us communion with Christ' so that we die increasingly to sin in fellowship with Christ's death.[33] Owen was drawing from Romans 6, where Paul teaches that even though the reign of sin's power is destroyed by the believer's connection to Christ in his death, sin's ongoing presence must be put to death.

In explaining the sanctifying change that the Spirit works in believers, Puritan theologians stressed the importance of habit. This concept had been basic in explaining spiritual life at least since Thomas Aquinas (1225–74), though Reformed and evangelical Christians today might opt for the word 'orientation', or 'disposition'. Likewise, Puritan theologians viewed habit as a behavioural pattern. So, love, peace and other fruits of the Spirit are habits of acting and reacting to circumstances. The believer keeps rejoicing, whatever may be going on; he keeps loving, whatever may be happening; he remains at peace in himself before the Lord, whatever may be transpiring. He does not allow his conduct to be determined by what goes on around him; rather, he lives out the disposition of Jesus Christ in every circumstance, whatever that circumstance may be. He strives for what the eighteenth-century Scottish theologian Thomas Boston calls 'habitual holiness', that is, a habitual aversion of the soul to evil, and inclination to good.[34]

The Spirit works according to his sovereign will in this grace, which means that believers are entirely at his mercy. But they must not become passive. Mortification is a duty, an activity to be performed, required by God as an act of obedience. Peter Golding observes that, for Owen, 'the Spirit's method is not to work mortification in us so as to bypass our activity but rather to enlist it. We are not spectators in the work but participants'.[35] Believers work out their sanctification because the Spirit works it in them (Phil. 2.13), but the Spirit is involved in both the working in and the working out. Owen writes that the Holy Spirit 'works upon our understandings, wills, consciences, and affections, agreeably to their own natures he works *in us* and *with us*, not *against us* or

---

[32]Owen, *Πνευματολογια* (1674), 256–7, 280; *Works* (1965), 3:301–2, 329. For discussion, see Hodge, *Systematic theology*, 2:686–7; Cleveland, *Thomism in John Owen*, 69–120; Allen, *Sanctification*, 250–1; Beeke, *Living for God's glory*, 196–7. Owen's theology of sanctification is indebted to Thomas Aquinas's concept of infused habits, but Owen modifies the theological construct significantly in keeping with Reformed theology. He had a critical appreciation for Thomas and was eclectic in his use of him.
[33]Owen, *Of the mortification of sinne in believers* (1656), 39; *Works* (1965), 6:19.
[34]Boston, *An illustration of the doctrines of the Christian religion*, 2:303.
[35]Golding, 'Owen on the mortification of sin: 2', 20–5.

without us; so that his assistance is an encouragement as to the facilitating of the work, and no occasion of neglect as to the work itself'.[36] The Spirit equips the believer for victory in the fight against sin but he does not fight the battle for him. Owen's emphasis on the work on the Spirit in mortification guards his teaching from legalism while grounding it in evangelical principles.

The evangelical nature of sanctification

The foregoing discussion sheds light on Owen's definition of sanctification and helps us to appreciate its grounding in grace:

> Sanctification is an immediate work of the Spirit of God on the souls of believers, purifying and cleansing of their natures from the pollution and uncleanness of sin, renewing in them the image of God, and thereby enabling them, from a spiritual and habitual principle of grace, to yield obedience unto God, according unto the tenor and terms of the new covenant, by virtue of the life and death of Jesus Christ. Or more briefly: – It is the universal renovation of our natures by the Holy Spirit into the image of God, through Jesus Christ.[37]

I recommend that the reader should go back over that definition and read through it again attentively, paying attention to how the doctrine of God, especially the Trinity, forges the structure of Owen's doctrine. Notice also how the primacy of God's work ensures the graciousness of sanctification by safeguarding the supernatural dynamic of it. Though man's involvement is not neglected, the doctrine is God-centred rather than man-centred. The supernatural element rules out the possibility of sanctification being a work of man. It is a work of God in man and through man by the Spirit because of Christ.

Owen's theology stands very much united to the church's historical understanding. The patristic era is known for bequeathing to the church the doctrine of the Trinity, and the Reformation era handed down the doctrine of God's sovereignty and supremacy in grace. Owen unites these traditions, converges the Trinity with the sovereignty of grace, and (in keeping with the Puritan emphasis on experiential piety) brings both doctrines to bear on the doctrine of sanctification. His development of sanctification and mortification made an important contribution to the church's understanding of the Christian life.

Let us tease this out. Owen takes pains to teach that in addition to the Son's atonement and the Spirit's endowment, sanctification is trinitarian in structure

---

[36] Owen, *Of the mortification of sinne in believers* (1656), 40; *Works* (1965), 6:20.
[37] Owen, *Πνευματολογια* (1674), 338; *Works* (1965), 3:386.

and evangelical in nature due to its connection with the Father's election. The God of peace is the author of sanctification (1 Thess. 5.23): 'He is the eternal spring and only fountain of all holiness; there is nothing of it in any creature but what is directly and immediately from him.'[38] If we were to think that we could sanctify ourselves by our own efforts, we would be practically renouncing our dependence on God. The one who decreed to make us in his image is the one who by the same principle remakes us in his image: 'We may as wisely and rationally contend that we have not our *being* and our lives from God, as that we have not our *holiness* from him, when we have any.'[39]

As a work of new creation in expression of the Father's electing love, sanctification is a work of grace because it is enabled by monergistic regeneration. The Spirit is promised to the elect, and in regeneration, he is received by them to make them believers. In this reception, they are 'passive' and 'receive him only in a way of grace'. Regeneration is the Spirit's work in them 'wholly and entirely', Owen emphasizes.[40] The impartation of new life in them is effectual when so intended by God. Owen explains that 'in or towards whomsoever the Holy Spirit puts forth his power, or acts his grace for their regeneration, he removes all obstacles, overcomes all oppositions, and infallibly produceth the effect intended'.[41] There are no necessary preparatory qualifications that the elect must meet before receiving the grace of regeneration. Obedience is no qualifier. Faith is not even a qualifier, because faith does not cause regeneration, but regeneration causes faith (see 1 Jn 5.1). Owen argues that 'in order of nature, our receiving of the Spirit is antecedent to the very seed and principle of faith in us, as the cause is to the effect, seeing it is wrought in us by him alone'.[42] Even 'the act of believing, or faith itself, is expressly said to be of God, to be wrought in us by him, to be given unto us from him'.[43] Regeneration is the implantation of a vital principle of new life by the Spirit. This generates faith. And faith enables and appropriates sanctifying grace.[44]

But in what way does faith stand causally related to sanctification? Owen says that 'faith is the *instrumental cause* of our sanctification; so that where it is not, no holiness can be wrought in us'.[45] He makes his case from the testimony of Scripture. Acts 15.9 says God purifies our hearts by faith. Acts 26.18 speaks of those 'sanctified by faith' in Jesus. Romans 1.5 calls good works 'the obedience

---

[38] Owen, Πνευματολογια (1674), 322; *Works* (1965), 3:367–8.
[39] Owen, Πνευματολογια (1674), 322; *Works* (1965), 3:368.
[40] Owen, Πνευματολογια (1674), 357; *Works* (1965), 3:408.
[41] Owen, Πνευματολογια (1674), 270; *Works* (1965), 3:318.
[42] Owen, Πνευματολογια (1674), 358; *Works* (1965), 3:408.
[43] Owen, Πνευματολογια (1674), 372; *Works* (1965), 3:320.
[44] For more on Owen's theology of regeneration, see Barrett and Haykin, *Owen on the Christian life*, 163–79.
[45] Owen, Πνευματολογια (1674), 362; *Works* (1965), 3:414.

of faith'. And 1 Pet. 1.20-22 links faith in Christ with sanctification by the Spirit. Owen says, 'It is from faith in God through Jesus Christ, acting itself in obedience unto the Gospel, that we purify or cleanse our souls; which is our sanctification.'[46] The Spirit imparts faith and faith becomes active, yielding to God's revealed will. God takes the initiative in this work but faith appropriates, cultivates and works out Gospel holiness.

The real virtue by which faith saves and sanctifies comes from its object. Faith looks to Christ, and laying hold on him, it brings the believer into union with him. The Spirit sanctifies by uniting believers to Christ so that they may receive from the virtue of his saving graces. These graces reside in Christ with all fullness, for in him dwells the Spirit without measure (Jn 3.34). There are two reasons why Christ possesses this fullness, writes Owen. First, he in his 'own divine personal subsistence' as the eternal Son is the 'fulness of the Godhead' (Col. 2.9), fully divine. Second, God has appointed him as the head and mediator of the covenant of grace (Heb. 9.15).[47] Now, God 'communicates nothing that belongs properly to the covenant of grace, as our sanctification and holiness do, unto any, but in and through him. And we receive nothing by him but by virtue of relation unto him, or especial interest in him, or union with him'.[48] Mortification is carried out in union and communion with Christ; it is nothing less than a drawing from his resources. Not the least sin can be resisted apart from him, for without him we can do nothing (Jn 15.5-6).[49] Ferguson comments on Owen's Christ-centred theology of Spirit-empowered sanctification: 'The Spirit takes from the fullness of Christ and brings it to us in order that we may be transformed by his ministry into the likeness of Christ.'[50]

Sometimes believers may be tempted to think that once they believe in Christ for justification, they are left to their own strength to work out their sanctification. While mortification does require our sincere effort, Owen makes it clear that there is no successful mortification apart from having an intimate connection with Christ. After all, Christ is the heart of the Gospel, and sanctification is by the Gospel. Owen observes that 'this whole matter of sanctification and holiness is peculiarly joined with and limited unto the doctrine, truth, and grace of the Gospel; for holiness is nothing but the implanting, writing, and realizing of the Gospel in our souls'.[51] Hence in contrast to a so-called sanctification based on legal principles, Owen spoke of 'evangelical holiness'.[52] Sanctification

---

[46]Owen, Πνευματολογια (1674), 362; Works (1965), 3:414.
[47]Cf. Owen, *The doctrine of the saints perseverance* (1654), 172–3; Works (1965), 11:308–9.
[48]Owen, Πνευματολογια (1674), 363; Works (1965), 3:414.
[49]Owen, Πνευματολογια (1674), 363; Works (1965), 3:414. See Ferguson, *Pastors and teachers*, 252.
[50]Ferguson, *Pastors and teachers*, 252.
[51]Owen, Πνευματολογια (1674), 325; Works (1965), 3:370–1.
[52]See Kapic, 'Evangelical holiness', 97–114.

is the work of the Father, the Son and the Holy Spirit, effected by grace, made operative through a living faith that works by love, enjoyed in union with Christ, resulting in the humbling of sinners and the glory of God.

THE CHRISTIAN'S EMBRACE OF MORTIFICATION

The Christian's duty

The pre-eminence of the Lord's work in sanctification does not diminish the reality that mortification is a brutal fight unto death, Owen insists. In Romans 8:13, there is 'a *duty* prescribed', he observes. 'Mortify the deeds of the body.' The exhortation is addressed to believers, for whom 'there is no condemnation' (Rom. 8.1), signifying that they – not unbelievers – are charged with this task. Though all people should and must mortify sin or else face God's judgement, only believers can do so successfully. The fact that they are believers, already pardoned and purged by the blood of Christ, does not mean that the presence of sin in them has been removed. They are still subject to 'corruption' and 'depravity of nature' that uses the body as a 'seat' and 'instrument', using the corporeal faculties as weapons against God's will in the service of sin (Rom. 6.19). Addressing this, Owen's theology of mortification avoids religious externalism and calls for piety in the inward life of the heart – the thoughts, affections and will. The duty of mortification calls for obedience stemming from internal spirituality and Godward devotion. What needs to be mortified is not just sin in the act but in the root – both the *commission* of sin and *original* sin. 'The deeds of the flesh are to be mortified in their causes, from whence they spring.'[53]

Owen explains that in Rom. 8.13, there is a propositional condition ('if ye') subordinated to the promise of eternal life ('ye shall live'), indicating that mortification is the necessary means of ultimately experiencing the thing promised. To draw this out, he cites Col. 3.5, which presses believers with an imperative stressing their responsibility: 'Mortify therefore your members which are upon the earth.' This exhortation is followed by a list of sins, by way of example, that provoke God's wrath. Owen explains that the persons to whom these words are directed are believers, for they are those who 'were risen with Christ' (v. 1), were 'dead with him' (v. 3) and who 'will appear with him in glory' (v. 4). The fact that the command is issued to believers and that it calls for the killing of sin in their 'members' points to the reality of indwelling sin that needs continual mortification. Even Paul, though 'so incomparably exalted in grace, revelations, enjoyments, privileges, consolations, above the ordinary

---

[53]Owen, *Of the mortification of sinne in believers* (1656), 9; *Works* (1965), 6:8.

measure of believers', was impressed with his need for daily mortification (1 Cor. 9.27). If that is the case with Paul, Owen surmised, how much more must it be with the rest of us. The main proposition of Owen's treatise on *Mortification* is: '*The choicest believers, who are assuredly freed from the condemning power of sin, ought yet to make it their business all their days to mortify the indwelling power of sin.*' For the person in Christ, sin's penalty has been pardoned, but sin's power must be reckoned with and subdued.[54]

Killing indwelling sin

The reason for the necessity of continual mortification is due to the nature, power, deceit and prevalence of indwelling sin in believers – a subject to which Owen devoted an entire treatise in 1668. Paul confessed his own struggle with indwelling sin in Rom. 7.21: 'I find then a law, that, when I would do good, evil is present with me.' Owen understands this particular 'law' to be 'an *operative effective principle*, which seems to have the force of a law'.[55] 'There is an exceeding efficacy and power in the remainders of indwelling sin in believers', he observes, 'with a constant working towards evil'.[56] The influence of indwelling sin is always present, seeking to bend the will towards evil, though the force by which it exerts itself varies according to individual personalities and the circumstances of temptation. Even the best of our good works and holy duties are not free from its pull.

For believers, the rule of sin is broken but the influence of sin does not go away. Because of regeneration, through grace there is now a habitual, constant and ordinary 'prevailing will of doing good, notwithstanding the power and efficacy of indwelling sin to the contrary'.[57] The believer's renewed and sanctified will constantly struggle to overcome the influence of indwelling sin, 'for the flesh lusteth against the Spirit, and the Spirit against the flesh: and these are contrary the one to the other' (Gal. 5.17). J. I. Packer observes that 'regeneration makes man's heart a battlefield, where "the flesh" (the old man) tirelessly disputes the supremacy of "the spirit" (the new man). The Christian cannot gratify the one without interference from the other'.[58] This internal conflict highlights the indispensable duty of devoted and ceaseless mortification. Christopher Wynn comments on the logic of Owen's thinking:

---

[54]Owen, *Of the mortification of sinne in believers* (1656), 6; *Works* (1965), 6:7.
[55]Owen, *Indwelling sin* (1668), 2; *Works* (1965), 6:158.
[56]Owen, *Indwelling sin* (1668), 4; *Works* (1965), 6:159. Italics removed from original.
[57]Owen, *Indwelling sin* (1668), 6; *Works* (1965), 6:160.
[58]Packer, *A quest for godliness*, 197.

'The need for mortification becomes lucid after grappling with the personal reality of indwelling sin.'[59]

Sin is the great defiler, always seeking to steal our peace, kill our communion with God and destroy our life. We must kill sin, or else be killed by it. Owen paraphrases the imperative of Rom. 8.13: 'Do you mortify; do you make it your daily work; be always at it whilst you live; cease not a day from this work; be killing sin or it will be killing you.'[60] He provides six reasons as to why mortification is a daily duty for the believer:

(1) Indwelling sin is always present and never goes away in this world. Some people claim that mortification is unnecessary because they think they have attained a state of sinless perfection, Owen observes. Others deny original sin and, like the Pharisees that Jesus corrects in the Sermon on the Mount, degrade the spirituality of the law by lowering its standard to a level that is attainable by human effort. Owen insists that we have not yet attained or been made perfect (Phil. 3.12), that 'we know in part' (1 Cor. 13.12), and that we have a 'body of death' (Rom. 7.24) 'from whence we are not delivered but by the death of our bodies'. The practical import of this cannot be exaggerated because sin's dominion will go unchallenged or it will win the upper hand if left unchecked.[61]

(2) Sin is always 'acting', so it must always be mortified. The law of sin instigates within us desires that are contrary to the holiness of God. These desires, or lusts, constantly tempt and seek to conceive sin (Jas 1.14). Owen explains that 'in every moral action it is always either inclining to evil, or hindering from that which is good, or disframing the spirit from communion with God'. Of course, at times in the Christian life, sin's influence may not be consciously felt. But sin never calls a truce in this war, and such times of respite should cause us to be all the more alert: 'There is not a day but sin foils or is foiled, prevails or is prevailed on; and it will be so whilst we live in this world.' If the believer presumes all is well and neglects watching against temptation, sin may exert its power in unexpected ways and overtake them. 'There is no safety against it but in a constant warfare.'[62]

(3) If it is not mortified, sin's influence will increase and cause one to commit scandalous sins. Sin is parasitic – it feeds on our lifeblood and

---

[59] Wynn, *The essential psychology and theological foundations for John Owen's doctrine of mortification*, 69.
[60] Owen, *Of the mortification of sinne in believers* (1656), 14; *Works* (1965), 6:9–10.
[61] Owen, *Of the mortification of sinne in believers* (1656), 17; *Works* (1965), 6:10–11.
[62] Owen, *Of the mortification of sin in believers* (1668), third edition, 15; *Works* (1965), 6:11.

nourishes itself by depriving us of spiritual strength.[63] So-called little sins need to be mortified with just as much diligence as scandalous ones, or they may turn into scandalous ones. Owen explains that

> sin aims always at the utmost; every time it rises up to tempt or entice, might it have its own course, it would go out to the utmost sin in that kind. Every unclean thought or glance would be adultery if it could; every covetous desire would be oppression, every thought of unbelief would be atheism, might it grow to its head.

Sin deceives and hardens people by degrees (Heb. 3.13). No ground can be given to it that will not result in a corresponding degree of deception and hardening. It gains ground little by little, offering a 'little' incentive with a 'little' temptation. Believers may try to compromise with sin and indulge in it 'just a little', but in doing so they are relinquishing ground to their enemy so he can win that territory and gain more strength.[64] Mortification 'every hour' is the only means to resist the encroachment of sin's power on our hearts.[65]

(4) God gives us the Spirit to empower us to mortify sin. In Romans 7.23 Paul speaks of 'the law of my mind', received in regeneration, which opposes 'the law of sin' (cf. Jer. 31.33). Galatians 5:17 teaches that the Spirit exerts his will in us to produce holy affections in us that oppose the desires of the flesh. Owen argues that 'there is a propensity in the Spirit, or spiritual new nature, to be acting against the flesh, as well as in the flesh to be acting against the Spirit'. He admonishes his readers: 'The contest is for our lives and souls. Not to be daily employing the Spirit and new nature for the mortifying of sin is to neglect that excellent succour which God hath given us against our greatest enemy.'[66]

(5) Negligence in mortification will cause grace to wither and decay rather than being renewed and increasing in strength. Paul said his inward man was 'being renewed day by day' (2 Cor. 4.16). Like bodily exercise, mortification is a spiritual exercise that increases our strength in the fight against sin. '*Exercise* and *success* are the two main cherishers of grace in the heart; when it is suffered to lie still, it withers and decays.'[67] Spiritual sloth will only yield weakness and defeat.

---

[63]Plantinga, *Not the way it's supposed to be*, 89–90.
[64]Owen, *Of the mortification of sinne in believers* (1656), 20; *Works* (1965), 6:12.
[65]Owen, *Of the mortification of sinne in believers* (1656), 20; *Works* (1965), 6:12.
[66]Owen, *Of the mortification of sinne in believers* (1656), 21–2; *Works* (1965), 6:12–13.
[67]Owen, *Of the mortification of sinne in believers* (1656), 23; *Works* (1965), 6:13.

(6) It is the Christian's duty to grow in grace every day (2 Pet. 3.18). We must be 'perfecting holiness in the fear of God' (2 Cor. 7.1). Sin is opposed to every act and degree of holiness in us, so putting it to death is essential for thriving in spiritual growth. Owen writes: 'Let not that man think he makes any progress in holiness who walks not over the bellies of his lusts. He who doth not kill sin in his way takes no steps towards his journey's end.' Whether or not one is killing sin is an important indicator of the state of their soul. He warns that 'he who finds not opposition from it, and who sets not himself in every particular to its mortification, is at peace with it, not dying to it'.[68] And to be at peace with sin is to be at enmity with God.

The benefits of mortification and the dangers of unmortified sin

The assurance and joy of salvation depend on the believer's success and progress in this task. The vitality and health of our spiritual life are also contingent on our faithfulness in mortifying sin. Owen writes, *'the life, vigour, and comfort of our spiritual life depend much on our mortification of sin'*.[69] Contrary to the claims of the theologians at the Council of Trent, who taught that assurance is only possible by special revelation, and that to a handful of saints, Owen believed assurance and comfort should be pursued expectantly by the use of means. As Chad Van Dixhoorn notes, 'We must remind people that this assurance can be had without some "extraordinary revelation." We are only to rely on the Spirit, and show diligence in the pursuit of an assurance of salvation by a "right use of ordinary means" – means which God himself has established for the strengthening of our faith (Heb. 6.11, 12).'[70] Owen realizes that some, like Heman in Psalm 88, faithfully practise mortification and walk with God all their lives without enjoying any sweet comfort. So he clarifies that mortification does not necessarily bring about joy and assurance. Assurance is, after all, a benefit of adoption, not a necessary, immediate, automatic consequence of mortification. God is sovereign in granting and withholding his blessings. But he ordinarily grants the blessings of assurance and joy based on principles and patterns pertaining to the proper use of the means he has chosen to bless. For, as Owen puts it, 'The *use of means* for the obtaining of peace is ours; the *bestowing* of it is God's prerogative.'[71]

---

[68] Owen, *Of the mortification of sinne in believers* (1656), 25; *Works* (1965), 6:14.
[69] Owen, *Of the mortification of sinne in believers* (1656), 42; *Works* (1965), 6:21.
[70] Van Dixhoorn, *Confessing the faith*, 230.
[71] Owen, *Of the mortification of sinne in believers* (1656), 44; *Works* (1965), 6:21.

Mortification also results in spiritual flourishing. Owen compares the believer's heart to a garden. If choice plants are sown but not tended to, weeds will grow around them and sap the life and vigour out of them. The plants may survive but they cannot thrive. They will wither, bear little fruit and sometimes cannot even be spotted in the midst of the brush. Those who are slack in mortification are 'like the sluggard's field – so overgrown with weeds that you can scarce see the good corn'. It is difficult to see such plants among the weeds, to discern the fruit of salvation. Through neglect of rooting out the sins that suck the joy and strength out of their hearts, the souls of such people are withering and 'ready to die' (Rev. 3.2). On the other hand, mortification 'prunes all the graces of God, and makes room for them in our hearts to grow'. Diligence in it ordinarily yields great harvests of fruitfulness.[72]

To spur on his readers, Owen also specifies some of the dangers of unmortified sin. 'Every unmortified sin will certainly do two things', he writes. First, it 'weakens the soul, and deprives it of its strength'. Like an untuned musical instrument that cannot play a pleasant sound, unmortified sin untunes the heart from 'vigorous communion with God'. It entangles the affections and draws them out after carnal pleasures. It fills the imagination with thoughts about sin, defiling the mind, so that it is not filled with glorious thoughts about God. It hinders all duty and makes Christians weak in their service. Second, unmortified sin darkens the soul, and deprives it of comfort and peace. 'As sin *weakens*', Owen notes, 'so it *darkens* the soul. It is a cloud, a thick cloud, that spreads itself over the face of the soul, and intercepts all the beams of God's love and favour. It takes away all sense of the privilege of our adoption; and if the soul begins to gather up thoughts of consolation, sin quickly scatters them'.[73]

The meaning of mortification: What it is and is not

In *Mortification*, Owen's pastoral heart comes to the fore. He is concerned for the true believer who finds himself struggling with 'a powerful indwelling sin, leading him captive to the law of it, consuming his heart with trouble, perplexing his thoughts, weakening his soul as to duties of communion with God, disquieting him as to peace, and perhaps defiling his conscience, and exposing him to hardening through the deceitfulness of sin'.[74] How can such a one prevail in mortifying such sins? Owen proceeds to describe what mortification is before providing rules and directions for engaging in it.

---

[72]Owen, *Of the mortification of sinne in believers* (1656), 49–50; *Works* (1965), 6:23.
[73]Owen, *Of the mortification of sinne in believers* (1656), 47–8; *Works* (1965), 6:23.
[74]Owen, *Of the mortification of sinne in believers* (1656), 51; *Works* (1965), 6:24.

A mistaken understanding about mortification may lead believers to have false hopes or expectations. This would set them up for disappointment and failure. So Owen gives clarity by describing what mortification is not in five particulars. Philip Craig summarizes them:

> First, it is not the total destruction of the sin nature, for that will not occur until glorification. Secondly, neither does it consist in mere legal (or moral) reformation. . . . Thirdly, improvement of one's natural temperament does not qualify. Fourthly, exchanging one type of sin for another, as when an old man pursues wealth rather than youthful lusts, does not count as mortification. Finally, mortification does not consist in occasional victories over sin, especially when motivated by a dreadful bout of sin or pressing affliction.[75]

Some of these things may appear to be mortification, but they fall short. If counterfeits are mistakenly considered to be true mortification, they may convey false peace to the conscience. Such can cause believers' estimation of their spiritual condition to be much more favourable than it actually is, resulting in a soul-damning mistake.

What, then, is mortification? It consists of three elements, and all three will be present in all true mortification of sin: (1) the habitual weakening of sinful desires, (2) 'constant *fighting* and *contending* against sin' and (3) 'frequent success' against the lusts of the flesh when sinful impulses tempt us to yield to them. To mortify sin is to crucify the flesh with its affections and lusts (Gal. 5.24). The motions and temptations of particular indwelling sins can be strong. Mortifying them at the first will be difficult, but they can be progressively weakened as one grows in spiritual strength. The focus of our efforts to battle sin should not be primarily on the external expressions and fruits of it but on the internal workings and root of it.[76]

As sins are put to death, positive graces and virtues that supplant and replace our sinful tendencies should be studied out, sought, prayed for and pursued. We must 'cease to do evil' and 'learn to do well' (Isa. 1.16-17). We mortify pride by seeking humility, sexual impurity by occupying our minds with pure thoughts, and worldliness by meditating on heaven. As we die to sin, we are being renewed in God's image in Christ by the Spirit (Col. 3.5, 9-10).[77] Packer explains that, for Owen, as for other Puritan theologians, 'sanctification has a double aspect. Its positive side is vivification, the growing and maturing of the new man; its

---

[75]Craig, *The bond of grace and duty*, 188.
[76]Owen, *Of the mortification of sinne in believers* (1656), 61–73; *Works* (1965), 6:28–32.
[77]Owen, *Of the mortification of sinne in believers* (1656), 70–3; *Works* (1965), 6:32–3.

negative side is mortification, the weakening and killing of the old man'.[78] Any progress in mortification will always be accompanied and empowered by the renovative process of vivification. Calvin describes vivification as 'the desire to live in a holy and devoted manner, a desire arising from rebirth; as if it were said that man dies to himself that he may begin to live to God'.[79] Owen argues that vivification is by the habitual residence, cherishing, cultivation and growth of the principle of grace implanted in the children of God in their regeneration, a principle that is opposed to sin and is destructive to it.[80] We die to the flesh as Christ's resurrection power is realized in us, fashioning us into his image (2 Cor. 3.18).

So much for what mortification is and is not. The ultimate question, however, is not so much in terms and definitions, but in practice. How can the believer effectively mortify sin?

The fight of faith: Practical directives for mortification

Owen's take on mortification and sanctification reveals his penetrating knowledge of human nature and psychology. Thoroughly conversant with his own heart, his knowledge of God was accompanied by knowledge of human nature. Applying his Reformed experiential theology to the fight of faith, Owen offers wise counsel and practical directives for the believer engaged in the practice of mortification.

Diagnosing the symptoms: Discerning sin appropriately

When a professing believer battles with indwelling sin, Owen argues, the precise dynamic of an unmortified lust's temptations and manifestations ('motions') speaks to one's spiritual condition. Like a person with a festering wound, if deeply ingrained sins receive only superficial treatment, the infection may grow worse: 'Old neglected wounds are often mortal, always dangerous.'[81] So Owen operates like a wise master physician. Al Martin writes that Owen seeks 'to consider what symptoms accompany sin, and if it is of a deadly sort, what extraordinary remedies are to be used'.[82] He diagnoses the precise nature of the disease in order to prescribe the right method of treatment. Discerning carefully between the marks of a true work of grace and its counterfeits, he warns about sin's guilt, power and consequences. At the same time, he gives

---

[78]Packer, *A quest for Godliness*, 199.
[79]Calvin, *Institutes*, 3.3.5.
[80]Owen, *Of the mortification of sinne in believers* (1656), 72; *Works* (1965), 6:32.
[81]Owen, *Of the mortification of sinne in believers* (1656), 106; *Works* (1965), 6:44.
[82]Martin, 'Means of mortification', 98.

practical counsel on how to deal with sin in a manner that is both thorough and effective.

When dealing with a particularly strong inclination to sin ('indwelling lust'), one should examine the nature of the sin problem by observing the 'marks' and 'symptoms' that accompany it. While each and every sin is deserving of God's wrath and curse, some sinful practices can indicate that their practitioners are not merely struggling to subdue sin but are under its damnable dominion. So they should consider whether it is potentially a soul-destroying sin. The attempt to mortify this sin should be tailored to the precise nature of the problem. Indwelling sins and temptations that have 'deadly' characteristics about them require 'extraordinary' means to be used to conquer them.[83] Owen, in keeping with common Puritan emphases in theology, is concerned about the necessity of true conversion, the importance of a well-grounded assurance of faith, the dangers of carnal presumption and the prevalence of precarious professions of faith. Hence he breaks down a list of dangerous symptoms that his readers can use in sober self-examination.

Owen identifies six warning signs of deadly sin. The first is 'inveterateness', or the firm establishment of sinful behaviour as a habit by long persistence. David wrote, 'My wounds stink and are corrupt because of my foolishness' (Ps. 38.5). 'When a lust hath lain long in the heart, corrupting, festering, cankering, it brings the soul to a woful condition.'[84] The longer such sins fester, the worse they become. Second, if sin is accompanied by self-deception and false peace, one's condition is dangerous. To show mercy to unmortified sin rather than fighting it, or to countenance the sin by speaking peace to it, is to pervert the grace of God. Third, indwelling sin may have frequent success in tempting a person to yield to it. Even if one does not give outward expression to the sin, if his or her heart delights in it and the will consents to it secretly, the sin is prevailing. Fourth, greater concern for the punishment of sin than for the evil of sin itself is a dangerous sign. When tempted, what most restrains us from committing the sin? Is it only the consequences sin brings, such as shame before men, or eternal hell? Or is it because we treasure Christ, abhor evil and cherish our communion with God?[85] Fifth, when sin's temptations are strong and persistent, causing one to yield repeatedly due to personal weakness, it may be a sign of God's judgement. God may judicially hand over a person to temptation to afflict and humble them. He may permit one sin to disturb the conscience and afflict a person in chastisement in order to humble them for

---

[83]Owen, *Of the mortification of sinne in believers* (1656), 104; *Works* (1965), 6:43.
[84]Owen, *Of the mortification of sinne in believers* (1656), 104–5; *Works* (1965), 6:43–4.
[85]Owen, *Of the mortification of sinne in believers* (1656), 111–14; *Works* (1965), 6:47–8.

other sins.[86] Sixth, when one's sin has been confronted by the Lord numerous times, but has not been met with repentance, it is a dangerous symptom. A person may repeatedly suffer afflictions or experience divine desertion; or they may be repeatedly convicted by the power of the Spirit through the Word. But if none of these divine means for awakening people to the danger of sin prevails, their condition is perilous.[87]

Owen cautions that countenancing sin will rob our assurance because the true believer does not practise sin (1 Jn 3.9). If a person continues in sin with obstinance, how can they tell whether they are a true believer struggling with an 'unmortified lust' or unregenerate and held captive under the 'dominion of sin'?[88] In the case of persistent and prevailing sin, there may be no sure way to tell – the only safe course to secure assurance is to kill the sin.[89]

Owen insists that we must have right beliefs and proper affections towards sin. Of indispensable importance is to recognize how dangerous temptation can be. Owen counsels believers to 'get a clear and abiding sense upon thy mind and conscience of the guilt, danger, and evil of that sin wherewith thou art perplexed'.[90] People like to downplay their guilt through corrupt reasoning. But we must recognize that sin can harden the heart, sear the conscience, dull the affections, rob us of peace, deplete us of spiritual strength, grieve the Spirit, wound the heart of Christ, hinder our usefulness and subject us to divine judgement. John Hanna contends that 'the place to begin the mortification of a particular sin is for the believer to recognize sin for all its terrible potential, meditate on its destructive power, and load the conscience with the heavy weight of its guilt'.[91] This is not a popular message today, any more than it was likely to be a popular message among Owen's addressees, but the recognition of these truths will help foster a genuine abhorrence of sin as sin and instil in our hearts a healthy fear of God.[92]

In *A discourse on the great duty of mortification* (1701), Ezekiel Hopkins (1633–90) reiterates much of Owen's teaching. It makes for excellent supplemental reading alongside Owen's treatise. Hopkins warns of the propensity individuals have to downplay the gravity of sin: 'Take heed, lest through any deceitfulness of thy heart, thou excuse and lessen thy sin, when thou shouldst be dealing against it by a vigorous mortification.'[93] To treat sin

---

[86]Owen, *Of the mortification of sinne in believers* (1656), 114–15; Works (1965), 6:48.
[87]Owen, *Of the mortification of sinne in believers* (1656), 115–17; Works (1965), 6:48–9.
[88]Owen, *Of the mortification of sinne in believers* (1656), 105; Works (1965), 6:44.
[89]Owen, *Of the mortification of sinne in believers* (1656), 103–14; Works (1965), 6:43–7.
[90]Owen, *Of the mortification of sinne in believers* (1656), 120; Works (1965), 6:50. Italics removed from original.
[91]Hanna, 'John Owen and the "normal" Christian life', 17.
[92]Owen, *Of the mortification of sinne in believers* (1656), 135; Works (1965), 6:56.
[93]Hopkins, *A discourse on the great duty of mortification* (1701), 126; Works, 3:547.

lightly is a deception of the devil that may damn the soul or at least hinder a rigorous pursuit of mortification. 'It is the common method of Satan', writes Hopkins, 'in the height and fury of a temptation, to persuade the heart, either that it is no sin, or else a small and venial one. If this deceit prevail and take place, the work of mortification can never go on vigorously'.[94] Hopkins advises that individuals face the heinousness of sin, the reality of God's determination to punish it, and that they arm themselves with firm resolutions to oppose it using the law and the Gospel.[95]

Owen advises believers to be aware of the constitutional advantages that sin seeks to exploit. 'Consider whether the distemper with which thou art perplexed be not rooted in thy nature, and cherished, fomented, and heightened from thy *constitution*. A proneness to some sins may doubtless lie in the natural temper and disposition of men.'[96] By 'constitution', Owen refers to a person's makeup, personality, temperament, psychology and particular manner of thinking and feeling and being. Because of each person's unique differences, each one may be tempted in different ways with particular temptations that prey on weaknesses associated with their constitution. Such sins may seem natural, but they are only 'natural' in the sense that they correspond to fallen human nature, corrupted by the inherent moral depravity of indwelling sin.

In his treatise *Of temptation* (1658), Owen deals with this topic more extensively. He explains that 'men may have peculiar lusts or corruptions, which, either by their natural constitution or education, and other prejudices, have got deep rooting and strength in them'.[97] He offers some wise pastoral counsel about this. Not least of all, it necessitates serious self-examination – what Griffiths calls 'a self-critical mode of thinking'.[98] Owen counsels believers to 'labour to know thine own frame and temper; what spirit thou art of; what associates in thy heart Satan hath; where corruption is strong, where grace is weak; what stronghold lust hath in thy natural constitution, and the like'.[99] We must search and study our own hearts. As we do so, we should be as objective and impartial as possible. We must discern our sins clearly in spite of their propensity to hide from our mind's eye. And we must call out our sin for what it is rather than winking at it or giving it flattering names and titles. This takes time and effort. It requires humiliation, earnest prayer, the Spirit's presence and the searchlight of the Word. Owen's advice really follows Calvin's reasoning:

---

[94]Hopkins, *A discourse on the great duty of mortification* (1701), 127; *Works*, 3:547.
[95]Hopkins, *A discourse on the great duty of mortification* (1701), 127–30; *Works*, 3:548–51. Cf. Owen, *Of the mortification of sinne in believers* (1656), 136–9; *Works* (1965), 6:56–8.
[96]Owen, *Of the mortification of sinne in believers* (1656), 144; *Works* (1965), 6:60.
[97]Owen, *Of temptation* (1658), 126; *Works* (1965), 6:132.
[98]Griffiths, *Redeem the time*, 74.
[99]Owen, *Of temptation* (1658), 127; *Works* (1965), 6:132.

we can grow in the knowledge of God only as we grow in the knowledge of ourselves.[100] Because men are strangers to themselves, they do not recognize the nature and extent of indwelling sin.[101]

People are prone to give in to their weaknesses and excuse their negligence in these areas. But Owen cautions that the fact that a sin is facilitated by one's constitution does not lessen its guilt. The realization that it is so deeply ingrained in us should cause more, not less, alarm. He admonishes that since such besetting sins easily gain advantage there is a need for extraordinary watchfulness concerning them. There is also need for an increased effort of a more holistic nature. Observing this theme in Owen's writing, Daniel Wray notes that 'watchfulness is a major task which overlaps into every area of Christian experience'.[102] Owen says the only way to effectively deal with constitutional moral infirmities is what Paul describes concerning his own practice in 1 Cor. 9.17: 'I keep under my body, and bring it into subjection.' This is done by living in the purposeful cross-bearing of evangelical self-denial, in constant watching, through fasting and prayer, and by diligence in forcing one's entire constitution – body, mind and soul, with the thoughts, feelings, passions and affections – into submission to God's will. By taking circumspect dominion over our entire constitution, we yield ourselves to God and present our entire physiology and psychology as instruments of righteousness (Rom. 6.13).

Sin can also pry open the door into our lives through situational advantages. Owen writes, 'Consider what *occasions*, what *advantages* thy distemper hath taken to exert and put forth itself, and watch against them all.'[103] The Lord Jesus spoke of this when he commanded his disciples to 'watch' (Mk 13.37). They were to keep themselves from becoming ensnared by temptation when occasional circumstances would accentuate the appeal of sin. We must avoid sin and its ordinary occasions, including the attendant circumstances that may be an overture for a temptation that could strategically exploit our natural weaknesses. Sin calls for the violent hacking off of hands and the plucking out of eyes (see Mk 9.43-47), not for toying around with it or pandering to its company. 'Know that he that dares to dally with occasions of sin will dare to sin', says Owen.[104]

---

[100] Calvin, *Institutes*, 1.1.1. Owen elsewhere develops Calvin's teaching on knowing God and ourselves. He states, 'The sum of all true wisdom and knowledge may be reduced to these three heads: – I. The knowledge of God, his nature and his properties. II. The knowledge of ourselves in reference to the will of God concerning us. III. Skill to walk in communion, with God.' Owen, *Of communion with God* (1657); *Works* (1965), 2:80.
[101] Owen, *Of temptation* (1658), 127; *Works* (1965), 6:132.
[102] Wray, 'Spiritual man in the teachings of John Owen', 13.
[103] Owen, *Of the mortification of sinne in believers* (1656), 149; *Works* (1965), 6:61.
[104] Owen, *Of the mortification of sinne in believers* (1656), 150; *Works* (1965), 6:62.

The disease of indwelling sin is pervasive in human nature. Much care must be taken in ascertaining the signs and symptoms of this disease. Thorough examination is necessary, and regular checkups are crucial for good spiritual health. Compromises that would weaken our immunity to it should be avoided. How, though, does 'Dr. Owen' treat this disease once its true nature and extent have been diagnosed?

Dealing with the disease: Mortifying sin effectively

To have any degree of health, one must first be alive. One of the truths that Owen lays great stress on is the need for a person to be a true believer in Christ for effective mortification to take place. Believers are spiritually alive even though sin is at work within them. But unbelievers are spiritually dead, which means they are unwilling and unable to take any steps towards personal holiness. Without Christ's justifying righteousness, mortification would be but a 'glorious sin'. Or, as Thomas Brooks (1608–80) put it, 'Till men have faith in Christ, their best services are but glorious sins.'[105] And without the power of Christ's Spirit, we would all be helpless before sin's foreboding power. The remedy for sin and the key to mortifying it successfully are found, not in some secret formula, not in esoteric attainments, and not in extra-biblical rites and ceremonies, but in Christ and his Gospel. Adherents of false religion cannot truly mortify indwelling sin; they can only suppress its external manifestations. 'The truth' of the biblical Gospel is needful for spiritual sanctification to occur (Jn 17.17). Owen's prescription for indwelling sin is not something in addition to the Gospel, as if he intended to supplement it. The Gospel does not need supplementation; it is already complete. We must plug into the resources that are already there. Christ is all, and he is sufficient, for the believer is complete in him (Col. 2.10). Since mortification is caused by the Gospel, it is done by believing, repenting and appropriating the resources of grace that are already inherent in the Gospel.

Yet Owen would avoid a simplistic approach that would say 'just let go and let God', or 'have more faith'. He knew that overcoming temptation was not as simple as just wishing sin to go away by thinking beautiful thoughts about streets of gold. Effective mortification is like strategic warfare. The battle is unto death. The Christian's foe is mighty and astute. And in the case of indwelling sin, Owen reminded his readers, 'Your enemy is not only *upon* you, as on Samson of old, but is *in* you also.'[106] Some of Owen's principles and directives are particularly helpful in this regard, especially the ones found in the

---

[105] Brooks, *Works*, 1:148.
[106] Owen, *Indwelling sin* (1668), 11; *Works* (1965), 6:162.

latter half of his *Mortification*. What follows is a summary of some of the ones not already mentioned with some reflection.

(1) Meditate much on the greatness and glory of God. Owen encourages his readers to 'keep thy heart in continual awe of the majesty of God'.[107] God is excellent and full of majesty but our distance from him is inconceivably infinite. Thoughts of this should fill us with a sense of our own vileness, producing self-abasement and humility before his presence. This is what happened in the case of Job. After he summarized the amazing works of God, he exclaimed, 'Lo, these are parts of his ways: but how little a portion is heard of him? But the thunder of his power who can understand?' (Job 26.14). Further revelations of the divine glory would unveil the loftiness of God's infinite majesty and abase Job to the point of recognizing, lamenting and opposing his remaining sin (see Job 42.5-6).

The Christian should meditate on the being and glory of God, his works and especially his attributes. David Saxton published a summary of Puritan teaching on meditation in which he observed that 'the majority of Puritan instruction about meditating on God directed the believer to dwell upon God's specific perfections, characteristics, or attributes'.[108] This is important advice because sin can look formidable when we are facing it, like an indomitable giant that no-one can slay. But the size and power of sin dwindles in comparison to the grandness and power of the God who triumphs in the face of impossibility. The believer struggling with unbelief in the face of temptation, who wonders if it is even possible to overcome it, can find strength by thinking on the One who drowned Egypt's legions in the Red Sea and busted the jaws of death through a bloody cross. His holiness exposes our depravity, his justice rebukes our corruptions, his immensity shows our tininess, his faithfulness offers us hope and his compassion gives us relief. Even God's incommunicable attributes – such as his incomprehensibility, simplicity, omnipotence and eternity – are spiritually profitable subjects for meditation. They remind us that our struggles are not the ultimate reality; in fact, our 'reality' (i.e. the perception of our own experience and our evaluation of it) is very small compared to the ultimate reality of who God is. When we battle with sin, it is too easy to become consumed with ourselves; with our struggles, our temptations our difficulties. When this happens, we

---

[107]Owen, *Of the mortification of sinne in believers* (1656), 155; *Works* (1965), 6:64.
[108]Saxton, *God's battle plan for the mind*, 84.

must look up and gaze on the glory of God and allow his greatness to enrapture our souls with a sanctified sense of awe. Owen asks the rhetorical question, 'Will not a due apprehension of this inconceivable greatness of God, and that infinite distance wherein we stand from him, fill the soul with a holy and awful fear of him, so as to keep it in a frame unsuited to the thriving or flourishing of any lust whatever?'[109]

(2) Resolve to pursue and practise universal repentance. 'Universal' obedience is comprehensive in scope and embraces one's entire humanity and entire lifestyle with God's entire, revealed will. It is opposed to selective obedience, which is to obey in some things but not in others. The apostle called for universal obedience in 2 Cor. 7.1 when he wrote, 'Let us cleanse ourselves from all filthiness of the flesh and spirit, perfecting holiness in the fear of God.' That word, 'all', is all-embracing. It means every single stain of sin, every hint of pollution, every moral imperfection.

Owen explains that the believer's determination to overcome all sin (in general) is necessary for God's blessing to be upon their endeavours to overcome any sin (in particular): 'Without sincerity and diligence in a universality of obedience, there is no mortification of any one perplexing lust to be obtained.'[110] Otherwise, mortification would be pursued by wrong motives and selfish incentives that do not honour God. The sincerity of one's devotion is tried by the scope of their resolved obedience. True mortification must be carried out through true repentance, which cannot but be universal in scope.[111]

(3) Rise mightily against sin's first actings. As soon as temptation can be perceived, it must be violently opposed. Preemptive mortification is preferable to perilous procrastination. James 1.14-15 speaks of the progression of temptation from the incitement of evil desire to the manifestation of full-blown acts of sin: 'But every man is tempted, when he is drawn away of his own lust, and enticed. Then when lust hath conceived, it bringeth forth sin: and sin, when it is finished, bringeth forth death.' Owen says that James' point is that we would catch sin's influences where they first appear and deal with them before they gain the strength to occasion scandalous falls. If temptation has its way and sin breaks out, it will be much more difficult to check its course than it would have been to deal with the initial influences

---

[109]Owen, *Of the mortification of sin in believers* (1668), third edition, 143; *Works* (1965), 6:70.
[110]Owen, *Of the mortification of sinne in believers* (1656), 95; *Works* (1965), 6:40. Italics removed from original.
[111]Owen, *Of the mortification of sinne in believers* (1656), 95–103; *Works* (1965), 6:40–3.

of it in the first place. Again, Hopkins echoes Owen on this point. 'Another direction is this', he observes: 'resist strongly the first motions and first risings of thy corruptions. Crush them while they are in their infancy, before they get to a head, and gather strength against thee.'[112]

Part of the reason for getting to the bottom of sin's first conceptions is to get at the root of the sin itself, in order to target its mortification by identifying it clearly, rather than focusing one's efforts on related sins that are not as central to the problem. As Jonathan Edwards wrote in his *Resolutions*:

> Resolved, whenever I do any conspicuously evil action, to trace it back, till I come to the original cause; and then both carefully endeavor to do so no more, and to fight and pray with all my might against the original of it.[113]

Commenting on this passage, Steve Lawson observes that Edwards 'committed himself to battling the corruptions he discovered in his life. He was on an unending mission to put his sin to death'.[114] Hopkins, Edwards and Owen were resolved in their determination to trace out the workings of sin in their hearts so they could identify, mark out, strategically study and hone in on their indwelling sin with strategic, deliberate assaults and Scriptural truths. Following the proverb, they sought to wage war with strategic effectiveness by applying wise counsel to the battle against sin (Prov. 24.6).

(4) Believe with active faith in Christ crucified. Mortification, carried on in the right manner according to the right principles, has God's promise that it is a labour that will not be in vain. The Saviour who frees his people from the penalty of their sins also frees them from the power and stain of sin (Mt. 1.21). Everything else Owen has taught is preparatory or supplementary to this point. The proper activity of mortification is effected by faith in Christ. Owen encourages believers to 'set faith at work on Christ for the *killing* of thy sin. His blood is the great sovereign remedy for sin-sick souls. Live in this, and thou wilt die a conqueror; yea, thou wilt, through the good providence of God, live to see thy lust dead at thy feet.'[115]

---

[112]Hopkins, *A discourse on the great duty of mortification* (1701), 134; *Works*, 3:551.
[113]Edwards, 'Resolutions', in *Letters and personal writings*, 754–5.
[114]Lawson, *The unwavering resolve of Jonathan Edwards*, 86.
[115]Owen, *Of the mortification of sinne in believers* (1656), 198; *Works* (1965), 6:79.

This is done by trusting in Christ's provision and raising one's heart in expectation to receive from Christ's fullness. He is a compassionate High Priest who is full of tender mercies and is most willing to help (Heb. 4.15-16). Temptation may seem overwhelming at times; so much so that the believer can feel helpless before its power. But he must resolve to look to Christ and say to himself, 'Behold, the Lord Christ, that hath all fulness of grace in his heart, all fulness of power in his hand, he is able to slay all these his enemies. There is sufficient provision in him for my relief and assistance. He can take my drooping, dying soul and make me more than a conqueror.'[116] The needs occasioned by our sin will never exhaust the fullness of the mediator's gracious supply.

Owen encourages believers to look to Christ with faith that studies, understands, assents, trusts and appropriates his provision for the killing of our sin. This kind of faith will be actively engaged in seeking Christ through his appointed means of grace. These means, such as Bible reading, Scriptural meditation, the sacrament of the Lord's Supper and prayer, are vehicles through which Christ communicates himself to believers in the fullness of his grace. They provide a point of contact which enables a reciprocal bond of fellowship between the spiritual presence of Christ and his people. Through this spiritual communion, Christ provides real grace to helpless believers who wait eagerly for his mercy.[117] No one who has trusted in him has ever perished 'by the power of any lust, sin, or corruption'.[118] Christ will never disappoint or turn away those who seek him. He stands ready and eager to meet with us through God's appointed means.

CONCLUSION

Owen's Reformed, Christ-centred soteriology undergirds his theology of mortification and ensures that it is viewed from the perspective of God the Spirit's gracious work to free his people from the power of inbred sin. It stands in stark contrast to legalistic approaches to dealing with sin as well as approaches that whitewash sin's seriousness. Legalism and antinomianism are avoided by setting forth Christ in all of his holiness and in all of the sufficiency of his saving grace. The spiritual duty of mortification is not a work by which a sinner becomes his or her own saviour in part; it is a grace-empowered duty by which Christ through the Spirit exerts his redeeming power to actually subdue the power of sin in the hearts of God's people. The sufficiency of Christ's

---

[116]Owen, *Of the mortification of sinne in believers* (1656), 200; *Works* (1965), 6:79–80.
[117]Owen, *Of the mortification of sinne in believers* (1656), 198–203; *Works* (1965), 6:79–81.
[118]Owen, *Of the mortification of sinne in believers* (1656), 208; *Works* (1965), 6:82.

sacrifice ensures the certainty of Gospel mortification's ongoing progress and ultimate eschatological success. This assurance bolsters the believer's faith and hope in the midst of present duty (see 1 Jn 3.4). We fight our sin in hope, not to turn the tide to gain victory in spite of current defeat but to work out the victory already accomplished, because it is the fruition of Christ's once-for-all triumph.

Though often overlooked, a valuable contribution Owen makes to this subject is with respect to the relationship between sanctification and assurance. True Christians love God, hate sin and pursue holiness. But what does that look like, practically speaking? Truths like this are easier to affirm than they are to apply to the complexities of real-life situations. Owen helps us to bridge the gap from theological theory to experiential application. He explains what the pursuit of holiness looks like in the life of the believer as that pursuit brings the presence of indwelling sin into its scope. He describes how one's involvement or negligence in mortification speaks to their spiritual condition. Or, as Sinclair Ferguson put it,

> Owen once wrote that in a sense there are only two basic issues with which a minister of the Gospel has to deal. The first presents an evangelistic challenge: persuading those who are under the dominion of sin that this is the truth about them. The other? It is the pastoral challenge: persuading those who are no longer under sin's dominion that this is who they really are.[119]

Owen's counsel exemplifies how we may navigate these issues with pastoral wisdom and care. Those who serve in the church as counsellors to those struggling with sinful habits could glean lots of practical wisdom from a careful study of Owen.[120]

Finally, Owen would not want us to walk away without asking if his teaching finds a practical 'amen' in our own lives. Are we earnestly pursuing the 'holiness, without which no man shall see the Lord' (Heb. 1.:14)? We must not spare any choice lust but strike at every single one until all sin is effectively subdued in this lifelong battle. The duty of Gospel mortification calls us to be diligent, thorough and unrelenting in this task. With all our spiritual poverty, we cannot afford to be idle even for a second.

---

[119]Ferguson, *Devoted to God*, 91.
[120]See Deckard, *Helpful truth in past places*, 73–97; Martin, 'Practical helps to mortification of sin'.

CHAPTER 15

Exercitations on the epistle to the Hebrews (1668)

JOHN W. TWEEDDALE

John Owen viewed the world through the lens of the Bible. Commenting on the formative role that Scripture played in seventeenth-century England, the historian Christopher Hill quipped that 'the Bible was central to the whole of the life of the society: we ignore it at our peril'.[1] Hill's maxim is certainly true for Owen. Knowing how he viewed the Bible is essential for assessing his place in history. Like other Reformed theologians, Owen believed that the principle of *sola Scriptura* governed doctrinal formulations and practical reflections in the Christian faith. Seen from this vantage point, his entire literary corpus represents an extended application of the post-Reformation formula that Scripture is the cognitive foundation of theology.[2] But what is often overlooked is that approximately one-fourth of Owen's over eight-million-word canon is devoted to the analysis of the New Testament epistle to the Hebrews. As John Coffey observes, Owen's 'gargantuan' two-million-word commentary on Hebrews is 'twice as long as the Bible itself'.[3] The sheer size of the work suggests that Owen may have had more in mind when writing it than simply recording his thoughts on a single book of the Bible. The importance of Owen's

---

[1] Hill, *The English Bible and the seventeenth-century revolution*, 4.
[2] Muller, *Post-Reformation Reformed dogmatics*, 2:151–223; Tweeddale, *John Owen and Hebrews*, 37, 62.
[3] Coffey, 'The Bible and theology', 381.

commentary, therefore, goes beyond his exegesis of Hebrews. Over the course of his life, the writing of this commentary was integral to his entire theological enterprise.

As this chapter will argue, Owen's first volume on Hebrews is important not only for setting the trajectory of his overall commentary and introducing the main themes of the epistle but also for establishing Owen's credentials as an exegete and theologian. As such, Owen's commentary provides a window on his life as well as on the nature of biblical scholarship in seventeenth-century England. Throughout the work, he draws upon the latest methods of biblical interpretation, defends the central tenets of the Christian faith against various opponents, provides exegetical ammunition for his other writings and encourages fellow dissenting Christians. No other book in Scripture better served Owen's cause than Hebrews. As a result, Owen's commentary became an essential part of his literary career.

THE NEED FOR OWEN'S COMMENTARY

In 1668, Owen published the first volume of his extensive and wide-ranging commentary with the cumbersome title *Exercitations on the epistle to the Hebrews also concerning the Messiah . . . With an exposition and discourses on the two first chapters of the said epistle to the Hebrews*. The book was divided into two parts with a series of essays or 'exercitations' that introduced the principal themes of the epistle and an exposition of the first two chapters of Hebrews. Other volumes, covering the rest of the letter, emerged in 1674, 1680 and posthumously in 1684.

When Owen published the first volume on Hebrews, there was nothing like it available in his native tongue. In 1663, the bibliographer William Crowe produced a catalogue of 'English writers on the Old and New Testament' that included lists of 'Commentators, Elucidators, Adnotators, or Expositors' for every book in the Bible. The guide promised to be 'very usefull for any ones information as to what hath been writ upon any part of the Holy Scriptures'.[4] The design of the work was to showcase 'English writers of the holy Scriptures' who matched the 'eminent piety' and 'profound learning' of their European counterparts. By helping readers locate faithful biblical commentators in their own language, Crowe and his editorial colleagues wanted their catalogue to aid 'the advancement of [God's] glory, in the edification of this part of his true

---

[4][Crowe,] *An exact collection or catalogue of our English writers on the Old and New Testament* (1663), title page.

catholick church here in England'.[5] For those interested in studying the book of Hebrews, the reference guide itemizes multiple resources for each of the thirteen chapters of the letter. It also lists five commentaries 'on the whole' of the epistle by David Dickson, William Jones, Thomas Lushington, William Gouge and George Lawson.[6] Each of these works contributed to the emerging exegetical tradition of Hebrews commentating in English.[7] Dickson's exposition provided a solidly Reformed but 'short explanation' of the epistle.[8] Jones, whose commentary was subject to Laudian censorship prior to its publication, surveyed the letter along with Philemon and two of the Johannine epistles.[9] Lushington translated a controversial commentary on Hebrews attributed to Johann Crell and Jonas Schlichting that promoted Socinianism.[10] Gouge's exposition was substantial but mostly expository and homiletical in nature, based as it was on his thirty years of preaching on the epistle in London.[11] And Lawson's work provides a 'theo-political' exposition, which supplemented his larger project critiquing the political thought of Thomas Hobbes, along with a refutation of Socinianism.[12] While each of these commentaries, with the exception of Lushington, provided English readers with reliable Protestant interpretations of Hebrews, there was no single resource on offer that could exegete the text of Scripture, promote godly living, refute theological errors like Socinianism and match the level of technical sophistication seen, for example, by Johannes Oecolampadius's *In epistolam ad Hebraeos* (1534) or Johannes Cocceius's *Epistolae ad Hebraeos explicatio et eius veritatis demonstratio* (1659).[13] When the second edition of Crowe's catalogue appeared in 1668, the same five full-

---

[5] [Crowe,] *An exact collection or catalogue of our English writers on the Old and New Testament* (1663), sig. A5r, A5v, A6v, A7v.

[6] [Crowe,] *An exact collection or catalogue of our English writers on the Old and New Testament* (1663), 234. The list also includes a partial commentary 'on the first five chapters and part of the sixth' by Edward Deering; cf. Deering, *XXVII. Lectures, or readings, upon part of the epistle written to the Hebrues* (1576; Crowe lists 1590).

[7] On the history of commentaries on Hebrews in the Reformation and post-Reformation, especially in England, see Gatiss, 'Adoring the Fulness of the Scriptures in John Owen's commentary on Hebrews', 1–48; Knapp, 'Understanding the mind of God', 15–24; Padley, 'A Reception History of the Letter to the Hebrews in England, 1547–1685'.

[8] Dickson, *A short explanation of the epistle of Paul to the Hebrews* (1635).

[9] Jones, *A commentary upon the epistles of Saint Paul to Philemon, and to the Hebrewes, together with a compendious explication of the second and third epistles of Saint John* (1635; Crowe lists 1636).

[10] [Lushington,] *The expiation of a sinner in a commentary upon the epistle to the Hebrewes* (1640).

[11] Gouge, *A learned and very useful commentary on the whole epistle to the Hebrews wherein every word and particle in the original is explained* (1655; Crowe lists 1657).

[12] Lawson, *An exposition of the epistle to the Hebrewes wherein the text is cleared, theopolitica improved, the Socinian comment examined* (1662).

[13] Fisher, *A Christoscopic reading of scripture*; Lee, *Johannes Cocceius and the exegetical roots of federal theology*.

length commentaries remained. Although the title page announced that the volume had been 'enlarged with three or four thousand additional' resources, nothing new was listed that covered the epistle of Hebrews 'on the whole'.[14]

Owen felt the need for a new commentary. He opens his preface to the 'Christian reader' by expressing his desire to write such a work, saying that it had been 'sundry years since I purposed in my self, if God gave life and opportunity, to endeavour, according to the measure of the Gift received, an Exposition of the Epistle to the Hebrews'. He acknowledges that 'many eminent and learned men, both of old and of late' have written on Hebrews, including 'some entire Commentaries, composed with good judgment and to very good purpose' that have been published in 'our own Language', perhaps thinking of the ones listed in Crowe's catalogue.[15] Owen saw himself operating within the stream of the history of exegesis on Hebrews. He recognized that some commentaries excelled at making critical observations of the biblical text, others were useful for locating Old Testament references, some analysed the literary structure of the epistle, others had a practical orientation, some focused on difficult passages, and still others were designed to settle matters of religious controversy. Owen wanted to 'undertake the same work with them'.[16] But he did not want to limit himself to any one of these approaches. He believed that the subject matter of the epistle and the theological demands of his own day required a multifaceted commentary that incorporated each of these aspects of the exegetical tradition and that was written in English as opposed to Latin, the conventional language for scholarly works at the time.[17] In other words, Owen wanted to write a definitive commentary that appealed to English readers.

After a 'thorough perusal of all the Comments, Expositions, Annotations, or Observations on the Epistle' that he could obtain, Owen concludes that the time had come for 'executing my purpose, of casting my Mite into this Sanctuary' of Hebrews and writing a commentary on it.[18] He gives at least three reasons for doing so. First, since the epistle covers 'the whole body of Christian Religion', he believed additional reflections on these 'very fundamental Principles of our Christian Profession' would serve both 'the present Generation' and subsequent

---

[14][Crowe,] *An exact collection or catalogue of our English writers on the Old and New Testament*, second impression (1668), 254.
[15]Owen, *Hebrews* (1668), sig. a1r; *Works* (1850), 18:5. Crowe's work is listed in the auction catalogue of Owen's library, see Millington, *Bibliotheca Oweniana*, Divinity in Octavo, 16, no. 287; cf. Gribben, 'John Owen, renaissance man? The evidence of Edward Millington's *Bibliotheca Oweniana*'.
[16]Owen, *Hebrews* (1668), sig. a1v; *Works* (1850), 18:5.
[17]Gatiss, 'Adoring the fullness of the scriptures in John Owen's commentary on Hebrews', 42.
[18]Owen, *Hebrews* (1668), sig. a1v; *Works* (1850), 18:6. NB: Goold incorrectly records the phrase 'casting my Mite into this Sanctuary' as 'casting my mite into this treasury'.

generations 'unto the consummation of all things'.[19] The commentary, in other words, provided Owen with an exegetical foundation for extended theological reflection on the Christian faith. Second, the threat of Socinianism warranted fresh exegetical analysis on the epistle. He states, 'It is evident, that the principal things asserted and taught in this Epistle, such as is the Doctrine of the Person and the Priesthood of Jesus Christ, have received a more eager and subtle opposition, since the labours and endeavours of the most in the Exposition of it, than they had done before.'[20] Third, and perhaps most importantly for Owen, advances in biblical scholarship, particularly in Hebraic studies, helped him revaluate the text of Scripture and challenge the conclusions of previous commentators on the epistle. If progress in the 'human sciences' requires developments in scholarship, how much more should those who study the 'grand principles of supernatural revelation' strive to glean new insights from the 'sacred storehouse' of the biblical text.[21] With some bravado, Owen states,

> But that which most of all took off the weight of the discouragement that arose from the multiplied endeavours of learned Men in this kind, was an Observation that all of them being intent on the sense of the words, as absolutely considered, and the use of them to the present church, had much over-looked the direct respect and regard that the Author had in the writing of this Epistle to the then past, present, and future condition of the Hebrews, or church of the Jews.[22]

As Owen evaluated the state of the church, as well as his own gifts and personal interests, he realized there was a need for a new commentary. 'The common neglect of these things', referring to his three enumerated reasons, 'or slight transaction of them in most Expositors, was that which principally' motivated him to launch his project on Hebrews.[23] Despite experiencing 'impressions of failings, mistakes, and several defects in exactness, uncertainties, streights, and exclusion from the use of Books', a surprising confession given what he's already said about the literature on Hebrews in his preface, Owen maintains that in 'the good Providence of God' he has been prepared for such an undertaking.[24]

---

[19] Owen, *Hebrews* (1668), sig. a1v, a2v; *Works* (1850), 18:6, 7.
[20] Owen, *Hebrews* (1668), sig. a1v; *Works* (1850), 18:6. On the Socinian controversy in relation to Owen's commentary, see Gatiss, 'Adoring the fullness of the scriptures in John Owen's commentary on Hebrews', 49–98; cf. Lim, *Mystery unveiled*, 172–216; Mortimer, *Reason and religion in the English revolution*, esp. 194–232.
[21] Owen, *Hebrews* (1668), sig. a1v, a2v; *Works* (1850), 18:6, 7.
[22] Owen, *Hebrews* (1668), sig. a2r; *Works* (1850), 18:6. On the Jewish context of Owen's commentary, see Tweeddale, *John Owen and Hebrews*, 48–51.
[23] Owen, *Hebrews* (1668), sig. a2r; *Works* (1850), 18:7.
[24] Owen, *Hebrews* (1668), sig. a3r; *Works* (1850), 18:8.

Executing his task in the days and years following the Restoration, these 'impressions of failings' surprisingly created a culture of literary excellence for nonconformists like Owen. As N. H. Keeble has argued, 'political defeat was the condition of cultural achievement'.[25] Owen believed that everything he had done to date had prepared him for writing this commentary. 'I confess', he states, 'that I have had thoughts for many years to attempt something in [Hebrews], and in the whole course of my studies have not been without some regard thereunto'.[26] While the completion of his Hebrews commentary would occupy Owen for the remaining fifteen years of his life, there is evidence that the legwork of his commentary began during his early ministry in the 1640s. Seen in this light, his 'whole life' was devoted to teaching and defending the truths of the epistle to the Hebrews.

THE BEGINNINGS OF OWEN'S COMMENTARY

From his earliest publications in the 1640s to his death in 1683, Owen turned to the texts and themes of Hebrews throughout his ministry. In his work on *The duty of pastors and people distinguished* (1644), for example, Owen reflects on the teaching of the Old Testament law in a discussion on the importance of Bible reading for individuals and families. At the end of his analysis, he makes a passing reference that he had 'declared elsewhere' some of these matters. In a marginal note, he cites a 'not yet published' (*nondum edito*) treatise of his on the priesthood of Christ that was written 'against Arminians, Socinians, and Papists' (*Tractatu de Sacerdotio Christi, contra Armin. Socin. et Papistas*).[27] There is no record of this work ever being published, although William Goold theorizes that it might have become part of his essays on Hebrews. At the very least, the reference suggests that from the beginning of his ministry Owen was reflecting on the central role of the priesthood of Christ, a theme he would later argue is key for unlocking the epistle to the Hebrews, in relation to three of his major theological opponents.[28]

Owen develops the theme of Christ's priesthood in more detail in *Salus electorum, sanguis Jesu: or, The death of death in the death of Christ* (1648). In this work, he constructs a theology of the atonement along the lines of Christ's priestly duties of oblation and intercession. Significantly, he grounds this paradigm in his reading of Hebrews. He states,

---

[25]Keeble, *The literary culture of Nonconformity in later seventeenth-century England*, 22.
[26]Owen, *Hebrews* (1668), sig. a3r; *Works* (1850), 18:9; cf. Gribben, *John Owen and English Puritanism*, 237.
[27]Owen, *The duty of pastors and people distinguished* (1644), 16; *Works* (1850), 13:18.
[28]Tweeddale, *John Owen and Hebrews*, 32; cf. Goold, 'Prefatory Note', in *Works* (1850), 13:2; Orme, 'Memoirs of Dr. John Owen', in *Works* (1826), 1:37; Trueman, *John Owen*, 17–33.

> This the Apostle exceedingly cleares, and evidently proves in the Epistle to the Hebrews describing the Priest-hood of Christ in the execution thereof, of offering up himselfe in, and by the shedding of his bloud, and interceding for us to the utmost; upon the performance of both which, he presseth an exhortation to draw neere with confidence to the throne of grace.[29]

In the late 1640s, Owen relies on the biblical categories of Hebrews to build his doctrinal formulation of Christ's twofold work as priest. There is a direct link between the work Owen did on the priesthood of Christ in *The death of death in the death of Christ* and the resulting commentary on Hebrews that he produced later in life. As Edwin Tay has argued, 'It can reasonably be concluded that from the writing of *The Death of Death* in 1647 [sic] to his *Excercitations Concerning Christ's Priesthood* in 1674 [in the second volume of Hebrews], Owen's formation of Christ's priestly office remained consistent.'[30] Owen's commentary represents the culmination of thoughts on the priesthood of Christ that were introduced in seed form in *The death of death in the death of Christ*.

On 19 April 1649, Owen preached before the House of Commons on Heb. 12.27 ('And this word, Yet once more, signifieth the removing of those things that are shaken, as of things that are made, that those things which cannot be shaken may remain'). He opens the sermon with a summary of the epistle, noting especially the theme of backsliding.

> The main designe of the Apostle in this Scripture to the Hebrews, is to prevail with his Country-men who had undertaken the Profession of the Gospel, to abide constant and faithful therein, without any Apostasie unto, or mixture with Judaisme, which God and themselves had forsaken, fully manifesting, that in such backsliders the soul of the Lord hath no pleasure, chap. 10:38.[31]

Owen draws an explicit parallel between Jewish Christians in the first century and professing Christians in seventeenth-century England, noting the difficulty of persuading 'professors to hold out, and continue in the glory of their profession unto the end'.[32] The sermon is noteworthy for a number of reasons, as several scholars have observed. It provided the occasion for Owen's first encounter with Oliver Cromwell,[33] encapsulates his understanding of the epistle and grasp of the exegetical tradition,[34] illustrates his use of a metaphorical

---

[29] Owen, *The death of death in the death of Christ* (1648), 31; *Works* (1850), 10:183.
[30] Tay, *The priesthood of Christ*, 112.
[31] Owen, *The shaking and translating of heaven and earth* (1649), 1; *Works* (1850), 8:253.
[32] Owen, *The shaking and translating of heaven and earth* (1649), 1; *Works* (1850), 8:253.
[33] Cooper, *John Owen, Richard Baxter and the formation of Nonconformity*, 106–7.
[34] Tweeddale, *John Owen and Hebrews*, 33–4.

reading of the text of Scripture,[35] embodies the political zeal of the 1640s[36] and captures his model of prophetic preaching.[37] Perhaps most importantly for Owen, the sermon gave him an opportunity to reflect on how the epistle to the Hebrews warns against backsliding and encourages perseverance in the faith. Crawford Gribben suggests that Owen revisited this theme later in life as he was concerned about the danger of backsliding among dissenters after the Restoration. Gribben explains, 'Declension was, of course, an important theme in Hebrews, and Owen may have figured his readers as being tempted, like the addresses of the epistle about which he was also thinking, to slip back into an easier pattern of religious conformity.'[38] Owen's sermon on Heb. 12.27 highlights the formative role of Hebrews in shaping his biblical, theological and political imagination in the first decade of his public ministry.

In the 1650s, Owen's battle with the Socinians provided him with another occasion to give sustained attention to the letter to the Hebrews, especially in relation to the doctrine of the person and work of Christ. Throughout his blistering critique of John Biddle and the Racovian Catechism in *Vindiciae evangelicae* (1655), Owen interacts extensively with Socinian readings of Hebrews. At one point, undoubtedly for rhetorical as well as polemical effect, he surveys the epistle's main passages on the priesthood of Christ to refute Socinian teaching. He states, 'Seeing all the proofes collected for this purpose are out of the Epistle to the Hebrews, I shall consider them in order as they lye in the epistle.'[39] Owen's verse-by-verse analysis of the relevant portions of Hebrews on the priesthood of Christ gave him exegetical ammunition to counter Socinian rejection of core doctrines such as the priestly work on Christ during his earthly ministry, his substitutionary work on the cross and his present heavenly ministry of intercession. As Owen will later argue in the second volume of *Hebrews* (1674), 'The greatest Opposition that ever was made among Christians unto the Doctrine of the Priesthood of Christ, or rather unto the Office it self, is that which at this day is managed by the Socinians.' Owen regarded Socinian rejection of traditional expressions of the priestly office of Christ as a theological 'crime' that must be answered through careful biblical exposition.[40] No other portion of Scripture helped him make his case against Socinian teaching more effectively than the letter to the Hebrews. As part of his larger anti-Socinian polemic, Owen's commentary continues and extends the exegetical arguments he first made in *Vindiciae evangelicae*.

---

[35] Gribben, *John Owen and English Puritanism*, 105.
[36] Toon, *God's statesman*, 35–6.
[37] Cowan, *John Owen and the civil war apocalypse*, 54–6.
[38] Gribben, *John Owen and English Puritanism*, 237.
[39] Owen, *Vindiciae evangelicae* (1655), 435–55; *Works* (1850), 12:403–11.
[40] Owen, *Hebrews* (1674), sig. *A1v–*A2r; *Works* (1850), 18:17.

Based on the literary arc of Owen's early, pre-Restoration writings, it is no surprise that as his career develops, he anticipates writing more extensively on Hebrews, especially as he interacts with the latest developments in biblical scholarship. What might be the earliest reference from Owen of plans for writing a commentary appears in his work *Of the integrity and purity of the Hebrew and Greek text of the Scripture* (1659), where he expresses concern over Brian Walton's London Polyglot Bible (1653–7). In the middle of an argument where Owen defends the inspiration of the Hebrew vowel points in the *autographa*, he makes a passing statement that he may one day, with 'God assisting' him, 'manifest my thoughts on the Epistle of Paul to the Hebrewes'.[41] The attribution of the Apostle Paul as the author of Hebrews in a book defending the inspiration of Hebrew vowel points might illustrate for modern readers the pitfalls of what is often referred to as 'pre-critical' exegesis and, as a result, cause some to dismiss Owen's observations on Hebrews as outdated.[42] In response to these concerns, however, Kelly Kapic rightly notes that 'those who dismiss Owen as naïve for some of his positions, such as defending the Hebrew vowel points as part of the original [autographs], do not understand his historical moment. Well into the eighteenth century, even leading biblical scholars who did not share Owen's brand of orthodoxy still defended the ancient historicity of the Hebrew vowel points'.[43] As the 1650s ended, Owen's polemical and scholarly activities were in part shaped by his reading of Hebrews. While Owen approached the biblical text with different assumptions than many people today, the development of his commentary was the result of his desire to interpret the text of Scripture in light of the best scholarship available to him, including the critical use of Walton's polyglot.[44]

This basic point is underscored in another statement by Owen, where he clearly expresses his intentions to write a commentary on Hebrews. In 1661, seven years before the release of the first volume on Hebrews, he published his Θεολογούμενα παντοδαπά, a vast, complicated work on theological prolegomena that, among other things, follows the redemptive plotline of covenant theology from Adam to Christ.[45] The book stemmed from Owen's lectures at the University of Oxford and reflects his broad range of scholarly interests.[46] In one instance, while discussing the Jewish background of Hebrews, Owen announces his plan to write a commentary. He states, 'But the apostle in

---

[41]Owen, *Of the integrity and purity of the Hebrew and Greek text of the Scripture*, in *Of the divine originall* (1659), 225; *Works* (1850), 16:376.
[42]Knapp, 'Understanding the mind of God', 1–13; Tweeddale, *John Owen and Hebrews*, 15–20.
[43]Kapic, 'John Owen's theological reading of Hebrews', 137; cf. Muller, *After Calvin*, 146–55.
[44]Gatiss, 'Adoring the fullness of the Scriptures in John Owen's commentary on Hebrews', 27–30; Gundry, 'John Owen on authority and Scripture', 210.
[45]Tweeddale, *John Owen and Hebrews*, 59–71.
[46]McGraw, *John Owen*, 157–87; Rehnman, *Divine discourse*, 18.

the epistle to the Hebrews is arguing from a basis which was formerly conceded among the Jews, as I will make clear, with God's help, in our commentary on the epistle.'[47] Θεολογουμενα is important not only because it marks Owen's overt desire to write on Hebrews but also because it illustrates another link between Owen's theological constructions developed earlier in his career and his later commentary. The dogmatic infrastructure mapped out in Θεολογουμενα gave Owen a framework for explaining what he calls the 'whole progress of divine revelation'[48] in his exposition on Heb. 1.1-2 ('By sundry parts, and in diverse manners God having formerly [or of old] spoken unto the Fathers in the Prophets, hath in these last dayes spoken unto us in the Son, whom he hath appointed heir of all, by whom also he made the worlds').[49] For help interpreting the gradual unfolding of the 'sundry parts' of Scripture, Owen encourages readers of his commentary to study his more programmatic work in Θεολογουμενα, which he calls 'my Discourse of the rise, nature and progress of Scripture Divinity or Theology'.[50] Owen's dependence on arguments made in Θεολογουμενα for his exegesis of Hebrews 1 demonstrates how his commentary must be read within the literary context of his other writings.

The textual relationship between Owen's early reflections on Hebrews and his later commentary points to an organic unity of his thought and suggests that Owen believed his project on Hebrews was central to his overall work as a biblical scholar and theologian. As he combated theological errors such as Arminianism and Socinianism, reflected on the spiritual health of his country, and engaged in the latest scholarship on biblical criticism and covenant theology, he found that few, if any, places in Scripture better served his purposes than the epistle to the Hebrews. So, when removed from leadership at the University of Oxford after the Restoration, one of the first major tasks Owen wanted to accomplish was the production of one of the most ambitious, even if ultimately unwieldy, commentaries in the history of the church.

THE DEVELOPMENT OF OWEN'S COMMENTARY

To publish a work of this magnitude, Owen needed help. For assistance in obtaining a licence to secure its public release, he garnered the support of Sir

---

[47] 'Apostolum autem ex principiis inter Judaeos olim concessis, in Epistola ad Hebraeos disputare, commentariis nostris ad eam epistolam (σὺν Θεῷ) ostendemus'. Owen, Θεολογουμενα παντοδαπα (1661), lib. 2, cap. 1, 130; *Works* (1850), 17:137, translation mine; cf. Owen, *Biblical theology*, 173.
[48] Owen, *Hebrews* (1668), lib. 2, 9 (comm. Heb. 1.1, 2); *Works* (1850), 20:17.
[49] This is Owen's translation of Heb. 1.1-2, see *Hebrews* (1668), lib. 2, p. 2 (comm. Heb. 1.1, 2); *Works* (1850), 20:5.
[50] Owen, *Hebrews* (1668), lib. 2, 10 (comm. Heb. 1.1, 2); *Works* (1850), 20:18; cf. Owen, Θεολογουμενα παντοδαπα (1661), lib. 2, cap. 1, 127; *Works* (1850), 17:134.

William Morice, who assisted in the restoration of Charles II, was knighted in 1660 and was subsequently appointed to political office as secretary of state, a position he held until he resigned in 1668 – the year Owen published the first volume of his commentary.[51] In addition to Morice, his successor, Sir John Trevor, whom Asty lists among 'several persons of honour . . . who very much delighted in [Owen's] conversation', may also have supported Owen in a similar capacity.[52] At the onset of his commentary, Owen appeals to Morice's reputation as a man known for 'Civil Prudence' and appreciating 'all manner of useful Literature'.[53] In the aftermath of the Restoration, Owen sees his 'wearisome Labours' in writing as the 'only way' for him 'to serve the Will of God, and the interest of the church, in my Generation'. To ensure that his work gains an audience with readers, Owen petitions Morice to approve its publication. He states, 'It was also through the countenance of your Favour, that this and some other Treatises have received Warrant to pass freely into the world.'[54] To return the favour, Owen dedicated his commentary to Morice.

Presumably with Morice's endorsement in hand, Owen also partners for the first time with bookseller Nathaniel Ponder – whose printshop 'at the Sign of the Peacock in Chancery Lane near Fleetstreet'[55] in London became a hub for Nonconformist literature – to publish the first volume of the commentary, and ultimately the other three volumes in the series. The relationship between author and publisher would continue for the duration of Owen's life, with Ponder publishing several of Owen's most well-known and important volumes, including *A practical exposition on the 130th Psalm* (1669), *Exercitations concerning the name, original, nature, use, and continuance of a day of sacred rest* (1671), *Πνευματολογια, or, A discourse concerning the Holy Spirit* (1674), *The nature of apostasie* (1676), *The reason of faith* (1677), *Σύνεσις πνευματική, or, The causes, waies & means of understanding the mind of God* (1678), *Χριστολογια, or, A declaration of the glorious mystery of the person of Christ, God and Man* (1679) as well as several others. Most famously, the connection between Owen

---

[51] Gribben, *John Owen and English Puritanism*, 236–7; Seaward, 'Morice, Sir William (1602–1676)', in *ODNB*, s.v.; Toon, *God's statesman*, 127, 149.
[52] Asty, 'Memoirs of the life of John Owen', xxix; Keeble, *The literary culture of Nonconformity in later seventeenth century England*, 118.
[53] Owen, *Hebrews* (1668), sig. A1v; *Works* (1850), 18:3. In his retirement, Morice evidently was known for erecting 'a fair library' and being 'very conversant in books, both ancient and modern'. One biographer states, 'For the increase [of his library], he had a great advantage by virtue of his office, having most of the books then published always presented to him; in the study and perusal whereof, was his principal divertisement, which yielded him the most sensible pleasure that he took, during the last years of his life.' Price, *Danmonii orientales illustres: or, The worthies of Devon*, 605.
[54] Owen, *Hebrews* (1668), sig. A2r; *Works* (1850), 18:3–4.
[55] Owen, *Hebrews* (1668), title page.

and Ponder would ultimately lead to the publication of John Bunyan's *Pilgrim's Progress* (1678), and the publisher being dubbed 'Bunyan Ponder'.⁵⁶ Like Bunyan's allegory, Owen's commentary represents one of the crowning achievements of the post-Restoration Nonconformist movement.

With a benefactor and publisher in place, Owen was able to execute his plan for a commentary on Hebrews. The overall project defies simple classification or explanation. The 1668 volume is structured in two parts with a series of twenty-four preliminary essays, called 'exercitations', along with an exposition of Hebrews 1–2. The essays cover introductory matters of the epistle such as its canonicity, authorship (whom Owen thought was Paul), historical setting (exercitations 1–7), hermeneutical matters concerning Old Testament messianic promises (exercitations 8–18) and biblical-theological matters relating to the Mosaic law (exercitations 19–24). Taken as a whole, the essays present a series of interlocking arguments that provide Owen with a biblical foundation to show that the promises of Scripture are fulfilled in the person and work of Jesus Christ. For Owen, the portrayal of Christ in Hebrews is predicated on the fundamental unity that exists between the Old and New Testaments. Consistent with Reformed orthodox hermeneutical approaches, Owen's essays aim to show that the Christ of Hebrews is both the *fundamentum Scripturae* and *scopus Scripturae*, and parallel similar arguments from Augustine, John Calvin, William Perkins, Francis Roberts and Johannes Cocceius.⁵⁷ Throughout the entire volume, Owen also follows more broadly in the tradition of the 'proof from prophecy' model of biblical interpretation that stretches back to Justin Martyr in order to counter both 'ancient and modern' Jewish arguments against a Christological reading of Scripture.⁵⁸ Owen's preliminary essays are important for his overall project. They not only structure the entire commentary project but also supply him with a set of guiding principles that inform his reading of Scripture. In short, Owen's exercitations are an important interpretive key for reading his exposition of Hebrews.

In his exposition on Hebrews 1–2, Owen aspired to go 'nakedly to the word itself' without imposing any 'prejudicate sense' – whether his own or

---

⁵⁶Lynch, 'Ponder, Nathaniel [called Bunyan Ponder] (1640–1699)', in *ODNB*, s.v.; Anne Dunan-Page states, 'Evidence of a connection between Ponder, Owen and Bunyan presents a strong case for suggesting that Owen might have introduced Bunyan to Ponder'. Dunan-Page, '"The Pourtraiture of John Bunyan" revisited: Robert White and Images of the Author', *Bunyan studies: A journal of Reformation and Nonconformist culture*, The International John Bunyan Society, 13 (2008), 7–39.
⁵⁷See discussion in Tweeddale, *John Owen and Hebrews*, 41–7; compare Owen, *Hebrews* (1668), sig. A2r and 1.8.1 (68); *Works* (1850), 18:7, 142 with Augustine, *Enchiridion*, cap. 4, in NPNF¹, 3:238; Calvin, *Institutes*, 2.11.1; Perkins, *The Arte of Prophecying* (1607), 7; Roberts, *Clavis Bibliorum* (1648), 470; Cocceius, *Summa theologiae*, 2nd ed. (1665), cap. 7, sec. 21, 93.
⁵⁸See Owen, *Hebrews* (1668), title page; *Works* (1850), 18:1; cf. Tweeddale, *John Owen and Hebrews*, 83–102; Skarsaune, *The proof from prophecy*.

others – onto the biblical text. Simply put, he wanted to 'learn humbly the mind of God in [Hebrews] and to express it as he should enable me'.[59] Owen divided his commentary roughly into three sections: textual, expository and practical.[60] This format was designed in part to broaden the appeal of the book to include 'Persons of Learning and Godliness'.[61] The idea was that readers could peruse sections of the commentary 'by the sole guidance of his Eye, without farther trouble than in turning the Leaves of the Book'.[62] Ultimately, the volume's design was to produce more faithful interpreters of Scripture. In the words of the biblical epigraph on the title page of each of the four volumes, Owen wanted his readers to 'search the Scriptures' (Jn 5.39).[63] His commentary demonstrates by precept and example how Christians should do just that. Above the epigraph, the subtitle of the commentary proper outlines Owen's exegetical steps for moving from textual and critical analysis to biblical-theological exposition to practical and pastoral observations:

The Original Text is Opened and Cleared.
Ancient and Modern Translations are compared and examined.
The Design of the Apostle, with the Reasonings, Arguments and Testimonies are unfolded.
The Faith, Customs, Sacrifices, and other Usages of the Judical Church are opened and declared;
The true sense of the Text is Vindicated from the wrestings of it by Socinians and others.
And lastly, Practical Observations are deduced and improved.[64]

---

[59]Owen, *Hebrews* (1668), sig. A3r; *Works* (1850), 18:9.
[60]Owen, *Hebrews* (1668), sig. A3r–A3v (*Works*, 18:9); Owen, *Hebrews* (1674), sig. A1r–A1v; *Works* (1850), 18:14–15). A similar threefold format was used by Wolfgang Musculus in his commentary on the Psalms, see *In sacrosanctum Davidis Psalterium commentarii* (1551); cf. Ballor, *Covenant, causality, and law*, 143.
[61]Owen, *Hebrews* (1668), sig. A3v; *Works* (1850), 18:9.
[62]Owen, *Hebrews* (1674), sig. A1r (misnumbered A2r); *Works* (1850), 18:14.
[63]This biblical text is also cited on the title page of Jones's commentary on Hebrews, see his *A commentary upon the epistles of Saint Paul to Philemon, and to the Hebrewes, together with a compendious explication of the second and third epistles of Saint John* (1635). The text may serve as a pedagogical marker that places these commentaries by Jones and Owen in the literary context of biblical study aides popular at the time. The call to 'search the Scriptures', in other words, reflects a print culture that was devoted to producing resources marketed to help a variety of readers interpret the Scriptures; cf. Green, *Print and Protestantism in early modern England*, 101–67. Gatiss notes that Jn 5.39 was used on the title page of several of Owen's works published by Ponder, see his 'Adoring the fullness of the Scriptures in John Owen's commentary on Hebrews', 6.
[64]Owen, *Hebrews* (1668), title page for *An exposition of the two first chapters of the epistle of Paul the apostle unto the Hebrews*. Note that the title page for the commentary proper is located in the second section of the volume, after page 218 of the exercitations.

Owen's exegetical method was typical for Puritan biblical scholarship. In the year following the publication of the first volume on Hebrews, for example, Owen wrote a preface for Henry Lukin's *An introduction to the Holy Scripture* (1669). Lukin designed his hermeneutical manual to help his own 'countrey men', who may not have the knowledge to read comparable works in other languages, develop the necessary skills to 'better understand the Scripture' and 'delight in the Word of God'.[65] Like Owen, Lukin encourages readers not to bend Scripture to their own 'preconceived opinions'. Rather, they must discover 'the true sense' of the biblical text and then deduce from the passage practical insights 'which may be of some use to us'. This approach applies to everyone who interprets Scripture. Even if some individuals struggle 'to resolve every Critical and Philological question', they may locate the basic meaning of the text by focusing on three components: 'First, the words and Phrases; Secondly, the circumstances of the place . . . thirdly, the *ratio rei*, or nature of thing treated of, that we may not contradict right reason, or those common Principles, generally agreed upon amongst Christians, according to the general scope of Scriptures, which are commonly called the Analogy of Faith.'[66] Lukin's guidelines correspond with Owen's exegetical method. Perhaps Lukin even had the first volume on Hebrews in mind as an example of these hermeneutical principles.

In the second edition of volume one, published in 1676, a new table listing 'practical observations drawn from the exposition' of Hebrews 1–2 is inserted between the preface 'to the Christian Reader' and the first exercitation, presumably to make the commentary more accessible to readers.[67] The second volume on *Hebrews* (1674) explicitly follows the template Owen established in the inaugural volume, with a series of ten exercitations on the priesthood of Christ along with an exposition of Hebrews 3–5.[68] This volume also provides a series of additional study aides to help readers navigate the bulky commentary, including the same list of 'practical observations' from the second edition of volume one, a new table of 'practical observations' on Hebrews 3–5, an 'alphabetical table' of topics covered in volume two and a Scripture index.[69] But

---

[65]Lukin, 'To the Reader', in *An introduction to the Holy Scripture* (1669), sig. A2r–A2v. Lukin especially has in view the work by the Lutheran scholar Salomon Glasius, *Philologiae sacrae, qua totius sacrosanctae veteris et Novi Testamenti scripturae* (1643).
[66]Luke, *An introduction to the Holy Scripture*, 31, 33.
[67]Owen, *Exercitations on the epistle to the Hebrews, also concerning the Messiah . . . With an exposition and discourses on the two first chapters of the said epistle to the Hebrews*, second edition (1676).
[68]Owen, *Hebrews* (1674), sig. A2r; *Works* (1850), 18:14.
[69]Owen, *Hebrews* (1674), these study aides are located between part 1 on the exercitations and part 2 on Hebrews 3–5.

Owen was not entirely convinced of the usefulness of these added resources. He gripes,

> Unto the whole there are Tables added, collected I confess in too much hast [*sic*], and not digested into so convenient a method as might be desired. But those who are acquainted with my manifold Infirmities, not to mention other Occasions, Employments, and Diversions, will not perhaps too severely charge upon me such failures in Accuracy and other Effects of strength and leisure as might otherwise be expected.[70]

In the preface to the third volume (1680), Owen states that he had to forego his practice of introducing the commentary with a series of exercitations, saying that his 'near Approach unto the Grave' rendered him 'insufficient for that labour'.[71] Instead, the third volume consists entirely of an exposition of Hebrews 6–10, including a controversial and meandering excursus on Heb. 8.6 where he delivers a 'minority report' on the Mosaic covenant.[72] The final volume (1684), published the year after Owen's death, covers the remaining portions of the epistle, including an exposition of Hebrews 11 on the 'efficacy and operation of faith in them that are justified . . . in times of persecution'.[73] The series concludes with Scripture and topical indexes for volumes three and four.

Owen's first volume on Hebrews both sets up the other three volumes and provides an exegetical basis for his other writings. For example, in Πνευματολογια (1674) Owen cites his exposition of Hebrews 1 to lend support for his articulation of the role of the Holy Spirit in Old Testament prophecy against the teaching of Maimonides.[74] He also relies on his commentary on Heb. 1.3 ('Who being the brightness of his glory, and the express image of his person, and upholding all things by the word of his power, when he had by himself purged our sins, sat down on the right hand of the Majesty on high') to augment his discussion on the kingly role of Christ in the church in Χριστολογια (1679).[75] This level of intertextuality between Owen's commentary and his general writings is carried throughout the entire *Hebrews* project, with evidence linking his essay on the covenant of redemption (1674) to his treatise on justification by faith (1677), his essay on the Sabbath (1671) to his exposition

---

[70] Owen, *Hebrews* (1674), sig. *Ar; *Works* (1850), 18:16.
[71] Owen, *Hebrews* (1680), sig. A2v; *Works* (1850), 18:19.
[72] Jones, 'The minority report: John Owen on Sinai', 293–303; Tweeddale, *John Owen and Hebrews*, 123–43.
[73] Owen, *Hebrews* (1684), title page.
[74] Owen, Πνευματολογια (1674), 105; *Works* (1850), 3:134.
[75] Owen, Χριστολογια (1679), 100; *Works* (1850), 1:96.

on Hebrews 4 (1674), and his essay on apostasy (1676) to his commentary on Hebrews 6 (1680).[76] It is also likely that Owen's hermeneutical manual on *The causes, waies & means of understanding the mind of God* attempts to codify his own approach to biblical interpretation that is implemented throughout his commentary.[77] These literary connections may suggest that Owen intended for his commentary and more occasional writings to be read together. His four volumes on Hebrews should be understood therefore both as the capstone of his literary career and as an exegetical basis for his theological writings.

THE RECEPTION OF OWEN'S COMMENTARY

Despite Owen's desire for a wide readership, his commentary was expensive and likely out of reach for many readers. The large folio volumes on Hebrews sold for 16s each, the same price for reference works such as the second edition of *A concordance to the Holy Scriptures* (1672) and scholarly works such as the latest printing of Francis Roberts's *Clavis Bibliorum* (1675).[78] Other titles by Owen were more affordable and typical of popular Nonconformist literature. *A brief declaration and vindication of the doctrine of the Trinity* (1669) in duodecimo sold for 1s; *A practical exposition on the 130th Psalm* (1669) in quarto sold for 4s; and *Exercitations concerning the name, original, nature, use, and continuance of a day of sacred rest* (1671) in octavo sold for 3s 6d.[79] By writing literature sold at these various price points, Owen was able to reach laity, pastors and scholars.[80] At the high end of the market, his commentary was one of the most sophisticated and expensive examples of Nonconformist literature available to the public. The publication of Owen's four-volume commentary on Hebrews was a statement of his reputation as one of England's leading Reformed theologians and biblical scholars.

There is reason to believe that Owen viewed the production of his commentary as his greatest literary achievement. At Owen's funeral, his assistant David Clarkson reported that Owen regarded his series on Hebrews as the conclusion of his writing career. Clarkson states, 'I have had credible Notice when that [commentary on Hebrews] was finish'd; (and it was a merciful Providence that

---

[76]For example, Owen, *The doctrine of justification by faith* (1677), 268; *Works* (1850), 5:191; Owen, *Sabbath* (1671), 5–6; *Works* (1850), 18:267. On *The nature of apostasie* (1676), see Tim Cooper's chapter in this volume.
[77]Knapp, 'Understanding the mind of God'; Tweeddale, *John Owen and Hebrews*.
[78]Arber, *The term catalogues, 1668–1709*, 1:113, 146, 200. NB: the catalogue only gives the price for the second volume of Hebrews.
[79]Arber, *The term catalogues, 1668–1709*, 1:8, 12, 65.
[80]See discussion in Keeble, *The literary culture of Nonconformity in later seventeenth-century England*, 134–5.

he lived to finish it.) He said, Now his Work was done, it was time for him to die.' Assessing Owen's contributions as a minister and author, Clarkson also recounts that Owen's 'Excellent Commentary upon the *Hebrews*' was esteemed by readers 'not only at Home, but in Foreign Countries'.[81] At the end of his life, Owen's stature was measured at least in part by the successful completion of his project on Hebrews.

There is evidence that Owen's commentary was read by a diverse audience. Crawford Gribben has shown how copies of the first two volumes on Hebrews (1668, 1674), located now in the Folger Shakespeare Library, were owned by multiple individuals, and apparently include personal annotations across several centuries.[82] Among his earlier readers were 'elite women' such as Anne Hamilton, the countess of Clanbrassil, who evidently acquired a copy of the third volume on Hebrews (1680) shortly after its publication.[83] One of the first individuals to interact with Owen's commentary in print was the Particular Baptist minister Nehemiah Coxe, who favourably cites the first and third volumes on Hebrews in *A discourse of the covenants that God made with men before the law* (1681) – a work also published by Nathaniel Ponder and brandished with the call for readers to 'search the Scriptures' (Jn 5.39) on the title page.[84] By the end of the century, the Dutch theologian Herman Witsius, in the third edition of his *De oeconomia foederum Dei cum hominibus libri* (1694), mentions Owen's exercitation on the 'personal transactions between the Father and the Son' in support of the doctrine of the covenant of redemption.[85] The citations by Coxe and Witsius illustrate how Owen's commentary set him apart as a leading voice among Puritan and Reformed exegetes and theologians, especially on the topic of covenant theology, and established his standing as a biblical scholar.[86]

Witsius's comment helps corroborate Clarkson's claim about the international readership of Owen's commentary. Along these lines, a Latin translation was

---

[81]Clarkson, 'A funeral sermon of the much lamented death of the late Reverend and learned divine John Owen, D. D.', in *Seventeen sermons*, 1:lxxiii.

[82]Gribben, 'Becoming John Owen', 319–20.

[83]Gribben, 'John Owen, Lucy Hutchinson and the experience of defeat', 179–90.

[84]Coxe, *A discourse of the covenants that God made with men before the law* (1681), A4v sig., 138. For discussion of Coxe and his use of Owen, see Renihan, *From shadow to substance*, 195–264.

[85]Witsius, *De oeconomia foederum Dei cum hominibus libri* (1694), lib. 2, cap. 2, 142; cf. Owen, *Hebrews* (1674), exercitatio IV, 49; *Works* (1850), 19:77.

[86]The notoriety of Owen's commentary may explain why he was asked to commend several scholarly works on biblical interpretation. As his volumes on Hebrews gave him an extended platform to advance nuanced readings of the Mosaic covenant and the covenant of redemption in particular, it is not surprising that during this season of life he also wrote prefaces for Samuel Petto's *The difference between the old and new covenant stated and explained* (1674) and Patrick Gillespie's *The ark of the covenant opened* (1677), which develop biblical arguments that align with Owen's viewpoints on the Mosaic covenant and the covenant of redemption, respectively.

proposed for publication in Amsterdam in 1700 but was never released.[87] However, in 1733, Simon Commeniq, a merchant in Rotterdam, oversaw the translation of *Hebrews* into Dutch.[88] In the transatlantic world, Owen's commentary was read by several Puritan luminaries in America.[89] On 2 January 1701, Samuel Sewall donated 'Dr. Owens two last Volumes on the Hebrews' to the Harvard College library. Before parting with the volumes, he read Owen's exegesis of Hebrews 8, focusing especially on verse 11 and the new covenant promise that the least to the greatest will 'know the Lord', but confessed, 'I read it over and over one time and another and could not be satisfied'.[90] Years later, on 20 March 1716, Sewall wrote to John Love, asking him to 'Send me Dr. Owen upon the Hebrews, all the 4 Books'.[91] This was perhaps to give them to his son. He writes in his diary on 29 September 1716, 'I received . . . Dr. Owen on the Hebrews for my Son, 4 volumes, *Laus Deo*.'[92] Also in Massachusetts, Increase Mather records reading during his morning and evening devotions from several of Owen's works, including Owen's exposition on Hebrews 2 and 4 along with his treatise on the Sabbath.[93] Increase's son, Cotton Mather, owned the first volume on Hebrews, perhaps the same edition as his father's. In the early nineteenth century, Cotton Mather's copy of *Hebrews* (1668) was brought by an American missionary to Damascus, Syria, but 'was lost in 1860 when the Christians of Damascus were massacred by the Moslems and the Christian Quarter was plundered and laid in ruins'. By 1899, the volume was recovered and presented to the library of the Chicago Theological Seminary and now resides in the Congregational Library in Massachusetts.[94] Cotton's son inscribed his copy of volume 1 with the simple ascription: 'Saml. Mather's Book. 1734.'[95] Jonathan Edwards also made frequent use of Owen's commentary. Edwards owned a complete four-volume set in his personal library, let a friend borrow two of the volumes and incorporated Owen's findings in several of his writings,

---

[87]Le Long, *Bibliotheca sacra in binos syllabos*, 2:889; cf. Tweeddale, *John Owen and Hebrews*, 3–4.
[88]Owen, *Eene uitlegginge van den sendbrief van Paulus den apostel aen de Hebreen* (1733–40); cf. Beeke, 'The reception of John Owen in early modernity', 85–90.
[89]Bearman, '"The Atlas of Independency": The ideals of John Owen (1616–1683) in the north Atlantic Christian world'.
[90]*Collections of the Massachusetts historical society*, vol. IV, fifth series, 28.
[91]*Collections of the Massachusetts historical society*, vol. II, sixth series, 53.
[92]*Collections of the Massachusetts historical society*, vol. VII, fifth series, 105.
[93]Green, ed., *Diary by Increase Mather*, 33–4.
[94]This account is taken from an inscription in the volume dated 'Feb 3rd, 1899' by John Crawford, missionary of the Presbyterian Church in Ireland, who served in Damascus, Syria. See 'Acquisition: Book owned by Cotton Mather' (7 March 2011), https://www.congregationallibrary.org/blog/201103/acquisition-book-owned-by-cotton-mather, accessed 5 August 2021.
[95]Tuttle, *Libraries of the Mathers*, 75.

including his sermon series on *A history of the work of redemption* (1739).[96] Despite this positive reception by early readers, Owen's bulky commentary was far from accessible, both in terms of its length and style. Reading habits and scholarly conventions were also changing. Only the most determined admirers of Owen would continue to revisit his essays and exposition on Hebrews in the modern world.[97]

In 1790, the Welsh Nonconformist minister Edward Williams edited a four-volume octavo abridgement of Owen's commentary that was approximately one-third the size of the original. Williams had high praise for Owen's voluminous work on Hebrews, calling it 'one of the most valuable systems of doctrinal, practical, and experimental divinity, that is to be met with in the English language'.[98] He notes, however, that a 'revolution in the mode of dressing thought' has altered the expectations of modern readers. 'In the present day', he adds,

> the very idea of an expository work, consisting of four volumes folio, on a single epistle, is enough to frighten the fashionable class of readers, who are never better pleased, as one observes, than when they peruse a book 'brief, gaudy, and superficial.' The difference between the taste of the last and present age, in this respect, is very striking.

Williams wanted to abridge an edition of Owen's outdated commentary for evangelical readers in the modern age.[99] A revised second edition of the abridgement was published in 1815, with the publisher acknowledging 'that the works of no Author will better admit of abridgment that those of Dr. Owen'.[100] Dissatisfied with Williams's abridgement, the Baptist minister George Wright produced in 1812 'a new edition' of Owen's commentary 'with a view of putting a valuable book into the hands of more readers, at a reduced price'. This seven-volume set rearranged Owen's exercitations, added his discourse on the Sabbath and placed the entire commentary proper together so that 'the continuity of the Exposition may not be broken'.[101] For several decades, Wright's edition was viewed as the best place for readers to access Owen's commentary. When Thomas Russell released his 21-volume collection of Owen's works in 1826, he omitted Owen's writings on Hebrews and simply

---

[96] See, e.g., *The works of Jonathan Edwards*, 9:554; 26:339; cf. Minkema, 'Jonathan Edwards reads John Owen', 97–108; Sweeney, *Edwards the exegete*.
[97] Tweeddale, *John Owen and Hebrews*, 4–5.
[98] Williams, 'Preface', in *An exposition of the epistle to the Hebrews* (1790), 1:iv.
[99] See discussion on Williams in Rivers, *Vanity faith and the celestial city*, 127–8.
[100] 'Advertisement', in *An exposition of the epistle to the Hebrews* (1815), 1:iii.
[101] Wright, 'Preface by the editor', *An exposition of the epistle to the Hebrews* (1812), 1:iv–v.

referred interested readers to the Wright edition.[102] These earlier editions of Owen's commentary were ultimately replaced by the twenty-four volumes of what would become the standard edition of *The works of John Owen* edited by William Goold in 1850–5. However, when the Banner of Truth republished the Goold edition of Owen's works in the 1960s, his commentary on Hebrews was not originally included and would not be released until nearly three decades later, in 1991. The separation of Owen's commentary from his collected works may help explain why over time Owen's theological writings have been read with little reference to his exegesis on Hebrews.[103]

CONCLUSION

Owen viewed the epistle to the Hebrews as a gateway into the rest of the Bible. He states, 'For my part, I can truly say, that I know not any portion of Holy Writ, that will more effectually raise up the heart of an understanding Reader to a holy Admiration of the Goodness, Love, and Wisdom of God, than this Epistle doth.'[104] For its depiction of the excellencies of the priesthood of Christ in particular, Owen believed that Hebrews was 'as Useful to the church as the Sun in the Firmament is unto the World'.[105] However, Owen's four-volume project on Hebrews does more than shed light on his reading of Scripture. It also illuminates how Owen saw himself as a biblical scholar. The publication of Owen's *Exercitations on the epistle to the Hebrews* in 1668 marked a definitive moment in his life. The book was the result of years of reflection on Hebrews in the early days of his career and officially began a project that would occupy him until his death. Indeed, Owen's 'whole life' revolved around the production of his commentary on Hebrews. Evaluation of his writings should not be limited to his commentary. Owen wrote plenty of things unrelated to Hebrews. However, he did comment in print on the epistle for most of his adult life. From this perspective, Owen's essays and exposition on Hebrews are not only important for their contribution to the history of exegesis but also for what they communicate about his biography. Central to understanding Owen's life and theology is his commentary on Hebrews. As Hill might even say, interpreters of Owen ignore it at their peril.

---

[102]'Advertisement', in *Works* (1826), n.p. [iii].
[103]Tweeddale, *John Owen and Hebrews*, 24, 146.
[104]Owen, *Hebrews* (1668), 1.1.24 [13]; *Works* (1850), 18:47.
[105]Owen, *Hebrews* (1674), 1.1.1 [1]; *Works* (1850), 19:3.

CHAPTER 16

Πνευματολογια

or, A discourse concerning the Holy Spirit (1674)

ANDREW M. LESLIE

John Owen's magisterial study, Πνευματολογια: *or A discourse concerning the Holy Spirit* (1674), has not unjustly been described as the 'greatest Reformed treatise' on the subject.[1] To Owen's mind, however, this may not be saying all that much. At least in his own day, Πνευματολογια might well have been bereft of any real comparison. As he nonchalantly admits in his prefatory introduction, 'I know not any who ever went before me in this design of representing the whole oeconomy of the Holy Spirit.'[2] In the seventeenth-century context, the greatness of his achievement is perhaps best measured, then, in terms of its originality. That is not to claim that Owen set out to deliver something particularly innovative, as measured by the standards of doctrinal orthodoxy. At the outset, he emphatically accents the continuity of his exposition with Scripture above all, of course, but also with more specific treatments of the Spirit's redemptive work, and especially with 'the ancient writers of the church'.[3] Indeed, the treatise is replete with numerous citations from Greek and Latin patristic authors, such as Justin Martyr, John Chrysostom, Basil the Great, Didymus, Cyprian, Jerome, Ambrose, Prosper of Aquitaine and,

---

[1] Webster, *The domain of the word*, 52.
[2] Owen, Πνευματολογια (1674), n.p. *iii; *Works* (1965), 3:7.
[3] '[M]y design was, not to handle these things in a way of controversie'. Owen, Πνευματολογια (1674), n.p. *vi; *Works* (1965), 3:9.

of course, Augustine. Owen even devotes an entire chapter to illustrating the experience of Christian conversion by deploying Augustine's own biographical depiction in his famous *Confessions*.⁴

Aside from underlining the orthodoxy of his exposition, there was surely an added contextual reason for this move. As Jean-Louis Quantin has illustrated, the Restoration establishment had a habit of defending its pedigree through explicit recourse to patristic precedent.⁵ While Owen denies having any particular polemical reason for writing Πνευματολογια, it is quickly apparent both from its preface and the opening chapters that certain quarters of the Restoration establishment are squarely in his sights.⁶ In this case, his chief interlocutor is undoubtedly the erstwhile puritan, later bishop of Oxford, Samuel Parker.⁷ Owen had already locked horns with Parker over the issue of Christian liberty in 1669.⁸ And among other things, Parker's acrimonious reply, *A defence and continuation of the ecclesiastical politie* (1671), goes out of its way to chide Owen for theological novelty in deviating from the teaching of the 'ancients'. While Parker supplies no real evidence for this charge, it is unsurprising that Owen is especially keen to cover his tracks. Indeed, the particularly heated tone of this exchange may help explain what his nineteenth-century editor fairly identifies as an abundance of 'Owen's usual prolixity' throughout Πνευματολογια. For all its theological precision, the argument is frequently repetitive and laborious in detail. At times it certainly suggests Owen was 'panoplied for conflict rather than girt for useful work', whatever his denials might have been to the contrary.⁹

In terms of substance, Owen's primary concern stems from a general neglect and even disdain he senses for the economy of the Holy Spirit in the public religious life of Restoration England.¹⁰ In the opening chapter of Book I, he situates this neglect in a long history of error concerning the person and work of the Spirit, through its most immediate antecedents, exemplified in the teachings

---

⁴See, Book 3, chapter 4: Owen, Πνευματολογια (1674), 287–311; *Works* (1965), 3:337–66.
⁵See, especially, Quantin, *The Church of England and Christian antiquity*, 252–326.
⁶Owen, *Works* (1965), 3:9.
⁷For brief discussions of Owen's exchange with Parker, see, Thomson, 'Life of Dr Owen by the Rev. Andrew Thomson, B.A., Edinburgh', [Owen, *Works* (1965), 1:lxxxviii–xc]; Toon, *God's statesman*, 136–7; Gribben, *John Owen and English Puritanism*, 247–8.
⁸Owen, *Truth and innocence vindicated* (1669); *Works* (1965), 13:343–506. *Truth and innocence vindicated* is Owen's response to Parker's initial attack on the nonconformists: Parker, *A discourse of ecclesiastical politie* (1671) [3rd ed., first published in 1669].
⁹Owen, *Works* (1965), 3:3.
¹⁰In a posthumously published set of discourses, *Several practical cases of conscience resolved*, which can be dated to the 1670s, Owen candidly remarks that a reproach of the Spirit is perhaps 'the peculiar sin of the nation at this day, and that the like has not been known, or heard of, in any nation under the sun'. Owen, *A complete collection of the sermons of the Reverend and learned John Owen* (1721), 543; *Works* (1965), 9:365.

of the Socinians, Quakers and medieval papacy, all the way back to the biblical era itself. Owen is particularly sensitive to what he perceives is a deleterious over-reaction to spiritual radicalism in the mainstream religious climate of England. To his mind, this fashionable, rationally enlightened opposition to 'vain enthusiasmes' more accurately disguises an outright, inexcusable reproach of the Spirit's indispensable work in our redemption. '[M]any pretending unto the belief and profession of the Gospel', he remarks, 'are so far from owning or desiring a participation of this Spirit in their own persons, as that they deride and contemn them who dare plead or avow any concern in him or his works'.[11] While it seems this reproach has thus far been most vigorously promoted by 'private persons', Owen fears it will soon take hold in the church. And if it does, he warns, it will be tantamount to the same apostasy that led the Jewish church into exile in Babylon.[12]

Certainly, even a quick glance at Parker's *A defence and continuation of the ecclesiastical politie* (1671) readily betrays the sort of derision Owen has in mind, with its relentless mockery of any accent on the supernatural work of the Spirit. And in the second half of Πνευματολογια, Owen will explicitly refute Parker's insistence that evangelical sanctification does not possess any distinctly supernatural character and is instead indistinguishable from natural 'moral virtue'.

While Parker's 'putid figment of moral virtue', as Owen disdainfully calls it, is never far from his sights, it is easy to overstate the significance of this polemical backdrop.[13] The structure of Πνευματολογια reveals a deliberate attempt to proceed more constructively, with the primary intention of outlining the Spirit's soteriological work.[14] After opening with some general theological principles and assumptions, Book I grounds the Spirit's soteriological economy in the context of his work in the 'old' or 'first' creation (Book I). Book II progresses to the Spirit's work in the 'new' creation, a discussion that includes lengthy digressions on the inspiration of Old Testament revelation and the person of Christ. The remaining bulk of the treatise (Books III–V) is then devoted to the supernatural application of Christ's redemptive work through regeneration and the dynamics of a believer's sanctification. This structure buttresses Owen's clear desire to ensure that the Spirit's supernatural, soteriological work is understood to be harmonious with his more general, natural economy. Again,

---

[11] Owen, Πνευματολογια (1674), 21; *Works* (1965), 3:39.
[12] Owen, Πνευματολογια (1674), 24–6; *Works* (1965), 3:42–4.
[13] Owen, Πνευματολογια (1674), n.p. *vii; *Works* (1965), 3:11.
[14] 'For my purpose is, through the permission and assistance of God, to treat from hence of the name, nature, existence, and whole work of the Holy Spirit, with the grace of God through Jesus Christ in the communication of him unto the sons of men.' Owen, Πνευματολογια (1674), 7; *Works* (1965), 3:22.

there are undoubtedly polemical factors at play here, with accusations of irrational and even seditious enthusiasm not far away.[15] But Owen also hints at a related pastoral concern. It is not that the Holy Spirit somehow needs defending against any assault on his work. The Spirit is, and has been, readily redeeming sinners despite opposition, and every spiritually regenerate believer will have ample testimony to that reality in their hearts (quoting 1 Jn 5.10). Rather, Owen targets his biblically reasoned apology at growing the assurance of the believer in the truths they readily profess.[16] To borrow the terminology of the Reformed prolegomena, Owen sees this dogmatic exercise as an application of the 'instrumental use' of human reason to a fundamentally supernatural and spiritual matter, with an explicit pastoral end.[17] The concern to defend this proper relationship between faith and reason is already on view in the preface to Πνευματολογια and will surface regularly throughout the treatise.[18] Indeed, so significant is this relationship that Owen will take it up much more expansively in the planned sequels to Πνευματολογια, eventually published as *The reason of faith* (1677) and Σύνεσις πνευματική: or, *The causes, waies, & means of understanding the mind of God* (1678).

BOOK I

To justify a work of this scope, Owen is keen to open the treatise by underlining the tremendous significance of the Spirit's work in the gracious administration of the gospel. 'It is', he says, 'the second great head or principle of those Gospel-truths wherein the glory of God, and the good of the souls of men are most eminently concerned' – second only to the gift of the Son for sinners. Indeed, so significant is the gift of the Spirit that it was the very context in which God chose to reserve the climactic disclosure of his triune nature.[19] Right at the outset, Owen introduces a principle that will remain a theme throughout the treatise, namely, that the Holy Spirit's work is so fundamental to the economy of salvation that Christ's redemptive accomplishments are virtually redundant without it. Another way of putting this is to say that the economy of the divine Word is inseparable from the economy of the Spirit. Owen then illustrates that

---

[15] Invoking the scars of England's recent past, Parker insinuates that the supernaturalism of Owen and his confrères renders them 'dangerous enemies to the publick peace'. Parker, *A defence and continuation of the ecclesiastical politie*, 332.
[16] Owen, Πνευματολογια (1674), 26–7; *Works* (1965), 3:45–8.
[17] Cf. e.g. Turretin, *Institutes of elenctic theology*, 1.8–10; Mastricht, *Theoretical-practical theology*, 1.2.34.
[18] Owen, Πνευματολογια (1674), n.p. *8–11; *Works* (1965), 3:11–13.
[19] Owen, Πνευματολογια (1674), 8; *Works* (1965), 3:23.

claim through a number of biblical testimonies,[20] before concluding the chapter by outlining the negative circumstantial factors that have pressed him to write the treatise (see earlier).[21]

Four foundational dogmatic propositions

The divine identity of the Spirit

The rest of Book I unfolds four dogmatic propositions which are foundational assumptions to all that follows. The first proposition concerns the precise identity of the Holy Spirit. So, in chapter 2, Owen expounds the various names that are given to the Spirit in Scripture, following this with a fuller statement of the divinity and personality of the Spirit in chapter 3. Throughout this discussion it is not so much the divine nature of the Spirit that he seeks to defend in detail – something he had already done when contesting with the Quakers[22] – but the distinct divine personality of the Spirit that the Socinians had denied.[23] The Socinians had typically regarded biblical references to the Spirit (e.g. the Hebrew term *ruach* [רוח] or the Greek term *pneuma* [πνεῦμα]; literally, 'breath' or 'wind') as mere expressions of divine power.[24] Owen singles out some of their rather idiosyncratic proof texts, such as an interpretation of the genitive construct in 1 Pet. 1.10-11, 'the Spirit of Christ', as a reference to the content of Old Testament prophecy rather than to the sovereign personal agent behind it – an interpretation that he labours to contest.[25] More positively, however, he draws attention to some general testimonies to the Spirit's personality, such as Christ's command to baptize in his 'name' (Mt. 28.19), or his bodily manifestation in the form of a dove (Mt. 3.16; Lk. 3.22; Jn 1.32).[26] Owen also

---

[20] Owen, Πνευματολογια (1674), 9–12; *Works* (1965), 3:24–8.

[21] Owen, Πνευματολογια (1674), 13–27; *Works* (1965), 3:29–47.

[22] See his extensive engagement with John Biddle: Owen, *Vindiciae evangelicae* (1655); *Works* (1965), 12:1–590.

[23] Owen does offer some very brief testimonies to the divinity of the Spirit towards the end of chapter 3: Owen, Πνευματολογια (1674), 64–6; *Works* (1965), 3:89–91.

[24] For a useful discussion of Socinian Christology, with respect to that of Owen, see Kapic, 'The Spirit as Gift', 115–27.

[25] Contrast, e.g. Crell, *Tractatus de Spiritu Sancto*, 12–13, with Owen, Πνευματολογια (1674), 40–2; *Works* (1965), 3:61–3. Owen also refutes the inference Crell will go on to draw from 1 Jn 4.3 in support of his reading of 1 Pet. 1.10-11, which interprets John's reference to the 'spirit of the antichrist' as merely a foreshadowing effect of the Antichrist who had not yet come into the world: so, Crell, *Tractatus de Spiritu Sancto*, 13–14. Cf. Owen, Πνευματολογια (1674), 41–2; *Works* (1965), 3:63–4.

[26] Owen, Πνευματολογια (1674), 50–5; *Works* (1965), 3:72–8. Owen again draws attention to and refutes Crell's inference from apparition of the dove that the Spirit must likewise be a non-rational and therefore impersonal being. Owen responds that it is sufficient that the dove is a 'subsisting substance' (i.e. a 'person' or 'hypostasis' in the technical sense): Owen, Πνευματολογια (1674), 44–5; *Works* (1965), 3:77–8. Cf. Crell, *Tractatus de Spiritu Sancto*, 73–80.

highlights various properties and economic activities that can only be said in reference to a person. On the one hand, the Spirit is ascribed 'understanding', a 'will' and 'power'.[27] On the other, he is said to 'teach', to 'witness' and to act as a 'comforter', or conversely, is capable of being tempted, lied to, grieved, resisted or blasphemed.[28]

The Spirit's personal order of subsistence

The second dogmatic proposition in Book I concerns the Spirit's order of subsistence in the divine nature as the 'third person' of the Trinity. With the orthodox theological tradition, Owen's key assumption here is that the order of 'operation' among the persons points to a natural order of subsistence as the foundation of their economic activity. And unsurprisingly, Owen believes the New Testament points to a Western order of processions: 'Thus the Father is said to send him [the Spirit], and so is the Son also (John 14:16, 26; 16:7). And he is thus said to be sent by the Father and the Son, because he is the Spirit of the Father and Son, proceeding from both.'[29] Yet, in a hint of the famous Augustinian maxim concerning the undivided operations of the divine persons, Owen goes on to reject any form of ontological subordination beneath this economic order: 'But as he is thus sent, so his own will is equally in and unto the work for which he is sent. As the Father is said to send the Son, and yet it was also his own love and grace to come unto us and to save us.' Owen states the precise connection between the order of subsistence and the economic order of operations as follows:

> The Father is the fountain of all, as in being and existence so in operation. The Son is of the Father, begotten of him, and therefore as unto his work is sent by him. . . . The Holy Spirit proceedeth from the Father and the Son, and therefore is sent and given by them as to all the works which he immediately effecteth.[30]

---

[27]Owen, Πνευματολογια (1674), 55–9; Works (1965), 3:78–83. Here Owen's Socinian interlocutor is Jonas Schlictingius. Among other things, Schlictingius argues that Paul's reference to the Spirit who searches all things in 1 Cor. 2.11 is not a divine person but an effect of divine power; likewise, that the attribution of a 'will' to the Spirit is merely a metaphor; and finally, that references to the Spirit's power are only a divine effect within our own spirits. Szlichtyng, De S.S. Trinitate, 605–6; 10; 13–15, respectively.

[28]Owen, Πνευματολογια (1674), 59–64; Works (1965), 3:83–9.

[29]All the quotations in this paragraph are taken from Owen, Πνευματολογια (1674), 66–7; Works (1965), 3:92.

[30]Again, in an emphatic attempt to trace an orthodox path between modalism and ontological subordination, Owen qualifies that the one divine will is equally personalized by each as the undivided principle of these distinct operations. He reiterates the principle even more explicitly at the beginning of chapter 4: 'I say not this as though one person succeeded unto another in their

The Spirit's agency in the 'old creation' and the formation of humanity

The trinitarian order of subsistence is, of course, confidently stated from the explicit order of operations revealed in the divine economy of redemption. But as a third prolegomenous doctrinal detail, Owen believes it is also worth providing an outline of the Spirit's agency in the 'old' or 'original' creation (chapter 4). This he divides up into two, bracketing together the inanimate and non-rational animate creation on the one hand and the 'rational or intelligent part' of creation on the other. His general point here is to insist, with abundant biblical allusion and explicit patristic precedent, that the economic order in redemption must also be consistently mirrored in creation. In this way it is right to contend that the 'forming and perfecting' of the heavenly host, the earth and everything contained within it, should be assigned 'peculiarly to the Spirit of God'.[31]

Of particular interest in this chapter are Owen's rudimentary theological assumptions about the original creation of humanity, assumptions which form the crucial foundation for Owen's discussion of the Spirit's work in our redemption. Following the broad outlines of an anthropology that early modern Protestants inherited from a late-medieval Augustinian consensus, Owen distinguishes between the natural and moral makeup of the first humans in their original integrity. In terms of Adam's original nature, he makes a standard appeal to Gen. 2.7. Here he differentiates Adam's bodily composition ('of the dust of the ground') from his immaterial 'quickening principle', the 'breath of life' granted immediately by God (otherwise known as his soul), which together mark out this creature as a rational hybrid, a 'living soul' somewhere between the purely spiritual angels above and the purely material beasts below.[32]

---

operation, or as though where one ceased and gave over a work, the other took it up and carried it on. For every divine work and every part of every divine work is the work of God, that is, of the whole Trinity unseparably and undividely. But on these divine works which outwardly are of God, there is an especial impression of the order of the operation of each person with respect unto their natural and necessarie subsistence, as also with regard unto their internal characteristical properties, whereby we are distinctly taught to know them and adore them.' Owen, Πνευματολογια (1674), 70; *Works* (1965), 3:94–5.

[31] So, Owen, Πνευματολογια (1674), 70–4, 78; *Works* (1965), 3:94–9, 104.

[32] Owen, Πνευματολογια (1674), 74–5; *Works* (1965), 3:100. On this, compare, e.g. Aquinas, *STh* 1a.q.90.a.3; q.91.a.2 (for Latin text and English translation: Aquinas, *Summa theologiae*); Calvin, *Commentaries on the first book of Moses, called Genesis*, 111–3. One of the most remarkable and exhaustive early modern Reformed precedents for the appropriation of this classical anthropological tradition is found in Jerome Zanchius's exposition of creation, *De operibus Dei*, part. 3, lib. 2., where he discusses the formation, constitution and unity of the body and soul in its original integrity: Zanchius, *Omnium operum theologicorum*, t.3 (cc.541–678). Zanchius's summary at the outset of this discussion captures the general point. As yet devoid of any creature through which he may be properly known, loved and worshipped, after six days of creation, Zanchius remarks that God 'willed to create the most perfect animal, namely a man, who was no less living than the plants,

As regards Adam's moral nature, Owen defines this in terms of the 'image of God' which primarily consisted in a state of 'original righteousness'. In Owen's words, this 'universal rectitude of nature consisting in light power and order in his understanding mind and affections, was the principal part of this image of God wherein he was created'.[33] Owen's definition of the image again aligns with the mainstream Augustinian tradition. Here the association of the image principally with Adam's original moral integrity stems largely from the way that the New Testament connects the soteriological renewal of a lost image to the righteousness of Christ.[34] In other words, if the restoration of the image consists chiefly in a transformation into Christ's likeness as the most perfect reflection of divine glory, it follows logically that the primary feature of the image in the beginning must also have consisted in a qualitative reflection of God's glory, manifesting itself above all in a morally upright nature. It is not that Owen reduces the image exclusively to this original righteousness, as the Lutheran theologian Matthias Flacius Illyricus had done. Flacius's notorious conclusion was that when Adam forfeited this righteousness at the fall, his image-bearing status was entirely lost and substituted with the 'image of Satan'.[35] Owen frequently speaks quite radically about the impact of the fall on the image, particularly in its loss of original righteousness, but he does admit that some 'feeble reliques' of the image remain even after the righteousness is relinquished, both in terms of the soul's spiritual nature and its remaining capacities.[36]

---

no less sentient and able to move itself than the brute animals, and yet no less able to understand and know both himself, other things and God himself than the angels'. Zanchius, *Omnium operum theologicorum*, t.3 (c.543). Unless otherwise indicated, translations of Latin texts are my own.

[33] Owen, Πνευματολογια (1674), 75; *Works* (1965), 3:101.

[34] Here Owen makes the logic of this connection explicit: 'And this appears as from the nature of the thing itself, so from the description which the apostle giveth us of the renovation of that image in us by the grace of Christ (Eph. 4:24; Col. 3:10)': Owen, Πνευματολογια (1674), 75; *Works* (1965), 3:101.

[35] So, e.g., Flacius Illyricus, *Clavis scripturae*, I:542; II:482.

[36] 'By the loss of the image of God, our nature lost its preeminence, and we were reduced into order amongst perishing beasts. For notwithstanding some feeble reliques of this image yet abiding in us, we have really, with respect unto our proper end, in our lapsed condition, more of the bestial nature in us, than of the divine.' Owen, Πνευματολογια (1674), 509; *Works* (1965), 3:580. Cf. this remark in an earlier work: 'We were created in the image of God. Whatever was good or comely in us, was a part of that image: especially the ornaments of our minds, the perfections of our souls. These things had in them a resemblance of, and a correspondency unto some excellencies in God, whereunto by the way of analogie they may be reduced. This being for the most part lost by sin, a shadow of it only remaining in the faculties of our souls; and that dominion over the creatures, which is permitted unto men in the patience of God.' Owen, *A practical exposition on the 130th Psalm* (1669), 220; *Works* (1965), 6:497. In Πνευματολογια Owen is more pessimistic about the 'right' to dominion post-fall, believing this is now 'lost' and that 'mankind scrambles' for it only 'with craft and violence'. Owen, Πνευματολογια (1674), 510; *Works* (1965), 3:580.

In this respect, Owen's position corresponds to that of his early modern Reformed contemporaries who adopted the fairly typical late-medieval retrieval of Augustinian anthropology when attempting to synthesize these inferior and superior aspects of the image.[37] Aquinas, for instance, ties the soul's structural divine likeness to a 'natural' dimension of the image, and the moral likeness or 'original righteousness' to a higher 'supernatural' dimension of the image.[38] Like Aquinas, Owen considers the uprightness of the soul, metaphysically speaking, to be an 'accidental' 'quality' or 'habitual disposition', distinguishable from the substance of the soul itself. Specifically, it provided Adam with three essential capacities: first, 'an ability to discern the mind and will of God, with respect unto all the duty and obedience that God required of him'; second, 'a free uncontrolled unintangled disposition to every duty of the law of his creation in order unto living unto God'; and finally, 'an ability of mind and will, with a readiness of complyance in his affections, for a due regular performance of all duties and abstinence from all sin'.[39] Owen also shares with Aquinas a belief that this quality was immediately 'concreated' with Adam's soul, explicitly distinguishing his position from a common renaissance view that postulated at least a hypothetical division between a disordered purely natural state (*pura naturalia*) and a subsequently added supernatural gift of righteousness (*donum superadditum*).[40] Like his Reformed contemporaries, Owen emphatically resists this later development.[41] Nevertheless, he is certainly content to speak of

---

[37]On this and the following, see Leslie, *The light of grace*, 161–71.
[38]Cf. Aquinas, *STh* 1a.q.93.a.4.
[39]Owen, Πνευματολογια (1674), 76; *Works* (1965), 3:102. On the Reformed adoption of the structural and qualitative dimensions to the image of God, compare, e.g. Zanchius, *Omnium operum theologicorum*, t3 (cc683–86); Leigh, *A systeme or body of divinity consisting of ten books*, 3.8 (288–91); Witsius, *The economy of the covenants between God and man*, I:53; Mastricht, *Theoretico-practica theologia* (1724), 3.9.29–30 (379a–80a).
[40]Aquinas, *STh* 1a.q.93.a.1, a.3, 4; q.95.a.1, a.3. On the later developments, see de Lubac, *Augustinianism and modern theology*, 240–62. As an example of the later development, Robert Bellarmine distinguishes between the 'image' of God (the nature of the soul), and the divine 'likeness' as a further gift of 'original righteousness' which was immediately added to stabilize the soul's purely natural disorder ('concupiscence') and fit it for a supernatural end: Bellarmine, *Opera omnia*, IV/1:18b–20a. The history of this development is complicated in part by historiographical debates about Aquinas's own understanding of the relationship between Adam's 'natural' and 'supernatural' ends, together with his later reception. While all agree that Aquinas believed that Adam was created in a supernatural state, some have argued (notably, against Henri de Lubac) that he clearly distinguishes between a 'purely natural' end and the 'supernatural' end he acquires by grace, setting things up for the more emphatic separation of these states that would come later: e.g. Mulcahy, *Aquinas' notion of pure nature and the Christian integralism of Henri de Lubac*, 49–122; Long, *Natura pura*, 10–51. For a balanced assessment of Aquinas's position, see Bauerschmidt, *Thomas Aquinas*, 128–34.
[41]'For although this rectitude of his nature be distinguishable and separable from the faculties of the soul of man; yet in his first creation they were not actually distinguished from them, nor superadded or infused into them when created, but were concreated with them': Owen, Πνευματολογια (1674),

some distinction between the nature of the soul and the 'quickning principle of spiritual life' that is 'inlaid . . . by especial grace', as he will later put it, which furnished Adam a 'supernatural' 'life', provided it is understood to have been naturally concreated with the soul.[42] Without this chief dimension of the image, his soul's natural powers alone were not adequate to equip him for the kind of vocation and covenantal relationship with God that he was intended to enjoy in the Garden.[43] In this way, then, Owen again exemplifies an Augustinian consensus which holds that while Adam was naturally created for an end of blessedness with God, the actual possibility of attaining that end could only be provided by gracious, supernatural means – for the simple reason that such an end is entirely out of proportion with any natural, creaturely capacity.[44] Of course, we must not miss the primary pneumatological observation that he seeks to make throughout this anthropological digression, which concerns the Spirit's immediate personal agency in Adam's physical and spiritual constitution.

The distinct manner of the Spirit's acts within the divine economy

Owen closes this 'short view' of the Spirit's work in the 'first creation' with a reference to his agency in the providential preservation of the old order.[45] However, before embarking on his exposition of the Spirit's work in the 'new creation', Owen sets out one last preliminary dogmatic statement concerning the general manner in which Scripture describes the acts of the Holy Spirit in

---

76; *Works* (1965), 3:102. The Reformed rejection of this development has little to do with more recent Protestant aversion to a 'nature-grace' paradigm, but stems in large part from a fundamental commitment to the inherent depravity of 'concupiscence': Turretin, *Institutes of elenctic theology*, 5.9; 5.11; Mastricht, *Theoretico-practica theologia*, 3.9.45 (383b-84a). Contra, e.g., Bavinck, *Reformed dogmatics*, 2:539–54. Moreover, Baschera has observed that some Reformed thinkers were happy to speak of 'original righteousness' as a 'supernatural' gift, even if they would insist that it was basic to Adam's originally created integrity; Baschera, 'Total depravity?'

[42]Owen distinguishes between the soul itself as a natural 'quickning principle' (as noted above), and what he calls a 'quickning principle of spiritual life': 'for in life natural the soul is the quickning principle, and the body is the principle quickened. . . . So in life spiritual the soul is not in and by its essential properties the quickning principle of it, but it is the principle that is quickened'; Owen, Πνευματολογια (1674), 243; *Works* (1965), 3:287.

[43]For the above, see, Owen, Πνευματολογια (1674), 76; *Works* (1965), 3:102. Cf. Owen, Πνευματολογια (1674), 240–1; *Works* (1965), 3:284–5.

[44]On the importance of distinguishing between the constitution of humanity physically and theologically, while retaining their naturally created union, note Turretin's parallel remark: 'The question is not whether original righteousness may be called natural constitutively *a priori* or consecutively *a posteriori* (as if it either constituted or followed the nature itself). No one of our divines asserts this. . . . But the question is – Is it natural with respect to the entire state, necessary to the perfection of the entire nature and pertaining to the native gifts of entire man? For thus man is not considered simply physically as man, but theologically and morally as sound and entire'; Turretin, *Institutes of elenctic theology*, 5.11.4.

[45]Owen, Πνευματολογια (1674), 77–8; *Works* (1965), 3:103–4.

the economy of God's works.⁴⁶ Consistent with his earlier observations, Owen deliberately structures this discussion in a way that points both to the Spirit's procession as the third person of the trinitarian *taxis*, as well as his full possession of the divine attributes. So, on the one hand, he draws attention to the ways in which the Father is said to 'give', 'send', 'minister' and 'pour' out the Spirit, or his gifts. On the other hand, he is keen to stress that this economic procession is a voluntary and free act of the Spirit (unlike his necessary 'natural' procession) so that he is equally the subject of his economic acts. Accordingly, as a free divine agent, he is said to 'come', to 'fall on', to 'rest on' and to 'depart from' some persons. Owen concludes the chapter with a final observation, refuting Crell's suggestion that the 'distributions' of the Spirit's 'gifts' (Heb. 2.4) represent different portions of the Holy Spirit. Of course, Crell does not think the 'Spirit' is anything more than an emanation of divine power.⁴⁷ In a sense, Owen agrees that the 'gifts' are effects of divine power but once again is keen to stress the Spirit's personal agency as the subject of these 'distributions'.⁴⁸

BOOK II

An overview of the Spirit's economy in the 'new creation'

The Spirit's agency in Old Testament revelation

Book II of Πνευματολογια proceeds with an overview of the Spirit's more conspicuous work in the 'new creation', or the economy of redemption. The Book falls into four key parts. It begins with an outline of the Spirit's operations in the Old Testament, preparatory to the New (Chapter 1). As he remarks at the outset, the vast majority of this work had 'a respect unto our Lord Jesus Christ and the Gospel, and so was preparatory unto the compleating of the great work of the new-creation in and by him'.⁴⁹ This discussion he divides up into two – focusing on the extraordinary works and those that improved and exalted existing abilities for the welfare of the church. Owen devotes most of the chapter to the former, and especially, to the Spirit's agency in revelation, both in terms of prophecy and biblical inspiration. This remarkable and detailed discussion offers the most extensive treatment of this issue in his entire corpus.⁵⁰

---

⁴⁶For the following, see, Owen, Πνευματολογια (1674), 79–95; *Works* (1965), 3:105–24.
⁴⁷Crell is, in fact, keen to emphasize the unity of the 'Spirit', but his unity is capable of being distributed into diverse parts (he uses the analogy of the water in the ocean): Crell, *Tractatus de Spiritu Sancto*, 94–126. Note especially his comments on Heb. 2.4: Crell, *Tractatus de Spiritu Sancto*, 99–101.
⁴⁸Owen, Πνευματολογια (1674), 93–5; *Works* (1965), 3:121–4.
⁴⁹Owen, Πνευματολογια (1674), 98; *Works* (1965), 3:126.
⁵⁰For a more detailed outline of Owen's discussion, see Leslie, *The light of grace*, 203–12.

There are a number of features worth noting. The first is Owen's explicit indebtedness to Aquinas for the broad outline of his account.[51] In particular, Owen refers to three specific modes of prophetic inspiration: sensible voices, impressions on the imagination (as in dreams and visions) and direct illustration or enlightenment of the mind.[52] Alongside this, Owen emphasizes that the minds of the prophets were 'acted guided and raised in a due manner by the Holy Spirit' for the receipt of any divine impression.[53] This granted the prophet an 'infallible assurance that it was himself [the Spirit] alone by whom they were acted', and not some satanic delusion.[54] Throughout his account, Owen clearly assumes something approximating Aquinas's adaptation of the peripatetic cognitive tradition, where all knowledge involves a concurrence of some input or evidence that results in a mental 'intelligible species', alongside a God-given capacity of the soul to perceive that input (a theory of illumination).[55] Moreover, he adds, having furnished this revelation, the Spirit also guided 'the very organs' of the prophet's body through which they then communicate 'the revelation which they had received by inspiration from him'.[56] In other words, the Spirit's special sovereign agency in prophecy did not stop with the mere inspiration of the prophet's mind, leaving the rest to a more general providential concurrence, but extended as far as the communication itself, ensuring it was not corrupted by the 'frailties or infirmities' of the prophet. The same principles apply to Owen's description of scriptural inspiration, which he labels a 'distinct species or kind of prophesie'.[57] There was a communication of revelation to the writer's mind alongside a spiritual elevation of the mind to grasp its truth with infallible certainty. And again, to preserve the inerrancy of the text, the Spirit specifically concurred with the actual process of inscripturation by the 'suggestion of words unto them to express what their minds conceived' and the 'guidance of their hands in setting down the words suggested'.[58]

As Richard A. Muller has observed, the Reformed tradition readily adopted medieval accounts of prophetic inspiration without any significant revision, and Owen is no exception.[59] Owen's reception of these ideas illustrates not simply a point of continuity with the older tradition but also a more fundamental concern to account for this supernatural inspiration in a way that coheres with extant

---

[51] Aquinas discusses inspiration in Aquinas, *STh* 2a2ae.qq.171–4.
[52] Owen, Πνευματολογια (1674), 106; *Works* (1965), 3:135. Cf. Aquinas, *STh* 2a2ae.q.174.a.1.ad3.
[53] Owen, Πνευματολογια (1674), 109; *Works* (1965), 3:138.
[54] Owen, Πνευματολογια (1674), 104; *Works* (1965), 3:133.
[55] Leslie, *The light of grace*, 207–9. For a brief overview of this cognitive theory, together with Owen's appropriation of it, see Leslie, *The light of grace*, 257–64. See also further below.
[56] Owen, Πνευματολογια (1674), 105; *Works* (1965), 3:134. Cf. Aquinas, *STh* 2a2ae.q.173.a.4.
[57] Owen, Πνευματολογια (1674), 113; *Works* (1965), 3:143.
[58] Owen, Πνευματολογια (1674), 113; *Works* (1965), 3:144.
[59] Muller, *Post-Reformation Reformed dogmatics*, 2:38–51, 61–2.

theories concerning the normal, natural processes of cognition. While Owen's theory of scriptural inspiration is undeniably more rigorous than others,[60] by no means is it a crude form of dictation theory, readily acknowledging, for instance, how the Spirit's sovereign choice of words worked through, not in spite of, the human author's personality, vocabulary and mental processes.[61]

More briefly, Owen finally concludes chapter 1 with an overview of the Spirit's parallel work in Old Testament times through extraordinary, miraculous acts, as well as in the elevation of existing powers for specific purposes in the life of the Jewish church.[62]

The general dispensation of the Spirit in the 'new creation'

Owen devotes the remainder of Book II to an extensive discussion of the Spirit's principal work in the new creation as it centres on Christ himself, the head of this new creation. In the meantime, however, he sets out some general foundational principles concerning the Spirit's work in the New Testament era of the church.[63] At the outset, he keenly accentuates the Old Testament prophetic expectation that the 'plentiful effusion of the Spirit' would be 'the great privilege and pre-eminence of the Gospel-church state',[64] a promise emphatically underlined by Christ himself the night before he died, in the famous upper room discourse of John's Gospel.[65] Conscious, yet again, of the way such an accent on the Spirit might be scorned by some of his contemporaries, Owen confidently underlines just how crucial the Spirit's work is to the vitality of the church and the ministry of the gospel, while denying predictable charges of enthusiasm and the like.

The agency of the Spirit with respect to the humanity of Christ

The identity and work of Christ is, of course, the focal point of God's work in the new creation. '[I]n and by him', Owen remarks, 'in his work of the new creation all the glorious properties of the nature of God are manifested and displayed incomparably above what they were in the creation of all things in the

---

[60] Cf. e.g., Herman Witsius, who stresses the dual authorship of Scripture more emphatically than Owen: Witsius, *Miscellaneorum sacrorum*, 1.11.11, 14 (84–5, 86–7); 1.22.19 (337). And Owen's position is clearly distinct from someone like the Renaissance exegete, Alfonso Tostatus (1410–55), who as Muller points out, believes that having enlightened the prophets' minds, the Spirit left the words and expression to themselves: Tostatus, *Operum tomus vigesimus*, 411b. Cf. Muller, *Post-Reformation Reformed dogmatics*, 2:46–7.
[61] Owen, Πνευματολογια (1674), 113–14; *Works* (1965), 3:144–5.
[62] Owen, Πνευματολογια (1674), 114–20; *Works* (1965), 3:145–51.
[63] Owen, Πνευματολογια (1674), 121–7; *Works* (1965), 3:152–9.
[64] Owen, Πνευματολογια (1674), 122; *Works* (1965), 3:153.
[65] Owen, Πνευματολογια (1674), 124–5; *Works* (1965), 3:156–7.

beginning'.⁶⁶ For the rest of Book II, therefore, Owen will outline the Spirit's eminent role in this Christological economy, beginning with the incarnation of the Son and concluding with his ultimate glorification in the life of his mystical body, the church. In a sense, this final stage will occupy Owen for the rest of Πνευματολογια and its thematic sequels, but here he first situates it specifically within the context of Christ's exaltation.

Owen is justly famous for his deliberate and carefully articulated 'Spirit-christology', but that is not to say it is dogmatically innovative or entirely unique, even within the early modern Reformed tradition.⁶⁷ Indeed, it is clear that he himself merely considers it to be an inevitable detail within the uncontroversial account of triune operations he has already sought to unfold. So, with due deference to the principle of undivided operations, he will assert that the Father's eminent role is in 'sending, giving, [and] appointing' the Son; 'in preparing him a body, in comforting and supporting him'; and 'in rewarding and giving a people unto him'. Yet, the 'actual operation' of these works belongs eminently to the Son himself: 'the Son condescendeth, consenteth, and engageth to do and accomplish in his own person, the whole work which in the authority, counsel and wisdom of the Father was appointed for him (Phil. 2:5-8)'. Likewise, the Spirit too is responsible for immediately putting into effect 'whatever was to be done in reference unto the person of the Son, or the sons of men, for the perfecting and accomplishment of the Father's counsel, and the Son's work'.⁶⁸

In relation to the latter, Owen notes how the Socinians reject as redundant a specific pneumatological economy that pertains to the human nature of Christ himself. Surely the Son, 'in his own person', can 'perform all things requisite both for the forming, supporting, sanctifying and preserving of his own nature, without the especial assistance of the Holy Ghost?'⁶⁹ In response, Owen's central contention throughout chapters 3 and 4 is that the 'only singular immediate act of the person of the Son on the human nature, was the assumption of it into subsistence with himself'. Apart from this, 'all other actings' of the Son on his human nature did not 'necessarily ensue on the union' itself but were put into effect immediately by the Spirit.⁷⁰ Beginning with the conception and formation of Christ's body and replete with biblical justification, Owen traces the Spirit's

---

⁶⁶Owen, Πνευματολογια (1674), 126; Works (1965), 3:157–8.
⁶⁷Recently, Dominic Legge has drawn attention to this distinctive in Aquinas's writings. Given Owen's familiarity with Aquinas, Owen himself may not have considered his own contribution to be quite as novel as contemporary scholarship has assumed: Legge, *The Trinitarian Christology of St Thomas Aquinas*. Cf. too, for other Puritan contributions, Beeke and Jones, *A Puritan theology*, 342–5.
⁶⁸Owen, Πνευματολογια (1674), 127; Works (1965), 3:158–9.
⁶⁹Owen, Πνευματολογια (1674), 129; Works (1965), 3:160.
⁷⁰Owen, Πνευματολογια (1674), 129–31; Works (1965), 3:161–2.

work through the sanctification of his humanity with habitual grace, his gradual acquisition of wisdom, the provision of specific gifts necessary for his kingly, priestly and prophetic ministry, together with an empowerment to perform miracles, resist temptation and ultimately undergo his death and resurrection.

Owen's contribution has been outlined in detail elsewhere, but several observations are in order.[71] The chief of these is his concern to bring together a consistent application of the trinitarian appropriations with a typically Reformed commitment to the fundamentals of the Chalcedonian Christological settlement, with its framing of the *communicatio idiomatum* between the two natures. On the one hand, the immediate operation of the Spirit on the formation and perfection of Christ's humanity represents the pre-eminent outworking of his designation as the 'immediate peculiar [and] efficient cause of all external divine operations'.[72] Far from being an exception to this principle, Christ's humanity embodies its pinnacle and perfection. On the other hand, the very same principle ensures the integrity of both natures is preserved without confusion or change to either, which was a particular concern among early modern Reformed theologians in the context of debates with their Lutheran counterparts.

Furthermore, Owen's insistence upon the Son's immediacy in the assumption itself is critical to protecting his Christology from any unwanted Nestorian implications. It upholds the Son's eminency as the immediate personal subject of his incarnate activity, notwithstanding the Spirit's immediacy as the agent who effects his divine will within the human nature itself.[73]

Finally, consistent with the Reformed pattern, this account of the Spirit's agency upon Christ's humanity not only distinguishes itself from Socinian and Lutheran alternatives but also from typical Catholic accounts of the so-called grace or theology of union, which attribute beatific perfection of wisdom to Christ's humanity from conception, simply by virtue of the hypostatic union itself.[74] There may even be a sense in which he modifies more typically

---

[71] For example, Spence, *Incarnation and inspiration*.

[72] Owen, *Πνευματολογια* (1674), 130; *Works* (1965), 3:161

[73] Oliver Crisp's critique of Owen's Christology misses the subtleties of Owen's formulation. At no point does Owen deny that the Son is the immediate personal subject of his incarnate activity. Yet with the Chalcedonian tradition, Owen clearly assumes that the person of the Son cannot act in abstraction, but only ever performs divine or human acts through his two respective natures. And therefore, Owen's point is simply that the divine nature of the Son (of which his divine will is an attribute) cannot operate directly on his human nature without the mediation of the Spirit, otherwise there would be a straightforward confusion of natures. Cf. Crisp, 'John Owen on Spirit Christology'.

[74] So, Owen, *Πνευματολογια* (1674), 138; *Works* (1965), 3:170–1. It should be noted that the Catholic position typically acknowledged Christ's gradual acquisition of wisdom too, as a function of possessing a humanity furnished with bodily senses, cognitive faculties and thus the potential

Reformed accounts of the theology of union. Like his Reformed counterparts, Owen certainly assumes an element of sanctification stemming from the hypostatic union itself, not least in the form of a human nature entirely free from original sin and adequately furnished with habitual grace: in other words, a human nature in its state of original integrity.[75] But Owen more emphatically distinguishes this grace from the specific prophetic, priestly and kingly gifts the Son receives from the Father via the Spirit, to accomplish his mediatorial work: gifts he received first in the womb, and then more fully at his baptism.[76] Arguably this is intended to ensure the Father's distinctive economy in the work of redemption is not side-lined or replaced by a function of the hypostatic union itself.[77]

The Spirit's agency with respect to the mystical body of Christ

In the final chapter of Book II, Owen completes his outline of the Spirit's economy in connection with the head of the new creation by attending to his operations, namely the exalted Christ's mystical body, the church. In general terms, 'this belongs unto the establishment of our faith, that he who prepared, sanctified, and glorified the human nature, the natural body of Jesus Christ, the head of the church, hath [also] undertaken to prepare, sanctify, and glorify his mystical body, or all the elect given unto him of the Father'.[78] As ever, Owen is keen to situate this work within an explicit articulation of the trinitarian economy in redemption. If the Father is the 'peculiar fountain' of the gracious economy, and the Son the 'great treasurer' of grace and mercy on account of his mediatorial work, the Spirit is the agent by whom the saving and sanctifying fruits of Christ's work are 'actually communicated unto us'.[79] Moreover, Owen once again stresses that this voluntary economy rests upon a necessary eternal *taxis* of persons, where in accordance with that *taxis*, each of the three persons

---

for acquiring knowledge. Yet, this gradual acquisition of wisdom was mysteriously juxtaposed alongside his possession of an actualized perfection of wisdom. Cf. Aquinas, *STh* 3a.q.9.aa.2–4.
[75] So, Owen, *Πνευματολογια* (1674), 136–7; *Works* (1965), 3:168–9.
[76] Owen, *Πνευματολογια* (1674), 138–41; *Works* (1965), 3:171–4; Cf. Owen, *Hebrews* (1668), 16–17; *Works* (1991), 20:28–31. Junius, for example, casts the 'theology of union' in a similar Trinitarian frame to Owen, where the Father sends the Son and endows him 'without measure'. Unlike Owen, however, he does not make a distinction between this gift flowing purely from the 'grace of union' versus discrete special gifts of the Spirit for his mediatorial work: Junius, *Opuscula theologica selecta*, 58; likewise, Alsted, *Praecognitorum theologicorum libri duo*, 1.6 (24–7).
[77] Cf. especially, Owen, *Hebrews* (1668), 16–17; *Works* (1991), 20:28–31. See, Leslie, *The light of grace*, 201–2. Cf. Spence, *Incarnation and inspiration*, 57, 116–7; Trueman, *The claims of truth*, 175–6.
[78] Owen, *Πνευματολογια* (1674), 155; *Works* (1965), 3:189.
[79] Owen, *Πνευματολογια* (1674), 163; *Works* (1965), 3:199.

freely consent to this work as the hypostatic subjects of the single divine will.[80] In terms of the Spirit's particular economy in all this, Owen has an eye to Christ's specific promises of his spiritual presence and provision for the church after his heavenly exaltation (e.g. Mt. 28.18-20; Jn 14.15-17; 16.13-15; Acts 1.4, 8), which is essential to its 'being', 'success' of its ministry and its 'edification'. Of course, if the vitality of the church and its ministry absolutely depends on Christ and the grace he supplies through the Spirit, this begs a question that Owen anticipates towards the end of the chapter: Does that render the meaningful agency of the individual believer essentially redundant?[81] Lurking in the background here is his sensitivity to the establishment disdain of any perceived over-emphasis on the Spirit's work. In the rest of Πνευματολογια, Owen will furnish a detailed outline of the individual's role within their sanctification. At this point, however, he is simply content to stress that the Scriptures see no conflict between our duty of obedience to the divine will and our wholescale dependence upon the Spirit's power.

At the end of Book II, Owen summarizes the Spirit's redemptive economy under three heads: '1. Of sanctifying grace; 2. Of especial gifts; 3. Of peculiar evangelical privileges.' The rest of Πνευματολογια is fundamentally concerned with the first of these. Book III is narrowly focused on regeneration, followed by a treatment of sanctification (Book IV), and it concludes with some motives that necessitate gospel holiness (Book V). Owen leaves the second and third aspects of the Spirit's redemptive economy to the eventual sequels of Πνευματολογια: *The reason of faith* (1677); *The causes, waies, & means of understanding the mind of God* (1678); *A discourse of the work of the Holy Spirit in prayer* (1682); *Two discourses concerning the Holy Spirit* (1693), on the Spirit as 'comforter' and as the 'author of spiritual gifts'.[82]

BOOK III

The nature of regeneration

An overview of the doctrine in the context of the 'new creation'

Owen begins his treatment of regeneration by comparing the Spirit's spiritual 'vivification' of a sinner to the original creation of light and life out of the formless 'void' of 'darkness and death'. While all three persons are involved in this work, the Spirit is eminently its 'efficient cause'. And in broad outline, Owen highlights a number of its key features. First, while he recognizes that the

---

[80]Owen, Πνευματολογια (1674), 162–3; *Works* (1965), 3:198–9.
[81]Owen, Πνευματολογια (1674), 166–8; *Works* (1965), 3:203–5.
[82]Each of these are published in volume 4 of the Goold edition.

revelation of this work is much more distinctly revealed in the New Testament, it was no less a reality for all God's elect under the Old Testament. There may be a variety of outward means and circumstances surrounding a person's regeneration, but Owen insists its essential character is the same. His theological reasons are simple: not only is the unregenerate condition of sinners 'absolutely the same', so too is the 'state whereinto men are brought', as is the efficient spiritual cause of the change.[83] Second, he is keen to clarify what regeneration is not. Against the Catholics, it cannot be collapsed into an outward sacramental ordinance like baptism,[84] nor, against some of his Protestant contemporaries, can it be thought of as a mere moral reformation or 'new course of actions',[85] let alone as 'enthusiastical raptures, exstasies, voices, or any thing of the kind'.[86] Rather, before any reformation of life or behaviour, to be regenerate is to be made a 'new creature' in Christ (cf. 2 Cor. 5.17).

Building upon the anthropological assumptions noted earlier, Owen provides a metaphysical synthesis of this theological reality which he will develop further in subsequent chapters. In brief, regeneration entails the spiritual infusion of a new 'habit of grace', reinstating that quality of righteousness lost at the fall and providing the indispensable foundation for a new life of true holiness. If Adam inherently possessed that quality as the chief dimension of the image of God in the beginning, the difference now is that the principle stems from the grace of Christ alone, and is fundamental both to Old Testament prophetic expectations of a 'new heart' (Ezek. 36.25-7; Jer. 31.33) and what the New Testament means by a renewal of the image after the likeness of Christ (so, Eph. 4.24; Col. 3.10). As always, Owen is clearly attempting to navigate past the Scylla and Charybdis of what he believes is an aridly moralistic, Spirit-less religion which severely underestimates the impact of original sin, on the one hand, and, on the other, the accusation of an overly spiritualized radicalism that despises the usual means of grace.[87] Indeed, in a pointed remark directed squarely at the established church, Owen begins the next chapter by confidently asserting that the 'substance' of his own position is that 'of the divines of the Church of England, at the Synod of Dort, two whereof died bishops' – the illustrious John Davenant and Joseph Hall – 'and others of them were dignified

---

[83] Owen, Πνευματολογια (1674), 178–9; *Works* (1965), 3:215–16.
[84] Owen, Πνευματολογια (1674), 179–81; *Works* (1965), 3:216–17.
[85] Owen, Πνευματολογια (1674), 181–6; *Works* (1965), 3:217–24.
[86] Owen, Πνευματολογια (1674), 186–7; *Works* (1965), 3:224–6.
[87] He quotes Parker's aspersions against those who 'set down nice and subtile processes of regeneration, to fill peoples heads with innumerable swarms of superstitious fears'. Owen, Πνευματολογια (1674), 189; *Works* (1965), 3:227. Cf. Parker, *A defence and continuation of the ecclesiastical politie*, 306–7.

in the hierarchy'. 'I mention it', he adds, 'that those by whom these things are despised, may consider a little whose ashes they trample on and scorn'.[88]

The fall and the necessity of regeneration

Over the next two chapters, Owen seeks to distinguish any preparatory works of the Spirit from the work of regeneration itself and then proceeds to overview the effects of sin that render that work necessary. In the first instance, he begins by acknowledging that while there is nothing within the fallen soul that provides a 'formal disposition' for regeneration, it is certainly true that the existing faculties of the soul provide the necessary 'material disposition'.[89] In other words, the infusion of sanctifying grace does not add to or alter the material substance of the soul, a misunderstanding that sometimes afflicts modern Protestant characterizations of the notion.[90] Rather, as an accidental quality, it radically re-orders its powers. Furthermore, Owen readily admits that the Spirit occasionally induces a partial illumination of the gospel truth, which might produce some conviction of sin and reformation of behaviour.[91] While those affected in this way are often the subject of an ensuing regeneration, it is formally distinct from that regeneration itself.[92] For whatever its superficial resemblance to genuine conversion, it nevertheless falls short of that reality and explains the phenomenon of an apparently temporary illumination famously described in Heb. 6.4.[93] By contrast, genuine saving illumination provides a 'direct intuitive insight and prospect into spiritual things, as that in their own spiritual nature they suit, please, and satisfie it. So that it is transformed into them, cast into the mould of them, and rests in them'.[94] Such a remark again betrays Owen's indebtedness to the late-medieval peripatetic cognitive tradition where intellection entails an adequation of the mind to the object of knowledge through the impression of an image or 'intelligible species' of that object. In this case the impression is no less than the supernatural and spiritual truth of the gospel, indeed, the very image of Christ himself (to support this argument Owen quotes his beloved 2 Cor. 3.18; 4.6, along with Rom. 6.7; 12.2; and 1 Cor. 2.13-15). And the rather illusive notion of 'intuitive' (versus

---

[88]Owen, Πνευματολογια (1674), 191; Works (1965), 3:229.
[89]Cf. Thomas Goodwin, Works, 6:209; Voetius, Selectarum disputationum theologicarum, 2:438–9.
[90]E.g., Alister E. McGrath, Reformation thought, 103.
[91]For the following, Owen, Πνευματολογια (1674), 193–203; Works (1965), 3:231–42.
[92]Quoting Augustine, Owen explicitly rejects the late-medieval Catholic notion (with Franciscan origins) that with the help of actual grace (gratia gratis data), a person might be able 'to do what is in them' (facere quod est in se) to merit in a congruent fashion, infused justifying grace (gratia gratum faciens): Owen, Πνευματολογια (1674), 202; Works (1965), 3:241.
[93]On Heb 6.4, see Calvin, Commentaries on the epistle of Paul the Apostle to the Hebrews, 135–8; Turretin, Institutes of elenctic theology, 15.15.1–15.
[94]Owen, Πνευματολογια (1674), 199–200; Works (1965), 3:238.

'abstractive') cognition, which is typically traced back to Duns Scotus, at the very least denotes a further immediate certitude of the cognitive object, 'a direct view', as Owen puts it.[95] In Owen's mind, then, authentic regeneration is distinguished by a full conformity of the soul to its spiritual object, which results in a unique effect on the conscience, will and affections that a partial or 'preparatory' illumination simply cannot produce.

Against what Owen perceives to be an excessively optimistic assessment of human nature among some of his contemporaries, whom he pejoratively labels 'Socinianized Arminians', in chapter 3, he is chiefly concerned to underline the depravity and helplessness of the fallen state. Owen clearly adopts a traditional faculty psychology where the mind is the 'guiding and leading' faculty and the will the 'ruling' or 'governing' faculty of the soul.[96] Sidestepping contested issues such as the possibility that the will might reject the object proposed by the mind, Owen describes the effects of sin on both faculties in detail.[97] Whereas God ought to be the mind's 'principal object', sin has distracted it from him and introduced 'vanity' in its wake. Even more corrupt than the mind are the understanding and the heart, which both consent to the mind's vanity and also obstinately reject any impression of truth.[98] Alluding to a classic Protestant doctrine of original sin, which is more severe than its Catholic

---

[95]Cf. Owen, *The nature of apostasie* (1676), 26–7; *Works* (1965), 7:21. On Scotus's admittedly vexed distinction between 'intuitive' and 'abstractive' cognition, see, for example, Day, *Intuitive cognition*, 1947); Boler, 'Intuitive and abstractive cognition'; Tachau, *Vision and certitude in the age of Ockham*, 68–81; Dumont, 'Theology as a science and Duns Scotus's Distinction between Intuitive and Abstractive Cognition'; Wolter, 'Duns Scotus on Intuition, memory, and our knowledge of individuals'; Wolter and McCord Adams, 'Memory and intuition'; Langston, 'Scotus's doctrine of intuitive cognition'; King, 'Thinking about things'.

[96]Owen, Πνευματολογια (1674), 199; *Works* (1965), 3:238. Here in chapter 3, Owen actually follows Paul's tripartite distinction between the 'mind', 'understanding' and the 'heart' in Eph. 4.17-18. While the 'heart' is the 'practical principle of operation', embracing the actual compliance of the will to the 'mind' and 'understanding', the 'understanding' is distinguished as the 'directive, discerning, judging-faculty of the soul, that leads unto practice. It guides the soul in the choice of the notions which it receives from the mind': Owen, Πνευματολογια (1674), 212; *Works* (1965), 3:252. Here Owen does not seem to have in mind a distinct faculty in the strict sense, but something akin to the Greek notion of *synderesis* (συντήρησις) which, like Aquinas, he considers to be a habit containing the principles which inform acts of practical judgement. Cf. his remark in his *Pro Sacris Scripturis* (1658): 'The Greeks call [it] Συντήρησιν, which is a natural habit by which the intellect of a man is born fit to give an assent to the first principles of moral operations. It is συνείδησις, or the necessary judgment of a man concerning himself conforming to that habit'. *Works* (1965), 16:471. Cf. Aquinas, *STh* 1a.q.79.a.12.

[97]Note, Owen, Πνευματολογια (1674), 236–7; *Works* (1965), 3:281.

[98]It is not that Owen's account of sin results in a radical inversion of the usual, mind-led operations of the faculties themselves, as Griffiths suggests, but it is true that Owen's accent on the particular depravity of the practical faculties reflects what Muller calls a 'soteriological voluntarism' that is typical among the Reformed: Cf. Griffiths, *Redeem the time*, 65; Muller, *The unaccommodated Calvin*, 159–73.

counterpart, Owen indicates that there is now not simply a 'natural' and 'moral' 'impotency' resulting from the absence of original righteousness, but also a pernicious depraved habit, a positive 'power' which entrenches the soul and the affections in wilful enmity towards God.[99] Consequently, Owen argues, when the fallen mind encounters the gospel, it is thoroughly incapable of embracing its uniquely supernatural, 'evangelical' truth and will stubbornly refuse it. At best it will simply latch on to any 'moral' accidents of the gospel, which reaffirm principles embedded in the natural law or light of nature and even then, without a proper regard for their spiritual ends.[100]

Such an account of the fallen state, then, leads naturally to the proposition at the beginning of chapter 4, affirming the 'necessity of an internal, powerful, effectual work of the Holy Ghost on the souls of men, to deliver them out of this state and condition by regeneration'.[101] But before devoting the last two chapters of Book III to regeneration itself, Owen expands on the anthropological assumptions he has already outlined by drawing an analogy between natural versus spiritual life and death.[102] Just as the soul is the quickening principle of the body, so too is the spiritual habit of grace the quickening principle of the soul. The separation of the soul from the body in natural death might leave it bereft of any active power, but a kind of 'passive' or 'remote' power remains, which may yet be activated again by the soul's return. Likewise, Adam's loss of habitual grace left his soul bereft of any active spiritual power – a point he keenly emphasizes in this chapter – but Adam still possessed a passive power to have it quickened through regeneration. Only this time, Owen reiterates his point that the habitual grace received in regeneration is not one's native possession, like it was for Adam in the beginning, but stems exclusively from Christ who renews the image of God after his specific likeness. Moreover, Owen also hints at a further, significant analogy between the natural, material *'vehicula gratiae'* (means of grace) – the gospel in its verbal 'promises' or 'exhortations' – and its spiritual form through which the Spirit delivers Christ's regenerative grace.[103] Determined, as always, to sidestep the dreaded spectre of enthusiasm, Owen insists that spiritual regeneration occurs in conjunction with the gospel word, not apart from it. Nonetheless, the formal, spiritual reality or substance of the gospel cannot be collapsed into its natural, material accidents, or else the ministry of the gospel amounts to no more than a kind of 'Pelagian'

---

[99]Owen, Πνευματολογια (1674), 225–37; Works (1965), 3:266–82. Catholics had typically limited original sin to the depravation of original righteousness which results in a disorder or concupiscence: not so much a sin itself, but rather something which inevitably leads the soul into sin.
[100]Owen, Πνευματολογια (1674), 220–4; 34–6; Works (1965), 3:261–6; 78–9.
[101]Owen, Πνευματολογια (1674), 239; Works (1965), 3:282.
[102]For this, see Owen, Πνευματολογια (1674), 238–42; Works (1965), 3:283–7.
[103]For this, see Owen, Πνευματολογια (1674), 243–5; Works (1965), 3:288–91.

moralism. In this way, then, just as the natural soul serves as the passive power for spiritual grace, so too is it naturally capable of comprehending the verbal material content of the gospel, the natural means through which the Spirit will perform his supernatural, regenerative work.

The nature, causes and means of regeneration

In chapter 5, this last clarification regarding the ministry of the gospel is sharpened in a polemical direction to form the backdrop to his own constructive account of regeneration. Owen is especially concerned to distance genuine spiritual regeneration from a view that reduces its efficacy to 'moral suasion' or the external proclamation of the gospel alone. The denial of the need for any 'physical' spiritual operation on the will in regeneration is recognizably a Molinist or Arminian distinctive, and Owen is clearly alarmed that it is gaining traction within the established church. In his mind, it amounts to no more than a revived form of Pelagianism that can be traced back through the Jesuits, the sophisms of Gabriel Biel, William of Ockham and Duns Scotus, to the eponymous bête noire himself. Indeed, by contrast, Owen emphatically underlines the continuity of his own alternative with the convictions of the mainstream Augustinian tradition, including the more 'sober school-men; and others of late without number'.[104] It is unlikely that any of Owen's interlocutors were crassly denying the need for the Holy Spirit to remove existing 'prejudices' and 'moral impediments' to belief, as Owen seems to concede.[105] Nonetheless, the thing that troubles him is how this concession is merely limited to restoring the natural neutrality of human reason, so that an indifferent will is left to respond to the external gospel offer of grace as it chooses, untouched by any further physical operation of the Spirit. Certainly, it is not difficult to find high-profile advocates of something like this among Owen's contemporaries in the established church.[106] In any event, the effect of this kind of claim, he believes, is to ascribe the 'whole glory of our regeneration and conversion unto our selves,

---

[104] Owen, Πνευματολογια (1674), 255; Works (1965), 3:301.
[105] So, Owen, Πνευματολογια (1674), 263, 64; Works (1965), 3:310, 11.
[106] Parker, for instance, limits the Spirit's work to an assistance in performing the duties of natural moral virtue: 'whatever assistances the Spirit of God may now afford us, they work in the same way, and after the same manner, as if all were perform'd by the strength of our own reason': Parker, *A defence and continuation of the ecclesiastical politie*, 334. In his sequel to Πνευματολογια, *The reason of faith* (1677), Owen will take issue with other prominent voices who more-or-less limit the Spirit's work at the foundation of Christian faith to a restoration of right reason, so that such faith is understood to proceed on purely rational grounds. See, for instance, Bishop Edward Fowler's denial of any 'immediate' operation of the Spirit in faith, other than an assistance against any prejudices that prevent a person from detecting the abundantly sufficient 'rational motives of credibility': Fowler, *The principles and practices of certain moderate divines of the Church of England*, 56–8. See further, Leslie, *The light of grace*, 37–65.

and not to the grace of God', destroying Christian assurance and contradicting the explicit testimony of Scripture.[107]

Owen responds to the inadequacy of collapsing the grace of conversion into 'moral suasion' by asserting the necessity of a real, physical operation of the Spirit on the faculties which irresistibly draw a person to faith in Christ. He spells out the effect of regenerative grace on the mind, will and affections, in a manner that directly answers the impact of original sin outlined in chapter 3. He cautiously avoids accounting for this work in a way that bypasses the ministry of the word or the authentic agency of the individual. On the one hand, the Spirit's illumination of the mind does not consist in any 'new revelations', but in a 'subjective' 'enabling' of the mind to grasp what is objectively proposed in the gospel.[108] As noted earlier, this illumination results in a conformity of the mind to the spiritual truth Christ graciously conveys through the gospel itself, or, as he puts it later, it 'is nothing but the word changed into grace in our hearts'.[109]

In technical terms, it is likely that Owen understands the Spirit's 'subjective' 'enabling' of the mind in a manner congruent with Aquinas's theory of illumination. Aquinas effectively defines illumination (whether natural or supernatural) as a subjective intellectual power, a habitual capacity that enables a person actively to acquire knowledge through the 'intelligible species' of an object, communicated to the mind through the senses. Nonetheless, in a nod to Augustine, Aquinas characterizes that capacity as itself a kind of 'participation' in the truth that is objectively revealed, creating an exact symmetry between the truth acquired by the senses and the intellect's habitual capacity to apprehend that truth, both of which are grounded in the divine origin of all truth.[110] When applied to the context of spiritual regeneration, the genius of this metaphysical construct is that it enables Owen to retain a union of word and Spirit along both objective and subjective axes, thereby avoiding any trace of 'enthusiasm'. The supernatural reality conveyed in the spiritually inspired gospel proclamation is exactly mirrored in the spiritual illumination required to perceive its truth through the senses, the conjunction of which actualizes a conformity between the mind and the gospel's doctrine.[111] With the mind illumined in this way,

---

[107] Owen, Πνευματολογια (1674), 262; Works (1965), 3:308–9.
[108] Owen, Πνευματολογια (1674), 281; Works (1965), 3:331.
[109] Owen, Πνευματολογια (1674), 412; Works (1965), 3:470; see also Owen, Πνευματολογια (1674), 18; Works (1965), 3:76.
[110] On natural illumination, see, Aquinas, STh 1a.q.84.a.5. On the parallel necessity of supernatural illumination, see, STh 1a2ae.q.62.a.3; q.110.a.3; 2a2ae.q.1.a.4.ad3; q.2.a.3.ad2; q.6.a.1; q.8.a.4, a.5.
[111] As he would later put it, 'it is nothing but the seed of the Gospel quickened in our hearts, and bearing fruit in our lives. It is the delivery up of our souls into the mould of the doctrine of it, so as that our minds and the word should answer one another, as face doth unto face in water';

a spiritually healed will is thus able to exercise faith in the gospel offer in a manner that thoroughly corresponds to its normal, natural operations, without any 'violence or compulsion'.[112] In other words, '[t]he power which the Holy Ghost puts forth in our regeneration, is such in its acting or exercise, as our minds, wills, and affections, are suited to be wrought upon, and to be affected by it according to their natures, and natural operations'.[113]

Before moving on to explore sanctification in Books IV and V, Owen concludes Book III by appropriating Augustine's account of his conversion in his famous *Confessions* as a vivid application of the principles he has unfolded so far. Undoubtedly this is a deliberate attempt to underscore the continuity of his own doctrine with that of the patristic giant. But Owen's theological commentary on Augustine's experience also allows him to explore the fallen nature's encounter with regenerative grace from the perspective of an individual's psychological experience, before finally concluding the chapter with a brief outline of the 'external manner' or outward means of regeneration, 'which many practical divines of this nation, have in their preaching and writings much insisted on and improved, to the great profit and edification of the church'.[114]

Owen, Πνευματολογια (1674), 446; *Works* (1965), 3:508. See also his parallel reflections elsewhere on the reference to 'light' (φῶς) in 1 Pet. 2.9 and 2 Cor. 4.4: 'Just as, indeed, that darkness from which we have been called, was not only objective, or a mere ignorance of the divine truth which had not yet been revealed [to us], but was chiefly internal, or a natural darkness of our mind; so the "wondrous" (θαυμαστόν) "light" (φῶς) into which we are called [cf. 1 Pet. 2.9] signifies not only the Gospel teaching [*doctrinam*], but also that spiritual light whereby we are rendered fit for duly understanding the glory of God. "The light of the Gospel of the glory of Christ" (2 Cor. 4.4) illuminates us. It is "light" (φωτισμός) in itself, and it "illumines" (αὐγάζει) our minds. The Holy Spirit sent Paul "to open the eyes" (ἀνοῖξαι ὀφθαλμοὺς) of the Gentiles, "to turn them from darkness to light" (Acts 26.18). The Gospel truth itself is "light" (φῶς); and "light" (φῶς) is also imparted within the ones who will come to faith, to open their eyes so they may see that light [*lucem*]; "light in the light of God" (Psalm 36:9)': Owen, Θεολογουμενα παντοδαπα (1661), 6.6 (493–4); *Works* (1965), 17:444.

[112]The fallen will is necessarily 'passive' in the 'first act of conversion', or in the healing of its spiritual impotency, Owen insists. But the Spirit's gracious work on the will is such that 'in the same instant of time wherein the will is moved [by the Spirit], it moves; and when it is acted, it acts it self, and preserves its own liberty in its exercise. There is therefore herein an inward almighty secret act of the power of the Holy Ghost, producing or effecting in us the will of conversion unto God, so acting our wills, as that they also act themselves, and that freely': Owen, Πνευματολογια (1674), 272; *Works* (1965), 3:319–20.

[113]Owen, Πνευματολογια (1674), 270; *Works* (1965), 3:318.

[114]Owen, Πνευματολογια (1674), 311; *Works* (1965), 3:366.

BOOK IV

The 'compleating and perfecting' of regeneration: Sanctification

If 'regeneration' is the 'second great work of the Spirit of God in the new creation', the final two books of Πνευματολογια are devoted to the 'compleating and perfecting' of this work in an individual's sanctification.[115] Owen is aware that the biblical language of sanctification may in the first instance refer to God's 'separation' or 'consecration' of 'persons' and 'things' unto his service. While he will touch on the ways in which regenerate believers are sanctified in this once-for-all sense, his particular interest in Books IV and V is with the 'consequent and effect' of this consecration, namely, a real, internal change stemming from the 'principle of holiness' communicated to us in our regeneration.[116] In broad terms, Owen defines this progressive dimension of sanctification as a divine work which fulfils God's gracious covenantal promises in the elect through the gradual renovation of their natures into the perfect image and likeness of Christ, a reality which will terminate with their resurrection and ultimate glorification. The continuity of sanctification with regeneration means that much of the theological foundation for this work has already been laid by Owen in the first three books of Πνευματολογια. And although he does not miss the opportunity to repeat these connections exhaustively in Book IV, we are now in a position to summarize them more briefly in terms of a conceptual outline of his overall argument.

The root and foundation of sanctification: The habit of grace

Owen essentially breaks up the Spirit's sanctifying work into two parts. Sanctification may either be thought of in terms of its root and foundation or in terms of its specific acts, two dimensions which are occasionally distinguished by Reformed theologians as 'habitual' versus 'actual' sanctification.[117] It is the habitual dimension which particularly underlines the continuity of sanctification with the effects of regenerative grace, something that Owen outlines in detail in chapter 6. If regeneration consists in a physical, recreative infusion of habitual grace within the fallen soul, it is this very same grace that forms the vital foundation of the sanctified life. The unity of regeneration and habitual sanctification is, of course, grounded in Christ, whose mediatorial work provides the soil out of which the image of God is renewed. Whereas the concreated righteous quality once furnished Adam's soul with the capacity he

---

[115]Owen, Πνευματολογια (1674), 321; *Works* (1965), 3:366–7.
[116]Owen, Πνευματολογια (1674), 324–5; *Works* (1965), 3:370.
[117]For example, Charnock, *The complete works*, 5:105–18; Voetius, *Selectarum disputationem theologicarum*, II:437; Mastricht, *Theoretico-practica theologia*, 6.8.25 (843b–44a).

needed to live in actual obedience to God, now that capacity is only restored to sinners through Christ, and a qualitative, habitual participation in his own righteous life. Unsurprisingly, this is something that Owen readily infers from the New Testament's references to an organic union with Christ's life as that which alone vitalizes Christian faith and obedience.[118] The restoration of habitual grace in Christ does not, however, merely amount to a return to Adam's pristine state. There are precepts and obligations in the gospel, Owen argues, which extend beyond what was the law of nature required of Adam in the beginning.[119] If Adam's concreated habitual grace enabled his illumined mind and will to discern and act upon what God required of him by the law, so the habitual grace supplied by Christ corresponds to what the gospel uniquely requires in its 'preceptive part'. In other words, the light of grace surpasses the light of nature.

What habitual sanctification provides the regenerate sinner, therefore, is a new, permanent 'disposition' and 'power' to act in willing conformity to the duties of sanctification outlined by the gospel in Scripture and exemplified in Christ himself.[120] And just as it is initially infused into a person by the Spirit, so too is it continually sustained and strengthened by his power.[121] As Owen argues earlier in Book IV, this abiding habitual renewal of a sinner is the subjective implication of what the Scriptures mean by a once-for-all sanctification, a cleansing or purification from the defiling effects of original sin (chapters 4 and 5). Just as the pollution of original sin cannot be reduced to discrete acts, but embraces a habitual inconformity of the soul to God's law, so the 'washing of regeneration' (cf., Tit. 3.5) removes this stain by giving a 'new understanding, a new heart, new affections, renewing the whole soul into the image of God (Eph. 4:23, 24; Col. 3:10)'.[122] To Owen's mind this purification is a necessary and immediate effect of a person's union to Christ. Without it, such a union, let alone any communion with Christ would be as inconceivable as the possibility of any fellowship between light and darkness.[123] Of course, the most obvious objection to this proposition stems from the ongoing presence

---

[118]For instance, among other places, Owen sees this as an implication of the Pauline 'body' metaphor or Christ's own metaphor of the 'vine' and the 'branches': Owen, Πνευματολογια (1674), 453–8; *Works* (1965), 3:516–23.
[119]Owen, Πνευματολογια (1674), 445–6; *Works* (1965), 3:507–8. Again, contra Parker: 'I humbly crave leave to remonstrate, that religion for the substance and main design of it . . . is the same now as it was in the state of innocence. . . . And therefore our Saviour came not into the world to give any new precepts of moral goodness, but only to revive the old rules of nature.' Parker, *A defence and continuation of the ecclesiastical politie*, 314–16; cf. 11–18.
[120]Owen, Πνευματολογια (1674), 422–8; 30–62; *Works* (1965), 3:482–8; 91–527.
[121]Owen, Πνευματολογια (1674), 435; *Works* (1965), 3:496.
[122]Owen, Πνευματολογια (1674), 383; *Works* (1965), 3:437.
[123]Owen, Πνευματολογια (1674), 406–9; *Works* (1965), 3:464–7.

of sin in a regenerate person's life. Owen responds to this by admitting that the habitual renewal of a person's faculties does not completely eradicate a 'contrary habitual principle', which 'the Scripture calls the "flesh," "lust," the "sin that dwelleth in us," the "body of death"; being what yet remaineth in believers of that vitious corrupted depravation of our nature, which cameth upon us by the loss of the image of God'.[124] Even so, such is the radical power of a person's sanctification that the 'habit of sin is weakened, impaired, and so disenabled, as that it cannot nor shall incline unto sin with that constancy and prevalency as formerly, nor press unto it ordinarily with the same urgency and violence'. In other words, alluding to Paul's argument in Romans 6, Owen insists that the power of sin is 'dethroned', albeit not entirely removed.[125]

With his robust theological account of habitual sanctification in place, Owen concludes chapter 6 on a polemical note objecting to those who are content to reduce sanctification to the 'practice of moral virtue', as if Christian obedience consists of no more than a call to heed what was originally required by the law and light of nature. Once again, Owen undoubtedly has in mind a prevailing cynicism towards any emphasis on the Spirit's supernatural work, as typified in Parker's writings.[126] To his mind, however, it is simply a 'Pelagian figment', repristinating 'the doctrine of the Quakers' by denying the fundamentally gracious character of sanctification as it grounded exclusively in the person and work of Christ.[127]

The acts and duties of sanctification

In chapter 7, Owen turns to the second dimension of the Spirit's work in sanctification, the specific 'acts and duties of holy obedience' which necessarily flow from the habitual life of Christ formed within a believer.[128] He is not particularly concerned to outline these duties in any detail so much as to insist upon the Spirit's special, effectual concursus in these acts, a concursus which cannot be adequately explained in terms of the Spirit's general providential operations.[129] Similarly, to 'walk by the Spirit' (cf., Gal. 5.16; Rom. 8.4) cannot be reduced to a merely external 'persuasion' of an otherwise indifferent will.

---

[124] Owen, Πνευματολογια (1674), 428; *Works* (1965), 3:488.

[125] Owen, Πνευματολογια (1674), 429; *Works* (1965), 3:489.

[126] For Parker's defence of 'moral virtue', see: Parker, *A defence and continuation of the ecclesiastical politie*, 301–75. See also his remark: 'there is nothing beyond the bounds of moral vertue but chimeras and flying dragons, illusions of fancy, and impostures of enthusiasm': Parker, *A defence and continuation of the ecclesiastical politie*, 338–9.

[127] Owen, Πνευματολογια (1674), 459–62; *Works* (1965), 3:524–7.

[128] Owen, Πνευματολογια (1674), 463; *Works* (1965), 3:527.

[129] For the following, see chapter 7, *passim*: Owen, Πνευματολογια (1674), 463–72; *Works* (1965), 3:527–38.

Rather, Owen is adamant that if we take the teaching of the New Testament seriously, the dependence on the Spirit in these acts has to be understood as far more radical and fundamentally supernatural in its character.[130] The same principle applies to the believer's corresponding duty to mortify the lingering presence of indwelling sin (chapter 8). The dependence on Christ's spiritual supply of grace in this duty corresponds to a dynamic within the regenerate that begins with faith in his promises of assistance and as an expression of that faith, and attends diligently to the means of mortification expressly outlined in Scripture.[131] Implied here is a familiar concern to relate the Spirit's work in all this to Christ and Scripture. In a sense, the promises and duties of mortification outlined in Scripture are no more or less than a reflection of Christ himself. Behind them resides the very efficacy of his crucifixion and out of a trust in its power to deliver from sin, Owen insists, will emerge a transforming love for Christ's person. In other words, through gazing on the beauty of Christ, represented exclusively in Scripture to the eyes of faith, the believer is gradually conformed into his image and likeness (2 Cor. 3.18).[132]

BOOK V

Several arguments for the necessity of Christian holiness

In the last Book of the treatise, Owen sets out several arguments for the necessity of Christian holiness. Throughout this discussion, he seeks to steer a course between the typical Socinian and Catholic charges of antinomianism levelled at those who uphold the satisfaction of Christ for sin and the imputation of his righteousness, on the one hand, and the sterile moralism he detects among his contemporaries, on the other.[133] Instead, he seeks to prove that the necessity of holiness is thoroughly 'consistent and compliant with the great doctrines of the grace of God', and naturally flows out of them. In broad terms, his demonstration will respect the essential nature of holiness, and its manifestation in the Christian life.[134] And the five arguments he deploys move logically from the nature of God, through his redemptive acts, terminating in the believer as the object of those acts.

The first argument stems from the nature of God (chapter 1).[135] Here Owen carefully distinguishes between the holiness of God absolutely speaking, and that

---

[130] Some of the texts he mentions include Eph. 2.10; Jn 15.5; 1 Cor. 15.10; 2 Cor. 3.4-5; 9.8; 12.9; Phil. 2.13.
[131] Owen, Πνευματολογια (1674), 481–93; *Works* (1965), 3:547–61.
[132] Owen, Πνευματολογια (1674), 493–6; *Works* (1965), 3:561–5.
[133] Owen, Πνευματολογια (1674), 497–9; *Works* (1965), 3:566–8.
[134] Owen, Πνευματολογια (1674), 499; *Works* (1965), 3:568.
[135] Owen, Πνευματολογια (1674), 497–519; *Works* (1965), 3:516–91.

which is manifest to us through Christ the mediator. It is undoubtedly true that God's holy character, absolutely considered, is itself a sufficiently compelling reason to demand holiness from his creatures. But Owen is conscious that the perversity of our fallen natures renders us thoroughly incapable of properly discerning and responding to that necessity on purely natural terms. Rather, it is now the peculiarly gracious manifestation of God's character in the person of Christ and his mediatorial office that is both 'directive' and 'effective' unto holiness. Once again, he frames this in terms of the restoration of the lost image in the believer after the likeness of Christ, through an exercise of faith and love towards its reflection in the gospel (2 Cor. 3.18–4.6).

In chapter 2, Owen moves from the holiness of God himself to the particular decree of election.[136] Election motivates holiness in two ways, Owen thinks. First, the decree itself necessitates holiness as its end or purpose (Eph. 1.4). Second, and by implication, the only way a believer can deduce their interest in this decree is through a kind of reflexive practical syllogism, since its transformative effects will inevitably manifest themselves in the elect. Far from inducing sloth-like resignation, then, Owen insists that the nature of the decree should act as an incentive for a Christian to entrust themselves to the strength God supplies his elect to pursue his will in their lives.

Owen's third argument (chapter 3) issues from the commands of God.[137] As with the holiness of God, Owen carefully distinguishes the nature of God's commands under the covenant of works from those 'annexed' to the covenant of grace. Under the former, the natural state of Adam provided adequate capacity for an individual to comply with the holiness they demanded. Now, however, the grace to comply with the requirements of God's commands is supplied exclusively by the mediator of the covenant, who writes the law on a person's heart and effectually concurs with their will to obey. While the new covenant clearly does not demand perfect obedience, nor anticipates an entirely uniform supply of grace at all times, Owen insists the divine authority upon which its commands rest remains as compelling a reason for holiness as it did under the old.

Owen then turns his attention to consider God's purpose in sending of Christ (chapter 4), which was 'to recover us into a state of holiness, which we had lost'.[138] Here he spells this out in terms of his threefold mediatorial office. While he only briefly touches on the atoning effects of Christ's priestly work, having elaborated on them extensively elsewhere, the prophetic and kingly offices receive special attention. Not even the 'greatest moralist' can proclaim

---

[136] Owen, Πνευματολογια (1674), 520–32; Works (1965), 3:591–604.
[137] Owen, Πνευματολογια (1674), 533–53; Works (1965), 3:604–28.
[138] Owen, Πνευματολογια (1674), 556; cf. 56–65; Works (1965), 3:628. Cf. 28–41.

such perfection of doctrine as Christ, let alone with the power, efficacy and authority to accomplish its ends in a person's life. By implication, then, the person who truly possesses 'any interest in Christ' will necessarily begin to manifest the sanctifying effects of this office in their lives.[139]

In chapter 5, Owen concludes by drawing attention to the necessity of holiness as the only solution to the effects of the fall in our lives.[140] However, far from instilling tranquillity, the introduction of divine grace to a person's life will result in an internal conflict with the remnants of fleshly 'lusts', and even with the more 'natural infirmities and distempers' that afflict a person in this world. The treatise ends with an impassioned exhortation that believers recognize the degree to which Christ's honour in the world is bound up with their individual holiness.

CONCLUSION

Even in its own day, Owen's Πνευματολογια represented a remarkable feat of constructive theological engagement. In many ways the project is unashamedly conventional, and its overall alignment with the Reformed orthodox confessional tradition is unmistakable. But as is evident in so much of his other post-Restoration output, Owen was no mere traditionalist.[141] And rather than offering a predictable and overtly partisan distillation of some Reformed consensus on the Spirit, Owen seeks to engage directly with Scripture in a way that is both catholic and intellectually compelling within its own context. There were clear polemical factors at play in this move, surfacing throughout the treatise and readily influencing its rather laboured gait. Even still, through its extensive dialogue with the patristic tradition and its careful metaphysical synthesis, Πνευματολογια is in the best sense a fresh and immensely learned illustration of the instrumental use of reason in unfolding a central tenet of the biblical, Christian faith. It is perhaps for this reason that the treatise won admiration – and, it must be said, a certain amount of opprobrium – in Owen's own context, as well as in subsequent centuries, in which it continues to capture the attention of dogmaticians.[142]

---

[139]Owen, Πνευματολογια (1674), 562–5; *Works* (1965), 3:638–41.

[140]Owen, Πνευματολογια (1674), 566–75; *Works* (1965), 3:641–51.

[141]Cf. Gribben's nuanced conclusions about Owen's distinctive contribution in his own biographical portrait: Gribben, *John Owen and English Puritanism*, 267–73.

[142]As Goold observes: Owen, *Works* (1965), 3:3. Very much in the mould of Samuel Parker's earlier censures, the restoration Anglican polemicist, William Clagett, responds to Owen's 'dangerous opinions' by explicitly seeking to refute Πνευματολογια's construal of the Spirit's supernatural work in the economy of redemption. Clagett is obviously sufficiently agitated by Owen's citation of patristic precedent that his reply seeks to dispute Owen's interpretation of these sources throughout. See Clagett, *A discourse concerning the operations of the Holy Spirit*.

CHAPTER 17

The nature of apostasie (1676)

TIM COOPER

The fortunes of Reformed orthodoxy profoundly shifted in seventeenth-century England. There were definite winners and losers. John Owen was not one of the winners. His every attempt to hold back successive waves of worrying theological and philosophical development ended in failure, and he was forced to observe the steady erosion of some of his most cherished beliefs. It seemed to him that England had abandoned and betrayed those evangelical truths that had marked out the sixteenth-century English Reformation, and that he had lived to witness the nation's Great Apostasy from the Gospel. Crawford Gribben is exactly right: 'Despite his best efforts, his extraordinary project of refining the Reformation had failed. He had published millions of words in the defence and development of doctrines that now met with indifference.'[1] *The nature of apostasie*, published in 1676, just seven years before he died, throws light on that drawn-out, acutely painful and seemingly implacable defeat. This chapter will use Owen's book to help understand and illuminate his life – a life that, on this score at least, ended in the shadow of failure and fruitless ambition.

---

[1] Gribben, *John Owen and English Puritanism*, 260. See also, Gribben, 'The experience of dissent'.

THE DEMISE OF REFORMED ORTHODOXY IN ENGLAND

One of the most unanticipated developments in the religious life of England during the seventeenth century was what G. R. Cragg called 'the overthrow of Calvinism'. 'At the beginning of the century', this system of theology 'had dominated the religious life of England; by the end its power had been completely overthrown'.[2] Such a stark assessment should be qualified, but it is not far wrong. Recent historiography has moved on from seeing the sixteenth-century Church of England as a middle way between Roman Catholicism on the one hand and Reformed orthodoxy on the other, and to place it with other churches on the Continent within a broad spectrum of Reformed ecclesial identities. 'In fact', says Anthony Milton, 'the Church of England was in some ways more "Calvinist" than the continent'.[3] Diarmaid MacCulloch identifies early and enduring links with the Swiss Reformation that allowed the Church of England to claim a genuinely Reformed Protestant identity. By 1600, the theological influence of John Calvin had come to dominate, but even then the church guided itself by patterns set in Zürich decades earlier. If there was a tension, then, it lay within the Reformed tradition, not against it.[4] For all its multiple identities and shifting complexities, the sixteenth-century Church of England can be seen as broadly Reformed.

But the church's identity changed during the following century. Under Charles I, the hierarchy of the established church experienced what has been termed 'the rise of Arminianism'. A new set of churchmen (not least William Laud, first bishop of London then archbishop of Canterbury) privileged a more sacramental style of church doctrine and practice along with a soteriological emphasis on good works and human responsibility in the economy of salvation.[5] Bundled up under the labels of 'Arminianism' and 'Laudianism', these changes and the polemical campaigns that surrounded them were devastatingly effective in making Reformed orthodoxy appear foreign and 'other' to the Church of England, largely by conflating Calvinist theology with Puritan Nonconformity – so that all Calvinists were now subsumed under that 'odious name'.[6] This generated heated tensions that, along with other complexities in ruling the three kingdoms, played a large part in provoking the civil wars that broke out in the early 1640s. Owen's first book, *Θεομαχία αυτεξουσιαστικη: or, A display of Arminianisme* (1643), appeared in that context. It was 'a *Bill of Complaint*,

---

[2]Cragg, *From Puritanism to the age of reason*, 13. See also Lee Gatiss's chapter in this book.
[3]Milton, 'Introduction', 25.
[4]MacCulloch, 'The Church of England and International Protestantism', see esp. 331.
[5]See Tyacke, *Anti-Calvinists*.
[6]Tyacke, *Anti-Calvinists*, 49.

against no small number in this Kingdome' who had sought to pit the 'old Pelagian *Idol Free-will*' and 'the new Goddesse *Contingency*' against God's sovereign will. The promoters of the new theology were part of a larger plot to oppose the Calvinists and so, by creating dissension, to *'reduce the people againe to Popery'*.[7] The high stakes could admit no leniency. As armed conflict broke out among the English people, Owen declared 'an holy warre, to such enemies, of *Gods providence, Christs merit, and the powerfull operation of the Holy Spirit'*.[8] He appeared on the scene, therefore, as an avowed defender of Reformed orthodoxy (or, as he would have it, of the 'truth, and the Gospel of Christ') against the ascendency of the Arminians.[9]

From one angle, Charles's defeat in the civil wars appeared to have broken that ascendency. When Owen preached his first sermon to Parliament, in April 1646, he asserted that God had acted decisively to rescue the Gospel from Arminian bondage, and he exulted in that victory. But from another angle, the broader theological and intellectual trends continued largely unchecked, and Owen was too shrewd an observer not to notice. For all his confidence, he issued a sharp warning to his auditors: if the nation were once more to draw back from the Gospel, it would 'finde again *cause* to depart, [and] it will not go by *steps*, but all at once'. There could be no going back to slavery in Egypt. This 'is *our* Day, wherein we must mend or end'.[10]

Indeed, two years later, when he published *Salus electorum, sanguis Jesu: or, The death of death in the death of Christ* (1648), Owen discerned a new enemy – 'cursed *Socinianisme*'.[11] This, of course, was another label of varying accuracy and applicability deployed as a short-hand to encompass a range of positions. Generally, Socinians read the Scriptures in a uniformly flat way to dissolve what they perceived to be an imposed doctrinal overlay of trinitarian Christology – a move that had dire implications for Reformed soteriology. During the 1630s, Socinian writings from the Continent had found a sympathetic reception among the 'Great Tew Circle', an intellectual network situated outside the two universities and centred on the country estate of Lucius Carey, Second Viscount Falkland, located just 18 miles from Oxford. They appreciated the Socinian objection to the Reformed understanding of predestination, the view of Christianity as an ethical religion in which one might choose for oneself,

---

[7] Owen, *A display of Arminianisme* (1643), title page and Dedicatory Epistle, sig. *2v and A2v; *Works* (1965), 10:1, 5, 7.
[8] Owen, *A display of Arminianisme* (1643), sig. A1v-A2r; *Works* (1965), 10:7.
[9] Owen, *A display of Arminianisme* (1643), Dedicatory Epistle, sig. *3; *Works* (1965), 10:5.
[10] Owen, *A vision of unchangeable free mercy* (1646), 32; *Works* (1965), 8:31.
[11] Owen, *The death of death in the death of Christ* (1648), preface to the reader, n.p.; *Works* (1965), 10:150.

and the high value that Socinians attached to human reason.[12] From the mid-1640s, Henry Hammond emerged as a defender of the Church of England with a vision that drew on ideas previously associated with the Socinians.[13] He is credited with fostering a 'golden age of High Anglican theology and apologetic' during the Interregnum.[14] Hammond believed that all of God's decrees were conditional, and that receiving Christ as Lord and Saviour was 'the condition of Scripture-election'. Any other view was 'the meer invention and fabrick of mens brains'.[15] In the early 1650s, John Biddle, perhaps England's most notorious Socinian, offered a sharper provocation. He translated into English a version of the Socinians' *Racovian Catechism* that was published in 1652.[16] In 1654, and in response to the mounting alarm, the Council of State asked Owen, now the vice-chancellor of the University of Oxford, to respond.[17] The result was the *Vindiciae evangelicae* (1655), a truly massive and prodigious demolition of Socinian doctrine. Yet for all off the book's size and weight, it was far from clear that Owen's war was any closer to being won.

Owen needed reliable allies among his fellow Puritans, surely the group most likely to hold firm to Reformed orthodoxy. Here he might have felt badly let down. First, Richard Baxter published *The aphorismes of justification* in 1649. The first ten pages of the book would have warmed the heart of any Calvinist; the remaining three-hundred-odd pages offered a distressing set of qualifications designed to banish any hint of Calvinism's dark shadow – antinomianism. In this and his many other subsequent publications, Baxter had a worrying knack of sounding exactly like the Socinians when he argued for a 'mere Christianity' based only and literally on the words of Scripture, and when he retained a place for human responsibility in the process of salvation and the centrality of human reason in his vision for the Christian life. Owen's relationship with Baxter was an exercise in mutual frustration at every turn.[18] John Goodwin was a second disappointment. A Puritan minister in London, Goodwin abandoned Calvinism altogether. In *Redemption redeemed* (1651), he argued for a universal atonement. He no longer accepted that the Calvinist doctrine of predestination was consistent with either Scripture or God's

---

[12]Mortimer, *Reason and religion in the English revolution*, ch. 3.
[13]Mortimer, *Reason and religion in the English revolution*, ch. 5.
[14]Wallace, *Puritans and predestination*, 125.
[15]Hammond, *Pacifick discourse of Gods grace and decrees*, 25.
[16]Mortimer, *Reason and religion*, 165. The Catechism had been published the year before in Latin.
[17]Smith, 'And if God was one of us', 175.
[18]For an assessment of Baxter's Calvinist credentials, see Wallace, *Puritans and predestination*, 136–40. For a fuller account of Baxter's relationship with Owen, see Cooper, *John Owen, Richard Baxter and the formation of Nonconformity*.

nature, and, like Baxter, he disliked its inclination towards antinomianism.[19] John Coffey explains that *Redemption redeemed* 'was the longest and most substantial defence of Arminianism yet published in the English language', which 'both epitomised and exacerbated the crisis of Calvinism', and yet it came from a Puritan author.[20] Owen replied to Goodwin in yet another massive work to appear in 1654, *The doctrine of the saints perseverance*. It is not that Owen was working entirely alone, but his battle through the 1650s was hardly helped by his having to fight on other fronts within the Puritan community – and all this while Puritans were politically in the ascendant.

And then occurred disaster and reversal. In 1659, the Cromwellian regime fell apart in chaos, and, ever after, the Calvinist cause was discredited as the fomenter of sedition, disorder, impiety, fanaticism and rebellion.[21] In *Aerius redivivus: or, The history of the Presbyterians* (1670), for example, the clergyman and historian Peter Heylyn connected the 'dangerous Doctrine . . . breathed and Broached by *Calvin*' with seditious activity across Europe and in England.[22] At the same time, within intellectual circles, there was a growing disillusionment with Reformed orthodoxy, a disinclination to pry into hidden mysteries such as predestination and election, and an aversion to anything that smacked of religious enthusiasm.[23] A new confidence in human reason took shape – illustrated by the Cambridge Platonists with their 'quiet Arminianism' – along with a broad shift of emphasis from grace to nature.[24] Latitudinarians focused on human reason, natural truths, moderation and moral duties in preference to obscure points of doctrine.[25] The result of all this was that earlier expressions of Calvinist orthodoxy were 'now rapidly becoming archaic' and 'outmoded'.[26] Herbert Thorndike, a biblical scholar and theologian at Cambridge, criticized the antinomian implications of the Calvinists' doctrine, declaring that the 'ground and substance of Christianity is utterly inconsistent with the Decree [of absolute predestination] that they imagine'.[27] When the clergyman and controversialist William Sherlock attacked Owen's Reformed soteriology in 1674 he 'presented a rather fair statement of Owen's actual

---

[19]John Coffey, *John Goodwin and the Puritan revolution*, 207–14. See also, Wallace, *Puritans and predestination*, 130–2.
[20]Coffey, *John Goodwin and the Puritan revolution*, 214, 226.
[21]Wallace, *Puritans and predestination*, 127.
[22]Heylyn, *Aerius redivivus* (1670), 23ff.
[23]Mortimer, *Reason and religion*, 212.
[24]Wallace, *Shapers of English Calvinism*, 31–2; Wallace, *Puritans and predestination*, 158.
[25]For a good discussion of the intellectual context of the Restoration period, see Wallace, *Shapers of English Calvinism*, ch. 1. See also, Spellman, *Latitudinarians and the Church of England*, and Tyacke, 'From Laudians to Latitudinarians'.
[26]Rivers, *Reason, grace and sentiment*, 139, 163.
[27]Thorndike, *Just weights and measures*, 56.

beliefs as though they were sufficiently absurd that their very recital would refute them'.[28] Doctrine that had once seemed so plausible to so many was now 'a rock of offence'.[29]

All of this presents a very bleak picture for the prospects of English Calvinism – but it was not all dark. Stephen Hampton argues that the demise of Calvinism in England has been exaggerated. If we take a broader and more generous view of what the Reformed tradition entailed, there is certainly a case for continuity. A range of influential figures within the established church was 'decidedly Reformed': English Calvinistm was not the 'moribund and marginal tradition that historians have led us to expect'.[30] Even Dewey Wallace, who has done so much to chart the declining fortunes of Calvinism, accepts that a moderate (if embattled) strain of Reformed orthodoxy persisted within the Church of England – and outside it.[31] The very potency of the attack provoked a significant number of defences and rich restatements of Reformed orthodoxy, many of them prefaced by Owen.[32] 'If the age of the Restoration was generally unreceptive to strict Calvinist theology, it was nonetheless a time for a great flowering of books of piety and devotion that explicated and applied personally the predestinarian theology of grace.'[33] Thus Hampton emphasizes not the disappearance but the 'tenacity of Reformed thought'.[34]

As we shall see, Hampton's perspective has much to commend, but it is much easier to see that tenacity in hindsight. At the time, Owen perceived no 'great flowering'. By the mid-1670s, he feared the tradition that he had done so much to defend sat precariously on the brink of extinction.[35] Admittedly, the mid-1670s offered a particularly brutal set of circumstances. In a matching pair of recent articles, Christopher Haigh has described at some length the 'theological wars' that generated numerous works of polemic in what looks like an unruly scrum: between 1675 and 1680 a total of fifty-three books were published in an extended controversy over justification that included thirty-four different authors, Owen among them.[36] Hardly helping his perspective, the decade was difficult for Owen personally. He was then 'in his late fifties, dogged by illness,

---

[28]Wallace, *Puritans and predestination*, 170.
[29]Wallace, *Puritans and predestination*, 132. Owen replied to Sherlock in *A vindication of some passages* (1674).
[30]Hampton, *Anti-Arminians*, ch. 1 (the quotes are on 18, 31).
[31]Wallace, *Puritans and predestination*, 144; Wallace, *Shapers of English Calvinism*, 26.
[32]Wallace, *Puritans and predestination*, 149.
[33]Wallace, *Puritans and predestination*, 182.
[34]Hampton, *Anti-Arminians*, 29.
[35]Owen, *The nature of apostasie* (1676), Epistle to the Reader, 4 (all quotes from the Epistle to the Reader have their italics removed); *Works* (1965), 7:4.
[36]Christopher Haigh, 'Theological wars' (the figures cited are on 341), and 'The Church of England, the Nonconformists and Reason' (Haigh assesses *The nature of apostasie* on 546).

and likely concerned about the health of his wife', Mary, who died in January 1677.[37] In 1676 he preached a sermon on 2 Tim. 3.1, which spoke of 'perilous times' in the 'last days'. Clearly, he and his auditors were living in just such a 'perilous season'. The 'glorious profession' of the Reformation had given way to a woeful state of affairs in which English religion was now 'half Arminian and half Socinian; half Papist and half I know not what'.[38] This was a nation poised for judgement:

> Will you hear the sum of all? Perilous times and seasons are come upon us; many are wounded already; many have failed. The Lord help us! the crown is fallen from our head – the glory of our profession is gone – the time is short – the Judge stands before the door.[39]

What this dangerous situation urgently required, therefore, was a lesson in the nature of apostasy. That is precisely what Owen delivered.

THE CONTEXT IN OWEN'S COMMENTARY ON HEBREWS

The nature of apostasie appeared in 1676 at a length of 612 pages in octavo with an 18-page epistle to the reader; altogether, it amounted to almost 135,000 words. The stationer was Nathaniel Ponder, whose first publication as a bookseller in 1668 had been Owen's *Exercitations on the epistle to the Hebrews . . . with an exposition on the two first chapters*; he remained Owen's principal publisher through the final fifteen years of the author's life. He more famously published works by Andrew Marvell and John Bunyan, focusing on Nonconformist concerns in the main, and always operating under the threat of prosecution.[40] *The nature of apostasie* was not entered in the Stationers' Register, though by then few books were.

The connection with Owen's four-volume commentary on the book of Hebrews is directly relevant. With parts appearing in 1668, 1674, 1680 and 1684, this project framed Owen's later years as a theologian and published author. And it clearly suited his mood: Hebrews was a letter written to an audience of Jewish Christians tempted under the threat of persecution to abandon their faith in Jesus and to revert to a conventional Judaism. Declension,

---

[37] Gribben, *John Owen and English Puritanism*, 253, 255.
[38] Owen, 'Perilous times' (1676); *Works* (1965), 9:329. The sermon is cited in Gribben, *John Owen and English Puritanism*, 255.
[39] Owen, 'Perilous times' (1676); *Works* (1965), 9:334.
[40] Lynch, 'Ponder, Nathaniel'.

then, was an important theme of the letter and of Owen's commentary.[41] While it did not make many references to current circumstances, for 'defeated nonconformists like Owen', his commentary on Hebrews offered important perspective, consolation and challenge.[42] One of those challenges lay in a central warning the anonymous author presented in Heb. 6.4-6:

> For it is impossible for those who were once enlightened, and have tasted of the Heavenly gift, and were made partakers of the holy Ghost, and have tasted the good word of God, and the powers of the world to come, if they shall fall away, (for any) to renew them again to repentance; seeing they crucifie again to themselves the Son of God, and put him to open shame.

This is Owen's translation in *The nature of apostasie from the profession of the Gospel, and the punishment of apostates declared in an exposition of Heb. 6. 4, 5, 6*, to give the book its fuller title and significance. So it was, in some measure, an early instalment on the next volume of his Hebrews commentary. The text of pages 2–71 in *The nature of apostasie* is identical to pages 38–52 in part three of Owen's commentary on the Hebrews.[43] Even the printer's errors in *The nature of apostasie* recur in the commentary;[44] and two cross-references to other parts of the commentary were, despite their redundancy, retained in *The nature of apostasie*.[45] But the cross-references extend beyond this section of identical text. On page 83 of *The nature of apostasie*, Owen made another passing reference to what he had said earlier in his commentary, and on page 511 he looked ahead: 'we shall (God willing) shew the *Manner* of it in our Exposition of the *seventh Chapter* of the *Epistle to the Hebrews*'.[46] Therefore, it is most likely that Owen gave to Ponder the manuscript of his exegesis of verses 4-6 initially intended for his commentary (and later replicated there) but now to be published in 1676. It seems that he added to his discussion of Heb. 6.4-6 some further text that he began writing with the intention of including in his Hebrews commentary before deciding to take it out and place it in this earlier work. He provided a reason in his epistle to the reader: 'the thoughts which arose thereon were drawn forth into such a length, as would have been

---

[41] Gribben, *John Owen and English Puritanism*, 237.
[42] Tweeddale, *John Owen and Hebrews*, 146–7.
[43] Owen, *A continuation of the exposition of the epistle of Paul the Apostle to the Hebrews* (1680).
[44] Six errors in pages 2–71 are listed on 612. Only one, an errant comma, is corrected in the commentary. It would seem that Ponder was working from the 1676 publication, not the original manuscript (and ignored or forgot the list of errors).
[45] Owen, *The nature of apostasie* (1676), 6, 52. These cross-references are retained by Goold in *Works* (1965), 7:13, 32.
[46] Owen, *The nature of apostasie* (1676), 83, 511; *Works* (1965), 7:45, 218.

too great a Digression from the context and design of the Apostle'.[47] Not an author known for his aversion to long digressions, even Owen realized that his broader discussion of Heb. 6.4-6, animated as we shall see by the urgency of the times, had departed from the intentions of the anonymous writer of Hebrews. Once he realized that his text was running away with him, he appears to have settled on a plan to publish a separate book. From that point on he was putting words together that were intended for that purpose and not for the commentary at all. In other words, what began as an integral component of his Hebrews commentary eventually became something different and distinct.[48]

What drove Owen to write a separate book? A concern that his nonconformist colleagues were in danger of returning to the Church of England under the pressure of persecution is certainly plausible, but that was not a move that could be said inherently to endanger anyone's salvation, and it was not the focus of Owen's alarm in this book. Instead, he was dismayed by 'the present Defection from the Gospel', and that is what he set out to address.[49] He also worried that his time was running out. He assured the reader that he fully intended to complete his exposition on Hebrews – he was not deserting or truncating his grand project – but 'I know not what I may attain unto, in the very near Approach of that Season, wherein I must lay down this Tabernacle, and the daily warnings which through many infirmities I have thereof'.[50] Therefore, under the shadow of what was beginning to feel like imminent death and desperately concerned by England's apparently headlong apostasy, Owen set out to offer his thoughts on its 'Nature, Causes, and Occasions'.[51]

This is most clearly borne out in the epistle to the reader, where Owen identified a 'grand Defection' and 'woful declension from the Power and Purity of Evangelical Truth'.[52] Everywhere he looked, Christianity had degenerated from its original pristine beauty. The narrow and hard way of faith and grace lay in neglect while the broad way of the flesh seemed crowded with people on their way to death and hell, so much so that true Christian faith was all but extinguished.[53] He had lived to see 'its most glorious Mysteries be abused or despised', 'its most important Doctrines be impeached of Error and False-hood' and 'the vain Imaginations and carnal Reasonings of the Serpentine wits of men be substituted in their Room'.[54] Somehow, the Socinians had managed to wrest

---

[47]Owen, *The nature of apostasie* (1676), Epistle to the Reader, 18; *Works* (1965), 7:9.
[48]Henry M. Knapp glimpses this in 'John Owen's Interpretation of Hebrews 6:4–6', 44, n. 39.
[49]Owen, *The nature of apostasie* (1676), Epistle to the Reader, 17; *Works* (1965), 7:8.
[50]Owen, *The nature of apostasie* (1676), Epistle to the Reader, 18; *Works* (1965), 7:9.
[51]Owen, *The nature of apostasie* (1676), Epistle to the Reader, 17; *Works* (1965), 7:8.
[52]Owen, *The nature of apostasie* (1676), Epistle to the Reader, 3, 14; *Works* (1965), 7:4, 7.
[53]Owen, *The nature of apostasie* (1676), Epistle to the Reader, 1–5; *Works* (1965), 7:3–4.
[54]Owen, *The nature of apostasie* (1676), Epistle to the Reader, 5; *Works* (1965), 7:4.

to themselves a reputation for wit and learning when their actual beliefs were far removed from reason, properly proportioned.[55] Worse still, he observed a similar declension among orthodox Protestants. Even they 'grow weary of the Truths which have been professed ever since the Reformation'. So it is that 'the Reformed Religion is by not a few, so taken off from its old foundations, so unhinged from those pillars of important Truths, which it did depend upon, and so sullied by a confused medly of Noysom Opinions, as that its loss in Reputation of Stability and Usefulness, seems almost irreparable'.[56] And that is why he wrote the book. He set out to uncover the 'Causes' and 'hidden Springs' of this great declension by examining the generic causes of apostasy across the ages, beginning with the exposition of Heb. 6.4-6 that he had lifted directly out of his commentary.

Immediately Owen met with an obstacle. These verses that he was expounding seemed to imply that true believers could fall away and lose their salvation – Why else would the writer address a supposedly Christian audience with such a stern warning? But that is not what Owen believed. Indeed, one of those 'most important Doctrines' of the Reformation was the infallible perseverance of the elect, the very doctrine he had maintained against John Goodwin two decades earlier and in many other places since. To circumvent this obstacle, Owen posited three types of people: those who possess a knowledge of spiritual things that is merely natural and that can be gained without any assistance of the Holy Spirit; those who have received some illumination from the Spirit, which brings a measure of delight and joy but has 'little or no Power upon the Soul'; and those who have received a 'saving, sanctifying Light and Knowledge'.[57] Owen made no attempt to justify this tripartite categorization; he simply asserted that the writer to the Hebrews was addressing the middle group of people, not the final group of genuine believers – the elect, who, by definition, could never finally fall away. In these verses the writer used five descriptions of those apostates who could never again be brought back to repentance: they had been enlightened, they had tasted the heavenly gift, they had partaken of the Holy Spirit, they had tasted the word of God and they had tasted the powers of the world to come. In each case, Owen essentially argued that these five descriptions matched those in the second category but fell short of those in the third category. They were like the Israelites referenced in Hebrews 3–4 who had left Egypt, who had sampled the grapes of the promised land, but who in the end had refused to go in.[58] Exegetically, Owen made much of verse 9:

---

[55]Owen, *The nature of apostasie* (1676), Epistle to the Reader, 9–10; *Works* (1965), 7:6.
[56]Owen, *The nature of apostasie* (1676), Epistle to the Reader, 12; *Works* (1965), 7:7.
[57]Owen, *The nature of apostasie* (1676), 24–7; *Works* (1965), 7:20–1.
[58]Owen, *The nature of apostasie* (1676), 397–8; *Works* (1965), 7:172.

'But we are perswaded of you, Beloved, better things, and such as accompany Salvation, although we thus speak.'[59] He contrasted the language used by the writer to describe the Hebrews with that used to describe these apostates, and once again concluded that they resided in quite different categories. Whoever the writer was addressing in Heb. 6.4-6, it was not members of the elect. Owen had preserved this essential element of Reformed orthodoxy. It remained to be seen whether he could convince all of his readers.

HISTORY AS DECLENSION

So much for that portion of the book that is identical to Owen's later commentary. Launching out into his 'digression', his next move was to tackle the Roman Catholics. Having established a claim for the infallibility of the elect, it would hardly do to allow a claim for the infallibility of the pope or of the Roman Catholic Church more generally. More than that, Roman Catholicism seemed to be steadily on the rise, helped along by the patronage at the court of James, the Duke of York and heir to the throne, who had publicly advertised his Roman Catholic faith by his non-compliance with the 1673 Test Act.[60] In 1677, Andrew Marvell attempted to counter this creeping Catholicism with his *Account of the growth of Popery and arbitrary government in England*, focusing particularly on the events of 1675, 1676 and 1677. In March 1679, Owen would go on to add his own contribution: *The Church of Rome, no safe guide*, which he cast as one small bucket of water 'to help allay the flames of a raging Fire'.[61] Thus the Roman Catholics were at the forefront of those groups that Owen set out to oppose.

These comments establish the strong sense of history running through *The nature of apostasie*. Naturally, the earliest years of the church were its best years, when the Christian religion modelled a 'Pristine Beauty and Glory',[62] and when the '*Primitive Church*' carefully walked in holiness.[63] Yet even at this early stage of the record, the New Testament proved that 'all sorts of Persons, all Churches are and always have been exceedingly prone to turn aside from the Mystery and Truth of the Doctrine of the Gospel'.[64] Paul issued his warnings;

---

[59]This is Owen's translation in *A continuation of the exposition of the epistle of Paul the apostle to the Hebrews* (1680), 86.
[60]Harris, 'Introduction: Revising the Restoration', 3.
[61]Owen, *The Church of Rome, no safe guide* (1679), Preface, sig. A2 (italics removed); *Works* (1965), xiv: 483.
[62]Owen, *The nature of apostasie* (1676), Epistle to the Reader, 2; *Works* (1965), 7:3.
[63]Owen, *The nature of apostasie* (1676), 6; *Works* (1965), 7:13.
[64]Owen, *The nature of apostasie* (1676), 124; *Works* (1965), 7:60–1. See also, pp. 128, 429; *Works* (1965), 7:62, 185.

the lifecycles of the churches in Corinth and Galatia bore them out.[65] The post-apostolic church fared no better: many of the church fathers neglected 'the Gospel and its simplicity'; heretics proliferated, not least the Arians and the Pelagians; and *'Monkish Fables'* took root, cultivating a proclivity in the church for foolish myth and superstition.[66] Then the *'Mystery of Iniquity'* rose up 'unto its height in the Papacy', and in Owen's telling it is almost as if the true church disappeared for a millennium or more. He allowed that faithful believers were hidden, driven into the wilderness and secretly nourished by the Spirit, but in the main the visible church had fallen into apostasy under the 'Rise and Progress of this Catholic Defection'.[67] Nevertheless, 'when the time came that God would again graciously visit the remnant of his Inheritance, he stirred up, gifted, and enabled many faithful Servants of Christ, by whom the work of Reformation was successfully begun and carried on in many Nations and Churches'.[68] Thus the church was brought into a state of *'Revalescency'*, or recovery from illness. 'But all men know what Care and Diligence is required to attain perfect Health and Soundness in such a Condition, and to prevent a Relapse, which if it should fall out, the last Error would be worse than the first.' Alas, even those involved in this recovery did not press on to a perfect reformation. Instead, the Protestant Reformation has 'visibly and apparently lost its force, and gone backwards on all Accounts', especially in what had 'of late years fallen out among our selves'.[69] Those beliefs once owned by all the prelates in England were how held in derision.[70] The heretics of old had resurfaced in a new guise: the Pelagians reappeared with a fresh layer of 'Varnish and gilding'; ancient *'Photinianisme'* and Arianism spread once more in the *'Leprosie* of *Socinianisme*, which secretly enters into the Walls and Timbers of the House, whence it will not be scraped out'.[71] Ominously he warned that 'the next Stage is down-right *Atheisme'*.[72]

The historical trajectory was, therefore, one of declension. The Reformation looked increasingly like a temporary reprieve: a season in which evangelical truths had been received, but a season only. Thus Owen saved his greatest agitation for the resurgence of Roman Catholicism, only because the current circumstance seemed to be working in its favour. 'Every slight Occasion, every Temptation of Pleasure, Profit, Favour, Preferment, turns men unto the *Papacy*',

---

[65] Owen, *The nature of apostasie* (1676), 128–30; *Works* (1965), 7:62–3.
[66] Owen, *The nature of apostasie* (1676), 142–7; *Works* (1965), 7:68–70.
[67] Owen, *The nature of apostasie* (1676), 148–50; *Works* (1965), 7:71.
[68] Owen, *The nature of apostasie* (1676), 150; *Works* (1965), 7:71.
[69] Owen, *The nature of apostasie* (1676), 150–3; *Works* (1965), 7:71–3.
[70] Owen, *The nature of apostasie* (1676), 301; *Works* (1965), 7:133.
[71] Owen, *The nature of apostasie* (1676), 162–5; *Works* (1965), 7:77.
[72] Owen, *The nature of apostasie* (1676), 299; *Works* (1965), 7:132.

which was now 'in fashion among men'. One way or another, 'many in all places fall off daily to the *Papacy*, and the old Superstition seems to be upon a new Advance, ready to receive another Edition in the world'.[73] For this reason Owen sought to demolish the credibility of Roman Catholicism, especially its piety. This was important, because the Restoration period witnessed a growing alarm at an apparent decline in public morality. The last thing Owen could afford was the idea that Reformed theology was a contributor to that decline or that Roman Catholicism might prove to be its remedy. So he went to great lengths to expose what he saw as the damage done by the Roman Catholic practice of penance, which was 'easie to Persons who never intend to leave their Sins'.[74] Since it was so vacated of those evangelical truths that alone can bring about true piety, Roman Catholicism was a religion that could never bring it to a genuine fruition.[75] Catholics had established only a form or image of faith, love and holiness – not the reality.[76] The decline in England's moral standards started when the evangelical truths of the reformation were traded in for *'novel Opinions* contrary to the Faith of the first Reformed Churches'.[77] Apostasy produced immorality. So if the country's moral condition was the problem, Roman Catholicism was hardly the answer.

JOHN GOODMAN'S *SERIOUS AND COMPASSIONATE INQUIRY* (1674)

In *The nature of apostasie*, Owen made it very clear what he felt he was responding to in general – the broad intellectual and theological trends that were steadily pushing England adrift of its Reformation moorings, as a boat slips away from its jetty. It is less clear what he was reacting to in particular. He did not name names, except in one instance in which he directly responded to John Goodman, the vicar of Watford and the author of *A serious and compassionate inquiry into the causes of the present neglect and contempt of the Protestant religion and Church of England*, first published in 1674.[78] Goodman's book provides a useful foil for Owen, in a curious way. In *The nature of apostasie*, Owen celebrated the English Reformation, deplored the possibility of a return

---

[73]Owen, *The nature of apostasie* (1676), 153–4; *Works* (1965), 7:73. See also Owen, *The nature of apostasie* (1676), 191; *Works* (1965), 7:88.
[74]Owen, *The nature of apostasie* (1676), 216–19, 224; *Works* (1965), 7:98–100, 102.
[75]Owen, *The nature of apostasie* (1676), 346–50, 355; *Works* (1965), 7:151–3, 154–5.
[76]Owen, *The nature of apostasie* (1676), 114–17, 379–87; *Works* (1965), 7:57–8, 165–8.
[77]Owen, *The nature of apostasie* (1676), 163; *Works* (1965), 7:77.
[78]*Clergy of the Church of England Database*, Person ID 89127. The title page of a posthumous collection of sermons suggests that he had been awarded a Doctor of Divinity degree; *Seven sermons preach'd upon several occasions . . . by John Goodman, D.D.* (1697).

of Roman Catholicism, lamented a general declension in the piety of English Christians, set out his diagnosis of the causes of the nation's dire condition and offered his prescription for its only possible cure. In his *Serious and compassionate inquiry*, Goodman celebrated the English Reformation, deplored the possibility of a return of Roman Catholicism, lamented a general declension in the piety of English Christians, set out his diagnosis of the causes of the nation's dire condition and offered his prescription for its only possible cure. The difference is that for Owen, Reformed theology was the solution, while for Goodman it was part of the problem.

Goodman's *Inquiry* appears to have been an influential and enduring book. Two further editions of the work appeared in 1675, and two further editions appeared in 1684 and 1693. In a way that suggests its lingering influence, Vincent Alsop replied to it in 1678 (with Alsop's reply itself running to three editions).[79] In essence, Goodman's work was an attack on the dissenters for their lack of moderation. As with Owen, Goodman couched his critique within a strong sense of history going all the way back to Jesus himself, who came into the world at a time of peace 'that he might find men in calm thoughts and at leisure to consider the reasonableness of his propositions'.[80] This is a Jesus who would appear to sit comfortably among early Enlightenment thinkers. For Goodman, the early church was a model of pristine beauty, piety, unity and, above all, obedience. But looking around at 'the present state of *Christendome*', one 'cannot choose but be astonished at the contrary face of things'.[81] To be sure, the rise of Roman Catholicism was a disaster for the church but, crucially, it was not all bad: 'it is certain all is not to be esteemed Popery, that is held or practised by the Church of *Rome*, and it cannot be our duty . . . to depart further from her than she hath departed from the truth'. There was much within the Roman Catholic Church that was held in common with all churches and that characterized it 'before it lay under any ill character'.[82] The English Reformation, therefore, was so good because it was so 'moderate and temperate': it purged only what needed to be purged.[83] But, alas, it was 'not well confirmed and swadled in its Infancy'. The reversal under Queen Mary drove many of its leaders into exile (to the Swiss territories, home to Reformed theology), where they were 'tempted with novelty'. They brought back home with them 'those foreign fashions, the fond singularity of which is still taking

---

[79]The editions are listed in Wing; Alsop replied in *A sober inquiry into the reasonings of the serious inquiry* (1679).
[80]Goodman, *A serious and compassionate inquiry* (1674), 110.
[81]Goodman, *A serious and compassionate inquiry* (1674), Introduction, sig. B1–B3v (all quotes from Goodman's introduction have had their italics removed).
[82]Goodman, *A serious and compassionate inquiry* (1674), 12, 13.
[83]Goodman, *A serious and compassionate inquiry* (1674), Introduction, sig. [C3]v.

with too many to this day'.[84] Thus the English Reformation lost its way: 'he that understands and considers what was the felicity of the first Age of our Reformation, and compares it with the present condition of our affairs, will have just cause to lament the difference'.[85]

And that was entirely the fault of the dissenters. They embodied the 'true and real Causes of the present disaffection to the *English* Reformation', because they had abandoned its essential moderation.[86] They were like physicians who never stopped meddling and purging, removing the good with the bad, even to the death of the patient.[87] Goodman's focus here lay mostly on liturgy and ceremony, which the first reformers had not scrupled to remove, but that was never Owen's main concern in *The nature of apostasie* – his focus was on doctrine, and that is where he tangled directly with Goodman.[88] When it came to doctrine, unlike 'common Arts and Sciences' that maintained their advancement through new ideas, Goodman believed that the oldest was the best: 'the elder any Doctrine of Christianity can be proved to be, it must needs be truer'. Thus the Thirty-nine Articles would always trump the Synod of Dort: 'Must a novel *Dutch Synod* prescribe Doctrine to the Church of *England*, and outweigh all Antiquity?'[89] Goodman's conception of God was nothing if not moderate. His was no 'captious Deity' who condemned men and women to hell on the basis of a choice he made before they were even born.[90] In this sense, Goodman embodied the tradition of moderate Anglicanism pioneered by Henry Hammond. In response, Owen strenuously objected to Goodman's sleight of hand in implying that Reformed theology was a novel departure at the Synod of Dort and not part of the English Reformation from the beginning:

> For look upon as it is contained in the [Thirty-nine] *Articles of Religion*, in the *Books of Homilies*, and declared in the Authenticated Writings of all the Learned Prelates and others for *sixty years* after the Reformation, wherein

---

[84]Goodman, *A serious and compassionate inquiry* (1674), 31–5.
[85]Goodman, *A serious and compassionate inquiry* (1674), Introduction, sig. C1v.
[86]Goodman, *A serious and compassionate inquiry* (1674), 31.
[87]Goodman, *A serious and compassionate inquiry* (1674), 2–3. In the same way, the dissenters love 'to be always reforming', 2.
[88]'I am not contending about *small things*'; Owen, *The nature of apostasie* (1676), 606; *Works* (1965), 7:257.
[89]Goodman, *A serious and compassionate inquiry* (1674), 3–7.
[90]Goodman, *A serious and compassionate inquiry* (1674), 7, 151–2. For other condemnations of the Reformed theology of predestination, see 23, 74. Beginning in 1675, the subsequent editions of Goodman's *A serious and compassionate inquiry* carried an 'Author's Post-script to the Reader', in which he elaborated on his view of predestination. He did not deny God's providence or his prerogative to distribute the means of salvation as he chose, but Goodman strongly denied any thought that God willed the eternal damnation of any person without regard to his or her behaviour.

the Doctrine taught, approved and confirmed in this Church was testified unto all the world.[91]

All Owen asked was that the original doctrine of the English Reformation be allowed to continue.[92] As for the Synod of Dort, there was no way it prescribed the doctrine for the Church of England because the influence flowed in exactly the opposite direction: it was the English delegates who took a leading role in the outcome.[93]

Goodman also took a swipe at Augustine. Not one of the Church Fathers preached a doctrine of predestination before Augustine, Goodman claimed, and in doing so the bishop of Hippo disagreed with himself as much as he did the Church of England. He was 'a devout good man . . . whose Piety was far more commendable than his Reason', pushed as he was to the extreme by Manicheans and Pelagians.[94] Owen objected to this disparagement of Augustine's reason that had been prompted only by 'Partiality and Prejudice' and that was hardly in keeping with 'the Learned men of all sorts in the Church for Twelve hundred years'. If anyone was novel and alone, it was Goodman.[95] He also swatted away Goodman's more substantive point that Augustine's doctrine of predestination was unprecedented. It was 'of little importance in this Cause', because Goodman was simply repeating what others had told him (though how Owen could be certain of this is unclear) and because essentially the same claim was made for the doctrine of the Trinity and that claim was just as worthless (though this argument sidestepped Goodman's point about Augustine's novelty on predestination).[96]

Each of these rival publications carried its own embedded sense of history, which shows just how contested that history was in these later seventeenth-century debates. Owen had to show that Reformed theology (not to mention orthodox trinitarianism) was no new thing but part of the inherent fabric of the faith, reaching back across the centuries to the church's very beginning. To make that argument, he had to place in their proper frame historical figures like Augustine and, more importantly, the sixteenth-century English reformers. Both Owen and Goodman posited an unwelcome declension from the true essence of the Reformation, but they cast the nature of that declension and essence in entirely different terms. Each one felt that he was witness to a grievous apostasy – but an apostasy from what?

---

[91] Owen, *The nature of apostasie* (1676), 157; *Works* (1965), 7:74.
[92] Owen, *The nature of apostasie* (1676), 158; *Works* (1965), 7:75.
[93] Owen, *The nature of apostasie* (1676), 162; *Works* (1965), 7:76.
[94] Goodman, *A serious and compassionate inquiry* (1674), 6–7.
[95] Owen, *The nature of apostasie* (1676), 160–2; *Works* (1965), 7:76.
[96] Owen, *The nature of apostasie* (1676), 159; *Works* (1965), 7:75.

THE CAUSES AND CURE OF APOSTASY

Both Owen and Goodman had written a book examining the nature of England's current apostasy, but each author offered a different diagnosis. Goodman latched on to the dissenters as the primary culprits for the church's decline. First, they unreasonably criticized the doctrine, liturgy and clergy of the Church of England because they had to represent the established church to be far worse that it really was in order to justify their departure from it.[97] The initial English Reformation had, as we have seen, gone awry, and the problem had been compounded by growing trade, civil war and the febrile condition of many corporations and parishes. That is where these new opinions were 'generally hatcht and nursed up', largely the product of their poorly educated and poorly chosen clergy.[98] It has to be said that Goodman's book might well have registered on Owen and his fellow dissenters with an infuriating complacency. It was easy enough for Goodman to chastise the dissenters for their unwillingness to conform to the requirements of the state church and to cry up the obedience of the early church to its own rulers when Goodman was happily aligned with those who dictated the privileges of ecclesiastical power in England. He also had a habit of blithely assuming that all reasonable men would agree with him. Given the poor repute of Calvinism in mid-1670s England, his presumption is perhaps understandable.

Second, Goodman claimed there was running through the Puritan and dissenting tradition an unmistakeable vein of legalistic Judaism (with its emphasis on ceremonial purity), of prejudice, of a want of piety and of the 'Rashness of popular Judgement'.[99] Goodman claimed that he had not set out to wound anyone, but no one could miss his sustained attack on the dissenters:[100] their aim was not to reform or amend but to 'destroy and lay waste'; they prosecuted 'endless scrupulosity and straining at Gnats' with 'censorious and rash judging [their] Betters and Superiours'; they ran from one extreme to the other, thus the 'middle opinion is condemned' by all; and their 'passion is such a Magnifying-glass as is able to extend a Mole-hill to a Mountain'.[101] Worse still, with their cries for toleration, they threatened a return of Roman Catholicism; and with their 'wounding and murdering' of the reputation of the Church of England, they diminished the Christian religion and inadvertently

---

[97]Goodman, *A serious and compassionate inquiry* (1674), 3.
[98]Goodman, *A serious and compassionate inquiry* (1674), 37.
[99]Goodman made this argument in ch. 3; the quote is from 56 (italics removed).
[100]Goodman, *A serious and compassionate inquiry* (1674), 56.
[101]Goodman, *A serious and compassionate inquiry* (1674), 12, 26, 59, 121.

but powerfully presented 'an Apology for the Atheism and Profaneness of the Age'.[102]

Goodman's diagnosis provides a striking contrast to that of Owen. On the one hand, many elements in their critique were common to both. Owen also observed how 'stupidly ignorant' the common multitudes were,[103] the lamentable quality of many of the clergy; the prejudice of those who held to opposing positions and the discrediting effect of disunity that served only to encourage the Roman Catholics and the atheists. On the other hand, it was precisely the kind of tendencies Owen would have discerned in someone like Goodman that pointed towards the fundamental fault. Goodman described the Christian religion as 'a plain, easie, intelligible and rational way of serving God'.[104] But Owen had little interest in a merely reasonable faith. His first question was not 'Is this reasonable?' or 'Is this moderate?' but 'Is this true?' He deduced an instinct in every human heart, one that played itself out again and again in the history of the Christian faith: a deep-seated aversion to the evangelical truths of the Gospel in preference for a self-sufficiency of human resource and reason. The problem was, at its root, for Owen, a spiritual condition. The tendency of the human mind was to render itself 'the sole and *absolute Judge* of what is Divinely proposed unto it, whether it be *true* or *false*, *good* or *evil*, to be received or rejected, without Desire or Expectation of any *supernatural Guidance* or Assistance'.[105] The mind in its natural state was established in pride: high and elevated, self-sufficient and standing in need of no assistance from outside. But the Gospel could be received only with humility and submission. A person must accept that, when it comes to salvation, 'we have *no sufficiency* of our selves, but that all our sufficiency is of God'.[106] So Owen had little interest in the language of moderation and temperance and reason, which served only to cushion the demands on a proud mind. The tools of reason and philosophy were designed to draw 'the Minds of men from the *simplicity of the Truth* as it is in *Christ Jesus*'.[107] The saving truths of religion, the doctrines of the incarnation and of the Trinity, were 'above Reason, as it is finite and limited, and some things contrary unto it, as it is deprav'd and corrupted'.[108] To say that 'we can be obliged to *believe no more* than we can comprehend ... or that we may reject what is really *above Reason*, on a Supposition that it is *contrary*

---

[102]Goodman, *A serious and compassionate inquiry* (1674), 16, 25. See also 232.
[103]Owen, *The nature of apostasie* (1676), 269 (italics removed); *Works* (1965), 7:120.
[104]Goodman, *A serious and compassionate inquiry* (1674), 144.
[105]Owen, *The nature of apostasie* (1676), 278; *Works* (1965), 7:123.
[106]Owen, *The nature of apostasie* (1676), 276–81; *Works* (1965), 7:123.
[107]Owen, *The nature of apostasie* (1676), 282–3; *Works* (1965), 7:125.
[108]Owen, *The nature of apostasie* (1676), Epistle to the Reader, 9; *Works* (1965), 7:5. See also Owen, *The nature of apostasie* (1676), 296; *Works* (1965), 7:131.

unto Reason, is to renounce the Gospel'. 'All ancient Heresies sprung from this Root.'[109] The radical cause of apostasy, therefore, was a deep aversion to the notion that we are not sufficient in ourselves. Goodman's diagnosis was hardly going to help with that.

That conviction underpinned Owen's analysis of the nature of apostasy, which began with a *'rooted Enmity'* in the mind against *'spiritual* things', those truths 'which the Mind disrelisheth'.[110] Error took root more easily than truth, and when the Gospel tried to do its work, that 'uncured *Enmity*' in the natural mind rose up at the provocation. What at first had seemed a promising friend now appeared as a judge; those principles that began as the subject of pleasant speculation now showed their true measure in the demand for a practical obedience; and thus the once-welcomed Gospel became a 'troublesome *Inmate*', and quickly ejected.[111] 'And herein lyeth the Danger of this Age. The great Design of the generality of men is to *live in sin* with as little Trouble at *present*, and as little Fear of what is *future* as they can arrive unto.'[112] That, of course, was the great danger of Roman Catholic piety that, in Owen's eyes, allowed such people to carry on their sin. His was no accommodating Christianity.

Ignorance and spiritual darkness presented a second cause of apostasy, one that also contributed to the 'Defection from the Truth which attends the dayes wherein we live'.[113] Yet this ignorance was cloaked in the cover of reason – once again it was a spiritual condition, not a cognitive one. Owen lived among 'a numerous Generation of *scepticks*'.[114] These people made a public profession of the Christian religion, and they may even have preached it or taught it, but they did not relish the goodness and beauty of it. They kept these truths at arm's length, as the object of intellectual scrutiny that is always subject to the dictates of reason in their own mind. For that reason, the moral standard of their lives was no better than that of Muslims or Roman Catholics, founded as it was on mere moral effort rather than the vital power of living truth received in a humble, teachable heart.[115] Conformity to the light of nature or human reason served to keep intelligent people in spiritual ignorance. What we would call the early Enlightenment was no friend to the Gospel in the terms that Owen perceived it.

---

[109] Owen, *The nature of apostasie* (1676), 288, 294; *Works* (1965), 7:128, 130.
[110] Owen, *The nature of apostasie* (1676), 176, 186; *Works* (1965), 7:82, 86.
[111] Owen, *The nature of apostasie* (1676), 180; *Works* (1965), 7:84. See also Owen, *The nature of apostasie* (1676), 281; *Works* (1965), 7:125.
[112] Owen, *The nature of apostasie* (1676), 219; *Works* (1965), 7:100.
[113] Owen, *The nature of apostasie* (1676), 234; *Works* (1965), 7:106.
[114] Owen, *The nature of apostasie* (1676), 234; *Works* (1965), 7:106.
[115] Owen, *The nature of apostasie* (1676), 238, 387–94; *Works* (1965), 7:107, 168–71.

The fundamental causes of apostasy are obvious, but there were still others. Love of the world prompted people to conform to the patterns around them, just as those first Hebrew Christians were tempted to revert to Judaism in the face of persecution from their Jewish brethren.[116] Satan, the archetypal apostate, worked steadily to keep people in their ignorance, blindness and aversion to the truth.[117] God himself, notwithstanding his patience and kindness, allowed people to have what they wanted if they did not want him: he could 'forsake them, and withdraw from them the Means of their Edification and Preservation'.[118] After all, Hebrews 6 made it clear that such apostates could never be brought back to repentance (though Owen was careful to present that as something short of absolute impossibility).[119] At its root, though, the causes of apostasy lay in the individual. People dismissed the usefulness of Christ's death, they lacked a spiritual view of the excellency of Christ and the experience of the power of the Holy Spirit, they remained oblivious to the holiness and otherness of God, they refused to submit to his sovereignty and they diminished the authority of the Scriptures.[120] That is quite a list. Taken together, it is easy to imagine how daunted Owen may have felt. Everything in Restoration England seemed designed to annul the Gospel of all its life and power:

> Do we see things any where in the World upon a *Recovery*, or any thriving Design for the retrieval of *Holiness*? The Name and Thing are growing more and more into Contempt. What Instance can be given wherein this *Apostasie* from the *Gospel* doth or may exert it self, be it in *Atheisme*, be it in *Popery*, in hatred of and scoffing at the *Mysteries of Evangelical Truth*, in Worldliness, Prophaneness, Vanity, and Sensuality of Life, in the Coldness in Love, and Barrenness among Professors, that is not openly in its *progress*?[121]

No wonder Owen decided to get his book out into the world just as quickly as he could.

It can hardly have been with much optimism that he presented the cure for this widespread apostasy. It seemed that only God could put a stop to it.[122] But there were means within people's reach, if only they would use them. Coercion was not one of them. Owen wrote his book at a time when dissenters were subject to the coercive power of the state. At first he resolved not to say

---

[116] Owen, *The nature of apostasie* (1676), 313–17; *Works* (1965), 7:138–9.
[117] Owen, *The nature of apostasie* (1676), 317–20; *Works* (1965), 7:139–41.
[118] Owen, *The nature of apostasie* (1676), 321; *Works* (1965), 7:141.
[119] Owen, *The nature of apostasie* (1676), 62–8; *Works* (1965), 7:36–8.
[120] Owen, *The nature of apostasie* (1676), ch. 7.
[121] Owen, *The nature of apostasie* (1676), 532; *Works* (1965), 7:226–7.
[122] Owen, *The nature of apostasie* (1676), 533, 534; *Works* (1965), 7:227–8.

anything at all on the subject,[123] but as the book went on he opened up, not just to protest what he saw as the un-Christian treatment of his fellow dissenters but also to show the futility of trying to use outward compulsion to cure an inward, spiritual condition.[124] Instead of force, England needed to return to what worked so well at the time of the Reformation: evangelical preaching. 'A diligent communication unto the body of the People through the Dispensation of the Word, or Preaching of it . . . will alone secure the Continuance of the Gospel in succeeding Generations. All other means will be ineffectual.'[125] The only cure for this widespread apostasy was conversion, and the main means of conversion was the word of God preached and proclaimed.[126] Spiritual darkness could be countered only by spiritual illumination.[127] Those truths of the Gospel had to be released to do their saving work.

Needless to say, Goodman would have disagreed. Dissenters, of course, were the problem, and he despaired at the way they side-lined the early Reformation's devotion to liturgy and venerated the sermon in its place, and how they made it 'the great point of Sanctity to scruple every thing' – his marginal reference to 'Mr. *Calv.*' made it clear where the trouble began.[128] He bemoaned the '*Babel* of a Church' that he witnessed around him, in contrast to the pleasing unity and obedience of the early church.[129] So the solution was certainly not comprehension or toleration but for dissenters to end their perverse scrupulosity and conform themselves 'to the Wisdom of our Superiours, and the interests of Society'.[130] This would present a more credible profession of Christianity that would prevent any further slide into Roman Catholicism and atheism. Goodman reinterpreted such high-stakes phrases as 'tender conscience' and 'Christian liberty' in such a way as to highlight the potentially chaotic implications of the way Calvinists appeared to throw those terms around.[131]

Perhaps this is why Owen went so far out of his way to stress not just the gracious generosity of the Gospel but also its severity. He was certainly careful to show that his prescription for England's ills did not entail the antinomianism and

---

[123] Owen, *The nature of apostasie* (1676), 192; *Works* (1965), 7:89.
[124] Owen, *The nature of apostasie* (1676), 204–5, 270–1, 473–80; *Works* (1965), 7:93–4, 120–1, 203–5.
[125] Owen, *The nature of apostasie* (1676), 197; *Works* (1965), 7:90–1. See also Owen, *The nature of apostasie* (1676), 198–200; *Works* (1965), 7:91–2. Not just any preaching would do, since many preached only out of their own natural talents and interests, but only the preaching of 'the *Mysteries* of the Gospel', 248–9; *Works* (1965), 7:111.
[126] Owen, *The nature of apostasie* (1676), 223; *Works* (1965), 7:101.
[127] Owen, *The nature of apostasie* (1676), 225–32; *Works* (1965), 7:102–5.
[128] Goodman, *A serious and compassionate inquiry* (1674), Introduction, sig. C2r-v.
[129] Goodman, *A serious and compassionate inquiry* (1674), Introduction, sig. B3r-v.
[130] Goodman, *A serious and compassionate inquiry* (1674), 98–104, 187.
[131] Goodman, *A serious and compassionate inquiry* (1674), ch. 7 and 8.

the kind of chaos that had, in the eyes of many, attended Reformed theology on its way through the seventeenth century. Those verses in Hebrews 6 pointed the way by presenting a stern warning. 'In the preaching of the Gospel, it is necessary to propose unto men, and to insist on the Severity of God.'[132] Careless security was in fact a cause of apostasy – it led to over-confidence and thus to the neglect of the use of means in persevering in the faith.[133] Owen was adamant about the high call of the Gospel: no unholy person could expect to gain 'the least Advantage' from it; the life of faith involved continual conflict and vigorous warfare and vigilance against sin; the only way to fix the boundaries of sin was the hard way; to accept Christ's mercy one was also required to accept his authority.[134] 'But these are the Terms of the *Gospel*; no one Duty is to be *neglected*; no one sin is to be *indulged*.... If we like not to be *Holy* on these Terms, we must let it alone, for on any other we shall never be so.'[135] Free grace did not mean a free ride.

And so, having presented his diagnosis of England's condition, Owen exhorted his readers to apply the cur that he prescribed. As the book headed towards its conclusion, Owen injected pastoral advice to help the believer to maintain his or her faith in these dismal conditions of hastening apostasy. His general prescription was 'a *watchfull Attendance unto all Gospel Duties, and a vigorous Exercise of all Gospel Graces*'.[136] He began by reminding the persevering believer that even they were not immune from the possibility of apostasy. A present freedom from temptation 'will not secure us from the Assaults of the next Hour', so in his advice he sought 'to excite men unto a due Apprehension of their *Danger*'.[137] If there was ever a time to stand firm and to watch carefully it was now, in an age of prevailing temptation.[138] Not every sin ended in apostasy, but a wilful and persistent course of sin would do so, thus the believer had to take a firm stand in holiness, taking heed to avoid any sort of sin that tended towards the erosion of their faith and any love of the world that might draw them off from the love of Christ.[139] For those who saw in themselves this sort of declension he advised them to find '*an able Spiritual Guide*', to do '*Violence*' even to themselves 'as unto all Occasions of sin' and to remain steadfast in prayer.[140] Owen held fast to the infallible perseverance of

---

[132] Owen, *The nature of apostasie* (1676), 72 (italics removed); *Works* (1965), 7:40. He repeated the point on Owen, *The nature of apostasie* (1676), 82; *Works* (1965), 7:44.
[133] Owen, *The nature of apostasie* (1676), 305–13; *Works* (1965), 7:135–8.
[134] Owen, *The nature of apostasie* (1676), 372, 396–7, 413, 599; *Works* (1965), 7:162, 171–2, 178–9.
[135] Owen, *The nature of apostasie* (1676), 407, 396; *Works* (1965), 7:176, 172.
[136] Owen, *The nature of apostasie* (1676), 568; *Works* (1965), 7: 241.
[137] Owen, *The nature of apostasie* (1676), 524, 525; *Works* (1965), 7:223, 224.
[138] Owen, *The nature of apostasie* (1676), 529, 537; *Works* (1965), 7:225–6, 229.
[139] Owen, *The nature of apostasie* (1676), 541, 543; *Works* (1965), 7:230, 231.
[140] Owen, *The nature of apostasie* (1676), 562–7; *Works* (1965), 7:239–41.

the elect, but that did nothing to ameliorate the demand he placed on believers rigorously to exert themselves towards the end of their own salvation.

The final chapter of the book offered *'Directions to avoyd the Power of a prevailing Apostasie'*, but it reads as a lament: England's apostasy really was prevailing. Owen mourned for his country, and he invited his readers to do the same. The vast majority of those who took the name of Christian lived in a dangerous idolatry, risking their eternal ruin. That should prompt a secret mourning in faithful believers as well as an open proclamation of those Gospel truths that were so sorely neglected, he insisted, all while believers should keep a stern watch on their own hearts.[141] There was really no hope at all, except as it lay in Jesus, 'the *Spring and Fountain* of all *Grace*, as He who alone is able to preserve us in *Faith* and *Obedience*, and doth communicate supplyes of *effectual Grace* unto Believers for that purpose'.[142] The faithful Christian was to trust in him, not in a form of church or visible profession, even one that is governed completely according to the institution of Christ.[143] They were to persist in the practice of private duties and they were to present to the world a credible witness to the truths they proclaimed.[144] Only such careful walking could preserve believers from the danger of apostasy that, while they walked in the world, would always be with them.

CONCLUSION

The nature of apostasie is testament to Owen's sense of defeat. For a lifetime he had laboured to secure the truths of Reformed theology. He was battling, but he was not winning. He looked all around and saw a growing disease, a spreading contagion: *'the whole World doth daily wax worse and worse'*. The apostasy he had warned against for decades had seemingly come to pass. 'I hope for better things, and pray for better things, but I have no certain Ground of Assurance that this Apostasie shall not *grow*, until in one Instance or other of it, it [will] swallow up all *visible Profession*.'[145] We can see his book, then, as one more effort in what appeared to be a losing cause, offered by a faithful combatant who was nearing the end of his energies. In the opening pages he presented himself as a person of 'mean condition in the World, disadvantaged by all imaginable circumstances that might prejudice the most sincere Endeavours'.

---

[141] Owen, *The nature of apostasie* (1676), 568–87; *Works* (1965), 7:241–9.
[142] Owen, *The nature of apostasie* (1676), 584; *Works* (1965), 7:248.
[143] Owen, *The nature of apostasie* (1676), 587–8; *Works* (1965), 7:249–50.
[144] Owen, *The nature of apostasie* (1676), 596–9, 607–12; *Works* (1965), 7:253–4, 257–9.
[145] Owen, *The nature of apostasie* (1676), 530, 533–4; *Works* (1965), 7:226, 227. For other expressions of Owen's dismay at the dire condition of English Christianity, see Owen, *The nature of apostasie* (1676), 378–9, 422–3, 454, 471, 572–3; *Works* (1965), 7:164–5, 182, 195, 202, 243.

This sounds like the customary humility we might expect of any early modern author, but in the conditions of the 1670s and this late in Owen's life it carries a good measure of plausibility. He felt in himself the 'daily warning' of his soon departure from the battlefield.[146] His pilgrimage was 'hastning unto its Period', and its end really was not far off.[147] Two days before he died, in 1683, Owen wrote to his long-time companion Charles Fleetwood that he was 'leaving the ship of the church in a storm', though the 'great Pilot' remained at the helm.[148]

As Owen approached his death, he might have felt an enormous despondency about the condition of Christianity. If so, that may have been too pessimistic. Just as he underestimated the continuation of a faithful church through the time of alleged papal domination, so he may also have missed the continuity of true faith around him. Even if there were no known replies to *The nature of apostasie*, his own book and others he wrote offered weighty defences of Reformed theology. And he was not as alone and embattled as he may have felt. Figures like John Edwards and Isaac Watts, along with plenty of others, helped to sustain Calvinist doctrine through its English nadir.[149] It is mistaken to see a dark and empty gulf between the great heights of Puritanism in the seventeenth century and the evangelical revivals of the eighteenth century. Yet that would have been difficult for Owen to see at the time. He had lived long enough to sense that his many efforts to counter that decline had come to nought.

Thus *The nature of apostasie* sheds light on Owen's career and his long defeat, not least when it is placed alongside a book such as John Goodman's *Serious and compassionate inquiry*. It is entirely possible there were other books more central to the concerns Owen addressed in *The nature of apostasie*, but in Goodman's *Inquiry* we gain a good sense of what Owen was facing, and we can be certain that it was, at the least, on his mind. We might note that Goodman was no Socinian or Roman Catholic. There is no reason to doubt his trinitarian orthodoxy or his Protestant credentials. So he was far from the worst that Owen felt he was up against, but even that was worrying enough. Goodman operated within an entirely different frame of reference, one that was above all focused on the Church of England, which had 'the countenance of the Laws, the support of Reason, the favour of Antiquity, the recommendation of Decency'.[150] Owen had no such regard. History showed that widespread conversion to the Gospel

---

[146] Owen, *The nature of apostasie* (1676), Epistle to the Reader, 15, 18; *Works* (1965), 7:8, 9.
[147] Owen, *The nature of apostasie* (1676), 346; *Works* (1965), 7:151.
[148] *The correspondence of John Owen*, 174.
[149] For John Edwards, see Wallace, *Shapers of English Calvinism*, ch. 6. For Isaac Watts, I am grateful to Daniel Johnson, a PhD candidate at the University of Leicester, for alerting me to the significance of Watts and to the significance of the post-Owen period for Reformed theology.
[150] Goodman, *A serious and compassionate inquiry* (1674), 51–2. Goodman looked to the worship of the Jewish synagogue as a model, which was 'wholly Governed by Prudence and the general reasons of Religion', (143).

gave way over time to a merely notional profession.[151] Excessive attachment to a particular form of the visible profession of Christianity was a cause of apostasy, not its solution. If that was true even when a church was governed according to the institution of Christ, how much more in the Church of England with its pompous worship and wealthy clergy?[152] Whatever the condition of the church, 'we doe not *rest in these Things*, the Name, Title, Priviledge, and outward Observance of them'.[153] In themselves, they did not save.[154] Instead, for Owen, what mattered most was the inward and spiritual – the Gospel.

We need to be careful not to privilege Owen against Goodman. Both men presented coherent frames of reality: Goodman, the church-centred moderate strain of Anglicanism in the tradition of Henry Hammond;[155] Owen, the gospel-centred, Word-focused strain of Congregational Puritanism. But their rival books suggest that these frameworks were essentially incompatible. Goodman was far from being a heretic but, even so, in Owen's eyes, his attachment to reason and moderation was quite capable of doing enormous damage to the cause of the Gospel in England. In that sense, Goodman embodied those trends that had Owen so much on the defensive. Furthermore, we should not be entirely taken in by Owen's rhetoric about England's degeneracy. Puritan jeremiads had a long and worthy tradition, and the tendency of every generation of Christians is to see themselves, as Owen did, in a Laodicean age.[156] But he was not wrong to be alarmed – as G. R. Cragg's comment about the 'overthrow of Calvinism' suggests. Whatever else he did, Goodman dismissed the doctrine of predestination, John Calvin and the Reformed tradition. That was why his attack on Dort and Augustine animated Owen to respond. Yet Goodman was just one voice among many. At the end of his life, Owen had good cause to be grievously worried. He had done so much, but had he done enough? We know that Reformed orthodoxy was not dead yet – far from it. What part *The nature of apostasie* played in keeping it alive is impossible to say. But we can be sure that in writing the book Owen aimed to uphold it. It is further testament to his willingness to fight what might have seemed a losing battle, even to his dying breath.

---

[151]Owen, *The nature of apostasie* (1676), 259–61, 268; *Works* (1965), 7:116, 119–20.
[152]Owen, *The nature of apostasie* (1676), 487–93; *Works* (1965), 7:208–11.
[153]Owen, *The nature of apostasie* (1676), 590–1; *Works* (1965), 7:251.
[154]Owen, *The nature of apostasie* (1676), 593; *Works* (1965), 7:252.
[155]The subsequent editions of Goodman's *A serious and Compassionate inquiry* ended with the stationer's list of the available works of Henry Hammond.
[156]Owen, *The nature of apostasie* (1676), 533; *Works* (1965), 7:227. The biblical allusion is to Rev. 3.14-22, the letter to the lukewarm church at Laodicea.

CHAPTER 18

The doctrine of justification by faith (1677)

WHITNEY GAMBLE-SMITH

If we lose the ancient Doctrine of Justification through Faith in the Blood of Christ, and the Imputation of his Righteousness unto us, publick profession of Religion, will quickly issue in Popery or Atheism.[1]

John Owen situates his explanation of the doctrine of justification by faith in a sweeping overview of the history of redemption, which begins with God's eternal plan of salvation determined before time. In over 350 pages of dense writing, Owen carefully elaborates the relationship between sin and grace, the law and the Gospel, justification and sanctification, justice and mercy, and the role of each member of the Trinity in bringing sinners to salvation. His goal is to explain how a guilty sinner could come to obtain favour and acceptance before God.[2] By the time Owen published *The doctrine of justification by faith*

---

[1] Owen, *The doctrine of justification by faith* (1677), 291; *Works* (1965), 5:207.
[2] Owen, *The doctrine of justification by faith* (1677), 6; *Works* (1965), 5:11. While a major study on Owen's doctrine of justification is yet to appear, the following chapters or articles are helpful: Trueman, *John Owen*, 101–21; Beeke and Jones, *A Puritan theology*, 491–506; Kapic, *Communion with God*, 109–46; Fesko, *Beyond Calvin*, 286–98; Hunsinger, 'Justification and mystical union

through the imputation of the righteousness of Christ; explained, confirmed, and vindicated (1677), he had spent over three decades lecturing, publishing and preaching on these themes. Owen's intention in writing this treatise – his most mature treatment of the doctrine of justification – was not to engage in controversy or produce yet another vitriolic text. He had already expended much ink and energy as a controversialist. Instead, his goal now was pastoral – to explain how a 'distressed sinner may attain assured peace with God through our Lord Jesus Christ'.[3] Owen offered this treatise to 'establish the minds of believers, to direct the consciences of them that inquire after abiding peace with God' and to 'extricate their minds' from the difficulties surrounding the doctrine.[4] Owen claims that he takes more pleasure in the 'steady Direction on one Soul in this enquiry, than in disappointing the Objections of twenty wrangling or fiery Disputers'.[5]

He expresses frustration that now, in 'these dark times', the church in England was so troubled and burdened by controversy that there was a need for a simple explanation of the doctrine of justification by faith, a cornerstone doctrine of the Reformation:

> Who would have thought that we should have come to an indifferency as to the doctrine of justification, and quarrel and dispute about the interest of works in justification; about general redemption, which takes off the efficacy of the redeeming work of Christ; and about the perseverance of the saints.[6]

The very nature of the doctrine of justification is directly concerned with practical Christian living, for in no other 'Evangelical Truth is the whole of our Obedience more concerned'. At its heart, the doctrine addresses how sinners can 'get and maintain peace with God' and to live before him in an acceptable manner.[7] Therefore, to carry the discussion of justification 'out of the understandings of ordinary Christians, by speculative notions and distinctions, is disserviceable unto the Faith of the Church'.[8]

Despite Owen's pastoral focus, he seemingly could not help but spend considerable time combatting familiar opponents – Socinians, Pelagians,

---

with Christ'; Baylor, 'One with him in Spirit'; and Barrett and Haykin, *Owen on the Christian life*, 185–218.

[3]Owen, *The doctrine of justification by faith* (1677), 'To the Reader', sig. A1v; *Works* (1965), 5:3.

[4]Owen, *The doctrine of justification by faith* (1677), 'To the Reader', sig. A1v–sig. A2r; *Works* (1965), 5:4.

[5]Owen, *The doctrine of justification by faith* (1677), 'To the Reader', sig. A1v; *Works* (1965), 5:3.

[6]Owen, 'Sermon V'; *Works* (1965), 9:459. This sermon was preached on 8 September 1682. Cf. Gribben, *John Owen and English Puritanism*, 260.

[7]Owen, *The doctrine of justification by faith* (1677), 5; *Works* (1965), 5:10.

[8]Owen, *The doctrine of justification by faith* (1677), 5; *Works* (1965), 5:10.

'Papists', Arminians and antinomians. However, Owen largely remains true to his goal to present the doctrine simply and without profligate references to current or past controversies, and he is critical of the fact that many works on justification spend more time on philosophical debates and definitions than on exegesis. In his treatise, he intends to present the 'Analogy of Faith', namely, the 'manifest scope and design of the Revelation of the Mind and will of God in the Scripture'.[9] His goal in this is to 'exalt the Freedom and riches of [God's] Grace, the Glory and Excellency of Christ and his Mediation; to discover the woful, lost, forlorn condition of man by Sin, to debase and depress everything that is in and of our selves, as to the attaining of Life, Righteousness and Salvation'.[10]

For Owen, in order to understand the biblical teaching on justification, one must first comprehend God as holy, great, majestic, sovereign and as a righteous judge; and second, understand humanity as possessing an apostate and guilty nature, inherited and imputed from Adam.[11] Once God and humanity were apprehended, one could begin to grasp the foundation of justification, which is the imputation of Christ's righteousness to sinners through their union with him by the Holy Spirit. This righteousness is received by the gift of faith alone. God's loving and gracious provision of a mediator to secure sinners' acceptance before him is the 'Substance of the Gospel, and the Centre of all the Truths revealed in it'.[12]

SUMMARY OF CONTENT

By the time Owen published his work in 1677, the basic Protestant content of the doctrine of justification had been established in England for over a century. Article 11 of both the Forty-two Articles (1552) and the Thirty-nine Articles (1562) state that justification is by faith alone. In the late decades of the 1500s and the first several of the 1600s, the doctrine received renewed attention as the rise of Arminianism and antinomianism, and later Socinianism, provided the impetus for new debates.[13] The venerable theologians William Pemble, John Davenant and George Downame each wrote classic treatments of the doctrine by 1634.[14] In 1643, as members of the Westminster Assembly set about their task

---

[9]Owen, *The doctrine of justification by faith* (1677), 426; *Works* (1965), 5:295. For a thorough treatment of Owen's exegetical method, see Knapp, 'Understanding the mind of God'.
[10]Owen, *The doctrine of justification by faith* (1677), 426; *Works* (1965), 5:295.
[11]Owen, *The doctrine of justification by faith* (1677), 8–13, 89; *Works* (1965), 5:13–20, 69.
[12]Owen, *The doctrine of justification by faith* (1677), 54; *Works* (1965), 5:45.
[13]For an excellent analysis of the rise of Arminianism in England, see Milton, *The British delegation and the Synod of Dort*; for antinomianism, Como, *Blown by the Spirit*, and Gamble, *Christ and the law*; and for Socinianism, see Mortimer, *Reason and religion in the English revolution*.
[14]Pemble, *Vindiciae fidei* (1625); Davenant, *A treatise on justification* (1631); Downame, *A treatise of justification* (1634).

to revise and expand the Thirty-nine Articles, it was the doctrine of justification that received the most spirited and lengthy debates on the floor.[15] Crafted out of the fire of debate, with its statement of justification as a result of the imputation of Christ's righteousness received by the instrument and gift of faith alone, the eleventh chapter of the assembly's confession of faith set the standard for the doctrine post-Reformation. Many English theologians continued to contribute to the growing pool of sources on the doctrine through the 1640s and 1650s.[16] Owen's theological conclusions on justifying faith, the role of faith and works, the abiding nature of the law and the work of Christ largely echo the Westminster Assembly's formulations. Owen, along with Thomas Goodwin, proved to be instrumental in an expanded and revised version of the Westminster Confession, known as the 'Savoy Declaration of Faith and Order'.[17] Though largely following the Westminster divines' chapter on justification, the Savoy Declaration further defined Christ's work of obedience in justifying sinners as both active and passive.[18] The Savoy Declaration on this point can be assumed to reflect Owen's theology. However, in this 1677 treatise, most likely due to Owen's pastoral aim, he adamantly declares that he does not wish to participate in the debate about the definition and nature of, or the difference between, active and passive righteousness.[19] Nevertheless, he spends considerable time arguing against Socinian views on the nature of Christ's obedience, centring his arguments on the person of Christ as the second Adam and as the 'surety' of his people.[20]

Owen's treatise on justification is developed around his treatment of four main topics: justifying faith, in chapters 1–3; justification itself, in chapters 4–6; imputation, in chapters 7–9; righteousness and faith alone, in chapters 10–15; and finally, detailed exegetical arguments and objections answered to the above topics, in chapters 16–20. Kelly Kapic notes that despite being a premier Reformed theologian committed to God's sovereign election, Owen chooses to begin his discussion of justification with, and concentrates heavily on, the

---

[15]See Gamble, *Christ and the law*, 87–108.
[16][Westminster Assembly], *The humble advice of the Assembly of Divines*. A complete listing and analysis of the many works on justification composed from 1600 to 1677 falls outside the scope of this chapter. See Trueman, *John Owen*, 101–21, for a concise summary.
[17]*Savoy Declaration*, ed. Matthews, highlights the differences between the Westminster Confession and the Savoy Declaration. For a historical introduction to the Savoy Declaration, see McGraw, *A heavenly directory*, 23–4.
[18]See Gamble, *Christ and the law*, 88–108 for the Westminster divines' debates and final decision on the wording of these phrases.
[19]Owen, *The doctrine of justification by faith* (1677), 81; *Works* (1965), 5:63.
[20]Owen, *The doctrine of justification by faith* (1677), 361–96; *Works* (1965), 5:251–75. See below for further analysis.

human role in faith rather than God's role in predestination.[21] This speaks to Owen's driving pastoral concern to provide comfort to believers instead of presenting a detached and polemical analysis of God's character.[22]

JUSTIFYING FAITH, CHAPTERS 1–3

Owen begins by outlining the nature of justifying faith, distinguishing it from a faith that does not justify. He argues that there were many examples in Scripture of people 'believing' and having 'faith', but their faith was not saving faith. People could give assent to divine truth, but mere assent was not justifying faith. Faith could be temporary, it could also wax and wane, and it could have various degrees of effect in a person's life.

Before sinners can exercise justifying faith, they must first come to a knowledge and conviction of their sin.[23] 'Let no man think to understand the Gospel, who knoweth nothing of the Law', Owen warns.[24] Justification is God's deliverance of the convicted sinner, one who is guilty before God and has a deep sense and conviction of that guilt.[25]

Owen holds up the example of Adam to illustrate the relationship between conviction of sin and justifying faith: after the fall, when Adam was convicted of his shame and guilt and was filled with fear, God promised redemption through Christ.[26] That pattern holds even now. When people are in their 'lost, forlorn, hopeless condition', God reveals the proper object of justifying faith by which men and women are to be justified: Christ himself.

Even in describing the necessity of conviction of sin as a first step, Owen is clear that God is still the one who graciously provides that conviction. Conviction of sin itself is a gift; it is a 'meer Act of Sovereign Grace' that is ordained by the infinite wisdom, love, grace and goodness of God to answer all the wants and needs of guilty sinners.[27] God is the one who provides deliverance and comfort to those in despair over their sin. The believer's regard of the work of Christ does not take anything away from the free grace, favour and love of God, for it was by God's ordaining plan that Christ become the sinner's

---

[21] Kapic, *Communion with God*, 111.
[22] Kapic's point appears to be contra Hunsinger, 'Justification and mystical union with Christ', 205, who claims that Owen took an approach that is more 'disputational than systematic'.
[23] Owen, *The doctrine of justification by faith* (1677), 99; *Works* (1965), 5:75.
[24] Owen, *The doctrine of justification by faith* (1677), 133; *Works* (1965), 5:98.
[25] Owen, *The doctrine of justification by faith* (1677), 99; *Works* (1965), 5:75.
[26] Owen, *The doctrine of justification by faith* (1677), 100; *Works* (1965), 5:76.
[27] Owen, *The doctrine of justification by faith* (1677), 105; *Works* (1965), 5:80.

mediator.[28] Christ 'brings nothing unto us, does nothing for us, but what God appointed, designed, and made him to be'.[29]

True justifying faith is that which 'receives' Christ, that which receives the promise, the word, the grace of God and the atonement. It is faith that 'cleaves' unto God. In the Old Testament, faith is generally expressed by trust and hope.[30] As sinners recognize their sin and have nowhere else to turn for relief, they renounce all else and rest fully upon God. This trust in God composes and quiets the soul; it is also the most frequent demonstration of true justifying faith in Scripture. All of the believer's rest in this world is from trust in God, and specifically, trust in the fact that he works to reconcile the world in Christ.[31]

This waiting and resting upon God produces an 'Acquiescency of the Heart' in God as the author and principal cause of salvation.[32] True faith is the consent of the will, where the soul comes to Christ and receives from him pardon of sin and righteousness before God. True faith acknowledges that there is no other way of attaining righteousness, life and salvation apart from Christ's pardon of sin and gift of righteousness before God.[33] Thus, justifying faith is the 'acting of the Soul towards God, as revealing himself in the Gospel for deliverance out of this state and condition, or from under the Curse of the Law applied unto the Conscience, according to his mind, and by the ways that he hath appointed'.[34]

True justifying faith will ascribe to God the glory that he is due. Owen argues that the design and end of the Gospel was not the salvation of sinners but God's own glory. In the Gospel, God designed the glory of his righteousness, the glory of his love, the glory of his grace, the glory of his wisdom, the glory of his power and the glory of his faithfulness.[35] True faith delights in 'all these glorious properties of the Divine Nature, as manifested in the provision and proposition of this way of life, Righteousness and salvation'.[36] Delighting in and ascribing unto God his glory is the essence of true faith.

Owen summarizes his understanding of justifying faith in trinitarian terms: the Lord Jesus Christ himself, in his work of mediation for the recovery and salvation of lost sinners, is the proper object of justifying faith. The grace of God is the cause of this faith, the pardon of sin is its effect and the promises of the Gospel are the means of communicating Christ and the benefits of his

---

[28]Owen, *The doctrine of justification by faith* (1677), 122; *Works* (1965), 5:91.
[29]Owen, *The doctrine of justification by faith* (1677), 122–3; *Works* (1965), 5:91.
[30]Owen, *The doctrine of justification by faith* (1677), 110; *Works* (1965), 5:83.
[31]Owen, *The doctrine of justification by faith* (1677), 137; *Works* (1965), 5:101.
[32]Owen, *The doctrine of justification by faith* (1677), 136; *Works* (1965), 5:101.
[33]Owen, *The doctrine of justification by faith* (1677), 137; *Works* (1965), 5:101.
[34]Owen, *The doctrine of justification by faith* (1677), 101–2; *Works* (1965), 5:77.
[35]Owen, *The doctrine of justification by faith* (1677), 133; *Works* (1965), 5:97.
[36]Owen, *The doctrine of justification by faith* (1677), 131; *Works* (1965), 5:97.

mediation unto sinners.[37] The true nature of faith consists in the heart's embrace of God's love, grace and wisdom and Christ's mediation, obedience, sacrifice, satisfaction and atonement.[38] Ultimately, true justifying faith is 'not found in any but those who are made partakers of the Holy Ghost, and by him united unto Christ, whose Nature is renewed, and in whom there is a principle of all Grace and purpose of Obedience'.[39] Owen concludes that any description of faith that did not include the above marks was 'vain speculation'.[40]

OF JUSTIFICATION, CHAPTERS 4–6

In chapters 4 through 6, Owen moves from outlining the nature of justifying faith to discuss the 'notion and signification' of the terms 'justification' and 'to justify' in Scripture.[41] The terms are forensic, denoting an act of jurisdiction, and their meaning is 'to Acquit, to Declare and pronounce righteous upon a Trial'.[42] He argues that adoption and justification are similar: in the case of adoption, there is no internal, inherent change made in the person adopted, but because of the adoption, the person is 'esteemed and adjudged as a true Son, and hath all the rights of a legitimate Son'. So, by justification, a person is esteemed, declared and pronounced righteous, as if he or she were completely so.[43]

Owen argues that in the Old Testament, there is no place where the Hebrew word צָדַק (*zadaq*) is used in the conjugation where it denotes an action towards another 'in any other sense, but to absolve, acquit, esteem, declare, pronounce righteous, or to impute righteousness'. The term is never used to signify 'to make inherently Righteous; much less to pardon for sin'.[44] Through an analysis of numerous passages in the New Testament, Owen argues that the Greek word δικαιόω (*dikaioō*) is also never used to signify the making of a person righteous by producing internal righteousness in the person himself.[45] Instead, it is always used either to absolve and acquit, to judge, esteem, and pronounce righteous or to condemn. The word is capable only of a forensic meaning.

Owen summarizes the nature of justification in courtroom terms: God himself is the judge who pronounces his judgement from his 'throne of grace'.

---

[37] Owen, *The doctrine of justification by faith* (1677), 115; *Works* (1965), 5:86–7.
[38] Owen, *The doctrine of justification by faith* (1677), 119; *Works* (1965), 5:89.
[39] Owen, *The doctrine of justification by faith* (1677), 141; *Works* (1965), 5:104.
[40] Owen, *The doctrine of justification by faith* (1677), 125; *Works* (1965), 5:93.
[41] Owen, *The doctrine of justification by faith* (1677), 169; *Works* (1965), 5:123.
[42] Owen, *The doctrine of justification by faith* (1677), 171; *Works* (1965), 5:124.
[43] Owen, *The doctrine of justification by faith* (1677), 172; *Works* (1965), 5:125.
[44] Owen, *The doctrine of justification by faith* (1677), 173; *Works* (1965), 5:125.
[45] Owen, *The doctrine of justification by faith* (1677), 176; *Works* (1965), 5:128.

There is a guilty person, with accusers ready to propose and promote the charges. The charge is admitted and laid before the judge's tribunal. The work of Christ is the gospel plea prepared for the guilty person, where the ransom is paid and atonement made. Eternal righteousness is brought in by the surety of the covenant. To this alone the sinner 'betakes himself', renouncing all other defences. To make the plea 'effectual', an advocate with the Father pleads his own propitiation for the sinner. The sentence then is absolution on the account of the ransom, blood, sacrifice and righteousness of Christ.[46]

Owen analyses and disputes the Roman Catholic idea of a first and a second justification as well as the Socinian notion of an evangelical, inherent personal righteousness as a necessary condition to justification. In the Catholic teaching, according to Owen, a sinner's mind is first prepared to receive a habit of grace. Then a second justification, which is dependent upon the first, occurs after the sinner has performed good works, which proceed from this first principle of grace.[47] Owen argues against these teachings by stating that 'justification is such a work as is at once completed in all the causes, and the whole effect of it, though not as unto the full possession of all that it gives Right and Title unto'.[48] All the believer's sins – past, present and future – were laid upon Christ. He will never do more than he has already done to expiate sin. His sacrifice was the 'meritorious procuring cause' of the sinner's justification and is never to be renewed. By the sinner's actual believing on Christ with justifying faith, he or she is at once completely justified. Once justified, all of the believer's sins are forgiven. There is nothing to be laid unto his or her charge, and he or she can delight in the blessedness of salvation. Owen concludes – there is only one justification, 'namely, that whereby God at once freely by his Grace justifieth a convinced sinner through Faith in the Blood of Christ'.[49]

IMPUTATION, CHAPTERS 7–9

In chapters 7 through 9, Owen discusses imputation and, particularly, the imputation of Christ's righteousness to sinners. For Owen, the doctrine of the imputation of Christ's righteousness is an 'Important Truth immixed with the most fundamental Principles of the mystery of the Gospel, and inseparable from

---

[46]Owen, *The doctrine of justification by faith* (1677), 188; *Works* (1965), 5:136.
[47]Kapic points out that the notion of a double justification became hotly contested even among Roman Catholic theologians, with the Council of Trent deciding against the inclusion of a theory of double justice because 'it sounded Lutheran', and they considered it a novelty. However, since Robert Bellarmine used the language, it became commonly associated with all Roman Catholic theology by Protestants. See Kapic, *Communion with God*, 126–37.
[48]Owen, *The doctrine of justification by faith* (1677), 199; *Works* (1965), 5:143.
[49]Owen, *The doctrine of justification by faith* (1677), 212; *Works* (1965), 5:152.

the Grace of God in Christ Jesus'.[50] He states that the 'life and continuance of any Church on the one hand, and its Apostasie or Ruine on the other', depends on the 'Preservation or Rejection of the Truth in this Article of Religion'.[51]

Quoting a definition from Davenant, Owen declares that the 'Righteousness of Christ (in his Obedience and Suffering for us) imputed unto Believers, as they are united unto him by his Spirit, is that Righteousness whereon they are justified before God, on the Account whereof their sins are pardoned, and a Right is granted them unto the Heavenly Inheritance'.[52] While this definition is preserved, Owen states, 'we need not trouble our selves about the Differences that are among Learned men, about the most proper stating and declaration of some lesser concernments of it. This is the Refuge, the only Refuge of distressed Consciences, wherein they may find Rest and Peace'.[53]

The first biblical expression of the nature of justification is by imputation, when Abraham believes and God 'accounts' it to him or 'imputes' it to him as righteousness in Genesis 15. In the New Testament, Paul provides a fuller explanation of the doctrine, proving that the righteousness by which sinners are justified comes by imputation, and specifically, the non-imputation of sin and the imputation of righteousness.[54]

Here, Owen reiterates his pastoral focus – in explaining the doctrine of imputation, he desires not to participate in the various disputes over definitions common among fellow Reformed theologians. He questions why he would challenge them when the substance of the doctrine itself was openly opposed and rejected: 'why should we debate about the order and beautifying of the Rooms in an House, whilst fire is set unto the whole'?[55] Instead, in this section, he seeks to explicate the doctrine of imputation from the abuses of the 'Papists and the Socinians . . . the design of one is to exalt their own Merits, of the other, to destroy the merit of Christ'.[56] Owen laments that the important doctrine, which is so vital as to have an 'immediate influence into [the believer's] whole present duty' as well as his or her eternal welfare or ruin, is 'so fallen out in our days, that nothing in Religion is more maligned, more reproached, more despised'.[57] Those who reject the doctrine of the imputation of righteousness by necessity bring in antinomianism and libertinism.[58] Owen identified

---

[50] Owen, *The doctrine of justification by faith* (1677), 245; *Works* (1965), 5:175.
[51] Owen, *The doctrine of justification by faith* (1677), 231; *Works* (1965), 5:165.
[52] Owen, *The doctrine of justification by faith* (1677), 293; *Works* (1965), 5:208. See below for further analysis of Owen's doctrine of union with Christ.
[53] Owen, *The doctrine of justification by faith* (1677), 294; *Works* (1965), 5:208.
[54] Owen, *The doctrine of justification by faith* (1677), 227; *Works* (1965), 5:163.
[55] Owen, *The doctrine of justification by faith* (1677), 230; *Works* (1965), 5:165.
[56] Owen, *The doctrine of justification by faith* (1677), 230; *Works* (1965), 5:165.
[57] Owen, *The doctrine of justification by faith* (1677), 227; *Works* (1965), 5:163.
[58] Owen, *The doctrine of justification by faith* (1677), 228; *Works* (1965), 5:163.

imputation as an 'ancient doctrine of the church of England', claiming that it was 'well-known' that the Reformed church taught the imputation of Christ's righteousness. Those who pretend otherwise were not his concern, 'for to what purpose is it to dispute with men who will deny the Sun to Shine, when they cannot bear the heat of its beams'?[59]

Owen then launches into a detailed explanation of the biblical definition and examples of imputation. First, he explains that things that are not one's own originally, personally and inherently may yet be imputed to him or her from someone else '*ex justitia*', or by the rule of righteousness. This may be done for two reasons: first, because of a covenant relation between the two parties, and second, because of a natural relation between them. The imputation of Adam's sin to all of his posterity is an example of this *ex justitia* imputation, because Adam stands as the head and representative of all humankind, as Paul describes in Romans 5. Adam's descendants became as guilty as he was, as if each individual person sinned along with Adam.[60]

Second, imputation can also take place when one person freely agrees to answer for another, where one undertakes the responsibility for something or someone as if he himself had originally made the agreement. This voluntary imputation is what Christ did for sinners, when he took their sins onto himself, to answer for what they had done against God and the law.[61]

Third, the imputation which Paul outlines in Romans 4 must be understood as a communication of that unto sinners which was before not theirs. Owen summarizes Pauline imputation both negatively and positively. Negatively, imputation is not a judging or esteeming of people to be righteous who truly and really are not so. God, as a righteous judge, cannot declare someone to be righteous who is not perfectly righteous. Paul's imputation also is not a transmission or transfusion of someone's righteousness to another.[62] It is impossible for the righteousness of one to be transfused to another. Positively, the imputation spoken of in Romans 4 involves God, out of his mere love and grace, and upon the consideration of 'the mediation of Christ', making an effectual grant and donation of a 'true, real, perfect Righteousness'. This true righteousness is that of Christ himself, and it is given to all who believe. God accounts it as theirs, and, on his own gracious act, 'both absolves them from sin, and granteth them Right and Title unto Eternal Life'.[63]

Finally, in order to understand imputation truly, Owen states that one must first comprehend the notion that Christ and the church are one mystical

---

[59] Owen, *The doctrine of justification by faith* (1677), 229; *Works* (1965), 5:164.
[60] Owen, *The doctrine of justification by faith* (1677), 237; *Works* (1965), 5:169.
[61] Owen, *The doctrine of justification by faith* (1677), 238; *Works* (1965), 5:170.
[62] Owen, *The doctrine of justification by faith* (1677), 242; *Works* (1965), 5:173.
[63] Owen, *The doctrine of justification by faith* (1677), 243; *Works* (1965), 5:173.

person.⁶⁴ Imputation is founded upon union. Through the uniting efficacy of the Holy Spirit, Christ and the church coalesce into one person, of which Christ is the head and the church is the body.⁶⁵ The work of Christ is imputed to the church so that it becomes as if the church did it. In the same way, what the church deserved due to her sin is charged upon Christ. Believers' sins are transferred to Christ and made his. He then undergoes the punishment due to them, all owing to the fact that he is united to them.⁶⁶

RIGHTEOUSNESS AND OBEDIENCE, CHAPTERS 10–14

At the beginning of chapter 10, Owen restates the point of his treatise, which is to seek out how sinners 'on their Believing obtain the Remission of sins, Acceptance with God, and a Right unto Eternal Life. And if this can no other way be done, but by the Imputation of the Righteousness of Christ unto them, then thereby alone are they justified in the sight of God'.⁶⁷

This assertion assumes that there is a righteousness required in order for a sinner to appear before God. Thus, from chapters 10 through 14, Owen outlines the nature of the righteousness and obedience necessary for a sinner to be declared righteous before God. His culminating summary, stated at the end of chapter 11, is that 'there is no other way whereby the original, immutable Law of God, may be established, and fulfilled with respect unto us, but by the Imputation of the perfect Obedience and Righteousness of Christ, who is the end of the Law for Righteousness unto all that do believe'.⁶⁸

Owen expounds this claim first by arguing that the required righteousness could not be an inherent, personal righteousness, for, as stated in Ps. 130.3-4, if the Lord marked iniquities, no-one could stand before him.⁶⁹ There is no-one righteous inherently; no-one whose obedience or good works could have any effect upon his or her justification before God.⁷⁰

God, out of his free, sovereign act, created humanity with the need to be governed by a law, and this 'necessary Law . . . did immediately and unavoidably ensue upon the constitution of our nature in Relation unto God'.⁷¹ The substance of this law was that humanity is to adhere to God 'absolutely, universally, unchangeably, uninterruptedly, in trust, love, and fear, as the chiefest

---

⁶⁴Owen, *The doctrine of justification by faith* (1677), 294; *Works* (1965), 5:209.
⁶⁵Owen, *The doctrine of justification by faith* (1677), 246; *Works* (1965), 5:176.
⁶⁶Owen, *The doctrine of justification by faith* (1677), 249; *Works* (1965), 5:178.
⁶⁷Owen, *The doctrine of justification by faith* (1677), 315–16; *Works* (1965), 5:223.
⁶⁸Owen, *The doctrine of justification by faith* (1677), 348; *Works* (1965), 5:250.
⁶⁹Owen, *The doctrine of justification by faith* (1677), 317; *Works* (1965), 5:224.
⁷⁰Owen, *The doctrine of justification by faith* (1677), 318; *Works* (1965), 5:225.
⁷¹Owen, *The doctrine of justification by faith* (1677), 341; *Works* (1965), 5:241.

good, the first Author of his being, of all the present and future advantages whereof it was capable, should yield Obedience unto him'.[72] This law eternally and unchangeably obliges all humans to obedience to God, for it is built into humanity's very essence. If one is human, he or she is obliged to obey God.

Owen argues that the law of sinless, perfect obedience with its sentence of punishment and death to all transgressors abides in force forever in this world. Nowhere does Scripture indicate that it has been altered or abrogated. Thus, 'every rational Creature is eternally obliged from the Nature of God, and its Relation thereunto, to love him, obey him, depend upon him, submit unto him, and to make him its End, Blessedness, and Reward'.[73]

Owen acknowledges that with the entrance of sin at Adam's fall, the original covenant established between God and man was annulled. Once humanity became sinful, men and women could not keep the original law of obedience, trust and love.[74] However, as the whole of the law is an 'Emanation of Eternal Right and Truth, it abides and must abide in full force for ever'.[75] The law is a representation to humanity of God's holiness and righteousness in the government of his creatures. So 'there can be no Alteration made herein, seeing with God himself there is no variableness nor shadow of changing'.[76] Thus, because all humankind has fallen under the penalty of death given in the first covenant, 'it is utterly impossible that any one individual person of the posterity of Adam should be justified in the sight of God, accepted with him or blessed by him, unless this Penalty be answered, undergone, and suffered, by them or for them'.[77]

Furthermore, it is a dishonour to Christ to assert that God would accept a lesser righteousness for a sinner's justification than that which he required upon humanity's creation.[78] Owen states that

> if it were necessary that the Lord Christ, as our surety, should undergo the penalty of the Law for us, or in our stead, because we have all sinned; then it was necessary also that, as our surety, he should yield obedience unto the preceptive part of the Law for us also; And if the Imputation of the former be needful for us unto our Justification before God, then is the Imputation of the latter also necessary unto the same End and Purpose.[79]

---

[72] Owen, *The doctrine of justification by faith* (1677), 341–2; *Works* (1965), 5:241.
[73] Owen, *The doctrine of justification by faith* (1677), 376; *Works* (1965), 5:261.
[74] Owen, *The doctrine of justification by faith* (1677), 346; *Works* (1965), 5:244.
[75] Owen, *The doctrine of justification by faith* (1677), 345; *Works* (1965), 5:244.
[76] Owen, *The doctrine of justification by faith* (1677), 346; *Works* (1965), 5:250.
[77] Owen, *The doctrine of justification by faith* (1677), 347; *Works* (1965), 5:245.
[78] Owen, *The doctrine of justification by faith* (1677), 346; *Works* (1965), 5:250.
[79] Owen, *The doctrine of justification by faith* (1677), 361; *Works* (1965), 5:251.

Christ was made under the law for the church – to become the surety of the covenant and representative of the whole: 'He was born to us, and given to us, lived for us, and died for us, obeyed for us, and suffered for us; that *by the obedience of one, many might be made Righteous.*'[80]

Owen further elaborates that the original law that bound humankind to obedience is summarized by the words, 'Do this and live'. The law has two parts. First, it requires obedience, hence the phrase, 'do this, and live'. It also requires sanction in case of disobedience, summarized by God's statement that man should die on the day he disobeyed the law. When the law was broken, humans became liable for both aspects of the law: they inherited guilt for breaking the law's positive command, and also came under the law's curse.[81] Christ must come and answer the command of the law by his obedience to the law, and he must answer for the curse of the law by shedding his blood.[82] There must be a taking away of dirty clothes – sinners must be pardoned of sin. And then, they must be granted clean clothes – they must be declared righteous. Christ, by his suffering and perfect life of obedience, completed both requirements of the law.[83]

In this context, Owen then discusses the differences between the covenant of works and the covenant of grace.[84] The covenant of works – established between God and Adam at creation, with Adam representing all of humanity – consisted in this, 'that upon our personal obedience, according unto the Law and Rule of it, we should be accepted with God, and rewarded with him'.[85] There was no mediator in this covenant. All transactions were immediately between God and humanity. There was also no provision for sin in this covenant – nothing but perfect obedience could be accepted by God. On the other hand, the covenant of grace, being of grace, wholly excludes works. It had a mediator and surety – it is not upheld on the basis of the sinners' personal obedience but upon Christ's perfect obedience.

Owen turns to exegesis to prove that 'no Acts or Works of our own, are the Causes or Conditions of our Justification; but that the whole of it is resolved into the Free Grace of God, through Jesus Christ, as the Mediator and Surety

---

[80]Owen, *The doctrine of justification by faith* (1677), 371–2, italics in original; *Works* (1965), 5:258.
[81]Owen, *The doctrine of justification by faith* (1677), 383; *Works* (1965), 5:266.
[82]Owen, *The doctrine of justification by faith* (1677), 383; *Works* (1965), 5:266.
[83]Owen, *The doctrine of justification by faith* (1677), 386; *Works* (1965), 5:268. Although he does not cite it, Owen here echoes the language of the Westminster Assembly's confession of faith. See Gamble, *Christ and the law*, 101–8 for the divines' debates, and Gamble, *Christ and the law*, 133–54, for the final form in chapter 11 of the confession.
[84]See Beeke and Jones, *A Puritan theology*, 217–318, and Fesko, *The Covenant of redemption*, 47–81, for an overview of the complex landscape of the Puritan understanding of covenant theology.
[85]Owen, *The doctrine of justification by faith* (1677), 397; *Works* (1965), 5:275.

of the Covenant'.⁸⁶ Owen states that Paul, in his writings, excluded all works of the law in a sinner's justification – outward works, even those performed with an inward principle of faith were excluded; works that the law itself required were excluded; and the believer's good works performed after conversion were excluded.⁸⁷

Owen summarizes as follows: 'the Law intended by the Apostle, when he denies that by the Works of the Law any can be justified, is the entire Rule and Guide of our Obedience unto God, even as unto the whole frame and spiritual Constitution of our Souls, with all the Acts of Obedience or Duties that he requireth of us'. Second, the works of the law, 'which he so frequently and plainly excludeth from our Justification, and therein opposeth of the Grace of God, and the Blood of Christ, are all the Duties of Obedience, Internal, Supernatural, External, Ritual, however we are or may be enabled to perform them, that God requireth of us'. It is the 'Righteousness of Christ alone imputed unto us, on the account whereof we are justified before God'.⁸⁸

Owen comments that while the current debates over justification appeared to be new, due to their protagonists' use of 'Exotic Learning, with Philosophical Terms and notions', they in fact mirror those of Paul and the Jews in Galatia, Paul and the Pharisees, and Augustine and Pelagius: 'Controversies in Religion make a great Appearance of being new, when they are only varied and made different, by the new Terms and Expressions that are introduced into the handling of them.'⁸⁹

In chapter 15, Owen moves from the first section of the treatise's main point to the second. The first section stated that Christ's righteousness is imputed to sinners, by whose obedience they are made righteous. The second part is that this righteousness is made sinners' by faith alone. Owen then provides definitions of faith. Faith is illustrated in Scripture by how one interacts with Christ: justifying faith is the act of the hopeless, helpless and lost soul receiving Christ, looking to Christ, coming to Christ, fleeing to Christ for refuge, cleaving to Christ and leaning, trusting, hoping and resting on God.⁹⁰ Faith is a receiving of Christ as he is 'the Lord our Righteousness'. Conversely, unbelief is expressed by not receiving Christ, or rejecting Christ.

Since faith is a 'receiving of what is freely granted, given, communicated, and imputed to us, that is, of Christ, of the Atonement, of the Gift of Righteousness, of the forgiveness of sins', then there can be no other influence into a sinner's justification. Not any 'other Graces, our Obedience, Duties, Works, no

---

⁸⁶Owen, *The doctrine of justification by faith* (1677), 400; *Works* (1965), 5:278.
⁸⁷Owen, *The doctrine of justification by faith* (1677), 406–10; *Works* (1965), 5:282–4.
⁸⁸Owen, *The doctrine of justification by faith* (1677), 416–17; *Works* (1965), 5:289.
⁸⁹Owen, *The doctrine of justification by faith* (1677), 417–18; *Works* (1965), 5:289–90.
⁹⁰Owen, *The doctrine of justification by faith* (1677), 422–5; *Works* (1965), 5:292–4.

influence into our Justification, nor are any Causes or Conditions thereof. For they are neither that which doth receive, nor that which is received, which alone concur thereunto'.[91] True justifying faith consists 'in a mans going out of himself, in a complete Renunciation of all his own Duties and Righteousness, and betaking himself with all his Trust and Confidence unto Christ alone, and his Righteousness, for pardon of sin, acceptance with God, and a right unto the Heavenly Inheritance'.[92]

In summary, Owen stated that the faith

> whereby we believe unto the Justification of Life, or which is required of us in a way of Duty that we may be justified, is such an Act of the whole Soul whereby convinced Sinners do wholly go out of themselves to rest upon God in Christ for Mercy, Pardon, Life, Righteousness and Salvation, with an acquiescency of Heart therein.[93]

EXEGETICAL ARGUMENTS AND OBJECTIONS ANSWERED, CHAPTERS 16–20

Chapters 16 through 20 present a biblical theology of the former issues. Owen's purpose in writing his treatise was to provide a thoroughly Scriptural and non-philosophical or controversial outline of the doctrine of the justification of sinners through the imputation of Christ's righteousness by faith alone. While Owen analysed Scripture throughout, these final chapters present an almost overwhelming amount of Scriptural support for his arguments. He traces the themes through the Old Testament, the Gospels; spends a considerable amount of time in Romans; and concludes with a comparison of Paul and James. As he exegetes, Owen reiterates the definitions of key terms and theological points made earlier.

PRINCIPAL THEMES

Throughout his treatise, Owen seeks to answer the following questions, some combination of which were raised by Socinians, antinomians and Catholics: if Christ's passive righteousness is imputed to believers, is there no need for his active righteousness? If all sin is pardoned, is there no need for Christ's

---

[91] Owen, *The doctrine of justification by faith* (1677), 422; *Works* (1965), 5:292.
[92] Owen, *The doctrine of justification by faith* (1677), 423–4; *Works* (1965), 5:293.
[93] Owen, *The doctrine of justification by faith* (1677), 425; *Works* (1965), 5:294. See Beeke and Jones, *A Puritan theology*, 443–61, on the Puritan idea of the necessity for 'preparation' for justification.

righteousness to be imputed? If sinners believe that their sins are pardoned, does that mean their sins are already pardoned before they believe? If Christ's righteousness is imputed to his people, are they esteemed to have done and suffered what they never actually did and suffered? If sinners' sins are imputed to Christ, was Christ sinful? If good works are excluded from justification, are they of no use?[94] Despite the breadth of these questions, Owen subsumes his answers to them under two reoccurring themes: union with Christ and the relationship between faith and works.

Union with Christ

It can be argued that Owen is unmatched among his contemporaries in his focus on the doctrine of union with Christ.[95] For Owen, the doctrine of justification and all its accompanying benefits is founded upon the believer's union with Christ.[96] The believer's participation in Christ, while it does not receive a chapter of its own in the treatise, is a theme that runs throughout.[97] In the 'General considerations' at the start of the work, Owen quotes Albertus Pighius, whose words, he stated, for their 'worth and truth' bore repeating at length:

> In him [Christ] therefore we are justified before God, not in ourselves, not by our own, but by his Righteousness, which is imputed unto us now communicating with him. Wanting Righteousness of our own, we are taught to seek for Righteousness without ourselves in him . . . we are made Righteous in Christ, not with our own but with the Righteousness of God. By what Right? The Right of friendship, which makes all common among friends, according unto the ancient celebrated proverb. Being ingrafted into Christ, fastened, united unto him, he makes his things ours, communicates his Riches unto us, interposeth his Righteousness between the Judgment of God and our unrighteousness, and under that, as under a shield and buckler, he hides us from that divine wrath which we have deserved; he defends and

---

[94]See Owen, *The doctrine of justification by faith* (1677), 68; *Works* (1965), 5:54–5, where he poses these questions.

[95]Allison, *The rise of moralism*, 262; Baylor, 'One with him in Spirit', 428.

[96]Owen, *The doctrine of justification by faith* (1677), 246; *Works* (1965), 5:176; Fesko, *Beyond Calvin*, 290. There is great debate among American scholars of the Reformation and post-Reformation era regarding whether John Calvin and subsequent Reformed theologians held union with Christ as the 'priority' in redemption or whether justification should be prioritized. See Edwards, 'John Flavel on the priority of union with Christ', 34 n. 3 for the many works on this. Beeke and Jones, *A Puritan theology*, 481–9, argue that union holds priority among the Puritans.

[97]Hunsinger, 'Justification and mystical union with Christ', 205, claims that 'the idea of mystical union with Christ appears with remarkable infrequency' in the treatise. Yet, it appears early in the 'General Considerations' and continues throughout; see citations in the following footnotes.

protects us therewith, yea he communicates it unto us and makes it ours, so as that being covered and adorned therewith, we may boldly and securely place our selves before the divine Tribunal and Judgment, so as not only to appear Righteous, but so to be.[98]

Owen continually rests his treatment of imputation, righteousness, sin, the law, Adam and justification upon the notion that a sinner becomes united to Christ by the power of the Holy Spirit. A sinner's justification is due to this union, where Christ and believers become 'one spiritually animated Body, Head, and Members'.[99] What Christ did for believers, in their stead, is imputed and communicated to them as they become one with him by faith – and 'thereon' they are justified before God.[100] No one can be a true believer and not be justified, and no one can be justified who is not united to Christ, as union is the 'foundation of our Justification'.[101] Owen comments that all that Paul requires unto the sinner's justification is that he or she be found in Christ and not in him or herself.[102] The reality 'that there is such a Union between Christ and Believers, is the faith of the Catholick Church, and hath been so in all Ages', and 'those who seem in our days to deny it [union as foundational] or question it, either know not what they say, or their minds are influenced by their Doctrine, who deny the Divine Persons of the Son, and of the Spirit'.[103]

Owen explains his understanding of union by describing Christ's work of redemption in detail. First, the spring, or the cause, of Christ's union with his people lies in Christ's agreement to take on the redemption of fallen humanity in the eternal compact made with his Father.[104] The ultimate function of the covenant is to bring men and women into union with Christ.[105]

Second, integral to this covenant agreement is Christ's promise to be the mediator and surety for sinful humanity. A surety is an undertaker for another, or others, who 'thereon is justly and legally to answer what is due to them'.[106] Christ voluntarily becomes the surety for sinners in order to bring them into the new covenant.[107] In the first covenant made with Adam, there was no need for a mediator; God and Adam were the only participants. Adam was created

---

[98] Owen, *The doctrine of justification by faith* (1677), 46; *Works* (1965), 5:39.
[99] Owen, *The doctrine of justification by faith* (1677), 302; *Works* (1965), 5:222.
[100] Owen, *The doctrine of justification by faith* (1677), 314; *Works* (1965), 5:222.
[101] Owen, *The doctrine of justification by faith* (1677), 217; *Works* (1965), 5:156.
[102] Owen, *The doctrine of justification by faith* (1677), 538; *Works* (1965), 5:371.
[103] Owen, *The doctrine of justification by faith* (1677), 294; *Works* (1965), 5:209.
[104] Owen, *The doctrine of justification by faith* (1677), 251; *Works* (1965), 5:179.
[105] Ferguson, *John Owen on the Christian life*, 32.
[106] Owen, *The doctrine of justification by faith* (1677), 253–5; *Works* (1965), 5:181–2.
[107] Baylor, 'One with him in Spirit', 433, states that against 'the Socinian argument that Christ is a surety from God to the elect – a kind of sign or assurance that God will keep his promise, Owen

with the ability to keep the covenant in and of his own strength. When he broke it, there was a need for a new covenant with new members.[108] In the new covenant, Christ takes on the original obligations of the covenant and incorporates into himself his own people. He does not become the surety for a nameless mass of people, but for the church.[109]

Third, Christ's obedience is the surety of the covenant. This obedience and perfect righteousness with respect to the law is granted to believers and made theirs by the 'gracious Constitution, Sovereign Appointment, and Donation of God'.[110] It is due to Christ's work that believers are 'judged and esteemed to have answered the Righteousness of the Law', as righteousness is imputed to sinners by virtue of their union with Christ.[111] The 'principal Foundation' of imputation is that 'Christ and the church . . . were one mystical Person'.[112] This union, centred in the communion of Christ's Spirit, provides the 'complete foundation of the Imputation of their sins unto him, and of his Righteousness unto them'.[113]

Fourth, in Christ's agreement to take on human flesh, he was predestined and foreordained to grace and glory. He was foreordained as the head of the church to gather all things to him, to gather all of the elect of God and bring them into this everlasting covenant.[114]

Owen draws from the rich imagery used in Scripture to describe the union between Christ and his church: it is like that as of a husband and wife; that of Eve and Adam, where she shared in Adam's very flesh and bone; that of a head and members of the same body; that of a political union between a ruling leader and his subjects; that of a vine and its branches; that of Adam and his posterity. Owen stated that this mystical union is difficult to comprehend, but by the use of all of these representations in Scripture, the Holy Spirit seeks to illustrate that the church's union with Christ cannot be reduced to any one of them.[115]

The means by which the church becomes mystically united to Christ as her surety is through the work of the Holy Spirit. The same Spirit who dwells in Christ is sent to the church to abide in, animate and guide the whole body and all its members. To be made the righteousness of God in Christ, as he was made sin for his people, can be accomplished through no other way but to be

---

maintains that Christ is principally a surety for the church to God, since Christ undertakes to make restitution for the debt of sin and to endow us with his righteousness'.
[108] Owen, *The doctrine of justification by faith* (1677), 261; *Works* (1965), 5:186.
[109] Baylor, 'One with him in Spirit', 433.
[110] Owen, *The doctrine of justification by faith* (1677), 348; *Works* (1965), 5:245.
[111] Owen, *The doctrine of justification by faith* (1677), 348; *Works* (1965), 5:245.
[112] Owen, *The doctrine of justification by faith* (1677), 246; *Works* (1965), 5:175.
[113] Owen, *The doctrine of justification by faith* (1677), 275; *Works* (1965), 5:198.
[114] Owen, *The doctrine of justification by faith* (1677), 253; *Works* (1965), 5:180.
[115] Owen, *The doctrine of justification by faith* (1677), 250; *Works* (1965), 5:179.

made righteous through the imputation of Christ's righteousness as his people are united to him.[116] For Owen, to deny the reality of Christ's union with his church is to 'overthrow the Church and the Faith of it'.[117]

Faith and works

Owen admits that he desired to forgo a detailed explanation of the necessity of good works post justification, as he already treated the topic at length in Πνευματολογια: or, A discourse concerning the Holy Spirit (1674). Yet, he repeatedly addresses the subject throughout the treatise. Owen defends himself from the charge of holding to a form of antinomianism which denies the connection between justifying faith and the 'necessity of Holiness, Righteousness or obedience, but that we are by Grace set at liberty to live as we list'. He is accused of holding to the idea that 'if we are made Righteous with the Righteousness of another, we have no need of any righteousness of our own'.[118] Owen appears to be at once sensitive to and tired of the charge of antinomianism, first levelled against him by Richard Baxter in 1649.[119] He dryly commented that 'it were well if many of those who make use of this plea would endeavour by some other way also to evidence their esteem of these things; for to dispute for the necessity of Holiness, and live in the neglect of it, is uncomely'.[120]

Owen states that sinners are justified by faith alone, but not by a faith that is alone. Faith is alone in its influence towards justification, but it is not alone in its nature and existence. Justifying faith must be accompanied by a 'principle of spiritual Life and universal Obedience, operative in all the works of it, as Duty doth require'.[121] By its very nature, true faith manifests itself in the disposition and actions of the believer.[122] Owen disparages those who call themselves 'Solifidians', but at the same time oppose the necessity of good works or obedience to the law. He argues: 'we allow no Faith to be of the same kind or nature with that whereby we are justified, but what virtually and radically contains in it universal Obedience, as the effect is in the cause, the fruit in the root'.[123] No faith can be justifying which is not itself, and in its

---

[116]Owen, *The doctrine of justification by faith* (1677), 508; *Works* (1965), 5:351.
[117]Owen, *The doctrine of justification by faith* (1677), 302; *Works* (1965), 5:214.
[118]Owen, *The doctrine of justification by faith* (1677), 544; *Works* (1965), 5:375.
[119]Baxter, *Aphorismes* (1649), 'Appendix'. See Boersma, *A hot pepper corn*, for Baxter's doctrine of justification. See Gribben, *John Owen and English Puritanism*, 115–17, and Trueman, *John Owen*, 115–18, for Owen and Baxter's theological debate. See Cooper, *John Owen, Richard Baxter and the formation of Nonconformity* for an overview of Owen and Baxter's relationship.
[120]Owen, *The doctrine of justification by faith* (1677), 544; *Works* (1965), 5:375.
[121]Owen, *The doctrine of justification by faith* (1677), 95; *Works* (1965), 5:73.
[122]Kapic, *Communion with God*, 112.
[123]Owen, *The doctrine of justification by faith* (1677), 96; *Works* (1965), 5:73.

own nature, a 'spiritually vital principle of Obedience and Good Works'.[124] Justifying faith, with this accompanying principle of good works, is a special type of faith, wholly different in character and type from any other faith.

Wherever true faith is found – faith that has a 'cordial, sincere approbation of the way of salvation by Jesus Christ, proposed in the gospel' – it will 'infallibly produce both repentance and obedience'.[125] Owen states that it was 'utterly impossible that a man should be a true Believer, and not at the same instant of time be truly penitent'.[126]

Because of Christ's work, all duties of obedience – internal, external and ritual – are excluded from the believer's justification.[127] There is no personal, inherent righteousness in any believer by which he or she can be justified before God because sin remains in the believer.[128] Yet, one's justification does not render personal righteousness needless.[129] God has ordained that his people should 'walk in good Works', and thus good works are necessary from God's will and command.[130]

Once justified, believers are obliged unto universal obedience to God, as the law is not abolished, but established by faith, and it reflects God's nature.[131] The commanding power of the law shows justified people their sins and obliges them to obedience.[132] To be under the curse of the law and to be justified are opposite states. But to be under the commanding power of the law and to be justified are not. Justification dissolves the obligation of the sinner to receive punishment due to the curse of the law, but it does not 'annihilate the commanding Authority of the Law'.[133]

The means of the continuation of a sinner in his or her justified state is through the work of Christ and his Spirit in sanctification. Justification and sanctification are inseparable – to suppose that one could exist without the other is to 'overthrow the whole Gospel'.[134] Owen defines sanctification as 'the inherent Renovation of our Natures, exerting and acting it self in newness of Life, or Obedience unto God in Christ, and works of Righteousness'.[135] It is by the grace of sanctification that a believer's nature is spiritually washed, purified

---

[124] Owen, *The doctrine of justification by faith* (1677), 96; *Works* (1965), 5:73.
[125] Owen, *The doctrine of justification by faith* (1677), 129; *Works* (1965), 5:96.
[126] Owen, *The doctrine of justification by faith* (1677), 300; *Works* (1965), 5:213.
[127] Owen, *The doctrine of justification by faith* (1677), 417; *Works* (1965), 5:289.
[128] Owen, *The doctrine of justification by faith* (1677), 317; *Works* (1965), 5:225.
[129] Owen, *The doctrine of justification by faith* (1677), 540; *Works* (1965), 5:372.
[130] Owen, *The doctrine of justification by faith* (1677), 552; *Works* (1965), 5:380.
[131] Owen, *The doctrine of justification by faith* (1677), 201; *Works* (1965), 5:145.
[132] Owen, *The doctrine of justification by faith* (1677), 202; *Works* (1965), 5:145.
[133] Owen, *The doctrine of justification by faith* (1677), 202; *Works* (1965), 5:146.
[134] Owen, *The doctrine of justification by faith* (1677), 553; *Works* (1965), 5:381.
[135] Owen, *The doctrine of justification by faith* (1677), 215; *Works* (1965), 5:155.

and endowed with a principle of life, holiness and obedience towards God.[136] By sanctification, a sinner is 'made meet' for glory.

Justification will always have as its accompaniment the sanctification of a sinner, for walking in holiness is required of justified sinners. However, 'Godly sorrow, Repentance, Humiliation for sin, and confession of it' are not duties required for justification, as that would make a sinner's continuation in a justified state a matter of his or her own obedience and good works. Instead, 'all other works and duties of obedience do accompany Faith in the continuation of our justified estate, as necessary effects and fruits of it, but not as causes, means, or conditions whereon that effect is suspended'.[137] God requires a sincere obedience from all who believe, to be performed in and by their own persons though through the aids of grace supplied to them by Christ, 'but the consideration of them which are performed before believing is excluded by all from any causality or interest in our justification before God'.[138]

CONCLUSION

In seeking to provide 'direction, satisfaction, and peace' to distressed sinners' souls concerning their relation to God, for Owen, the only answer could be found in a simple yet profound explanation of the doctrine of justification through God's triune work of redemption. The questions driving Owen's treatise specifically were: 'what that is upon the account whereof, God pardoneth all their [i.e., guilty sinners] sins, receiveth them into his favour, declareth or pronounceth them Righteous, and acquitted from all Guilt, removes the Curse, and turneth away all his wrath from them, giving them Right and Title unto a blessed Immortality or life Eternal'?[139] Further, is it anything in 'our selves, as our Faith and Repentance, the Renovation of our Natures, inherent habits of Grace, and actual works of Righteousness which we have done or may do' that provides sinners acceptance before God?[140]

In his process of answering these questions, Owen provides a biblically rich, exegetically robust, logically reasoned account of the work of Christ in saving sinners by his obedience, righteousness, satisfaction and merit, as well as the work of the Holy Spirit in 'expressing the most eminent Acts in our Justification, especially as unto our Believing, or the acting of that faith whereby we are justified'.[141] He summarizes:

---

[136]Owen, *The doctrine of justification by faith* (1677), 180; *Works* (1965), 5:130.
[137]Owen, *The doctrine of justification by faith* (1677), 207, 210–11; *Works* (1965), 5:151.
[138]Owen, *The doctrine of justification by faith* (1677), 214; *Works* (1965), 5:154.
[139]Owen, *The doctrine of justification by faith* (1677), 2; *Works* (1965), 5:8.
[140]Owen, *The doctrine of justification by faith* (1677), 3; *Works* (1965), 5:8.
[141]Owen, *The doctrine of justification by faith* (1677), 7; *Works* (1965), 5:12.

> Wherefore seeing that we had lost original righteousness, and had none of our own remaining, and stood in need of a perfect, compleat righteousness to procure our acceptance with God, and such a one as might exclude all occasion of boasting of any thing in our selves, the Lord Christ being given and made unto us, the Lord our Righteousness, in whom we have all our righteousness, our own, as it is ours, being as filthy rags in the sight of God, and this making an end of sin, and reconciliation for iniquity, and bringing in everlasting righteousness. It is by his Righteousness, by his only, that we are justified in the sight of God, and do glory.[142]

At the end of a long career, and experiencing the turmoil of tumultuous, confusing and distressing days, Owen harkens back to the Reformation of the previous century. He wishes that Martin Luther's prophetical words, that in the 'following Ages the Doctrine hereof would be again obscured', were not true.[143] As the time had come and the doctrine had once again fallen into obscurity, Owen viewed his efforts for the 'preservation of this doctrine of the gospel pure and entire' as following in the vein of the first reformers. However, his task was even more difficult than was theirs, for during the Reformation, 'under the power of Ignorance and Superstition', many men and women were affected with a deep sense of the guilt of sin. Now, the majority of people had become senseless of their sin and held the doctrine of justification with contempt. Others, out of ignorance of the knowledge of the righteousness of Christ and finding no respite from the troubles of their sin, were turning back to Rome.[144] Owen, himself speaking prophetically, cautioned that such mindsets could only lead to carelessness in sinning, and, eventually, would lead to atheism. Owen's treatise on justification was offered to the public in an attempt to prevent such a catastrophe. Indeed, for Owen, the stakes could not be higher. If the doctrine of justification were lost, so too was the totality of Christian doctrine.[145]

---

[142] Owen, *The doctrine of justification by faith* (1677), 430; *Works* (1965), 5:298.
[143] Owen, *The doctrine of justification by faith* (1677), 87; *Works* (1965), 5:67.
[144] Owen, *The doctrine of justification by faith* (1677), 90; *Works* (1965), 5:70.
[145] Owen, *The doctrine of justification by faith* (1677), 87; *Works* (1965), 5:67.

CHAPTER 19

Meditations and discourses on the glory of Christ (1684)

SUZANNE MCDONALD

John Owen died on 24 August 1683. *Meditations and discourses on the glory of Christ* (1684) is the last work that he personally prepared for publication.[1] He was already ailing as he was writing it, having already sent over seventy volumes to the press, and knew that it would be his final theological testament. On the morning of the day of his death, William Payne, who had oversight of the publication of *Meditations and discourses on the glory of Christ*, came to tell Owen that the first page had just gone through the press. Owen is said to have responded: 'I am glad to hear it; but O brother Payne! The long wished-for day is come at last, in which I shall see that glory in another manner than I have ever done, or was capable of doing, in this world.'[2]

---

[1] All references to *Meditations and discourses on the glory of Christ* are to the 1684 edition. A second part was published in 1691 (*Meditations and discourses concerning the glory of Christ*), consisting of two further chapters found among Owen's papers after his death, applying the themes to 'Unconverted sinners and saints under spiritual decays'. These additional chapters can be found in *Works* (1965), 1:417–61. Both parts were printed in a single volume in 1696.
[2] This account is given in Andrew Thompson's 'Life of Dr Owen', in *Works* (1965), 1:ciii, which cites it from an earlier account. See Middleton, *Evangelical biography*, 3:480. Goold gives slightly

For convenience, we will refer to this text by its abbreviated title, but the full title clearly summarizes its content and intent: *Meditations and discourses on the glory of Christ, in his person, office, and grace: with the differences between faith and sight. Applied unto the use of them that believe.* In this work, Owen largely presupposes, and occasionally refers his readers directly back to, the content of his Χριστολογια (1679). In that volume Owen engages the major issues in Christology, from the being of the eternal Son in the Trinity to his role in God's relationship with Israel, the nature of the hypostatic union and the incarnate life and ministry of Christ, his death, resurrection and ascension, his continuing work as reigning Lord, and the relationship between Christ and his people in glory. With this doctrinal foundation already in place from his earlier volume, Owen does not enter into detailed theological discussion or debate in *Meditations and discourses on the glory of Christ*, which is not primarily a doctrinal or polemical treatise. Instead, as Owen repeatedly states throughout, his main goals are to offer a multifaceted description of the glory of Christ in his person and work and to exhort his readers to meditate on it, with instructions on how to do this and why it is needful. The entire work could be seen as one long exhortation to take up what today might be called the 'spiritual practice' of Christ-focused scriptural contemplation, with only so much theological information as is required to keep a proper doctrinal framework for one's prayerful meditation.

Owen insists that the practice of meditating on the glory of Christ is essential for both this life and the next. As is the case throughout much of his corpus, but even more so in this work, he is deeply committed to urging his readers to apply theological truths – in this instance, properly theologically oriented contemplative practices – to the details of their daily lives. He is clear that the more we seek to gaze upon Christ by faith now, the more we will live in Christ-like love of God and neighbour, and the more we will be detached from the desire for worldly power and success. This is both a general goal for all Christians and one that almost certainly resonated with particularly poignancy for dissenters such as himself and his congregation in the hard decades following the Restoration.[3] *Meditations and discourses on the glory of Christ* also gives more sustained attention than we find elsewhere in Owen to orienting readers towards the eschatological consummation of our knowledge and experience of Christ in this life. Beholding the glory of Christ by faith now is practice for, and essential to the attaining of, the vision of the fullness of his glory in eternity,

---

different wording in his 'Prefatory Note' to *Meditations and discourses on the glory of Christ*; *Works* (1965), 1:274.

[3] For an account of the impact of the Nonconformist experience on Owen and his theology, see Gribben, *John Owen and English Puritanism*, chapters 7–9.

since, as Owen frequently remarks, we cannot expect to behold Christ in glory for eternity if we have not sought to meditate on the glory of his person and work by faith in the present life.

The theological concerns that undergird his exhortations to meditate on the glory of Christ reflect and repeat the nexus of key ideas found in his theology as a whole. We see Owen once again vigorously upholding Chalcedonian Christology and trinitarian orthodoxy against the threats of Socinianism and rationalism. The beating heart of this text, as of Χριστολογια, is a passionate insistence on the centrality of the two natures of Christ, and in particular his divinity, since the latter was under the most under threat. In key sections he also reminds his readers of the axiomatic trinitarian principle that the works of the triune God *ad extra* are the expression of the being and relations of the triune God *ad intra*. We also find his repeated insistence that Scripture is the sole authoritative source for knowledge of God and the Christian life, and that the person and work of Christ is the hermeneutical key to rightly interpreting the whole of Scripture. In this way he continues his resistance from earlier works to any tendencies to elevate reason over Scripture, as well as any claims to an authoritative 'inner light' from Quakers and other 'enthusiasts'. He also continues his attacks on aspects of Roman Catholic belief and practice, particularly, in this volume, any attempt to depict and behold the glory of Christ through works of art when it is to be seen only in the mirror of Scripture. In addition, he reiterates his objections to interpretations of sanctification and the Christian life that reduce these to mere morality, rather than rooting them in union with Christ and the transforming work of the Holy Spirit. Finally, he offers one last account of the contours of a Reformed understanding of election. While there is no anti-Arminian polemic here, vigorously maintaining key facets of the approach to election encapsulated in the Canons of Dort is a priority for Owen since his first published volume in 1643.

Perhaps because of the haste with which Owen was seeking to finish this text, and his significantly declining health and strength for the task, *Meditations and discourses on the glory of Christ* is highly repetitive, and not always clearly structured within and between chapters. For the following summary, I have chosen to group the chapters according to a structure that is not explicitly Owen's, but which is suggested by his chapter titles, in order to highlight key themes and to make the progression of his thought somewhat clearer.

- **The preface to the reader and chapter 1** outline the major themes of the whole work;
- **Chapters 2–3** focus on the glory of the person of Christ;
- **Chapters 4–7** describe the glory of Christ in the exercise of his office as mediator, and his exaltation on successfully accomplishing this;

- Chapters 8–11 explain the relationship of God's people with Christ in the old and new covenants, and the recapitulation of all things in Christ; and
- Chapters 12–14 identify some differences between beholding the glory of Christ by faith and by sight.

PREFACE TO THE READER AND CHAPTER 1

The preface begins with Owen declaring that the glory of Christ as revealed in Scripture should be 'the principal Object of our Faith, Love, Delight, and Admiration', even though its fullness is beyond what we can currently conceive and express.[4] Almost immediately he turns to a theme that will loom large throughout the work, castigating those who reject Scripture as the revelation of God and prefer other sources and kinds of knowledge. For Owen, the revelation of Christ in the Gospel is greater than all the knowledge attainable from the rest of creation. He insists that, without true knowledge of Christ, regardless of how people pride themselves on other 'Inventions and Discoveries', our minds are lost in darkness and confusion.[5]

Owen speaks of *Meditations and discourses on the glory of Christ* as being intended first for 'the exercise of my own mind' and then for the edification of his congregation, but urges that all people are 'under the highest Obligation to betake themselves unto this *Contemplation of Christ and his Glory*'.[6] Christ alone shows us that our nature, even though it has been so utterly debased by sin, is able to be exalted to heaven; and that the image of God in which we were created, but which has been so hideously defaced, can be renewed and restored. Because of the hypostatic union, the true glory of our human nature is safe with Christ and indissolubly united to God in him. In turn, as we are united to Christ so our relationship with God is eternally secure. In our personal union with Christ, we share in the glory of the union and communion of his human nature with the triune God, and we have the pledge that our glorified humanity will be made fit for eternal life in the fullness of the presence of God.[7]

Meditating on the glory of Christ is not simply important for the eschatological future, however; it is also vital for living well now, and for dying well. Taking the time to behold the glory of Christ by faith now 'will alleviate all our Afflictions, make their burden light, and preserve our Souls from fainting

---

[4] Owen, *Meditations and discourses on the glory of Christ* (1684), 'Preface to the Reader', fol. A3r; *Works* (1965), 1:275.
[5] Owen, *Meditations and discourses on the glory of Christ* (1684), fol. A3v; *Works* (1965), 1:275.
[6] Owen, *Meditations and discourses on the glory of Christ* (1684), fol. A4r; *Works* (1965), 1:276.
[7] Owen, *Meditations and discourses on the glory of Christ* (1684), fol. A4v–A6v; *Works* (1965), 1:276–7.

under them. . . . He that can at all times retreat unto the contemplation of this Glory, will be carried above the perplexing prevailing sense of any of these evils, of a confluence of them all'.[8] Moreover, in extended reflections on death and dying for Christians, and acknowledging his own weakness and weariness as death approaches, Owen assures his readers that assiduously contemplating the glory of Christ is what will 'carry us cheerfully and comfortably into [death], and through it'.[9]

In the first chapter Owen introduces the foundational Scripture text for the whole treatise: 'Father, I will that they also whom thou hast given me, be with me where I am: that they may behold my Glory which though hast given me' (Jn 17.24).[10] From that verse, Owen declares that his sole focus is the petition 'that they may behold my glory', remarking that Jesus' intent in this phrase is that they behold his glory not for his own sake, but for their benefit.[11] Owen sees this glory of Christ as the believer's true north, such that their compass needle cannot rest until it is directed towards beholding it. He proclaims that 'the Foundation of the ensuing Meditations [is] in this one assertion, namely, *That one of the greatest Priviledges and Advancements of Believers, both in this World, and unto Eternity, consists in their* BEHOLDING THE GLORY OF CHRIST'.[12]

Over the course of the chapter, Owen introduces many of the themes that will dominate the rest of the treatise. Above all, Owen emphasizes that a true beholding of Christ's glory requires a full acknowledgement of his two natures, and in particular his divinity, since this is under significant attack by those who oppose it 'under a pretence of *Sobriety of Reason*'.[13] Owen's aim here, however, is less to engage in theological disputes than to strengthen true believers, and encourage them to meditate on the glory of Christ in his person and work by giving an account of 'the Experience which they . . . may have of the Power and Reality of these things' even now.[14] Owen stresses the present transforming power of beholding the glory of Christ to move us away from worldly obsessions and anxieties towards living more fully for Christ, and experiencing peace in Christ. His primary desire, therefore, is not to enable his readers to win theological arguments, but to lead them 'into the more retired walks of Faith, Love, and Holy Meditation'.[15]

---

[8] Owen, *Meditations and discourses on the glory of Christ* (1684), fol. A7r; *Works* (1965), 1:278.
[9] Owen, *Meditations and discourses on the glory of Christ* (1684), fol. A10v; *Works* (1965), 1:279.
[10] Owen, *Meditations and discourses on the glory of Christ* (1684), 1; *Works* (1965), 1:285.
[11] Owen, *Meditations and discourses on the glory of Christ* (1684), 2; *Works* (1965), 1:285–6.
[12] Owen, *Meditations and discourses on the glory of Christ* (1684), 3; *Works* (1965), 1:286.
[13] Owen, *Meditations and discourses on the glory of Christ* (1684), 5; *Works* (1965), 1:287.
[14] Owen, *Meditations and discourses on the glory of Christ* (1684), 5; *Works* (1965), 1:287.
[15] Owen, *Meditations and discourses on the glory of Christ* (1684), 12; *Works* (1965), 1:291.

More than this, contemplating the glory of Christ is also the 'Spring and Cause of our Everlasting Blessedness' – that is to say, it is a salvation matter.[16] Meditation on Christ's glory will make us fit for heaven, and, as Owen points out, this is not the case for everyone, even though most blithely assume it. People are no more fit to be with Christ for eternity without beholding the glory of Christ now than a fish is able to survive out of water in the heat of the sun.[17] While our salvation is from the will and grace of God from beginning to end, God has nevertheless 'ordained ways and means whereby [we] may be made *meet receptive subjects* of the Glory so to be communicated unto [us]', and one of these is the beholding of the glory of Christ by faith. 'This, therefore, should excite us unto this Duty; For all our *present* Glory consists in our Preparation for *future* Glory.'[18]

As this indicates, there is a direct link between beholding the glory of Christ by faith now and by sight in eternity. With some asperity, he remarks that 'most . . . will say with confidence . . . *that they desire to be with Christ, and to behold his Glory*; But they can give no Reason, why they should desire any such thing' – except, of course, that it is vastly better than the alternative of eternal hell.[19] It is axiomatic for Owen, however, that no one 'shall ever behold the Glory of Christ by *Sight* hereafter, who doth not in some measure behold it by *Faith* here in this World. *Grace* is a necessary preparation for *Glory*, and *Faith* for *Sight*'.[20]

Equally deceived are those who equate beholding the glory of Christ with images and paintings. Owen frequently critiques what he considers to be a Roman Catholic identification of beholding the glory of Christ with artistic images of Christ. Instead, we should hold exclusively to the glory of Christ as it has been revealed to us in Scripture, to be received by faith.[21] To seek to behold it by other means will take us away from true contemplation of Christ's actual glory, and therefore jeopardize our salvation.

The culmination of our salvation is the beatific vision in heaven. Owen points out that while we cannot fully know what this will be like, even then

---

[16]Owen, *Meditations and discourses on the glory of Christ* (1684), 14; *Works* (1965), 1:292.
[17]Owen, *Meditations and discourses on the glory of Christ* (1684), 12–13; *Works* (1965), 1:291–2.
[18]Owen, *Meditations and discourses on the glory of Christ* (1684), 13; *Works* (1965), 1:292.
[19]Owen, *Meditations and discourses on the glory of Christ* (1684), 7; *Works* (1965), 1:288.
[20]Owen, *Meditations and discourses on the glory of Christ* (1684), 7; *Works*, (1965), 1:288.
[21]Owen, *Meditations and discourses on the glory of Christ* (1684), 7–9; *Works* (1965), 1:289. The frequent and highly repetitive attacks on Roman Catholic art in *Meditations and discourses on the glory of Christ* are an expression of Owen's lifelong hostility towards Roman Catholic beliefs and practices, now intensified by his fears of the undoing of the Protestant Reformation in England, with the prospect that Charles II's openly Roman Catholic brother, James, would succeed to the throne. Only a few years before, Owen had published the highly polemical *The Church of Rome, no safe guide* (1679). For the possibility that Owen was involved in the Rye House plot, see Gribben, *John Owen and English Puritanism*, 260–1, and the chapter by Gribben in this volume.

it will be Christ-centred: 'God in his *Immense Essence* is *invisible* unto our Corporeal Eyes, and will be so to Eternity; as also *incomprehensible* unto our Minds. For nothing can perfectly comprehend that which is Infinite, but what is itself Infinite. Wherefore the Blessed and *Blessing Sight* which we shall have of God, will be always *in the face of Jesus Christ*.'[22] While we cannot yet truly speak of such things, for those who devote themselves to meditating upon the glory of God in the face of Jesus Christ by faith now, there can be a 'fore-sight and fore-taste of this Glorious Condition. There enters sometimes by the Word and Spirit into their Hearts such a sense of the *uncreated Glory* of God, shining forth in Christ, as Affects and Satiates their Souls with ineffable Joy'.[23]

CHAPTERS 2–3

After his overview of the themes of the whole treatise in chapter 1, these next two chapters turn to the foundational theme of the glory of Christ in the hypostatic union. Chapter 2 ('The Glory of the Person of Christ, as the onely Representative of God unto the Church') opens with the blunt assertion that 'The *glory of Christ* is the Glory of the Person of Christ'.[24] This is so both essentially (the eternal glory of the Son in the Trinity) and in the exercise of his office in the incarnation. Referring frequently to a seminal text for the whole treatise, it is as we contemplate the hypostatic union that we behold the light of the knowledge of the glory of God in the face of Jesus Christ (2 Cor. 4.6). Jesus Christ is the self-revelation of God to us: he represents God to us 'in person', so to speak. While we might be able to discern some truths about God more obscurely in other ways, he is radiantly manifest in Christ, who is the image of

---

[22]Owen, *Meditations and discourses on the glory of Christ* (1684), 14–15; *Works* (1965), 1:292. For Owen's highly Christological account of the beatific vision, see McDonald, 'Beholding the glory of God in the face of Jesus Christ', 145–54, and Boersma, *Seeing God*, 321–7. In my essay I contrast Owen's approach to the beatific vision, in which the redeemed will not see or apprehend the triune God except as mediated by the glorified Christ in his two natures (and Owen's corresponding insistence on the place of our glorified physical eyesight in the beatific vision – see further below), with that of Aquinas. For a defence of Aquinas's account of the beatific vision as more Christ-centred than I give him credit for, see Gaine, 'Thomas Aquinas and John Owen on the beatific vision', 432–46. As Gaine concedes, Aquinas has no role for the glorified humanity of Christ in the beatific vision, and to my mind, Gaine's wider Christological defence of Aquinas does not materially alter the claim that Owen's understanding of the beatific vision – as the beholding of Christ himself, rather than the immediate intellectual apprehension of the essence of God – is far more radically Christological than that of Aquinas and the tradition that follows him. See also Boersma, *Seeing God*, 159–60 for an engagement with Gaine's article, in which he asserts the 'christological deficit' of Aquinas on the beatific vision in the context of a comparison between Aquinas and Gregory Palamas, and 327, fn. 24, where he returns to Gaine's article in his discussion of Owen.
[23]Owen, *Meditations and discourses on the glory of Christ* (1684), 15; *Works* (1965), 1:293.
[24]Owen, *Meditations and discourses on the glory of Christ* (1684), 16; *Works* (1965), 1:293.

the invisible God, and who reveals to us the nature and character of God, in particular God's wisdom and love.

Beholding and meditating upon the glory of Christ in his divine–human person is therefore the source of all true knowledge of God. Owen is particularly keen to stress that neither the rational capacities of the human mind nor any claim to personal revelations or 'inner light' can ever be adequate for true knowledge of God. Referencing Romans 1, Owen insists that because of sin, these will lead only to idolatry. Our only sure access to true knowledge of God is God's self-revelation in Jesus Christ through the proper interpretation of the Scripture, which is the mirror in which we behold the face of Christ. As he trenchantly puts it, 'men may talk what they please of a *Light within them*, or of the Power of Reason, to conduct them unto that Knowledg of God, whereby they may live unto him', but without the light of divine revelation in Scripture, and in particular, the light of the revelation of the glory of God in the face of Jesus Christ, they remain in utter darkness.[25] As this suggests, beholding of the glory of Christ in his divine as well as human nature is the touchstone for true faith and therefore for salvation. Whoever denies the divinity of Christ is an unbeliever.[26]

In Chapter 3 ('The Glory of Christ in the Mysterious Constitution of his Person'), Owen refers his readers to his Χριστολογια for a detailed account and defence of Christ's two natures. Here, his primary aim is to show believers how deeply this truth matters. As he points out, this profound mystery to which we now have access (and into which even the angels long to look) is the 'only Spring of present Grace, and future Glory', the overthrow of Satan and his kingdom, and the foundation of the church.[27] With this in mind, much of the chapter is an exhortation to his readers to spend more time in daily, focused meditation on Christ in his two natures, and the significance of this for the Christian life now and into eternity.

The way to do this, says Owen, is through engagement with Scripture, with the intention of discerning the revelation of the glory of Christ's person throughout. Picking up from his account in the previous chapter of how the divine–human person of Christ is the source of all true knowledge of God, and of how this is to be found in Scripture above all other sources, Owen here insists that a proper understanding of Christ's two natures is the hermeneutical key to a true understanding of the whole of Scripture. There are 'such *Revelations* of the Person and Glory of Christ treasured up in the Scripture, from the beginning unto the end of it, as may exercise the Faith and Contemplation of believers in

---

[25] Owen, *Meditations and discourses on the glory of Christ* (1684), 22; *Works* (1965), 1:296–7.
[26] Owen, *Meditations and discourses on the glory of Christ* (1684), 19–20; *Works* (1965), 1:295.
[27] Owen, *Meditations and discourses on the glory of Christ* (1684), 47–8; *Works* (1965), 1:310–11.

this world; and shall never during this life be fully discovered or understood; and in Divine Meditations of these Revelations, doth much of the *life of Faith* consist'.[28] This ability to discern the glory of the person of Christ throughout Scripture is the pearl of great price, which makes Scripture become a spring of living water, and this should inspire us to be diligent in reading and meditating upon it every day.

Not surprisingly, there are many shared themes across these two chapters. In particular, Owen laments that 'unbelief of [Christ's] Divine Person ... maketh havock of Christianity at this day in the world'.[29] As well as many who outright deny the incarnation, others are simply indifferent to it, finding the notion of Christ's divinity either unnecessary, irrational or both. And yet, as Owen passionately and frequently asserts, without true knowledge of God in Christ there is no salvation. Belief in the incarnation is the 'Foundation of our Religion, the *Rock whereon the Church is built*, the Ground of all our Hopes of Salvation, of Life and Immortality'.[30] Even so, while it is obviously better to believe in the divinity of Christ than to deny it, Owen insists that mere intellectual assent to the doctrine of Christ's two natures is insufficient without personal experience of its transforming power: 'But herein it is required, that we rest not in the *Notion of this* Truth, and a bare assent unto the Doctrine of it. The affecting Power of it upon our Hearts, is that which we should aim at.'[31]

Beholding the glory of God in the face of Jesus Christ is also the God-ordained means of our sanctification. Across both chapters Owen holds together two central verses for the whole treatise: 2 Cor. 3.18 and 2 Cor. 4.6. In the first, it is by beholding the glory of the Lord that we are transformed by the Spirit 'from glory to glory', and in the second, as we have already seen, we behold the glory of God in the face of Jesus Christ. Holding together these verses, and with Rom. 8.29 in the background, Owen reminds his readers that beholding the glory of God in the face of Jesus Christ is the means 'whereby the Image of God is renewed in us, and we are made like unto the first-born'.[32]

It is therefore not possible to follow Christ simply by striving to imitate his example and attempting to live a moral life.[33] Instead, we need the transforming work of the Spirit within us to conform us to Christ. For this to take place, we must spend dedicated daily time meditating on the glory of Christ in the fullness of his divine–human personhood, and also seek to reflect on it in passing at

---

[28]Owen, *Meditations and discourses on the glory of Christ* (1684), 55; *Works* (1965), 1:315.
[29]Owen, *Meditations and discourses on the glory of Christ* (1684), 33; *Works* (1965), 1:302.
[30]Owen, *Meditations and discourses on the glory of Christ* (1684), 18; *Works* (1965), 1:294.
[31]Owen, *Meditations and discourses on the glory of Christ* (1684), 42, see also 58, 66–7; *Works* (1965), 1:307, see also 317, 321–2.
[32]Owen, *Meditations and discourses on the glory of Christ* (1684), 38; *Works* (1965), 1:305.
[33]Owen, *Meditations and discourses on the glory of Christ* (1684), 35; *Works* (1965), 1:304.

other times in the day.[34] This is not an optional extra for the hyper-pious, but a requirement for anyone who would live for Christ now and expect to live with him eternally. Regularly beholding the glory of God in the face of Jesus Christ through meditation upon his divine–human personhood is

> so far from being unnecessary unto . . . *the sanctified duties of Morality*, that he knows not Christ . . . who imagines that they can be performed acceptably without it. Yea, this is the root whence all other *Christian duties* do spring . . . whereby they are distinguished from the works of Heathens. He is no Christian who believes not that faith in the Person of Christ is the spring of all Evangelical obedience.[35]

Owen acknowledges that most Christians are 'strangers unto this duty', which also explains why there is so little evidence of transformed lives among professing Christians.[36] If Christians were to spend more time meditating on the glory of Christ in his full personhood, 'our life in walking before God would be more sweet and pleasant unto us . . . [and] we should more represent the Glory of Christ in our ways and walking than usually we do'.[37] For many, however, spending time meditating on the fullness of Christ's personhood seems like a waste of time:

> Some will say they understand not these things, nor any concernment of their own in them. If they are true, yet are they *notions* which they may safely be without knowledg of; for so far as they can discern, they have no influence on Christian practice, or Duties of Morality. And the preaching of them doth but take off the minds of men from more necessary duties.[38]

But if there is no acceptance of Christ's divinity, all other Gospel truths are 'useless unto our souls'.[39] As Owen points out, we recognize the need to learn and practise skills for 'a secular Art or Trade', but reject the idea of meditating on the glory of Christ, which is the means God has ordained for us to live rightly before him.[40] Moreover, we can find an inordinate amount of time for meditating on how to be successful in this life and to accomplish our desires. As

---

[34] E.g., Owen, *Meditations and discourses on the glory of Christ* (1684), 36–7; 58–60; *Works* (1965), 1:304–5; 316–19.
[35] Owen, *Meditations and discourses on the glory of Christ* (1684), 38; *Works* (1965), 1:305.
[36] Owen, *Meditations and discourses on the glory of Christ* (1684), 35; *Works* (1965), 1:303–4.
[37] Owen, *Meditations and discourses on the glory of Christ* (1684), 36; *Works* (1965), 1:304.
[38] Owen, *Meditations and discourses on the glory of Christ* (1684), 37; *Works* (1965), 1:305.
[39] Owen, *Meditations and discourses on the glory of Christ* (1684), 37; *Works* (1965), 1:305.
[40] Owen, *Meditations and discourses on the glory of Christ* (1684), 40; *Works* (1965), 1:306.

Owen frequently points out, we are transformed into the image of what most occupies our minds.[41] If that is worldly matters rather than eternal glory, then it will be to our eternal loss.

CHAPTERS 4–7

In these chapters, Owen shifts from reflecting on Christ's person to focus on various facets of his work as mediator. As he remarks at the start of chapter 4 ('The Glory of Christ in his Susception of the Office of a Mediator. First in his Condescention'), it can be hard for those not used to contemplative practices to focus on something as seemingly abstract as the person of Christ. Dwelling on his role as mediator is likely to be more accessible to many, and in this 'doth the exercise of Faith in this life principally consist'.[42]

After a brief reminder of the importance of Christ's two natures for the exercise of his office – no mere creature could mediate between sinful humanity and God, and neither could this be done 'by God himself, absolutely considered'[43] – Owen turns to the principal theme of this chapter: the glory and wonder of Christ's condescension, with Phil. 2.1-10 constantly in the background. The paradox at the heart of the Gospel is that the eternal Son's free and gracious decision to enter into his state of humiliation in the incarnation is one of the greatest manifestations of the glory of Christ. There is infinite condescension in God deigning to take any notice of creaturely things, says Owen, let alone the Son freely choosing to enter into the midst of the situation of sinful humanity as one of us – and indeed as one of the lowliest among us – in order to redeem. As Owen puts it,

> if such be his self-sufficiency unto his own Eternal Blessedness, as that nothing can be taken from him, nothing added unto him, so that every regard in him unto any of the Creatures, is an act of *Self-Humiliation* and *Condescention* from the prerogative of his being and state; what heart can conceive, what tongue can express the Glory of that *Condescention* in the Son of God, whereby he took our Nature upon him, took it to be his own, in order unto a discharge of the Office of Mediation on our behalf?[44]

Owen is careful to remind us, however, that the Son's taking on our human nature 'did not consist in a *laying aside, or parting with* or *separation from* the

---

[41]For example, Owen, *Meditations and discourses on the glory of Christ* (1684), 40–1; *Works* (1965), 1:307.
[42]Owen, *Meditations and discourses on the glory of Christ* (1684), 69; *Works* (1965), 1:322.
[43]Owen, *Meditations and discourses on the glory of Christ* (1684), 70; *Works* (1965), 1:323.
[44]Owen, *Meditations and discourses on the glory of Christ* (1684), 74–5; *Works* (1965), 1:325.

Divine Nature, so as that he should cease to be God, by being man'.[45] This is both in his incarnate state, in which he 'became what he was not, but he ceased not to be what he was', and also in Owen's upholding of the *extra Calvinisticum*: that during the incarnation, the eternal Son nevertheless continues to exist in the fullness of his divine nature with the Father and the Spirit in heaven.[46]

Owen also briefly walks his readers through the inadequate alternative Christologies that are dismissed by the Chalcedonian formula to ensure that his readers do not diminish the full integrity of either nature in the one person of Christ. Above all, however, Owen is once again keen to continue to combat any denial of Christ's divine nature. Those who reject Christ's divinity have lost any sense of his condescension, and so have lost sight of this facet of his glory and its saving efficacy. He laments that many supposed Christians

> are willing to grant him to be a Prophet sent of God, who do not, who will not, who cannot, believe the Mystery of this *Condescention* in the susception of our Nature, nor see the Glory of it. But take this away, and all our Religion is taken away with it. Farewell Christianity as to the Mystery, the Glory, the Truth, the Efficacy of it; let refined *Heathenism* be established in its Room.[47]

Even so, as is the case throughout, Owen is less concerned with theological disquisition than with giving a basis for the practice of meditation and contemplation, to the end that his readers will live more fully for Christ now and be assured of beholding him in glory to all eternity. In particular, pondering the glory of Christ in his condescension readies us for self-denial and the cross in our own lives, since this is grounded in the glorious self-giving of the Son. For, he asks, perhaps with the experiences of his fellow dissenters in mind, what are 'our Goods, our Liberties, our Relations, our Lives' when required of us for the sake of the Gospel, in comparison to the self-surrender of Christ?[48]

Beholding Christ's glory in this way is also a deep comfort because it means we can know Christ as a refuge in distress. 'Are we . . . burdened with a sense of sin? Are we perplexed with Temptations? Are we bowed down under the Oppression of any Spiritual Adversary? . . . One View of the Glory of Christ herein is able to support us and relieve us.'[49] Since the eternal Son has undertaken such condescension for us we can know both his will and his power to help and to save, as the fully divine and fully human person he is. Even so,

---

[45] Owen, *Meditations and discourses on the glory of Christ* (1684), 75; *Works* (1965), 1:325.
[46] Owen, *Meditations and discourses on the glory of Christ* (1684), 75–6; *Works* (1965), 1:325–6.
[47] Owen, *Meditations and discourses on the glory of Christ* (1684), 80–1; *Works* (1965), 1:328.
[48] Owen, *Meditations and discourses on the glory of Christ* (1684), 88; see 87–8; *Works* (1965), 1:332; see 332–3.
[49] Owen, *Meditations and discourses on the glory of Christ* (1684), 85; *Works* (1965), 1:331.

this condescension of the eternal Son is beyond what we are able to conceive and express. We must simply rest in 'an Holy Admiration of what we cannot comprehend'.[50] Owen remarks:

> I know in the Contemplation of it, it will quickly overwhelm our *Reason*, and bring our Understanding into a loss: But unto this *loss* do I desire to be brought every day; For when Faith . . . finds the Object it is fixed on too great and glorious to be brought into our Minds and Capacities, it will issue . . . in holy *Admiration*, humble *Adoration*, and joyful *Thanksgiving*. In and by its actings in them, doth it fill the soul with *Joy unspeakable and full of Glory*.[51]

Although it might surprise many readers, chapter 5 ('The Glory of Christ in his Love') is devoted to the eternal electing decree of God, and its outworking in the mediating work of the Son. As the triune God is love in himself, so God's first outwardly oriented act (the decree of election) is one of love. This is the 'Eternal Election of a Portion of mankind to be brought unto the enjoyment of himself, through the Mystery of the blood of Christ, and the Sanctification of the Spirit'.[52] From his first published work, Θεομαχία αυτεξουσιαστικη: or, A display of Arminianisme (1643), to this final volume that he saw to the press, Owen remained a staunch and frequent defender of the Reformed position on election articulated in the Canons of Dort, here combined with his later understanding of the inner-trinitarian covenant of redemption. In keeping with his overall aims, he does not give a detailed defence of the doctrine but focuses on how it relates to the mission of the Son, and how from its inception to its outcome, it is a glorious manifestation of the free love of the triune God, as the saving will and choice of the Father is enacted in the Son and applied to those whom the Father has chosen for salvation by the Holy Spirit.

Election is rooted in the love of the Father, whose choice to save some from the consequences of their sin is free and undeserved. It is also the enacting of the infinite love and goodness of the Son that he chooses to effect the will of the Father by condescending to come among us to suffer and die for the redemption of those whom the Father has chosen. Indeed, for Owen, the Son demonstrates his love by becoming what he was not in the incarnation, and he exercises that love in ways that are only possible for a human being, even as these acts of love are also the expression of the love that is integral to his divine nature. Owen explains,

---

[50] Owen, *Meditations and discourses on the glory of Christ* (1684), 84; *Works* (1965), 1:330.
[51] Owen, *Meditations and discourses on the glory of Christ* (1684), 88–9; *Works* (1965), 1:333.
[52] Owen, *Meditations and discourses on the glory of Christ* (1684), 90; *Works* (1965), 1:334.

> WHEREFORE this Love of Christ which we inquire after, is the *Love of his Person*; that is, which he in his own Person acts in and by his Distinct Natures according unto their distinct Essential Properties. And the acts of love in these distinct Natures are infinitely distinct and different; yet are they all acts of *one* and the *same Person*. So then, whether that Act of Love in Christ which we would at any time consider, be an Eternal Act of the *Divine* Nature in the Person of the Son of God; or whether it be an act of the *Humane* performed in time by the Gracious Faculties and Powers of that Nature, it is still the *Love of one and the self same Person, Christ Jesus*.[53]

While the depths of this love are incomprehensible to us now, it will be a large part of our blessedness in heaven to understand this more fully, and gratefully contemplate the fruits of it. In the meanwhile, Owen's intent, as always, is to urge us to cultivate habits of mind that will enable us to contemplate this facet of the glory of Christ now, even though we can grasp so little of the depths of it. He returns to how eager we are to ponder everyday matters, but not Christ and his love, but he also urges us once again not to be content with a vague intellectual assent, but to seek after a true taste of the glorious love of Christ:

> All who believe his Divine Person, profess a valuation of his Love. . . . But they have only *General Notions*, and not any distinct Conceptions of it. . . . Be not content to have *right Notions* of the love of Christ in your minds, unless you can attain a Gracious *Tast* of it in your Hearts; no more than you would be to see a Feast or Banquet richly prepared, and partake of nothing of it unto your refreshment.[54]

Chapter 6 ('The Glory of Christ in the Discharge of his Mediatory Office') reflects on the paradox that Christ's glory shines most brightly where it is seemingly most obscured: in his humble obedience and humiliating sacrificial death. 'An unseen Glory accompanied him in all that he did, in all that he suffered. *Unseen* it was unto the eyes of the World, but not in his who alone can judg of it. Had men seen it, they would not have *Crucified the Lord of Glory*.'[55] The glory of Christ's obedience throughout his life is that it is a free, willing obedience even unto a death that was not for himself but for us, springing from his love for the Father and for those whom the Father has given him to save. It is also the obedience of perfect, sinless holiness, as well as of perfect love. This is why his obedience makes many righteous (Rom. 5:19): 'Herein . . . did

---

[53] Owen, *Meditations and discourses on the glory of Christ* (1684), 93–5; *Works* (1965), 1:335–6.
[54] Owen, *Meditations and discourses on the glory of Christ* (1684), 97–8; *Works* (1965), 1:337–8.
[55] Owen, *Meditations and discourses on the glory of Christ* (1684), 100; *Works* (1965), 1:338.

God give him Honour and Glory, that his Obedience should stand in the stead of the perfect Obedience of the Church as unto Justification.'[56] Even though our hearts and minds recoil from it, we are therefore called to contemplate the glory of Christ even in his suffering for our sake, as he takes on the full, horrific consequences of our sins: 'Let us, then, behold him as poor, despised, persecuted, reproached, reviled, *hanged on a Tree;* in all laboring under a sense of the *Wrath of God* due unto our sins . . . what *Glory* is in these things?'[57] With 1 Cor. 1.18-25 in mind, Owen points out that while others stumble at this, the cross is precious and glorious in the sight of believers, showing forth not only the power and wisdom of God but also the glory of Christ.

Chapter 7 ('The Glory of Christ in his Exaltation, after the Accomplishment of the work of Mediation in this world') turns to the culmination of Christ's role as mediator in the ascension, 'whereby the whole Glory of his Person in itself, and in the work of Mediation is most illustriously manifested'.[58] Owen is at pains to point out that this is still not the same as seeing the essential glory of the Son – the glory of his divine nature per se. Owen suggests that even in eternity we will be incapable of seeing the fullness of Christ's divine nature except as it is mediated through his ascended and glorified humanity. His divine glory was veiled by his humanity while he was in the world – Owen uses the analogy of a solar eclipse to illustrate how it was a reality during his life and ministry, but hidden from our perception – but we will behold it shining forth through his glorified humanity in his exaltation.[59]

As this suggests, that Christ has ascended in his humanity matters greatly to Owen, not only because through it we will behold his divine–human glory to eternity but also because it is the '*Exemplar*' of that Glory which he will bring all those unto who believe in him'.[60] To deny that Christ has ascended in his human nature is a '*Socinian* Fiction'.[61] While no one can as yet fully comprehend what the glorification of Jesus' or our human nature will be like, 'that he is still in the same *Humane Nature,* wherein he was on the earth, that he hath the same Rational Soul and the same Body is a Fundamental Article of the Christian Faith'.[62]

Taking a Reformed understanding of the ascended humanity of Christ, Owen insists that Christ's exalted humanity retains its creaturely integrity. There is

---

[56]Owen, *Meditations and discourses on the glory of Christ* (1684), 102; see 100–3; *Works* (1965), 1:339; see 338–40.
[57]Owen, *Meditations and discourses on the glory of Christ* (1684), 106; see 106–7; *Works* (1965), 1:342.
[58]Owen, *Meditations and discourses on the glory of Christ* (1684), 110; *Works* (1965), 1:343.
[59]Owen, *Meditations and discourses on the glory of Christ* (1684), 110–11; *Works* (1965), 1:343–4.
[60]Owen, *Meditations and discourses on the glory of Christ* (1684), 111; *Works* (1965), 1:344.
[61]Owen, *Meditations and discourses on the glory of Christ* (1684), 112; *Works* (1965), 1:344.
[62]Owen, *Meditations and discourses on the glory of Christ* (1684), 112; *Works* (1965), 1:344–5.

no mingling of the natures, or communication of properties, in the ascended humanity of Christ. So, while Christ's glorified human nature is *'filled with all the Divine Graces and Perfections* whereof a limited, created Nature is capable. It is not *Deified*, it is not made a God; It doth not in Heaven coalesce into one Nature with the Divine by a composition of them; It hath not any Essential Property of the Deity communicated unto it . . . it is still a Creature'.[63] As such, Christ's glorified humanity is the pattern for our own. By implication, we will experience the highest possible glorification of our bodies and our faculties, and the deepest possible union and communion with God in Christ, but we will remain creatures and will not become God or be dissolved into God.

As we have come to expect, Owen urges that we seek to behold something of this glory now by faith. The way to do this is not by works of art purporting to depict Christ in glory, such as are encouraged in Roman Catholic piety, but by regular meditation on the glimpses of Christ's ascended glory that we find in Scripture. He also returns to a theme first strongly articulated in chapter 1: we cannot expect to enjoy eternally what we have never sought or found any enjoyment in now. So, he complains that many 'care neither *where* Christ is, nor *what* he is, so that one way or other they may be saved by him. They hope, as they pretend, that they shall see him and his glory in Heaven'. Nevertheless, for anyone who has not sought to behold something of the glory of Christ by faith now, any expectation of beholding him with the redeemed in heaven 'is mere *Fancy* and Imagination'.[64]

CHAPTERS 8–11

With Chapter 8 ('Representations of the Glory of Christ under the Old Testament'), Owen transitions to several chapters that focus on the glory of Christ as he makes himself known to, and is in relationship with, his people. With regard to the Old Testament, Owen both sums up and expands his remarks about a Christological hermeneutic for the whole of Scripture from earlier in the treatise. Christ and his glory are the 'line of Life and Light, which runs through the whole Old Testament'.[65] Picking up on 2 Cor. 3.14-16, Owen asserts that we are blind to its meaning if we neglect to discern Christ there, and that it is only when faith discovers the glory of Christ in the Old Testament that the veil of darkness when reading it is removed.

He then enumerates various ways in which the retrospective light of the Gospel reveals glimpses of Christ's person and office. These include worship

---

[63] Owen, *Meditations and discourses on the glory of Christ* (1684), 112–13; *Works* (1965), 1:345.
[64] Owen, *Meditations and discourses on the glory of Christ* (1684), 115–16; *Works* (1965), 1:346–7.
[65] Owen, *Meditations and discourses on the glory of Christ* (1684), 119; *Works* (1965), 1:348.

and the details of the tabernacle and temple; the Song of Songs, which he summarizes as giving a *'Mystical Account* . . . [and] Gracious Record . . . of the Divine Communications of Christ in Love and Grace unto his Church, with their returns of love unto him, and delight in him';[66] personal appearances of Christ in theophanies (which he is careful to say are only preludes to the incarnation, and not yet taking human nature); all anthropomorphic expressions about God (such as his anger, grief and repentance), which Owen sees as anticipations of the incarnation; the giving of the law with the blessings and curses, pointing to Christ's fulfilment of it; and the many hints about his person and work in the prophets.[67] While all of these might have been obscure at the time, they are clear now that we read the Old Testament in the light of the Gospel and with the Christological hermeneutic that the New Testament exemplifies and requires of us. 'Nor can we read, study, or meditate on the writings of the Old Testament unto any Advantage, unless we design to find out and behold the Glory of Christ declared and represented in them. For want hereof they are a *sealed book* to many unto this day.'[68]

As the title indicates, chapter 9 concerns 'The Glory of Christ in his intimate Conjunction with the Church'. The particular focus here is the glory of Christ in the wondrous exchange. Everything Christ did in the discharge of his mediatorial office is 'esteemed, reckoned, and imputed unto us, as unto all the fruits and benefits of it, as if we had done and suffered the same things ourselves . . . wherein he is ineffably glorious'.[69] Recognizing that many in his time consider the transfer of the punishment of our sins to Christ to be unreasonable and unjust, Owen is at pains to describe how it is a fitting expression of God's love and righteousness. He begins with election: the whole church having fallen in Adam, and being unable to rescue itself, God in his eternal electing decree to save the church intends the punishment due to their sins to be transferred from those who deserved it to the one who did not, but who could bear it. 'A supposition of this *Translation of punishment* by Divine dispensation, is the foundation of Christian Religion, yea of all supernatural Revelation contained in the Scripture.'[70] This is prefigured in the sacrificial system of the Old Covenant, and also in the transfer of the punishment of sins from fathers to children. Owen points out that this transfer of punishment is not random but requires a particular 'conjunction' (relationship or union) between those who sin and those who are punished for their sin.

---

[66]Owen, *Meditations and discourses on the glory of Christ* (1684), 121; *Works* (1965), 1:349.
[67]Owen, *Meditations and discourses on the glory of Christ* (1684), 119–26; *Works* (1965), 1:348–51.
[68]Owen, *Meditations and discourses on the glory of Christ* (1684), 126; *Works* (1965), 1:351.
[69]Owen, *Meditations and discourses on the glory of Christ* (1684), 128; *Works* (1965), 1:353.
[70]Owen, *Meditations and discourses on the glory of Christ* (1684), 130; *Works* (1965), 1:353.

Christ is the supreme example of this, Owen claims, to which all earlier instances in Scripture point. There is a more intimate union between Christ and the church than any other relation in the world, so that it is indeed 'just and equal in the sight of God, that he should suffer for us, and that what he did and suffered should be imputed unto us'.[71] He then outlines a threefold conjunction of Christ with believers, which he describes as natural, moral or mystical, and federal. The natural conjunction Christ has with believers is that he freely chooses to take on human nature (which in itself unites all human beings to one another), and with it the consequences of their sin. This, then, is not an ordinary person being punished for other people; it is uniquely related to Christ's divine–human person and office. The moral, or 'mystical', conjunction between Christ and the elect is the intimate union and communion that believers enjoy with him, picking up on the Scriptural analogies of the vine and branches, husband and wife. Owen sees this union as the foundation of the fittingness of his suffering in their stead, but again reminds us of its uniqueness beyond any other creaturely union. This is not the transfer of punishment from one creature to another, but the divine condescension to come among us as one of us for no other reason than to accomplish this transfer of sin and righteousness, rooted in the eternal election of God. Finally, Owen describes the federal conjunction between Christ and the church, in which he covenantally undertakes to stand surety for the elect. He 'tendred himself unto God to do and suffer for them, in their stead, and on their behalf, whatever was required, that they might be sanctified and saved'.[72]

With Rom. 3.24-26 very much in mind, Owen sees the wondrous exchange, rooted in this threefold conjunction of Christ and the church, as the glorious manifestation of both the righteousness justice of God and the grace-filled love of God. Turning to an exhortation to meditation, he remarks:

> This is the glory which ravisheth the hearts, and satiates the souls of them that believe . . . whereof one view by faith will scatter all the fears, answer all the objections, and give relief against all the Despondencies, of poor tempted, doubting souls; and an *Anchor* it will be unto all believers, which they may cast within the Vail, to hold them firm and steadfast in all Trials, Storms, and Temptations, in Life and Death.[73]

Chapter 10 ('The Glory of Christ in the Communication of Himself unto Believers') elaborates on the glory of what in the previous chapter Owen

---

[71] Owen, *Meditations and discourses on the glory of Christ* (1684), 133; *Works* (1965), 1:355.
[72] Owen, *Meditations and discourses on the glory of Christ* (1684), 138; *Works* (1965), 1:358.
[73] Owen, *Meditations and discourses on the glory of Christ* (1684), 141–2; *Works* (1965), 1:359.

referred to as the 'mystical conjunction' between Christ and the elect. Referring to the Song of Songs, he explains this 'mystical union' as that by which 'he becomes theirs as they are his; which is the Life, the Glory and Consolation of the church'.[74] Before Owen explains the way Christ communicates himself to the church, he reflects more generally on the topic of divine communications. It is God's constant communication of being, goodness and power to all things that sustains them in being. As is the case with all of God's acts *ad extra*, this communication of God to all things is from the Father, through the Son, by the Spirit. This same pattern is the basis of God's self-communication to believers in salvation and new creation, which is from the Father's electing will, enacted through the person and work of the incarnate Son, and applied to the elect by the Holy Spirit. In this way, God manifests

> his ineffable glorious *Existence* in three Persons, by the order of the communication of these things unto the Church. . . . And herein is the glorious truth of the *Blessed Trinity*, which by some is opposed, by some neglected, by most looked on as that which is so much above them, as that it doth not belong unto them, made precious unto them that believe, and becomes the Foundation of their Faith and Hope. In a view of the glorious order of those Divine Communications, we are in a steady contemplation of the ineffable Glory of the existence of the Nature of God in the Three distinct Persons of Father, Son, and Holy Ghost.[75]

Owen then focuses particularly on the glory of our union with Christ by the Holy Spirit through faith. Christ gives the Holy Spirit to his elect to abide in them, and it is by the power of the Holy Spirit that the elect come to faith. From this follows 'an *ineffable Union* between him and them. For as in his Incarnation he took our *Nature* into personal Union with his own; so herein he takes our *Persons* into a *Mystical Union* with himself'.[76] There is nothing else comparable to the union of Christ and believers in the whole of creation, and Owen describes it as the glory, exaltation, honour and eternal security of the church, to the praise of the grace of God in Christ.

This union with Christ by the Spirit also effects a transformation in us. The Spirit communicates Christ to us, thereby forming a new nature in us – Christ's own nature – and conforming us more and more into the image of Christ:

---

[74]Owen, *Meditations and discourses on the glory of Christ* (1684), 143; *Works* (1965), 1:360.
[75]Owen, *Meditations and discourses on the glory of Christ* (1684), 150; *Works* (1965), 1:363.
[76]Owen, *Meditations and discourses on the glory of Christ* (1684), 153; *Works* (1965), 1:365.

On this communication of Christ unto us by the forming *of his own nature* in us, depends all the purity, the beauty, the holiness, the inward Glory of the Church. Hereby is it really, substantially internally separated from the world, and distinguished from all others, who, in the outward form of things, in the profession and duties of Religion, seem to be the same with them. Hereby it becomes the *first fruits of the Creation unto God*, bearing forth the renovation of his Image in the world; Herein the Lord Christ is, and will be, *glorious* unto all eternity.[77]

In chapter 11 ('The Glory of Christ in the Recapitulation of all things in him'), Owen gives an account of how 'the Lord Christ is peculiarly and eminently Glorious in the Recapitulation *of all things in him,* after they had been scattered and disordered by sin'.[78] Owen considers that the intent of God to gather all things in heaven and on earth under one head (e.g. Eph. 1.10; Col. 1.20) refers to Christ becoming the head of the re-gathered family of unfallen angels and elect human beings. This is something that no mere creature could have done, and neither could God in himself, and so it redounds uniquely to the glory of Christ. As God-man, all things depend on Christ, and are in subjection to him, and there is no communication between God and creation except by and through him who holds both together in himself. 'This glory God designed unto his Son incarnate, and it was the greatest, the highest that could be communicated unto him.'[79]

While this recapitulation of all things has indeed been accomplished in Christ, we and every part of creation currently groan, awaiting its consummation along with the full manifestation of Christ's glory as its head. Owen looks forward to the time when the full restoration of all things will be accomplished and the 'whole curious frame of the divine creation is rendered more beautiful than it was before', when it will rejoice in the unshakeable security of the new creation achieved by Christ's recapitulative work. The first creation was ruined by sin, but now, 'every thing that belongs unto this new Creation, even every believer in the world as well as the Angels in heaven, being gathered together in this one head, the whole and all, and every part and member of it, even every particular believer are secured from ruin, such as befell all things before'.[80]

---

[77] Owen, *Meditations and discourses on the glory of Christ* (1684), 155–6; *Works* (1965), 1:366.
[78] Owen, *Meditations and discourses on the glory of Christ* (1684), 158; *Works* (1965), 1:367.
[79] Owen, *Meditations and discourses on the glory of Christ* (1684), 167; see 161–7; *Works* (1965), 1:372; see 368–72.
[80] Owen, *Meditations and discourses on the glory of Christ* (1684), 170; *Works* (1965), 1:374.

CHAPTERS 12–14

Chapter 12 ('Differences between our beholding the Glory of Christ by Faith in this world and by sight in Heaven. The first of them explained') marks a final transition in the work, from describing aspects of Christ's glory to giving an account of how we apprehend it. Taking up Paul's analogy in 1 Cor. 13.12, Owen speaks of how in this life we can only see Christ's glory as if reflected in a mirror.[81] That mirror is Scripture (and once again, emphatically not any artistic representations of Christ such as are promoted in Roman Catholic piety).[82] Owen is at pains to add that it is not as if the representation of the glory of Christ that we have in the Gospel is inadequate in itself, but rather, our faith is imperfect and so we do not apprehend the fullness of it. Moreover, as he will point out later in the chapter, both our sin and our current creaturely limitations mean that we could not yet cope with beholding more of Christ's glory than we can discern by meditation on Scripture. To see that glory in its fullness now would destroy us.[83]

The chapter is punctuated with urgent and often extended pleas for believers to seek to perceive more and more of Christ and his albeit still veiled glory, even if we cannot cope with a prolonged and steady sight of it.[84] Like the spouse in the Song of Songs (2.9), who only catches a glimpse of her husband through the window, we should be searching after more and more glimpses of Christ and his glory through meditation on Scripture, and those glimpses ought to make us long for the time when we will behold him face to face for all eternity.

For the moment, however, our beholding of Christ's glory by faith is of necessity weak, transient and imperfect. The vision we shall have of it in heaven, however, will be '*immediate, direct, intuitive*; and therefore *steady*, eaven and constant'.[85] This will be both because of the object we behold and our glorified capacities. We will see Christ face to face: the object of our vision 'will be *real*

---

[81] While acknowledging that Paul refers to a mirror, Owen also reflects on Scripture as being like the recently invented telescope, which enables us to see very distant objects. The Gospel brings Christ closer to us, but we are still very far from apprehending the fullness of his glory; Owen, *Meditations and discourses on the glory of Christ* (1684), 174–5; *Works* (1965), 1:376.

[82] Owen, *Meditations and discourses on the glory of Christ* (1684), 174, 182–3; *Works* (1965), 1:376, 380.

[83] This becomes a reason for Owen to reject the millennial views of those of his contemporaries who were anticipating the reign of Christ on earth before the full consummation of the eschaton: no-one will be able to withstand the fullness of the presence of Christ in glory who has not yet been eschatologically transformed; Owen, *Meditations and discourses on the glory of Christ* (1684), 181–2; *Works* (1965), 1:380.

[84] See e.g., Owen, *Meditations and discourses on the glory of Christ* (1684), 176–8; 180–1; 189–91; 193–7; *Works* (1965), 1:377, 379–80; 384–5; 386–9.

[85] Owen, *Meditations and discourses on the glory of Christ* (1684), 179, see 178–9; *Works* (1965), 1:378.

and substantial. Christ himself in his own person with all his glory, shall be continually with us. . . . We shall no longer have an *Image*, a Representation of him, such as is the delineation of his Glory in the Gospel'.[86] Crucially, and unlike the earlier, highly intellectualized theological tradition on the beatific vision, Owen has a prominent and substantial place for our glorified bodies and senses.[87] While the beatific vision is indeed primarily about the glorified capacities of our minds to apprehend the fullness of the glory of Christ in his two natures, it remains central to Owen that we come to know the glory of Christ in his whole personhood through our whole glorified creaturely personhood. In a key passage, he asserts:

> There will be use herein of our bodily *eyes*. . . . That corporeal sence shall not be restored unto us, and that glorified above what we can conceive, but for this great use of the eternal beholding of Christ and his Glory. Unto whom is it not a matter of rejoycing, that with the *same eyes* wherewith they see the tokens and signs of him in the Sacrament of the Supper, they shall behold himself immediately, in his own person.[88]

In addition to the glorification of our senses, our minds will also be glorified. Just as our natural capacities now could not come to true knowledge of God without the illuminating grace of the Holy Spirit, so believers will need – and receive – the additional light of glory. And just as '*the Light of Grace* doth not destroy or abolish the *Light of nature*, but rectifie and improve it; so the *Light of Glory* shall not abolish or destroy *the Light of Faith and Grace*, but, by incorporating with it, render it absolutely perfect'.[89] Moreover, as it has been by beholding the light of the knowledge of the glory of God in the face of Jesus Christ by faith here that the Holy Spirit has transformed us from one degree of glory to another, so when we behold Christ in glory face to face, we will be fully and finally transformed. The first instant of encountering the fullness of the glory of Christ '*perfectly transforms the soul into the Image and Likeness of Christ*'.[90] To make sure that we do not reduce the beatific vision of Christ in glory to intellectual apprehension, Owen once again insists on the importance of the glorified body in this regard:

---

[86]Owen, *Meditations and discourses on the glory of Christ* (1684), 179; *Works* (1965), 1:378.
[87]For an account of this aspect of Owen on the beatific vision, see McDonald, 'Beholding the glory of God', 154–7, and Boersma, *Seeing God*, 321–7.
[88]Owen, *Meditations and discourses on the glory of Christ* (1684), 179–80; *Works* (1965), 1:379.
[89]Owen, *Meditations and discourses on the glory of Christ* (1684), 186; *Works* (1965), 1:382.
[90]Owen, *Meditations and discourses on the glory of Christ* (1684), 186; *Works* (1965), 1:383.

The body as glorified, with its senses, shall have its use and place herein. After we are cloathed again with our flesh, we shall *see our Redeemer with our eyes*. We know not here what power and spirituality there will be in the acts of our glorified bodies. Such they will be, as shall bear a part in eternal Blessedness.[91]

If this is what lies ahead of us, says Owen, returning to a well-worn theme, why is it that so few are willing to find time to meditate now on the glory to come – Christ's and our own? Far too many are more than willing to find the time to meditate upon how to gain worldly advantage, and so are transformed into the image of what most occupies their minds:

Hereby many deceive their own Souls. Good, Lands, Possessions, Relations, Trades . . . are the things whose image is drawn on their minds . . . so these persons beholding the beauty of the world, and the things that are in it, in the cursed glass of self-love, they are in their minds changed unto the same image. . . . But we have not so learned Christ Jesus.[92]

The heart of chapter 13 ('The Second Difference between our beholding the Glory of Christ by Faith in this world and by Sight in Heaven') is that while in the life to come our vision of Christ's glory will be steady and constant, in this life our glimpses of Christ's glory are fleeting and fluctuating. In particular, Christ sometimes deliberately withdraws himself from us, so that even those who diligently seek to meditate on Christ's glory sometimes find 'little of *Reallity* or *Power* in the exercise of this Grace, or the performance of this Duty'.[93] This may simply be because of his sovereign wisdom – Christ does not have to make his reasons clear to us about anything that he does. It might also be for our spiritual growth, to jolt us out of spiritual sloth and negligence, or because our minds are too preoccupied with worldly matters. Whatever the reasons, Christ's withdrawing of our experience of his presence is a 'sanctified ordinance' for our spiritual health.[94]

Only those who have come to know and experience the intimacy of Christ's presence can recognize his withdrawal, and are cast down by it, and there is only one remedy for it: the discipline of seeking to behold the glory of Christ whether we feel like it or not:

Do any of us find *decays in grace* prevailing in us; deadness, coldness, lukewarmness, a kind of Spiritual Stupidity and senseless coming upon us?

---

[91] Owen, *Meditations and discourses on the glory of Christ* (1684), 187; *Works* (1965), 1:383.
[92] Owen, *Meditations and discourses on the glory of Christ* (1684), 198; *Works* (1965), 1:389.
[93] Owen, *Meditations and discourses on the glory of Christ* (1684), 200; *Works* (1965), 1:390.
[94] Owen, *Meditations and discourses on the glory of Christ* (1684), 203, see 202–3; *Works* (1965), 1:392, see 391–2.

> ... And would we have our souls recovered from these dangerous diseases? Let us assure ourselves there is *no better* way for our healing and deliverance, yea, *no other* way but this alone, namely, the *obtaining a fresh view of the Glory of Christ by faith, and a steady abiding therein*. Constant contemplation of Christ and his Glory, putting forth its transforming power unto the revival of all Grace, is the only relief in this case.[95]

Owen recognizes that only the Holy Spirit can work this in us but reminds his readers that the Spirit has ordained particular means. In this case we have explicit instructions that it is by beholding the glory of Christ in the mirror of Scripture that the Spirit will transform us from glory into glory.[96] What we emphatically must not do, says Owen, with yet another attack on Roman Catholicism, is try to reinvigorate our love to Christ by seeking to behold his glory through crucifixes and paintings. As he bluntly puts it, 'an imaginary Christ will effect nothing in the minds of men, but imaginary Grace'.[97]

Many, however, see no need to seek to behold Christ's glory at all. To Owen, without some experience of the spiritual peace, consolation, joy and assurance that communion with Christ and beholding his glory bring, someone's profession is 'heartless, lifeless, useless; and Religion itself is a dead carcass without an animating soul'.[98] Some outright scorn the idea that it is possible to experience the glory of Christ in union with him in this life as 'distempered fancies and imaginations'.[99] Others may not deny such things, but assume that while some might experience them, or might have done in past eras of the church, it is not for them or for believers now. They live in hopes of heaven and future glory, but content themselves with performing token outward religious duties in the meanwhile. As such, they 'countenance themselves in their spiritual sloth and unbelief', and by seeking refreshment and satisfaction in temporal things, Owen suggests, they can expect to be sorely disappointed in eternity.[100]

With Mk 10.29-30 in mind – and very probably the circumstances of the dissenting community – Owen also reminds his readers that true faith is 'usually accompanied with outward troubles, Afflictions, Persecution, and Reproaches', but insists that the inward consolations and divine refreshment from meditating on the glory of Christ in this life 'outballance all those evils which we may undergo

---

[95] Owen, *Meditations and discourses on the glory of Christ* (1684), 210, see also 218; *Works* (1965), 1:395, see also 400.
[96] Owen, *Meditations and discourses on the glory of Christ* (1684), 210–11; *Works* (1965), 1:395–6.
[97] Owen, *Meditations and discourses on the glory of Christ* (1684), 205, see 205–8; *Works* (1965), 1:393, see 393–5.
[98] Owen, *Meditations and discourses on the glory of Christ* (1684), 213; *Works* (1965), 1:397.
[99] Owen, *Meditations and discourses on the glory of Christ* (1684), 215; *Works* (1965), 1:398.
[100] Owen, *Meditations and discourses on the glory of Christ* (1684), 217; *Works* (1965), 1:399.

upon the account of it'.[101] This is sufficient to sustain us in the meanwhile, in anticipation of fully beholding his glory in eternity, when there will be no sin, trouble or temptation to distract us, and no withdrawing of Christ's intimate presence, 'but the mind being made perfect in all its faculties, powers, and operations, with respect unto its utmost end, which is the enjoyment of God, is satisfied in the beholding of him for evermore'.[102]

In chapter 14 ('Other Differences between our Beholding of the Glory of Christ by Faith in the World and by sight in Heaven') the main theme is the contrast between our piecemeal view of Christ now, which is as much as our creaturely and sinful capacities can cope with, and apprehending the fullness of his person and work all at once in heaven. Now we have glimpses of Christ's glory distributed throughout Scripture, for which we must diligently seek (with yet further reminders that Scripture alone is the place to find these glimpses, not in any personal revelations outside of Scripture, nor in paintings and images). Even then, our minds still fail us in trying to hold together all that we can know of his glory in all the themes that Owen has enumerated in the preceding chapters, which he briefly lists.

In the beatific vision in heaven, however, the 'whole Glory of Christ will be at *once* and *alwaies* represented unto us; and we shall be enabled in one act of the Light of Glory to comprehend it'.[103] Moreover, as he has already noted earlier, this vision of Christ in which we fully apprehend the glory of his person and work will fully and finally transform us. This is our instantaneous glorification, unlike the gradual and incomplete process of sanctification in this life. 'The Vision which we shall have of the Glory of Christ in Heaven, and of the Glory of the immense God in him, is perfectly and absolutely *transforming*. It doth change us wholly into the Image of Christ. *When we shall see him, we shall be as he is, we shall be like him, because we shall see him*' (1 Jn 3.2).[104] Even so, Owen reminds us that our sanctification is still a genuine foretaste of the glorification to come. It is a *'previous Participation* of future Glory, working in them *Dispositions* unto, and *Preparation* for the enjoyment of it'.[105]

We do not enjoy the fullness of the beatific vision immediately after death, however. Owen upholds the traditional understanding of a disembodied intermediate state in which believers already experience greater intimacy with Christ, but not yet the fullness of the beatific vision that will come after the general resurrection. Then, our glorified minds and bodies together will behold Christ's glory in such a way that there can be neither satiety nor weariness, for

---

[101] Owen, *Meditations and discourses on the glory of Christ* (1684), 217; *Works* (1965), 1:399–400.
[102] Owen, *Meditations and discourses on the glory of Christ* (1684), 229; *Works* (1965), 1:406.
[103] Owen, *Meditations and discourses on the glory of Christ* (1684), 237; *Works* (1965), 1:410.
[104] Owen, *Meditations and discourses on the glory of Christ* (1684), 238; *Works* (1965), 1:410.
[105] Owen, *Meditations and discourses on the glory of Christ* (1684), 246; *Works* (1965), 1:415.

not only the *Object* of our sight is absolutely Infinite, which can never be searched into the bottom; yea, is *perpetually new* unto a finite understanding; so our *subjective* blessedness consisting in continual fresh Communications from the infinite fulness of the Divine Nature, derived unto us through Vision, is alwaies *new*, and alwaies will be so to Eternity. Herein shall all the Saints of God drink of the *Rivers of Pleasure* that are at his Right Hand, be satisfied with his likeness, and refresh themselves in the eternal Springs of Life, Light, and Joy for evermore.[106]

We cannot yet begin to understand how it is that God will communicate himself to us in this way – we can barely even grasp how God communicates to us in this life – but what we do know, says Owen, is that to all eternity God will make himself known to us and communicate himself to us only in and through Jesus Christ:

All *Communications* from the Divine Being and Infinite fullness in Heaven unto glorified Saints, are in and through Christ Jesus, who shall for ever be the *Medium* of Communication between God and the Church, even in Glory . . . this order shall never be dissolved. . . . And on these Communications from God through Christ depends entirely our continuance in a state of Blessedness and Glory. We shall no more be self-subsistent in Glory than we are in Nature or Grace.[107]

And now, says Owen, in the final words of the treatise:

There is nothing farther for us to do herein but that now and alwaies we shut up all our Meditations concerning it, with the *deepest self-abasement* out of a sense of our unworthiness and insufficiency to comprehend those things, *Admiration* of that excellent Glory which we cannot comprehend, and *vehement longings* for that season when [we] shall *see him as he is*, be *ever with him*, and know him, even as we are known.[108]

---

[106] Owen, *Meditations and discourses on the glory of Christ* (1684), 245–6; *Works* (1965), 1:414.
[107] Owen, *Meditations and discourses on the glory of Christ* (1684), 245; *Works* (1965), 1:414.
[108] Owen, *Meditations and discourses on the glory of Christ* (1684), 247; *Works* (1965), 1:415.

PART III
Owen today

CHAPTER 20

Retrieving Owen

KELLY M. KAPIC

Enigmatic historical figures can easily slip out of history and into the realm of legend. For figures like Francis of Assisi or Winston Churchill, the exaggerated stories that get enlarged at each telling often shape impressions more than careful scholarship. This is, of course, not usually the fault of the historical figures themselves, although they can play a complicating role if they deliberately manipulate their public images or intentionally edit the personal information they leave behind. Their friends and foes also shape the impressions of following generations, sometimes deepening our understanding of the person, at other times increasing the power of the myths that surround them.

John Owen may not be as revered as Francis nor as well remembered as Churchill, but he nevertheless has captured the imagination of many, not only in previous eras but also in the present. Prompted by Owen's 400th birthday, in 2016, several international conferences were convened in the Netherlands and in the United States to honour his memory and revisit his thought, not many years after a similarly lively conference in his honour in Cambridge. Participants at these gatherings came from all over the globe, including America, Australia, Belgium, Canada, England, Germany, Indonesia, Netherlands, New Zealand, Poland, Romania, Scotland and beyond. Publications about Owen have increased over the last two decades as scholars, pastors and a more general audience have continued to study the man and his thought. Owen's writing and the secondary literature that addresses his life and work has been published not only in English but also in Dutch, Portuguese, Korean, Russian and Simplified Chinese Script.

Given the range of Owen's writings and interests, we should not be surprised to discover that he has attracted different kinds of audiences. During his life, he was involved in passionate theological debates, political intrigue and demanding pastoral work – and that during a century filled with turbulence that pervaded the nation, academy, and religious institutions within and beyond England. Owen knew what it was to be highly valued and praised, and he knew what it was to be dismissed and censured. He was an educator, theologian, pastor, political powerbroker, husband and father. But how did these various – and sometimes competing – roles play out in his life and thinking? When did they reinforce one another, and when were they in tension? Here was someone who displayed impressive abilities in dogmatics and offered surprising insights into the complexity of human psychology – a combination for which theologians are not commonly known. As we will see, this overlap of interests is one factor that helps explain Owen's ongoing appeal among modern audiences. This current interest, however, which is largely divided between the popularity of Owen's academic treatises among theologians and his devotional works among a more popular audience, has itself sometimes increased the difficulty of discerning the historical person behind his writings.

Owen's full life and massive literary output have left plenty of material for people to use in constructing vivid and sometimes contradictory portraits of his character – and these portraits have not always been favourable. George Vernon, one of Owen's opponents, warned of an 'enthusiastic Owenistical spirit' and worried that 'Owenists' were maintaining his distinctive ideas.[1] In fact, although Owen was certainly read and appreciated during his lifetime, his popularity grew after his death.[2] That ongoing popularity is also why he remains a concern to those who opposed his views. For example, over 200 years after Owen's death, an anonymous author published *Under Calvin's yoke: Dr John Owen's three invincible questions answered by Bereana* (1900). Drawing from Acts 17.10-11, this author believed that a careful examination of the relevant biblical texts would reveal that Owen had been importing foreign and corrupting ideas into his treatment of Scripture. The author's decision to employ Owen's name so prominently in the book's title suggests that his theology was still being taken seriously. But while Owen always had supportive readers, that support was not always unquestioned or naïve, even from his co-religionists. To this day, criticism of Owen comes not just from outside the Reformed tradition but also from within: most significant points under

---

[1] This citation from Vernon, *A letter to a friend concerning some of Dr Owen's principles and practices*, is quoted in Haigh, 'Theological wars', 331.
[2] Gribben, 'Becoming John Owen', 311–25.

dispute are probably Owen's particular unpacking of 'limited atonement' and his flirtations with 'hyper-Calvinism'.[3]

Today's Owen enthusiasts not only preserve his memory and read his books but also wear t-shirts and drink from mugs that display his likeness or a quotation from his writings. Besides the movement of the 'Young, Restless, and Reformed' crowd that has done much to promote the rediscovery of Owen, first-rate international theologians such as Colin Gunton, John Webster, George Hunsinger and Kevin Vanhoozer have also discovered in Owen an able and stimulating conversation partner. Professional theologians are now taking Owen very seriously and engaging with his thought in a way that has not happened in a very long time. Scholars are giving more and increasingly detailed attention to Owen's carefully constructed theology, considering afresh his place as a dogmatician. This is not because they agree with all of Owen's philosophical moves or presuppositions, but because they recognize his depth and creativity, and they appreciate his goal of examining the practical effects that his dogmatic reflection has for its audience. Even among those who occasionally disagree with Owen's theological or pastoral conclusions, many say that his voice deserves more careful attention.[4]

Given Owen's propensity towards applying theology pastorally, it should not surprise us that non-specialist pastors and 'Christian readers', as Owen might say, have also been delighted with this renewed attention to his work, sometimes leading the charge and not just standing back while waiting for scholars to advance the discussion. There is a steady flow of primary and secondary literature on Owen that is aimed towards a non-academic audience. Sometimes it presents Owen in a romanticized or idealized form, cleansed of the messiness of politics and personal ambition. Some readers and admirers of Owen's writings even at times appear to express a desire to return to an unrealistic, Eden-like Puritan environment (which, it should go without saying, never really existed) rather than trying to apply his conclusions in a complex, modern world. We see this even in the way that the word 'Puritan' is sometimes employed in these discussions, especially when it is used to point to Owen as a primary example of being a Puritan, or only with reference to those who basically agreed with Owen's version of Reformed theology. This sentimental

---

[3] For example, Foord, 'John Owen's Gospel offer', 283–6; Chambers, 'A critical examination of John Owen's argument for limited atonement in *The death of death in the death of Christ*', which though not published is noteworthy for an extensive treatment that others have drawn upon; cf. from a non-Reformed but evangelical perspective, Allen, *The extent of the atonement*, critically engages Owen throughout.
[4] Colin Gunton, George Hunsinger and John Webster are examples of contemporary theologians who on various points differ from Owen (e.g. his particular atonement theology or various aspects of his view of predestination) but yet still mined his thought for insight and support.

kind of writing does justice neither to the complexity of that label nor to Owen's own distinctness. Owen clearly was a Puritan, but so were others with whom he greatly disagreed – a point we will revisit later.

Part of what is so surprising about this overall renewed interest in Owen is its breadth, encompassing historians, theologians, pastors and laity. As we consider some examples of the retrieval work on Owen in recent years, we will examine some of the promising themes and projects that have been developing and hint at possibilities for further exploration. I will divide the rest of the chapter into three categories: first considering Owen in history, then Owen in theology and finally discussing Owen's pastoral appeal. I will combine a brief commentary on recent attempts at retrieval in Owen studies with some suggestions about areas in which future inquiry might open further work. I will intentionally write with a broad audience in mind, since interest in Owen studies includes academics, clergy and laity alike. From his trinitarian theology to his hermeneutical strategy, from his anthropology to his advice on resisting temptation, Owen's work in these varied fields remains relevant. Further, precisely because we are dealing here with someone whose value and influence span several centuries, we must remember that he was a real historical person who was complicated, evolving and active. The current enthusiasm is thus not without dangers, which is why we must take some caution in further attempts at retrieval. Finally, while I take full responsibility for this chapter, numerous leading scholars who either are Owen specialists or at least have seriously engaged his work have been immensely helpful in my preparation, and I am deeply grateful for their insights, feedback and suggestions.[5]

OWEN IN HISTORY

The need for better biographies

The early attempts to recount the life of John Owen after his death were mostly unsatisfactory by modern standards, either omitting relevant material, flirting with hagiography or focusing so much on his thought that they rarely presented a reliable view of this concrete, particular seventeenth-century man. Some of the more scholarly attempts in the twentieth century not only retained some of these defects but also were usually written for a limited, dissertation-reading

---

[5] At risk of leaving some names out, the following scholars provided valuable feedback in preparation for the composition of this chapter: Michael Allen, Matthew Barrett, Timothy Baylor, J. M. Burger, Christopher Cleveland, Tim Cooper, Oliver Crisp, John Fesko, Danny Hyde, Michael Horton, Mark Jones, Ty Kieser, Jenny-Lyn de Klerk, Henry Knapp, Suzanne McDonald, Ryan McGraw, David Murray, Justin Taylor, Derek Thomas, Carl Trueman, John Tweeddale, H. Van den Belt, Kevin Vanhoozer, Willem van Vlastuin, Tyler Wittman and John Yates.

audience, never reaching broader readership.⁶ Because of this situation, it has been fairly common for theologians, pastors and laity who are interested in Owen to rely on vague generalizations and uncritically positive portrayals of his life. Even if it was unintentional, this often presented a romanticized or unrealistic portrait. Fortunately, over the past twenty years we have started to see significant progress in correcting these errors. Three main practices have been used to help produce a better understanding of Owen, the man. In this work, Owen has been more fully located within his immediate social, political and religious environments in England; his thought has been placed more fully against the backdrop of a larger international theology; and some studies have attempted to locate Owen's work within a longer historical trajectory. Taken together, these three methods, which still need to be built upon, are helping us better appreciate both the man and his thought. Current practice, increasingly, is to anchor his ideas within his concrete historical context. What emerges is the picture of a well-read, vigorous and sometimes offend-able and offending person who continues to capture people's imagination.

One difficulty for modern readers is that some important terms are used and understood inconsistently in recent writing on Owen, giving the impression of greater agreement and unity among 'Puritans' than was historically the case. For example, while we can rightly describe Owen as a 'Puritan' and 'Reformed orthodox' according to current usage, John Goodwin (1594–1665) is more ambiguous, easily fitting within the Puritan movement without being 'Reformed'. Richard Baxter (1615–91), on the other hand, who had significant differences from Owen,⁷ has been labelled 'Arminian' in his beliefs by modern interpreters of his work, but has been nevertheless held to be 'a Reformed Orthodox divine'.⁸ We simply note that such categories are not as rigid or well defined as many have often assumed. This problem is sometimes exacerbated when, in the twentieth century, selective editing and publication of 'Puritan' works (e.g. by Banner of Truth) may have given readers the impression that Owen, Baxter and all of their peers basically agreed on most matters.⁹ But in truth, as in any moment of history, and especially during times of heated

---

⁶The most helpful biographical account of Owen in the twentieth century was Toon, *God's Statesman*. Thankfully, however, more complete work has appeared in recent years. For a general review of the literature (much of it in dissertation form) on John Owen up until 2000, see my *Communion with God*, 12–48. For more recent material, see especially the exhaustive bibliography of Tweeddale, 'A John Owen bibliography', 297–328; and the impressive recent online bibliography – especially good on primary source material – by Burden, 'John Owen: Learned Puritan'.
⁷Including differences on the very important topic of justification.
⁸Pederson, 'Reformed Orthodoxy in Puritanism', 52. See also Trueman, 'Puritan theology as historical event', 253–75; Coffey, 'A ticklish business', 108–36.
⁹One thinks here, for example, of Banner of Truth's decisions regarding Richard Baxter, whom they selectively publish. This publisher's known commitment to a form of Reformed orthodoxy, and its

religious debate, friend and foe were far more complicated to pick apart than later readers may realize. And when the issues particularly involve doctrinal precision, the distance of centuries can make it much more difficult for us to recognize the similarities and differences, especially when current re-publication is as selective as it has been. This is where the work of historians like Tim Cooper and Crawford Gribben has proven invaluable.

In 2008, Tim Cooper wrote a thoughtful and probing review essay titled, 'John Owen unleashed: Almost', to describe the current state of Owen studies. He expressed his appreciation of the current revival of interest in Owen but also expressed some serious doubts. Having reviewed four recent monographs on Owen, Cooper respected their mainly theological or pastoral discussions, but he also expressed his unease that each of them, in its own way, tended to present Owen as a floating idea rather than a unified, real concrete person.[10] He concluded, 'I suspect that the effort to rescue Owen from undue neglect has given us a view of him that is too uncritical, frequently defensive and abstracted from historical context.'[11] Cooper's essay represents the beginning of fresh attempts to enter more deeply and deliberately into the muddy waters of history, and this work is producing a more accurate but also more complicated portrayal of Owen. Cooper has gone on to raise incisive questions about Owen's work, personality and conflicts – usually by showing his tense relationship with Baxter, not least in his monumental work, *John Owen, Richard Baxter and the Formation of Nonconformity* (2011).[12] By comparing and contrasting these two fiery figures, Cooper demonstrates how temperamental, theological and political differences like theirs can at times prove unitive, although maybe more often divisive.[13] Owen could get jealous and frustrated, not merely opining about communion with God but also in wondering how to best a rival who brought out his competitive nature.

The most notable contribution since Cooper's field-shaping work has been Crawford Gribben's ground-breaking book, *John Owen and English Puritanism* (2016). Informed and inspired in part by Cooper's methodology, Gribben offers a much-needed full-length scholarly biography of Owen. As in Cooper's

---

decision only to reprint those works by Baxter that fit with that perspective, may prevent readers from understanding the extent to which Baxter abandoned Reformed orthodoxy.

[10] Cooper, 'John Owen unleashed: Almost', 226–2. Responses by each of the authors followed Cooper's extended review, and pages are thus included. The four works in the order in which they were reviewed: Trueman, *John Owen* (242–4); Spence, *Incarnation and inspiration* (244–6); Kay, *Trinitarian spirituality* (246–50); Kapic, *Communion with God* (250–7).

[11] Cooper 'John Owen unleashed: Almost', 228.

[12] Cooper, *John Owen, Richard Baxter and the Formation of Nonconformity*; cf. Cooper, 'Owen's personality', 215–26.

[13] For a further example of these tensions and differences, see Cooper, 'Why did Richard Baxter and John Owen diverge?', 496–516.

work, Owen is no longer simply an unblemished godly hero who only does good and right from pure motives. Instead, now we see Owen as a more layered figure who cares not only about theology but also about his wardrobe, his struggling book sales and his reputation. Owen could be easily offended, intensely political and calculating, and he could be swept up with optimism in one season while feeling defeated in another. In all of this we begin to see a more well-rounded historical person emerge. While this work has made some Owen fans uncomfortable, it is nevertheless a helpful step in moving away from a docetic vision of the seventeenth-century dean of Christ Church, vice-chancellor of the University of Oxford, author and pastor. Certainly, all Owen scholarship must now take Gribben's work into account. As to be expected, Gribben, by unearthing neglected material and making connections that were previously ignored or downplayed, has opened as many questions as he solves; even though some disagreements with Gribben's portrayal of Owen will develop, the state of Owen scholarship is much stronger as a result of his monumental work.

A few examples of others trying to connect the man, his thought and his social setting can show the current state of Owen studies. Martyn Cowan's recent study of Owen's preaching helps us see Owen more clearly and make sense of the interconnections between his life and thought.[14] Whereas Owen's sermons had been, for the most part, either appreciated for devotional purposes or ignored altogether, Cowan demonstrates their historical–political significance. This enables us to see Owen's strongly eschatological view of England and the world. Soaked in the Scriptures, Owen's imagination and rhetoric draw upon the 'Israelite paradigm' as he speaks out to England's leaders and seeks to inform the nation as a whole.[15] While Owen did not simply equate Israel and England (though he comes close at times), he saw the stories of the Old Testament as a pattern for offering both comfort and warning. From the 'decade of negligence' (1630s) to the season when England was 'backsliding' and 'sick' (after 1660), Owen produced a theology and political theory that were tightly intertwined. His preaching skill and his governmental involvement always urged his audience to repentance and greater faithfulness – faithfulness of the sort that conformed to his Reformed–orthodox–Puritan vision for England. Further, whereas some have rightly observed changes in Owen's thought, Cowan also recognizes a surprising level of consistency in his politics, even amid the shifts.[16] But as times

---

[14]Cowan, *John Owen and the civil war apocalypse*. For my full review of this work, from which some of the following sentences are drawn, see *Church History* 87 (2018), 904–7.
[15]Cowan, *John Owen and the civil war apocalypse*, 18–27.
[16]For examples of changes noted, see Gribben, *John Owen and English Puritanism*, 10–11; for more on changes in Owen's thought, see Trueman, 'John Owen's *Dissertation on divine justice*', 87–103; Trueman, 'The necessity of the atonement', 204–22; Hyde, 'John Owen on public prayer', 246.

changed, so did Owen's emphasis and focus. As Cowan demonstrates, changing times did not mean for Owen that God had stopped working; instead, the challenge was for believers to be able interpreters of the times, which required both wisdom and skill in biblical understanding to make sense of events as they unfolded. God might be 'hardening' some, exposing others and further transforming or sanctifying his children.[17] Owen's theology gave him flexible categories for evaluating and responding to the events of history.

Further historical work might more fully place him within his English context, as is happening in academic dissertations that compare Owen's view of the kingdom of God to political reform movements in England.[18] But aspects of Owen's own life also need further attention. For example, one scholar wrote me, and his quip captured lingering tensions felt by Owen readers, even after Gribben's monograph: 'how could a former chaplain to Cromwell find favour with Charles II in the 1660s? There's being a survivor and then there's John Owen!'[19] While Gribben helpfully has laid the groundwork, I still regularly hear questions about the relative ease with which Owen lived his last two decades. Even though 'defeated', Owen still was not completely cast out like so many others. More work on Owen's navigating these years would prove illuminating. Similarly, Owen's earlier relationship to Cromwell remains intriguing, especially in terms of how the invasion and brutal subjugation of Ireland might have affected Owen. How might this experience, his relationship to power, his view of government, liberty and the tension between hierarchical authority and the value of local communities all relate to these dynamics? We can be grateful that both John Coffey and Manfred Svensson have helped us better appreciate the complexities of Owen's view of liberty and toleration.[20] More recently, Robert Wilken's *Liberty in the Things of God* (2019) has placed Owen's work within a much larger and longer trajectory of increasing religious freedom. He notes that Owen moved beyond the idea that religious freedom was a privilege to argue that 'liberty is necessary unto human nature'.[21] More work on how Owen used

---

[17] See Cowan, *John Owen and the civil war apocalypse*, esp. ch. 6.
[18] For example, Kelly, 'Reformed and reforming: John Owen on the kingdom of Christ'. Cf., Kelly, 'Reformed or reforming?', 3–30.
[19] Personal correspondence with Derek Thomas, 29 May 2020, slightly edited. Used by permission. Thomas appears to be referencing the fact that Owen was evidently brought in for a nearly two-hour dialogue with Charles II, which may have been the occasion for his often-quoted reference about John Bunyan. Asty reports that Charles assured Owen of 'his favour and respect'. Whether one speaks of 'favour' could be debated, but Thomas's point remains an interesting question. On Owen's interaction with Charles II, see Asty, 'Memoirs of the life of John Owen', xxix.
[20] Coffey, 'John Owen on toleration in the Puritan revolution', 227–48; Svensson, 'The alms of authority?', 690–709.
[21] Wilken, citing Owen, in *Liberty in the things of God*, 164; for his full treatment of Owen, see 155–64.

this theme to bring together theology, personal conscience and social structures could prove instructive.

Finally, while there has been legitimate concern that in the past the pendulum was too far on the side of hagiographical portrayals of Owen in earlier accounts, we need to ask whether more recent efforts have started to push us too far the other way so that we only read Owen in historical context. I suspect Gribben's newest volume will help ease concerns as it seeks to combine a healthy balance of appreciation and fair-minded commendation with incisive and impartial assessment.[22] This has always been a challenge for Christians (and historians) who deal with figures from the past: presenting them as genuinely human, while acknowledging that they might be driven by complicated desires, sometimes even pressed by motivations that would be difficult for the subject to recognize or articulate. Unpacking a person's internal world centuries after the fact is always a chancy business. However, by carefully filling in the details of Owen's setting, relationships and contexts, we can make better-informed judgements about both his actions and intentions. I expect that this ongoing discussion will significantly advance our knowledge of this area. Putting Owen in context and honouring his true (though fallen) humanity will inevitably produce a portrait that is less consistent and less heroic than many were hoping for, but maybe also more compelling.

Owen and the theological conversations of his time

Some authors have made serious progress in placing Owen more accurately within the larger intellectual world of the international setting of Reformed orthodoxy. They have produced fresh insights and continue to provoke the need for further research. For example, Carl Trueman has led efforts to see Owen not merely as a local figure nor isolated theologian, but as a 'Reformed Catholic, Renaissance man'. His training, friendships and vision all require this larger framework for making sense of Owen's place and contributions. Fresh efforts to place Owen within his larger international context have also been urged and practised by others, including Ryan McGraw.[23] Occasionally calling on Owen's readers to dampen our enthusiasm regarding his uniqueness, McGraw asks how many times claims of Owen's singularity are based more upon our ignorance of non-translated works from the continent than they are grounded upon an informed judgement. Similar biblical and theological insights – both in terms of style and content – can be found by Owen's continental Reformed peers.[24] Advocates of Owen's theology must recognize the multiple connections between

---

[22]Gribben, *An introduction to John Owen*.
[23]Esp., McGraw, *John Owen*; cf., McGraw, *A heavenly directory*.
[24]For example, McGraw, *John Owen*, 152.

Owen's ideas and those of others, and as well as an appreciation for Owen's insights. This requires an increased acquaintance with the other theologians, continental as well as British, of Owen's era.

Owen was aware of the theological works of his contemporaries on the continent, and he seems to have assumed or mirrored them at points. Clearly he was a giant intellectual figure in his own right, so this more sober-minded approach to Owen studies should not lessen our appreciation for Owen's work. And, precisely because of his knowledge of many continental authors, it appears a fair question to inquire, as one Dutch scholar asked me, 'Why did Owen so often write in English when his counterparts, who had his intellectual range and abilities, more often wrote in Latin?' While it may be true that Owen is overestimated for his historical importance, in part because his English writings are accessible (although his writing style has rarely been described as reader-friendly!), what might his preferred language choice tell us? If method and content cannot simply be separated, what does Owen's decision to write mostly in English communicate? What does it demonstrate about his priorities and purposes? As we know, he was more than capable of Latin prose, and yet, apparently from his desire to reach a broader audience beyond merely the academy, he wrote most of his more technical writing in English. Further attention to this dynamic would help us better understand not just Owen in comparison to his continental counterparts but also the legacy he intended to leave behind.

Owen and his theological heritage

A greater appreciation of Owen's place in history requires not merely that we unearth material about his relationship to Cromwell or Bunyan, nor only that we observe his similarities to his continental counterparts: it also requires that we understand his intellectual debts to those who preceded him. Along these lines, a great deal of debate was spent over the past fifty to seventy-five years on the 'Calvin and the Calvinists' debate, which occasionally included references to Owen. Alan Clifford's volume *Atonement and Justification* (1990), for example, attempted to draw a historical contrast between the theology of Geneva ('authentic Calvinism') and that of the Puritan theologian whom he deemed to be unduly indebted to Aristotle. Clifford's study – which suggests that Richard Baxter and Archbishop Tillotson were possibly closer to Calvin's original ideas – also included a theological judgement comparing Owen to John Wesley, who was born twenty years after Owen died.[25] In response, Trueman demonstrated Clifford's consistent misrepresentation of Owen and his relationship to the

---

[25]Clifford, *Atonement and justification*.

tradition of Calvin, raising questions about both the methodology employed and the conclusions that he reached.[26] Cooper has also demonstrated some of the factors in 'Calvin's decline' by the end of the seventeenth century, using Owen and Baxter for illustrative purposes.[27]

Thankfully, as the conversation about later 'Calvinism' has matured and deepened, the discussion has been better framed. Historical theologians are no longer simply interested in how later thinkers match Calvin's particular constructs, but also how they fit into the broader international scene of Reformed orthodoxy as it, too, developed. The tendency of historical theologians to reduce every question to a simple focus on Calvin skewed the conversation and therefore also distorted judgements about later theologians. Richard Muller in particular has helped us see figures like Owen as part of a larger Protestant scholastic theological movement: we must now frame questions of continuity and discontinuity not simply in terms of Calvin, nor even the Reformation in general, but also by going back even further to the medieval scholastic tradition.[28] As we noted already, the work currently being done to examine Owen's thought against his continental contemporaries is a step forward, but this can also include looking further back in history.

This new focus on Owen's intellectual context is not simply about looking beyond the shores of England, but also beyond the boundaries of the seventeenth century. Given how well read he was in the tradition, our efforts to understand his context require us to pay greater attention to his incorporation of his intellectual heritage. Christopher Cleveland, for example, has written a fair-minded volume on *Thomism in John Owen* (2016), demonstrating just how Catholic (Thomistic) Owen's doctrine of God and Christology was, while also recognizing key modifications and differences in his idea of 'infused habits'.[29] Much more work remains to be done, of course. For example, Owen's drawing upon the early fathers is far from fully understood. Owen's reading of patristic sources is easily missed, for he often makes these references only in his footnotes, and often he does not translate the relevant quotations. Because of this, they are too easily overlooked. Neglected figures like Didymus the Blind play a significant role in his doctrine of the Holy Spirit, but this has not been fully explored.[30] His reliance on figures such as Gregory of Nazianzus and Basil

---

[26] Trueman, *The claims of truth*.
[27] Cooper, 'John Owen, Richard Baxter and the battle for Calvin in later seventeenth-century England', 63–78.
[28] See esp. Muller's magisterial four-volume work, *Post-Reformation Reformed dogmatics*; cf. Muller, *The unaccommodated Calvin*.
[29] Cleveland, *Thomism in John Owen*.
[30] For example, Owen, Πνευματολογια (1674), 12, 20, 21, 30, 34, 37, 38, 47 (x2), 86, 131, 138, 182; *Works* (1965), 3:28, 37, 38, 48, 54, 58, 59, 68, 69, 113, 162, 170, 220.

has been observed, but, again, without careful study.³¹ Further, Augustine's conversation narrative in his *Confessions* appears to have almost canon-like status in Owen's Πνευματολογια (1674). While some have hinted at Owen's engagement with Augustine's work, far more could be done.³² In fact, a full survey of Owen's employment of patristic sources would help us better locate him within the longer tradition of Nicene orthodox Christianity. But also, what about John of Damascus and scholastics like Scotus and Anselm? Whom does Owen utilize, and when and how, while developing his points? Some good spadework has occurred in recent decades, but a great deal more remains to be unearthed.

Owen and his theological legacy

In an ideal world we would soon see a volume or two, or at least individual studies, that examine not only the historical figures who influenced Owen but also those whom Owen influenced. This would greatly move the conversation forward. Many who have written about later figures have also hinted at the influence that reading Owen had on them, but few have developed these explorations. Joel Beeke has nicely outlined 'The reception of John Owen in early modernity', giving much-needed attention to readers outside of England and including examples from recent centuries. But where he could only give a sentence or paragraph about specific readers, we would benefit from a fuller study. Beeke, for instance, cites early Dutch translations that enabled Owen's work to serve as part of the 'Further Reformation' (*Nadere Reformatie*) in the Netherlands.³³ Similarly, it is known that his work, especially on the Sprit, was deeply influential on Abraham Kuyper (1837–1920); but we really would benefit from a more detailed treatment of ways that Kuyper both incorporated and modified Owen's ideas in his own work. Within their significant theological overlap there also appear to be questions about 'whether Owen would have approved of Kuyper's program for the redemption of culture', questions that are still unanswered.³⁴ Does Herman Bavinck come closer to Owen's perspective than Kuyper? Here we admit a movement away from historiography and towards theological judgements. Yet, rather than picking between the right or wrong option, further historical study could provide a telling example of how two theologians with similar theological presuppositions nevertheless applied them in their respective settings with somewhat different results. Twenty-first-century tensions

---

³¹For example, Kapic, *Communion with God*, 79, 164; McGraw, 'Seeing things Owen's way', 192.
³²For example, Knapp, 'Augustine and Owen on perseverance', 65–88.
³³Beeke, 'The reception of John Owen in early modernity', 83–106.
³⁴Beeke, 'The reception of John Owen in early modernity', 96–7.

between 'Kuyperians' or 'neo-Calvinists' and 'two-kingdom' advocates recognize their differences in debate within their shared Reformed history. In those debates it is possible that many, who believe Owen was less concerned to emphasize 'common grace insights' than was Kuyper, fail to recognize how Owen still held (for a time) a real optimism regarding social and political changes: he desired that the early kingdom should more faithfully reflect the kingdom of God. Might this be partly why a social reformer like William Wilberforce found Owen worth reading even in the nineteenth century?[35] However one might imagine the dangers or benefits in Owen's theo-political assumptions, there may be more overlap between Owen and Kuyper than contemporary practitioners would at first imagine. Historians and theologians working together can help us map this complicated terrain. Real differences, shaped by their particular contexts, remain between Owen and Kuyper; we would be helped by careful treatments that help us better trace out similarities, differences and developments.

Others have hinted at Jonathan Edwards's interest in Owen, even claiming he was 'one of Owen's most active early American readers'.[36] A great deal of fascinating theological and historical work comparing the two men's theology within their respective socio-political contexts remains far from fully explored. Owen and Edwards approach the doctrine of the Trinity differently and develop different nuances:[37] So how might these two theologies relate?[38] And how do they compare in their accounts of believers who experience the Holy Spirit? Both authors wrote about what they considered to be a healthy understanding of the experience of the Spirit and about the character of what they believed to be the extremes of their day.[39] Further studies comparing and contrasting these two leading lights of the Reformed tradition would help us understand the organic development of doctrine within this tradition. But beyond – and before – Edwards, a great deal more could be done to compare Owen to other American Puritans. Why did they consider him to be a good candidate for serving in America, whether as president of Harvard College or as minister in a large church?[40] How did later generations in America draw upon Owen, and what circumstances led them to distance themselves from his work and influence?

---

[35]Cf., Wilberforce, *A practical view of the prevailing religious system of professed Christians, in the higher and middle classes in this country, contrasted with real Christianity*, 240–1.
[36]Gribben, 'Becoming John Owen', 316. For an example of where hints are dropped but left undeveloped, see Pauw, *The supreme harmony of all*, 5–7, 146–7, 156.
[37]On Owen, see, e.g., Kapic, *Communion with God*, esp. ch. 5; Letham, 'John Owen's doctrine of the Trinity in its Catholic context'. On Edwards, see, e.g., Pauw, *The supreme harmony of all*.
[38]Cf. Cunnington, 'A critical examination of Jonathan Edwards's doctrine of the Trinity', 224–40.
[39]Cf. Martin, 'Violent motions of carnal affections', 99–116.
[40]Gribben, *John Owen and English Puritanism*, 226–7.

Owen and multi-dimensional analysis

One final example demonstrates how studying the interplay of Owen's local context, his intellectual heritage and his own theological contributions leads to a fuller understanding of each. Focusing on the controversies Owen was embroiled in during his life and the debates that followed his death, Paul Lim's work provides a brilliant example of seeing a theological discussion as part of a larger context. By focusing on trinitarian debates, Lim places Owen and his peers within a particular conversation that was occurring in England in the second half of the seventeenth century.[41] Rather than falling into the trap of thinking that these were arguments that simply divided the faithful from unbelievers, Lim shows that the struggle was really about hermeneutics. John Biddle, for example, knew and valued the Scriptures deeply; but his Socinian and rationalistic intuitions strongly contrasted with the Nicene-hermeneutical assumptions of those, like Owen, who read the sacred text in light of the *depositum fide*: this difference meant that Owen ended up in the trinitarian camp while Biddle and others landed elsewhere. Yet these arguments with Biddle were not just theological, because they had much to do with questions of religious toleration within England at the time. It is not easy to separate politics, theology and sociological pressures in these situations, nor is it necessarily helpful. But an awareness of the various competing pressures and influences does aid us in gaining a more complete picture of what was happening.

Careful nuances of this kind are not only deeply helpful for historical purposes but also for modern debates. Thus Lim's work – with Owen as a prime example – proves to be especially insightful into the contemporary resurgence of what is often now called the 'theological interpretation of Scripture'.[42] This descriptor is a fair designation of Owen's general hermeneutical method, and further investigation into his assumptions for faithful interpretation may produce not only greater light on seventeenth-century debates but also for similar debates in the twenty-first century.[43] Michael Allen and Scott R. Swain, in *Reformed Catholicity* (2015), draw from Owen in current proposals built on this past hermeneutic.[44] To date, probably the best effort to expand our

---

[41]Lim, *Mystery unveiled*. Owen plays too significant a role in this volume to simply point to a few pages; cf. Lim, 'The Trinity, *adiaphora*, ecclesiology, and reformation', 281–300.

[42]For introductions to this approach, see Fowl (ed.), *The theological interpretation of Scripture*; Treier, *Theological interpretation of Scripture*; Vanhoozer (gen. ed.), *Dictionary for theological interpretation of the Bible*.

[43]Cf. Kapic, 'Typology, the Messiah, and John Owen's theological reading of Hebrews'. For an example of showing the tension in ways some attempts to employ Owen for a theological reading of Scripture (e.g., Francis Watson), see Sutanto, 'On the theological interpretation of Scripture', 337–53, esp. 346–50.

[44]Allen and Swain, *Reformed Catholicity*, esp. ch. 1.

understanding of Owen's hermeneutics is John W. Tweeddale's excellent volume *John Owen and Hebrews* (2019), which offers a series of careful reflections on ways in which Owen engages the Scriptures, from his general treatment of the Old Testament to his understanding of the Law.[45] But as Tweeddale himself indicates, a great deal more work can be done on Owen's massive Hebrews commentary, including looking more closely at his hermeneutical assumptions. Likewise, Henry Knapp's unpublished dissertation indicates some of the careful distinctions Owen made with regard to handling questions of typology; even so, more could be done to connect this more fully to his theological construction in general, and not only to his hermeneutical method.[46]

Finally, because of Owen's conservative conclusions regarding the Hebrew vowel point controversy (he imagined the vowels were part of the original text, which is now known to be untrue) there is often an under-appreciation of Owen's mastery of the Hebrew language as well as his pneumatologically driven framework for authenticating the original texts.[47] Owen's engagement with Old Testament texts and his view of illumination warrant further attention.[48] Was he merely affirming a dictation theory of inspiration, or is his work more nuanced than that? How does his particular understanding of the ancient near east inform both his hermeneutic and his political view of questions regarding how to treat seventeenth-century Jews? These considerations illustrate for us the connections between Owen's *Sitz im Leben* and his writings. A greater appreciation of the complexities of his life can help future Owen studies. But do all discussions of Owen's thought need to have such an extensive historical focus? To that question, we now turn.

OWEN IN THEOLOGY

While we can be thankful for the recent and much-needed explorations of Owen's social and political circumstances and the way they frame his thought within a larger historical and international setting, contemporary scholars usually draw upon his thinking, not because they want to return to the seventeenth century, but because they believe that it can help their own constructive theological work. Therefore, while it is necessary and fruitful to see Owen in his historical context, theological engagement with him often

---

[45] Tweeddale, *John Owen and Hebrews*.
[46] Knapp, 'Understanding the mind of God'; Knapp, 'The criticism and reassessment of seventeenth-century exegesis'.
[47] Cf. Reedy, 'The reception of a science of texts in England, 1658–1740', 402–22, esp. 407–9; Fuller, 'John Owen and the traditional Protestant view of the Old Testament', 79–99; Muller, 'The debate over the vowel points and the crisis in orthodox hermeneutics', 146–55.
[48] Cf. McGraw, 'The foundation of the Old Testament', 3–28.

asks a different set of questions and therefore approaches him from a different direction. And, although there are risks in limiting one's approach, this need not always be dismissed as inappropriate.

Theologians, like philosophers, would do well to be more mindful of the historical circumstances surrounding figures of the past, even though they are primarily interested in deriving theological insight from those figures and not in historical reconstruction. Of course, theologians in the twenty-first century are most interested – and legitimately so – in the formation, function and coherence of Owen's theological constructs and in obtaining insights from his work that they can use for contemporary proposals. But it is precisely for this reason that the historical context is useful, since historical perspectives enable theologians to understand what Owen was actually getting at, and therefore to see what aspects of Owen's thought can be used and what needs to be left behind.

Timothy Baylor helpfully identifies the tension between theologians and historical theologians on just this point. While he praises recent efforts to map Owen's thought onto the continuities and discontinuities within the historical Reformed tradition, Baylor worries that following a line of 'Muller-style historiography' too narrowly will not allow for engagement with more fruitful dogmatic discussions.

> Such a narrowly historical method prevents us from engaging theologians like Owen precisely as theologians. To do that would require us to analyze the deeper structures of Owen's own thought and to assess their faithfulness to the Gospel. In short, to treat him as a figure who not only strove to hold others accountable to the Word of God, but as a man *himself* accountable to the Gospel.[49]

Baylor is exactly right here. Theologians need to listen to and learn from historians but without being restricted to historical conversations. True, sometimes Owen has been seriously misunderstood or misrepresented by theologians who appear not to be concerned with the historical complexities that provide the necessary background to his thought.[50] But this does not mean that all conversations about Owen must be chiefly historical to be legitimate.

Suzanne McDonald, for example, has written a fair-minded assessment of Owen's historical-intellectual context, and then used that as background for

---

[49] Baylor, 'Review of Ryan M. McGraw, *A heavenly directory*', 379. Original emphasis.
[50] For example, Torrance presents Owen as if 'justice is the essential attribute of God', while love is arbitrary or at best secondary, in 'The incarnation and "limited atonement"', 32–40, esp. 33, 37. But given Owen's view of divine simplicity and other factors common in his historical period, such an assessment appears either not fair-minded or at best not historically nuanced.

theological discussion.[51] McDonald thus provides a model for fairly interpreting Owen within his historical setting while also drawing from him to construct a contemporary proposal.[52] Her efforts emerged not from attacking strawmen, but from deep engagement with primary sources.

Yet, as Baylor was reminding us, one need not become entangled in seventeenth-century politics or historical debates about continuity to use Owen as a powerful resource for current theological conversations. In other words, it is legitimate to debate Owen's ideas themselves, how they fit together, when they are useful and when they are not. One of the encouraging signs in recent years has been the increased interest of contemporary theologians in Owen's work. Let me briefly mention a few examples. Colin Gunton was no expert on the Puritans, but through the influence of his PhD students (e.g. Alan Spence) he eventually came to appreciate Owen's work. Gunton was not particularly interested in historical nuances about Owen, but he found him to be a neglected theological figure who offered real possibilities as a resource in dogmatics.[53] Gunton was especially interested in Owen's possible usefulness in constructing a Spirit-Christology and his attempt to hold together election and ecclesiology.[54] Since Gunton's time, a great deal of debate has broken out regarding Owen's Spirit-Christology: there is some doubt as to whether Spence and Gunton may have misunderstood Owen.[55] Was Owen trying to move beyond or solve tensions inherent within Chalcedon, or did he intend his own constructive work to be a straight reaffirmation of classic Western orthodoxy?[56] Among philosophers and theologians there is also debate about how Owen viewed the Spirit's function in the humanity of Christ. Oliver Crisp, for example, has raised questions about the eager use some theologians have made of Owen's apparent 'Spirit-Christology', asking whether their interpretation may be at

---

[51]McDonald, *Re-imaging election*, esp. chapters 1 and 7; cf. McDonald, 'Evangelical questioning of election in Barth', 250–68, esp. 254–62.

[52]Cf. McDonald, 'Beholding the glory of God in the face of Jesus Christ'. Cf., Farris and Brandt, 'Ensouling the beatific vision', 67–84, esp. 78–83.

[53]Gunton was somewhat notorious for drawing from past theologians for positive or negative examples, but not always using those figures in ways that fairly represented them within history. Probably most sinned against in this respect was Augustine, whom Gunton accused of many things that most historians (and theologians!) would now say often grow out of his misunderstanding or misrepresentation of Augustine. See, e.g., Green, *Colin Gunton and the failure of Augustine*; McNall, *A free corrector*.

[54]For a full treatment, see Kapic, 'Colin Gunton on John Owen'.

[55]Spence, 'John Owen and trinitarian agency'; 'Christ's humanity and ours'; *Incarnation and inspiration*; 'The significance of John Owen for modern Christology'. For an example of a critique of Spence's representation of Owen on these points, see Wittman, 'The end of the incarnation', 284–300, esp. 286–7.

[56]Cf. Kiser, 'Theandric and triune'.

risk of undermining the incarnate Son's full divinity.[57] As we will see later, John Webster raises similar cautions on this point. By seeming to limit the Son's immediate work in the incarnation to the assumption of a human nature, and then leaning so heavily upon the Spirit as mediating the natures, have they produced a new set of problems?

Contemporary theologians have adopted some of Owen's ideas (or interpretations of them) in order to produce fresh proposals. Bruce L. McCormack uses some Owenian ideas to explore how God in Christ reveals what the assumption of a human nature means for the reality of the eternal Son of God.[58] Keith Johnson, while differing from a proposal like McCormack's, finds promising guidance in Owen for maintaining a trinitarian form of understanding the distinct work of the Spirit in the life of the incarnate Christ.[59] Owen's ecclesiology linked the Spirit to the questions of schism and Congregationalism, and this connection has attracted the interest of theologians like Ephraim Radner.[60] Gunton, McCormack and others are examples of theologians who dip into Owen's theology as they have use for it, rather than offering any sustained reading or systematic engagement with him, but they do demonstrate the growing interest in his work.

One of the leading English-speaking theologians in the past fifty years, John Webster, also came to appreciate Owen's theology. In an autobiographical note, Webster mentions his 'conversion from watery suburban Methodism into a tough version of Calvinistic Christianity',[61] which some of his students interpreted to point to his early acquaintance with Owen; sadly, Webster never clarified that point. He did mention to them that, during his time at university, he found nourishment in Owen's writings. While I was studying in London in the late 1990s, he relayed to me a delightful story that others have since independently confirmed: Webster had originally considered doing his doctoral research on Owen, and so he wrote to Peter Toon, who had recently been researching Owen's life and thought. Webster apparently received from this correspondence the strong impression that Owen was now covered, and he should look elsewhere (too crowded a field?). The result was that Webster ended up working on the twentieth-century German theologian Eberhard Jüngel instead. Webster told me that, in many ways, he wished he had gone with his original plan. One is left to wonder what might have happened had this gifted theologian started his academic career by focusing on Owen rather than Jüngel. Whatever the historical accuracy of his personal stories, it would

---

[57]Crisp, 'John Owen on Spirit Christology', 5–25.
[58]McCormack, 'With loud cries and tears', 37–68.
[59]Johnson, 'The work of the Holy Spirit in the ministry of Jesus Christ', 147–67, esp. 160–6.
[60]Radner, 'The Holy Spirit and unity: Getting out of the way of Christ', 207–20, esp. 214–17.
[61]Webster, 'Discovering dogmatics', 129.

be years before Webster turned back to Owen and took him seriously again. Yet, as Webster's focus shifted through the years from twentieth-century theology to more engagement with earlier orthodox classics, he started to dive more deeply into the Protestant scholastics, especially Owen. In fact, his rediscovery of Owen appears to have made Aquinas more appealing to him: Webster saw Owen as a kind of bridge between Barth and Aquinas, and others have followed Webster's lead in this. The sheer theological weightiness of the methods of Owen and Aquinas, among others, appear to have inspired and encouraged Webster in the final season of his scholarship. Webster supervised dissertations on Owen (including Christopher Cleveland, Timothy Baylor, Kendall Cleveland) and encouraged his students not to treat Owen as a pietist preacher, nor as a devotional writer, but as a top-tier dogmatician. He wanted to press them to explore the structure and coherence of Owen's doctrinal system, learning from his connections even as they explored the weaknesses. In this way, while Webster didn't significantly care about Owen's political environment, he worried that too many twentieth-century theologians didn't take Owen seriously enough, thus dismissing an intellectual giant without adequately understanding his work. Most of Webster's references to Owen took a positive tone, such as his assessment of Owen as 'great', not only for having intellectual gifts that put him at the top of seventeenth-century English theology 'but also a man of deep spiritual perception: a capacious and discriminating mind broken and remade by love of the Gospel'.[62] And Owen appears more often in Webster's later writings and thinking, including throughout the two volumes of *God without Measure* (2018).[63] But Webster was also willing to criticize, even when he was uncertain whether problems originated with Owen or with his later interpreters: we see this, in particular, in the Kantzer lectures, where he offers strong reservations about some formulations of Spirit-Christology that related to Owen's work.[64]

---

[62]Webster, *Holiness*, 97–8.
[63]Webster, *God without measure*: vol. 1, esp. 50–1, 84–98; *God without measure*: vol. 2, esp. 4–6, 104, 107, 112–17.
[64]In the fourth of his Kantzer Lectures, 'Immanuel', Webster concludes: 'This is not to fall back into the Nestorian or Zwinglian segregation of God and creation so deplored by many contemporaries. The redemptive effectiveness of Jesus' Spirit-directed human struggle and his victory over sin enjoys some prominence amongst readers of Owen, for example, especially those who discover there something which accords with the two-fold structure of the covenant (Gunton, Spence, Horton). Such accounts are sometimes exegetically under-determined, particularly in their pneumatology; and they commonly under-value the retrospective component of a theology of the Word made flesh (not Horton), its reach back into eternity. Much hangs on retaining this retrospective element as an operative factor in a theology of incarnation; without it, the presence of God in Christ loses something of its incomprehensible difference. "He who has seen me has seen the Father" (Jn 14.9); "No-one has ever seen God; the only Son, who is in the bosom of the Father, he has made him known" (Jn 1.18). A theology of the incarnate presence of the perfect God must observe and be ruled by that tension, which is not abolished even in the coming of the Son to the world', 17. This

Though not backing away from this concern, Webster later positively employed Christological judgements from Owen in his essay 'The place of Christology in systematic theology'.⁶⁵ Webster also mined fresh insights from Owen to shape his own view of 'illumination'.⁶⁶ Webster's former students are continuing to navigate constructive theology through intensive engagement with Owen. In particular, Timothy Baylor's dissertation, once published, will advance this conversation.⁶⁷

Although a less prolific writer than Webster, Susan Hardman Moore was another key supervisor who, although a historian, has overseen a number of significant studies on Owen that assess theology in historical context, while leaning heavily in the theological direction. In addition to supervising my own work (co-supervised with Colin Gunton) and that of Tweeddale mentioned earlier, she oversaw a carefully crafted work on Owen's view of the authority of Scripture written by Andrew M. Leslie, as well as Edwin Tay's careful analysis of how the priesthood of Christ shaped Owen's atonement theology.⁶⁸ While each of these was heavily theological in nature, they did to varying degrees attempt to account for the historical context of Owen's work. Although not all supervisors and Owen dissertations can be mentioned here, it does seem noteworthy that a great deal of fruitful dissertation work on Owen has been coming out of the Netherlands,⁶⁹ as well as from other institutions such as Westminster Theological Seminary and Calvin Theological Seminary, where Richard Muller served as a supervisor.⁷⁰ But many more institutions and works could be discussed.⁷¹

Debates about Owen's theology continue, and result in both positive and negative assessments of his achievements. For example, there is some contention about Owen's careful account of the doctrine that the external works of the Trinity are inseparable, that is, attributable to all three persons. Current discussions of that account relate not merely to seventeenth-century

---

transcript was supplied by Michael Allen, who also was invaluable in helping me locate references to Owen in Webster's work.
⁶⁵Webster, 'The place of Christology in systematic theology', 611–27 (esp. 619).
⁶⁶Webster, 'Illumination', 50–64.
⁶⁷Baylor, 'A great king above all gods'.
⁶⁸Leslie, *The light of grace*; Tay, *The priesthood of Christ*.
⁶⁹For example, some mentioned already include Ryan Kelly and Ryan McGraw, but also there are a number of current students working on dissertations there on John Owen. See also Renihan, 'From shadow to substance', who gives Owen heavy attention throughout.
⁷⁰For example, Knapp has already been mentioned, but see also Lee, 'All subjects of the kingdom of Christ'. Cf. Woo, 'The *pactum salutis* in the theologies of Witsius, Owen, Dickson, Goodwin, and Cocceius'.
⁷¹For example, Tucker, 'Safeguarding the treasure: John Owen and the analogy of faith'; Mutisya, 'Divine sovereignty in John Owen's doctrine of atonement'; Caughey, 'Puritan responses to antinomianism in the context of Reformed covenant theology', which engages heavily with Owen.

debates, but to a current resurgence of disagreement about it.[72] Tyler R. Wittman, another student of Webster's, employs Owen and Aquinas not only to demonstrate Owen's debt to Aquinas but also to make his arguments more understandable for those less versed in classic scholastic nuances.[73] His brilliant essay shows how Owen creatively follows the tradition. While many today fear that affirming divine simplicity undermines the distinctiveness of the persons of the Trinity, Owen employs the doctrine of simplicity to support his claims as a way to honour the three divine persons without undermining the one divine essence: 'the Father, Son, and Holy Spirit, as subsisting principles of operation, demonstrate the one will of the divine nature in accordance with their mode and order of subsistence'.[74] Put differently, each divine person applies God's one will in ways distinctive to their personhood. Thus, while only the Son becomes incarnate, 'Owen maintains the incarnation was an undivided act of the Father, Son, and Holy Spirit, which had its appropriative *terminus* on the Son alone'.[75] In other words, Tyler R. Wittman demonstrates that Owen follows the approach taken from Augustine through Aquinas and into the Protestant scholastic tradition. Other studies look at topics like Owen's exploration, critique and defence of the covenant of redemption.[76] Other debates look at Owen's views of church government and baptism, with some Baptists strongly identifying with Owen,[77] while Lee Gatiss offers a counter-narrative, claiming that Owen really was 'an Anglican'.[78]

Finally, we look at one last area of Owen studies, namely, his function as a hinge between the older orthodoxy and the rise of modernism, showing characteristics of both worlds.[79] Both Owen's theology and his approach to the Christian life reflect this transition. For example, signs of a growing individualism surface throughout his work, and yet he is far more communal in his liturgy and instincts than people often realize.[80] Along similar lines, D. Glenn Butner has offered creative readings of Heinrich Bullinger, John Owen and Abraham Kuyper in dialogue with the ideas of Henri de Lubac,

---

[72]E.g., Claunch, 'What God hath done together', 781–800.
[73]Wittman, 'The end of the incarnation', 284–300.
[74]Wittman, 'The end of the incarnation', 292.
[75]Wittman, 'The end of the incarnation', 300.
[76]See, e.g., Cleveland, 'The covenant of redemption the Trinitarian theology of John Owen'; Bird, 'The covenant of redemption according to John Owen and Patrick Gillespie', 5–30; Loftin, 'A Barthian critique of the covenant of redemption', 203–22, esp. 207–10.
[77]Cf. Gribben, 'John Owen, baptism, and the Baptists', 53–72.
[78]Gatiss, 'Anglicanism and John Owen', 44–53. See Gingerich, 'John Owen was not an Anglican', and the chapter by Gatiss in this volume.
[79]See Kapic and van Vlastuin (eds), *John Owen between Orthodoxy and modernity*, esp. chapters 1–3.
[80]Cf. Trueman's 'John Owen and modernity', 35–54, and McGraw, 'Seeing things Owen's way', 189–204.

demonstrating connections between limited atonement and a social Reformed theology that resists the claims of undue individualism.[81] Owen will not fit nicely into a simple historical or theological pigeonhole, and so, necessarily, the conversation continues.

OWEN'S PASTORAL APPEAL

As important as careful historical investigation and rigorous theological construction are, Owen remains widely read by non-academics. We should not too quickly discount or ignore this audience. Starting in 1958, J. I. Packer was a key voice in the revival of Reformed theology that reintroduced evangelicals to the Puritans in general and to John Owen in particular.[82] His enthusiasm spread as he inspired many new students through his writings and teachings, often pointing them back to Owen for his balanced perspective, which appealed to many amid the shallowness of much evangelicalism in the twentieth century. Building on Packer, Sinclair Ferguson – who is an expert in John Owen's work – has probably done more than anyone else to make this Puritan's theology both accessible and relevant to pastors and laity. Providing a rich overview of Owen's theology as it relates to the Christian life and an approachable summary of the devotional nature of his trinitarian insights, these resources and others have helped many who were too intimidated to read Owen themselves.[83] This type of work helped spur on paraphrases and abridgements of Owen's treatises, which now abound.[84] Furthermore, volumes that commend Owen as a positive pastoral example or model for the Christian life continue to surface as accessible offerings for the non-specialist.[85] My own efforts have often aimed to demonstrate that Owen's presentation of evangelical holiness is closely interrelated to his carefully constructed theological edifice.[86] His trinitarian theology, holistic attempt at anthropology, particular approach to Christology

---

[81]Butner, Jr., 'Reformed theology and the question of Protestant individualism'.
[82]For example, Packer's famous 1958 introduction to the reprint of Owen's *The death of death in the death of Christ*, 'Saved by his precious blood', reprinted many times and is widely available online. But it was also reprinted (ch. 8), along with other chapters that point to Owen in Packer, *A quest for godliness*, esp. ch. 5, 8, 12 and 13.
[83]Ferguson, *John Owen on the Christian Life*; Ferguson, *The Trinitarian Devotion of John Owen*.
[84]For example, 'Reformed Anglican' Robert J. K. Law (a former medical doctor who became a pastor) abridged and paraphrased many of Owen's works with Banner of Truth, publishing at least six of them in the 'Puritan Paperbacks' series. Christian Focus has more recently also published a series of seven volumes of Owen's works, each arranged in a more visual friendly font and style than is found in the Goold editions, although other scholarly apparatuses or other helps are largely left out. The two most common authors to write prefaces for these abridgments and reprints are J. I. Packer and Sinclair Ferguson.
[85]For example, Piper, *Contending for our all*, 77–114.
[86]Kapic, 'Evangelical holiness', 97–114.

and pneumatology combine to form a framework for guiding the Christian life.[87] Similar work is found in the recently published volume *Owen on the Christian Life*, by Matthew Barrett and Michael Haykin, which in some ways updates Ferguson's earlier book by surveying key topics in Owen's thought that have practical relevance for everyday living.[88]

Most of the more popular resources pay more attention to Owen's teachings than to his life. Some potential confusion comes when commentators and readers assume that what Owen advocates he must have personally mastered. Readers need to recognize that preachers inevitably speak about what they still occasionally struggle with. That is not actually hypocrisy: hypocrisy is pretending one is something that one is not. Because Owen doesn't write much about himself, we rarely know about his own personal struggles and shortcomings. He does, however, give hints that the insights he advocates often arise from an awareness of his own ongoing struggles, not just in practices, but in beliefs. My favourite example of this is probably in his short treatment on distinctive communion with the Father. His reflections bristle with psychological complexity, reflecting his awareness of people who imagine the Father as cruel, distant, always angry and dissatisfied.[89] Clearly as a pastor Owen met and knew such people, but his tone also seems to reflect his own personal experience, not merely in spiritual struggles from the distant past, but in ongoing difficulties where he might still have 'hard thoughts' of God the Father.[90] Is he preaching here to himself? It could be that he gained these deep psychological insights from listening to and counselling others (university students?), but it remains hard for me to imagine that they don't also reflect his own internal life. This is why even at the end of his life he eagerly awaits a reality far better than anything he described in his writings: he longs to move past attempts at description and into the actual experience of fully satisfied worship and delight in Christ's presence in glory.[91] He writes about and longs for this experience, not because he is perfect or heroic, but because he recognizes how far short of it he and all sinners fall. We do Owen no favours when we try to elevate him out of such struggle. This takes us back to ongoing tensions between perception and historical reality.

---

[87]See also Kapic, 'Worshiping the triune God', 17–46; Kapic, 'Life in the midst of battle', 23–35.
[88]Barrett and Haykin, *Owen on the Christian life*.
[89]Owen, *Of communion with God* (1657), 1–40; *Works* (1965), 2:5–39, esp. part 1, ch. 3–4 (pp. 17–39).
[90]Owen, *Of communion with God* (1657), 34–5; *Works* (1965), 2:34–5. For more on this and related themes, see Kapic, 'Worshiping the triune God', 17–46.
[91]Early biographers reported that, on the morning of the day of Owen's death, and upon hearing that his volume, *Meditations on the glory of Christ*, was about to be published, Owen exclaimed, 'the long wished-for day is come at last, in which I shall see that glory in another manner than I have ever done, or was capable of doing, in this world'; Owen, *Works* (1965), 1:ciii.

In the United Kingdom and the United States, popular culture still circulates negative stereotypes of Puritans. Those with only a vague knowledge of Owen may assume that he mostly focused on a troubling account of Christ's death that seems to ignore the whole 'world', while others assume he is just another Puritan legalist, preaching only about strict adherence to moral standards. And yet, ironically, in Owen's own day, he was far more often accused of being an antinomian than he was of being a legalist.[92]

In 1677, for example, an antagonist addressed 'J.O. (two terrifying letters, the like are not to be found in all the ABC)', and derided him by means of slander and mischaracterizations.[93] Owen's account of union with Christ and the imputation of Christ's righteousness were believed by William Sherlock and his supporters to undermine the value of morality, so they charged Owen with antinomianism. Owen, however, thought it was clear that his opponents had, in their zeal for moral accountability, undermined the good news of the Gospel. Rather than ignoring or minimizing the ethical demands of the law, however, Owen saw himself and his Reformed party as keeping the right balance between the indicative and the imperative: believers were guilty of sin, and only as they are united to Christ by the Spirit are they then liberated to follow God's commandments. Thus obedience to the law was not a road to God's favour but a response to his love, grace and forgiveness. Owen was not one to encourage ignorance of the revealed law, nor did he dismiss its ongoing relevance for the Christian life. But he worried about the rise of moralism in his day, which seemed related to the loss of a strong account of imputation, which completely depended upon union with Christ. Former Episcopal bishop C. FitzSimons Allison traced this debate in history from Hooker to Baxter; while giving little attention to Owen, FitzSimons demonstrates that in the middle of the seventeenth century a growing concern with one's personal ethical advancement, combined with uneasiness or outright rejection of the doctrine of imputation, created an environment of growing moralism.[94] Pastors and laity who currently employ Owen in their sermons or personal devotions should be aware of differences between today's environment and Owen's: different temptations affect the church and individual believers in different eras. Applying insights of the past to circumstances of the present requires a careful look at the historical context of those insights, lest, for example, Owen become a tool of moralism, something he would have strongly opposed.

---

[92]Haigh, 'Theological wars', 325–50, esp. 340–4.
[93]Originally from *A vindication of Mr Sherlock and his principles*, 10. Cited in Haigh, 'Theological wars', 338.
[94]Allison, *The rise of moralism*.

Another matter that is currently being discussed is the extent to which Owen's theology was influenced by his temptation to blend his theology of the kingdom of God with the political events of his day. For example, Daniel Hyde's work shows that Owen's liturgical discussions, including the place of public prayer, need to be understood as a political act since the kingdom of God and the nation of England are at times so difficult to distinguish in Owen's thought.[95] Likewise, if readers today want to appreciate Owen's theology and practice of corporate fasting, for example, they must not just observe his exegesis of relevant biblical passages, but also the hermeneutic of his era, which often assumed such calls for fasting were not merely for individuals or the church but even the state could call for fasting. If readers ignore the contextual moment in which Owen is writing, they run the risk of misrepresentation and misapplying his thought. Therefore, when modern pastors and Christians want to draw from Owen, they must be aware of this tension. On the one hand, some will deeply dislike Owen's theological calls because they carry socio-political overtones that are meant to influence the state; while others will look at the same passages and see Owen's resistance to the early signs of modernist Christianity that reduced the Gospel to personal salvation and ignored social consequences. And, even though Owen may have had a different set of 'political' concerns in mind, there might be strange alliances possible here. Those who have concerns about injustice and greed in economic systems, racism in the church and society, or other problems that are widely recognized in our current historical moment may find in Owen someone who sees the kingdom of God not merely as an influence that changes hearts, but as a dynamic reality that also has social implications. And yet, the preachers and laity who use him to address contemporary issues would need to understand that our voices are not advocating particular issues that concerned Owen (e.g. he never wrote about racism); rather, they are applying his teachings on the kingdom of God and the complexity of the human heart to address current issues. Readers who do this must be aware of the dangers posed by attempting to apply Owen's hope that the kingdom of God would influence the kingdom of this world for good, because it often went in the opposite direction: such interaction may give the power of the political age a greater (and more negative) influence on the church than the church might have on the power structures of our age. But then they must also resist the temptation to reduce the kingdom of God to mere psychological change, with no relevance for the church and world.

---

[95] See Hyde, 'John Owen on public prayer', 238–54.

WORKS OF OWEN

One of the most exciting and promising developments in upcoming Owen studies is a massive new project by Crossway: *The Complete Works of John Owen*. Given that this was last attempted in the middle of the nineteenth century, this is good news indeed. Aiming for a fairly broad audience, the project's editors hope that its volumes will prove useful both to the church and academy. Following roughly the basic framework of two earlier, freshly edited volumes of Owen's work, this series proposes both to make the volumes more accessible (especially to an American audience) and to improve their usefulness to scholars.[96] While academics might have wished for a more critical edition and may not appreciate every change, the new *Works* will be a great improvement over Goold. The new editions will avoid paraphrasing Owen, but will make his work more accessible by adding the following features: checking and correcting the treatises according to the best original editions available; regularizing Owen's Scriptural citations; changing older verb forms to their modern equivalents (e.g. 'seeth' becomes 'sees'); dividing extremely long paragraphs; providing definitions of archaic words; and Americanizing English word forms (e.g. 'colour' becomes 'color'). In a further effort to help modern readers and non-specialists, the following helps will also be added: outlines of the original works; headings throughout that aim to make Owen's order in the treatises more apparent; translations of Latin, Greek and Hebrew terms and texts; explanatory footnotes of people and works that Owen mentions as well as providing references to material that he quotes; with lengthy introductions placing the work in its historical and theological context for modern readers. Lee Gatiss and Shawn Wright are serving as the general editors overseeing the massive project. They have a team of fourteen other editors who are working on individual volumes (or multiple volumes). The complete project should run to thirty-eight volumes. In addition to the material in the original Goold edition and the Hebrews commentary, this series will include almost everything else by Owen that is known to be extant, including new English translations of his Latin works, introductions that he prepared for other books, his correspondence and material related to the Savoy Declaration. The goal is for these volumes to start rolling off the press in 2022. Such a massive project put together by a publishing house that primarily targets pastoral and lay readers means that Owen's reception in the non-academic world will only increase for decades to come.

---

[96]Owen, *Overcoming sin and temptation*; *Communion with the triune God*.

CONCLUSION

Sometimes what you see depends on the vantage point from which you are looking. Some wonder why this verbose Puritan with his sometimes tortured sentences is still read by anyone. Others, however, look to Owen as a doctor of the soul who applies surprisingly effective cures to their abiding problems. On a fairly regular basis I receive emails from pastors and laity who have stumbled upon a work by Owen – often dealing with sin and temptation – and they speak as if he saved their lives. His early modern psychological insights combined with a thick doctrine of sin and salvation appear to be the medicine many need to address the malady they face. Similarly, some theologians bemoan Owen's ongoing influence, especially in terms of his advocacy of particular redemption; while others have found in him valuable nuance for the ongoing task of dogmatics, seeing riches to apply to contemporary theological debates. Whatever one's current opinion of this Puritan divine, it is clear that his influence remains broad and that interest in his life and theology seems only likely to increase.

BIBLIOGRAPHY

*All sections are listed alphabetically except for the section of Owen's works, which are listed chronologically.
*For full titles and abbreviations of Owen's works, see pages xi–xxv.
*Unless otherwise stated, all primary sources listed here that were printed before 1800 were published in London.

MANUSCRIPTS

Edinburgh, New College, MS Comm 1.
London, British Library (BL) Add Ms 23622.
London, Dr Williams's Library (DWL), MSS L6/2, L6/3, L6/4.
London, The National Archives, SP 9/26.
Oxford, Bodleian Library, MSS. Don.

OWEN SOURCES

Owen, John, Θεομαχία αυτεξουσιαστικη: or, a display of Arminianisme (1643).
Owen, John, *The duty of pastors and people distinguished* (1644).
Owen, John, *The principles of the doctrine of Christ unfolded in two short catechismes* (1645).
Owen, John, *A vision of unchangeable free mercy, in sending the means of grace to undeserved sinners* (1646).
Owen, John, *Eben-ezer: a memoriall of the deliverance of Essex, county, and committee* (1648).
Owen, John, *Eshcol: a cluster of the fruit of Canaan* (1648).
Owen, John, *Salus electorum, sanguis Jesu: or, The death of death in the death of Christ* (1648).
Owen, John, *A sermon preached to the Honourable House of Commons, in Parliament assembled: on January 31* (1649).

Owen, John, *Certaine treatises written by John Owen M.A. Sometimes of Queens College in Oxford, now pastor of the church at Coggsehall in Essex. Formerly published at severall times, now reduced into one volume* (1649).
Owen, John, *Ουρανων ουρανια. The shaking and translating of heaven and earth* (1649).
Owen, John, *The branch of the Lord, the beauty of Sion: or, The glory of the Church, in its relation unto Christ* (Edinburgh, 1650).
Owen, John, *Of the death of Christ, the price he paid, and the purchase he made* (1650).
Owen, John, *The stedfastness of promises, and the sinfulness of staggering* (1650).
Owen, John, *The advantage of the kingdom of Christ in the shaking of the kingdoms of the world* (Oxford, 1651).
Owen, John. 'The Epistle Dedicatory', in Henry Whitfield, *Strength out of weakness; or, A glorious manifestation of the further progress of the gospel among the Indians in New England* (1652).
Owen, John, *The labouring saints dismission to rest* (1652).
Owen, John, *The primer: or, An easie way to teach children the true reading of English* (1652).
Owen, John, *The humble proposals of Mr. Owen, Mr. Tho. Goodwin, Mr. Nye, Mr. Sympson, and other ministers, who presented the petition to the Parliament, and other persons, Febr. 11. under debate by a committee this 31. of March, 1652. for the furtherance and propagation of the Gospel in this nation* (1652).
Owen, John, *A sermon preached to the Parliament, Octob. 13. 1652. A day of solemne humiliation* (Oxford, 1652).
Owen, John, *Diatriba de justitia divina* (Oxford, 1653).
Owen, John, 'Preface', in William Twisse, *The riches of God's love unto the vessells of mercy, consistent with his absolute hatred or reprobation of the vessels of wrath* (Oxford, 1653).
Owen, John, *The doctrine of the saints perseverance, explained and confirmed* (Oxford, 1654).
Owen, John, 'Preface', in George Kendall, *Sancti sanciti, or, The common doctrine of the perseverance of the saints* (1654).
Owen, John, 'To the Reader', in William Erye, *Vindiciæ justificationis gratuitæ* (1654).
Owen, John, *Vindiciae evangelicae: or, The mystery of the Gospell vindicated, and Socinianisme examined* (Oxford, 1655).
Owen, John, *God's work in founding Zion, and his peoples duty thereupon. A sermon preached in the Abby Church at Westminster, at the opening of the Parliament Septemb. 17th 1656* (Oxford, 1656).
Owen, John, *God's presence with a people, the spring of their prosperity; with their speciall interest in abiding with Him. A sermon, preached to the Parliament of the Commonwealth of England, Scotland, and Ireland, at Westminster, Octob. 30. 1656. A day of solemn humiliation* (1656).
Owen, John, *Of the mortification of sinne in believers: the necessity, nature, and meanes of it* (Oxford, 1656).
Owen, John, 'Preface', in Lewis Du Moulin, *Paraenesis ad aedificatores imperii in imperi* (1656).
Owen, John, *A review of the annotations of Hugo Grotius, in reference unto the doctrine of the deity, and satisfaction of Christ* (Oxford, 1656).
Owen, John, *Of communion with God the Father, Sonne, and Holy Ghost, each person distinctly; in love, grace, and consolation* (Oxford, 1657).

Owen, John, *Of schisme. The true nature of it discovered and considered, with reference to the present differences in religion* (Oxford, 1657).

Owen, John, 'Preface', in George Kendall, *Fur pro tribunal* (Oxford, 1657).

Owen, John, *A review of the true nature of schisme, with a vindication of the congregationall churches in England, from the imputation thereof unjustly charged on them by Mr D. Cawdrey, preacher of the Word at Billing in Northampton-shire* (Oxford, 1657).

Owen, John, 'An answer to a later treatise of Daniel Cawdrey about the nature of schisme', in John Cotton, *A defence of Mr. John Cotton from the imputation of selfe contradiction, charged on him by Mr. Dan. Cawdrey written by himselfe not long before his death. Whereunto is prefixed, an answer to a late treatise of the said Mr. Cawdrey about the nature of schisme. By John Owen: D.D.* (Oxford, 1658).

Owen, John, *Of temptation, the nature and power of it* (Oxford, 1658).

Owen, John, *Pro Sacris Scripturis adversus hujus tempom Fanaticos exercitaliones apologeticae Quatuor fanaticos* (1658).

Owen, John, *A declaration of the faith and order owned and practiced in the Congregational churches in England* (1659).

Owen, John, *The glory and interest of nations professing the Gospel. Opened in a sermon preached at a private fast, to the Commons assembled in Parliament* (1659).

Owen, John, *Of the divine originall, authority, self-evidencing light, and power of the Scriptures* (Oxford, 1659).

Owen, John, 'Preface', in William Guild, *The throne of David: or, An exposition of the second of Samuell* (Oxford, 1659).

Owen, John, *Unto the questions sent me last night, I pray accept of the ensuing answer, under the title of two questions concerning the power of the supream magistrate about religion, and the worship of God; with one about tythes, proposed and resolved* (1659).

Owen, John, Θεολογουμενα παντοδαπα. *Sive de natura, ortu, progressu, et studio veræ theologiæ libri sex* (Oxford, 1661).

Owen, John, *Animadversions on a treatise intituled Fiat lux* (1662).

Owen, John, *A discourse concerning liturgies, and their imposition* (1662).

Owen, John, *A vindication of the animadversions on Fiat lux* (1664).

Owen, John, *A brief instruction in the worship of God, and discipline of the churches of the New Testament, by way of question and answer with an explication and confirmation of those answers* (1667).

Owen, John, *Indulgence and toleration considered. In a letter unto a person of honour* (1667).

Owen, John, *A peace-offering in an apology and humble plea for indulgence and liberty of conscience. By sundry Protestants differing in some things from the present establishment about the worship of God* (1667).

Owen, John, *Exercitations on the Epistle to the Hebrews, also concerning the Messiah. . . . With an exposition and discourses on the two first chapters of the said epistle to the Hebrews* (1668).

Owen, John, *The nature, power, deceit, and prevalency of the remainders of indwelling-sin in believers* (1668).

Owen, John, *A brief declaration and vindication of the doctrine of the Trinity: as also of the person and satisfaction of Christ* (1669).

Owen, John, 'Christian Reader', in Henry Lukin, *An introduction to Holy Scripture, containing the several tropes, figures, proprieties of speech used therein* (1669).

Owen, John, 'Christian Reader', in T[heophilus] G[ale], *The true idea of Jansenisme, both historick and dogmatick* (1669).

Owen, John, *A practical exposition on the 130th Psalm* (1669).
Owen, John, 'To the Reader', in James Durham, *Clavis cantici: or, An exposition of the Song of Solomon, by James Durham* (1669).
Owen, John, *Truth and innocence vindicated* (1669).
Owen, John, *An account of the grounds and reasons on which Protestant dissenters desire liberty* (1670).
Owen, John, *Reflections on a slanderous libel* (1670).
Owen, John, *Exercitations concerning the name, original, nature, use, and continuance of a day of sacred rest* (1671).
Owen, John, *A discourse concerning evangelical love, church-peace and unity* (1672).
Owen, John, 'Preface', in Joseph Caryl, *The nature and principle of love, as the end of the commandment* (1673).
Owen, John, 'Preface', in Vavasor Powell, *A new and useful concordance to the Holy Bible* (1673).
Owen, John, 'To the reader', in Edward Polhill, *The divine will considered in its eternal decrees and holy execution of them* (1673).
Owen, John, 'Christian Reader', in Samuel Petto, *The difference between the old and new covenant stated and explained: with an exposition of the covenant of grace in the principal concernments of it* (1674).
Owen, John, *Exercitations on the epistle to the Hebrews, concerning the priesthood of Christ. . . . With a continuation of the exposition on the third, fourth, and fifth chapters of said epistle to the Hebrews* (1674).
Owen, John, 'Preface', in Thomas Gourge, *The surest and safest way of thriving* (1674).
Owen, John, 'Preface', in Increase Mather, *Some important truths about conversion, delivered in sundry sermons* (1674).
Owen, John, 'To the Reader', in Henry Scudder, *The Christians daily walk, in holy security and peace* (1674).
Owen, John, *A vindication of some passages in a discourse concerning communion with God, from the exceptions of William Sherlock, rector of St. George Buttolph-Lane* (1674).
Owen, John, *Πνευματολογια: or, A discourse concerning the Holy Spirit* (1674).
Owen, John, 'The testimony of the church is not the only, nor the chief reason, of our believing the Scripture to be the word of God', in *The morning-exercise against popery, or, The principal errors of the Church of Rome* (1675).
Owen, John, 'How may we bring our hearts to receive reproofs', in *A supplement to the morning-exercises at Cripplegate: or, Several more cases of conscience practically resolved by sundry ministers* (1676).
Owen, John, *The nature of apostasie from the profession of the Gospel, and the punishment of apostates declared, in an exposition of Heb. 6. 4, 5, 6* (1676).
Owen, John, 'To the Reader', in James Durham, *The law unsealed, or, A practical exposition of the Ten Commandments* (1676).
Owen, John, *The doctrine of justification by faith through the imputation of the righteousness of Christ, explained, confirmed, & vindicated* (1677).
Owen, John, 'Preface', in Samuel Corbyn, *An awakening call from the eternal God to the unconverted* (1677).
Owen, John, *The reason of faith: or, An answer unto that enquiry, wherefore we believe the Scripture to be the word of God* (1677).

Owen, John, 'To the Reader', in Patrick Gillespie, *The ark of the covenant opened: or, A treatise of the covenant of redemption between God and Christ, as the foundation of the covenant of grace* (1677).
Owen, John, 'To the Christian Reader', in Elisha Coles, *A practical discourse of God's sovereignty: with other material points deriving thence* (1678).
Owen, John, Σύνεσις πνευματική: *or, The causes, waies & means of understanding the mind of God as revealed in his word, with assurance therein* (1678).
Owen, John, Χριστολογια: *or, A declaration of the glorious mystery of the person of Christ, God and Man* (1679).
Owen, John, *The Church of Rome, no safe guide* (1679).
Owen, John, *A brief vindication of the non-conformists from the charge of schism* (1680).
Owen, John, *A continuation of the exposition of the Epistle of Paul the Apostle to the Hebrews viz, on the sixth, seventh, eight, ninth, and tenth chapters* (1680).
Owen, John, 'Preface', in Stephen Lobb, *The glory of free grace display'd: or, The transcendant excellency of the love of God in Christ unto believing, repenting sinners in some mea-sure describ'd* (1680).
Owen, John, *Some considerations about union among Protestants, and the preservation of the interest of the Protestant religion in this nation* (1680).
Owen, John, *An enquiry into the original, nature, institution, power, order and communion of evangelical churches* (1681).
Owen, John, *An humble testimony unto the goodness and severity of God in his dealing with sinful churches and nations* (1681).
Owen, John, 'To the Reader', in Bartholomew Ashwood, *The best treasure: or, The way to be truly rich* (1681).
Owen, John, Φρόνεμα του πνεύματου: *or, The grace and duty of being spiritually-minded, declared and practically improved* (1681).
Owen, John, *A brief and impartial account of the nature of the Protestant religion* (1682).
Owen, John, *A discourse of the work of the Holy Spirit in prayer* (1682).
Owen, John, *The chamber of imagery in the Church of Rome laid open*. In *A continuation of morning exercises questions and cases of conscience, practically resolved by sundry ministers* (1683).
Owen, John, 'Preface', in Samuel Clark, *The New Testament of our Lord and Saviour Jesus Christ, with annotations* (1683).
Owen, John, 'To the Reader', in William Benn, *Soul prosperity, in several sermons* (1683).
Owen, John, *A continuation of the exposition of the Epistle of Paul the Apostle to the Hebrews viz, on the eleventh, twelfth & thirteenth chapters, compleating that elaborate work* (1684).
Owen, John, *Meditations and discourses on the glory of Christ, in his person, office, and grace, with the differences between faith and sight* (1684).
Owen, John, *A treatise of the dominion of sin and grace* (1688).
Owen, John, *The true nature of a Gospel church and its government* (1689).
Owen, John, *Seasonable words for English Protestants* (1690).
Owen, John, *Meditations and discourses concerning the glory of Christ applyed unto unconverted sinners, and saints under spiritual decayes* (1691).
Owen, John, *A guide to church-fellowship and order, according to the Gospel-institution* (1692).

Owen, John, *Two discourses concerning the Holy Spirit, and his work* (1693).
Owen, John, *Gospel grounds and evidences of the faith of God's elect* (1695).
Owen, John, *An answer unto two questions: by the late judicious John Owen, D.D.* (1720).
Owen, John, *Seventeen sermons preach'd by the late Reverend and learned John Owen, D.D.* 2 volumes (1720).
Owen, John, *A complete collection of the sermons of the Reverend and learned John Owen, D.D.* (1721).
Owen, John, *The works of the late Reverend and learned John Owen, D.D.* (1721).
Owen, John, *Eene uitlegginge van den sendbrief van Paulus den apostel aen de Hebreen*, 4 vols., ed. Simon Commincq (Rotterdam, 1733–1740).
Owen, John, *Thirteen sermons preached on various occasions* (1756).
Owen, John, *Twenty-five discourses suitable to the Lord's Supper, delivered just before the administration of that sacred ordinance* (1760).
Owen, John, *A treatise on the extent of the death of Christ. Being an abridgement of Dr. Owen's Death of death in the death of Christ, with a recommendatory preface by the Rev. Charles de Coetlogon* (1770).
Owen, John, *An exposition of the epistle to the Hebrews; with the preliminary exercitations, by John Owen, D.D., revised and abridged, with a full and interesting life of the author*, 4 vols., ed. Edward Williams (1790).
Owen, John, *Marweiddiad pechod mewn credinwyr* (Mwythig, 1796).
Owen, John, *An exposition of the epistle to the Hebrews, with the preliminary exercitations*, 7 vols., ed. George Wright (Edinburgh, 1812–1814).
Owen, John, *The works of John Owen*, 21 vols., ed. Thomas Russell (London: Paternoster, 1826).
Owen, John, *Evangelical theology: a translation of the sixth book of Dr. Owen's Latin work entitled* Theologoumena, trans. John Craig (Edinburgh: M. Paterson, 1837).
Owen, John, *The works of John Owen*, 24 vols., ed. William H. Goold (Edinburgh: Johnstone and Hunter, 1850–1855).
Owen, John, *Hebrews: the epistle of warning*, ed. M. J. Tryon (Grand Rapids, MI: Kregel, 1953).
Owen, John, *The Holy Spirit: his gifts and power, exposition of the Spirit's name, nature, personality, dispensation, operations and effects* (Grand Rapids, MI: Kregel, 1954).
Owen, John, *The death of death in the death of Christ* (Edinburgh: Banner of Truth, 1959).
Owen, John, *The works of John Owen*, 23 vols., ed. William H. Goold, reprint (Edinburgh: Banner of Truth, 1965 [vols. 1–16]; 1991 [vols. 17–23 on Hebrews]).
Owen, John, *The correspondence of John Owen (1616–1683): with an account of his life and work*, ed. Peter Toon (Cambridge: James Clarke, 1970).
Owen, John, *The Oxford orations of Dr. John Owen*, ed. Peter Toon (Cornwall: Gospel Communications, 1971).
Owen, John, *Sin and temptation: the challenge of personal godliness*, ed. James M. Houston (Portland, OR: Multnomah, 1983).
Owen, John, *Hebrews*, eds Alister McGrath and J. I. Packer (Wheaton, IL: Crossway, 1988).
Owen, John, *Thinking spiritually [from The grace and duty of being spiritually minded]* (London: Grace Publications, 1989).

Owen, John, *Communion with God*, ed. R. K. Law (Edinburgh: Banner of Truth, 1991).
Owen, John, *Apostasy from the gospel*, ed. R. J. K. Law (Edinburgh: Banner of Truth, 1992).
Owen, John, *Christians are forever* [from *The doctrine of the saints' perseverance explained and confirmed*], ed. H. Lawrence (Darlington: Evangelical Press, 1993).
Owen, John, *The glory of Christ*, ed. R. J. K. Law (Edinburgh: Banner of Truth, 1994).
Owen, John, *Biblical theology: the history of theology from Adam to Christ*, trans. Stephen P. Westcott (Morgan, PA: Soli Deo Gloria, 1994).
Owen, John, *The mortification of sin: a Puritan's view of how to deal with sin in your life* (Fearn, UK: Christian Heritage, 1996).
Owen, John, *The Holy Spirit*, ed. R. J. K. Law (Edinburgh: Banner of Truth, 1998).
Owen, John, *The Spirit and the church*, ed. R. J. K. Law (Edinburgh: Banner of Truth, 2002).
Owen, John, *The Holy Spirit: his gifts and power* (Fearn, UK: Christian Heritage, 2004).
Owen, John, *Meditations on the glory of Christ* (Fearn, UK: Christian Heritage, 2004).
Owen, John, *The doctrine of justification by faith: with an introductory essay by Carl R. Trueman* (Grand Rapids, MI: Reformation Heritage Books, 2006).
Owen, John, *Overcoming sin and temptation: three classic works by John Owen*, eds Kelly M. Kapic and Justin Taylor (Wheaton, MI: Crossway, 2006).
Owen, John, *Communion with God* (Fearn, UK: Christian Heritage, 2007).
Owen, John, *Communion with the Triune God*, eds Kelly M. Kapic and Justin Taylor (Wheaton, IL: Crossway, 2007).
Owen, John, *Spiritual-mindedness*, ed. R. J. K. Law (Edinburgh: Banner of Truth, 2009).
Owen, John, *The priesthood of Christ* (Fearn, UK: Christian Heritage, 2010).

PRIMARY SOURCES

'The life of the late Reverend and learned John Owen', in *Seventeen sermons preach'd by the late Reverend and learning John Owen* (London: William and Joseph Marshall, 1720).
'Truthsbye, Thomas', *A serious letter to Dr. John Owen, sent by a small friend of his* (1659).
[Cane, John Vincent], *An epistle to the authour of the Animadversions upon Fiat lux in excuse and justification of Fiat lux against the said animadversions* (Douai: s.n., 1663).
[Cane, John Vincent], *Fiat lux or, a general conduct to a right understanding in the great combustions and broils about religion here in England. Betwixt Papist and Protestant, Presbyterian & Independent to the end that moderation and quietnes may at length hapily ensue after so various tumults in the kingdom* (Douai: s.n., 1661).
[London Provincial Assembly], *An exhortation to catechizing* (1655).
[Racovian Catechism], *Catechesis ecclesiarum quae in regno Poloniae & magno ducatu Lithuaniae, & aliis ad istud regnum pertinentibus provinciis, affirmant, neminem alium praeter patrem Domini nostri Iesu Christi, esse illum unim Deum Israëlis: hominem autem illum Iesum Nazarenum, qui ex virgine natus est, nec alium, praeter*

aut ante ipsum, Dei filium unigenitum & agnoscunt & confitentur (Racov [London: William Dugard], 1652).

[Savoy Declaration], *A declaration of the faith and order owned and practised in the Congregational Churches in England* (1658).

[Savoy Declaration], *The Savoy declaration of faith and order, 1658*, ed. A. G. Matthews (London: Independent Press, 1958).

[Savoy Declaration], *The Savoy declaration*, in *The creeds of Christendom*, ed. Philip Schaff and rev. David S. Schaff (1931; rpr. Grand Rapids, MI: Baker, 1983).

[Walton, Brian], *Biblia sacra polyglotta, complectentia textus originales Hebraicum, cum Pentateucho Samaritano, Chaldaicum, Graecum*, 6 vols (1653–1657).

[Westminster Assembly], *The humble advice of the Assembly of Divines . . . concerning a shorter catechism* (1648).

[Westminster Assembly], *The humble advice of the Assembly of Divines . . . concerning part of a Confession of Faith, presented by them lately to both Houses of Parliament* (1646).

[Westminster Assembly], *The minutes and papers of the Westminster Assembly, 1643–1652*, 5 vols., ed. Chad van Dixhoorn (Oxford: Oxford University Press, 2012).

A declaration of the Lords and Commons assembled in Parliament concerning the papers of the Scots Commissioners (1648).

A dialogue between the pope and the devil, about Owen and Baxter (1681).

Concerning some of Dr. Owens principles and practices (1670).

A new confession of faith, or the first principles of the Christian religion necessary to be laid as a foundation by all such as desire to build on unto perfection. Represented by a committee of divines ... unto the Grand Committee on Religion as fitt to be owned by all such ministers as are or shall be allowed to receive publique maintenance for their works in the ministry. Propounded to the Parliament 12 Dec. (1654).

A Vindication of Mr Sherlock and his principles (1677).

Acts and ordinances of the Interregnum, 1642–1660, eds C. H. Firth and R. S. Rait (London: H.M. Stationery Office, 1911).

Alsop, Vincent, *Melius Inquirendum, or A sober inquiry into the reasonings of the serious inquiry* (1679).

Alsted, Johann, *Praecognitorum theologicorum libri duo: naturam theologiae explicantes, & rationem studii illius plenissime monstrantes* (Frankfurt, 1614).

Alvarez, Diego, *De auxiliis gratiae et humanae arbitrii viribus et libertate* (Rome, 1610).

Alvarez, Diego, *Disputationes theologicæ in primam secundæ S. Thomæ, in quibus præcipua omina quæ adversus doctrinam ejusdem et communem Thomistarum a diversis auctoribus impugnantur, juxta legitimum sensum præceptoris angelici explicantur et defenduntur* (Trani, 1617; Cologne, 1621).

Alvarez, Diego and Domingo Banez, *Apologetica fratrum praedicatorum in provincia Hispaniae sacrae theologiae professorum, adversus novas quasdam assertiones cujusdam doctoris Ludovici Molinae nuncupate* (Madrid, 1595).

An essay towards settlement (1659).

Aquinas, Thomas, *Summa theologiae: Latin text and English translation* (London: Blackfriars with Eyre and Spottiswoode, 1964–81).

Aquinas, Thomas, *Summa theologica*, trans. the Fathers of the English Dominican Province, 5 vols (1911; repr. Westminster, MD: Christian Classics, 1981).

Augustine, *Confessions*, in Philip Schaff (ed.), *Nicene and Post-Nicene Fathers, First Series*, vol. 1 (Grand Rapids, MI: Baker, 1994).
Austen, Ralph, *The spirituall use of an orchard, or garden of fruit-trees* (Oxford, 1657).
Bacon, Francis, *The works of Francis Bacon*, ed. Graham Rees et al (Oxford: Oxford University Press, 1995-present).
Ball, John, *A treatise of the covenant of grace* (1645).
Banez, Domingo, *Scholastica commentaria in primam partem Summae Theologiae S. Thomae Aquinatis* (Salamanca, 1584).
Barclay, Robert, *Universal love considered and established upon its right foundation* (1677).
Barrow, Henry, *A brief discoverie of the false church* (Dordrecht, 1590).
Baxter, Richard, *A paraphrase on the New Testament* (1685).
Baxter, Richard, *An apology for the nonconformists ministry* (1681).
Baxter, Richard, *Aphorismes of justification, with their explication annexed* (1649).
Baxter, Richard, *Calendar of the correspondence of Richard Baxter*, 2 vols., eds N. H. Keeble and G. F. Nuttall (Oxford: Clarendon Press, 1991).
Baxter, Richard, *A Christian directory, or, A summ of practical theologie and cases of conscience* (1673).
Baxter, Richard, *Church-history of the government of bishops and their councils* (1680).
Baxter, Richard, *Five disputations of church-government and worship* (1659).
Baxter, Richard, *Methodus theologiae christianae* (1681).
Baxter, Richard, *R. Baxter's confession of his faith* (1655).
Baxter, Richard, *Reliquiae Baxterianae*, gen. ed. N. H. Keeble, 5 vols (Oxford: Oxford University Press, 2020).
Baxter, Richard, *Reliquiae Baxterianae: or, Mr. Richard Baxters narrative of the most memorable passages of his life and times*, 3 vols (1696).
Baxter, Richard, *The Christian religion. Expressed I. briefly, in the ancient creeds, the ten commandments, and the Lords prayer* (1660).
Baxter, Richard, *The reasons of the Christian religion. The first part, of godliness: proving by natural evidence the being of God, the necessity of holiness, and a future life of retribution; the sinfulness of the world; the desert of hell; and what hope of recovery mercies intimate. The second part, of Christianity: proving by evidence supernatural and natural, the certain truth of the Christian belief: and answering the objections of unbelievers. by Richard Baxter ... also an appendix defending the soul's immortality against the Somatists or Epicureans and other pseudo-philosophers* (1667).
Baxter, Richard, *Which is the true church?* (1679).
Bellarmine, Robert, *Opera omnia* (Naples: Josephum Giuliano, 1856–62).
Bentley, Richard, *The folly and unreasonableness of atheism* (1693).
Boyle, Robert, *New experiments physico-mechanical, touching the air. Whereunto is added a defense of the author's explication of the experiments, against the objections of Franciscus Linus and Thomas Hobbes* (1662).
Boyle, Robert, *Occasional reflections upon several subjects, whereto is premis'd a discourse about such kinds of thoughts* (1665).
Bradshaw, William, *English Puritanisme* (1641).
Bradshaws ultimum vale (1660).
Brooks, Thomas, *The complete works of Thomas Brooks*, 5 vols., ed. A. B. Grosart (Edinburgh: James Nichol, 1866).

Bunyan, John, *Grace abounding to the chief of sinners* (1666).
Bunyan, John, *The holy war*, eds Roger Sharrock and James F. Forrest (Oxford: Oxford University Press, 1980).
Burges, Cornelius, *Baptismall regeneration of elect infants professed by the Church of England, according to the Scriptures, the primitive church, the present Reformed churches, and many particular divines apart* (1629).
Burgess, Anthony, *The true doctrine of justification in two parts* (1655).
Burroughs, Jeremiah, *Irenicum, to the lovers of truth and peace. Heart-divisions opened in the causes and evils of them: with cautions that we may not be hurt by them, and endeavours to heal them* (1645).
Calvin, John, *Commentaries on the Epistle of Paul the Apostle to the Hebrews*, trans. John Owen (Edinburgh: Calvin Translation Society, 1853).
Calvin, John, *Commentaries on the first book of Moses, called Genesis*, trans. John King (Grand Rapids: Eerdmans, 1948).
Calvin, John, *Institutes of the Christian religion*, ed. John T. McNeill, trans. Ford Lewis Battles (Louisville, KY: Westminster John Knox Press, 2006).
Caryl, Joseph, *The nature and principles of love* (1673).
Casaubon, Meric, *A vindication of the Lords prayer, as a formal prayer, and by Christ's institution to be used by Christians as a prayer: against the antichristian practice and opinion of some men. Wherein, also their private and ungrounded zeal is discovered, who are very strict for the observation of the Lords Day, and make so light of the Lords prayer* (1660).
Cawdrey, Daniel, *Independencie a great schism proved against Dr. Owen, his apology in his tract of schism: as also an appendix to the former discourse, shewing the inconstancy of the Dr. and the inconsistency of his former and present opinions* (1657).
Charleton, Walter, *Physiologia Epicuro-Gassendo-Charltoniana* (1654).
Charnock, Stephen, *The complete works of Stephen Charnock* (Edinburgh: James Nichol, 1864–6).
Cheynell, Francis, *The divine Triunity of the Father, Son, and Holy Spirit, or, the blessed doctrine of the three coessentiall subsistents in the eternall Godhead without any confusion or division of the distinct subsistences or multiplication of the most single and entire Godhead acknowledged, beleeved, adored by Christians, in opposition to Pagans, Jewes, Mahumetans, blasphemous and antichristian hereticks, who say they are Christians, but are not* (1650).
Chillingworth, William, *The religion of Protestants a safe way to salvation* (Oxford, 1638).
Cicero, *De officiis* (Paris: Antonium Augustinum Renouard, 1796).
Clagett, William, *A discourse concerning the operations of the Holy Spirit together with a confutation of some part of Dr. Owen's book upon that subject* (1678).
Clarkson, David, 'A funeral sermon of the much lamented death of the late reverend and learned divine John Owen, D. D.', in *Seventeen sermons preached by the late reverend and learned John Owen, D.D.*, 2 vols (London: William and Joseph Marshall, 1720).
Claude, John, *An essay on the composition of a sermon: translated from the original French of the Revd. John Claude, minister of the French Reformed Church at Charenton. With notes by Robert Robinson*, 2 vols (Cambridge, 1779).
Cotton, John, *Certain queries tending to an accommodation and communion of Presbyteriall and Congregational churches* (1654).

Cotton, John, *The keyes of the kingdom of heaven, and power thereof, according to the word of God* (1644).
Coxe, Nehemiah, *A discourse of the covenants that God made with men before the law* (1681).
Crell, Johann, *Tractatus de Spiritu Sancto qui fidelibus datur* (s.l.: s.n., 1650).
Crippen, T. G., 'Dr. Watts's church-book', *Transactions of the Congregational Historical Society* 1 (1901).
Cromwell, Henry, *The correspondence of Henry Cromwell*, ed. Peter Gaunt (Cambridge: Cambridge University Press, 2008).
Cromwell, Oliver, *A declaration of the Lord Lieutenant of Ireland, for the undeceiving of deluded and seduced people* (1649).
Crowe, William, *An exact collection or catalogue of our English writers on the Old and New Testament, either in whole, or in part* (1663).
Crowe, William, *An exact collection or catalogue of our English writers on the Old and New Testament, either in whole, or in part*, second impression (1668).
Cudworth, Ralph, *The true intellectual system of the universe. Wherein all the reason and philosophy of atheism is confuted and its impossibility demonstrated* (1678).
d'Ewes, Simonds, 'Journal of the House of Commons: April 1571', in *The journals of all the Parliaments during the reign of Queen Elizabeth* (1682), 155–80.
Davenant, John, *A thesis on the death of Christ*, in *An exposition of the epistle of St. Paul to the Colossians*, vol. 2, trans. Josiah Allport (London: Hamilton, Adams and Co., 1832).
Davenant, John, *A treatise on justification, or The disputatio de justitia habituali et actuali* (1631).
Davenant, John, *Animadversions written by the Right Reverend Father in God, John, Lord Bishop of Salisbury, upon a treatise intituled, Gods love to mankinde* (1641).
Davenant, John, *Dissertationes duæ: prima De morte Christi . . . altera De prædestinatione & reprobatione. Quibus subnectitur ejusdem sententia de Gallicana controversia* (Cambridge, 1650).
de Molina, Luis, *Liberi arbritrii cum gratiae donis, divina praescientia, providential, praedestinatione et reprobatione concordia* (Lisbon, 1588).
Debates of the House of Commons, from the year 1667 to the year 1694, ed. A. Grey (London, 1763).
Dell, William, *The tryal of Spirits both in teachers & hearers* (1653).
Deering, Edward, *XXVII. Lectures, or readings, upon part of the epistle written to the Hebrues* (1576).
Dickson, David, *A short explanation of the epistle of Paul to the Hebrews* (Aberdene [sic], 1635).
Downame, George, *A treatise of justification: wherein is first set down the true doctrine in the causes effects fruites consequents of it, according to the word of God* (1634).
Durham, James, *Clavis cantici: or, An exposition of the Song of Solomon* (Edinburgh, 1668).
Edwards, Jonathan, *Letters and personal writings. The Works of Jonathan Edwards.*, ed. George S. Claghorn (Yale: Yale University Press, 1998).
Edwards, Jonathan, 'The wisdom of God, displayed in the way of salvation', in Samuel Hopkins, *The life and character of the late Reverend Mr. Jonathan Edwards, President of the College at New-Jersey. Together with a number of his sermons on various important subjects* (Boston: S. Kneeland, 1765).

Edwards, Jonathan, *True grace distinguished from the experience of devils* (New York, 1791).
Eleutherius, Theodorus, *Historia controversarium de divinæ gratiæ auxiliis sub Summis Pontificibus Clement VIII et Paulo V* (Venice, 1742).
Episcopius, Simon, *Antidotum contines pressiorem declaratioem propriae et genuine senetentiae quae in Synodo Nationali Dordracena est et stabilita* (Leiden, 1620).
Faces about, or, A recrimination charged upon Mr. John Goodwin (1644).
Ferguson, Robert, *The interest of reason in religion with the import & use of scripture-metaphors, and the nature of the union betwixt Christ & believers: (with reflections on several late writings, especially Mr. Sherlocks Discourse concerning the knowledg of Jesus Christ, &c.) modestly enquired into and stated* (1675).
Fisher, Edward, *The marrow of modern divinity* (1645).
Fisher, Samuel, *Rusticus ad academicos in exercitationibus expostulatoriis, apologeticis quatuor* (1660).
Flacius Illyricus, Matthias, *Clavis scripturae, seu de sermon sacrarum literarum* (Basil, 1567).
Flavel, John, *Vindiciæ legis & foederis: or, A reply to Mr. Philip Cary's solemn call wherein he pretends to answer all the arguments of Mr. Allen, Mr. Baxter, Mr. Sydenham, Mr. Sedgwick, Mr. Roberts, and Dr. Burthogge, for the right of believers infants to baptism, by proving the law at Sinai, and the covenant of circumcision with Abraham, were the very same with Adam's covenant of works, and that because the gospel-covenant is absolute* (1690).
Fowler, Edward, *The principles and practices of certain moderate divines of the Church of England, (greatly mis-understood) truly represented and defended; wherein (by the way) some controversies, of no mean importance, are succinctly discussed: in a free discourse between two intimate friends* (1670).
Fox, George, *The journal of George Fox*, ed. John L. Nickalls (Philadelphia, PA: Religious Society of Friends, 1985).
Gale, Theophilus, *The court of the gentiles, or, A discourse touching the original of human literature, both philologie and philosophie, from the Scriptures and Jewish church. in order to a demonstration of 1. The perfection of Gods word and church light, 2. The imperfection of natures light and mischief of vain philosophie, 3. The right use of human learning and especially sound philosophie* (Oxford, 1670).
Gassendi, Pierre, *Animadversiones in decimum librum Diogenis Laertii qui est de vita, moribus placitiisque Epicuri* (Lyon, 1649).
Glasius, Salomon, *Philologiae Sacrae, qua totius sacrosanctae Veteris et Novi Testamenti scripturae: tùm stylus & literatura, tùm sensus & genuinae interpretationis ratio expenditure*, second edition (Jena, 1623).
Goodman, John, *A serious and compassionate inquiry into the causes of the present neglect and contempt of the Protestant religion and Church of England* (1674).
Goodwin, John, *Apolytrosis apolytroseos, or, Redemption redeemed* (1651).
Goodwin, Thomas, *The works of Thomas Goodwin* (Edinburgh: John Nichol, 1861).
Gouge, William, *A learned and very useful commentary on the whole epistle to the Hebrews wherein every word and particle in the original is explained* (1655).
Gregory of Nyssa, *Gregory of Nyssa: Contra Eunomium I. An English translation with supporting studies*, ed. Miguel Brugarolas (Leiden: Brill, 2018).
Grevinchovius, Nicolaas, *Dissertatio theologica de duabus quaestionibus hoc tempore controversis . . . inter Gvilielmum Amesium theologum anglum, & Nicolaum Grevinchovium, ecclesiastem Roterodamensenm* (Rotterdam, 1615).

Grotius, Hugo, *Defensio fidei catholicae de satisfactione Christi, adversus Faustum Socinum Senensem* (Leiden, 1617).
Hall, Joseph, *The arte of divine meditation profitable for all Christians* (1606).
Hammond, Henry, *Charis kai eirene, or, A pacifick discourse of Gods grace and decrees* (1660).
Harrab, Thomas, *Tessaradelphus, or The four brothers* ([Lancashire?], 1616).
Henry, Lukin, *An introduction to the Holy Scripture, containing the several tropes, figures, proprieties of speech used therein; with other observations, necessary to the right understanding thereof* (1669).
Henry, Matthew, *An account of the life and death of Mr. Philip Henry, minister of the gospel near Whitechurch in Shropshire, who dy'd June 24, 1696, in the sixty fifth year of his age* (1698).
Herbert, George, *The temple: Sacred poems and private ejaculations* (Cambridge, 1633).
Heylyn, Peter, *Aerius redivivus: or, The history of the Presbyterians* (Oxford, 1670).
Heylyn, Peter, *Ecclesias restaurata*, ed. J. C. Robertson (Cambridge, 1849).
Heylyn, Peter, *Theologia veterum: or, The summe of Christian theologie, positive, polemical, and philological, contained in the Apostles Creed, or reducible to it: according to the rendries of the ancients both Greeks and Latines. In three books* (1654).
Hoard, Samuel, *Gods love to mankind manifested, by dis-prooving his absolute decree for their damnation* (s.l.: s.n., 1633).
Hobbes, Thomas, *Considerations upon the reputation, loyalty, manners & religion of Thomas Hobbes of Malmsbury written by himself* (1680).
Hobbes, Thomas, *Dialogus physicus* (1661), trans. Simon Schaffer, in *Leviathan and the air pump* (Princeton, NJ: Princeton University Press, 1985).
Hobbes, Thomas, *Three papers presented to the Royal Society against Dr. Wallis together with considerations on Dr. Wallis his answer to them* (1671).
Hopkins, Ezekiel, and Josiah Pratt, *The works of the right reverend father in God, Ezekiel Hopkins* (London: C. Whittingham, 1809).
Howe, John, *The works of the Rev. John Howe, M. A.* (New York: John P. Haven, 1838).
Hutchinson, Lucy, *On the principles of the Christian religion, addressed to her daughter; and Of theology* (London: Longman et al., 1817).
Hutchinson, Lucy, *Order and disorder*, ed. David Norbrook (Oxford: Blackwell, 2001).
Hutchinson, Lucy, *The works of Lucy Hutchinson*, gen. ed. David Norbrook (Oxford: Oxford University Press, 2011–present).
Ireland, Thomas, *Momus elencticus* (1654).
Jackson, Thomas, *A treatise of the divine essence and attributes*, 2 parts (1628–1629).
Johnston, Archibald, of Wariston, *Diary*, 3 vols (Edinburgh: Scottish History Society, 1911).
Jones, William, *A commentary upon the epistles of Saint Paul to Philemon, and to the Hebrewes, together with a compendious explication of the second and third epistles of Saint John* (1635).
Journal of the House of Commons: volume 7, 1651–1660 (London: HMSO, 1802).
Junius, Franciscus, *De theologia vera; Ortu, natura, formis, partibus, et modo* (Lugduni Batavorum, 1594).
Junius, Franciscus, *Opuscula theologica selecta recognovit et praefatus est D. Abr. Kuyperus* (Amsterdam: Frederick Muller, 1882).

Lawson, George, *An exposition of the epistle to the Hebrewes wherein the text is cleared, theopolitica improved, the Socinian comment examined* (1662).

Lechford, Thomas, *Plain dealing: or, Newes from New-England* (1642).

Leigh, Edward, *A systeme or body of divinity consisting of ten books: wherein the fundamentals and main grounds of religion are opened, the contrary errours refuted, most of the controversies between us, the papists, Arminians, and Socinians discussed and handled, several Scriptures explained and vindicated from corrupt glosses: a work seasonable for these times, wherein so many articles of our faith are questioned, and so many gross errours daily published* (1654).

Leigh, Edward, *A systeme or body of divinity: consisting in ten books wherein the fundamentals of religion are opened; the contrary errours refuted; most of the controversies between us, the Papists, Arminians, and Socinians discussed and handled; several Scriptures explained, and vindicated from corrupt glosses* (1654; second edition, corrected and enlarged, 1662).

Lewgar, J., *The only way to rest of soule in religion here, in heaven hereafter* (1657).

Locke, John, *Some thoughts concerning education* (1693).

Locke, John, *The educational writings of John Locke*, ed. James L. Axtell (Cambridge: Cambridge University Press, 1968).

Lombard, Peter, *The Sentences*, trans. Giulio Silano (Toronto: Pontifical Institute of Medical Studies, 2008).

Lucius, Ludovicus, *De satisfactione Christi, pro peccatis nostris iustitiae divinae praestita, inter Michaelem Gittichium socinianum, et Ludovicum Lucium orthodoxum, scholastica & epistolica disceptatio: coniuncta est, nova hac editione, Synopsis antisociniana, qua tota Fausti Socini disputatio, de Servatore, breviter excutitur ac refutatur* (Basel: Henric-Petrinos, 1628).

[Lushington, Thomas,] *The expiation of a sinner in a commentary upon the epistle to the Hebrewes* (1646).

Marshall, Walter, *The gospel-mystery of sanctification* (1692).

Marvell, Andrew, *Remarks upon a late disingenuous discourse, writ by one T.D. under the pretence de causa Dei* (1678).

Mastricht, Petrus van, *Theoretical-practical theology* (Grand Rapids, MI: Reformation Heritage, 2018-).

Mastricht, Petrus van, *Theoretico-practica theologia, qua, per singula capita theologica, pars exegetica, dogmatica, elenchtica & practica, perpetua successione conjugantur. Editio nova, accedunt: historia ecclesiastica plena fere, quanquam compendiosa: idea theologiae moralis: hypotyposis theologiae asceticae &c* (Utrecht: W. van de Water, 1724).

Mather, Increase, *Diary by Increase Mather, March, 1675–December, 1676. Together with extracts from another diary by him, 1674–1687*, introduced and edited by Samuel A. Green (Cambridge: John Wilson and Son, 1900).

Millington, Edward, *Bibliotheca Oweniana, sive catalogus librorum plurimus facultatibus insignium, instructissimae bibliothecae Rev. Doct. Vir. D. Joan Oweni, (quondam Vice-Cancellarii & Decani Edis-Christi in Academia Oxoniensi) nuperrimè defuncti, cum variis manuscriptis Grecis, Latinis &c. propria manu doct. patric. junii aliorumq conscriptis, quorum auctio habebitur Londini apud domum auctionariam ex adverso Nigri Cygni, in vico vulgò dicto Ave-Mary-Lane, propè Ludgate-Street, vicesimo sexto die Maii* (1684).

Milton, John, *Letters of state written by Mr. John Milton, to most of the sovereign princes and republicks of Europe, from the year 1649, till the year 1659; to which is* added, an account of his life; together with several of his poems, and a catalogue of his works, never before printed (1694).

Milton, John, *Of education* (1644).

Milton, John, *The complete poetry and essential prose of John Milton*, eds William Kerrigan et al (New York: The Modern Library, 2007).

Moderation a vertue, or, A vindication of the principles and practices of the moderate divines and laity of the Church of England represented in some late immoderate discourses, under the nick-names of Grindalizers and Trimmers (1683).

Moore, Thomas, *The universallity of God's free-grace in Christ to mankind* (1646).

More, Henry, *The second lash of Alazonomastix, laid on in mercie upon that stubborn youth Eugenius Philalethes* (Cambridge, 1651).

Musculus, Wolfgang, *In sacrosanctum Davidis Psalterium commentarii* (Basel: Johannes Herwagen, 1551).

Osborne, Francis, *The private Christians non vltra, or, A plea for the lay-man's interpreting the Scriptures* (Oxford, 1656).

Parker, Samuel, *A defence and continuation of the ecclesiastical politie by way of letter to a friend in London: together with a letter from the author of The friendly debate* (1671).

Parker, Samuel, *A discourse of ecclesiastical politie wherein the authority of the civil magistrate over the consciences of subjects in matters of external religion is asserted: the mischiefs and inconveniences of toleration are represented, and all the pretenses pleaded in behalf of liberty of conscience are fully answered* (1671).

Pemble, William, *Vindiciae fidei: or, A treatise of justification by faith* (1625).

Perkins, William, *A golden chaine: or, The description of theologie containing the order of the causes of salvation and damnation* (1591).

Petto, Samuel, *The difference between the old and new covenant stated and explained with an exposition of the covenant of grace in the principal concernments of it* (1674).

Polanus, Amandus, *Syntagma theologiae Christianae ab amando Polano a Polansdorf* (Hanoviae, 1610).

Preston, John, *The doctrine of the saints infirmities* (1637).

Proposals for the furtherance and propagation of the Gospel in this nation. As the same were humbly presented to the Honourable Committee of Parliament by divers ministers of the gospell, and others. As also, some principles of Christian religion, without the beliefe of which, the Scriptures doe plainly and clearly affirme, salvation is not to be obtained. Which were also presented in explanation of one of the said proposals (1652).

Ray, John, *The wisdom of God manifested in the works of creation* (1691).

Roberts, Francis. *Clavis Bibliorum, the key of the Bible, unlocking the richest treasury of the Holy Scriptures: whereby the ¹order, ²names, ³times, ⁴penmen, ⁵occasion, ⁶scope, and ⁷principall parts, containing the subject-matter of every book of Old and New Testament, are familiarly and briefly opened: for the help of the weakest capacity in the understanding of the whole Bible* (London, 1648).

Roberts, Francis, *Mysterium & medulla Bibliorum: the mysterie and marrow of the Bible, viz. God's covenants with man in the first Adam before the fall, and in the last Adam, Jesus Christ, after the fall, from the beginning to the end of the world* (1657).

Rogers, John, *Ohel or Bethshemesh* (1653).

Rollock, Robert, *A treatise of effectual calling* (1603).

Rush, Benjamin, 'To Thomas Jefferson from Benjamin Rush, 6 October 1800', *Founders Online*, National Archives, https://founders.archives.gov/documents/Jefferson/01-32-02-0120, accessed 26 August 2019.
Schlichting, Jonas, *De SS. Trinitate, de moralibus N.& V. Testamenti praeceptis; itemque de sacris, Eucharistiae & baptismi ritibus; adversus B. Meisnerum disputatio* (s.l.: s.n., 1637).
Schlictingius, Jonas, *Confessio fidei Christianae edita nominee Ecclesiarum quae in Polonia* (1651).
Scrivener, Matthew, *A course of divinity: or, An introduction to the knowledge of the true Catholick religion; Especially as professed by the Church of England* (1674).
Sedgwick, Joseph, *A sermon, preached at St. Marie's in the University of Cambridge May 1st, 1653. Or, An Essay to the discovery of the spirit of enthusiasme and pretended inspiration, that disturbs and strikes at the universities* (1653).
Serry, J. H., *Historia Congregationum de auxiliis* (Louvain, 1700).
Shaw, John, *No reformation of the established reformation* (1685).
Sherlock, William, *A discourse about church-unity being a defence of Dr. Stillingfleet's Unreasonableness of separation, in answer to several late pamphlets, but principally to Dr. Owen and Mr. Baxter* (1681).
Sherlock, William, *A discourse concerning the knowledge of Jesus Christ, and our union and communion with him, &c.* (1674).
Socinus, Faustus, *De Jesu Christo servatore* (1594).
Sphinx Lvgdvno-Genevensis, sive, Reformator proteus, containing the true character of sanctified legion: together with his relations, associates, and retinue, viz. jealousies, fears, scruples, qualms, liberty, property, sack-possets, candles, guns, pikes, trumpets, drums, colours, ordinance (of both kinds), desolation, plunder, anarchy, thorough-Gospel-reformation, etc (1683).
Sprat, Thomas, *The history of the Royal Society of London for the improving of natural knowledge* (1667).
Stout, Harry S., *The Works of Jonathan Edwards*, vol. 16 (New Haven, CT: Yale University Press, 1998).
Stubbe, Henry, *Campanella revived, or An enquiry into the history of the Royal Society* (1670).
Suarez, Francisco, *Defensio fidei Catholicae et Apostolicae adversus Anglicanae sectae errores* (Coloniae Agrippinae, 1614).
Szlichtyng, Jonasz, *De S.S. Trinitate, de moralibus & N. & V. Testamenti praeceptis* (s.l.: s.n., 1637).
Taylor, Jeremy, *ΘΕΟΛΟΓΙΑ ΕΚΛΕΚΤΙΚΗ: a discourse of the liberty of prophesying* (1647).
The Anglican canons, 1529–1947, ed. Gerald Bray (Woodbridge: Boydell Press, 1998).
The commonwealth of England: documents from the English civil wars, the commonwealth and protectorate, 1641–1660, ed. Charles Blitzer (New York: Putnam, 1963).
The constitutional documents of the Puritan revolution, 1625–1660, ed. S. R. Gardiner, third edition (Oxford: Clarendon Press, 1906).
The memoirs of Edmund Ludlow, lieutenant-general of the horse in the army of the Commonwealth of England, 1625–1672, 2 vols (Oxford: Clarendon Press, 1894).
The Racovian catechisme (Amsterdam, 1652).
The register of the Visitors of the University of Oxford, from A.D. 1647 to A.D. 1658, ed. Montagu Burrows (Westminster: J. B. Nichols and Sons, 1881).
The weekly intelligencer of the Common-wealth.

Thorndike, Herbert, *Just weights and measures* (1662).
Thorndike, Herbert, *Of religious assemblies, and the publick service of God a discourse according to apostolicall rule and practice* (Cambridge, 1642).
Thurman, Henry, *A defence of humane learning in the ministry, or, A treatise proving that it is necessary a minister (or preacher) should be skill'd in humane learning* (Oxford, 1660).
Tostatus, Alfonso, *Commentaria in tertiam partem Matthaei, cum indicibus copiosissimis. Operum tomus vigesimus* (Venetiis: ex Typographica Balleoniana, 1728).
Turretin, Francis, *Institutes of elenctic theology*, 3 vols, trans G. M. Giger (Phillipsburg, NJ: Presbyterian & Reformed, 1994).
Twisse, William, *The riches of Gods love unto the vessells of mercy, consistent with his absolute hatred or reprobation of the vessells of wrath, or, An answer unto a book entituled, Gods love unto mankind* (Oxford, 1653).
Twisse, William, *Vindiciae gratiae, potestatis ac providentiae Dei, hoc est, ad examen libelli Perkinsiani de praedestinationis mode et ordine, institutum a Jacobo Arminio, responsio scholastica* (Amsterdam, 1632).
Tyndale, William, *The practice of prelates*, in *The works of William Tyndale*, ed. Henry Walter (1850; rpr. Edinburgh: Banner of Truth Trust, 2010).
Tyndale, William, *The practyse of prelates whether the kinges grace maye be separated from hys quene, because she was his brothers wyfe* (Antwerp, 1530).
Ussher, James, *A body of divinity, or the sum and substance of Christian religion* (1645; sixth edition, 1670).
Ussher, James, *The reduction of episcopacie unto the form of synodical government received in the antient church: proposed as an expedient for the compromising of the now differences and the preventing of those troubles that may arise about the matter of church-government* (1660).
Vernon, George, *A letter to a friend concerning some of Dr Owen's principles and practices* (1670).
Vincent, Thomas, *Words of advice to young men delivered in two sermons at two conventions of young men, the one Decemb. 25, 1666, the other Decemb. 25, 1667* (1668).
Voetius, Gijsbert, *Selectarum disputationum theologicarum pars prima (Quinta. Accedunt dissertatio epistolica de termino vitæ. Exercitatio de prognosticis cometarum. Antehac seorsim editæ)*, 5 vols (Utrecht: J. a Waesberge, 1648–67).
Wallis, John, *The correspondence of John Wallis (1616–1703)*, ed. Philip Beeley and Christoph J. Scriba (Oxford: Oxford University Press, 2003).
Walton, Brian, *The considerator considered: or, a brief view of certain considerations upon the Biblia Polyglotta* (1659).
Watson, Thomas, *A body of practical divinity consisting of above one hundred seventy six sermons on the lesser catechism composed by the reverend assembly of divines at Westminster: with a supplement of some sermons on several texts of Scripture* (1692).
Webster, John, *Academiarum examen, or, the examination of academies wherein is discussed and examined the matter, method and customes of academic and scholastic learning* (1654).
Wesley, Samuel, *A letter from a country divine to his friend in London concerning the education of the Dissenters in their private academies in several parts of this nation* (London, 1703).

Whitelock, Bulstrode, *The diary of Bulstrode Whitelocke, 1605–1675*, ed. Ruth Spalding (Oxford: Oxford University Press for the British Academy, 1990).

Wilkins, John, *A discourse concerning the gift of prayer . . . Whereunto may be added, Ecclesiastes, or, A discourse concerning the gift of preaching* (1647).

Witsius, Herman, *De oeconomia foederum Dei cum hominibus libri*, third edition (1694).

Witsius, Herman, *Miscellaneorum sacrorum Libri IV. Quibus de prophetis & prophetia, de tabernaculi Levitici mysteriis, de collatione sacerdotii Aaronis & Christi, de synedriis Hebraeorum, de IV bestiis Danielis, de cultu Molochi, de seculo hoc & futuro, de sensu Epistolarum Apocalypticarum, de schismate Donatistarum* (Utrecht: F. Halmam, 1692).

Witsius, Herman, *The economy of the covenants between God and man* (Edinburgh: Thomas Turnbull, 1803).

Zanchius, Girolamo, *Omnium operum theologicorum* (Geneva: Samuel Crispin, 1619).

SECONDARY SOURCES

Allen, David L., *The extent of the atonement: a historical and critical review* (Nashville, TN: Broadman & Holman, 2016).

Allen, Michael and Scott R. Swain, *Reformed Catholicity: the promise of retrieval for theology and Biblical interpretation* (Grand Rapids, MI: Baker Academic, 2015).

Allen, Michael and Scott R. Swain (eds), *Sanctification* (Grand Rapids, MI: Zondervan, 2017).

Allison, C. F., *The rise of moralism: the proclamation of the Gospel from Hooker to Baxter* (1966; rpr. Vancouver: Seabury Press/Regent College Publishing, 2003).

Alston, William P., *Perceiving God: the epistemology of religious experience* (Ithaca, NY: Cornell University Press, 1991).

Arber, Edward, *The term catalogues, 1668–1709, A.D.; with a number for Easter term, 1711 A.D. A contemporary bibliography of English literature in the reigns of Charles II, James II, William and Mary, and Anne*, 3 vols. (London, 1903).

Asty, John, 'Memoirs of the life of John Owen', in *A complete collection of the sermons of the Reverend and learned John Owen* (London: John Clark, 1721).

Bac, J. Martin, *Perfect will theology: divine agency in Reformed Scholasticism as against Suarez, Episcopius, Descartes, and Spinoza*, Brill Series in Church History 42 (Leiden: Brill, 2010).

Backus, Irena, 'The Fathers in Calvinist Orthodoxy: Patristic scholarship', in Irena Backus (ed.), *The reception of the Church Fathers in the West: from the Carolingians to the Maurists*, 2 vols (Leiden: Brill, 1997).

Bangs, Carl, *Arminius: a study in the Dutch Reformation* (Nashville, TN: Abingdon Press, 1971).

Ballor, Jordan J., *Covenant, causality, and law: a study in the theology of Wolfgang Musculus* (Göttingen: Vandenhoeck & Ruprecht, 2012).

Barbour, Ashley Reid, David Norbrook, and Maria Cristina Zerbino, 'Introduction', in *The Works of Lucy Hutchinson* (Oxford: Oxford University Press, 2011).

Barnes, Ambrose, *The memoirs of the Life of Mr. Ambrose Barnes, late merchant and sometime alderman of Newcastle upon Tyne*, ed. William Longstaffe (Durham: Surtees Society, 1867).

Barrett, Matthew and Michael A. G. Haykin, *Owen and the Christian life: living for the glory of God in Christ* (Wheaton, IL: Crossway, 2015).
Baschera, Luca, 'Total depravity? The consequences of original sin in John Calvin and later Reformed theology', in Herman J. Selderhuis (ed.), *Calvin Clarissimus Theologus: papers of the Tenth International Congress on Calvin Research* (Göttingen: Vanderhoek & Ruprecht, 2012).
Bates, Matthew, *The birth of the Trinity: Jesus, God, and Spirit in New Testament and early Christian interpretations of the Old Testament* (Oxford: Oxford University Press, 2015).
Bauerschmidt, Frederick Christian, *Thomas Aquinas: faith, reason, and following Christ* (Oxford: Oxford University Press, 2013).
Bauman, Richard, *Let your words be few: symbolism of speaking and silence among seventeenth-century Quakers* (Cambridge: Cambridge University Press, 1983).
Bavinck, Herman, *Reformed dogmatics*, 4 vols, trans. John Vriend (Grand Rapids, MI: Baker Academic, 2008).
Baylor, Timothy Robert, '"He humbled himself": Trinity, covenant, and the gracious condescension of the Son in John Owen', in Michael F. Bird and Scott Harrower (eds), *Trinity without hierarchy: reclaiming Nicene Orthodoxy in evangelical theology* (Grand Rapids, MI: Kregel Academic, 2019).
Baylor, Timothy Robert, 'One with him in Spirit: Mystical union and the humanity of Christ in the theology of John Owen', in Michael J. Thate et al (eds), *'In Christ' in Paul: explorations in Paul's theology of union and participation* (Tübingen: Mohr Siebeck, 2014).
Baylor, Timothy Robert, 'A great king above all Gods: Dominion and divine government in the theology of John Owen' (unpublished PhD thesis, University of St Andrews, 2016).
Baylor, Timothy Robert, 'Review of Ryan M. McGraw, *A heavenly directory: Trinitarian Piety, public worship and a reassessment of John Owen's theology* (Göttingen: Vandenhoeck & Ruprecht, 2014)', *Journal of Reformed Theology* 10 (2016): 378–80.
Baylor, Timothy Robert, '"With him in heavenly realms": Lombard and Calvin on the merit and exaltation of Christ', *International Journal of Systematic Theology* 17, no. 2 (2015): 152–75.
Bearman, Alan, '"The Atlas of Independency": The ideas of John Owen (1616–1683) in the north Atlantic Christian world' (unpublished PhD dissertation, Kansas State University, 2005).
Beeke, Joel R., *Living for God's glory: an introduction to Calvinism* (Lake Mary, FL: Reformation Trust Publishing, 2008).
Beeke, Joel R., 'The reception of John Owen in early modernity', in Kelly M. Kapic and Willem van Vlastuin (eds), *John Owen between orthodoxy and modernity* (Leiden: Brill, 2019).
Beeke, Joel R. and Mark Jones, *A Puritan theology: doctrine for life* (Grand Rapids, MI: Reformation Heritage Books, 2012).
Beeke, Joel R. and Randall J. Pederson, *Meet the Puritans: with a guide to modern reprints* (Grand Rapids, MI: Reformation Heritage Books, 2006).
Beeke, Jonathon D., *Duplex Regnum Christi: Christ's twofold kingdom in Reformed theology* (Leiden: Brill, 2020).
Beeley, Christopher A., *The unity of Christ: continuity and conflict in Patristic tradition* (New Haven, CT: Yale University Press, 2012).

Bird, Benedict, 'John Owen and the question of the eternal submission of the Son within the ontological Trinity', *Westminster Theological Journal* 80, no. 2 (2018): 299–334.

Bird, Benedict, 'The covenant of redemption according to John Owen and Patrick Gillespie', *Foundations* 70 (May 2016): 5–30.

Blair, Ann and Kaspar von Greyerz (eds), *Physico-theology: religion and science in Europe, 1650–1750* (Baltimore, MD: Johns Hopkins University Press, 2021).

Bobick, Michael William, 'Owen's razor: The role of Ramist logic in the covenant theology of John Owen (1616–1683)' (unpublished PhD thesis, Drew University, 1996).

Boersma, Hans, *Seeing God: the beatific vision in Christian tradition* (Grand Rapids, MI: Eerdmans, 2018).

Boler, John, 'Intuitive and abstractive cognition', in Norman Kretzmann et al (eds), *The Cambridge history of later medieval philosophy* (Cambridge: Cambridge University Press, 1982).

Booty, John E., 'Tradition and traditions', *Anglican and Episcopal history* 59 (1990): 453–66.

Bozeman, T. D., *The precisianist strain: disciplinary religion and antinomian backlash in Puritanism to 1638* (Chapel Hill, NC: University of North Carolina Press, 2004).

Bradshaw, David, 'The Logoi of beings in Greek patristic thought', in Bruce Foltz and John Chryssavgis (eds), *Toward an ecology of transfiguration: Orthodox Christian perspectives on environment, nature and creation* (New York: Fordham University Press, 2013).

Brink, Gert van den, 'Impetration and application in John Owen's theology', in Kelly M. Kapic and Mark Jones (eds), *The Ashgate research companion to John Owen's theology* (Burlington, VT: Ashgate, 2012).

Brooke, John Hedley, et al, 'Introduction', in John Hedley Brooke et al (eds), *The Oxford handbook of natural theology* (Oxford: Oxford University Press, 2013).

Brown, Peter, *Augustine of Hippo: a biography* (Berkeley, CA: University of California Press, 1967).

Burden, Mark, 'John Owen: Learned Puritan', https://earlymodern.web.ox.ac.uk/john-owen-learned-puritan.

Burden, Mark, *A biographical dictionary of tutors at the dissenters' private academies, 1660–1729* (London: Dr Williams's Centre for Dissenting Studies, 2013).

Butler, Charles, *The life of Hugo Grotius: with brief minutes of the civil, ecclesiastical, and literary history of the Netherland* (London: John Murray, 1826).

Butner, D. Glenn Jr., 'Reformed theology and the question of Protestant individualism: A dialogue with Henri de Lubac', *Journal of Reformed Theology* 10 (2016): 234–56.

Calloway, Katherine, 'A "metaphorical God" and the book of nature: John Donne on natural theology', *Studies in Philology* 116, no. 1 (2019): 124–58.

Calloway, Katherine, '"Rather theological than philosophical": John Ray's seminal Wisdom of God manifested in the works of creation', in Anne Blair and Kaspar von Greyerz (eds), *Physico-theology: religion and science in Europe, 1650–1750* (Baltimore, MD: Johns Hopkins University Press, 2021).

Calloway, Katherine, *Natural theology in the scientific revolution: God's scientists* (London: Pickering & Chatto, 2014).

Campbell, John Wesley, 'John Owen's rule and guide: A study in the relationship between the Word and the Spirit in the thought of Dr John Owen' (unpublished MTh thesis, Regent College, Vancouver, 1991).

Carmichael, Casey B., *A continental view: Johannes Cocceius's federal theology of the Sabbath* (Göttingen: Vandenhoek & Ruprecht, 2019).
Carroll, Kenneth L., 'Early Quakers and "going naked as a sign",' *Quaker History* 67 (1978): 69–87.
Carroll, Kenneth L., 'Quaker attitudes towards sign and wonders', *The Journal of the Friends' Historical Society* 54 (1976–1982): 70–84.
Carroll, Kenneth L., 'Sackcloth and ashes and other signs and wonders', *The Journal of the Friends' Historical Society* 53 (1972–1975): 314–25.
Carter, Edmund Carter, *The history of the University of Cambridge, from its original, to the Year 1753* (London: Privately published, 1753).
Caughey, Christopher E. 'Puritan responses to antinomianism in the context of Reformed covenant theology, 1630–1696' (unpublished PhD thesis, Trinity College Dublin, 2012).
Cefalu, Paul, *The Johannine renaissance in early modern English literature and theology* (Oxford: Oxford University Press, 2018).
Chambers, Neil, 'A critical examination of John Owen's argument for limited atonement in *The death of death in the death of Christ*' (unpublished ThM thesis, Reformed Theological Seminary, 1998).
Chenu, Marie-Dominique and Ellen Bremner, 'The plan of St. Thomas Aquinas' *Summa theologiae*', *CrossCurrents* 2, no. 2 (1952): 67–79.
Clark, J. C. D., 'Providence, predestination and progress: Or, did the Enlightenment fail?' *Albion* 35 (2003): 559–89.
Clarke, Elizabeth, 'Re-reading the Exclusion Crisis', *The Seventeenth Century* 21 (2006): 141–59.
Claunch, Kyle, 'What God hath done together: Defending the historic doctrine of the inseparable operations of the Trinity', *Journal of the Evangelical Theological Society* 56 (2013): 781–800.
Cleveland, Christopher, *Thomism in John Owen* (Burlington: Ashgate, 2013).
Cleveland, Kendall Beau, 'The covenant of redemption in the Trinitarian theology of John Owen' (unpublished PhD thesis, University of St Andrews, 2016).
Cliffe, Trevor, *The Puritan gentry besieged, 1650–1700* (London: Routledge, 2002).
Clifford, Alan C., *Atonement and justification: English evangelical theology, 1640–1790: an evaluation* (Oxford: Oxford University Press, 1990).
Coffey, John, 'A ticklish business: Defining heresy and orthodoxy in the Puritan revolution', in David Loewenstein and John Marshall (eds), *Heresy, literature, and politics in early modern English culture* (Cambridge: Cambridge University Press, 2010).
Coffey, John, 'The Bible and theology', in John Coffey (ed.), *The Oxford history of Protestant dissenting traditions*, vol. 1: *the post-reformation era, c.1559–c.1689* (Oxford: Oxford University Press, 2020).
Coffey, John, *John Goodwin and the Puritan revolution: religion and intellectual change in 17th-century England* (Woodbridge: Boydell Press, 2006).
Coffey, John, 'John Owen and the puritan toleration controversy, 1646–59', in Kelly M. Kapic and Mark Jones (eds), *The Ashgate research companion to John Owen's Theology* (Farnham, UK: Ashgate, 2012).
Coffey, John, *Persecution and toleration in Protestant England, 1558–1689* (London: Pearson, 2000).
Collins, Jeffrey R., *The allegiance of Thomas Hobbes* (Oxford: Oxford University Press, 2005).

Collinson, Patrick, 'Biblical rhetoric: The English nation and national sentiment in the prophetic mode', in Claire McEachern and Debora Shuger (eds), *Religion and culture in Renaissance England* (Cambridge: Cambridge University Press, 1997).

Collinson, Patrick, *The Elizabethan Puritan movement* (Oxford: Clarendon Press, 1967).

Como, David R., *Blown by the Spirit: Puritanism and the emergence of an antinomian underground in pre-civil-war England* (Stanford, CA: Stanford University Press, 2004).

Cook, Sarah Gibbard, 'A political biography of a religious Independent: John Owen, 1616–83' (unpublished PhD thesis, Harvard University, 1972).

Coolahan, Marie-Louise, 'Redeeming parcels of time: The aesthetics and practice of occasional meditation', *The Seventeenth Century* 22 (2007): 124–43.

Cooper, Tim, *Fear and polemic in seventeenth-century England: Richard Baxter and antinomianism* (Aldershot, UK: Ashgate, 2001).

Cooper, Tim, 'John Owen, Richard Baxter and the battle for Calvin in later seventeenth-century England', *The Southern Baptist Journal of Theology* 20 (2016): 63–78.

Cooper, Tim, *John Owen, Richard Baxter and the formation of Nonconformity* (Farnham, UK: Ashgate, 2011).

Cooper, Tim, 'John Owen unleashed: Almost', *Conversations in Religion and Theology* 6 (2008): 226–42.

Cooper, Tim, 'Owen's personality: The man behind the theology', in Kelly M. Kapic and Mark Jones (eds), *The Ashgate research companion to John Owen's theology* (Farnham, UK: Ashgate, 2012).

Cooper, Tim, 'Why did Richard Baxter and John Owen diverge? The impact of the first civil war', *Journal of Ecclesiastical History* 61 (2010), 507–11.

Cowan, Martyn, *John Owen and the civil war apocalypse: preaching, prophecy and politics* (London: Routledge, 2018).

Cragg, G. R., *From Puritanism to the age of reason: a study of changes in religious thought within the Church of England, 1660–1700* (Cambridge: Cambridge University Press, 1966).

Craig, John, 'Sermon reception', in Peter McCullough et al (eds), *The Oxford handbook of the early modern sermon* (Oxford: Oxford University Press, 2011).

Craig, Philip A., *The bond of grace and duty in the soteriology of John Owen* (Cape Coral, FL: Founders Press, 2020).

Crisp, Oliver D., 'John Owen on Spirit Christology', *Journal of Reformed Theology* 5 (2011): 5–21.

Cunnington, Ralph, 'A critical examination of Jonathan Edwards's doctrine of the Trinity', *Themelios* 39 (2014): 224–40.

Daniel, Richard, *The Christology of John Owen* (Grand Rapids, MI: Reformation Heritage Books, 2004).

Davies, Michael, *Graceful reading: theology and narrative in the works of John Bunyan* (Oxford: Oxford University Press, 2002).

Day, Sebastian, *Intuitive cognition: a key to the significance of the later scholastics* (St. Bonaventure, NY: Franciscan Institute Press, 1947).

De Krey, Gary S., 'London radicals and revolutionary politics, 1675–1683', in Tim Harris et al (eds), *The politics of religion in restoration England* (Oxford: Oxford University Press, 1990).

De Krey, Gary S., *London and the Restoration, 1659–1683* (Cambridge: Cambridge University Press, 2005).

de Lubac, Henri, *Augustinianism and modern theology*, trans. Lancelot Sheppard (London: Geoffrey Chapman, 1969).
Deckard, Mark, *Helpful truth in past places: the puritan practice of Biblical counseling* (Fearn, UK: Mentor, 2010).
Denault, Pascal, *The distinctiveness of Baptist covenant theology* (Vestavia Hills, AL: Solid Ground Christian Books, 2013).
Dennison, James T., *Reformed confessions of the 16th and 17th centuries in English translation, Volume 4: 1600–1693* (Grand Rapids, MI: Reformation Heritage Books, 2014).
Dieleman, Kyle J., *The battle for the Sabbath in the Dutch Reformation: devotion or desecration?* (Göttingen: Vandenhoeck & Ruprecht, 2019).
Dixon, Philip, *Nice and hot disputes: the doctrine of the Trinity in the seventeenth century* (London: T&T Clark, 2003).
Donnelly, John Patrick, 'Calvinist Thomism', *Viator* 7 (1976): 441–55.
Duff, John H., 'A knot worth unloosing': The interpretation of the new heavens and earth in seventeenth-century England* (Göttingen: Vandenhoeck and Ruprecht, 2019).
Dumont, Stephen D., 'Theology as a science and Duns Scotus's distinction between intuitive and abstractive cognition', *Speculum* 64 (1989): 579–99.
Dunan-Page, Anne, '"The Pourtraiture of John Bunyan" revisited: Robert White and Images of the Author', *Bunyan Studies: a Journal of Reformation and Nonconformist Culture*, The International John Bunyan Society, 13 (2008): 7–39.
Durston, Christopher, 'By the book or with the Spirit: The debate over liturgical prayer during the English revolution', *Historical Journal* 79 (2006): 50–73.
Dzelzainis, Martin, 'Marvell and science', in Martin Dzelzainis and Edward Holberton (eds), *The Oxford handbook of Andrew Marvell* (Oxford: Oxford University Press, 2019).
Edwards, William R. 'John Flavel on the priority of union with Christ: Further historical perspective on the structure of Reformed soteriology', *Westminster Theological Journal* 74 (2012): 33–58.
Englert, Walter, 'Introduction', in Lucretius, *On the nature of things* (Newburyport, MA: Focus Publishing, 2003).
Fallon, Stephen M., *Milton among the philosophers: poetry and materialism in seventeenth-century England* (Ithaca, NY: Cornell University Press, 1991).
Farr, David, *John Lambert, Parliamentary soldier and Cromwellian Major-General, 1619–1684* (Woodbridge, UK: Boydell and Brewer, 2003).
Farris, Joshua R. and Ryan A Brandt, 'Ensouling the beatific vision: Motivating the Reformed impulse', *Perichoresis* 15 (2017): 67–84.
Feingold, Mordechai, 'The Humanities', in Nicholas Tyacke (ed.), *Seventeenth-Century Oxford* (Oxford: Clarendon Press, 1997).
Ferguson, James, *Robert Ferguson, 'the plotter'* (Edinburgh: D. Douglas, 1887).
Ferguson, Sinclair B., *Devoted to God: Blueprints for sanctification* (Edinburgh: Banner of Truth, 2016).
Ferguson, Sinclair B., *John Owen on the Christian life* (Edinburgh: Banner of Truth, 1987).
Ferguson, Sinclair B., *Some pastors and teachers: reflecting a Biblical vision of what every minister is called to be* (Edinburgh: Banner of Truth, 2017).
Ferguson, Sinclair B., *The Holy Spirit* (Downers Grove, IL: IVP Academic, 1996).

Ferguson, Sinclair B., *The trinitarian devotion of John Owen* (Orlando, FL: Reformation Trust Publishing, 2014).
Ferrell, Lori Anne, *Government by polemic: James I, the king's preachers and the rhetoric of conformity 1603–1625* (Stanford, CA: Stanford University Press, 1998).
Ferrell, Lori Anne and Peter McCullough (eds), *The English sermon revised: religion, literature and history, 1600–1750* (Manchester: Manchester University Press, 2000).
Fesko, J. V., *Beyond Calvin: Union with Christ and justification in early modern Reformed theology (1517–1700)* (Göttingen: Vandenhoeck & Ruprecht, 2012).
Fesko, J. V., *The covenant of redemption: origins, development, and reception* (Göttingen: Vandenhoeck & Ruprecht, 2016).
Fesko, J. V., 'The doctrine of Scripture in Reformed Orthodoxy', in H. J. Selderhuis (ed.), *A companion to Reformed Orthodoxy* (Leiden: Brill, 2013).
Fisher, Jeff, *A Christoscopic reading of Scripture: Johannes Oecolampadius on Hebrews* (Göttingen: Vandenhoeck & Reprecht, 2016).
Foord, Martin, 'John Owen's gospel offer: Well-meant or not?' in Kelly M. Kapic and Mark Jones (eds), *The Ashgate research companion to John Owen's theology* (Aldershot, UK: Ashgate, 2012).
Forbes, Eric G., 'The comet of 1680–1681', in Norman J. W. Thrower (eds), *Standing on the shoulders of giants: a longer view of Newton and Halley* (Berkeley, CA: University of California Press, 1990).
Fowl, Stephen E. (ed.), *The theological interpretation of Scripture: classic and contemporary readings* (Oxford: Blackwell, 1997).
Fuller, Russell T., 'John Owen and the traditional Protestant view of the Old Testament', *The Southern Baptist Journal of Theology* 20 (2016): 79–99.
Gaine, Simon Francis, 'Thomas Aquinas and John Owen on the beatific vision: A reply to Suzanne McDonald', *New Blackfriars* 97 (2016): 432–46.
Gamble, Whitney G., *Christ and the law: Antinomianism at the Westminster Assembly* (Grand Rapids, MI: Reformation Heritage Books, 2018).
Gascoigne, John, 'The religious thought of Francis Bacon', in Carole M. Cusack and Christopher Hartney (eds), *Religion and retributive logic: essays in honor of Professor Garry W. Trompf* (Leiden: Brill, 2010).
Gathercole, Simon J., *The preexistent Son: recovering the Christologies of Matthew, Mark, and Luke* (Grand Rapids, MI: Eerdmans, 2006).
Gatiss, Lee, 'Adoring the fullness of the Scriptures in John Owen's commentary on Hebrews' (unpublished PhD thesis, University of Cambridge, 2013).
Gatiss, Lee, 'Anglicanism and John Owen', *Crux* 52, no. 1 (2016): 44–53.
Gatiss, Lee, 'From life's first cry: John Owen on infant baptism and infant salvation', in Lee Gatiss, *Cornerstones of salvation: foundations and debates in the Reformed Tradition* (Welwyn, UK: Evangelical Press, 2017).
Gatiss, Lee, 'Socinianism and John Owen', *Southern Baptist Journal of Theology* 20 (2016): 43–62.
Gatiss, Lee, 'The autobiography of a "meer Christian": Richard Baxter's account of the Restoration', *Churchman* 122, no. 2 (2008): 159–75.
Gatiss, Lee, *The tragedy of 1662: the ejection and persecution of the Puritans* (London: Latimer Trust, 2007).
Gatiss, Lee, *The true profession of the gospel: Augustus Toplady and reclaiming our Reformed foundations* (London: Latimer Trust, 2010).

Gaunt, Peter, '"To create a little world out of chaos": The Protectoral ordinances of 1653–1654 reconsidered', in Patrick Little (ed.), *The Cromwellian Protectorate* (Woodbridge, UK: Boydell, 2007).

Getz, Evan Jay, 'Analogy, causation, and beauty in the works of Lucy Hutchinson' (unpublished PhD thesis, Baylor University, 2008).

Gibson, Jonathan, 'Textual introduction', in *The works of Lucy Hutchinson,* vol. 2: *theological writings and translations: part 1 introduction and texts*, eds Elizabeth Clarke et al (Oxford: Oxford University Press, 2018).

Glassey, L. K. J., 'Shaftesbury and the exclusion crisis', in John Spurr (ed.), *Anthony Ashley Cooper, first earl of Shaftesbury, 1621–1683* (Aldershot, UK: Ashgate, 2011).

Gleason, Randall C., *John Calvin and John Owen on mortification: a comparative study in Reformed spirituality* (New York: Peter Lang, 1995).

Goldie, Mark, 'The Hilton Gang and the purge of London in the 1680s', in Howard Nenner (ed.), *Politics and the political imagination in later Stuart Britain* (Rochester, NY: University of Rochester Press, 1997).

Golding, Peter, 'Owen on the mortification of sin: 2', *Banner of Truth* 322 (1990): 20–5.

Gomes, Alan W., 'De Jesu Christo servatore: Faustus Socinus on the satisfaction of Christ', *Westminster Theological Journal* 55 (1993): 209–31.

Gomes, Alan W., 'Faustus Socinus' De Jesu Christo Servatore, Part III: Historical introduction, translation, and critical notes' (unpublished PhD thesis, Fuller Theological Seminary, 1990).

Gomes, Alan W., 'The rapture of the Christ: The "pre-ascension ascension" of Jesus in the theology of Faustus Socinus (1539–1601)', *Harvard Theological Review* 102, no. 1 (2009): 75–99.

Greaves, Richard L., *Enemies under his feet: radicals and nonconformists in Britain, 1664–1677* (Stanford, CA: Stanford University Press, 1990).

Greaves, Richard L., 'Fletcher, Elizabeth', in R. L. Greaves and Robert Zaller (eds), *Biographical dictionary of British radicals in the seventeenth century*, 3 vols (Brighton, UK: Harvester Press, 1982).

Greaves, Richard L., *Glimpses of glory: John Bunyan and English dissent* (Stanford, CA: Stanford University Press, 2002).

Greaves, Richard L., *John Bunyan and English Nonconformity* (London: Hambledon, 1992).

Greaves, Richard L., 'Owen, John (1616–1683)', *ODNB*, s.v.

Greaves, Richard L., 'Puritanism and science: The anatomy of a controversy', *Journal of the History of Ideas* 30 (1969): 345–68.

Greaves, Richard L., *Secrets of the kingdom: British radicals from the Popish Plot to the revolution of 1688–1689* (Stanford, CA: Stanford University Press, 1992).

Greaves, Richard L., *The Puritan revolution and educational thought: background for reform* (New Brunswick, NJ: Rutgers University Press, 1969).

Green, Bradley G., *Colin Gunton and the failure of Augustine: the theology of Colin Gunton in light of Augustine* (Eugene, OR: Pickwick Publications, 2011).

Greenslade, S. L., 'The faculty of theology', in James McConica (ed.), *The Collegiate University* (Oxford: Clarendon Press, 1986).

Gribben, Crawford, *An introduction to John Owen* (Wheaton, IL: Crossway, 2020).

Gribben, Crawford, 'Becoming John Owen: The making of an evangelical reputation', *Westminster Theological Journal* 79 (2017): 311–25.

Gribben, Crawford, *God's Irishmen: theological debates in Cromwellian Ireland* (New York: Oxford University Press, 2007).
Gribben, Crawford, 'John Owen, baptism, and the Baptists', in Ronald S. Baines et al (eds), *By common confession: essays in honor of James M. Renihan* (Palmdale, CA: Reformed Baptist Academic Press, 2015).
Gribben, Crawford, *John Owen and English Puritanism: experiences of Defeat* (Oxford: Oxford University Press, 2016).
Gribben, Crawford, 'John Owen, renaissance man? The evidence of Edward Millington's *Bibliotheca Oweniana*', *Westminster Theological Journal* 72 (2010): 321–32.
Gribben, Crawford, 'Polemic and apocalyptic in the Cromwellian invasion of Scotland', *Literature & History* 23 (2014): 1–18.
Gribben, Crawford, 'Samuel Rutherford and liberty of conscience', *Westminster Theological Journal* 71 (2009): 355–73.
Gribben, Crawford, 'The experience of dissent: John Owen and congregational life in England', in Michael Davies et al (eds), *Church life: pastors, congregation, and the experience of dissent in seventeenth-century England* (Oxford University Press, 2019).
Gribben, Crawford, *The Irish Puritans: James Ussher and the reformation of the church* (Darlington, UK: Evangelical Press, 2003).
Griesel, Jake, 'John Edwards of Cambridge (1637–1716): A reassessment of his position within the later Stuart Church of England' (unpublished PhD thesis, University of Cambridge, 2019).
Griffiths, Steve, *Redeem the time: the problem of sin in the writings of John Owen* (Fearn, UK: Mentor, 2001).
Guelzo, Allen C., 'John Owen, puritan pacesetter', *Christianity Today* 20, no. 17 (May 21, 1976).
Guy, Nathan, *Finding Locke's God: the theological basis of John Locke's political thought* (London: Bloomsbury Academic, 2020).
Haigh, Christopher, '"Theological wars": "Socinians" v. "Antinomians" in Restoration England', *Journal of Ecclesiastical History* 67, no. 2 (2016): 325–50.
Haigh, Christopher, 'The Church of England, the nonconformists and reason: Another Restoration controversy', *Journal of Ecclesiastical History* 69, no. 3 (2018): 531–56.
Halcomb, Joel, 'The examination of ministers', in *The Minutes and Papers of the Westminster Assembly, 1643–1652*, vol. 1: *Introduction*, ed. Chad Van Dixhoorn (Oxford: Oxford University Press, 2012).
Hall, David D., *The Puritans: a transatlantic history* (Princeton, NJ: Princeton University Press, 2019).
Hampton, Stephen, 'Confessional identity', in Anthony Milton (ed.), *The Oxford history of Anglicanism*, vol. 1: *reformation and identity, c.1520–1662* (Oxford: Oxford University Press, 2017).
Hampton, Stephen, *Anti-Arminians: the Anglican Reformed tradition from Charles II to George I* (Oxford: Oxford University Press, 2008).
Hanna, John D., 'John Owen and the "normal" Christian Life, or sanctification in an Era of Confusion', *Modern Reformation* 5, no. 6 (November/December 1996): 14–18.
Harris, Tim, 'Introduction: Revising the Restoration', in Tim Harris et al (eds), *The politics of religion in Restoration England* (Oxford: Blackwell, 1990).

Harris, Tim, *London crowds in the reign of Charles II: Propaganda and politics from the Restoration until the exclusion crisis* (Cambridge: Cambridge University Press, 1990).
Harrison, Peter, 'Religion and the early Royal Society', *Science & Christian Belief* 22 (2010): 3–22.
Harrison, Peter, 'Religion, the Royal Society, and the Rise of Science', *Theology and Science* 6 (2008): 255–71.
Harrison, Peter, *'Religion' and the religions in the English Enlightenment* (Cambridge: Cambridge University Press, 1990).
Harrison, Peter, *The Bible, Protestantism, and the rise of natural science* (Cambridge: Cambridge University Press, 1998).
Harrison, Peter, *The fall of man and the foundations of modern science* (Cambridge: Cambridge University Press, 2007).
Harrison, Peter, *The territories of science and religion* (Chicago: University of Chicago Press, 2015).
Harwood, John T., *The early essays and ethics of Robert Boyle* (Carbondale, IL: Southern Illinois University Press, 1991).
Haugaard, William P., *Elizabeth and the English reformation: the struggles for a stable settlement of religion* (Cambridge: Cambridge University Press, 1968).
Haykin, Michael A. G., 'The great beautifier of souls', *Banner of Truth* 242 (1983): 18–22.
Helm, Paul, *Calvin at the Centre* (Oxford: Oxford University Press, 2006).
Helm, Paul, *Human nature from Calvin to Edwards* (Grand Rapids, MI: Reformation Heritage Books, 2018).
Helm, Paul, 'Thomas Halyburton and John Locke on the grounding of faith in Scripture', in Aaron Clay Denlinger (ed.), *Reformed Orthodoxy in Scotland* (London: Bloomsbury Academic, 2015).
Henry, John, *The scientific revolution and the origins of modern science* (New York: Palgrave, 2008).
Henry, John, 'Voluntarist theology at the origins of modern science: A response to Peter Harrison', *History of Science* 47 (2009): 79–113.
Henry, John, 'Wilkins, John', *ODNB*, s.v.
Hill, Christopher, 'Puritans and the "dark corners of the land"', *Transactions of the Royal Historical Society*, 5th Series, 13 (1963): 77–102.
Hill, Christopher, *The English Bible and the seventeenth-century revolution* (London: Allen Lane, 1993).
Hill, Christopher, *The experience of defeat: Milton and some contemporaries* (New York: Penguin, 1984)
History of parliament.
Hodge, Charles, *Systematic theology*, 3 vols (Peabody, MA: Hendrickson, 2011).
Hoglund, Jonathan, *Called by Triune grace: divine rhetoric and the effectual call* (Downers Grove, IL: IVP Academic, 2016).
Holberton, Edward, *Poetry and the Cromwellian Protectorate: culture, politics, and institutions* (Oxford: Oxford University Press, 2008).
Holmes, Clive, 'The trial and execution of Charles I', *Historical Journal* 53 (2010): 289–316.
Hughes, Ann, '"The public profession of these nations": The national church in Interregnum England', in Christopher Durston and Judith Maltby (eds), *Religion in Revolutionary England* (Manchester: Manchester University Press, 2006).

Hunsinger, George, 'Justification and mystical union with Christ: Where does Owen stand?' in Kelly M. Kapic and Mark Jones (eds), *The Ashgate research companion to John Owen's theology* (Farnham, UK: Ashgate, 2014).
Hunter, Michael, *Boyle: between God and science* (New Haven, CT: Yale University Press, 2009).
Huntley, F. L., *Bishop Joseph Hall and Protestant meditation in seventeenth-century England* (Binghamton, NY: Medieval and Renaissance Texts and Studies, 1981).
Hyde, Daniel R., 'John Owen on public prayer: A critical reading', in Willem van Vlastuin and Kelly M. Kapic (eds), *John Owen between orthodoxy and modernity* (Leiden: Brill, 2019).
Jackson, T. G., *The Church of St Mary the Virgin, Oxford* (Oxford: Clarendon Press, 1897).
Jacob, James R., *Henry Stubbe, radical Protestantism and the early Enlightenment* (Cambridge: Cambridge University Press, 1983).
James, Jean, 'The doctrine of the church in the theology of John Owen' (unpublished MA thesis, Durham University, 1975).
Johnson, Keith, 'The work of the Holy Spirit in the ministry of Jesus Christ: A trinitarian perspective', *Trinity Journal* 38 n.s. (2017): 147–67.
Jones, Mark, 'The minority report: John Owen on Sinai', in Joel R. Beeke and Mark Jones (eds), *A puritan theology: Doctrine for life* (Grand Rapids: Reformation Heritage Books, 2012).
Kapic, Kelly M., 'Colin Gunton on John Owen', in Murray Rae et al (eds), *The T&T Clark handbook of Colin Gunton* (London: T&T Clark, 2021).
Kapic, Kelly M., 'Communion with God: Relations between the divine and human in the theology of John Owen' (unpublished PhD thesis, King's College London, 2001).
Kapic, Kelly M., *Communion with God: the divine and the human in the theology of John Owen* (Grand Rapids, MI: Baker Academic, 2007).
Kapic, Kelly M., '"Evangelical holiness": Assumptions in John Owen's theology of Christian spirituality', in Jeffrey P. Greenman and George Kalantzis (eds), *Life in the Spirit: Spiritual formation in theological perspective* (Downers Grove: IVP, 2010).
Kapic, Kelly M., 'Introduction: Worshiping the triune God: The shape of John Owen's trinitarian spirituality', in Kelly M. Kapic and Justin Taylor (eds), *Communion with the triune God: a classic work by John Owen* (Wheaton, IL: Crossway, 2007).
Kapic, Kelly M., 'Life in the midst of battle: John Owen's approach to sin, temptation, and the Christian life', in Kelly M. Kapic and Justin Taylor (eds), *Overcoming sin and temptation: three classic works by John Owen* (Wheaton: Crossway Books, 2006).
Kapic, Kelly M., 'The Spirit as Gift: Explorations in John Owen's Pneumatology', in Kelly M. Kapic and Mark Jones (eds), *The Ashgate research companion to John Owen's theology* (Farnham, UK: Ashgate, 2012).
Kapic, Kelly M., 'Typology, the Messiah, and John Owen's theological reading of Hebrews', in Jon C. Laansma and Daniel J. Treier (eds), *Christology, hermeneutics, and Hebrews: profiles from the history of interpretation* (London: Bloomsbury, 2013), 135–54.
Kapic, Kelly M., 'Worshiping the triune God: The shape of John Owen's trinitarian spirituality', in Kelly M. Kapic and Justin Taylor (eds), *Communion with the triune God: a classic work by John Owen* (Wheaton, IL: Crossway, 2007).

Kapic, Kelly M. and Mark Jones (eds), *The Ashgate research companion to John Owen's theology* (Farnham, UK: Ashgate, 2012).
Kapic, Kelly M. and Willem van Vlastuin (eds), *John Owen between orthodoxy and modernity* (Leiden: Brill , 2019).
Kay, Brian, *Trinitarian spirituality: John Owen and the doctrine of God in western devotion* (Carlisle, UK: Paternoster, 2007).
Keeble, N. H., *The Restoration: England in the 1660s* (Oxford: Blackwell, 2008).
Kelly, Ryan T., 'Reformed or reforming? John Owen and the complexity of theological codification for mid seventeenth-century England', in Kelly M. Kapic and Mark Jones (eds), *The Ashgate research companion to John Owen's theology* (Farnham, UK: Ashgate, 2012).
Kelly, Ryan T., 'Reformed and reforming: John Owen on the kingdom of Christ' (unpublished PhD thesis, Vrije Universiteit Amsterdam, 2015).
Kelsey, Sean, 'The death of Charles I', *Historical Journal* 45 (2002): 727–54.
Kelsey, Sean, 'The trial of Charles I', *English Historical Review* 118 (2003): 583–616.
Kieser, Ty, 'Theandric and triune: John Owen and a case for classically Reformed Christological agency' (unpublished PhD thesis, Wheaton College, 2020).
Killeen, Kevin, 'Chastising with scorpions: Reading the Old Testament in early modern England', *Huntington Library Quarterly* 73 (2010): 491–506.
Killeen, Kevin, *The political Bible in early modern England* (Cambridge: Cambridge University Press, 2017).
Killeen, Kevin, 'Veiled speech: Preaching, politics and Scriptural typology', in Peter McCullough et al (eds), *The Oxford handbook of the early modern sermon* (Oxford: Oxford University Press, 2011).
King, Peter, 'Thinking about things: Singular thought in the middle ages', in Gyula Klima (ed.), *Intentionality, cognition, and representation in medieval philosophy* (New York: Fordham University Press, 2015).
Kishlansky, Mark, 'Mission impossible: Charles I, Oliver Cromwell and the regicide', *The English Historical Review* 125 (2010): 844–74.
Knapp, Henry M., 'Augustine and Owen on perseverance', *Westminster Theological Journal* 62 (2000): 65–88.
Knapp, Henry M., 'John Owen on schism and the nature of the church', *Westminster Theological Journal* 72 (2010): 333–58.
Knapp, Henry M., 'John Owen's interpretation of Hebrews 6:4–6: Eternal perseverance of the saints in Puritan exegesis', *Sixteenth Century Journal* 34 (2003): 29–52.
Knapp, Henry M., 'The criticism and reassessment of seventeenth-century exegesis', in Jordan J. Ballor et al (eds), *Church and school in early modern Protestantism: studies in Honor of Richard A. Muller on the maturation of a theological tradition* (Leiden: Brill, 2013).
Knapp, Henry M., 'Understanding the mind of God: John Owen and seventeenth-century exegetical methodology' (unpublished PhD thesis, Calvin Theological Seminary, 2002).
Knights, Mark, *Politics and opinion in crisis, 1678–81* (Cambridge: Cambridge University Press, 1994).
Lake, Peter, *Anglican and Puritans? Presbyterianism and English conformist thought from Whitgift to Hooker* (London: Unwin Hyman, 1988).
Langston, Douglas C., 'Scotus's doctrine of intuitive cognition', *Synthese* 96 (1993): 3–24.

Lawson, Steven J., *The unwavering resolve of Jonathan Edwards* (Lake Mary, FL: Reformation Trust Publishing, 2008).

Lee, Brian J. *Johannes Cocceius and the exegetical roots of federal theology: reformation developments in the interpretation of Hebrews 7–10* (Göttingen: Vandenhoeck & Reprecht, 2009).

Lee, Francis, *John Owen represbyterianized* (Edmonton, Canada: Still Waters Revival Books, 2000).

Lee, Sungho, 'All subjects of the kingdom of Christ: John Owen's conceptions of Christian unity and schism' (unpublished PhD thesis, Calvin Theological Seminary, 2007).

Legge, Dominic, *The trinitarian Christology of St Thomas Aquinas* (Oxford: Oxford University Press, 2018).

Leslie, Andrew M., *The light of grace: John Owen on the authority of Scripture and Christian faith* (Gottingen: Vandenhoeck & Ruprecht, 2015).

Letham, Robert, 'John Owen's doctrine of the trinity in its catholic context', in *The Ashgate research companion to John Owen's theology* (Farnham, UK: Ashgate, 2012).

Levering, Matthew, *The theology of Augustine: an introductory guide to his most important works* (Grand Rapids, MI: Baker, 2013).

Lewalksi, Barbara Kiefer, *The life of John Milton: a critical biography* (Oxford: Blackwell, 2000).

Lim, Paul C. H., *Mystery unveiled: the crisis of the Trinity in early modern England* (Oxford: Oxford University Press, 2012).

Lim, Paul C. H., *In pursuit of purity, unity, and liberty: Richard Baxter's Puritan ecclesiology in its seventeenth-century context* (Leiden: Brill, 2004).

Lim, Paul C. H., 'The Trinity, *adiaphora*, ecclesiology, and reformation: John Owen's theory of religious toleration in context', *Westminster Theological Journal* 67 (2005): 281–300.

Lloyd, R. Glynne, 'The life and work of the Reverend John Owen D.D., the Puritan divine, with special reference to the Socinian controversies of the seventeenth Century' (unpublished PhD thesis, University of Edinburgh, 1942).

Locke, John, *The correspondence of John Lockei*, ed. Esmond de Beer (Oxford: Clarendon Press, 1976–89).

Loftin, R. Keith, 'A Barthian critique of the covenant of redemption', *Trinity Journal* 38 (2017): 203–22.

Long, Stephen A., *Natura pura: on the recovery of nature in the doctrine of grace* (New York: Fordham University Press, 2010).

Lucci, Diego, 'Ante-Nicene authority and the Trinity in seventeenth-century England', *International History Review* 28 (2018): 101–24.

Ludlow, D. P., 'Leavens, Elizabeth', in R. L. Greaves and Robert Zaller (eds), *Biographical dictionary of British radicals in the seventeenth century*, 3 vols (Brighton, UK: Harvester Press, 1983).

Lynch, Beth, 'Ponder, Nathaniel [called Bunyan Ponder] (1640–1699)', *ODNB*, s.v.

Lynch, Michael J., *John Davenant's hypothetical universalism: a defense of Catholic and Reformed orthodoxy* (Oxford: Oxford University Press, 2021).

Lynch, Michael J., 'Richard Hooker and the development of English hypothetical universalism', in W. Bradford Littlejohn and Scott N. Kindred-Barnes (eds), *Richard Hooker and Reformed Orthodoxy* (Amsterdam: Vandenhoek & Ruprecht, 2017).

MacArthur, John F. Jr., 'Mortification of sin', *The Master's Seminary Journal* 5 (1994): 3–22.

MacCulloch, Diarmaid, *The boy king: Edward VI and the Protestant reformation* (Berkeley, CA: University of California Press, 1999).

MacCulloch, Diarmaid, 'The Church of England and international Protestantism', in Anthony Milton (ed.), *The Oxford History of Anglicanism*, vol. 1: *reformation and Identity, c. 1520–1662* (Oxford: Oxford University Press, 2017).

MacCulloch, Diarmaid, *The reformation: a history* (New York: Penguin, 2004).

MacLean, Donald John, *James Durham (1622–1658) and the Gospel offer in its seventeenth-century context* (Göttingen: Vandenhoeck and Ruprecht, 2015).

Macleod, Jack N., 'John Owen and *The death of death*', in *Out of bondage* (London: Westminster Conference, 1983).

MacPhail, Kelly, '"This peculiar constitution of our nature": John Owen's perception of death, ontology, and the *isangeloi*', *The Seventeenth Century* 36 (2020): 1–16.

Maitland, David Johnston, 'Three Puritan attitudes toward learning: An examination of the Puritan controversies over a learned ministry, 1640–1660, and the consequences of this struggle for Puritan concern about the reformation of learning' (unpublished PhD thesis, Columbia University, 1959).

Mandelbrote, Scott, 'Early modern Biblical interpretation and the emergence of science', *Science and Christian Belief* 23 (2011): 99–113.

Mandelbrote, Scott, 'The uses of natural theology in seventeenth-century England', *Science in Context* 20 (2007): 451–80.

Manfred, Svensson, 'A dirty word? The Christian development of the traditional conception of toleration in Augustine, Aquinas, and John Owen', in Vyacheslav Karpov and Manfred Svensson (eds), *Secularization, desecularization, and toleration: cross-disciplinary challenges to a modern myth* (Cham: Palgrave Macmillan, 2020).

Martin, Albert N., 'Practical helps to mortification of sin', *Banner of Truth* 106–107 (1972): 23–33.

Martin, Ryan J., '"Violent motions of carnal affections": Jonathan Edwards, John Owen, and distinguishing the work of the Spirit from enthusiasm', *Detroit Baptist Seminary Journal* 15 (2010): 99–116.

Matava, R. J., 'A sketch of the *Controversy de auxiliis*', *Journal of Jesuit Studies* 7 (2020): 417–46.

Matava R. J., *Divine causality and human free choice: Domingo Báñez, physical premotion and the controversy de auxiliis revisited* (Leiden: Brill, 2016).

Matthew, Nancy L., *William Sheppard, Cromwell's law reformer* (Cambridge: Cambridge University Press, 2004).

Matthews, A. G., *Calamy revised: being a revision of Edmund Calamy's Account of the ministers and others ejected and silenced, 1660–2* (Oxford: Clarendon Press, 1934).

McCormack, Bruce L., '"With loud cries and tears": The humanity of the Son in the epistle to the Hebrews', in Richard Bauckham et al (eds), *The Epistle to the Hebrews and Christian Theology* (Grand Rapids, MI: Eerdmans, 2009).

McDonald, Suzanne, 'Beholding the glory of God in the face of Jesus Christ: John Owen and the "reforming" of the beatific vision', in Kelly M. Kapic and Mark Jones (eds), *The Ashgate research companion to John Owen's theology* (Farnham, UK: Ashgate, 2012).

McDonald, Suzanne, 'Evangelical questioning of election in Barth: A pneumatological perspective from the Reformed heritage', in Bruce L. McCormack and Clifford B. Anderson (eds), *Karl Barth and American Evangelicalism* (Grand Rapids: Eerdmans, 2011).

McDonald, Suzanne, *Re-imaging election: divine election as representing God to others and others to God* (Grand Rapids: Eerdmans, 2010).

McDonald, Suzanne, 'The pneumatology of the "lost" image in John Owen', *Westminster Theological Journal* 71 (2009): 323–35.

McDonough, Sean M., *Christ as creator: origins of a New Testament doctrine* (Oxford: Oxford University Press, 2010).

McDowell, Nicholas, *The English radical imagination: culture, religion, and revolution, 1630–1660* (Oxford: Clarendon Press, 2003).

McGrath, Alister E., *Reformation thought: an introduction*, third edition (Oxford: Blackwell, 1999).

McGraw, Ryan M., '"The Foundation of the Old Testament": John Owen on Genesis 3:15 as a window into Reformed Orthodox Old Testament exegesis', *Journal of Reformed Theology* 10 (2016): 3–28.

McGraw, Ryan M., *'A Heavenly Directory': Trinitarian piety, public worship, and a reassessment of John Owen's theology* (Göttingen: Vandenhoeck & Ruprecht, 2014).

McGraw, Ryan M., *John Owen: trajectories in Reformed Orthodox theology* (Cham: Palgrave MacMillan, 2017).

McGraw, Ryan M., 'Seeing things Owen's way: John Owen's trinitarian theology and piety in its early-modern context', in Kelly M. Kapic and Willem van Vlastuin (eds), *John Owen between Orthodoxy and Modernity* (Leiden: Brill, 2019).

McNall, Joshua, *A free corrector: Colin Gunton and the legacy of Augustine* (Minneapolis: Augsburg Fortress, 2015).

Meli, Domenico Bertolini, 'Wallis, John', *ODNB*, s.v.

Mendelson, Sara H., 'Rich [née Boyle], Mary, countess of Warwick', *ODNB*, s.v.

Merton, Robert K., 'Science, technology and society in seventeenth-century England', *Osiris* 4 (1938): 360–632.

Middleton, Erasmus, *Evangelical biography: or, An historical account of the lives & deaths of the most eminent and evangelical authors or preachers, both British and foreign, in the several denominations of protestants, from the beginning of the reformation to the present time*, 4 vols (London: W. Baynes, 1816).

Miller, John, *Popery and politics in England, 1660–1688* (Cambridge: Cambridge University Press, 1973).

Milton, Anthony (ed.), *The British delegation and the Synod of Dort (1618–1619)* (Woodbridge, UK: Boydell Press, 2005).

Milton, Anthony, 'Introduction', in *The Oxford History of Anglicanism*, vol. 1: *reformation and identity, c. 1520–1662*, ed. Anthony Milton (Oxford: Oxford University Press, 2017).

Milton, Anthony, *Catholic and Reformed: The Roman and Protestant churches in English Protestant thought, 1600–1640* (Cambridge: Cambridge University Press, 1995).

Moffatt, James, *The golden book of John Owen* (London: Hodder & Stoughton, 1904).

Moore, Jonathan D., *English hypothetical universalism: John Preston and the softening of Reformed theology* (Grand Rapids, MI: Eerdmans, 2007).

Morgan, John, *Godly learning: Puritan attitudes towards reason, learning, and education, 1560–1640* (Cambridge: Cambridge University Press, 1986).
Morrissey, Mary, 'Elect nations and prophetic preaching', in Lori Anne Ferrell and Peter McCullough (eds), *The English sermon revised: religion, literature and history, 1600–1750* (Manchester: Manchester University Press, 2000).
Morrissey, Mary, 'Scripture, style and persuasion in seventeenth-century English theories of preaching', *Journal of Ecclesiastical History* 53 (2000): 686–706.
Morrissey, Mary, 'Sermon-notes and seventeenth-century manuscript communities', *Huntington Library Quarterly* 80 (2017): 293–307.
Mortimer, Sarah, *Reason and religion in the English revolution: the challenge of Socinianism* (Cambridge: Cambridge University Press, 2010).
Mulcahy, Bernard, OP, *Aquinas' notion of pure nature and the Christian integralism of Henri De Lubac* (New York: Peter Lang, 2010).
Muller, Richard A., *After Calvin: studies in the development of a theological tradition* (Oxford: Oxford University Press, 2003).
Muller, Richard A., *Calvin and the Reformed tradition: on the work of Christ and the order of salvation* (Grand Rapids, MI: Baker Academic, 2012).
Muller, Richard A., *Christ and the decree: Christology and predestination in Reformed theology from Calvin to Perkins* (Durham, NC: Labyrinth Press, 1986).
Muller, Richard A., *God, creation, and providence in the thought of Jacob Arminius: sources and directions of Scholastic Protestantism in the era of early Orthodoxy* (Grand Rapids, MI: Baker, 1991).
Muller, Richard A., *Post-Reformation Reformed dogmatics: the rise and development of Reformed Orthodoxy, ca. 1520 to ca. 1725*, 4 vols (Grand Rapids: Baker, 2003).
Muller, Richard A., 'The Christological problem in the thought of Jacobus Arminius', *Nederlands Archief voor Kerkgeschiedenis* 68 (1998): 145–63.
Muller, Richard A., *The unaccommodated Calvin: studies in the foundation of a theological tradition* (New York: Oxford University Press, 2000).
Muller, Richard A., 'Toward the *pactum salutis*: Locating the origins of a concept', *Mid-America Journal of Theology*, 18 (2007): 11–65.
Mulsow, Martin, and Jan Rohls (eds), *Socinianism and Arminianism: Antitrinitarians, Calvinists, and cultural exchange in seventeenth-century Europe* (Leiden: Brill, 2005).
Murray, John, *Redemption accomplished and applied* (Grand Rapids, MI: Eerdmans, 1955).
Mutisya, Joseph U., 'Divine sovereignty in John Owen's doctrine of atonement' (unpublished PhD thesis, Dallas Theological Seminary, 2015).
Nelson, Eric, *The Hebrew republic: Jewish sources and the transformation of European political thought* (Cambridge, MA: Harvard University Press, 2010).
Newman, John Henry, *Apologia pro Vita Sua* (London: Oxford University Press, 1964).
Nichols, Aidan, *Discovering Aquinas: an introduction to his life, work, and influence* (Grand Rapids, MI: Eerdmans, 2002).
Norbrook, David, 'Atheists and republicans', in David Norbrook et al (eds), *Lucretius and the early modern* (Oxford: Oxford University Press, 2015).
Norbrook, David, 'Introduction', in Elizabeth Clarke et al (eds), *The works of Lucy Hutchinson*, vol. 2: *theological writings and translations: part 1 introduction and texts* (Oxford: Oxford University Press, 2018).
Nuttall, Geoffrey F., 'Milton's churchmanship in 1659: His letter to Jean de Labadie', *Milton Quarterly* 35 (2001): 227–31.

Nuttall, Geoffrey F., *The Holy Spirit in Puritan faith and experience* (Oxford: Basil Blackwell, 1946).
Oberman, Heiko A., 'Quo Vadis? Tradition from Irenaeus to Humani Generis', *Scottish Journal of Theology* 16 (1963): 225–55.
Oh, Changlok, 'Beholding the glory of God in Christ: Communion with God in the theology of John Owen (1616–83)' (unpublished PhD thesis, Westminster Theological Seminary, 2006).
Oliver, Robert W. (ed.), *John Owen: the man and his theology* (Darlington, UK: Evangelical Press, 2002).
Oliver, Robert W., 'John Owen (1616–1683): His life and times', in Robert W. Oliver (ed.), *John Owen: the man and his theology* (Darlington, UK: Evangelical Press, 2002).
Ollerton, Andrew, 'The crisis of Calvinism and the rise of Arminianism in Cromwellian England' (unpublished PhD thesis, University of Leicester, 2016).
Orme, William, *Memoirs of the life, writings, and religious connexions of John Owen, D.D.* (London: T. Hamilton, 1820).
Packer, J. I., *A quest for godliness: The Puritan vision of the Christian life* (1990; rpr. Wheaton, IL: Crossway, 2010).
Packer, J. I., 'Arminianisms', in J. I. Packer (ed.), *Honouring the people of God: collected shorter writings of J. I. Packer*, vol. 4 (Carlisle, UK: Paternoster, 1999).
Packer, J. I., '"Keswick" and the Reformed doctrine of sanctification', *Evangelical Quarterly* 27 (1955): 153–67.
Padley, Kenneth, 'A reception history of the letter to the Hebrews in England, 1547–1685' (unpublished DPhil thesis, The University of Oxford, 2016).
Patterson, Annabel M., *Censorship and interpretation: the conditions of writing and reading in early modern England* (Madison, WS: University of Wisconsin Press, 1984).
Patterson, W. B., *King James VI and I and the reunion of Christendom* (Cambridge: Cambridge University Press, 2000).
Patterson, W. B., *William Perkins and the making of a Protestant England* (Oxford: Oxford University Press, 2012).
Pauw, Amy Plantinga,*'The supreme harmony of all': the trinitarian theology of Jonathan Edwards* (Grand Rapids: Eerdmans, 2002).
Paver, Jonathan David, 'Union with Christ in the theology of Dr. John Owen (1616–1683): With special emphasis on its impact on sanctification and a Christian's duty' (unpublished MA thesis, Trinity Evangelical Divinity School, 1996).
Pederson, Randall J., 'Reformed Orthodoxy in Puritanism', *Perichoresis* 14 (2016): 45–59.
Peterson, Brandon, 'Paving the way? Penalty and atonement in Thomas Aquinas' soteriology', *International Journal of Systematic Theology* 15 (2013): 265–83.
Picciotto, Joanna, *Labors of innocence in early modern England* (Cambridge, MA: Harvard University Press, 2010).
Pipa, Joseph A., Jr. and J. Andrew Wortman (eds), *Sanctification: growing in grace* (Taylors, SC: Southern Presbyterian Press, 2001).
Piper, John, *Contending for our all: defending truth and treasuring Christ in the lives of Athanasius, John Owen, and J. Gresham Machen* (Wheaton, IL: Crossway, 2011).
Platinga, Jr. Cornelius, *Not the way it's supposed to be: a breviary of sin* (Grand Rapids, MI: Eerdmans, 1995).

Poole, William, *Milton and the idea of the fall* (Cambridge: Cambridge University Press, 2005).
Porter, Roy, *The creation of the modern world: the untold story of the British Enlightenment* (New York: W.W. Norton & Company, 2000).
Powell, Hunter, '"Promote, protect, prosecute": The Congregational divines and the establishment of church and magistrate in Cromwellian England', in Elliot Vernon and Hunter Powell (eds), *Church polity and politics in the Britain Atlantic world, c. 1635–66* (Manchester: Manchester University Press, 2020).
Price, John, *Danmonii Orientales Illustres: or, The worthies of Devon. A work, wherein the lives and fortunes of the most famous divines, statesmen, swordsmen, physicians, writers, and other eminent persons, natives of that most noble province, from before the Norman conquest, down to the present age, are memorized, in an alphabetical order, out of the Most Approved Authors, Both in Print and Manuscript* (London, 1810).
Quantin, Jean-Louis, *The Church of England and Christian antiquity: the construction of a confessional identity in the 17th century* (Oxford: Oxford University Press, 2009).
Radner, Ephraim, 'The Holy Spirit and unity: Getting out of the way of Christ', *International Journal of Systematic Theology* 16 (2014): 207–20.
Reece, Henry, *The Army in Cromwellian England, 1649–1660* (Oxford: Oxford University Press, 2013).
Reedy, Gerard, 'The reception of a science of texts in England, 1658–1740', *Harvard Theological Review* 105 (2012): 402–22.
Rehnman, Sebastian, *Divine discourse: the theological methodology of John Owen* (Grand Rapids, MI: Baker Academic, 2002).
Rehnman, Sebastian, 'John Owen: A reformed scholastic at Oxford', in Willem J. van Asselt and E. Dekker (eds), *Reformation and Scholasticism: an ecumenical enterprise* (Grand Rapids, MI: Baker Academic, 2001).
Reid, James, *Memoirs of the lives and writings of those eminent divines who convened in the famous Assembly at Westminster, in the seventeenth century*, 2 vols (Paisley: Stephen and Andrew Young, 1811–1815).
Renihan, S. D., 'From shadow to substance: The federal theology of the English Particular Baptists (1642–1704)' (unpublished PhD thesis, Vjrie University Amsterdam, 2017).
Rivers, Isabel, *Reason, grace and sentiment: a study of the language of religion and ethics in England, 1660–1780*, vol. 1: *Whichcote to Wesley* (Cambridge: Cambridge University Press, 1991).
Rohls, Jan 'Calvinism, Arminianism, and Socinianism in the Netherlands until the Synod of Dort', in Martin Mulsow and Jan Rohls (eds), *Socinianism and Arminianism: Antitrinitarians, Calvinists, and cultural exchange in seventeenth-century Europe* (Leiden: Brill, 2005).
Rose, Jacqueline, *Godly kingship in Restoration England: the politics of the royal supremacy, 1660–1688* (Cambridge: Cambridge University Press, 2014).
Sangha, Laura, 'Ralph Thoresby and individual devotion in late seventeenth- and early eighteenth-century England', *Historical Research* 92 (2019): 139–59.
Saxton, David W., *God's battle plan for the mind: The Puritan practice of Biblical meditation* (Grand Rapids, MI: Reformation Heritage Books, 2015).
Schendel, Joshua D., '"A learned dispute among friends": William Twisse (1578–1646) and John Owen (1616–1683) on the necessity of the Christ's satisfaction' (unpublished PhD thesis, St. Louis University, 2020).

Scott, Jonathan, *Algernon Sidney and the Restoration crisis, 1677–1683* (Cambridge: Cambridge University Press, 1991).
Seaward, Paul, 'Morice, Sir William (1602–1676)', *ODNB*, s.v.
Seaver, Paul S., *Wallington's world: A Puritan artisan in seventeenth-century London* (Stanford: Stanford University Press, 1986).
Serjeantson, Richard, 'Francis Bacon and the "interpretation of nature" in the late Renaissance', *Isis* 105 (2014): 681–705.
Sewel, William, *The history of the rise, increase and progress of the Christian people called Quakers* (New York: Baker & Crane, 1844).
Shapin, Stephen and Simon Schaffer, *Leviathan and the air-pump: Hobbes, Boyle and the experimental life* (Princeton, NJ: Princeton University Press, 1985).
Shapiro, Barbara, *John Wilkins, 1614–1672: an intellectual biography* (Berkeley, CA: University of California Press, 1969).
Simon, Irène, *Three Restoration divines: Barrow, South, Tillotson: selected sermons* (Paris: Société d'édition 'Les Belles Lettres', 1976).
Skarsaune, Oskar, *The proof from prophecy: a study in Justin Martyr's proof-text tradition: text-type, provenance, theological profile* (Leiden: Brill, 1987).
Smith, David L., 'Oliver Cromwell and the Protectorate parliaments', in Patrick Little (ed.), *The Cromwellian Protectorate* (Woodbridge, UK: Boydell, 2007).
Smith, Nigel, '"And if God was one of us": John Biddle and Socinianism in seventeenth-century England', in David Lowenstein and John Marshall (eds), *Heresy, literature and politics in early modern English culture* (Cambridge: Cambridge University Press, 2006).
Snoddy, Richard, 'A Display of Learning? Citations and Shortcuts in John Owen's *Display of Arminianisme* (1643)', *Westminster Theological Journal* 82 (2020): 319–35.
Snoddy, Richard, *The soteriology of James Ussher: the act and object of saving faith* (Oxford: Oxford University Press, 2014).
Southern, R. W., 'From schools to university', in Jeremy Catto (ed.), *The early Oxford schools* (Oxford: Oxford University Press, 1984).
Spellman, W. M., *The Latitudinarians and the Church of England, 1660–1700* (Athens, GA: University of Georgia Press, 1993).
Spence, Alan, 'Christ's humanity and ours: John Owen', in C. Schwobel and C. Gunton (eds), *Persons: divine and human* (Edinburgh: T&T Clark, 1991).
Spence, Alan, *Incarnation and inspiration: John Owen and the coherence of Christology* (London: T&T Clark, 2007).
Spence, Alan, 'John Owen and trinitarian agency', *Scottish Journal of Theology* 43 (1990): 157–73.
Spence, Alan, 'The significance of John Owen for modern Christology', in Kelly M. Kapic and Mark Jones (eds), *The Ashgate research companion to John Owen's theology* (Farnham, UK: Ashgate, 2012).
Spurlock, R. Scott, 'Cromwell's Edinburgh press and the development of print culture in Scotland', *Scottish Historical Review* 90 (2011): 179–203.
Spurlock, R. Scott, *Cromwell and Scotland: conquest and religion, 1650–1660* (Edinburgh: John Donald, 2007).
Spurr, John, 'Religion in Restoration England', in L. K. J. Glassey (ed.), *The reigns of Charles II and James VII & II* (London: Palgrave, 1997).
Stanglin, Keith D., '"Arminius *avant la lettre*": Peter Baro, Jacob Arminius, and the bond of predestinarian polemic', *Westminster Theological Journal*, 67 (2005): 51–74.

Stanglin, Keith D., *Arminius on the assurance of salvation: the context, roots, and shape of the Leiden debate, 1603–1609* (Leiden: Brill, 2007).
Stanglin, Keith D. and Thomas H. McCall, *Jacob Arminius: Theologian of grace* (New York: Oxford University Press, 2012).
Stephens, Isaac, *The gentlewoman's remembrance: Patriarchy, piety, and singlehood in early Stuart England* (Manchester: Manchester University Press, 2016).
Stevenson, Jane, 'Introduction', in *The works of Lucy Hutchinson*, vol. 2: *theological writings and translations*, eds Elizabeth Clarke et al (Oxford: Oxford University Press, 2018).
Strype, John, *Annals of the Reformation and establishment of religion*, volume 2, part 1 (Oxford: Clarendon Press, 1824).
Sutanto, Nathaniel Gray, 'On the theological interpretation of Scripture: The indirect identity thesis, Reformed Orthodoxy, and trinitarian considerations', *Westminster Theological Journal* 77 (2015): 337–53.
Svensson, Manfred, 'John Owen and John Locke: Confessionalism, doctrinal minimalism, and toleration', *History of European ideas* 43 (2017): 302–16.
Svensson, Manfred, 'The alms of authority? John Owen's understanding of toleration', *Journal of Church and State* 58 (2016): 690–709.
Sytsma, David S. *Richard Baxter and the mechanical philosophers* (Oxford: Oxford University Press, 2017).
Tachau, Katherine H., *Vision and certitude in the age of Ockham: optics, epistemology and the foundation of semantics, 1250–1345* (Leiden: Brill, 1988).
Tadmor, Naomi, *The social university of the English Bible: scripture, society, and culture in early modern England* (Cambridge: Cambridge University Press, 2010).
Tay, Edwin E. M., *The priesthood of Christ: the atonement in the theology of John Owen* (Milton Keynes, UK: Paternoster, 2014).
The register of the Visitors of the University of Oxford, ed. M. Barrows (London, 1881).
Thomson, Andrew, 'Life of Dr Owen', in William H. Goold (ed.), *The works of John Owen* (Edinburgh: T&T Clark, 1862), vol. 1.
Todd, Henry John, *Memoirs of the life and writings of the Right Rev. Brian Walton*, 2 vols (London: Rivington, 1821).
Todd, Margo, 'Justifying God: The Calvinisms of the British delegation to the Synod of Dort', *Archiv für Reformationsgeschichte* 96 (2005): 272–90.
Toon, Peter, *God's statesman: the life and work of John Owen* (Exeter, Paternoster, 1971).
Torrance, James B., 'The incarnation and "limited atonement"', *The Scottish Bulletin of Evangelical Theology* 2 (1984): 32–40.
Treier, Daniel J., *The theological interpretation of Scripture: recovering a Christian practice* (Grand Rapids, MI: Baker, 2008).
Trueman, Carl R., 'Atonement and the covenant of redemption: John Owen on the nature of Christ's satisfaction', in David Gibson and Jonathan Gibson (eds), *From heaven he came and sought her: definite atonement in historical, Biblical, theological, and pastoral perspective* (Wheaton, IL: Crossway, 2013).
Trueman, Carl R., 'John Owen's *Dissertation on divine justice*: An exercise in Christocentric scholasticism', *Calvin Theological Journal* 33 (1998): 87–103.
Trueman, Carl R., 'John Owen and modernity: Reflections on historiography, modernity, and the self', in Kelly M. Kapic and Willem van Vlastuin (eds), *John Owen between Orthodoxy and modernity* (Leiden: Brill, 2019).

Trueman, Carl R., *John Owen: Reformed Catholic, Renaissance man* (Aldershot, UK: Ashgate, 2007).
Trueman, Carl R., 'Puritan theology as historical event: A linguistic approach to the ecumenical context', in Willem J. van Asselt and Eef Dekker (eds), *Reformation and scholasticism* (Grand Rapids, MI: Baker, 2001).
Trueman, Carl R., *The claims of truth: John Owen's trinitarian theology* (Carlisle, UK: Paternoster, 2002).
Trueman, Carl R., 'The necessity of the atonement', in Mark Jones and Michael A. G. Haykin (eds), *Drawn into controversie: reformed theological diversity and debates within seventeenth-Century British Puritanism* (Göttingen: Vandenhoeck & Ruprecht, 2011).
Tuck, Richard, *Natural rights theories: their origin and development* (Cambridge: Cambridge University Press, 1998).
Tucker, Thomas J., 'Safeguarding the treasure: John Owen and the analogy of faith' (unpublished PhD thesis, University of Aberdeen, 2006).
Turner, G. Lyon, 'Williamson's spy book', *Transactions of the Congregational Historical Society* 5 (1911): 301–17.
Tuttle, Julius Herbert, *Libraries of the Mathers. Proceedings of the American antiquarian society at the semi-annual meeting, April 1910* (Worcester, MA: The Davis Press, 1910).
Tweeddale, John W., 'A John Owen bibliography', in Kelly M. Kapic and Mark Jones (eds), *The Ashgate research companion to John Owen's theology* (Farnham, UK: Ashgate, 2012).
Tweeddale, John W., 'John Owen's commentary on Hebrews in context', in Kelly M. Kapic and Mark Jones (eds), *The Ashgate research companion to John Owen's theology* (Farnham, UK: Ashgate, 2012).
Tweeddale, John W., *John Owen and Hebrews: the foundation of Biblical interpretation* (London: T&T Clark, 2019).
Tyacke, Nicholas (ed.), *A history of the University of Oxford*, vol. 4: *Seventeenth-Century Oxford* (Oxford: Clarendon Press, 1997).
Tyacke, Nicholas, *Anti-Calvinists: the rise of English Arminianism, c. 1590–1640* (Oxford: Clarendon Press, 1987).
Tyacke, Nicholas, 'From Laudians to Latitudinarians', in Grant Tapsell (ed.), *The later Stuart church, 1660–1714* (Manchester: Manchester University Press, 2012).
Under Calvin's yoke: Dr. John Owen's three invincible questions answered by Bereana (London: Elliot Stock, 1900).
Van Asselt, Willem J., 'Covenant theology as relational theology: The contributions of Johannes Cocceius (1603–1669) and John Owen (1618–1683) to a living Reformed theology', in Kelly M. Kapic and Mark Jones (eds), *The Ashgate research companion to John Owen's theology* (Farnham, UK: Ashgate, 2012).
Van den Belt, Henk, '*Vocatio* as regeneration: John Owen's concept of effectual calling', in Kelly M. Kapic and Willem van Vlastuin (eds), *John Owen between orthodoxy and modernity* (Leiden: Brill, 2019).
Van der Meer, Jitse M. and Richard J. Oosterhof, 'God, Scripture, and the rise of modern science (1200–1700): Notes in the margin of Harrison's hypothesis', in *Nature and Scripture in the Abrahamic Religions: up to 1700*, eds. Jitse M. van der Meer and Scott Mandelbrote (Leiden: Brill, 2008).
Van Dixhoorn, Chad, *Confessing the faith: a reader's guide to the Westminster Confession of Faith* (Edinburgh: Banner of Truth, 2014).

Van Dixhoorn, Chad, *God's ambassadors: The Westminster Assembly and the reformation of the English pulpit, 1643–1653* (Grand Rapids, MI: Reformation Heritage Books, 2017).

van Leeuwen, Marius, Keith D. Stanglin, and Marijke Tolsma (eds), *Arminius, Arminianism, and Europe: Jacobus Arminius (1559/60–1609)* (Leiden: Brill, 2009).

van Loon, Hans, *The Dyophysite Christology of Cyril of Alexandria* (Leiden: Brill, 2009).

VanDrunen, David, *Natural law and the two kingdoms: a study in the development of Reformed social thought* (Grand Rapids, MI: Eerdmans, 2010).

Vanhoozer, Kevin (gen. ed.), *Dictionary for theological interpretation of the Bible* (Grand Rapids, MI: Baker, 2005).

Vernon, Elliot, 'Introduction: Church polity and politics in the British Atlantic world, c. 1635–66', in Elliot Vernon and Hunter Powell (eds), *Church polity and politics in the British Atlantic world, c. 1635–66* (Manchester: Manchester University Press, 2020).

Wallace, Dewey D., 'The life and thought of John Owen to 1660: A study of the significance of Calvinist theology in English Puritanism' (unpublished PhD thesis, Princeton University, 1965).

Wallace, Dewey D., *Puritans and predestination: Grace in English Protestant theology, 1525–1695* (Chapel Hill, NC: University of North Carolina Press, 1982).

Wallace, Dewey D., *Shapers of English Calvinism, 1660–1714: variety, persistence, and transformation* (New York: Oxford University Press, 2011).

Warfield, B. B., *Studies in Tertullian and Augustine* (Oxford: Oxford University Press, 1930).

Webster, John B., 'Discovering dogmatics', in Darren C. Marks (ed.), *Shaping a theological mind: theological context and methodology* (New York: Routledge, 2017).

Webster, John B., *God without measure: working papers in Christian theology*, 2 vols (London: T&T Clark, 2018).

Webster, John B., *Holiness* (Grand Rapids, MI: Eerdmans, 2003).

Webster, John B., *The domain of the Word: Scripture and theological reason* (London: T&T Clark, 2012).

Webster, John B., 'The place of Christology in systematic theology', in Francesca Aran Murphy (ed.), *The Oxford handbook of Christology* (Oxford: Oxford University Press, 2015).

White, Peter, *Predestination, policy and polemic: conflict and consensus in the English Church from the Reformation to the civil war* (Cambridge: Cambridge University Press, 1992).

Whiting, C. E., *Studies in English Puritanism* (London: SPCK, 1931).

Wilberforce, William, *A practical view of the prevailing religious system of professed Christians, in the higher and middle classes in this country, contrasted with real Christianity*, eighteenth edition (London: T. Cadell, 1830).

Wilbur, Earl Morse, *A history of Unitarianism in Transylvania, England, and America* (Cambridge, MA: Harvard University Press, 1945).

Wilken, Robert Louis, *Liberty in the things of God: The Christian origins of religious freedom* (New Haven, CT: Yale University Press, 2019).

Williams, George Huntston, *The Polish Brethren: documentation of the history and thought of Unitarianism in the Polish-Lithuanian Commonwealth and in the diaspora, 1601–1685*, 2 vols. (Missoula: Scholars Press, 1980).

Wilson, John F., *Pulpit in Parliament: Puritanism during the English civil wars, 1640–1648* (Princeton, NJ: Princeton University Press, 1969).

Wilson, Walter, *The history and antiquities of dissenting churches and meeting houses, in London, Westminster, and Southwark*, 4 vols (London, 1808–1814).

Winship, Michael P., *Hot Protestants: a history of Puritanism in England and America* (London: Yale University Press, 2018).

Winship, Michael P., 'Weak Christians, backsliders, and carnal gospelers: Assurance of salvation and the pastoral origins of Puritan practical divinity in the 1580s', *Church History* 70 (2001): 462–81.

Wintroub, Michael, 'The looking glass of facts: Collecting, rhetoric, and citing the self in the experimental natural philosophy of Robert Boyle', in Tina Skouen and Ryan Stark (eds), *Rhetoric and the early Royal Society* (Leiden: Brill, 2015).

Wisse, Maarten and Hugo Meijer, 'Pneumatology: Tradition and renewal', in Herman J. Selderhuis (ed.), *A companion to Reformed Orthodoxy* (Leiden: Brill, 2013), 465–518.

Wittman, Tyler R., 'The end of the incarnation: John Owen, trinitarian agency and Christology', *International Journal of Systematic Theology* 15 (2013): 284–300.

Wojcik, Jan W., 'The theological context of Boyle's *Things above Reason*', in Michael Hunter (ed.), *Robert Boyle reconsidered* (Cambridge: Cambridge University Press, 1994).

Wolter, Allan B., 'Duns Scotus on intuition, memory, and our knowledge of individuals', in Marilyn McCord Adams (ed.), *The philosophical theology of Duns Scotus* (Ithaca: Cornell University Press, 1990).

Wolter, Allan B. and Marilyn McCord Adams, 'Memory and intuition: A focal debate in fourteenth-century cognitive psychology', *Franciscan Studies* 53 (1993): 175–230.

Woo, Byunghoon, 'The *pactum salutis* in the theologies of Witsius, Owen, Dickson, Goodwin, and Cocceius' (unpublished PhD thesis, Calvin Theological Seminary, 2015).

Wood, Anthony, *Athenæ Oxonienses: an exact history of all the writers and bishops who have had their education in the University of Oxford* (London, 1692).

Woolford, Thomas, 'Natural theology and natural philosophy in the late Renaissance' (unpublished PhD thesis, University of Cambridge, 2011).

Woolhouse, Roger, *Locke: a biography* (Cambridge: Cambridge University Press, 2007).

Woolrych, Austin, *Britain in revolution, 1625–1660* (Oxford: Oxford University Press, 2002).

Worden, Blair, 'Cromwellian Oxford', in Nicholas Tyacke (ed.), *Seventeenth-Century Oxford* (Oxford: Clarendon Press, 1997), 733–72.

Worden, Blair, *God's instruments: political conduct in the England of Oliver Cromwell* (Oxford: Oxford University Press, 2012).

Worden, Blair, 'Toleration and the Cromwellian protectorate', in W. J. Sheils (ed.), *Persecution and toleration* (Oxford: Blackwell, 1984).

Worden, Blair, *The Rump Parliament, 1648–1652* (Cambridge: Cambridge University Press, 1974).

Wray, Daniel, 'The spiritual man in the teachings of John Owen', *Banner of Truth* 182 (1978): 10–21.

Wynn, Christopher G. R., 'The essential psychological and theological foundations for John Owen's doctrine of mortification' (unpublished MTh thesis, Dallas Theological Seminary, 2003).

Zachman, Randall C., *The assurance of faith: conscience in the theology of Martin Luther and John Calvin* (Louisville, KY: Westminster John Knox Press, 2005).

Zook, Melinda S., *Radical Whigs and conspiratorial politics in late Stuart England* (University Park, PA: The Pennsylvania State University Press, 1999).

OWEN'S WORKS INDEX

Note: Works are listed in chronological order. For full titles, see the list of abbreviations on pp. xi–xxv.

A display of Arminianisme (1643)   7, 26, 28, 48–9, 56, 58, 60–1, 85, 119, 190–1, 200–5, 235, 256–7, 275–302, 305–6, 310, 314, 415, 473

The duty of pastors and people distinguished (1644)   26–7, 59, 67, 72, 86, 121, 123, 125, 132, 246, 369

Two short catechismes (1645)   27, 59–60, 137

A vision of unchangeable free mercy (1646)   27, 61, 86–7, 90, 121, 133–5, 141, 192, 240–1, 243, 416

Eben-ezer (1648)   16–17, 28, 61, 88, 121–2, 125, 133, 141

Eshcol (1648)   121, 125

The death of death in the death of Christ (1648)   7, 16, 28–9, 35, 47, 51, 58, 61, 64, 88, 120–1, 205–6, 257, 298, 302, 303–335, 338–9, 369–70, 416, 491, 510

A sermon preached to the Honourable House of Commons, in Parliament assembled: on January 31 (1649)   29, 89–90

The shaking and translating of heaven and earth (1649)   29, 91, 126, 133, 137, 370

The branch of the Lord, the beauty of Sion (1650)   29, 92, 133

Of the death of Christ (1650)   18, 29, 61–2, 137, 200, 332–4

The advantage of the kingdome of Christ (1651)   132–5, 137

The labouring saints dismission to rest (1652)   30, 93, 134–5, 137, 141

The primer (1652)   151

A sermon preached to the Parliament, Octob. 13. 1652 (1652)   30, 93–4, 133, 135

Diatriba de justitia divina (1653)   30, 35, 51, 64, 253–4, 260–1, 263, 266, 316, 322, 328

The doctrine of the saints perseverance (1654)   18, 31, 47, 63, 94, 269, 301, 345, 418

Vindiciae evangelicae (1655)   26, 31, 64–5, 74, 95, 153–6, 179, 208–10, 213, 255, 301–2, 310, 332, 334, 371, 388, 417

Of the mortification of sinne in believers (1656)   7, 14, 31, 33, 44, 47, 51, 68, 123, 156–9, 162, 256, 263, 336–63

A review of the annotations of Hugo Grotius (1656)   65

God's work in founding Zion (1656)   31, 96–7, 128, 133, 135, 138
God's presence with a people (1656)   31, 68, 128, 133–4, 138
Of communion with God (1657)   21, 32, 35, 38–9, 42, 45, 68, 70, 75–6, 78, 97, 123, 127, 132, 154, 156, 158–60, 216, 328, 357, 511
Of schisme (1657)   14, 33, 66–7, 82, 188, 190, 196, 241, 243
A review of the true nature of schisme (1657)   14, 33, 67, 82, 190
An answer to a later treatise of Daniel Cawdrey about the nature schism (1658)   67
Of temptation (1658)   97–8, 135, 138–9, 156–8, 163, 256, 263, 356–7
Pro Sacris Scripturis (1658)   21, 33, 65, 403
Of the divine originall (1659)   34, 65–6, 70, 241, 247, 372
The glory and interest of nations professing the Gospel (1659)   34, 99–100, 142
Two questions (1659)   34, 102, 181–3
Θεολογουμενα παντοδαπα (1661)   32, 35, 51, 59, 68–70, 153–4, 160–7, 226, 234, 372–3, 407
Animadversions on Fiat lux (1662)   36, 49, 71–2, 78, 103–5, 188–9, 192
A discourse concerning liturgies (1662)   35, 71, 104, 130, 183–5
A vindication of the animadversions on Fiat lux (1664)   36, 71, 78, 105–6, 185, 188, 191
Indulgence and toleration considered (1667)   37, 71, 107–8
A peace-offering (1667)   37, 71, 106–8, 186–7, 191
A brief instruction in the worship of God (1667)   36, 71, 106, 185
Hebrews (1668)   37, 72–3, 213–4, 364–83, 399, 420
Indwelling sin (1668)   19, 37, 44, 71, 108, 139, 256, 263, 347, 358
A practical exposition on the 130th Psalm (1669)   38, 71, 121, 124, 139, 263, 374, 379, 391
Truth and innocence vindicated (1669)   38, 71, 191, 193, 243, 246, 385

A brief declaration and vindication of the doctrine of the Trinity (1669)   39, 71, 74–5, 207, 211–4, 379
Sabbath (1671)   38, 71, 73, 75, 247, 334, 374, 378–9, 381, 382
A discourse concerning evangelical love, church-peace and unity (1672)   39, 112, 189
A vindication of some passages (1674)   38, 75–6, 419
Πνευματολογια (1674)   8, 24, 39, 41, 45, 68, 76–8, 119–20, 154, 158, 242, 258–9, 262–7, 270, 313, 334, 340–5, 374, 378, 384–413, 457, 499–500
Hebrews (1674)   310, 371, 376–8, 380, 383
The nature of apostasie (1676)   8, 37, 47, 193, 235, 374, 379, 403, 414–38
The doctrine of justification by faith (1677)   24, 40, 45, 192, 252, 266–8, 338, 379, 439–60
The reason of faith (1677)   39–41, 77, 236, 246–7, 271–2, 374, 387, 400, 405
The causes, waies & means of understanding the mind of God (1678)   39, 41, 77, 166, 242, 374, 379, 387, 400
Χριστολογια (1679)   41, 43, 51, 68, 76–8, 111, 215–20, 242, 247, 374, 462–3, 468
The church of Rome, no safe guide (1679)   41, 78, 143, 243, 424, 466
Some considerations about union among Protestants (1680)   42, 78–9, 111–12, 194
A brief vindication of the non-conformists (1680)   67, 112, 182
Hebrews (1680)   50, 328, 378, 380, 421, 424
An enquiry into evangelical churches (1681)   42
An humble testimony (1681)   42, 113, 123
The grace and duty of being spiritually-minded (1681)   42, 45, 47, 140, 242
A discourse of the work of the Holy Spirit in prayer (1682)   21, 39, 77, 400

A brief and impartial account of the nature of the Protestant religion (1682)   43, 78, 113–15, 145
The chamber of imagery in the Church of Rome laid open (1683)   41, 47, 78
Meditations and discourses on the glory of Christ (1684)   8, 24, 43, 45, 48, 51, 77, 124, 159, 169, 215, 220, 222, 237, 461–86
Hebrews (1684)   43, 378
Bibliotheca Oweniana (1684)   63, 65, 198, 367
A treatise of the dominion of sin and grace (1688)   44
The true nature of a Gospel church and its government (1689)   44, 79
Seasonable words for English Protestants (1690)   113, 144
Meditations and discourses concerning the glory of Christ (1691)   77, 214, 220–2, 243–4, 248
Two discourses concerning the Holy Spirit, and his work (1693)   39, 76–7, 400
Gospel grounds and evidences of the faith of God's elect (1695)   44
An answer unto two questions (1720)   45
Seventeen sermons (1720)   94, 380
A complete collection of the sermons of the Reverend and learned John Owen (1721)   45, 91, 124, 128, 131–5, 137–9, 142–3, 184, 385
Thirteen sermons (1756)   45, 112–13, 119, 130, 140, 144
Twenty-five discourses suitable to the Lord's Supper (1760)   45
Hebrews (1790)   382
Hebrews (1812)   382
Works (1826)   1, 45, 369, 382–3
Works (1850, 1965, 1991)   xxiv, xxv
The correspondence of John Owen (1970)   2, 23, 24, 45–6, 94, 95, 129, 131, 152, 188, 196, 223, 229, 231, 233, 437
The Oxford orations (1971)   2, 26, 45–6, 149, 151, 152, 153, 157, 165, 230, 234

AUTHOR AND SUBJECT INDEX

Act of Oblivion (1660)   105
Act of Supremacy (1559)   215
Act of Toleration (1689)   171, 187, 195
Act of Uniformity (1662)   22, 34–6, 38, 104, 183, 188
Aesop   248
Ainsworth, Henry   74
Albert the Great   252
Aldersey, Thomas   124, 128, 156, 168
Alleine, Joseph   151 n.30, 168
Allen, Michael   502
Allison, C. FitzSimons   512
Alsop, Vincent   427
Alston, William P.   245
Alvarez, Diego   252, 278, 299
Ambrose   77, 384
Ames, William   60, 203
Amyraut, Moses   50, 70, 79, 211, 261
Andrewes, Lancelot   281
Anglesey, Arthur Annesley, earl of   234
Anselm   323, 500
Antichrist   15, 91, 94, 96, 113, 130, 132, 145, 192
antinomianism   8, 88, 204, 332–4, 337, 362, 411, 417, 418, 434, 441, 447, 453, 457, 508, 512
Aquinas   26, 30, 33, 202, 206, 209, 211, 212, 215, 217, 222, 252, 253, 255, 258, 259, 265, 268, 288, 289, 301, 342, 392, 395, 406, 467 n.22, 499, 507, 509

Aratus of Sicyon   251
Archimedes   286
Aristotle   162, 198, 229, 230, 252, 254, 258, 259, 268, 498
Arius   173, 209, 425
Arminianism   5, 6, 8, 25, 26, 31, 33, 40, 54, 57, 72, 85, 88, 120, 151, 172, 177, 198, 199, 201, 202, 252, 275–302, 316, 403, 405, 415, 416, 418, 493
Arminius, Jacobus   58, 199, 202, 203, 205, 267, 277, 279–81, 291
Asty, John   109, 110, 112, 374, 496 n.19
Athanasius   213
atheism   28, 87, 138, 179, 202, 203, 227, 239, 240, 242, 245, 248, 349, 425, 431, 433, 434, 460
atonement   7, 26, 28–31, 38, 48, 65, 75, 120, 280, 296, 302–35, 338, 339, 343, 369, 417, 444–6, 452, 491, 508, 510
Augustine   77, 201, 204, 206, 207, 209, 212, 213, 215, 217, 252, 261, 276–8, 286, 287, 301, 375, 385, 406–7, 429, 438, 452, 500, 509
Austen, Ralph   249, 250

Bacon, Francis   149, 225, 230, 236, 237, 240, 242, 245, 249, 250
Bañex, Domingo   278
Banner of Truth   xxiv, 1, 45, 383, 493

Baptists and Baptist churches   13, 18, 88, 100, 150 n.23, 171, 172, 187, 188, 195, 221, 380
Barker, Matthew   101
Barlow, Thomas   151, 190, 198, 229, 254
Baro, Peter   58
Barrett, Matthew   511
Barrow, Henry   148
Barth, Karl   335, 507
Basil the Great   384, 499
Bavinck, Herman   500
Baxter, Richard   5, 7, 28, 29, 31, 40, 42, 44, 53, 61, 62, 64, 67, 70, 100, 129, 178, 180, 182, 189, 190, 197, 199–200, 208, 211, 221, 229, 238, 239, 245, 246, 306, 331, 333, 335, 417, 457, 493, 498, 512
Baylor, Timothy   7, 504, 505, 507, 508
Beeke, Joel   7, 500
Bernard of Clairvaux   288
Beza, Theodore   79, 283
Bible, London Polyglot   34, 65, 66, 70, 74, 372. *See also* Walton, Brian
Biddle, John   31, 63, 64, 154, 155, 179, 207–10, 213, 302, 371, 417, 502
Biel, Gabriel   211, 405
Blasphemy Act (1648)   28, 87–9
Boersma, Hans   217
Bolton, Samuel   50, 189
Book of Common Prayer   22, 33, 36, 104, 175, 182–4, 190, 215, 220, 221, 229. *See also* Church of England
Booth, Sir George   101
Boyle, Robert   7, 163, 223, 224, 227, 228, 233, 235, 236, 245, 248, 249
Bradwardine   204
Bricot, Thomas   268
Bridge, William   22
Brooks, Thomas   358
Brown, Peter   276
Browne, Robert   148
Bucer, Martin   288
Bullinger, Heinrich   509
Bunhill Fields, London   24
Bunyan, John   13, 22, 204, 239, 248, 375, 420, 498
Burgess, Anthony   40
Butner, D. Glenn   509
Byfield, Richard   28

Calamy, Edmund   15, 189
Calloway, Katherine   6
Calvin, John, and his legacy   3, 5, 6, 13, 15, 28, 54, 79, 82, 85, 120, 132, 156, 171–3, 189, 195, 196, 198–206, 208–11, 215, 219, 221, 225, 227, 234, 236–40, 244, 245, 253, 261, 267, 269, 271, 275, 278, 279, 281–3, 288, 289, 292, 301, 303, 304, 353, 356, 375, 415–19, 430, 434, 438, 472, 491, 498, 499, 501
Cambridge, University of   59, 147–9, 167, 199, 230, 418, 489
Cameron, John   50, 261
Cane, John Vincent   71–2, 103–5
Cardell, John   126
Carey, Lucius   416
Cartwright, Christopher   74
Caryl, Joseph   42, 101, 129, 130
Casaubon, Méric   184
Cawdrey, Daniel   33, 63, 66–7, 95
Chalcedon, Council of   216, 398, 463, 472, 505
Charles I   6, 15, 17, 29, 34, 89, 104, 110, 133, 198, 231, 281, 415, 416
Charles II   6, 13, 22, 34, 54, 71, 83, 84, 103, 105–6, 111, 114, 132, 197, 220, 230, 371, 374
Charleton, Walter   228
Charnock, Stephen   95, 189
Cheynell, Francis   38, 54, 67, 208
Christ Church, Oxford   6, 29, 62, 68, 79, 127, 146, 150–2, 160–1, 189, 336. *See also* Oxford, University of
Chrysostom, John   213, 384
Churchill, Winston   489
Church of England   4, 33, 36, 47, 56–8, 76, 82, 85, 104, 105, 111, 130, 132, 170–96, 215, 216, 221, 251, 254, 289, 292, 295, 296, 306, 401, 415, 417, 419, 422, 426, 429, 437, 438, 448. *See also* Book of Common Prayer; Thirty-nine Articles
Church of Scotland   89–90
Cicero   198, 285, 286
Civil Wars   15, 27, 85, 90, 93, 101, 114, 118–19, 133, 134, 140, 141, 146, 198

Clanbrassil, Anne Hamilton, countess of 380
Clarkson, David 45, 196, 380
Clerical Disabilities Act (1642) 94
Cleveland, Christopher 3, 7, 202, 499, 507
Cleveland, Kendall 507
Clifford, Alan C. 3, 259, 498
Cocceius, Johannes 69, 80, 269, 366, 375
Coffey, John 27, 49, 171, 364, 418, 496
Coggeshall 16, 27, 68, 125
Colchester 16, 28, 88, 125
Collinson, Patrick 131, 171, 197
comets 144
Commeniq, Simon 381
Congregationalism 16, 18, 44, 67, 129, 171, 180, 187, 195–6, 221, 230, 262, 438
Conventicle Acts 109, 129–32, 143, 191, 215
Cook, Sarah Gibbard 2, 115
Cooper, Tim 3, 8, 494, 499
Corvinus, Joannes Arnoldi 58, 203, 205, 281, 291, 297
Cotton, John 16, 27, 60, 87, 180, 182
Council of State 95, 126, 129, 154, 182, 417
Covenanters 111. *See also* Solemn League and Covenant
Coverdale, Myles 173
Cowan, Martyn C. 3, 6, 495, 496
Coxe, Nehemiah 380
Cragg, G. R. 415, 438
Craig, Philip 352
Crell, Johann 76, 366, 394
Crisp, Oliver 505
Cromwell, Oliver 17, 18, 21, 83, 99, 126, 176, 182, 195, 198, 229, 370
Cromwell, Richard 99–101, 116, 230
Crossway 2, 46, 514
Crowe, William 365
Curcellaeus 210
Cyprian 77, 384

Dallas Theological Seminary 4
Davenant, John 5, 53, 59, 61, 199, 257, 306, 441, 447
Dell, William 228, 230

de Lubac, Henri 509
Desborough, John 100, 115
Descartes, René 259
Dickson, David 366
Didymus the Blind 77, 384, 499
dissenting academies 167
Dominicans 278, 299
Dort, Synod of 57, 58, 62, 193, 199, 200, 210, 269, 281, 283, 306, 401, 428, 429, 438, 463, 473
Downame, George 441
Dr Williams's Library, London 2
Du Moulin, Louis 130
Dunbar 133
Duns Scotus 403, 405, 500
Durandus 211, 288
Durham, James 74, 76
Dutch war, second (1665–1667) 109

Edinburgh 92
Edwards, John 437
Edwards, Jonathan 43, 45, 159, 218, 361, 381, 501
Edwards, Thomas 200
Edwards, William 382
Eliot, John 23
Elizabeth I 170, 172–4, 194, 199, 215
Enlightenment 40, 202, 279, 427, 432
Epimenides of Cnossos 251
Episcopius, Simon 58, 190, 203, 205, 210, 279–81, 291
Erasmus 205
Eusebius of Caesarea 288
Exclusion Crisis (1679–1681) 112, 113, 143, 144, 197

Fairfax, Sir Thomas 57, 61, 88
Feingold, Mordechai 163
Ferguson, Robert 84, 111, 115
Ferguson, Sinclair B. 2, 341, 345, 363, 510, 511
Fifth Monarchists 96, 101
Fire of London (1666) 109, 142–4
Fisher, Samuel 81
Five Mile Act (1665) 191, 215
Flavel, John 50
Fleetwood, Charles 23, 24, 100, 102, 128–30, 196, 437
Fleetwood, Smith 100

Fletcher, Elizabeth   19–20
Folger Shakespeare Library   380
Fordham   16, 26, 60, 86
Forty-two Articles (1552)   441
Fox, George   20
Francis of Assisi   489

Gaine, Simon Francis   467 n.22
Gale, Theophilus   166–8
Gamble-Smith, Whitney   8
Gatiss, Lee   6, 509, 514
Gibson, Jonathan   124
Gillespie, Patrick   75
Glanvill, Joseph   228, 235, 236, 244
Glorious Revolution (1688–1689)   43, 84, 187–94
Goffe, William   101, 102
Golding, Peter   342
Gomarus, Francis   75, 79, 199, 201, 280, 283
Goodman, John   192, 193, 426–32, 434, 437, 438
Goodwin, John   31, 47, 51, 63, 177, 178, 301, 336, 418, 423, 493
Goodwin, Thomas   1, 22, 67, 95, 98, 152, 189, 230, 336, 442
Goold, William H.   xxiv, xxv, 1, 2, 26, 30, 31, 33, 35, 36, 38, 39, 46, 64, 66, 68, 70, 72, 76, 254, 255, 260, 269, 367 n.18, 369, 383, 461 n.2, 514
Gouge, William   189, 365
Great Ejection (1662)   71, 104, 189
Greaves, Richard L.   224–5, 228
Greenville Presbyterian Theological Seminary   4
Gregory of Nazianzus   198, 499
Gregory of Nyssa   218
Gregory the Great   287
Grevinchovius, Nicolaas   58, 203, 205, 281, 291
Gribben, Crawford   3, 5, 6, 15, 18, 24–9, 34–6, 40, 42, 44, 48–52, 62, 72, 123–6, 129, 130, 136, 140, 142, 182, 190, 191, 195, 200, 282, 371, 380, 414, 494–7
Grotius, Hugo   31, 63–5, 72, 74, 200, 210, 221, 325–7, 329
Gunton, Colin   491, 505, 506, 508

Haigh, Christopher   419
Hall, Joseph   248, 401
Hammond, Henry   417, 428, 438
Hampton, Stephen   173, 419
Hampton Court Conference   175
Hanna, John   355
Hardman Moore, Susan   508
Harrab, Thomas   171–4, 188, 196
Harrison, Peter   225–6, 250
Hartlib, Samuel   148, 249
Hartopp, Sir John   124, 130, 144
Harvard College/University   2, 23, 381, 501
Haugaard, William   174
Haykin, Michael A. G.   5, 511
Helm, Paul   7
Henry VIII   172, 189, 215
Henry, John   225
Henry, Matthew   168
Henry, Philip   153, 167, 168
Herbert, George   172
Heylyn, Peter   172, 418
Hilary of Poitiers   209, 286
Hill, Christopher   2, 364, 383
Hoard, Samuel   58–9, 63, 282–3
Hobbes, Thomas   7, 83, 225, 227, 228, 231–4, 240–2, 366
Holcot, Robert   268
Homer   284
Hooke, Robert   228
Hooker, Richard   59–60, 76, 306, 512
Hooper, John   173
Hoornbeeck, Johannes   32, 79
Hopkins, Ezekiel   355–6, 361
Howe, John   40
Humble Petition and Advice (1657)   176–7
Hume, David   250
Hunsinger, George   491
Hunter, Michael   236
Hutchinson, Lucy   7, 69, 124, 130, 228, 234, 239, 240, 245
Hyde, Daniel   513
Hyde, Edward, earl of Clarendon   36, 103
hypothetical universalism   61, 62, 64, 257, 297, 298, 306, 307, 314, 316, 317, 321, 339

Ignatius   287

Illyricus, Matthias Flacius   391
Independent churches. *See* Congregationalism
Indulgence, Declaration of (1672)   37, 71, 106, 108, 130, 192, 215
Instrument of Government (1653)   176, 207
Ireland   14, 17, 18, 30, 91, 92, 94, 104, 118, 121, 126, 133, 135, 137, 172, 176, 496
Ireton, Henry   30, 92, 115, 127, 134, 135, 137, 141
Isham, Elizabeth   204
Islam   180, 211, 214, 432

Jackson, Arthur   16
Jackson, Thomas   26, 58, 282
James I   187, 194, 199
James II (James, Duke of York)   6, 78, 84, 112–14, 191, 197, 424
Jefferson, Thomas   117
Jerome   286–7, 289, 384, 390
Jesuits   30, 173, 197, 203, 276, 278, 288, 289, 405
John of Damascus   286, 500
Johnston, Archibald, of Wariston   92, 95, 100
Johnston, Keith   506
Jones, William   366
Joseph of Arimathea   188
Judaism   72, 94, 211, 368, 378, 433. *See also* Hebraic learning under Owen, John
Junius, Franciscus   35, 69, 79, 252, 261, 399 n.76
Justin Martyr   375, 384

Kant, Immanuel   202
Kapic, Kelly M.   8, 9, 372, 442
Keeble, N. H.   369
Kelly, Ryan   181
Knapp, Henry   503
Kuyper, Abraham   500–1, 509

Lambert, John   102, 177
Lambeth Articles (1595)   292
Latinity   xxiv, xxv, 2, 5, 21, 25, 30, 32, 33, 38, 45, 51, 63, 69, 171, 228, 232, 252, 254, 260, 272, 285, 323, 367, 380, 384, 498, 514

Laud, William   6, 15, 57, 132, 151, 175, 282, 305, 415. *See also* Laudianism
Laudianism   6, 57, 58, 63, 119, 132, 133, 139, 174, 176, 191, 366, 415, 418. *See also* Laud, William
Lawson, George   366
Lawson, Steve   361
Leavens, Elizabeth   19
Leighton, Robert   117
Leslie, Andrew M.   3, 8, 508
Levellers   83, 91, 126, 133
Levering, Matthew   276
Licensing Order (1643)   85
Lightfoot, John   74
Lilburne, Robert   126
Lim, Paul C. H.   6, 180, 502
Locke, John   82, 84, 139, 168
London   2, 6, 15, 22, 24, 42, 83, 101–3, 105, 108, 109, 111, 112, 115, 120, 127, 129–31, 142, 144, 167, 179, 229, 230, 234, 282, 366, 374, 415, 417, 506
Louis XIV, of France   111
Lovelace, John Lord   15
Lucius, Ludovicus   64
Lucretius   225, 228, 234, 239–42
Ludlow, Edmund   100
Lukin, Henry   74, 377
Lushington, Thomas   366
Luther, Martin   172, 189, 205, 288, 460
Lutheranism   50, 108, 172, 175, 195, 289, 391, 398

McCormack, Bruce L.   506
Maccovius, Johannes   199, 201, 261
MacCulloch, Diarmaid   415
McDonald, Suzanne   8, 221, 340, 504–5
McGraw, Ryan M.   3, 5, 7, 497
Maclean, Donald John   120
Mandelbrote, Scott   235
Manton, Thomas   67, 189
Marshall, Stephen   67
Marston Moor   16–17, 133
Marvell, Andrew   420, 424
Mary I   427
Massachusetts   23, 188, 381
Mather, Cotton   381
Mather, Samuel   381
Menander   251

Milton, Anthony 199, 415
Milton, John 148–9, 154, 182, 199, 226
Moffatt, James 14
Molina, Luis de 261, 278, 405
Monck, George 22, 101–2
Monmouth, James Scott, Duke of 114–15, 197
Moore, Thomas 28, 61, 305
Morice, Sir William 373–4
Morrissey, Mary 121, 122, 124
mortalism 88
Mortimer, Sarah 178
Muller, Richard A. 3, 5, 395, 499, 504, 508
Murray, John 339
Musculus, Wolfgang 261

Naseby 16–17, 133
natural law theory 227, 404
Nelson, Eric 84
Nestorianism 398
Newman, J. H. 173
Newton, Eric 6
Nicaea Councils of 207–9, 215–16, 219, 500, 502
Nicole, Roger 13
Nuttall, Geoffrey F. 207
Nye, Philip 22, 67, 98, 100

Oates, Titus 113
Oberman, Heiko 216
Oecolampadius, Johannes 366
Oldenburg, Henry 228, 233, 238
Oliver, Robert 24
Origen 213, 287
Osborne, Francis 150
Ovid 285
Owen, Dorothy D'Oyley (Owen's second wife) 24
Owen, Henry (Owen's brother) 14, 83, 84, 96, 115
Owen, Henry (Owen's father) 14, 251
Owen, John. *See also the Index of Owen's works*
   and anthropology 7, 252, 254, 256–60, 269, 271, 272, 290–2, 353, 393, 403, 492 (*see also* sin)
   and apostasy 8, 37, 47, 138, 139, 142, 192, 193, 235, 242, 339, 374, 386, 414–38, 441

and Arminianism 5, 6, 8, 25, 26, 31, 33, 40, 54, 57, 72, 78, 86, 132, 139, 190, 196, 199–206, 209, 256, 257, 269, 275–335, 337, 373, 420, 441 (*see also* Arminianism)
assurance 5, 15, 38, 48 n.125, 120, 203–4, 271, 350, 354, 355, 363, 387, 395, 406, 484
atonement 7, 16, 30, 31, 48, 75, 79, 120, 205, 209, 214, 219, 269, 296, 297, 302–35, 338, 444, 446, 452, 491
audiences 25, 54, 490
baptism 26, 49, 50, 88, 172, 175, 188, 190, 296, 399, 401, 509
beatific vision 43, 45, 48, 217–18, 221–2, 398, 463, 466, 482, 485
biography 13–24, 260, 492–7
Christology 8, 25, 27, 32, 37, 41, 46, 48, 50, 55, 60, 73, 79, 154, 157, 158, 166, 168, 169, 215–22, 311, 345, 368–71, 396–9, 412, 451, 455, 456, 461–86, 505, 507
church covenants 47
classical literature 162–3, 165, 166, 284–5
Congregationalism 27, 34, 60, 66, 78, 79, 98, 221, 231, 262
conspiracies against government 24
correspondence 2, 26, 45, 46
covenant, new 41, 47, 50, 60, 258, 297, 318, 328, 343, 381, 412, 456
covenant of grace 50, 60, 108, 269, 334, 345, 412, 451
covenant of redemption 26, 41, 47, 48, 50, 69, 201, 205, 310, 313, 315, 318, 328, 330–1, 333, 334, 378, 380, 455, 473
covenant of works 27, 49, 60, 162, 334, 412, 450, 451, 455
covenant theology 35, 41, 45, 49, 69, 187, 188, 269, 270, 373, 380
covenant with Abraham 50, 69, 134
covenant with Moses 27, 49, 50
and Cromwell, Oliver 18, 83, 91, 96, 98, 496, 498
and Cromwell, Richard 82, 83, 116
death 1, 9, 23, 24, 42–4, 46, 56, 57, 84, 116, 140, 235, 248, 254, 369

ecclesiology 16, 26–8, 33, 48, 49, 54, 59, 79, 96, 180, 190, 255, 336, 339, 399, 505
education 54, 146–69
eschatology 118, 133, 204, 214, 255, 259, 363, 462, 464, 485, 495
Eucharist 27, 45, 49, 190, 192, 362, 482
faith 8, 16, 33, 37, 43–5, 67, 98, 99, 134, 136, 137, 144, 148, 150, 153, 154, 160, 163, 190, 192, 204, 212, 217, 218, 220, 227, 243, 244, 246, 247, 249, 250, 252–3, 267, 268, 271, 283, 287, 288, 295–300, 306, 307, 314, 317, 320, 332–5, 342, 344–5, 350, 354, 358, 361–4, 371, 378, 387, 399, 406, 407, 409, 411–13, 420, 422, 431, 435, 439–49, 460–86 (*see also* assurance)
glorification 243, 352, 397, 399, 408, 464, 475, 476, 481, 482, 485
Hebraic learning 38, 51, 65, 73–4, 147, 155, 165, 241, 372, 388, 445, 503, 514
Hebrew vowel points 34, 66, 70, 241, 372, 503
hermeneutics 41, 476–7, 491, 502
illness 24, 140, 419, 425
Imago Dei 164, 217, 221, 237, 246, 343, 344, 353, 391–2, 401–12, 464, 469, 483, 485
innovations in theology 32, 54–5, 115, 155, 384, 397
justification 8, 24, 28, 31, 40, 41, 45, 56, 64, 75, 139, 181, 192, 193, 200, 204, 252, 253, 266, 268, 319, 331–5, 338, 339, 345, 358, 378, 417, 419, 439–60, 475
law and legalism 59, 60, 85, 192, 287, 296, 306, 310, 311, 323–4, 347–51, 362, 369, 375, 412, 439, 442–4, 446, 449, 451, 452, 454, 455, 458, 477, 512
lay preaching 121, 125, 150
legacy and translations 56, 69, 379–83, 489–515
literary style 36, 41, 50–4, 272, 382, 498

liturgy 104, 170–1, 176–7, 183–5, 190, 195, 220, 428, 430, 434, 509, 513 (*see also* Book of Common Prayer)
medieval theology 3, 33, 54–6, 198, 211, 217, 252, 284, 286–8, 306, 323, 386, 390, 392, 395, 402, 499
meditation 8, 24, 43, 45, 48, 51, 68, 77, 124, 160, 184, 215, 220, 222, 227, 243, 244, 248–50, 267, 352, 355, 359, 362, 461–86
mortification (*see* sanctification)
neologisms 51
Oxford, University of 18, 29, 33, 35, 50, 69, 72, 94, 95, 118, 121, 146, 149–51, 160–1, 167, 169, 198, 207, 212, 225, 249, 260, 305, 336, 372, 373, 417, 495
as pastor 2, 5, 8, 9, 14, 16, 25–7, 44, 45, 48, 54–9, 67–8, 86, 100, 118, 119, 123–5, 183, 220, 222, 251, 336, 351, 356, 363, 369, 376, 387, 435, 440, 442, 443, 447, 489–95, 510–14
patristic sources 3, 54, 55, 69, 70, 76, 198, 209, 211, 213, 216, 252, 269, 284, 286–7, 343, 385, 390, 407, 413, 499
philosophy 5, 7, 35, 54, 55, 69, 70, 147–9, 154, 160–3, 165, 166, 185, 198, 202, 215, 221, 223–36, 240, 241, 245, 251–72, 414, 431, 441, 452, 453, 491, 504, 505
piety 3, 14, 32, 43, 47, 55, 68, 71, 92, 152, 156, 157, 169, 201, 215, 336, 343, 346, 365, 418, 419, 426, 429, 432, 470, 476, 481
pneumatology 7, 16, 19, 25, 46, 50, 57, 76, 119–20, 150, 193, 253, 261, 262, 269–70, 272, 298, 300, 313, 338–43, 345, 382–413, 445, 505, 507
politics 30, 36, 71, 81–117
prayer 35, 39, 41, 77, 93, 94, 119, 126, 178, 179, 183, 184, 196, 312, 314, 356, 357, 362, 400, 435, 462, 513
preaching 1, 4, 13, 19, 60, 61, 94, 118–45, 150, 157, 194, 255, 371, 434, 435, 470, 495, 511, 512

preaching to Parliament 6, 17, 27, 91, 370, 371, 416
preaching to students 19, 31, 32, 138, 139, 263
predestination 28, 57, 120, 139, 190, 192, 199, 201–5, 257, 276, 281, 282, 283, 285, 289–91, 295, 296, 300, 301, 304, 306, 307, 316, 317, 318, 321, 322, 332, 333, 334, 344, 412, 416, 417, 418, 429, 438, 442, 463, 473, 477, 478, 505
prolegomena 35, 66, 69, 74, 160, 165, 372, 387, 390
Protestant union 5, 54, 57, 79, 129, 191
providence 17–19, 59, 85, 99, 104, 118, 133, 134, 140–4, 153, 157, 201–5, 216, 218, 237–8, 244, 248, 289, 293–300, 328, 340, 361, 368, 416, 428
public worship 3, 17, 21, 22, 26, 29–43, 45, 47, 59, 67, 71, 75, 88, 89, 91, 99, 101, 102, 104, 106, 107, 116, 125, 132, 133, 135, 154, 155, 158, 165, 169–71, 176, 183, 184, 190, 192, 193, 208, 211, 212, 214, 215, 217, 220, 242, 438, 476, 511
regeneration 39, 76, 119–20, 258, 262–7, 270, 271, 299, 300, 342, 344, 347, 349, 352, 353, 355, 386, 387, 400–7
religious toleration 6, 27–30, 33, 37, 40, 42, 43, 45, 47, 49, 57, 61, 67, 71, 82, 83, 85, 87, 89, 90, 92, 97–9, 102, 104–9, 112, 113, 116, 170, 171, 178, 180, 181, 187, 188, 194, 195, 208, 210, 232, 385, 430, 434, 496, 502
repentance 42, 120, 121, 140, 141, 257, 339, 355, 358, 360, 421, 423, 433, 458, 459, 477, 495
resurgence of interest in his works 8
and Roman Catholicism 41, 43, 56, 66, 76, 79, 113, 114, 130, 132, 139, 143, 144, 191, 192, 206–15, 262, 337, 386, 411, 420, 424, 426, 432, 434, 441, 446, 447, 453, 466, 476, 481, 484

Sabbatarianism 37, 38, 71, 73, 75, 88, 184, 247, 378, 381, 382
sanctification 8, 156, 258, 262–5, 267, 269–71, 332, 335–63, 386, 399, 400, 408–13, 439, 458–9, 463, 469, 485
scholasticism 7, 35, 55, 119, 124, 211, 217, 219, 251, 253, 255, 256, 262, 266–9, 286–7, 294, 336, 405, 499, 507, 509
science 223–50
scripture 34, 40, 56, 65, 150, 192, 271, 336, 362, 364–83, 463, 464, 468, 481, 484, 485, 503
and Socinianism 41, 48, 50, 56, 61, 63, 64, 72, 75, 77, 79, 95, 139, 154, 155, 178, 182, 196, 200, 208, 213, 220, 260, 279–80, 309, 324, 337, 368, 371, 373, 386, 388, 397, 411, 422, 440, 446, 447, 453, 463, 502
soteriology 3, 174, 256–60, 386, 411, 418
speculation 321
theological method 7
and Thomism 26
trinitarianism 25, 29, 31, 37, 46, 50, 55, 74, 77–9, 158, 192, 193, 206–15, 247, 309, 340, 343, 387, 397, 429, 439, 444, 463, 492
union with Christ 32, 156, 164, 169, 222, 329, 345–6, 398, 409, 441, 454–7, 464, 476, 478, 479, 484
unpublished work 2, 6, 26, 37, 46, 72, 124, 142, 145
vivification (*see* sanctification)
Owen, Mary (Owen's first wife) 24, 420
Owen, Philemon 14
Owen, William 251
Oxford, University of 6, 18, 29, 94, 211, 219. *See also* Christ Church, Oxford

Packer, J. I. 13, 173, 347, 352, 510
Pagitt, Ephraim 200
Pannenberg, Wolfhart 335
Pareus, David 211, 261
Parker, Samuel 76, 121, 262, 385, 386, 387 n.15, 410
Parliament, Barebones/Nominated Assembly 127, 149

Parliament, Cavalier   103, 106, 183
Parliament, Exclusion   143, 144
Parliament, first Protectorate   83, 90, 94, 95, 207
Parliament, Long   89, 102, 103, 148, 282, 416
Parliament, Rump   6, 93, 100–2, 127, 129, 134–6, 370
Parliament, second Protectorate   14, 83, 96, 128, 137, 142, 144
Parliament, third Protectorate   82, 83, 99, 128
Patterson, W. B.   199
Payne, William   461
Perkins, William   60, 189, 199, 292, 375
perseverance of the saints   31, 37, 47, 63, 94, 147, 269, 301, 336, 371, 418, 423, 435, 440
Petto, Samuel   50
Piscator, Johannes   211, 261, 283
plague (1665)   109, 142–4
Plato   198, 288, 418
Pococke, Edward   182, 229, 231
Polanus, Amandus   32, 79, 252
Ponder, Nathaniel   374, 375, 380, 420, 421
Porter, Roy   202
Powell, Hunter   183, 195
Presbyterianism   15, 16, 26–8, 33, 35, 36, 44, 47, 48, 50, 58–61, 66, 67, 79, 84, 87, 88, 90, 96, 99–101, 103, 111, 129, 171, 180, 187, 188, 196, 221, 230, 418. *See also* Blasphemy Act (1648)
Pride's Purge   29, 89, 125
Prosper of Aquitaine   286–7, 384
Puritan Reformed Theological Seminary   4
Pyott, Edward   20

Quakers   6, 19–21, 30, 33, 65, 129, 149, 150, 180, 198, 214, 215, 218, 220, 386, 388, 410, 463
Quantin, Jean-Louis   216, 385
Queen's College, Oxford   15, 57, 151, 190, 251

Racovian Catechism   31, 63, 64, 208, 371, 417. *See also* Socinianism

Radner, Ephraim   506
Reformed Theological Seminary, Jackson, MS   4
Regicide of Charles I. *See* Charles I
Rehnman, Sebastian   3
resistance theory   6, 105, 113, 114, 116
Restoration of Charles II. *See* Charles II
Reynolds, Edward   26, 189, 288
Rich, Mary Boyle   248
Rivetus, Andreas   75, 211, 261
Roberts, Francis   69, 70, 375, 379
Robinson, Robert   122
Roman Catholicism   7, 36, 40, 71, 88, 92, 111, 113, 114, 172, 173, 180, 197, 262, 275, 386, 415, 427, 431, 437, 466
Root and Branch Petition (1640)   176
Royal Society   7, 223, 225, 226, 228–35, 237, 238, 250
Rush, Benjamin   117
Russell, Thomas   xxiv, 1, 45, 382
Rutherford, Samuel   27, 30, 63, 64, 73, 253, 256, 288
Rye House Plot (1683)   6, 14, 83, 115, 466 n.21

Sams, John   125
Savoy Declaration   22, 49, 98, 102, 112, 180–2, 185–6, 442, 514
Saxton, David   359
Schlinctingius, Jonas   208, 366, 389 n.27
Scotland   89, 91, 92, 101, 102, 104, 118, 126, 172, 489
semi-Pelagianism   58, 76, 173, 190, 200–1, 206, 275–7, 286, 287, 298, 404, 405, 410, 416, 425, 429, 440, 452
Servetus   49
Sewall, Samuel   381
Shaftesbury, Anthony Cooper, earl of   114, 197
Sheppard, William   135
Sherlock, William   38, 42, 71, 75, 76, 218, 418, 419, 512
Sibbes, Richard   189
Simpson, Sydrach   67
sin   8, 19, 26, 31–3, 35, 37, 44, 49, 59, 64, 71, 79, 99, 108, 139, 140, 155, 157, 169, 177, 193, 200,

205, 209, 210, 214, 219, 242, 256, 258, 263, 265, 278, 286, 296, 316, 319, 322–63, 385, 391, 399, 401–4, 406, 409–11, 432, 435, 439, 441, 443–51, 453, 456, 458–60, 464, 468, 473, 477, 478, 480, 481, 485, 507, 512, 514, 515
Sindercombe plot   138
Smalcius, Valentine   208
Snoddy, Richard   284 n.33
Socinianism   5, 6, 25, 26, 28, 30, 31, 33, 37, 39–41, 43, 48, 50, 51, 54, 56, 61, 63–5, 68, 70–9, 95, 139, 154, 155, 173, 177, 178, 180, 196, 200, 207–15, 219–22, 252, 253, 260, 279–80, 302, 309, 324–6, 337, 366, 368, 371, 376, 386, 388, 389, 397, 403, 411, 416, 417, 420, 422, 425, 437, 440–2, 446, 453, 455, 463, 475, 502. *See also* Racovian Catechism
Solemn League and Covenant   90, 102, 137, 176. *See also* Covenanters
South, Robert   122
Spence, Alan   3, 159, 505
Sprat, Thomas   228
Spurlock, Scott   92
Stadhampton   14, 24, 129
Star Chamber   85, 148
Stephens, Philemon   28
Stillingfleet, Edward   42, 67, 112, 228, 235, 244–6
Strickland, Sir William   174–5, 177
Stubbe, Henry   7, 228, 231–2
Suarez, Franciscus   30, 173, 196, 202, 252
Svensson, Manfred   496
Swain, Scott R.   502
Swift, Jonathan   223, 249
Sydenham, William   100
Sylvester, Edward   121, 229

Tay, Edwin E. M.   3, 370, 508
Taylor, Jeremy   180
Test Act (1673)   130, 424
Thirty-nine Articles (1562)   6, 58, 85, 111, 112, 171, 174, 176, 186, 187, 190, 191, 193–6, 281, 289, 295, 296, 428, 441, 442. *See also* Church of England

Thoresby, Ralph   130
Thorndike, Herbert   59, 418
Thornton, John   233
Thurman, Henry   150
Tillotson, John   498
Todd, Margo   199
Toon, Peter   2, 16, 21, 26, 46, 229, 251, 506
Toplady, Augustus   340
Trent, Council of   278, 350
Trevor, Sir John   374
triers and ejectors   127
Trueman, Carl   3, 259, 277, 280, 288, 340, 497, 498
Turretin, Francis   80, 211
Tweeddale, John   3, 8, 503, 508
Twisse, William   30, 40, 53, 63, 64, 72, 253, 256, 261, 288
Tyacke, Nicholas   199
Tyndale, William   163

Ussher, James   183

Van den Belt, Henk   120
Van Dixhoorn, Chad   350
Vanhoozer, Kevin   491
van Mastricht, Petrus   80
Veal, Edward   167
Venning, Ralphe   189
Vermigli, Peter Martyr   79
Vernon, Elliot   170
Vernon, George   231, 490
Vincent, Thomas   167, 168
Vines, Richard   67
Virgil   285
Voetius, Gisbertus   32, 80, 211, 269
Vorstius, Conrad   33, 58
Vossius, Gerardus Johannes   261

Wadham College, Oxford   229–30
Wales   88, 121, 135, 382
Wallace, Dewey D.   419
Wallingford House   83, 100, 102, 128
Wallington, Nehemiah   204
Wallis, John   228, 229, 231, 232, 241
Walton, Brian   34, 65, 70, 372
Ward, Seth   228, 229
Warwick, Robert Rich, earl of   235
Watts, Isaac   437

Webster, John, modern theologian 491, 506–8
Webster, John, Parliamentary army preacher 228, 230
Wesley, John 1, 498
Wesley, Samuel 167
Westcott, Stephen 2, 35
Westminster Assembly 27–8, 30, 61, 66, 87, 125, 176, 177, 231, 289, 441, 442, 451 n.83
Westminster Assembly, Confession of Faith 22, 27, 87, 98, 102, 112, 177, 180–2, 189, 195, 269
Westminster Assembly, Directory for Public Worship 171
Westminster Assembly, Shorter Catechism 226
Westminster Theological Seminary 4, 508
Westrow, Thomas 27
Whalley, Edmund 101, 102
Wharton, Lord Philip 22–3
Whigs 106, 114
Whitelock, Bulstrode 125
Whitgift, John 59
Wilberforce, William 1, 501
Wilken, Robert 496
Wilkins, John 7, 121, 128, 225, 228–31, 239, 245, 248
William and Mary 171, 187, 195
William of Ockham 405
Winship, Michael 195
Witsius, Herman 269, 380
Wittman, Tyler R. 509
Wood, Anthony 122
Woolrych, Austin 92
Worcester 127, 133
Wray, Daniel 357
Wren, Christopher 228
Wright, Shawn 514
Wynn, Christopher 347

Zanchius, Jerome 79, 283, 289, 390 n.32

www.ingramcontent.com/pod-product-compliance
Lightning Source LLC
Chambersburg PA
CBHW080932300426
44115CB00017B/2789